Home
Fires

Also by Donald Katz

THE BIG STORE:
INSIDE THE CRISIS AND REVOLUTION AT SEARS

HOME FIRES

An Intimate Portrait of One Middle-Class Family in Postwar America

DONALD KATZ

HarperPerennial
A Division of HarperCollins*Publishers*
Aaron Asher Books

Acknowledgments appear on p. 617.

A hardcover edition of this book was published in 1992 by HarperCollins Publishers.

HarperCollins books may be purchased for educational, business, or sales promotional use. For information please write: Special Markets Department, HarperCollins Publishers, Inc., 10 East 53rd Street, New York, NY 10022.

First HarperPerennial edition published 1993.

Designed by Ruth Kolbert

The Library of Congress has catalogued the hardcover edition as follows:

Katz, Donald, 1952–
    Home fires : an intimate portrait of one middle-class family in postwar America / Donald Katz. — 1st ed.
        p. cm.
    ISBN 0-06-019009-4
        1. Family—United States—History. 2. United States—Social conditions—1945– .
3. Middle classes—United States. I. Title.
HQ535.K38   1992   91-58347
306.85'0973—dc20

ISBN 0-06-099502-5 (pbk.)

93 94 95 96 97 ❖/RRD 10 9 8 7 6 5 4 3 2 1

For Leslie, Chloe, and Austin

Keep the home fires burning,
While your hearts are yearning...

PREFACE

I first heard some of the stories in this book while jogging. Between 1983 and 1988, I ran through Manhattan's Riverside Park several times each week beside a talented young composer named Ricky Ian Gordon. Ricky and I talked incessantly during those long runs, about his latest musical scores and about my writing—and, as friends do, we talked about our families.

Ricky described his father, Sam Goldenberg, who returned from World War II determined to establish a "normal" family untouched by the trauma of immigration, by Depression poverty, or by the household discord that had marred his own family. Sam came back to a pretty New York City girl named Eve, a professional singer, who'd become his wife during the urgent, romantic year 1942, and had since given up singing to "make a home" for Sam and the children. Sam worked very hard as an electrician, Ricky said. His parents decided to change the family name, and in 1952 the Gordons ascended in triumph from the ethnic Bronx to a brand-new house in a new suburb, a place that looked to Sam and Eve for all the world like the Promised Land. They were an all-American dynamo of a postwar family, the very embodiment of the American Dream.

But then things changed.

Like some Boswell in running shoes, I listened to stories of a family strained and torn by centrifugal forces that Ricky chose to call "the times." The Gordon family seethed, and soon Gordon children began to career out into the changing culture, touching an uncanny array of experiences in Greenwich Village, Harlem, Mississippi, London, San Francisco, Berkeley, Ann Arbor, Woodstock, Altamont. The list went on and on. Costume changes commenced at a startling pace: rocker, beat, Ivy Leaguer, radical, hippie, feminist, dealer, unwed mother, divorcée, gay, yogi, healer. Daughters named Susan, Lorraine, and Sheila presented Sam and Eve with grandchildren named Shuna, Shiva, and Gopal.

By the time I first heard Ricky's stories, his oldest sister, the one with a degree from Vassar, whose articles I'd read in early issues of *Rolling Stone* and *Ms.*, was a junkie roaming city streets. His second sister was living in poverty and was about to gather up her children, leave her boyfriend, a retired motorcycle outlaw, and return to the fold with her guru in Yogaville, Virginia. His mother, Ricky said, had become "skittery and sad." Ricky believed his father had never been able to accept that his only son was gay, and because of this and the rest of the story, had become so introverted he rarely spoke to his children at all.

A psychic told Ricky not to lose heart. "Your family will still have a happy ending," she said.

After several years, as I began a family of my own and found less time to jog with Ricky, I noticed that Gordon stories kept coming back to me, often evoking shivers like those inspired by the opening chords of old songs or by particular bits of documentary film. Ricky's stories made me think of my own father, an infantryman who'd served at the European front like Sam Gordon, and who died when I was twenty. But the stories came back to me most powerfully as I considered the whys and wherefores of being a husband and a father to my own daughter and son—a man with a family. Along with millions of other Baby Boom children born of the postwar middle class, I came to believe that nothing in my life was as important or potentially rewarding as creating a family, as raising children—albeit in a culture that family social historian Barbara Dafoe Whitehead has lately described, with some understatement, as "unfriendly" to families.

As Ricky's stories crowded together in retrospect, they began to appear both as vivid annotations on a historical time line and as parts of a grand family saga of the sort usually found in novels.

Four years ago, shortly before I began to write to the Gordons about my idea of chronicling a single American family through the postwar era, I recalled what anthropologist Margaret Mead had said about the famous 1973 documentary *An American Family*. A California family, the Louds, had agreed to let a film crew record their lives over several months, and Mead thought that the intimate results of the project were perhaps as "important for our times as were the inventions of drama and the novel for earlier generations." The stunning comparison was appropriate, Mead contended, because the literary genres and the ground-breaking documentary both offered new ways "to help people understand themselves."

⸻◆⸻

A recent opinion poll indicated that ninety-seven of every one hundred Americans want more than anything else—more than clean air, close friends, a good income, and (by twenty-four percentage points) good sex—to have what the poll-takers called a "happy family life." A study commissioned by the Massachusetts Mutual Life Insurance Company revealed that family is "the central element in the lives of most Americans." We devour how-to and self-help books about parenting and about the myriad impediments—the dependencies and addictions—carried into adult lives from our families of origin. Television brims with family recollections and confessional revelations of family trouble. Experts and policymakers shuffle through available political, social, economic, and psychological templates in search of the configurations that will help make families work.

The family is the primary lens that filters the early and lasting light of every life.

But was it indeed, as Ricky argued, "the times" that so roiled and even ruined many families of the postwar era? Or was it genetics; or the miniature historical forces of psychological formation; or the complex valances of invisible family structure; or the "myth of the 1950s family"; or the luck of the draw, or rock and roll; or, as several Gordons would attest at one point, was it karma?

When I formally approached the Gordon family and asked them to let me tell their story, I said that I was sure only that every family—happy and unhappy, intact and fragmented, functional and dysfunctional, the ones you make and the ones you come from—overflows with unanswered questions. I told all of them that I knew they had very good stories to tell, and that perhaps if they let me reconstitute their lives in a book, readers might learn something about themselves and their own lives over the decades.

For reasons as intelligent and varied as the members of this wonderful family, Sam and Eve Gordon, their four children, and hundreds of others all agreed to help out.

I have talked to most of the outside witnesses to Gordon family events described in this book. My account draws upon four years of regular interviews with the Gordons and several thousand pages of transcribed discussions with childhood friends, ex-spouses, lovers, teachers, mah-jongg partners, colleagues, psychologists, band members, commune associates, rabbis, and many other individuals who were most generous with their time and reminiscences. I also talked to many of the public figures and experts who either appear in or helped inform the ensuing narrative.

There are no composite characters in this book. Four last names have been omitted, and four names have been changed. "Gil" is not the real name of the boy Ricky encounters in 1968, and "Ahmad" and "Jimmy" are pseudonyms of young men who enter Susan Gordon Lydon's life during the early 1980s. The Gordon family friend "Gina Schick" requested that her name be changed so as to protect the privacy of the baby boy she gave up for adoption in 1967.

One or two readers of early drafts of this book—noting my description of profound changes within the Gordon family over the four years I was asking them to recapitulate their experiences—have asked if I thought the process of writing the book altered family events. I was reminded of Heisenberg's uncertainty principle, which holds that in the process of observation the thing observed will be changed.

I do not know whether or to what extent the writing of this book has changed the Gordons' lives. I can only say that if the final chapters of this story contain the subtle effects of my tape recorder and notebook, then all but four years of the half-century I describe do not. And if my questions have made for a happier ending, that argues for the ameliorative force of carefully reconsidering the course of a life—as novelists, psychotherapists, adherents of "twelve-step" programs, and various religious figures have claimed for quite a while. I freely admit that I have not been so "objective" as to envisage a happier ending for this family as a bad thing. At one point, Eve Gordon took to calling me her "fifth child," and that made me proud.

As I suspected from my earliest jogs with Ricky, all the Gordons turned out to be terrific storytellers, each possessed of a powerful memory that usually stood up quite well to the record contained in journals, diaries, correspondence, photographs, and tape recordings, as well as to eyewitness descriptions of events.

As with any family, there was often a consensual version of certain events that stood in as "the truth" through the sheer force of the story's retelling. Descriptions of other shared events were so dissimilar that they recalled the Japanese film classic *Rashomon*. In cases where individuals offered profoundly differing versions of the same event, I have tried to allow the narrative to reflect the divergence.

In the end, all perspectives and memories inside a family have a claim to an integrity not unlike the truth.

Here is the story of a real family.

Home
Fires

1945

Staff Sergeant Samuel Goldenberg walked down the gangplank of his Liberty Ship in the first week of November 1945, during a pre-Christmas homecoming crush occasioned by the fact that a soldier was returning from Europe every five seconds of the day.

President Roosevelt and General Marshall, and then the new president, Truman, had all agreed that a point system was the fairest way to bring the soldiers home. A point was awarded for each month a soldier had served, five points for each campaign, five points for being a father. Eighty-five points was said to be a ticket home. Sam had 136 points to his name the day the Reich fell, but as every soldier knew by that time, the army was run as much by exception as by the rule. Sam was ordered to the supply lines leading into Frankfurt, Germany, for five months while many more than a million others went home before him.

Sam easily balanced his heavy barracks bag on his shoulder with one hand. He kept patting his front pocket with the other, as if to reassure himself that he was not only home alive three months short of his twenty-seventh birthday but home flush with a stake, thanks to the uncanny consistency with which a pair of dice kept coming to rest between the exposed girders of a lower deck of the Liberty Ship. He was wearing twelve hundred dollars in that front pocket, more than he'd made through an entire childhood of hard work and the beginning of his apprenticeship as an electrician. Sam inflected "hard work" as "hard *woik*." At mid-century his Bowery Boys accent was still shared with considerable pride by movie stars, college professors, novelists, and many other urban tough kids made good.

Sam bulled through the crowd and hailed a taxi. The cab motored north through the warm autumn day as he groped for feelings appropriate to being back home alive from a terrible war. By the time the cab crossed into familiar neighborhoods, Sam—"one tough hombre from the Bronx," as some of his army buddies called him—was breathless in the back seat, nearly panting under the weight of fear. *Home alive and flush with a stake,* he kept thinking, patting the splayed silver money clip in his front pocket. *Back home alive with a stake, married to a girl I haven't seen since 1943...father of a child I've never seen at all.*

Sam pressed into the strong springs under the taxi seat, thinking back into the war and wondering if he had ever experienced such terror under fire.

Sam would always refuse to turn the Second World War into dinner table allegory. He wouldn't sugarcoat it, and he wasn't sure how to make sense of it, so he left the war stories untold. As a result, one of his daughters, the second-born—Lorraine—would believe many years later that Sam's job during the war was carrying the mangled and the dead from battlefields. It wasn't clear how this had come to Lorraine, but it served her as an explanation of why her father seemed unable to miss a single television show featuring a Nazi, and why he often seemed injured by things Lorraine couldn't quite see. Sam's decision not to speak of the war fostered many apocryphal assumptions about his experiences overseas. It turned his war into a highly decorated family myth.

Over the years Sam occasionally wondered, silently—*secretly,* his wife and his children would contend—at how much easier it was to talk to his family about his childhood poverty on the Lower East Side than it was to tell them an appropriate war story. For some reason the lessons born of surviving the Depression came back as stories about life, while Sam's vivid recollections of war came back as absurd illustrations of how suddenly people can die. He figured these were stories a family couldn't use.

Of the forty million lives lost in World War II, Sergeant Samuel Goldenberg returned home quite sure he would always remember the end of more than a few. He would never forget a single thing about the sight, sound, or even the strangely acrid smell of a monster German V-bomb falling upon the twelve-hundred-year-old Belgian town of Liège. An entire square block of the ancient city rose as a single piece not twenty feet from where Sam stood in a cobbled street. The great chunk of Liège—full of Gothic spires and quaint homes and children—unfurled before him like a picnic blanket hovering above a square of earth. Then, within what seemed to be a tiny fraction of an instant, the entire block at Sam's feet collapsed into dust and screams.

How could you tell somebody what that was like—especially your own kids? How could you ever figure out what it was supposed to mean?

What could it possibly benefit others, Sam wondered, to know how it felt when you learned that all your friends in your original infantry division were killed on the beach at Peleliu Island in the fall of 1944—after you were transferred out to Europe? Japanese soldiers garrisoned at Peleliu were ensconced in a dense honeycomb of deep caves; they hid behind walls made of oil drums filled with powdered coral. American planes dropped great belly tanks of a new compound called napalm. An infantryman was sent up the rise to explode the tanks with a phosphorus shell, setting much of the top of Peleliu Island and even the coral on fire.

But the guys in Sam's old unit never made it off the beach. Most of them were New York City boys too, tough Hell's Kitchen Irishmen, born at the rough edge of one island and killed at the tropical edge of another.

Sam never found the right time to tell Eve or the kids how cold he was during the vicious winter nights of December 1944, around the time of the Battle of the Bulge. Sam's unit had pulled back out of Belgium to the French town of Sedan, where he slept under ten khaki blankets yanked from a passing supply truck and yet was colder than during any one of his childhood nights in the shoulder-wide tenement on the Lower East Side when he had slept curled around his clothes to keep them warm for morning, dreaming all night about pieces of coal.

Fifty years after he went to war, Sam would wonder if perhaps his reluctance to talk about his experiences was somehow connected to his own father's romantic stories of the cavalry. Sam's war had turned out to be nothing—nothing at all—like the wars his father had described. Some of Sam's earliest memories included Yosef Goldenberg's heated descriptions of galloping deep into Mexico in search of the legendary bandit Pancho Villa. Joe Goldenberg, who served on horseback once again during World War I, loved adventure and horses. Yetta Goldenberg, Sam's mother, feared horses more than Christians, and the mere sight of one of the half-blind old workhorses that shambled down the streets of Sam's childhood caused her to shudder with distinct memories of Cossacks coming over the rise. All his life Sam heard his mother declare that she couldn't understand a man who could love a horse, and whenever his father was in town—back from an adventure or another long journey in search of work—Papa Joe wondered aloud about the value of a woman who could hate animals so entirely worthy of a man's love.

A year before Pearl Harbor, Secretary of War Henry L. Stimson donned a blindfold and began to pull capsules containing slips of paper out of an immense glass bowl. Sam's birthday—February 2, 1919— appeared on the eighteenth of 7,836 reaches inside. Franklin Roosevelt, Sam's hero, stood beside Stimson. The president said, "Only the strong may continue to live in freedom and in peace."

Sam volunteered to join the cavalry and chase the Nazis across Europe on a horse—as did Papa Joe. Both of the Goldenberg men were informed that the cavalry did not figure in the military's future plans, so Joe went off to a unit based in California, and Sam joined the infantry.

Sam was the best sharpshooter in any of his several units, but his job at the front was keeping the roads open. Sam directed the endless lines of trucks and the longer lines of civilians carrying huge packs on their heads and backs. He watched families trudge through the deep mud to avoid the fighting, and he watched them turn around when the fighting shifted and trudge back the other way. Sam figured they were able to turn around like that, remaining emotionless and strong under their loads, because their parents and grandparents had made the exact same journeys. "Fleeing," Sam said, "was like a habit, a natural thing."

"Stop here," Sam told the cabbie. He grabbed his barracks bag and walked to the nearest corner, close to the wall, soldier-style. He peered around the corner in the direction of 1052 Kelly Street. The stoops and sidewalks in front of the two- and three-story houses on the block where Eve's mother lived teemed with women and children. A few of the toddlers sat in sturdily wrought steel strollers with lawnmower-style handles, but most of the younger children were clinging to their mothers. A carriage or a stroller was as hard to find by the middle of the war as a tricycle or a toy train. One of the chief complaints heard on the front stoops of the Bronx was that so many young mothers had to cart their babies around in their arms.

Sam spotted a little girl in a stroller. Though the woman standing beside the stroller was turned away, her head bobbing in conversation, Sam knew her to be his wife.

Sam darted back behind the wall and thought about the first time he saw Eve smiling at him. The luminous eight-by-ten portrait tacked to Sid Samberg's footlocker at Fort Dix, New Jersey, was of the type favored by professional entertainers of the time; it was a black-and-white photograph that had been hand-colored in the confectionery hues of storybook clouds and flowers. Rich piles of dark hair reflected a silvery luster; the girl's cheeks bore a slight flush of innocence, while deep-red lipstick highlighted a knowing but unaffected smile. Her glowing shoulders rose from a seemingly diaphanous powder-blue gown.

But best of all, Sam thought the photograph was full of laughter. It depicted a woman who was "lighter than air."

"My sister," Sid Samberg explained in the mess hall. "She sings."

When Sam finally met Sid's little sister during a weekend leave, he noticed that Eve's eyes were hazel instead of the eggshell blue of the portrait. He was surprised that she was barely five feet tall, and he knew that no photograph could have prepared him for the way he felt when he watched her move. What was precisely the same about the real Eve and the one Sam had imagined from the picture was the utter lightness of heart and spirit. Even when she wasn't telling jokes—and she told jokes all the time, in English or Yiddish (the language she spoke until entering school), the clean version or the standard "off-color" one, depending on the audience at hand—Eve Samberg's voice sounded like laughter, and her phrasing was rich with the syncopated turns of the Catskill *tummlers* she'd studied at the big Borscht Belt hotels.

During his next visit to the Samberg home, Sam heard Eve sing. She had a pure, trilling voice that she styled to sound slightly distracted. It was a voice that said "it's okay" to a man; it said "relax." When Sam listened to the sexy girl sing of "tropical nights so tender" and "orchestras playing in the swaying palms," he could feel the sweetness of happy evenings stretching out forever.

Sam was crazy in love.

The courtship was like many others conducted during 1942. Seven hundred and fifty miles separated the Samberg home in the Bronx from the training camp in South Carolina where Sam was stationed, and the train fare ate up most of the twenty-one dollars he was paid at the end of the month—a perfectly reasonable commute, Sam thought. They wrote "hot" letters back and forth, until the dark day in the early summer of 1942 when Sam opened a "Dear John" from Eve. She was having quite a summer in the Catskill mountains, it seemed.

Sam rushed home on furlough during the first week of November. He was prepared to dispense with his considerable sense of pride in pursuit of this girl, but before he could say a thing, Eve Samberg said, "Okay, Sammy, let's get married."

"I'm almost twenty-two," Eve told her friends. "I've had my fun."

During her regular Blue Network radio broadcast, Eleanor Roosevelt warned against the "hasty marriages" of the moment. The First Lady directed her comments to the nation's "eligible young women." She implored them not to curtail their "preparations for life" out of misplaced "patriotic fervor."

Yetta Goldenberg agreed, though she was less delicate in her analysis of the genesis of the young couple's fervor. "Just wait," Sam's formidable mother pleaded to her son. "This war will be over in two weeks! You can't wait two weeks?"

"Our Sammy," Yetta and Sam's older sister Sylvia told the rest of the family, "has fallen in love with a glossy."

Without parental approval, but with so many soldiers and girlfriends on every block similarly willing to seize the day, Sam and Eve picked up a ring, shed a bit of blood for the test, and eloped to a dingy registry office on November 7 in the company of Eve's brothers. Sid, Louis, and Buddy Samberg took the newlyweds to a restaurant and tried without success to get Sam drunk. The couple spent their first night as man and wife at the Concourse Plaza Hotel, where visiting ball teams stayed when in town to play the Yankees.

Eve was five months pregnant when Sam went overseas in July 1943. He carried the famous picture everywhere he went. Eve sent him a record featuring her own version of Bing Crosby's hit song "Ac-cent-tchuate the Positive" and another hit she'd altered slightly, "I'm Just Wild About Sammy."

Sam sent Eve sprigs of heather from Scotland. ("To a gal who is dearest to the heart of this guy. A sprig of bonnie heather.") He wrote her all the time. ("And please give a kiss to little Sue," he'd add, feeling strange each time he wrote the name of a baby girl he couldn't see or hold.) Sam continued to write even after he discovered that he was losing his capacity to conjure up the subtle way his wife's face moved when she talked to him or when she smiled. He used the picture as a prop for a while, but soon her happy eyes stopped moving. For a time he clung fast to the sound of her wonderful voice, but eventually, as the war progressed, the songs left him too. Sam played the record when he could, and he stared at the picture when there was enough light.

But now, home again, gazing at Eve's back, peering out at her like a man assessing the immediate future from a foxhole, Sam could no longer imagine his wife's face at all. He felt himself begin to turn away from the scene. It was as if some force over which he had no control—like those primal sensations that climbed from your belly each time a bomb or a rocket landed nearby—was impelling him. Sam was surprised at himself, but it certainly felt like he was about to run away.

Eve Goldenberg was a "nervous wreck," though none of the other young mothers and wives of the neighborhood whose spirits she elevated regularly could tell. They didn't seem to notice that Eve had been losing weight by the day. She hadn't slept well for several months, but she still managed to navigate the long afternoons of street-corner conversation, telling jokes as if nothing was bothering her at all. "Evie," one of her neighbors had said a few days before Sam came home and stared at her from behind a wall, "you're gonna live to be two hundred years old. If I had a husband still stuck overseas, I couldn't be so high. Nothing gets to you, Eve. You're one lucky girl."

Eve didn't consider herself so lucky. The army that won the war— the same organization that had presented her with an ancient wooden baby cradle shaped like a coffin—had kept her husband while almost every other soldier from the neighborhood was repatriated. Every single day since the war ended she'd expected to see him—communications from Europe had been sporadic—and now the streets of New York City were bare of the confetti and other detritus from the mass celebrations of the surrender days. War Department officials had expected that more than a year would pass between the European victory and the defeat of Japan, but with the nuclear destruction of Hiroshima and Nagasaki, even men from the Pacific front were returning home. Other families were already "looking ahead," as Eve's magazines often put it, but by late October she had received not so much as a hint about when Sam would return.

"The worst of it's always having to be ready," Eve confided to a woman who was in the same limbo. But every day Eve cranked her face into a smile and went out behind Susan's stroller, greeting the neighbors and telling jokes, and every day she felt more physically ill from her abiding fear of Sam coming home.

The dread was heightened by Eve's compulsive reading of magazine stories describing ruined husbands and young families that would never be the same. For over a year the young wives of the Bronx had been poring over articles about the "readjustment" dilemmas of returning servicemen. They studied these texts like the content analysts and code breakers who assigned numerical weight to each word in Nazi propaganda in hopes of seeing into the author's unconscious. Eve riffled past the tales about mere tricks of time—soldier boys leaping from the gangplanks into the arms of the wrong girl—and turned directly to the much darker reports of broken men, of husbands "maimed in heart, in mind, and in spirit," as one magazine put it, of soldiers bearing secret wounds that might be hidden at first, only to resurface as family chaos.

Some of the professionals quoted in the women's magazines seemed most concerned about the effect of readjustment on the future of the nation as a whole. "The focal point of life after the war will be the home. It was from a family circle that most of the boys and girls were called into the armed forces. It will be to the same family circle that most of them, now grown old beyond their years, will return," observed Coleman R. Griffith, a professor of education at the University of Illinois. "If the family fails," Griffith warned, "it might well be impossible for industry and government to succeed."

By November, the divorce rate was already double that of prewar times. The letters pages of the newspapers Eve read were filled with I-told-you-so testimonials from parents who'd tried—as Yetta Goldenberg had tried—to warn their children away from the hasty, passionate marriages so often produced by wars.

"Let's say it was love, right from the start," conjectured one wholly patronizing writer named Irene Stoke Culman in a spring *Good Housekeeping* Eve read. "Or let's say it was something in the air—a current, a shaft of light, a sudden swirl of patriotic fervor, a modicum of pathos for him in uniform, a touch of pity for yourself, a bit of being lonely for both of you. Whatever it was you got married....You begin to wonder— did you make a gigantic mistake? Could be. *But you're married to him*. Give him, and yourself, a chance. That takes time—lots of it, probably years and years....You took your soldier, young woman; he's yours. In heaven's name stick with him. Let's reinvest marriage in this wonderful country of ours with some of its departed dignity."

"The family," observed Dr. Margaret Mead, an anthropologist who'd "spent a good part of her life making studies of primitive peoples," according to a biographical note inserted by the editors at *Harper's* magazine, "has survived polygamy and polyandry, it has survived social codes under which a husband never saw his wife except at breakfast, in which wives were all years younger than the husbands who reared them or years older than the husbands whom they reared." Responding to the contagion of concern for the future of young American war families, Dr. Mead noted that "the family is a very tough institution and has survived a long time."

But Mead's solace did not permeate the popular reading material that so agitated Eve Goldenberg and her neighbors. The magazine articles Eve could not stop rehashing late into the night were the ones describing how time, distance, and war could transfigure passion. "Will it feel the same to kiss him? Will you be able to make love again?"

Eve never doubted that she and Sam would want to reclaim their shared prewar desire to make a happy family together. They both came from families that were noisy and argumentative, and they'd talked about their dream of a home life less fraught than theirs had been. They'd agreed that they wanted a family that was calm as well as happy.

Rebecca Samberg, Eve's mother, was a quiet woman who spent many hours of each day sitting in a gray kitchen surrounded by gray mounds of clothes. Her father, Simon Samberg, was well educated in the cultural realm of things Yiddish and Polish, but in the New World he labored as a fish-smoker, a latter-day Tantalus of the chubs and herring, who stood knee-deep in ice water all day long, lugging massive crates of fish onto tables to be filleted. Simon came home to drink homemade cherry schnapps until his head rolled back. He would bang on the table and growl for more wine like an angry bear.

Eve and Sam would make a different home. They would leave their families behind and start a better one of their own. But the thought that Sam might have lost his passion for her made everything seem tenuous to Eve.

Even so, she was not concerned about the sorts of wartime infidelities that were now the mainstay of conversation among her neighbors in the Bronx. She was friendly with a woman named Frieda Brown, who had come by Kelly Street every day since they realized that Sam and Frieda's husband, Barney, were serving in the same outfit. Frieda had a job in a fancy hat shop, and after work she would show up on Eve's stoop dressed to kill. (Eve had wanted desperately to work. She wanted to sing to bring in some money, but Sam, Yetta, and Rebecca insisted this was the wrong thing for a young mother to do.) Frieda Brown would stand there on Kelly Street in her fine clothes and hats, weeping mechanically and moaning ceaselessly about the terrible things she planned to do to Barney Brown if she found out that he'd so much as looked crosswise at some Jezebel across the Atlantic. "I'll divorce him, Evie," Frieda would cry. "I swear it. I really will."

Eve consoled Frieda warmly, thinking all the while that her friend—from her gorgeous chapeaux to her fine leather shoes—was something of an ass. Never had it crossed Eve's mind that a man of Sam Goldenberg's extreme passions had practiced celibacy for two and a half years. Eve was almost twenty-five years old, and she had several social seasons in the Catskills under her belt. The more she'd talked to other wives during the war, the more she considered herself sophisticated in the ways of men. Eve agreed completely with Miss Dorothy Dix, the seventy-five-year-old newspaper columnist and literary "sob sister." Dix was the author of the famous book *How to Win and Hold a Husband,* and her specific advice concerning wartime infidelity was known to some sixty million readers. While countless husbands "had solaced themselves from the horrors of war by having little affairs with the attractive women they met in their wanderings," Dix wrote, married men "do not take their philandering seriously." Miss Dix (a pen name the columnist had derived years earlier from "Dick," the name of a family slave who saved the ancestral silverware from rampaging Yankee troops) was sure that it was entirely possible for a man to remain "true in heart" even in the act of making love to another woman.

Eve Goldenberg did not believe for a second that this same fidelity of heart prevailed in a woman who made love to another man, nor did anyone advise the soldiers that wifely infidelity over long absences didn't mean much. Some 2,500 New York City soldiers had filed for divorce on grounds of adultery before they even got home.

Eve had never approved of the fickleness of the well-to-do women deposited at Grossinger's or the Edgemont Inn or the other Catskill resorts where she had worked. Husbands would leave, and right away Eve would see their wives flirting with the boys on the staff.

"If I'm going to marry, I will be a true-blue wife," Eve declared. One of the reasons she'd been so hesitant about marrying Sam Goldenberg was that she was determined to be a wife forever.

Eve was sitting directly behind an ornate column at Broadway's Empire Theater the night she suddenly decided to marry Sam. Those who could see were watching Lindsay and Crouse's *Life with Father*— "amusing sketches" about a "despotic parent," as *New York Times* critic Brooks Atkinson described the play. Atkinson said that what made the play's raging father so "hilarious" was the "violence of his temper....He is rugged individualism in full flower...the civilized male in awful grandeur."

For some reason, at the end of the performance, Eve looked at her date for the evening—another young man named Sam—and decided to marry Sam Goldenberg, whom she'd known, from the moment she saw him look at her, was a man madly in love.

Several of Eve's old friends disapproved of her decision. Eve was one of the Bronx girls destined to transcend the neighborhood. Evie Samberg (she used the stage name Eve Saunders) was beautiful, chosen, a golden songbird, a "natural" before she was seven. At ten she won first prize in an open-air singing competition in Central Park with her rendition of the 1924 ballad "Indian Love Call." Eve's heroes were the opera stars Lily Pons and Gladys Swarthout. Pons, a coloratura soprano, was one of the first truly chic modern divas. Swarthout had been considered one of the best-dressed women in America when Eve was younger, the prettiest Carmen ever to grace a stage. Both were small and voluptuous, like Eve. Eve's life was meant to be an adventure.

"How in the world can you marry somebody as plain as Sam Goldenberg?" Eve's friend Nicky asked her.

"Well," Eve said, hiding her irritation, "for one thing, I don't think he's plain."

All Sam's life people told him how much he looked like Humphrey Bogart—especially as Sam and Bogey approached middle age—but to Eve, the match was the actor and future politician George Murphy. Sam wasn't handsome in the blond, sleek Jazz Age style of some of the sharpies Eve had dated back in the Catskills, but there was such a manly force about him that people always looked up when he entered a room. His big, handsome head, topped by an interesting high-crested pompadour, was usually cocked slightly to the side. And he had a similarly cocky, off-center smile that rearranged his face all the way up past brown eyes that could fill a room with light—especially, Eve noticed, when she was in the room.

Sam was stationed at Fort Jackson, Mississippi, when Eve found out she was pregnant. A friend had told her about diaphragms, but Eve only learned later that they had to fit. Camp-following wives, war wives, and younger urban wives in general were not unaware of abortion. The *New York Times* reported the various trials of rogue doctors and other proprietors of "abortion mills." Almost all the trials—three were currently in the news, of a Dr. Elster, a Dr. Frankel, and a Dr. Nisonhoff—concerned botched abortions from which women had died. By some estimates, more than ten thousand women were dying each year from attempted abortions, some of them involving lethal overdoses of quinine drug mixtures that many women believed would end their pregnancies.

Eve pondered an abortion for several weeks, but she couldn't stop thinking that her own mother had considered an abortion when she was pregnant with Eve. Rebecca Samberg told Eve that she'd had a vision in the waiting room of the doctor's office. "My mother—your grandmother—she came to me and told me to go home and have you," Rebecca said.

One evening, when Eve was eight months pregnant, a strong limb rose high and swift from within her, propelling an open copy of *Gone with the Wind* off her swollen belly and onto the floor. Years later Eve would recall the swift kick as a forewarning.

Her water broke halfway through *Holy Matrimony*, a movie starring

Monty Woolley and Gracie Fields, the actress whose heavy English accent—especially when she sang "White Cliffs of Dover"—Eve could mimic almost perfectly. Eve was sitting beside Sam's younger sister, Blanche, in the middle of the last row of the balcony at the crowded Loew's Paradise Theater. She was so close to the theater's great ceiling glittering with tiny lights that she felt like she was up with the stars.

A young soldier rose to help clear the way out of the theater. For all twenty-four hours of the labor that followed, Eve was certain she was dying. Not once had anyone informed her that it hurt to bear a child. Eve cried out and waited for death at the Bronx Hospital while thirty Russian divisions broke through Nazi lines at the Dnieper Bend; she screamed for mercy while American subs sank seven Japanese vessels.

Late on November 14, 1943, Eve named her baby for Susan Hayward, the beautiful daughter of a Coney Island carnival barker. Hayward had only just missed the chance to play Scarlett O'Hara, and Eve loved the way the actress wore her hair and the hint of wickedness she saw when she watched her on screen.

Eve and the ever-circling grandmothers agreed that Susan was beautiful. Rebecca, Yetta, and Eve were also sure that Susan was brilliant. Susan was their little Scarlett, all petulant and precocious and adored.

Susan was almost two on the November day her father came home. She was old enough to toddle at her mother's feet and laugh as if she understood her mother's jokes.

Frieda Brown dropped by that day, and "Miss Full-of-It," as Eve referred to her, once again threatened to divorce Barney if he'd been anywhere near another woman.

"Has Your Husband Come Home to the Right Woman?" taunted a recent *Ladies' Home Journal.* "Will you know how to kiss him? Will making love be strange? Will the passion be gone?"

Questions of passion had so overtaken Eve's thoughts that when she heard her mother scream from the top of the stoop, and when she looked at the women she was talking to and saw their hands covering their mouths and their eyes cast over her shoulder, full of tears, she knew what was happening but felt nothing at all.

She finally managed to turn toward the nearby street corner where Sam Goldenberg seemed to be moving in circles. He made a final round and began to walk toward her, each stride longer and faster than the one before it, a huge duffel bag up on his shoulder as though it weighed nothing at all. As he came closer, she could see his eyes moving down to the baby stroller.

People seemed to be piling out of all the houses on Kelly Street; they were running down the block to surround the little family in front of 1052. Several women were weeping out loud by the time Eve found her husband's gaze.

Sam started grinning, patting his front pocket. "We got a stake," he said.

Then he opened his arms.

Less than an hour later, Eve went into her bedroom to change. She looked at the big-shouldered red woolen suit with the bright buttons and the little crossed bars over the pockets, the one she'd worn to the registry office when the war had barely begun. She was reaching for the slate-blue dress Sam loved when she felt strong hands encircle her from behind.

"The communion between two bodies, the ultimate symbol of their oneness with each other and the testless stuff of life," Betsy Barton had suggested to the readers of *McCall's*, "can heal all the wounds of mind and heart."

Afterward Eve stared at Sam. "Okay, Sammy, I don't want a list of names. I just want to know the name of the country."

Sam saw the smile she was holding inside, so he began to laugh, hugging his true-blue war wife. They laughed together for a long time as Sam told Eve just enough to assure her that it hadn't really mattered, just as Dorothy Dix promised. Everything—everything—would be fine.

"So was there anybody who didn't fool around?" Eve asked.

"Only one guy in the whole unit that I can think of," Sam said. "Some character from around here named Barney Brown."

———✦———

Sam slept hard for a few hours and awoke as his little girl strolled into the room. "She carries herself like some kind of debutante or something," Eve had said in a letter. Eve wrote that Susan regularly amazed passengers on New York City buses and subways by "reading" out loud, as rapidly and clearly as an adult, from memorized books she occasionally held upside down.

Sam smiled down at Susan, and her brown eyes flashed back full of defiance. In a voice almost unnaturally duplicating the force and cadence of adult speech, Susan declaimed, "Don't...you...*touch* my mommy's pajamas!"

She never stopped staring at her father as she spoke, and Sam felt himself reeling away, even though he couldn't move at all. He looked down at his daughter and saw the eyes of war. He felt those eyes backing him close to what he knew was the edge of his own family. It made him think back to France in the winter of 1944.

One frigid morning, Sam had awakened to find that he could barely walk because his feet were so cold. He saw smoke rising from a chimney atop a tiny stone farmhouse and hobbled to the door. Inside, dozens of GIs were sleeping in a space no more than twenty-five feet square. Sam crawled over them to the fireplace, where a French family of five huddled together in silence.

Sam moved close to their fire. He turned to warm his back, and after a moment he felt the family staring at him. Some of the other soldiers were staring at him too. Sam looked down at his left pocket and noticed a dark blue stain. His bar mitzvah pen, the Sheaffer with the gold tip and the white dot, had frozen and cracked during what may have been the coldest night of his life. Sam watched as the dark stain spread over his heart, and then he looked up at the French children cowering close to their parents. He stared at them staring back at him with their family eyes of utter fear.

Family.

A family, to Sam's mother, was something formed and managed under siege. Yetta Goldenberg seemed to believe a family required any number of rules and immutable orthodoxies. Sam, Sylvia, Blanche, and little Freddy, nine years younger than Sam, all grew up with the sound of their parents in full "tiger fight" in the background whenever Joe was around. Papa Joe and Yetta both came from families at once glacial and volcanic, families in which relatives didn't speak for decades over slights that nobody could quite recall.

As a little boy Sam dreamed of a family that didn't fight. He dreamed of a wife who knew how to kiss and make up, one adept at drawing joy from a day. This, Sam had thought so many times during the long war, he surely had. Some of the young army fathers told him that the "modern" way was to treat your children like friends. Fathers need not hold forth as if from the mount. New thinking—informed by the slight leaching of psychoanalytic dogma from professional spheres— indicated that a father and his kids could be buddies. Sam liked the sound of that.

Sam Goldenberg came back alive from the war, and now that he had broken the ice with Eve he was able to say that there was only one thing he wanted from the rest of his life: a normal family. That was all a million other guys who'd survived the family degradations of the

Depression and the harrowing experience of the war wanted too. Sam wasn't after greatness or fame or more wealth than was required to create a family success story.

But as he lay on the bed the day he came home, Sam looked into a pair of eyes just twenty-eight inches from the floor, and he saw nothing familial there at all. He thought he saw violence in his little girl's eyes.

Sam hadn't seen any of the articles about "getting a good start with your baby." One doctor, speaking on behalf of the Rehabilitation Division of something called the National Committee for Mental Hygiene, told a writer for the *New York Times* that the returning soldiers must give their relationships with their kids some time. A lot of men had suddenly turned from boyfriends into husbands into fathers, with very little in between. A *McCall's* article, "A Father Comes Home," featured a soldier named Bill Gordon and his daughter, Susan: "Susan was only a baby when her father went to war. She isn't afraid of him now, but she must have time to welcome him in her own way."

All Sam knew was that in the family he craved, a father loved and was loved right back again.

Sam couldn't take his eyes from Susan's. He was back home in the womb of the familiar, to make the best American family of all time. And yet, just like a thousand other soldier-fathers looking down at a thousand other daughters that day, Sam felt Susan stare him against the ropes. In a voice clear and sure, she said, "Go away!"

1946

Twelve hundred dollars in craps winnings was not insignificant to a family man who'd gone back to work—less than a day after civilian reentry—for a dollar an hour (with twenty hours' overtime guaranteed). "This money is gonna help us get a jump on things," Sam had assured Eve when they talked about their plans. But now, as Sam pondered the painful reason for his visit to Mount Sinai Hospital in Manhattan, he faced the prospect of parting with a major portion of his winnings to get his behind repaired.

"I insist that my patients register in the private pavilion of the hospital," Dr. A. A. Berg said, jotting some notes on a pad. "I will agree to perform this procedure for one thousand dollars."

Sam, Eve, and Sam's sister Sylvia all looked over to Yetta Goldenberg, who'd carefully assembled a demeanor at once humble and unashamed before leading the family delegation to see Albert Berg, a man still regarded as one of the finest surgeons in the country at the age of seventy-three. Chief of surgery at Mount Sinai and president of the International College of Surgeons, an institution he'd helped found, A. A. Berg was a sainted patron of the New York Public Library on Fifth Avenue. During the two years before the attack on Pearl Harbor alone, Berg had donated some 24,000 rare books to the library, a magnificent collection worth many millions of dollars.

A. A. Berg was born in America seven years after the end of the Civil War. The doctor now lived in a brownstone on East Seventy-third Street, a few doors off Fifth Avenue. His clubs were the woody and overstuffed Harmonie and Grolier.

The Goldenbergs sat quietly before Dr. Berg, an "uptown Jew" (his working-class coreligionists' shorthand for his assimilated station). Sam looked at the surgeon's carefully trimmed beard, at the tiny red rose in his lapel, and at his rather skeptical expression.

"Why didn't you have the cyst removed in the army?"

"There wasn't time," Sam said. "There was the war. Since then I've been at work."

First and foremost, Sam believed, a family must be financed.

A few weeks before the cyst—a legacy, most vets agreed, of too many nights sleeping on frozen ground—finally made it impossible for Sam to stand as well as sit, he was working deep in a subcellar beneath the garment district in Manhattan. Sam glanced away as his partner opened a reddish iron vault crammed with oversized electrical switches. Apparently the heavy latch briefly spanned the tops of two copper bars inside the box. Even with his back turned, Sam knew that the white flash produced by the inadvertent error was brighter than the aerial flares that had turned night into day during the war. The flash instantly made Sam's partner a blind man for a day.

"Sit here!" Sam barked, leaning the man against a wall. Sam sprinted off in search of a six-hundred-amp fuse. He knew the flash was only the most spectacular manifestation of an electrical short that had surely shut down all the sewing machines on the floors above. The machines were never shut down.

Sam had still been biding his time in Frankfurt when Harry Truman ended most of the rationing programs, unleashing a long-impacted national will to retail purchasing. The economic consequences meant that the tricks of Sam's trade had to be performed fifteen hours a day without a net. The "juice"—the flow, the light—could never be cut off. Sam's specialty was "working live," which meant that he spent most of his long days in the dark, inches away from a pyrotechnical death.

It was an old buddy from the neighborhood, Harry Green, who had first told Sam about the trades growing up around what Depression kids still called the "miracle" of electricity. Harry was a tough kid like Sam. Maybe even tougher. Harry's name was briefly inscribed in *Ripley's Believe It or Not!* because he once flattened his opponent in a Golden Gloves boxing competition while the opening bell was still ringing. For several years Harry held the record for fastest amateur knockout of all time.

Harry had a philosophy of economic advancement that was shared by many boys who were poor and Jewish during the 1930s. "If you want to move up quick," was how Harry put it, "you gotta find work that other people are scared to death of."

At the time, the three-wire, hot-legged DC current that ran into most New York City buildings and homes was so rich with amperage that it could weld a careless soul to a wall. Many city dwellers of the first half of the century feared electrocution as generations before them feared disease and generations to come would fear atomic incineration.

If there was such a thing as a natural electrician, Sam Goldenberg probably qualified. Confronted by any man-made artifact he didn't understand, Sam would take it apart and put it back together until the mystery was gone. It was known all over the Springhurst district of the South Bronx, where the Goldenbergs moved from the Lower East Side when Sam was eight, that if you brought Sammy Goldenberg an orange crate and a roller skate he could throw together a superior scooter. He wouldn't even charge. Sam dazzled fellow trainees in the army by stripping and rebuilding an M-1 rifle behind his back while blindfolded, only a day or two after the weapons were handed out.

At seventeen, Sam had dropped out of Stuyvesant High School, the elite alma mater of James Cagney and various winners of the Nobel Prize in medicine and chemistry. The test scores that helped him gain admission to Stuyvesant were among the highest in New York City, but Papa Joe was unemployed again and the family needed money.

The cavalryman Joe Goldenberg had helped shovel out several of the subway tunnels underneath Manhattan Island, and he'd shoveled again in front of coal fires aboard the Staten Island ferry. But for most of Sam's childhood his father worked less than two months of the year. Few family memories came back to Sam quite as wintry and sad as the sight of Papa Joe leaving early for the New York fur district—"the markets"—there to "shape up" in long lines, waiting for the chance to sew or scrape skins for a day or two.

Sam was born close to a time of factory childhoods, when the rights of parents extended morally and legally to the earnings of their children. Sam always figured it was because of this sense of entitlement and the specter of starvation that Yetta Goldenberg told him to quit school and go to work full-time.

By the time he was twelve he'd already had a part-time job carting sacks of buttons around midtown Manhattan. The loads were so heavy that one of his shoulders would droop slightly for the rest of his life. Sam would hand his two dollars in earnings over to Yetta, and Yetta would give him back a nickel. Sam later said that his recollections of being young and poor were like "permanent scars" on his body, but those who got close to him thought the memories were more like open wounds.

As a vet and father, Sam could have collected ninety dollars a month while attending college under the GI Bill. But Sam was not alone in thinking another depression was coming after the war. He was determined never to be cold and poor again, so when an old buddy from the electric trade called to say a job was open wiring up factories for the Electric Wiring Installation Company in midtown, Sam went to work— his first morning back home.

Roosevelt had talked about sixty million new jobs after the war, and because Sam loved FDR he wanted to believe it, but Roosevelt was dead by the time Sam got home. He'd died on April 12, 1945, a sunny day in central Germany that Sam would never forget because he stopped working long enough to cry. In a time when too many fathers had been beaten down by circumstances in full sight of their sons, Roosevelt was a father who would not bend. He was a giant of a man in Sam's estimation—even in a wheelchair. During coffee breaks (a new feature of the work day gleaned from the British, who seemed irritated if they couldn't stop fighting during tea time), Sam often interjected that at twenty-seven he'd lived to see the worst president of the United States (Hoover) and the best. Sam would observe in later years that he was only half right.

Every time Sam heard Roosevelt's elegant speaking voice replayed over the radio, he'd "get a glow."

"And I say all this about Roosevelt as a man whose family never took anything from the New Deal," he'd add. The public largess was for other families, Yetta Goldenberg said—those less proud than hers.

"A thousand dollars?" Yetta said quietly, as if she was considering Dr. Berg's kind offer. "*Doc*-tor Berg," she continued in her more typical tone of adamantine resolve, "my son Sammy has only just returned home from the war in Europe. He doesn't have one thousand *pennies*, let alone one thousand dollars. We don't have that kind of money."

There was defiance in Yetta's voice. Eve sat across from her mother-in-law, amazed by how indifferent Yetta was to the courtly refinements of Dr. A. A. Berg. Yetta's self-possession was hard to figure in light of her inability to shed the tribal fears and superstitions that Eve knew to dominate her mother-in-law's days.

Yetta kept the dietary laws of her shtetl childhood and expected the same of others, but she never went to synagogue. Eve endeavored to prepare kosher food for Yetta—which meant groveling theatrically before a kosher butcher everyone in the neighborhood knew to be a crook (the same man was clearly terrorized by the sight of Yetta entering his store)—but nothing was ever good enough. Yetta's constantly offended dignity, her prideful unhappiness, seemed a natural state that she returned to out of instinct.

"You know what the worst of it is?" Eve would complain to Sam. "She doesn't think being Jewish is funny."

In her Catskill days, Eve would come on stage during a vaudeville act in a tight white dress, singing in full voice, "I'm burning! I'm burning!"—at which point two guys would enter with seltzer bottles and spray her down. The crowds dissolved. They screamed with joy.

"We wrote the book on humor. It's how we deal with life," Eve would say to Sam. "If I had to give up all but one of my senses, I would hold on to my sense of humor. Not being able to laugh, even at myself—this would kill me." Eve thought many great Americans—look at Mark Twain, look at Will Rogers—would also have died without humor, and they weren't even Jews.

Sam had spent more time trading punches over being Jewish than laughing about it. As a little boy he'd been in plenty of inter-ethnic street brawls, and in the army he'd fought with a semiliterate anti-Semitic coal miner, a veteran of bloody miners' strikes in Harlan County, Kentucky. Sam might have otherwise admired the man—an officer—for his capacity for hard work if he hadn't hated Jews.

"Hey, Jew!" he kept yelling at the only other Jewish guy in Sam's company. "Go get my cap!"

"How can you let him talk to you like that?" Sam raged at the victim.

"Because I don't care," the soldier said.

The burly Kentuckian ordered Sam to scrub down the barracks with a toothbrush. Sam approached until he was inches away from the man. "No," he said.

Conviction on the insubordination charges enumerated during Sam's court-martial carried a six-month sentence in the stockade, but because of the exigencies of war Sam got a bad mark on his military record and was fined a sum equivalent to three months' pay.

Two years later, when German snipers began a systematic decimation of the American officer corps—second lieutenants were tearing the insignia off their helmets and uniforms and still getting shot down so often that Sam figured the Nazis were offering a bonus—General Eisenhower ordered all soldiers of Sam's grade with an IQ above 110 to be sent through Officer Training School. Sam considered the order an invitation to graduate as a duck in a shooting gallery.

"I can't be an officer, sir," Sam said to a Jewish kid fresh from West Point, the major who had handed him his orders. "I've been court-martialed, sir. Check my record."

"You have to go," the major said. "I mean...you ought to go."

"I've been court-martialed," Sam said.

"I can't make you become an officer, but you should...because you're Jewish," the young major said. "This war is being fought for the Jews."

By the summer of 1946 everyone in the country was talking about the war against the Jews. As details about the European concentration camps emerged, Sam and Eve talked about the horror every night. "I didn't believe it when I first heard," Eve admitted.

"Neither did I, even while I was overseas," said Sam. "I thought human beings were civilized."

Neither Sam nor Eve discussed what would come to be known as the Holocaust with Mama Yetta Goldenberg, but they often wondered what she was thinking while she hunkered down next to the radio speaker as it poured out the proceedings of the Nuremberg Trials. Yetta was twelve when she came to America from Poland, a nation with a prewar Jewish population of 3.5 million, currently home to less than one hundred intact Jewish families—not one of which included any of Yetta's brothers, cousins, aunts, uncles, or childhood friends.

As the visual images of corpse mountains were added to the sound of the voices of Goering and Keitel (whom Hitler had once complimented for being "faithful as a dog"), the issue of a Jewish state in Palestine was also much in the news. Despite all the moral reconsideration apparently prompted by the plight of the Jews, Sam was not in the least surprised to read about a poll indicating that one in five GIs based in Europe believed the Germans were justified in persecuting the Jews.

But for all the persistent evidence of anti-Semitism, Sam and Eve sensed that in general the economic mainstream had never before been so accessible to people like them. The young Goldenbergs entertained no fantasies of rising to the status of a Dr. A. A. Berg. Sam didn't even allow himself to dream of being part of the American middle class—which at the time, to a young Jewish workingman like Sam, meant "private property" and security that could be measured in dollars. Sam, Eve, and many of their young friends in the Bronx wanted a "private life" insofar as that meant freedom from the abiding fears and constraints of the past. Sam's aspiration was to feed his family regularly through hard and steady work. "Economics," he said, "is the science of having enough to eat." If his economic freedom had once been limited by hatred and fear, the hope for a private, prosperous future appeared strangely bright by the middle of 1946. Perhaps it was a function of Gentile guilt, a kind of mass atonement, but for great numbers of young American Jews like Sam and Eve, who'd grown up with the fact and constant assumption of anti-Semitism, the terrible images of corpses coexisted with a gathering sense of hope.

"Well...all right," said Dr. Albert Berg, chuckling slightly. "This boy went off to fight for me. I suppose I should do something for him."

Berg operated on Sam for one hundred dollars, though the balance of Sam's craps winnings went to defray the cost of his two-week recuperation in what he called "that overpriced hotel," Mount Sinai Hospital. From his bed, Sam often spied his famous surgeon bounding across the hall to pinch a passing nurse. Sam also noticed that the old doctor worked all the time. Some nights Berg slept in an empty bed at the hospital.

Sam respected a man who knew how to work. His forced two weeks of idleness kept him up late into the night. Work had ordered Sam's days for most of his life. Not working made him jumpy. Religion or war or love might baffle, but at work a man could take control. Sam couldn't wait to get out of the hospital. He'd never had so much to do.

Eve believed her second experience of childbirth was much less traumatic than the first because Sam was out in the waiting room with the other fathers. The abiding terror of Susan's birth did not return, though for some reason the violent struggle of labor caused Eve's neck to swell with a hideous goiterlike protuberance worthy, she thought, of a full page in *National Geographic*.

Lorraine—named for Laraine Day, a rising movie star of the moment, and Sam's current favorite next to the mysterious Paulette Goddard—was dragged out into the light of the delivery room at the end of a pair of lengthy "high" forceps. She looked like a little Eskimo. Lorraine's thick hair was shiny and black; her skin was darker than any other Goldenberg or Samberg child's; and she had what one of the nurses called "exotic eyes" (though one eye would always droop slightly from the harsh application of sterile pliers).

Eve had once again been at the movies when she went into labor.

Tyrone Power's character in the epic film version of W. Somerset Maugham's *The Razor's Edge* was on the verge of discovering the lofty, spiritually essential stuff of a brand-new life when Eve's water broke. Lorraine was born on Friday the thirteenth of December. She weighed in at seven eleven. "Look at the lucky little Eskimo," another nurse said.

Eve brought Lorraine home on a day cold enough for Susan to wear the luxurious coat Papa Joe Goldenberg had made for her at the little fur ranch he owned before the war. After so many years of either doing or being turned away from the putrid work of scraping future mink stoles and coats, the patriarch had been determined to raise the elite carnivores himself, in a rural county two hours north of the Bronx. The brief business venture was something Sam Goldenberg would have loved, but he was too much the responsible young man to stake his future on an old man who confused work and dreams.

Susan loved the feel of fabric and fur. She was also in love with her dolls. Nobody—not even Eve—was allowed to touch Susan's dolls. "Get *away* from my children!" she'd yell at anyone who came too close. Susan was a pretty, slender three-year-old with brown bangs that stopped halfway down her forehead. In the summer you could see that her skin had an olive tint like Sam's.

The consensus in baby Lorraine's extended family was that she was "adorable." She was not, however, "precious." Only Lorraine's cousin—a daughter born within a few days of her to Sam's sister Sylvia—was precious. Officially named Carol, the baby everyone called "Presh" was as blond, blue-eyed, and Scandinavian-looking as Lorraine was dark and exotic.

Eve watched closely when Sylvia and Yetta looked down at Lorraine. "Hmm…charming," they'd say. "Gorgeous! Precious!" they would enthuse after turning to gaze into the other cradle, their expressions changing so radically as to suggest the twin masks of Drama.

"She can see them smirking," Eve said to Sam after Yetta, Sylvia, and Presh went home. Tears filled her eyes. "Young as she is, she can feel it. I'm sure of it, Sam."

Eve couldn't forgive Yetta for her overt condescension to Eve's parents over the five years of her marriage. The Goldenberg women still referred to the Sambergs' dank and depressing apartment, where Sam and Eve lived, as "the nightmare." Now Eve stood by as Yetta, normally consistent in her preference for all things Jewish, seemed to choose one grandchild over another simply because Presh looked like a Kewpie doll parody of a non-Jew, like a baby shiksa.

The rejection made Eve want to circle the nuclear family wagons. She wanted to move away or scream out that family love should be withheld from no child.

Eve worried herself to the point of tears over the love she believed others were denying Lorraine. Sam worried constantly about family sustenance and had to keep reminding himself not to lose his concentration while working amid live wires.

1947

Nineteen forty-seven was a big year for worrying about family.

There was a spate of interrogative articles—"Whither Family Life?" "Can the Home Be Saved?" "Are Families Passé?" "What's Wrong with the Family?"—though usually in intellectually oriented magazines Sam and Eve and their friends didn't "take." It wasn't until a long article appeared in *Life* magazine—"The American Family in Trouble"—that many novice postwar families realized what dire straits they were in.

For one thing, *Life* reported that the American family was becoming "tiny." There were simply not enough new babies to keep a great nation great. Beyond that, the family was "atomizing," losing its cohesive character and breaking up into its component parts: "Its members do little more than sleep and eat together....The individual now looks outside his home for his interests," the article lamented.

Though a number of family experts feared the consequences of an apparently plummeting postwar birth rate, the concept of the "atomized," newly individualistic American family was borrowed by *Life's* editors from a Harvard sociologist named Carle Zimmerman, who'd recently predicted in his book *Family and Civilization* that if "familistic" values were not restored the institution would disintegrate by the end of the twentieth century. From there, Zimmerman contended, American civilization as a whole would experience a fall on the order of the decline of classical Greece or Rome.

The first twelve pages of the widely discussed jeremiad in *Life* were given over to visual and literary depictions of Zimmerman's "three main types of American family." A very large and sober-looking Ozark Mountain family represented the homey, hokey, loving, multigenerational "trustee" family type ("... to ease his womenfolks' work Russell also bought an electric washing machine"). A churchgoing family from Enid, Oklahoma, represented Zimmerman's "domestic type": The Frantzes of Enid were "cohesive not from economic necessity, but by choice." By praying, shopping, fishing, and reading *together,* as the photographs and text underscored, the Frantz clan was "consciously" close-knit.

The third type of American family was represented by the "atomistic" Parkers of a Long Island suburb outside New York. The Parkers were shown sitting together in their living room, each of them wearing what could charitably be described as a hollow expression. They were all staring at the family telephone, which dominated the foreground of a full-page photograph. "As the telephone rings," the caption writer noted, "the Parker family look up in unison, wondering which member of the family is being paged for a bridge game, a golf date, or a baby sitting arrangement. The telephone has made the modern home a communications center for outside activities and clearing house for outside services."

The Parkers were a family, it seemed, only out of some soulless expediency. Antifamilial suburban automatons, modern Americans filled with self-love, they lived only to atomize. Never a magazine to abjure judgment at this high point in its popular sway, *Life* passed a harsh condemnation on the Parkers of Long Island, though as time passed, it would appear weirdly prescient.

Thirteen pages into this unsettling article, an austere photograph of Carle Zimmerman accompanied his claim that unbridled individualism was at the root of the epidemic "nihilism in family behavior." On the next page Zimmerman's distinguished Harvard colleague Pitirim Sorokin prophesied that "the main sociocultural functions of the family will further decrease, until the family becomes a mere incidental cohabitation of male and female, while the home will become a mere overnight parking place, mainly for sex relationships."

The anguished family experts speaking out during the first years after World War II—sociologists, psychologists, social workers, medical doctors, and government policymakers among them—represented the latest in a pattern of intermittent bouts of intense professional concern over the "sweet asylum" of family dating back to the eighteenth- and nineteenth-century founding of modern social science. Observations similar to Professor Zimmerman's had been made by Emile Durkheim, the "father of sociology," who worried toward the end of the nineteenth century over the new French families dominated by what he called "personal motives."

The debate flared up again in the postwar era, with the intellectual middle ground as empty as always. Something about the nature of family—"society's bulwark," the "bedrock," the "anvil," the "cradle," the "irreducible cell"...the list goes on—had caused powerfully concentrated minds to be drawn to intellectual extremes.

Within five years the American family would be celebrated and extolled as never before, and Cassandras like Zimmerman would be relegated to the library stacks for another twenty years.

———◆———

The young mother of two, Eve Goldenberg—and most of the other moms steering carriages and strollers through the handsome parks of the Bronx—felt well insulated from the imminent decline and fall of *the* American family because *her* American family had the aid and comfort of a forty-four-year-old pediatrician with a few years of psychiatric training: Benjamin Spock.

Three years before the publication of Spock's *Common Sense Book of Baby and Child Care*, Eve had defied conventional wisdom by picking Susan up whenever she cried. "It makes me nervous," she'd explain to relatives when they urged the rigid behaviorist dispensation of cuddles and bottles prescribed by psychologist John Watson, who had counseled two generations of parents never to "hug and kiss" their children and to "shake hands with them in the morning," and who believed picking up a bawling infant would create a grown-up with no self-control.

"I'm sorry," Eve would say, "but nothing that hurts me so much can be good for the baby."

And then came Spock. His book was only a year old, but it would be sold eight million times over the next nine years. The text was so ubiquitous by 1956—when Eve's last baby was born—that an estimated one in four children was being raised by "Spock-doting parents."

Dr. Spock, Eve read, believed she'd done the right thing by trusting her "instincts" when Susan cried. Dr. Spock's own mother "gave herself completely" to young Benjamin and his siblings, and his baby book, full of intimations that it was okay for a mother to unleash the full force of her love, read as if it had been written with that doting mother looking over her son's shoulder.

The proper "management" of children and family, Dr. Spock and Eve's own instincts agreed, would emerge organically. Eve would respond to a year of family worry by making a home that was clean and beautiful, and by doting on her little doll queen, her Eskimo baby, and her passionate husband who worked day and night for them.

But since Eve considered being a good mother her job—her part of the deal, like Sam's hard labor—she knew she would have to get away from the larger Samberg and Goldenberg families. Unlike Mama Spock, Eve's mother and mother-in-law glared gloomily over her own shoulder. Carle Zimmerman's admonitions notwithstanding, Eve and Sam became convinced that family happiness required them to get a place of their own.

Eve wandered with Susan and Lorraine in tow for miles in search of a vacant apartment. Most of the Bronx buildings she visited still contained families "doubled up" by a nationwide housing shortage of nearly five million units in the wake of the war.

Eve Goldenberg was in the habit of singing out loud everywhere she went. She'd fill elevators and bakeries with Jeanette MacDonald love songs, buses and subways with Al Jolson tunes. But after many weeks of looking for a place to live, she found she couldn't sing. She would approach the inevitable circles of mothers and children on each of the colorful residential blocks, alive with flowers and bright paint, and she would try to tell a joke or chat. "I'm desperate," she'd blurt out. "Does anyone know of a vacant place?"

"I do," a lady finally said. "It's on a good block on Hunt's Point Avenue. But the furniture's for sale." This last euphemism meant that a secondary cash transaction would be required to secure the lease. But Eve knew Hunt's Point Avenue, which bisected the peninsular section of the Bronx that protruded into the East River just below the mouth of Long Island Sound.

Number 737 faced a grassy vacant lot. It wasn't far from the end of the trolley line. "There's even a little park," Eve told Sam when he grimaced at the thought of parting with five hundred dollars under the table.

"It stinks of urine," Sam said when they walked through the big fourth-floor apartment. "Some real pigs have lived here."

But the apartment was full of sunlight, and Sam believed a family needed light. Toward the end of the war, he had befriended a little French boy who took him to meet his parents and his sisters. They had recently emerged from three years in a windowless room in a house owned by someone who had decided to risk hiding a Jewish family. "All of them had turned this terrible shade of white," Sam told Eve, breaking his silence on the war because of the obvious application at hand. "They were the color of milk—like they'd been bleached of life."

After they moved in Sam would come home from work and continue replacing all the fixtures in the apartment. He patched the holes in the walls, painted, and Eve joined him in scrubbing away an odor Sam called "the smell of people who don't care." Whenever Sam resurrected old things—machines he found in the trash or the work of some forgotten craftsman—he would pause to lament the lost nobility of a job done right. Most people didn't appreciate quality anymore, but Sam knew he always would, whether it cost him time and money or not.

While Sam worked, Eve assembled her first kitchen. It was a long, narrow cooking space, but Eve couldn't wait to make her first batch of mashed potatoes, so laden with fragrant fried onions and pepper that they had been known to make people moan. In her new kitchen Eve would take command.

When curtains were up and plants positioned in each square of sunlight, the neighbors from the other floors of 737 Hunt's Point Avenue were invited in to look. "You've turned a filthy apartment into a dollhouse," one neighbor said.

After they were gone, Sam went over to stand by the window, just to take in the light. The windows of Sam's childhood were dark. The windows of one frigid family apartment back on Houston Street looked out on a five-story tenement an arm's length across the alley.

Sam closed his eyes and allowed himself to feel that the family was about to soar.

Since the end of the war, J. Edgar Hoover, director of the FBI, had been warning the "unwitting" veteran about impulsive purchases. The bulldog-jowled crime fighter in Washington decried "unscrupulous fakers, who have been cudgeling their brains for evil little tricks with which to dupe the veteran."

Sam was not a young man easily duped, at least in the realm of machines, but he still ended up the owner of a rattling heap of scrap metal that had once upon a time, back in 1936, been a brand-new two-door Plymouth. It was gray as an old sewer grating, and the sole hint of a designer's hand was an ever so slight backward sweep of the vertical strips on the front grille.

Sam paid out every spare cent he had to get that Plymouth, and then he poured in another two hundred dollars to rebuild the engine.

But when it was all done, the family Goldenberg had an automobile fit to "motorize" into the finest of autumn afternoons.

Sam, Eve, Susan, Susan's family of selected dolls, and baby Lorraine would pile into the Plymouth and take off on long drives on Sunday afternoons when Sam didn't have to work. They would pause for "auto trunk picnics" along the way, just one of the "adventures" that were part of "driving pleasure." They rode along parkways snaking out from the Bronx and specifically designed for "recreational driving." They followed the landscaped old parkways to Westchester County and similar places—the suburbs—where the inhabitants were rich enough to live far away from work.

Soon there would be great "superhighways" of the sort Sam had read about in articles describing the General Motors Futurama exhibit at the 1939 World's Fair. Sam was excited by the thought of a future of broad highways—straight shots through Zion. With a car and clean stretch of road, a man and his family could be free of *all* former moorings.

If they stopped at a park or a zoo, Sam would often stand as close as he dared to Susan, wondering as he wondered so often if she'd finally "decided to accept him." By now Sam had compared notes with many other men whose children had "latched onto others" during the war. His was not the only two-year-old who'd turned against her father, but she was four now, and Sam thought it was high time for Susan to come back to him. It was still hard to tell where she stood, and Sam—veteran of a family that withdrew from shared feeling and even the most basic aspects of civility for years on end—simply could not force himself to be the first to show his hand.

So he glanced often into the rearview mirror or gazed across tables and picnic blankets at his little girl's eyes, telling himself that all a father could do was keep looking and hope.

1948

Once a week Eve sang sweet songs to the madmen at the Veterans Administration Hospital a few trolley stops away on Kingsbridge Road. She held hands gone pillowy-soft from disuse and whispered jokes in ears that had never stopped ringing from the sound of bombs. Eyes haunted, encircled by bruises from the drugs Eve saw attendants forcing on the young vets, they shuffled along the feculent hallways of the old hospital because their shoes had no laces, and they walked with one hand holding up their pants because they weren't allowed to have belts.

Eve took home an image of their mouths still agape, still amazed by whatever horror had made them this way.

As soon as she walked into the apartment she would start to weep. She couldn't stop crying for such a long time that she began to wonder if everything that terrified her about World War II was coming back through the demented eyes of those boys. She felt such a terrible pain for them that she sometimes wondered if she was going mad too.

"Eve, please," Sam said when she'd get home. "You don't have to go back. Eve, you're a volunteer."

Eve had writhed in her seat throughout *The Snake Pit*, an Olivia de Havilland movie about an insane asylum. "When there's more sick ones than well ones," the head nurse in the movie says, "then, by golly, the sick ones will lock the well ones up."

"It's like I got a casualty on my hands, Eve," Sam said one day when she burst into tears after coming home from the VA hospital. "What if you break down? Huh? How'm I gonna work and take care of the children at the same time?"

Eve looked at Sam and saw that he was scared.

Harry Truman spoke to the nation on the radio: "The moral force of women has always had a wholesome influence upon the character of civilization," the president said. "Women care more for people than for dollars, more for healthy children than fat dividends.…Women want a world in which we sow and harvest the seeds of a good life instead of the seeds of war."

Facing a strong challenge from Republican Thomas E. Dewey, governor of New York, Truman wanted the good women of America to vote for him come November, but this was not the first time he'd argued that women could mitigate the harshness of a world that was essentially the responsibility of men. Noting the barely audible talk of "women's rights" in certain elite realms of the Republic, Harry Truman dismissed the idea as "a lot of hooey." Women should see to the work of shoring up "fundamental human values." What women did best, the President believed, was to care.

The American Hospital Association was currently organizing some three hundred thousand American women into a new volunteer force dedicated to helping injured vets. Three hundred national organizations now had wings for women willing to take care of hospitalized GIs. Remembering with sadness how veterans were "forgotten" so quickly after World War I, General Omar Bradley, war hero and former director of the Veterans Administration, was quoted as saying that Americans "don't mean to forget."

Eve wanted to keep helping. If just one of the boys who could have been Sam heard just one of her songs, she thought the pain worth her while, but her behavior alarmed Sam. She wondered if that was fair. If she was so unhappy only after going to the hospital, it might have been different, but it seemed she lost control more often than that.

Every few weeks Eve got so "nervous," as she put it, that she felt as though some seismic force were shaking her face and hands. She felt the walls closing in like some scene in a movie, and when she cried her tears came in great crashing waves that just wouldn't stop. For fifty years psychiatrists had been writing articles about "the nervous housewife" that neither Eve nor any of her friends had ever seen, and "nervousness" was still an all-purpose clinical and theoretical term. At a conference of family professionals in Los Angeles, Dr. Harry Friedgood of UCLA reported that epidemic nervousness in American women might cause a physiological reaction leading to sterility.

It would be another twenty years before Eve recognized these black episodes as aspects of "premenstrual syndrome," a far from rare biological phenomenon that might have had something to do with the strange thoughts that came to her in 1948: harsh reminiscences of a chaotic childhood and vivid daydreams that she was hurting Sam.

Not long after Eve agreed to give up at the VA, she put her coat on and told Sam she was going out to the movies.

"Nah," he said, "come on, stay in."

Baby-sitters were hard to come by for young couples who struck out from their parental homes. Sam and Eve took turns going to the movies.

"It's my turn!" Eve yelled. Then she stormed out the door and stomped to the bus stop.

Eve was holding her ticket when she was struck by what she suddenly considered her consummate selfishness. She cashed in the ticket and rushed home. Sam was sitting clenched and defensive on the horse-hair sofa. It took longer than usual to draw him out of the Goldenberg mire. It took longer than usual to replenish the light in his eyes.

⋯⋯

During June Sam drove Eve and the girls to a resort in the Catskills. A few weeks earlier Lorraine had scratched a chicken pox scab hidden under her thick, dark hair, and before the resulting infection finally responded to massive doses of penicillin, Eve could part her little girl's hair and gaze so far into a small hole that she was certain she could see Lorraine's skull. Eve stayed up night after night holding moist compresses to her one-year-old's head. She thought about how her own mother's concept of motherhood might have been formed by living in a time when children so often died.

Eve had also begun to have recurrent nightmares about hurting Sam—or at least she would find him hurt and assume, still inside the dream, that it was she who'd caused his injury.

"You deserve a rest," Sam said, dropping Eve and the girls off before driving back to the city and his job. "Take it easy."

So Eve tried to rest in the mountains where she had befriended old masters like Eddie Cantor and Phil Foster. One summer the famous hotel matron Jenny Grossinger had handed Eve a wad of bills. "Here, kid. Go buy yerself some clothes." It was during the long nights of dancing at the big hotels that Eve became so adept at following a man's lead.

Asked to describe herself in 1948, Eve Goldenberg still said, "I'm a singer."

Susan and Lorraine seemed happy to be able to run through the woods, and Eve would have enjoyed a month in the country with the family if only Sam had been there too. They were all glad to see him when he arrived on weekends. Susan liked to dance on the tops of his shoes when the families gathered in the evening. One afternoon she ventured into a deep section of the slender stream where the vacationers came to swim, and Sam jumped in to pull his sputtering daughter up onto the bank. Sam would be unable to recall the incident in later years, but Susan would always remember the summer day her father saved her as an instant when there was no ambivalence between them at all.

After the girls were in bed, Eve listened to other wives whose husbands rarely appeared. Most of them claimed to be happy the men were out of their hair. One evening Eve saw a woman massage the crotch of a man who was not her husband. She was appalled.

Marital dissolution was a prime topic of conversation these days. Of the one million marriage vows exchanged in 1948, family specialists—and divorce lawyers, formerly regarded as denizens of a sleazy reach of the legal profession, now quoted at length in women's magazines—estimated between three hundred thousand to a half million of them would not take. Divorce had replaced death as the primary solvent of marriage for the first time in American history.

With the avidity of sports fans, millions of Americans had followed the wartime Supreme Court case involving two North Carolinians who had walked out on their respective spouses, driven to Nevada in the *same car*, obtained two of the "quickie" divorces available in that most demonic of states, and proceeded to live together in a tourist camp for the period stipulated by local statute for one of Nevada's equally notorious "quickie" marriages. The newlyweds went on to redefine "unmitigated gall" in the estimation of many by moving back to North Carolina to resume life as an apparently respectable American family. Divorce had become all but automatic, and the highest court in the land did nothing to contradict the general impression that the institution of marriage was now vulnerable to passing sexual whims and a drive down one of the new highways.

At the same conference of family professionals where Dr. Friedgood characterized female nervousness as yet another blow to the national birth rate, the director of the American Institute of Family Relations, Paul Popenoe, contended that "no one can escape the conclusion that the divorced population represents to some extent a biologically inferior part of the population."

Sylvia, Sam's sister, was now divorced from the father of Precious. Sylvia often dropped Presh off for a day with her cousins so she could make it to her job in the diamond district in Manhattan. In June, Sylvia and her daughter came to stay with Eve, Susan, and Lorraine in the Catskills, and the three girls presented quite a contrast—Presh in her starched pinafores and golden curls, Lorraine and Susan in muddy jeans, geared for action.

Yetta and Papa Joe were not officially divorced, but they were no longer living in the same apartment. Eve enjoyed Papa Joe's visits. He always brought kippers and sat at her table chatting amiably with his hat on. One day before Eve and the girls left town, Yetta arrived while Joe was still there. "He's wearing a hat," Yetta observed. "What are you wearing a hat for?" she asked her husband, making no attempt to mask her scorn. "He's wearing a hat," she announced, turning to Eve, "because he's *bald*. That's why! Look at him, the man has to wear a hat indoors he's so bald."

In Eve Samberg's senior yearbook Minnie "Freckles" Levenstein wrote, "First comes graduation, then comes marriage, then comes Evie wheeling a baby carriage." That was precisely how Eve had always imagined it. The sound of the baby crying had prevailed over the smell of the proverbial greasepaint all along. Family sociologists debated whether marriage was a "social institution" or a "human instinct," and strict Freudians defended the master's axiom that women only transcended their regressive penis envy through adjustment as mothers and wives. Eve wasn't sure how it had started, but she'd known since she was a little girl that all she wanted was to be happily married.

What she hadn't bargained for were the bad dreams and bouts of extreme unhappiness.

"Happiness," Dorothy Dix advised her millions of readers, "is largely a matter of self-hypnotism. You can think yourself happy or you can think yourself miserable. It's up to you." The first of the famous "Ten Rules for Happiness," according to Dorothy Dix—who'd suffered something of a nervous collapse and a divorce—was "Make up your mind to be happy."

"Happiness," wrote a family sociologist trying to address the apparent family unrest of the moment, is a "psychological state of adjustment." Self-adjustment within the rigors of organized living was the stuff of several current best-selling books, notably two by the modern oracles of human management technique, Dr. Norman Vincent Peale and the irrepressible Dale Carnegie, whose *How to Stop Worrying and Start Living* was standard reading for millions of Americans attempting to cope decades before their children came to self-help programs thinking themselves pioneers.

Central to Carnegie's advice was the injunction "Live in day-tight compartments," his own variation on the older "Do one thing at a time." "We are all dreaming of some magical rose garden over the horizon—instead of enjoying the roses that are blooming outside our windows today," Dale Carnegie wrote.

When Eve experienced physical pain as a young girl, Rebecca Samberg would instruct her to chant, *"Mich hart nicht! Mich hart nicht!"* It doesn't matter! It doesn't matter! When Rebecca was upset, she would seize a broom and sweep her kitchen until dust clouded the air. Eve's mother had always sworn by cleaning to alleviate tension and pain, and her daughter tried to carry on the tradition.

After returning from her summer vacation, Eve would go to her kitchen to clean if she felt the walls closing in or the tears spilling over. But sometimes it didn't help, and one day she was so hysterical that she went to her cupboard and grabbed a china plate. She reared back like Dizzy Dean in his heyday and smashed the dish against the wall. Then she grabbed another and threw it even harder.

Who would have guessed how much a few shattered plates helped? Eve braved family gossip about her diminishing supply of chinaware and suffered a nagging sense that her B-movie outburst was far from original. But Eve had spent enough time in front of the footlights to know that she was lost if she couldn't work with the props at hand.

By the fall of the year, Eve was sure she would never end up in dim madhouse corridors holding her pants up with one hand—as long as there were dishes in her cupboard.

———◆———

Nearly three dozen neighbors gathered in the cheery Goldenberg apartment on the fourth floor of 737 Hunt's Point Avenue to watch Sam— one of "today's pioneers," as the advertisements put it—carefully position a small walnut-colored box on an end table. A loud click silenced the assembled witnesses and moved them in an excited semicircle closer to one of 975,000 televisions sold in America in 1948. It was the year Orville Wright died and the year the public learned that a fellow named Chuck Yeager had broken the sound barrier in a rocket-powered X-1 Orville would have been hard put to recognize as a plane.

Two years earlier the little ten-inch RCA now glowing hazily in the corner had come on the market at $374, when most other models were still well over $500. Only seven thousand sets of any sort were sold in 1946. The RCA was under $300 now but still represented half a month of Sam's wages. Sam had struck a deal with his boss, a man whose entrepreneurial aspirations went beyond rewiring to opening an appliance store at the corner of West Forty-seventh Street and Ninth Avenue. Sam could take television back to Eve and the girls for a few dollars off his paycheck every week.

"Televiewers"—Americans lucky enough to own television sets already—spent an average of three and one-half hours a day watching the machines, according to a New Jersey professor who had a hunch the invention would catch on. Forty-six percent of the owners in his study said that television "killed" conversation of the traditional sort while creating a "new kind of rapid discourse carried on during commercials."

The Goldenberg neighbors exchanged bits of conventional wisdom after the building's first set lit up—that doctors would soon diagnose diseases via television, that Americans would "tour the world" in their homes, that television would educate the nation's children by day and "provide a new occasion for the American family to get together and get better acquainted at night" (this from a vice president of the Columbia Broadcasting System, who also said he was quite sure that television would "re-cement" the American family, still so much a cause of popular concern).

Susan felt a thrill of intense anticipation every time the RCA let loose the piercing squeal that meant it was coming to life. Some of the people on television reminded Susan of her beautiful mother because they sang or told jokes (*Riddle Me This* and *Stop Me If You've Heard This One* were popular shows in this early year of programming).

The television was on far more than the radio, and over the next few years it would seem to bring more and more of the world into Susan's family, into her bedroom, into the realm of her imagination that occasionally conjured up fear. Sometimes she would wake up panting, the RCA still blaring ominous voices and music through her bedroom wall. Then Susan would look around and realize she was still at home, in the little apartment she shared with her mother, her father, her baby sister, and the new TV.

1949

On too many Sunday afternoons, Eve thought, Sam met his life-long pal Frankie Huber to wander through the old neighborhood. Neither Eve nor Frankie's wife could fathom the allure of what Sam called his "fantasy" afternoons with Frankie—roaming around like ten-year-olds again, walking for hours through an injured South Bronx neighborhood with fewer inhabitants, buildings, and even trees each time they went.

"What are you guys looking for?" Eve asked in exasperation when Sam came home one Sunday after dark.

Frankie Huber was tall and quiet, and though they didn't talk about it much, Sam believed Frankie would never quite recover from having his heart broken by a local girl just before he shipped out for the South Pacific. Still, Frankie had managed to fall in love again after the war, and Sam was honored when his oldest friend asked him to be his best man.

Just before the wedding, as they were sauntering through the Springhurst neighborhood where they'd fought and played and raised homing pigeons on the roofs, Frankie stopped and turned to Sam. "Listen, Sammy," he said, "you know she's Catholic. They won't even let a Presbyterian like me marry her in the damned church. We're supposed to do it in some rectory off to the side. But the priest, he says the best man can't be—"

"It's okay, Frankie," Sam said.

"I'm gonna tell her no. We'll move the damned wedding."

"Nah," said Sam. "I understand."

Sam and Eve didn't even go to the wedding, and the Hubers and the Goldenbergs rarely socialized. But Sam still left Eve and the girls on

Sunday afternoons so that he and Frankie could hunt down members of the old gang, some of them living in buildings with many black, uncurtained windows.

Sam had sensed since he first came back from Europe that the Bronx was inexorably pushing settlers of his vintage to the north and west. Many immigrant families who'd escaped Manhattan ghettos during the brief economic expansion after the last world war (the Goldenbergs had finally departed the Lower East Side in 1925) were now moving from the southeastern corners of the forty-two square miles of the Bronx to the once ritzy upper and central reaches of the Grand Concourse. Northern Bronx residents were said to be moving up near Pelham Parkway, into Yonkers, or crossing the border into southern Westchester County, or even vaulting into old upper-class suburbs like Bronxville.

"It's disintegrating, Frankie," Sam said as they toured. "It's an Exodus."

The old friends mounted a staircase leading up through an apartment building to a rooftop pigeon loft still maintained by one of their buddies. "I'll say it again," Sam said. "The Jews shoulda bought the Bronx. They coulda come and fixed the place up and made it beautiful. I mean, what have they got now? They're gonna make a homeland in the middle of some desert full of Arabs—people who still own slaves?"

In August the prime minister of the infant state of Israel came to town. "We are only nine hundred thousand Jews in Israel," David Ben-Gurion said. "Our next task will not be easier than the creation of the Jewish State. It consists of bringing all Jews to Israel....We appeal to the parents to help us bring their children here. Even if they decline to help, we will bring the youth to Israel, but I hope that this will not be necessary."

All the current talk of a "Jewish" state and a "Jewish" flag sounded strange to Sam and Eve. Zionism had always seemed like a family matter before, like keeping kosher. Zionist ideology was also a popular avenue for secularized, educated, progressive young American Jews to distinguish themselves from parochial parents and grandparents. To a degree, Sam was sympathetic to the Israeli cause. "But I've had my war and my D-Day," he said. May 14, 1948, was a good day for the Jews—no doubt about that—but on the whole Sam believed they would have done better in the Bronx.

The visits to the pigeon lofts were the highlight of Sam and Frankie's fantasy afternoons. Sam was aware that for every American who knew enough to regard a pigeon with respect, there were hundreds—thousands—who loathed the birds both in fact and as living metaphors for all things urban, ungainly, and unclean. Sam's own wife had only unkind words for pigeons. Sam Goldenberg and Frankie Huber could talk pigeons on the rooftops of the dying neighborhood for hours, so long that Eve was often upset when Sam finally came home. She would never understand how a family man just turned thirty, a husband and father away from home far too often during the week, could squander a Sunday afternoon on some filthy old birds.

<hr />

Susan, almost six, was allowed to lean out of the fourth-floor windows. Lorraine, almost three, was not allowed within ten feet of a window— not that she acknowledged the proscription. The alert building superintendent had recently retrieved Lorraine from the Goldenbergs' window ledge. Lorraine was known around 737 Hunt's Point Avenue as "hell on wheels." Her dark little face was always swollen and bruised from her most recent high-speed collision with a table or a wall. Bills, letters, and other documents existed so Lorraine could make confetti.

Susan didn't like it when Lorraine refused to hold her hand, and she was jealous because she believed Lorraine feared nothing at all.

The day the green van pulled up, Susan was hanging out the window. She saw the words DYNAMIC ELECTRIC emblazoned on the side. A jagged white lightning bolt flashed across the vehicle close to the painted letters. She watched a man climb out of the driver's side of this beautiful spaceship and walk around to make sure the back door was locked. Then he glanced up long enough for her to see that the man was Sam.

Susan Goldenberg was by no means the only girl on the block who wondered what her father did during his days and nights away from home. Whatever preoccupied her father, Susan imagined that it couldn't possibly be as glamorous as her uncle Buddy Samberg's line of work. Buddy played guitar in nightclubs and restaurants, and Susan told her friends that he was a "genius." Susan reasoned that whatever made Sam too tired to talk on the rare nights when he got home before she was in bed could not begin to approach Uncle Sid Samberg's job. Sid worked down the road at the wondrous Hunt's Point Market, and Susan had found herself in the company of jealous friends on several occasions when Sid rode by atop a truckload of bananas.

"That's my uncle!" she'd scream.

But the arrival of this new van, complete with lightning bolt, was cause for serious reconsideration. Perhaps there was glamour in her father's secret life after all. And did the new van indicate that the family would no longer be so poor?

Susan coveted the expensive dolls other girls had, dolls with hair you could comb and wardrobes of the finest fabrics. When the rowdy boys from downstairs broke her favorite doll, their mother went to a department store and bought Susan a far superior doll, but Eve forbade her to accept it.

Beyond nonessentials the family couldn't afford, there were things Susan couldn't have for reasons connected to complicated emotions she couldn't quite understand.

The meat shortages and rapid doubling of food and clothing prices a year earlier had coincided painfully with Sam's loss of overtime. His twenty to thirty hours of overtime pay had become a requirement of a balanced family budget, but the economy's transitory sag left him only his straight time, and the family was floundering by the middle of the year, wanting for basics.

Other families in the building were riding high on the carefully butchered but unequally distributed postwar hog, almost all of them—or so Sam firmly believed—supported by men who'd avoided going to war. One neighbor on a lower floor "soaked up so much money it leaked out his backside," according to Sam. The man's income came from buying up lifeless hulks of discarded refrigerators, refurbishing them, and then selling them to appliance-mad "bargain hunters" at an immense profit. Galling as it was, the man's success helped to confirm Sam's hunch that only by being "in business" and independent would he ever drag his family off the shoals and into the stream.

Sam claimed that many working men with a talent for a trade like his—people said all the time that he had a gift for "electric"—lived well because of the protection of a trade union. Sam had by now given up on getting into the closed world of fathers and sons that was the International Brotherhood of Electrical Workers. He had taken several jobs since 1938 because of promises of a union card, and after more than ten years he knew it would never happen. Sam now looked back on his father's near religious fealty to the fur workers' union as yet another cause of his childhood deprivation.

Sam would have voted for Harry S. Truman even if Truman hadn't inherited his job from "the president" (as Sam still called FDR). He would have voted for Truman if he'd been a *Republican*, for that matter, because Truman had called out the army instead of letting the railroad workers shut down the trains. Sam often wondered if he was the only man in the country who hadn't gone out on strike since the war. So many: steel workers, auto workers, coal miners, meat processors, the phone guys, the electrical workers—even the Pittsburgh Pirates had gone out on strike for a piece of the pie too long denied.

But during 1948 Sam had begun to think that unions represented "the right not to work as hard as the next shmuck in line." And by the middle of 1949, he had decided to break out on his own and become what men he'd grown up respecting resented and even loathed. He would be a boss.

A scant three out of twenty American workers ran businesses of their own in 1949; just fifteen percent of all workers owned the tools of their trade—the same proportion who did *not* own their means of production a century earlier. A two-man "electric shop" like the one Sam and a longtime colleague named Louis Bernstein had in mind would have to start small, but there were plenty of jobs to be had converting individual New York apartments from the old DC system to the AC method of delivering current for all those new televisions and refrigerators.

Sam and Louis agreed they wouldn't miss the outlandish corruption of some of their garment center jobs. "I already have a partner" was Sam's standard comeback when the palms were presented for payoffs.

Sam believed that he and Louis would do well simply by being fair. He now knew he had an almost animal capacity to work harder than most men, and he figured that this, plus the scarcity in his line of "real human beings"—by which he meant honest people—would be the key to success.

Sam and Louis agreed to pitch in five hundred dollars apiece, but Sam and Eve only had four hundred in savings, so he threw in the wreckage of his thirteen-year-old Plymouth. After the partners bought new tools and the Ford van, they had enough left over to pay for the futuristic handiwork of an inspired sign painter who needed some extra cash.

DYNAMIC ELECTRIC.

Electricity was the future. Nearly half of all the electricity ever generated was coursing through the nation's wires on any given day. Half of the world's manufactured goods and half of the world's controlled flow of electrons were serving less than six percent of the world's population in the United States. Americans were told that dinner would soon be served by "throwing a switch." Futuristic extrapolation suggested that many of the fifteen million new homes made possible by electricity would be built of plastic. A citizen could order a house from Macy's in the morning, and workmen would "set it up" that afternoon.

This gleaming promise seemed far removed from Sam's constant labor and the ever present anxiety of keeping a family afloat and a new business too. The material dreams pumping through the culture did not include the sight of Eve coming home from another attempt to bring in extra money by peddling clothing and small accessories (as the man downstairs moved his refrigerators). Eve would collect orders from the ladies in her weekly mah-jongg game and take the bus down to Manhattan to purchase blouses and stockings on consignment.

Not long after the green van rolled up new and hopeful in front of 737 Hunt's Point Avenue, around Mother's Day, Susan Goldenberg found five dollars on the sidewalk. She took it home and handed it to her mother. "Buy something pretty to wear," Susan demanded.

Eve did. She went out and bought a black-and-white-checked skirt made of a rustling sort of taffeta embellished with tiny dots of black velvet flock. No other mother in America could have looked so beautiful in the skirt, Susan thought, just as nobody else could sing "I'm Wishing," from *Snow White*, quite so perfectly.

If there was less luxury in her life than a student of luxury like Susan would have preferred—if her mother still broke plates now and then and her father stayed away so long and so often that she wondered if she was being punished—then there were also sweet songs, the rustle of taffeta, the promise in a bolt of lightning flashing jagged and wild across a van, and a new sister too.

———◆———

Sheila Claire Goldenberg, big-eyed and calm, was born on September 12. She arrived at the end of a great year for babies. By the close of 1949 babies were the talk of the town.

Babies grinned down from billboards all over the city and up from the ever more colorful packaging of items filling the grocery stores. After worrying darkly over the future of the American family, *Life* magazine had run five covers featuring babies during the first half of 1949 alone. Eve noticed that the gossip dominating her now twice-weekly mah-jongg games had ceased to revolve around family troubles left over from the war.

It was as if the victorious postwar aura had been transferred to a celebration of children. Five years of peace would forever be symbolized by the millions of infants born at the time. Statistics finally available at the turn of the decade indicated that Professor Carle Zimmerman's concerns about the narcissistic young married couples of the 1940s were baseless.

The birth rate had in fact soared by almost twenty percent from 1945 to 1946, and had increased another twelve percent in 1947, a year during which one American citizen was added to the population every eleven and a half seconds.

The divorce rate that so worried the family professionals—rising as it had since the 1920s—had peaked in 1946 and was now in decline. The tendency of women to marry younger than their mothers would continue through 1953, when nearly one-third of American women taking their wifely vows would be under nineteen. Only one of four mothers still worked outside the home; the wartime working women had handed their tools over to men and returned to a domesticity that was now, if not fashionable, certainly "the right thing to do."

Sheila slept in the bedroom with her older sisters, the communal blue-and-red-plaid baby blanket that was first Susan's and then Lorraine's deposited in her crib.

Now they were five.

1950

Without warning, Susan's usually placid first-grade teacher whirled on her students: "Drop! *Drop!*" she bellowed.

Susan and the other stunned children began to spill from their desk chairs to the linoleum floor. They tried to balance in a pose that required them to kneel, clasp their hands behind their necks, and cover their eyes with their elbows so that the imminent atomic flash wouldn't turn their little faces to ash.

In the New York public schools the atomic air raid drills demanded by the state civil defense authorities were called "sneak attack drills." All students were required to participate. It had been more than a year since a worldly six-year-old like Susan learned that the Russians had the Bomb. By January of 1950 Susan knew too, in her own way, that President Truman was building a bomb that would make the one dropped on Hiroshima seem conventional—a "super-bomb," as Truman called the hydrogen-based device.

Albert Einstein appeared on television to say that this fervid bomb-making could lead to the "annihilation of all life on earth," but for the benefit of Americans so uninformed and naïve as to believe Einstein, or so deluded as to think "a falling A-bomb means the end of everything," the *Saturday Evening Post* published a "remarkable report" in January. "How You Can Survive an A-Bomb Blast" was written by Richard Gerstell, an early expert on atomic war and now an adviser to the Secretary of Defense. "Although repeatedly subjected to radiation on the Bikini ships," Gerstell had "suffered no physical damage, not even losing a hair." Mr. Gerstell advised readers that after the blast, a careful citizen would do well to keep his eyes closed, lest "five minutes or so of blindness...result from looking into the explosion's dazzling burst of light." Cotton clothing in light colors, he added, would help shield against the heat.

At the end of 1950, after the Federal Civil Defense Administration was established and Congress had allocated three billion dollars for a new defense plan, *Life* carried an article entitled "How You Can Prepare for Atomic War": "The blunt truth at this moment is that not one American city has so far made even a fair start toward minimum preparedness," the editors claimed. So *Life* did its part by presenting an urban civil defense plan designed by MIT mathematician Norbert Wiener, whose maps and drawings indicated that circular highways and Quonset hut hospitals would at least alleviate public panic after the attack. Civil defense manuals began appearing on coffee tables, and Geiger counters were available in appliance stores. Though the administrators of Susan's school adopted the kneeling posture, there were those who argued loud and long for the fetal position, while other experts recommended lying flat on your stomach with your face buried in your arms.

Susan would soon be issued a set of dog tags so that civil defense officials could identify her if she died or got lost during an atomic attack. Occasionally called "identification necklaces," these "heat and corrosion resistant" metal plates were recognized by the children of the Bronx as the same artifacts of war that their fathers wore home from overseas.

For many years to come, the dog tags, the sound of air raid sirens during afternoon tests, the sudden, hysterical commands of teachers ordering her to fall to the floor, would merge into a single continuum of terror that arched over all of Susan's days.

Shortly after the concentration camp images presented during the Nuremberg Trials were shown on television in 1949, Susan began to dream that Nazi storm troopers came into her first-grade class to take her away forever. Wearing the purple corduroy jumper and yellow organdy blouse she received for her sixth birthday, she would be escorted from her desk by the Nazis, their jackboots clicking down the halls of Public School 48. Now, less than a year later, the Nazis and their televised horrors had fused with the Russians and their bombs, which the children knew—whatever *Life* or the *Saturday Evening Post* might claim—would rain down an all-consuming fire.

By the time Susan turned seven in November, she knew her dog tags were there to identify her corpse after the Bomb ended the world.

Susan's identification tags actually differed substantially from Sam's army issue. Sam's dog tags said "Goldenberg, Staff Sgt. Samuel, 32010340." But his daughter's tags said "Susan Gordon," because her parents had decided that the family would forge into the new half century with a new name.

"What does it really matter, Eve?" Sam said when the name change was first discussed. "A couple of your uncles don't have the same name as your father." (One of Simon Samberg's brothers was Zimberg; another was Simberg.) "Because some donkey Irishman sitting at a desk on Ellis Island gave them out that way, half the families in New York don't have the right name," Sam argued.

The name Goldenberg had come to Sam by way of a Romanian border guard, Sam's grandfather, who executed an about-face one day and crossed the border himself in search of America, his new name borrowed from a cousin who'd already made it to the other side.

The idea of changing names came up as business began to take off for Dynamic Electric. Some of the big new jobs Sam and Louis got were controlled by the Little Sisters of the Poor, a Catholic organization. Sam thought they might be more amenable to the kind of long-term working relationship he was after if the signature on the contracts were something other than Goldenberg. The name eluded people anyway, especially non-Jews. Sam was as often called Goldberg or Goldberger as Goldenberg.

Eve agreed to the change because she decided upon reflection that leaving your name behind was something of "an American tradition." Unlike the forced immigrants from Africa who were deprived of identity by being assigned the last names of their owners, many of the Americans Eve admired most had smoothed and celebrated their emergence from the past by shedding Kaminsky for Kaye (Danny), Levitch for Lewis (Jerry), and Berlinger for Berle. There was even a Goldenberg (Emanuel) who went so far as to become Robinson (Edward G.). Eve had always planned to be a professional singer under the name Eva Lynn, though at the time Sam met her she'd been appearing for years as Eve Saunders (her brother Buddy used Saunders, and they occasionally went on as a sibling act). By now Eve had been a Samberg for twenty-two years, an intermittent Saunders for eight, and Eve Goldenberg for eight. "Another name is not such a big deal," she said, giving Sam the go-ahead.

So they would be the Gordons: Sam, Eve, Susan, Lorraine, and little Sheila. Sam chose the name of a Scots clan associated with a decent gin. Gordon was still popular in various parts of Central Europe, perhaps derived from the Russian *gorodin,* "townsman." Sam had a cousin who'd become a Gordon, and he'd always considered the choice relatively euphonic, brief, and "simple enough for any idiot to spell it."

"Gordon's the kind of name a person could remember," Sam explained to his furious mother.

Yetta's outrage might have been expected, but Sam wasn't prepared for the look of devastation that spread over his father's face. Neither Sam nor Joe could even remember the original family name, but Sam had to live with the fact that Papa Joe was deeply hurt by his son's decision to erase his brand.

Eve put the documents legalizing the change in a drawer, but in less than two weeks Lorraine had found them. The family's "little terror" had recently discovered the recording Eve made, the one Sam had carted safely across Europe. Lorraine had played with it for a while and then smashed it to pieces. Now Lorraine came out to display the tiny scraps of paper with her customary look of pride, tossing them in the air like a kid at a parade.

<hr />

By 1950 exemplary television families came to life every evening in millions of homes. The former Goldenbergs of 737 Hunt's Point Avenue in the Bronx considered themselves personal friends of the Goldbergs of 1030 East Tremont Avenue in the Bronx. The Goldbergs had been reborn from radio in early 1949. Now, on Monday nights—on CBS, from eight o'clock to eight-thirty—a man named Jake Goldberg worked hard in the apparel business, and Molly Goldberg worked just as hard at being a housewife, a mother to two adolescents, and something of a compulsive gossip, though her interest in the human dilemmas befalling her neighbors was nothing if not warmhearted and generous.

But during the year Jake Goldberg was purged from the family.

As soon as Sam and Eve began to read about the House Un-American Activities Committee scouring Hollywood for Communists, Sam, in particular, assumed it was only a matter of time before the likes of Joseph McCarthy emerged from the morass. The leering junior senator from Wisconsin, like Sam, had the kind of forearms you wouldn't want to lose track of during a fight. But Sam didn't shuffle around like a slob and drink during the day, nor did he fake a limp or lie about war wounds when he never came close enough to the battlefront to get hit.

Later Joe McCarthy couldn't quite recall whether it was fifty-seven

Communists or two hundred or more of them, but in 1950 the senator set out to make himself famous by claiming to have in his possession the names of "card-carrying Communists" who'd managed to infiltrate the State Department and other important government offices.

McCarthy terrified and infuriated urban children of the Depression years like Sam and Eve. Sam often commented within the safe confines of the apartment that if the Goldenbergs had only had a bit more money when he was growing up, and if Yetta had been less unwilling to let him leave home except to work, he might have joined some of his friends at one of the Communist summer camps of the very sort McCarthy now claimed had turned red-blooded American boys into godless Reds. Sam knew of soldiers who'd come home and joined veterans' organizations that were now being caught in McCarthy's insidious web, and the men were scared.

"It's crazy," Sam would say to Eve, turning away from the television news. "When we were kids the Communists were just followers of another political party—like the Democrats."

Sam and Eve ached as if for close relations as the names of so many fine performers turned up on "blacklists" by the day. They both felt they knew actors like Zero Mostel, Larry Parks, Lew Ayres, and Lee J. Cobb, now virtually unemployable, and they empathized in some part because they realized that they themselves could have been pilloried in public as "do-gooders" and "bleeding hearts."

McCarthy and the witch-hunt committees reminded Sam of his court-martial (he wasn't allowed to testify about the epithets the officer had unleashed before Sam disobeyed his order). The hearings also made him think about secret blackballings by corrupt labor unions.

Sam and Eve were stunned when CBS canceled *The Goldbergs* because Philip Loeb, who played Molly's husband, Jake, had been named on a long list (which also included conductor Leonard Bernstein, playwright Arthur Miller, newsman Howard K. Smith, and dozens of others) published in *Red Channels: The Report of Communist Influence in Radio and Television*, a book written by several former FBI agents. Philip Loeb's crime was having supported the desegregation of professional baseball.

The Goldbergs moved to NBC and the Goldenbergs continued to watch, but a different actor played Jake. Philip Loeb had been purged from the show and the television industry for good. A few years later, out of work since becoming "controversial," Loeb checked into a hotel and killed himself with a massive overdose of sleeping pills.

Eve Goldenberg would enter the second half of the century without her mother, Rebecca Samberg, who died at the age of fifty-nine on Yom Kippur, the Day of Atonement.

Eve was chatting with Rebecca in her gray kitchen one morning when she noticed a strange expression cross her mother's face. Rebecca groped for Eve's hand. "Susala," Eve heard her mother say in obvious confusion.

Eve rushed her to the hospital. Pneumonia was mentioned as a possible cause of death, though one of the doctors thought it could have been a brain tumor. Eve would later say that if Rebecca had lived into the time of CAT scans and MRIs, perhaps science might have located a tumor or a lesion to help explain her mother's constant sadness.

People had always come to the many Samberg apartments of Eve's youth—each darker and more unpleasant than the last—so that Rebecca could read their fortunes. It was said that she was something of a Gypsy, and though Eve was sure Rebecca had dreams that came true, she would remember her as the depressed and docile wife of a volatile man, as a woman who "needed help" she never received. Eve never forgot the day she came home from elementary school to find Rebecca slumped at the kitchen table. She was positive that her mother had finally taken poison and killed herself. She stood frozen on the other side of the table for several minutes, until Rebecca woke up and asked her what was wrong. Long past her mother's death, she often dreamed that Rebecca was threatening to hurt herself and Eve couldn't get to her across the table.

In the early evening of the day Rebecca died, Eve began to iron. When she finished one load, she found another. Eve didn't stop pressing her family's clothes, most of which were already ironed, until sunrise. It was a full month later that she began to cry so hard that it made her sick. The same thing had happened a month after Sam left for the war.

Eve was good at drawing her husband out of the darkness of his Goldenberg moods, but the power of her own family sadness paralyzed her every thought.

━━◆◆◆━━

Paralysis in the face of family pain was most certainly not a personality trait exhibited by the fiercely emotional family man Harry Truman. On December 6, 1950, the president opened his morning *Washington Post* to read that the paper's music critic, Paul Hume, had not been at all impressed with the singing talents of Truman's daughter, Margaret, who'd made her debut at Constitution Hall the previous night.

Harry Truman sat down and fired off a handwritten letter in which he called the thirty-four-year-old music critic a "frustrated old man....Some day I hope to meet you," Truman raged in full paternal sway. "When that happens, you'll need a new nose, a lot of beefsteak for black eyes, and perhaps a supporter below."

This was the sort of thing about Harry Truman that people like Sam Gordon loved. Perhaps there were urban sophisticates who tittered at the hokey protective sentiments of a father toward the injured feelings of his only child, but in 1950 there could not have been many. Harry Truman's political fortunes would soon begin to decline, but still, Americans like Sam had to respect the president's style.

Sam knew that Harry Truman was a poor boy with only a high school education. He was at various times a railroad man, a newspaper man, a banker, a soldier in France during World War I, a farmer (for ten years in partnership with his father), and by age thirty-seven, a bankrupt Missouri haberdasher. But he'd beaten all that and become—only in America—the president of the United States. The job was his by default at first, true, but in 1948 Truman had won the office himself, against all predictions of a Dewey victory.

Truman predicted at the beginning of 1950 that if all went according to plan, his Fair Deal program would give the average American family an annual income of twelve thousand dollars by the year 2000. The government, if Truman had anything to say about it, would keep large firms from absorbing or damaging small firms. Americans would work less, produce more, play more, and spend more time close to family hearths in what Harry Truman called "adequate" homes.

———◆———

"Eve, I'm sweatin'," Sam said as he watched the RCA. "I'm sure I'm not eligible anymore. I'm out of the inactive reserves, but with the army you never know."

Harry Truman was somber as he addressed the nation only nine days after coming to his daughter's defense. He announced that some 3.5 million men must soon be under arms in defense of democracy. "All things we believe in," Truman said, "are in great danger."

The Americans were in quick retreat in Korea. Some thirty-three Communist Chinese divisions had attacked the United Nations force and, according to historian Ronald Oakley's later analysis, had simply "ripped it to pieces." Brilliant World War II commanders had been outfoxed by their Chinese counterparts.

Within three weeks of Truman's announcement of a military and economic mobilization, the Korean capital city of Seoul would be evacuated. The Communist assault would be halted, but a war many Americans considered impossible to win because of political machinations in Washington—many of them Harry Truman's—would drag on until more than fifty thousand Americans had been killed.

Such a slender span of national innocence had separated the Big War from the new war. To the baby-filled hopefulness of the year, to an abiding fear of the Bomb, there was added before Christmas the possibility of national humiliation.

1951

Like the Sooners of Land Rush days streaming forth to lay claim to a piece of virgin territory—wagon wheel to wagon wheel across the rough prairie—thousands of young Bronx families took to the roadways almost every weekend, all of them sharing a fierce determination to be first in line when a new model home was unveiled. The stampede of so many cars at once created some of the first traffic jams ever seen on an open road. Often, from makeshift offices in the newest Shangri-la, a line of anxious families stretched out for a mile. Weekend house-hunters like the Gordons spun out from the city with an urgency inspired by daily rumors and official reports of a flurry of down payments on new homes, some of them priced as low as seven thousand dollars.

Only *new* homes were even considered by the Gordons and their neighbors in 1951. A *Saturday Evening Post* poll indicated that one in five Americans was willing to inhabit an apartment or a "used house," but it was hard to locate a would-be evacuee from the Bronx who would admit to such a thing. After all, not a week went by without news of another development about to rise from some farmer's field in Long Island or some swamp in New Jersey.

The Gordons rushed toward "a new life" in a used Pontiac made possible by Dynamic Electric's thriving business. "Now that we have a decent car, we can start looking farther away," Sam had announced when he drove up in his first General Motors car.

Over the course of the decade, over 1.5 million residents of New York City would leave for the surrounding suburbs, and to hear her in-laws tell it, not one of them sought the contemporary dream house more avidly than Eve Gordon. Yetta and sister Sylvia had seen the first signs after Rebecca died, and by the middle of 1951 they had pronounced Eve certifiably "house-crazy."

"Out…of…her…*mind*," said Sylvia, who tended toward loud emphasis of every syllable of every word she uttered. Sylvia had taken it upon herself to chaperone Sam, Eve, and their children on their weekend quests. She followed Eve closely from one house to another. One day they looked at a house on Long Island that was an apparent afterthought and only fit into a corner of a small development because it was shaped like an isosceles triangle.

Even Sam seemed shocked when Eve said, "It's…it's okay. It could be okay. I like it a lot. I think it's good."

"What are you? You are kah-*razy!*" Sylvia replied, low to high, like a staccato police siren. "Eve, it's a tah-*ri*-angle. You'll get up in the morning and think you're dah-*runk!*"

"I think it's…lovely," Eve sniffed. "Besides," she said, narrowing her eyes at Sylvia, "if I listen to you, I'll never get my house."

On the way home, Eve declared passionately, "I want to leave the Bronx. I have to leave, and I don't *ever* want to go back."

Even when the Puerto Rican men who now gathered along Hunt's Point Avenue weren't making ugly, sibilant noises or kissing the air, Eve could feel them staring as she passed by. "One thing a girl learns from show business is when the men are looking." Even if she was on her way to the store with all three girls, Eve could feel the ugliness in their eyes.

"I am not about to change the way I look. I won't let them force me to do that," Eve would say when other women suggested protective measures. Décolletage, boned brassieres, and the sweater-girl look were all the vogue this year, and besides, Eve was a sexy woman—that was who she was. She wore her black hair sort of like Hedy Lamarr these days, though her sweaters occasionally evoked comparisons to Lana Turner. The red sweater she'd made, with the white angora trim, was particularly eye-catching. Eve also had what might be called a "way of walking," which to her was simply the way she walked.

"Am I supposed to walk differently so I can feel safe going to the store?" she'd ask her friends. "The way I look and walk is me."

Then Eve began to think that the Latin men who stood outside the new bodega that had opened beside the nearby church—now occupied by a Puerto Rican congregation—were leering at her children.

Susan had a new set of nightmares because of the changing streets. She would dream that men picked her up and dragged her into one of the many courtyards or alleys in the neighborhood. Then she would be raped, like a local girl Susan had read about in the newspaper. Susan thought being raped meant being taken away from your mommy.

Susan and Lorraine loved the corner candy store because it was run by an old man who said "mine goodness" instead of "my goodness," making them giggle uncontrollably. Lately Susan had grown afraid of the short walk.

But the idea of leaving the Bronx scared her too. Susan would later talk constantly of the extended Bronx family of grandparents, aunts, uncles, and cousins that had swirled around her and adored her back on Kelly Street before Sam came home. She would describe the dark apartment on Kelly Street as "paradise." She would claim that for years after Sam returned she'd imagined herself a "princess in exile." Sam's younger sister, Aunt Blanche, was the one who had taught Susan to read before she started school and had taken her to museums and musical recitals. Eve's brother Buddy painted her pictures and played the guitar. Yetta cooked exquisite kosher meals. Susan would often close her eyes and see Rebecca reaching down as her own baby arms reached up. Her maternal grandmother was as soft and accessible as her father was hard and absent. But now Rebecca was gone.

The Bronx was indeed becoming scary, but Susan didn't want to leave. She would lie in bed at night and listen to the music that seeped through the wall like her fear of the evil lurking outside the apartment building. A new television show called *Dragnet* began with a theme song—"Dum-dah-*dum*-dum"—that kept Susan awake for hours. She would snuggle close to Lorraine in the bed they shared, wanting to stay in the Bronx with all the other relatives, wishing she was as utterly fearless as her little sister.

The neighborhood was beginning to remind Sam of the Lower East Side in the pushcart days when his own family moved to the Bronx. He'd seen men he believed to be hustlers or pimps, and he'd witnessed street fights.

"A slum is a beautiful thing," Sam liked to say, though most of his friends never quite understood what he meant. "The slums are full of old buildings made when people worked from the heart." But a man with a wife and children had little time for preservationist aesthetics. Sam was convinced he should leave the city "for the good of the family."

Sam's motivation differed from that of the middle-class merchants who'd migrated to some of the earlier suburbs in that he wasn't looking to distinguish himself from the lower classes. Sam called himself a "workingman," and if he sought social distance from those poorer than himself, it was only to get away from people who might hurt Eve or the kids. He didn't want to emigrate to one of the vast tracts of prefabricated housing out of some desire to assimilate or to lose his ethnic roots, or even to "conform"—a word that had lately filtered down to mahjongg tables and coffee breaks from complex sociological analyses of changing national character like David Riesman's *The Lonely Crowd*, published the previous year. But he did admit to a sense of meaning and even pleasure when he looked forward to the new suburbs and then back at his family in the Bronx.

"You know, I'm the first member of my family to own a car, and now it looks like I'll be the first to own a house," he said to Eve.

The beauty of the whole thing—this "boom"—was that an electrician could now reach out and grasp a portion of the beauty and comfort previously glimpsed from the car on weekend drives. In the new suburbs, where Sam and Eve now talked day and night of finding a home, a boy tossed newspapers through the clean dawn—a far cry from lugging a crushing weight of buttons down a crowded midtown street. In the new suburbs, the American family would pray together and so stay together, it was said. If life could really be as sentimental and sweet as Sam and Eve dreamed, if they were lucky enough to find a place they could afford, they really were headed for Shangri-la.

The most positive thing Yetta could bring herself to say about Sam and Eve's plan to leave the city was that it was "too soon." "Just wait, things will get cheaper," she said, her fleshy arm undulating as she waved her hand in a "Whadda you kids know?" gesture. "Just wait."

From Eve Gordon's perspective, the coming liberation of her brood from the extended family was almost as powerful a reason for househunting as the danger of the streets.

Eve knew Yetta had said some cruel things about her: that she had swept Sam off his feet, that she got pregnant "not two minutes" after they married. But what Eve could not abide was the way Yetta treated Sam. Eve would say, "Everyone in the world knows how brilliant Sam is," but she regularly watched Yetta cut Sam off in front of his children. "Whadda you know?" Yetta would sneer. If Sylvia criticized Sam, Yetta would cut her off too. "Leave him alone," she'd say. *"Er hot nisht keyn sechel."* He has no sense.

The venerable Dorothy Dix, approaching the end of a life of advicegiving, told young couples that they would indeed be better off away from the in-laws. Family scholar Robert F. Winch, in a textbook called

Selected Studies of Marriage and the Family, noted that many analysts of domestic tranquillity believed that for the first-generation American child, "breaking away" from "immigrant families" was "a necessary prelude to growth and assimilation into American society."

Economists supported the mass flight from parents and city as an aspect of the mobility required by expanding economies. Newspaper editorialists helped developers win zoning battles against local authorities by weighing in on behalf of "homeless vets" and "young wives with babies in their arms." The federal government stood ready to weigh in most mightily of all with mortgage guarantees for everyone.

And all the while the young families kept hunting, covering the changing suburban landscape in droves. They lined up to see models of a new future promising a way of life as different from the tenements as turn-of-the-century cities of America were from the shtetls of Eastern Europe.

As the war marked the 1940s, the new decade would be remembered as a time when millions of Americans found a new house in a new place designed specifically for a family looking to begin anew. The Gordons were bound to be homeowners, with a fixed address shared by none but themselves. They were searching for Big Rock Candy Mountain this year, and "house-crazy" or not, Sam and Eve would not rest until they arrived.

1952

They found it in the early spring.

House-hunting on the southern shore of Long Island, no more than five miles past the New York City limits in the village of Island Park, Sam spotted a small handmade sign fitted at an angle to a wooden stick. In block capital letters were the evocative words HARBOR ISLE.

Sam cajoled the Pontiac up and over the camelback rise of a slender old wooden bridge. A road of bleached sand and powdered clam shells continued along the edge of a boggy inlet. Through heavy reeds the tops of abandoned shanties were visible on an opposite shore until the road veered inland, snaking through an expanse of towering wild grass.

The road ended in a clearing full of parked cars. Sam opened the door to the sweet smell of marshland and intermittent whiffs of the open sea. Eve, Susan, Susan's dolls, Lorraine, Sheila, Mama Yetta, Papa Joe, and sister Sylvia climbed out of the Pontiac into an overcast day still so bright with a high ocean light that they all stood blinking beside the car for a moment. Then Sam strode quickly toward the long-abandoned island's only new home.

A portion of Island Park, just on the other side of the humpbacked bridge, was formerly called Barnum Island, after its onetime owner, the master manipulator of modern publicity Phineas T. Barnum. In 1889 the great showman had built a house there for his frail sister, Phoebe. Barnum would have been in the final year of a long life in 1891, when locals claimed he brought his famous circus to winter on their island. After a time the huckster struck camp and moved to new quarters in

Connecticut, leaving the sickly Phoebe behind until her home was turned into an almshouse.

This story was no more true than P. T. Barnum's profitable claim that Joice Heth, the septuagenarian black woman he carted across the Republic for years, was in fact the 161-year-old former nurse to baby George Washington. It was actually a real estate man, P. C. Barnum, who named the island for himself in 1921. An early wave of upwardly mobile suburban flight was heading P. C. Barnum's way that year, and the P. T. conceit was apparently part of the lesser Barnum's pitch.

In 1951 the lie entered local history when it was written into an official pamphlet for house-hunters enticed over the camelback bridge to a smaller, overgrown island that employees of the Brill-Tishman Development Company were renaming Harbor Isle—"future home of Harbor Isle Estates."

"It's on an honest-to-God island, Sam," a Bronx neighbor named Jack Binder had told him some weeks before he spotted the sign. Binder had put a down payment on a split-level home he claimed was far superior to the renowned "Levitt" houses not far away.

Five years earlier William J. Levitt, a second-generation home builder, had changed the name of Island Trees, Long Island, to Levittown. He filled identical tract houses with rent-paying war veterans until he got the idea of selling the houses to the vets for less than eight thousand dollars apiece. By the time Sam drove onto Harbor Isle, Levittown was home to more than fifty thousand pioneers. Other Levittowns were in the works, and Bill Levitt was quite famous and extremely rich.

The Brill-Tishman ads in the New York papers claimed that Harbor Isle's eighty-five acres of boggy ground—with its three full-time residents, a handful of ancient summer houses, hundreds of wild ducks (in season), geese, rabbits, and a significant population of bats—would in short order boast two hundred ninety of the finest brand-new homes on Long Island, each with "thirteen-foot bedrooms," and each facing a vernal tree-lined street. A portion of shoreline would eventually be groomed so residents could enjoy a "private beach."

Easy terms were available.

"Jew nails," Sam said as the family watched him inspect the model home. He was using the term favored by practitioners of the building trades for hardware connections largely made with a particularly cheap cliplike fastener. Sam took no offense, any more than he meant offense by calling a cheap, quick piece of electrical wiring an "Italian job."

Sam circled the house slowly, moving in to study the intersection of planes and surfaces, noting that the frame was made of two-by-fours instead of the sturdier three-by-five beams of prewar times. Everyone traipsed behind him, knowing that his professional appraisal was the first step. The structure was entirely typical of the houses going up at a rate of 150 per day in Nassau County, the fastest-growing county in the nation.

"Everything's simple," Sam said, still scrutinizing the outside of the house. Before the war it took at least twelve weeks to build even the smallest home. Now they were being tossed up in less than six weeks—half the time—to create a quantity of housing stock that would soon be as large as the number of standing homes "built by craftsmen," as Sam put it, over nearly three hundred years. "Lumpers" had framed out the house, not carpenters.

Sam studied the asbestos shingles that had allowed untrained sheathers to lay the roof instead of union men. He peered inside to see sheetrock on the walls, a recent innovation that was making the artistry of lathers and plasterers obsolete—men whose skill Sam had admired since he was a boy. This was not a well-made house by Sam Gordon's standards, but it would do. And it was the kind of shell that a man with Sam's know-how could vastly improve over time. It had a crawl space underneath instead of a concrete slab platform like the Levittown homes. Storage, thought Sam.

After circling the house several times, Sam nodded.

Eve rushed inside.

"The first *true* split-level homes on Long Island," an agent announced. He meant that the central rooms were connected by abbreviated staircases, offering an illusion of space and a real sense of separation between each level and each smaller room.

Eve noticed that one bedroom on the second floor had a dormer window. She wandered from level to level in a daze, trying to contain a giddy outburst of house madness.

After ten minutes Eve and Sam finally locked eyes. They realized they were both excited and afraid.

The agent said the basic house could be had for $12,999, a sum pushing the upper limit of the Veterans Administration mortgage guaranteed to Sam through the GI Bill. "For an extra thousand we have some corners available," the seller said, "and for another thousand you can have a house on the water."

"I'd love to live on a corner, Sam," Eve said. Waterfront property was out of the question. If a child could climb out of a fourth-floor window when your back was turned, Eve knew she would have drowning dreams every night if they lived on the water.

With a mortgage at four percent (almost no down payment required), Sam figured the corner house would run him eighty-seven dollars a month. Along with three of every four hardworking Americans, Sam had yet to crack the five-grand-a-year barrier. The new house meant that Sam would become an entirely different kind of American; like the vice-presidential candidate Richard Nixon, who would soon bare his finances before the whole nation and ask to be judged, Sam would owe more money than he had.

"I love this house, Sam."

"Me too," he said.

Papa Joe and Mama Yetta—who had converged on the Pontiac from their separate dwellings in order to come along, for Sam and for history—were standing outside with Sylvia. The Gordon girls were playing nearby.

Sylvia was already nodding when Sam and Eve emerged from the house. "It's bee-*yoo*-tiful," Sylvia said.

"Do you think we could borrow fifty bucks for the down payment?" Sam asked his father.

Joe handed over the cash.

Throughout the late spring and summer, young fathers drove their families out to Harbor Isle on weekends. They would all clamber up great mounds of friable earth and lay out picnic blankets. They'd look down into several hundred huge holes and watch men and machines build their island town atop the sand.

When the tall grass was cut away they could see how flat Harbor Isle really was. There were no trees, no telephone poles, no walls. One Sunday everyone got out of their cars to find surveyors' stakes marking out square lots on what would be twenty-six rectangular blocks.

Families met in troughs between hills of rubble, bearing brownies and cans of beer. They made connections based on common fields of combat. Eve met a woman who also had three girls. They exchanged lot numbers and chatted excitedly above the roar of the earthmovers. Eve sensed immediately that the woman would be a friend.

"It's like everyone who's gonna live here is the same," Sam enthused on the way home one Sunday night. "Hundreds of families, and it's like we all have the same kind of life."

It was true that most of the adults were the same age. The fathers had fought in the war, and when families exchanged names in search of friends in common, they occasionally came across men who hadn't come back. Most of the families atop the hills were Jewish. All of the adults, as far as Sam could tell, had grown up poor. Nobody seemed to have made anything like big money in the meantime, but there were company men and professionals in the crowd. Those who worked with their hands were by and large skilled craftsmen. If there were differences in the nature of their work, they in no way overshadowed the aspects of their lives that made the young men feel good because they were the same.

"And we all *look* the same," Sam said with wonder. "I can see a kid wandering around and I know who the parents are—already." Sam practiced. Even though all the boys had those drill-sergeant crew cuts, hair so short that a sunbeam lit up pink circles on their heads, Sam would draw upon his powerful memory to place them. It was as if all these families had been struck from a mold cast in homage to their common desire for the same things. That most of them shared the same religion was secondary to the fact that they were a generation who'd decided to live like Americans in ways their parents never had.

Sam and Eve were so excited they were sleepless all week. No esprit de corps Sam had experienced during the war had engendered such a profound and instant loyalty to an ideal. Sam felt a physical surge watching the houses rise, a sense of power, an élan, a limitlessness of possibility.

An article in a coming issue of *Life* would attempt to define the sense of boundlessness observable in certain parts of the country, this feeling that something fundamental and systemic had led Americans to a bountiful reward. The *Life* writer would claim it was the result of "capitalism tempered by democracy." But as Sam and Eve looked across the sand with the others, he thought he was seeing real democracy for the first time—democracy untempered and as it was meant to be. He couldn't have been more excited if the workmen below him had been building Athens. For years to come he would read occasional critiques decrying the "conformity" of suburban culture, and he would wonder how anyone could so misrepresent a singular moment for democracy at its best.

"Eve," Sam said when the walls started going up, "This will be heaven…heaven on earth."

❈

When news broke about a secret eighteen-thousand-dollar "slush fund" collected from his political supporters, Senator Richard M. Nixon, General Eisenhower's energetic running mate, stopped his campaign train dead in its tracks. Nixon disembarked in Marysville, California, to meet the press. "The Communists, the left-wingers, have been fighting me with every smear that they have been able to do," he said. "They have told you, and you can be sure that the smears will continue to come and the purpose of those smears is to make me, if possible, relent and let up on my attack on the Communists and the crooks in the present administration. I'm going to tell you this: As far as I'm concerned, they've got another guess coming."

Richard Nixon tended to talk that way.

Four days later, on September 23, some fifty-six million Americans gathered before their television sets and many millions more tuned in their radios to see and hear the defense of Richard Nixon, a humble, injured man "whose honesty and integrity has been questioned." A man, moreover, on the verge of being dumped from the Republican ticket.

As his blond wife sat in a nearby chair wearing a Mona Lisa smile, Nixon explained away the eighteen thousand dollars, told the story of his life of hardship and his military service in the South Pacific "when the bombs were falling," and went on to talk himself back into Eisenhower's good graces, swearing that the only gift he had accepted as a public servant was "a little cocker spaniel dog" from a man in Texas. It was "black-and-white-spotted," and "our little girl—Tricia, the six-year-old—named it Checkers. And you know the kids love the dog and I just want to say this right now, that regardless of what they say about it, we're gonna keep it."

Most Americans believed that a rolling wave of love for children, dogs, and country caused the tough-guy candidate to cry at this point. Only one in 350 who wrote or phoned after the speech had anything bad to say about Richard M. Nixon.

Some of the vets Sam knew went out to cheer for General MacArthur after Truman fired him for insubordination. Sam found it ironic that though he loathed the bureaucratic inhumanity of the military—he had seen it up close at its worst—he still found himself among a minority of vets who believed that obeying orders was prime among what soldiers were paid to do, and that MacArthur had overstepped himself in Korea. Even General Eisenhower, MacArthur's onetime speechwriter, agreed that the uniform carried certain restrictions on a man's latitude.

Sam was less than easy with the fact that he found himself seriously considering a Republican candidate. "If it wasn't Eisenhower it'd be different," he'd say to Eve, who had already been won over by the heroic general with the winning smile. His opponent, Adlai Stevenson, seemed to have too much to say, Eve thought. Eisenhower knew when to speak and when to smile.

Sam thought Eisenhower might have the stuff of "greatness" that Sam knew to be within the grasp of American presidents because he had lived in the time of Roosevelt. Sam considered Eisenhower, with his bad knee from trying to tackle the legendary Jim Thorpe during a college football game, and his fifth star awarded after a rather more successful onslaught against the Germans in Normandy, a decent American and a former employer (his 29th Infantry Regiment was at one point attached to Eisenhower's Supreme Allied Command headquarters).

Come November, Sam and Eve would steel themselves in the ballot box, and along with millions of other Depression children who decided they "liked Ike," they would both vote Republican for the first time.

———◆———

The new house fronted a street named for the first Republican President: 221 Lincoln Avenue, at the corner of Lincoln and Kent Road. It was precisely the same as the house next door, finished the day before.

Sam and Eve stood in the middle of the empty, unpaved street. "My fourth child," said Eve.

The Gordons were pioneers among Harbor Isle pioneers, since only a handful of houses had been completed when they moved in. Some of the stronger members of Sam and Eve's extended family assembled to roll the heavy moving barrels into the house. Eve burst into tears when she saw the barrels clogging her newly painted living room, but eventually everything found its place.

Every time a family moved in, the neighbors gathered to celebrate and help out. A new homeowner would drag a little shrub out into the sandy dirt and begin to dig, and all of a sudden a crowd would gather, laughing and congratulating, offering tips and assistance.

As soon as there were enough people around, regular parties were held. The first of the Saturday Night Beach Dances convened on what would be the town beach when the builders got around to it. The Barn Dance planned by newcomer Bunny Allen and her "social committee" was held in the recently established Jewish Center across the bridge in Island Park.

The parties grew louder and longer every week, only in part because of the swelling population. Perhaps one hundred first-wave Harbor Isleites (as they called themselves, borrowing the suffix from the oft-repeated "suburbanites") would gather to swirl away the evening, all of them neighbors, new friends, and terrific dancers too. Eve and Sam had long cut a figure on any dance floor because of the elegant way they moved. Sam's powerful frame became light and graceful whenever the music started, as he and Eve whirled through the crowd displaying a wide selection of steps and gazing into each other's eyes.

Sam had learned to dance as a kid "because dancing was something you could do without money." He'd danced to the best of the big bands. "People are already forgetting that those bands got so big as a way to give poor musicians the chance to work," he'd say. "For a quarter I used to dance to those bands all night long."

Eve had learned her moves from some of the best professional dancers of the day up at the Catskill resorts, but like many of the new Harbor Isle couples, she and Sam had begun going to one of Arthur Murray's studios to pick up the latest steps. The popularity of the jazzy free-form dances of the immediate postwar years was fading now, and the dancing on television was becoming more regimented. Arthur and Katherine Murray were in the process of becoming millionaires several times over by teaching Americans to sway to and fro in the same way.

For several years the parties continued as the people of Harbor Isle celebrated their triumphant arrival. They joined together like a happy tribe to dance lightly into a beautiful American dream.

1953

The Gordons pitied the Rosenbergs, especially the two little boys. "If they weren't Jewish…" Sam Gordon said, his voice trailing away.

On Friday, June 19, Julius and Ethel Rosenberg went calmly to the electric chair after spending the previous twenty-six months in the "death house" at Sing Sing prison. Julius, an electrical engineer, had been born in New York City a few months before Sam, and Ethel was "a housewife" known to millions of Americans who had followed the Rosenberg espionage case as a young woman who "wanted to be a singer." The execution, the newspapers reported, was scheduled so that it would be over before the Jewish Sabbath began on Friday night.

Two years earlier the Rosenbergs had been convicted under the Espionage Act of 1917 of supplying atomic secrets to the Russians back in 1944–45. Neither Sam nor Eve had heard or read a suitable reason to doubt that documents had indeed passed between Julius, then an employee of the army, and some Russian spy. Ethel's own brother, David Greenglass, had testified against her and Julius (according to a poll, eight of ten Americans now believed it was important to "report to the FBI relatives and acquaintances suspected of being Communists"). But the Gordons were among the observers of the case who thought the death sentence was as much a consequence of hysteria generated by the Korean War and fear of the Bomb as it was of the nature of the crime. "And being Jewish," Sam would add. "If they were Gentiles, the Rosenbergs wouldn't have got the chair."

The judge presiding over their case, Irving R. Kaufman, described the crime as "worse than murder" because the Rosenbergs had helped those who would start a nuclear conflagration. "They may have condemned to death tens of millions of innocent people all over the world," said President Eisenhower at the beginning of his term.

Personal views about the fate of the Rosenbergs were best expressed with extreme caution the year they died. Senator McCarthy and his minions were cleansing library shelves of subversive material. McCarthy said Communists were out to assassinate him. If there was a general opinion the new friends in Harbor Isle considered safe to share, it was only that Communists and executions were aspects of the urban life so recently left behind.

———◆———

"You will have a greater chance to be yourself than any people in civilization," the suburban readers of *House Beautiful* were told.

One hundred sixteen families were living in Harbor Isle by early summer, with another 131 on their way. On weekends men carrying tools could be seen darting in and out of every house, followed by children scurrying to keep up like excited ducklings. Six-year-old Lorraine Gordon was arguably the most eager assistant on the island. Strong, agile, and attentive, Lorraine was always around when there was wallpaper to be hung or cement to be mixed, ready to sprint off on a new mission at her father's every command.

Lorraine thought the way her father could make beautiful things appear from pieces of junk and rough boards was magic pure and simple. He could also calm animals—she'd seen it on their drives to the country. Horses and cows would come up to nuzzle her father's hand. And he could make anything grow, this father of Lorraine's, even things that were dead. Lorraine cried the day Sam cut off the top of a withering mulberry tree he'd transplanted to the front yard, leaving only a lifeless stump.

"Don't worry, Lorraine," her father said. "Just wait."

And just as he'd promised, a few weeks later a tiny shoot appeared on the trunk. Magic.

Lorraine would put her boots on, and she and her father would walk down to one of the piers to fish. Sometimes Frankie Huber came out from the Bronx with his pole to join them. Lorraine would walk along the beach with her father, listening to his stories: about why horseshoe crabs dragged themselves across the sand, about poor kids on the Lower East Side going to the store and holding out their hands for a piece of paper loaded with rich peanut butter scraped from a big barrel—better than any peanut butter now.

Lorraine couldn't wait for her weekend work details. The joy she felt at her father's side was so complete that it obscured her terror of...the crawl space.

"Keep going!" Sam would bark at Lorraine and Susan. "Start passing them back."

Every time Sam came home with another truckload of bricks destined for the patio he planned to build, both girls began to feel the same choking sensation in their throats. The crawl space under the new house was too small for Sam, so Lorraine and Susan had to ferry the bricks across jagged gravel, deep into the lightless tunnel of fear. Over and over again they were told to belly into the blackness. "Stack them carefully," Sam would call, but the girls could only see the wall at the far end of the crawl space when his flashlight caught the angle just right.

Halfway through the dreaded mission, Lorraine imagined that she was about to disappear like Alice in Wonderland. The house was on top of her, pushing down, pushing all the air and light from the tomblike passage. Sometimes she thought the house was collapsing. It made noise. The walls were closing in, and the hole where her daddy was waiting with the light was closing up behind her. But still Lorraine crawled back and forth with the bricks, and so did Susan. Their father had told them to do it, sometimes in a voice so full of frustration because he couldn't do it himself that the girls knew he would yell at them if they showed their fear.

One midsummer day, Sam made them take most of the inventory out of the crawl space, but a few hours later he decided he wasn't ready to use the bricks after all. "Okay, girls, let's put 'em back," he said.

It was almost too much to bear.

Susan still thought that Lorraine wasn't scared of anything. "Not even the witch in *The Wizard of Oz*," she would say, with envy and respect for her stolid sister's response to the cackling green visage that haunted a generation of children. Before they moved to Harbor Isle, Eve had taken Lorraine and a little girl from the building next door to see the famous movie. The girl screamed and cried, but Lorraine, who was in fact terrified by the witch, betrayed nothing of her fear.

Lorraine was also terrified by the collection of what she called "Daddy's war books"—books and magazines full of pictures of dead people. Some were families caught in bed or in the kitchen or at the table when a bomb hit their home. One book showed skinny people lying in piles.

Susan wasn't the only one who had Nazi dreams. Storm troopers and Nazi dogs came to torture Lorraine at night too. By the middle of 1953, most of Lorraine's bad dreams were set in the crawl space.

If Sheila woke up scared (she was four now), she would pad onto the landing and into her sisters' bedroom. She always approached Susan first. Susan took Sheila on long walks through Harbor Isle. They would stop in front of the Tolans' house a few blocks away, and Susan would always say, "We're here. We're in California now." They would walk a few more blocks. "Now we're in China," Susan would say with authority.

"Can I get in bed with you?"

"No," Susan would say.

Then Sheila would ask Lorraine.

"Come on in."

Sheila had one sister who took her in when she was scared and one sister who did not. She had a father who worked, at home and away, and a mother who sang so loud as she pushed the stroller through the tree-less town that people would come to their windows. Her mother sang about noodles or garlic when she was in the kitchen. She sang when she hung the laundry on the line. And sometimes she sang sweet, sad songs, though Sheila couldn't understand the words.

⤛⧫⤜

Eve returned to the stage that summer.

It was opening night for the Harbor Isle Beach Club fund-raiser production of *Guys and Dolls*. Eve was to star as Sarah, the saintly Salvation Army soldier. She had already been a hit as Sharon in the Harbor Isle *Finian's Rainbow*, a 1947 musical that used the story of a leprechaun who comes to the American South to search for his stolen crock of gold as a vehicle to condemn racial bigotry.

Sam fidgeted while he waited for his wife to appear. The girls rocked back and forth in their chairs, excited and nervous.

Eve had been in rehearsal every night after dinner for weeks. She had refused to read articles about stage actors, and she hadn't seen a Broadway show in several years; it seemed that reminders of the professional theater made her regretful or "just plain jealous."

But being a star of the stage in Harbor Isle fell outside the "show biz" realm she'd ambivalently left behind. Eve, along with every other woman in Harbor Isle she knew, was determined to be "active." Women in the rapidly expanding American suburbs were "joining up" with the zeal of Colonial Americans, who had formed thousands of organizations of every kind years before they thought of federating their new society as a whole.

Active residents had formed the Harbor Isle Civic Association in May. The first order of business was the publication of a mimeographed newsletter, the *Harbor Isle Beacon*. "With enlightened information, we can all work together for the best community in the USA," the first issue suggested. The newsletter also offered advice. How best to cope with the noisy, "whirling, swirling blades of your Venetian blinds on windy nights?...Raise the blinds above the windows."

The *Beacon* reported Harbor Isle's first bar mitzvah (Harold Levy) and the first mortgage paid in full (Murray Levy, Harold's dad). Concern was voiced in its pages that "urgent calls" might be impeded by "the kids" clogging the telephone party lines. The newsletter chronicled the frustrating efforts of the new homeowners—like their counterparts all over the country—to pressure Harbor Isle's developers, Brill-Tishman, to hurry up and finish the town.

In addition to the theater group, Eve was active in the Jewish Center Sisterhood and several regular mah-jongg games with Harbor Isle women who had names like Dot, Esther, Bunny, and Daisy. Eve had learned to play a mean round of the ancient Chinese game—which employs ivory or bone tiles etched with delicate Oriental images, and which could turn a tableful of otherwise sweet-tempered Jewish ladies into sharks and assassins—from Mattie Kriendler, whose family owned the elegant 21 Club in Manhattan. "Siddown," Mrs. Kriendler had commanded Eve one afternoon up at Grossinger's. "I need a fourth."

Eve's Harbor Isle mah-jongg game—part child-rearing seminar, part communications system, part Greek chorus, and in no small part secret club every bit as gender-loyal as the Masonic lodge Sam would eventually join—was an essential feature of the week. The game was an organization with a purpose, like the PTA or the electrical workers' union, and for Eve it ranked right up there with the theater club.

As soon as Eve appeared on stage and her big bell of a voice filled the little auditorium, Sam eased back in his seat and let her singing take him away.

Sam loved to eavesdrop after the show. The men in particular couldn't stop complimenting Eve awkwardly. "You were so, so...I don't know." Sam would back up and listen proudly, just as Eve enjoyed the hint of jealousy she heard when the other wives talked about Sam and his knack for home improvement. "He can build anything. He can make anything work."

Everyone in Harbor Isle knew Sam was the guy over on Lincoln Avenue who was making a brick patio enclosed by an elegant iron railing. Sam was said to be finishing his attic, and he'd already fitted a substantial new front door in place of the flimsy standard issue. Men with superior educations and much bigger incomes sauntered over to ply him for information when Sam appeared on Sundays in his old army fatigue sweater, a White Owl cigar crushed casually between his teeth. Was it true that he was planning a new dormer window for the front façade?

The first blades of lawn were just beginning to poke through the dirt during the cool grass-growing days of autumn. There were a few knee-high shrubs, some finger-thin sycamore saplings, and little three-pronged birch trees in front of the Gins and Goldstein properties, but Sam Gordon had had himself a big mulberry tree until he had to cut it back. Brill-Tishman had yet to pave all the streets and sidewalks, but Sam Gordon had already built four sections of rough-hewn split-rail fence—with hand-bored mortises—at the corner of Lincoln Avenue and Kent Road.

If there was any incongruity in a weathered corral-style fence set so close to a fancy wrought-iron railing, itself only a few feet from the neighborhood's first cast-iron rendition of a beaming, black-faced, high-booted lawn jockey with a lantern in his hand, then none of the other Harbor Isle settlers chose to point it out to the industrious creator at 221 Lincoln.

Prospective buyers of Harbor Isle homes were regularly brought by the Gordons' to see what a homeowner could do with old-fashioned, all-American know-how and the will to personalize a simple, straightforward structure through the agency of his own hands. None of them could know how truly resourceful Sam had been. Many of his bricks had been "rescued" from skids near construction sites (they weren't going to be used, so he was saving somebody some stiff haulage fees). Sam found the front railing, which reminded everyone in Harbor Isle of an East Side townhouse, in a junkyard. The big mulberry tree came from an abandoned residential district that would soon be a new runway at Idlewild International Airport. Sam figured the tree had a two-hundred-pound gnarl of root fiber, and when he cinched it up onto the roof of the van, the branches completely covered the sides. On the way home the girls were amazed that he could find the road through the forest in front of the windshield.

Sam believed that if a man couldn't afford twelve bucks a month for the commuter train to the city—which he decided he could not—he certainly couldn't afford store-bought landscaping or building materials.

And he believed that a man who could use tools and build from things he found was ahead of the game anyway.

Sociologist Erving Goffman would later describe the singularly American proclivity for what he called "ritual competence." For an American, a display of conscientiousness was "perhaps the most fundamental socialization of all." No application of Sam's vast body of knowledge and careful attention to detail—not even the orange-crate scooters he'd made in the old neighborhood—had ever brought him so much joy.

"Anniversary greetings to Eve and Sam GORDON," wrote Bunny Allen, gossip columnist for the *Harbor Isle Beacon*. The Gordons "celebrated 11 yrs. of married bliss Nov. 7th," Bunny reported. "Birthday congrats to daughter Susan who will be 10, Nov. 14th....Sam finally finished his front patio."

A week later, a Brooklyn man named Sam Randsman was driving through Harbor Isle, engaged in debate with his wife, Bernice. He and Bernice liked the Harbor Isle houses okay, but Sam Randsman still wasn't sure. He pulled up in front of a house where a man chewing on a White Owl was standing in a newly dug garden, a dark little girl in big boots by his side.

"I'm trying to find out more about this place," he said, leaning out the window. "What's this community like?"

"You'd better ask somebody else," the homeowner said in an accent Sam Randsman was able to place within a few subway stops.

"Why's that?"

"Because I love it so much. I just love this place. I'm prejudiced, but that's the way I feel. Everyone says it's a great place for kids, you know, but it's a great place for adults too. But you'd really do better asking somebody else."

Randsman looked up at the lawn jockey and the well-wrought patio. "No need for that. What you've said is good enough for me."

Sam Randsman turned his car around in the driveway and went to buy his house in Harbor Isle.

1954

When Mr. Jules Bilash, Susan's fifth-grade teacher, pointed to the American flag jutting from his classroom wall, Eve Gordon rose along with other visiting Harbor Isle and Island Park mothers to recite the Pledge of Allegiance.

Within a few weeks, on Flag Day, June 14, the words "under God" would be added to the Pledge. The addition of the Deity was President Eisenhower's idea. The "American way of life" would not exist "without God," the president reasoned, and besides, by the most essential current measure of America's moral condition—whether or not we could whip the Russians if push came to shove—a nation "under God" was in a far better strategic position than a "godless" one.

Hand over her heart, standing at her desk near the front of the room, Susan glanced back at Eve, who had dressed for Parents' Night in a tight black skirt and a gleaming white blouse that opened on a delta of tanned neck and chest—nothing remarkable by urban nightclub standards, perhaps, but entirely scandalous according to the buttoning conventions observed by most Harbor Isle wives.

Jules Bilash was extremely frustrated by the absence of fathers at Parents' Night. As an elementary school teacher, he was conversant with the emerging case for more paternal involvement in the life of the "emotionally healthy" child. Even articles outside "the literature," Bilash noted, had taken up the cause of the "new fatherhood." Even Madison Avenue was doing its part by depicting dads not just behind the wheel but behind supermarket shopping carts and baby strollers.

When Bilash made his annual visit to each of his students' homes, he rarely saw a father, but that didn't stop him from expounding the case for paternal participation to the mothers, nor from invoking the growing body of educational theory that emphasized the importance of the home to the essential mission of the school. "Conversely," Bilash would explain, "I believe my classroom must also be like a home...*in loco parentis*, if you will."

Though Jules Bilash of the Radcliffe Road School was clearly an extremely serious pedagogue, Eve had a hunch that he also had an eye for the ladies.

For his part, Bilash thought the mother of the troublemaker Susan Gordon, the mother with the décolletage, was pleasantly flamboyant and in general "quite a woman."

Susan thought Jules Bilash—a youngish Brooklyn man who had been wounded twice during the war—was as old as Grandpa Simon Samberg or Papa Joe Goldenberg. She also thought Mr. Bilash had extremely bad breath, and she'd found his rendition of "Ol' Man River," presented to the class in a quavering baritone, so inept that she started to giggle.

Mr. Bilash paced theatrically before his audience of mothers and children, demonstrating a typical geography lesson. He wheeled away from them and addressed the blackboard, where he inscribed the names of several South American nations in three-inch-high letters. The chalk was still squeaking across the board when he heard the familiar, slightly whiny voice of his second-brightest and least polite pupil.

"Hey! Mr. Bilash."

He turned around, pointedly ignoring the bright-eyed girl flapping her hand in the air. It was evidently not the first time he'd tried to ignore her.

"*Mr. Bilash!*"

The teacher kept talking about South America.

"Mr. Bilash, you're wrong," Susan Gordon persisted. "You misspelled Colombia. You wrote it with a *u*, like the university, but the country has an *o*."

A loudly whispered "oy vey" was heard from a desk a few rows back. The other mothers turned to see Eve Gordon burying her face in her hands.

"Did you have to make a monkey out of the man?" Eve complained as they walked quickly home.

"But he was wrong," Susan said, more quizzical than defiant.

"Susan, sometimes...some things just are not...necessary."

Susan shrugged. "He was wrong."

* * *

By now Susan had taken to condemning her father's errors of fact, judgment, and opinion in no uncertain terms. When Sam listened to his daughter at the dinner table, he heard the hateful gaze she had trained on him the day he came back from the war flowering into words.

"She's saying I'm not what I should be as a father!" Sam would rage to Eve when they were alone. "Well, she's not what she should be as a daughter either."

The image of an American family gathered around the dinner table was beginning to assume the near religious significance of the crucifix or the Star of David. During the spring of 1954, *McCall's* magazine, perhaps recalling the dire predictions of Carle Zimmerman, gave a name to the spirit symbolized by a family at table: "togetherness"—arguably the first of postwar American "buzz words." For the next six years "togetherness" would be woven into countless ads, editorials, and speeches delivered by any politician who hoped to win. *McCall's* would soon begin promoting itself on its cover as "The Magazine of Togetherness."

This golden age of the family coincided with the cry from the pulpits of popular culture that wives and children must begin the reclamation of the hardworking but distant American father. Articles entitled "Father as a Family Man" or "Man's Place Is in the Home" (both in the *New York Times Magazine*) or "Fathers Are Parents Too" or "Have Fathers Changed?" appeared one after another. If the culture reflected any of the equivocal feelings churned up by this clarion call to the new father, moviegoers might have been among the first to see it when *Rebel Without a Cause* opened in 1955. In one of this popular movie's most dramatic scenes, the upper-middle-class father played by Jim Backus appears in an apron, utterly feminized and quickly humiliated by his son, who is troubled not by poverty but by his family's way of life.

Sam could not help thinking of the dinner table as a proving ground when the Gordons now sat down to an evening of television full of normal, happy, well-governed families eating a meal together. In 1954 some American families would fan around the vacuum-tube hearth in crescents of pleasure while consuming a brilliant frozen invention from C. A. Swanson & Sons of Omaha, Nebraska. Though Eve Gordon would have cut off her chopping hand before serving a TV dinner to the family she loved, by the late months of the year certain family television shows rarely aired without several Gordons—and usually the family's terrier puppy, Cleo—looking on. They watched *The Adventures of Ozzie and Harriet*, *Make Room for Daddy*, and *I Love Lucy*. (The Goldbergs were still on too, though they would soon leave the Bronx for a suburb called Haverville.)

Sheila's favorite was *Father Knows Best*. She imagined that she was the Gordon family's very own "Kitten," little sister to the glamorous and worldly Betty, known on the show as "Princess," who reminded Sheila of Susan Gordon. Kitten's father, Jim Anderson, worked in insurance, though he never seemed to mention his job or to drag himself home close to midnight smelling like an electrical fire. Unlike Sam, Jim Anderson came home at a reasonable hour; he put on his sweater, and over dinner, before the eyes of his and millions of other families, he turned into King Solomon, adjudicating quarrels and philosophizing easily about the essential stuff of family life.

The adjective often applied to these perfect television families was "wholesome," a quality that served as moral mortar for the great protective wall of "togetherness." Gone was the "zany domesticity" of the not so distant past, when everything from infidelity to divorce was fair game in movies like *Holiday* (1930), *The Awful Truth* (1937), *My Favorite Wife* (1940), and *The Palm Beach Story* (1942). The nuclear family, calm and normal and having dinner together at home, was cast in bronze and fixed like some glorious hood ornament to the front of the national automobile.

As Sam watched Jim Anderson, he found it more and more difficult to fathom Susan's hostility at dinner. Jim would not have remained so calm, Sam was sure, if Susan Gordon had ever had a go at him.

On the rare occasions when Sam was home for dinner, he was invariably the target of Susan's assaults because of a vestigial quirk of Eve's from the Bronx, or for all Sam knew, from the shtetl. Eve would not sit down. She would flutter around the table while everyone urged her to join them. "Eve, sit." "Mom, sit." But Eve believed she was mistress of the feast. "Eat," she'd say. And when the fighting started, she'd serve more food, piling it on as if to cushion the blows.

"Oh yeah?" Sam would reply to one of Susan's pronouncements, narrowing his eyes in the direction of his eleven-year-old daughter. "Who told you *that*? Your *teacher*?"

Susan would not back down. "Yes, that's what my teacher said."

"You know what?" Sam might say. "You're *stupid*. How come you're so smart at school and so dumb at home?"

Then Susan would begin to cry.

Sam was by no means the first smart self-made man to resent the education that some people flaunted like a badge. Harry Truman had rarely passed up the chance to take a crack at "the ivory tower of academe."

But what Susan came home with was worse. It sounded as if she believed that all authority resided in her school. The Gordon house was not the only place where parents felt reduced to lay associates of the professionals bringing up their kids.

For decades past, the family had been regarded as the "little school," but early in the century American educational reformers began to argue that the schools should care for "the whole child" because parental authority had failed. Shortly after World War II, Frank Tannenbaum, a Columbia University professor who'd once ridden *with* Pancho Villa instead of *after* him, like Papa Joe, wrote a fascinating essay tracing the long history of power struggles between the "irreducible" human institutions, "perennial through time": state, church, and family. "Each of the institutions in its own inner logic," said Tannenbaum, "tends to be all-embracing, laying claim to the entire man, and showing an impelling tendency to assume all responsibility for the governance of society." In China, Brazil, Scotland, "even in Kentucky," the family once held "complete control" over the individual. In a complex modern society institutional tension was inevitable, Tannenbaum concluded, but Sam Gordon thought the state was turning him into the enemy. Every class and every library book gave Susan new ammunition. Every day was like a war.

"She questions my whole life," Sam said to Eve. "There's nearly seven hundred kids at that school. Do you think they all come home and stick it to the old man? She aggravates the shit out of me—on purpose."

Eve thought Sam "had a temper." She didn't have to read Simone de Beauvoir's analysis of the modern male's marital "anchorage in immanence" in *The Second Sex*, published in English last year, to know that he was, after all, a man. Away from Susan and the dinner table, he would calm down. She figured this was a "phase."

But Sam's ire and confusion were deeper than she knew. Unlike some Harbor Isle fathers who resented challenges from their children because they'd brought them out of the city and given them a new life, Sam did not feel Susan owed him because of anything he'd done for her. She owed him because of who he was—her father.

She doesn't accept me, fine, Sam would think to himself after a mealtime argument. *You don't accept me. I don't accept you. That's it.*

"I'm sorry, Eve," Sam would say after losing his temper, "but she's just too much for me to handle."

Before school started in the fall, a "runaway hurricane" named Carol slammed into Harbor Isle. If the town had been older, its trees might have been tall enough to number among the thousands destroyed on Long Island. Water was rushing through the still unfinished streets, and the power was out.

Lorraine watched Sam wire a light bulb to a car battery. She was proud when neighbors were drawn to Harbor Isle's only working light. Then he filled the big black kettledrum of a suburban barbecue with charcoal and dragged it into the garage. He lit a Coleman stove and opened a can of beans. Some people brought food to cook over the fires, and the sense of adventure reminded everyone of the early days of Harbor Isle, which felt distant though they were only two years past.

Lorraine was happy to see her father in control, grinning his huge handsome grin, away from the dinner table. All summer, Sam had assigned Lorraine and Susan jobs like trimming the hedge, and it seemed to both of them that whatever they did their father said it was wrong.

Susan still couldn't understand why Sam got so angry when she talked about school. She knew she had a tendency to be sneaky and tell lies—reasonable cause for parental distress—but school was an essential component of her life. School was the thing she did best. It was the only place Susan thought she could be like Sam, who knew almost everything. Aunt Sylvia had told Susan that Sam was always in trouble when he was in school. Sylvia said Mama Yetta had to go see his teachers all the time. Susan figured school had bored him, and she assumed that as father and daughter they shared an inability to suffer fools.

At dinner she would try to show him how alike they were, but he always got angry. "Why does he look at me like that?" Susan asked Eve.

Sam's eyes would crease, his lips would purse, and a strange smile would spread over his face. Then came the arrows of sarcasm that made Susan cry. But she kept talking. She'd never get his attention back if she stopped.

One day Susan fell all the way down the steep basement stairs. Lying there stunned, she looked up to see her father rushing toward her, his face shining with concern. He swooped down like a dancer and swept her up in his arms. Many years later Susan could still remember the blissful feeling of his arms around her, strong and gentle as he carried her up the stairs.

* * *

Sam was turning the garage into a playroom by the end of the year. By any standard—rumpus rooms, rec rooms, television rooms, or dens improvised by professional builders or inspired do-it-yourselfers all over Long Island—Sam Gordon's playroom would be a work of art. His plan was to build a large semicircular wet bar entirely of hardwoods he would shape by hand. A huge console would control recessed colored lights that could be adjusted to flood the bar with any shade on the spectrum. The floor would be red, made of a grade of "battleship linoleum" that Sam announced was "all but guaranteed to last a hundred years."

Sam thought of the new room as a place of celebration and refuge. He'd taken to calling this elegant chamber his "drinking room," not that he liked to drink—he didn't—but because the phrase connoted joyous crowds, happy faces, people gathered together in neighborly concert in his hand-crafted room, trying out the subtle new steps of the cha-cha, dancing the night away to Les Baxter and Benay Venuta records playing loud on the hi-fi Sam had assembled from spare parts.

Lorraine stood by in her usual helper's pose during the construction of the playroom, though her father had grown increasingly exacting ever since the project began. "Quick, get the level," he would order, but never said which level. Sam grew frustrated if Lorraine asked, and even more frustrated if she brought all the levels or took a chance and chose the wrong one. Lorraine, almost eight, had also noticed that her father wasn't very excited or complimentary anymore when she got things right.

Lorraine and Susan were both present when Sam proclaimed the playroom finished. The final touch was a sign, designed to capture the hybrid of Old West saloon and private club Sam had in mind, cut and lettered with a woodburning pen by the master's own hands. The girls watched him hang the sign on the wall, and then they all stood back and stared at the words: "Gordon's Hacienda."

1955

In 1955 cracks appeared in Harbor Isle. Thirty-nine houses had leaky foundations, and half the sidewalks and driveways in town were in dire need of repair by late summer. Many homeowners had septic-tank problems and grass growing in their crawl spaces. Like other developers of the new suburbs, Brill-Tishman had suddenly gone out of business, with several streets still unpaved. The town ended up floating a fifty-thousand-dollar bond issue to complete the job.

When the broad streets were finally finished and had proper curbs, safety issues became the talk of Harbor Isle. A contingent of concerned citizens called for stop signs at every corner and a ten-mile-per-hour speed limit to control reckless drivers. Had there been a stop sign at the corner of Lincoln and Kent, then maybe Cleo, the Gordons' beloved dog, would not have been run down.

Their neighbor, Al Barden, head of the Harbor Isle Safety Committee, wrote an admonitory eulogy in the *Beacon* entitled "Cleo Was a Dog": "To some of us, the dogs running around loose are a nuisance and an annoyance. They may have mistreated your lawns or your shrubs.... But Cleo was a living thing, and was killed by a vehicle....Cleo was a dog, but it could have been your child or mine."

An actuary might have noted that the three Gordon girls were at greater risk than other Harbor Isle children because they were pedestrians far more often. If they had been unable to speak English, or if they had had black skin (two white families had recently been asked to leave Levittown because they had dared to have black guests in broad daylight), Susan, Lorraine, and Sheila thought they could hardly have been more different from the other children in town: their mother did not know how to drive. They were constantly being picked up and delivered by other mothers, and Eve could not reciprocate. They often walked for what seemed to them like miles and miles, while their friends were never seen to walk anywhere at all.

Susan lamented to Lorraine that having a mother who didn't drive in Harbor Isle was like being "an orphan or a waif." But Eve's daughters never told her how terribly deprived they felt, because it was easier to bear their humiliation than to make their mother feel guiltier or sadder or more different than she already did. All the girls—even five-year-old Sheila—knew that there were certain things their mother did not want to see or hear or know.

Susan tried to control her grief over Cleo's death, and Eve held her tight. "She's not in pain, Susan." But Susan couldn't stop crying. The mourning continued for weeks. Susan was forty-seven years old when she first realized that it was Al Barden, and not she, who had written "Cleo Was a Dog" for the *Beacon.* A new teacher had recently introduced Susan to the world of creative writing, and all her life she had regarded the obituary as her first published work.

Eve had injured her lower back just a few hours before Cleo was killed. Racked by spasms, she did her best to comfort Susan as the dizzying pain climbed down her legs and up behind her eyes. She was scheduled to check into the hospital first thing in the morning.

"Oh, Mommy, Mommy, Mommy!"

Finally Eve pushed Susan away, regarding her at arm's length. "That's it, Susan!" she said, cool and distant. "This…is…*too much.*"

Susan held her breath, but a sob rolled out anyway.

"That's it!" Eve yelled. "We are *never* going to have another dog ever again!"

<hr>

Eve Gordon began to wonder if there was something wrong with her. For several months she had been wrestling with "a feeling," and by the middle of the summer she was concerned that the feeling had won. *I don't fit,* Eve kept thinking. She'd banish the thought, but it would return. *I don't really fit into Harbor Isle.* The sense of doubt would hound her all the way to the beach, where friends always welcomed her with open arms.

In the company of dozens of other town mothers, Eve would drag a flimsy bridge table to one end of the tiny, vivid rectangle of American mid-decade leisure that was the Harbor Isle Beach Club. On warm summer days the long-awaited, newly opened beach club blossomed with

Caribbean colors. A quilt of beach towels glowed candy-bright in the sharp island light. Ladies paraded their cordial-hued coifs, in "Sherry," "Champagne," and "Apricot Brandy." There were always a few beauty-parlor "Mamie bangs" and professionally colored "poodle cuts" on display at the beach, but like six of ten American women who now agreed that retail dyes and other hair products could be safely and artistically applied at home, most of the Beach Club regulars did their hair themselves. Beauty parlors were now considered a waste of an active woman's time, and dyed hair—not so long ago a sign of easy virtue—had gone mainstream, as Clairol's hugely successful "Does she or doesn't she?" campaign would attest next year.

On weekends, fathers appeared on the beach, though Sam always seemed to be at work. ("You're not really married, admit it," her friends would occasionally tease Eve.) Many sported Harry Truman Hawaiian shirts and Bermuda shorts in the new fashion color of the American male circa 1955: pink. Just as men in other cultures grew their fingernails long as evidence of their distance from manual labor, suburban husbands of increasing leisure (three of four American men now claimed to be "middle-class") proudly wore the once ladylike color.

The island colors of the beach were joined by island sounds: loud laughter, the buzz of gossip, the generally gleeful cries rising from the startling concentration of kids overseen by three lifeguards. The sounds all fell into a syncopation ruled by the brittle clickety-click of mah-jongg tiles.

Eve Gordon was considered one of the island's better mah-jongg players. She had added one after-dinner game to her twice-weekly afternoon sessions but refused to be coaxed out for a second night. "I don't believe in women going out more than once a week without their husbands," Eve would say.

"You cater to him too much," her friends would object.

"What, I shouldn't be flattered he still wants me around?"

The girls would laugh—mah-jongg players were always "girls," even at ninety—but Eve would quietly fume. *And are you happier than me? Have you made such a success of things?* But she never stopped smiling.

There were five core players at most of the regular mah-jongg games, which meant that one would sit out and place bets on the others. The game required "card sense," and veterans like Eve, Rose Brown, and Esther Kreiner did not tolerate slow play, obvious play, talky play, or lapses from the transcendent balance between camaraderie and pitched combat that made mah-jongg so worthwhile.

You can't really talk during a serious hand of mah-jongg, but since

Eve knew the tempo and phrasing of the game as well as she knew hundreds of songs, she could inject one-liners, brief family stories, and the odd Borscht Belt routine without breaking the spell.

Sometimes Eve wondered why she found it impossible to be in the presence of more than one person without dragging a joke out of the pile. At the club on weekends, the men would gather around as soon as she stood up from the card table.

"Okay, okay. So the Negro runs up to the urinal and pulls out a shlong this long to have a pish. 'Phew,' he says, 'just made it.' 'Vell, darlink,' says a little Jewish guy standing next to him, 'can ya make me von in white?'"

The men roared. "Another! Another, Eve!"

"Tell one in Yiddish, Eve!"

"Tell the one about the whipper."

"Tell the one about pishing in the sand!"

Many of the men and women who loved Eve's shtick had worked hard to shed their parents' accents. They had left a raft of inflections behind in Brooklyn or the Bronx. But Eve Gordon refused to renounce the *Yiddishkeit* of old, and when she went into a turn on the beach, they all flocked around the flamboyant lady from Lincoln Avenue with the Liz Taylor hairdo, the tan, and the great figure, begging for more.

But even as she entertained, Eve could feel the distance between herself and the laughter. Often, as she walked toward the wooden bridge to shop in Island Park, that feeling of not fitting in would descend on her. It saddened her, though it didn't inspire the nervous anxiety she used to feel in the Bronx—she hadn't tossed a dish since the family's move to the suburbs. Still, not fitting in, or at least the sense that she didn't, induced a preoccupation with available options or adjustments. Eve would spend months mulling over a single question: *What*, she asked herself again and again, *should I do?*

When Eve thought about her attacks of nervousness back in the Bronx and her inability to "fit" in idyllic Harbor Isle, she sometimes recalled articles about the human mind she'd been reading lately. She couldn't help wondering if she was...if there was something wrong.

She would gaze around the Harbor Isle Beach Club, a place of safety only nine blocks from home, where people laughed at her jokes and children frolicked. She knew she had a good marriage, a beautiful house, and a wonderful family. Except for Susan Hayward, who had tried to commit suicide a few months earlier, it seemed to Eve that most Americans her age were happier than they'd ever been. A recent magazine quiz had offered a chart to assist in rating the precise extent of one's happiness: "extraordinarily happy," "decidedly more happy than average," "somewhat more happy than average," "just over happy," and so on.

But perhaps because of her acute sense of rhythm, Eve was sure she was "out of step." The sameness that Sam still considered one of Harbor Isle's strengths was like a dance routine she couldn't quite master.

Eve could tell that her determination to teach her daughters to "be themselves" and to "know their own minds" did not jibe with local norms. For instance, Eve allowed Susan to stay home from school whenever Fred Astaire movies were on TV. She and Susan would watch the former Fred Austerlitz and his smiling Ginger glide across the floor in *Top Hat* or *Follow the Fleet*. Eve thought that the sight of Fred Astaire in artless motion—getting the girl in the end as he offered a lesson in taste, style, and what in 1955 was still called "class"—was just as important to a girl's education as a day at school.

Eve's belief that she did not conform was confirmed when one of Susan's teachers summoned her for a meeting.

"I think you should make it your business to do something about Susan's personality," the woman said.

"What do you mean by that?"

"Well, she talks back. She's too aggressive and too smart for her own good."

All this Eve knew to be quite true. She remained entirely composed. "So, you're saying you don't like the way her *personality* and yours work together?"

"No, I don't."

"*Well, change yours, then!*" Eve roared at the startled teacher. "Try to get along with your students instead of asking me to turn my daughter into something else…like she's a robot!"

And with that, Eve marched out of the room.

Susan could be "a precocious little pain in the ass," as Eve was willing to admit to the girls over mah-jongg, but she did not trust the current assumption that misbehavior was a sign of "maladjustment." "What's the difference between being maladjusted and having a strong personality?" Eve would ask. "I mean, a strong personality can save a girl's life."

But when Eve went back to thinking about her own problems, when she tried to plumb her feelings of doubt and drift, she still kept wondering if there was something wrong with her. Sometimes she asked herself if *she* was maladjusted, even crazy. Not crazy like the girls meant when they teased her—"You're so crazy, Eve!"—but crazy in the way implied by a word middle-class Americans were just beginning to toss around at cocktail parties: "neurotic."

Ever since the public discussion of "neuropsychiatric" war veterans with "adjustment" problems, the nomenclature of psychoanalysis had been gaining currency by the year, particularly in connection with unruly children and unhappy families. Since the war, filtered Freudianism had been reaching the general population via sociology (David Riesman and his fellow students of social type), anthropology (the magazine articles of Margaret Mead), pediatrics (Dr. Spock), and all manner of literary and artistic criticism. But the straight stuff was hard to come by for those not wealthy enough to become analysands, and especially for those who'd left the city to concentrate on raising families.

In 1953, under a gigantic banner headline—"DOES YOUR FAMILY HAVE A NEUROSIS?"—a Collier's magazine article had helped transport psychoanalytic terminology directly into the home. "Here is an advance report on a challenging new psychiatric concept which should deeply interest everyone concerned with family health—in short, just about all of us. Thus far very few laymen—indeed, few specialists—have heard of it but…a family may be what psychiatrists call hysterical, or mother-fixated, or compulsive, or sado-masochistic and so on.…Even happy, ambitious or devoted families may be neurotic, according to a prominent psychiatrist."

This last line was extracted from the body of the article and boldly highlighted at the top of a page featuring photographs of twenty-two Americans who managed to look both typical and tortured, shocked, manipulative, confused, euphoric, murderous, withdrawn, or otherwise demented. The writer, Morton Hunt, reported that a study of nearly four hundred middle-class families in the Boston area showed that a "compulsive pattern of excessive worry about neatness, quietness and social conformity turned up as a common source of tension contributing to the maladjustments and troubles of the children in those families."

In 1954 a large psychoanalytic field study conducted in Chestnut Lodge, Maryland, revealed that all the patients in the study group who suffered from manic-depressive psychoses came from "socially isolated" families that "felt themselves to be too little respected in their neighborhood." David Riesman had already described a "packaged sociability" that bore heavily on the lives of suburban women. That the nation demanded conformity as a test of fundamental Americanness was borne out by Samuel Stouffer's Communism, Conformity, and Civil Liberties, a fascinating study based on opinion polls conducted in 1954. According to Stouffer, most Americans who detected Communists in their midst did so almost entirely by observing personal or conversational styles not quite consonant with community norms.

Eve wasn't particularly interested in whether her family had a neurosis. Indeed, she would manage to avoid the psychoanalyzation of popular culture for some time to come. But the family did have its *tsuris*, an all-purpose Yiddish word that translates poorly as "trouble," and then there was the nagging need she felt to act, to take a step in the direction of the normal life of Harbor Isle. Eve loved Harbor Isle; she only wanted to be happier there.

So she continued to worry. She could no more stop singing or telling jokes than breathing, and besides, everyone seemed to like it. She didn't work, so she couldn't quit her job. And no matter what Morton Hunt of *Collier's* had to say, she would always keep her home neat and clean.

Finally, it came to her, as in a vision.

It was dinnertime in the early fall, a moment of Cold War thaw in the geopolitical arena. A few days ago, after playing twenty-seven straight holes of golf and some billiards, President Eisenhower had had a heart attack. Eve watched Sam eat all of a big dinner she'd set aside for him hours before, as she'd done so often since Dynamic Electric began to recover from rough times earlier in the year. She waited until they were alone in bed—the best of all places to talk to Sam Gordon. "Honey," she said. "I've made a decision. I've got to make a change. I want to learn how to drive."

Eve strained to peer over the looming dashboard. She was so small she couldn't even see the road. The rearview mirror mounted on the dash seemed miles away. "Well, I cannot believe this," she said. "You gotta shift. You gotta steer. And you gotta push down on the gas. All at the same time?"

"Yes!" Sam barked. "Yes, yes, yes!"

The much maligned "woman driver" had lately been given something of a boost when several of the nation's largest automobile insurance carriers decided to offer young female drivers discounts of up to thirty-two percent, while making no such concessions to young men. Soon thereafter Anthony Tramondo, a driver education instructor from White Plains, New York, claimed in the *New York Times* that even though "women approach an automobile with a good deal more respect than do men—if only because it is a mechanical mystery to them," that did not make them good drivers. In fact, Mr. Tramondo believed that "poor women drivers" fell into five distinct categories: The Scatter-brains ("deeply involved in personal problems"), The Frighteneds ("do not know what a car can do and are afraid to find out"), The Overconfidents, The Lookers ("does her window shopping while driving"), and of course The Conversationalists.

One of the most famous representations of an otherwise competent American wife becoming incapacitated by stupidity behind the wheel of a man-sized 1950s car was an episode of *Father Knows Best*. Confronted by Margaret's auto antics, even the steady Jim Anderson became exasperated—and Jim was a saint when it came to patience.

"I can't believe this!" Sam screamed, pitching violently back and forth in his seat after Eve's foot slipped off the clutch for the ninth or tenth time.

"Don't yell at me!" Eve screamed back, and with that the muscles of her lower back constricted around her injured disks. Within seconds she was paralyzed by pain.

Two hours later Eve was in the hospital, staked out in traction as if about to be vivisected. Before the leaves turned on the spindly Harbor Isle trees, she had "bloated out" by three dress sizes. She always blamed the rapid weight gain on the medication she was given for the pain. The extent of the fiasco was such that no one in the family ventured to mention Eve's driving in her presence for many years.

Once out of traction and back on her feet, Eve remained determined to change her routine. All she needed was a new plan.

1956

Eve eventually addressed complications of spirit, vicissitudes of psyche, subtle details of assimilation and socialization, and her persistent identity crisis—even at the age of thirty-five—by having a baby boy.

"Of all the accomplishments of the American woman," it said right there in *Life* magazine, "the one she brings off with the most spectacular success is having babies."

Eve delivered on Mother's Day. "I haven't felt so good in months!" she rejoiced. "Something's popped in my back. Right in the middle of everything, when I started pushing. Sam, I think I'm cured."

Sam scrutinized the birth certificate. "Ricky? Not Richard or Rick?"

"Ricky," she said.

Eve had in mind Bogart's romantic if introverted Rick in *Casablanca*, but like so many new mothers, she wanted something catchy. Fathers had names like Sam, and boys had names like Sammy. The name on the birth certificate—"Ricky Ian Gordon"—also had to do with show biz. Eve cast a drowsy smile at a head the size of a small grapefruit with ears the size of Sam's protruding from either side. "With a name like Ricky Gordon, he won't have to change it if he decides to go on stage."

Mama Yetta Goldenberg came out from the city to stay with Susan, Sheila, and Lorraine while their parents went to the hospital. The phone call came late. The radio in the corner of Lorraine and Susan's dark bedroom had finally fallen silent by the time Yetta entered and administered the extensive series of shakes required to wake Susan.

"Thank God!" Yetta said, her hand to her cheek.

"What? What happened?" Susan managed, jerking to a sitting position. "What?"

"*Finally*. Your mother managed to have a boy!"

Eve overheard Sheila telling her friend Freddy Baker that she could make her new baby brother smile. "It takes a while for them to learn how to smile," Eve told her six-year-old. "Ricky's only a few days old."

"I *will* make him smile," Sheila assured Freddy on the way up the stairs. They went into Sheila's room, where Eve had decided to put the baby's cradle.

Sheila stared down at her new brother, and as Freddy looked on, Ricky's face rearranged into a massive grin.

Sheila was quite sure that this new baby was meant for her.

❖

Yetta, as everyone in the family knew, did not in the least approve of the sounds she heard in her son's home these days. For almost a year Sam and Eve had also been listening to what came out of the girls' radio: music punctuated by wild, squawking chatter, with bass and drum backup that pulsated through several walls and three split levels.

Eve and Sam recognized the music immediately. It had been known to the relatively sophisticated as "race music" for some time. It was music of grief and joy, thrumming, daring music of passionate love. And it was the music of poor people, of pickers in the cotton fields back home, and of some of their black neighbors from the old days in the Bronx. As far as Sam and Eve knew, Susan and Lorraine had not even seen a "Negro" since they'd escaped the city. The girls were modestly well-off suburbanites whose acquaintance with cotton was limited to blouses and Q-Tips.

"It's no different from when I discovered jazz," Sam said, recalling that jazz had made his mother nervous too. "Music changes. This is all normal."

At first Eve agreed. Better willfulness beside the radio than at the dinner table. But after Susan decided she had to get closer to the sound—and Lorraine wanted to tag along—Eve, the family singer, wasn't so sure.

Susan passed over the iridescent navy blue taffeta circle skirt in favor of a pair of jet-black stretch pants so tight she could feel the blood whoosh to her head. She pulled on three pairs of white "elephant socks" from an army-navy store, one over the other, their ribbed tops gathered like great bladders around her ankles. She tied mirror-bright black-and-white saddle shoes purchased two sizes too big to accommodate the socks, and buttoned a delicate see-through nylon blouse over a cotton brassiere with padded conical cups.

Susan draped a black chiffon scarf over her head and tied it so that only certain pincurls peeked out in front. She unearthed a pack of Marlboros from one of her hiding places and slid it into her purse, glancing at Lorraine, who was soaking up each nuance of Susan's fashion ritual. Lorraine's dreams had recently been filled with the contents of her sister's closet. So dazzling was Susan's shopping prowess, so specific were her tastes, that she could navigate the vast indoor reaches of the brand-new Greenacres Mall, a place that made Lorraine dizzy, as if she'd grown up there.

Susan was the dresser in the family, and the brilliant sister too. If Lorraine was now on her way to a 97.2 average in Jules Bilash's class, Susan had a 99.2 when she had Bilash two years earlier. She was the smart one and she was the tease. When Lorraine was three she had to have an operation to straighten a crossed eye, and Susan convinced her that the doctors were going to remove her eye, cut it up a bit, and then see if they could fit it back into the hole. To Lorraine, being on the receiving end of Susan's jokes was like being "sent to the gas chamber."

At dinner, Lorraine sometimes resorted to hyperbole in the face of Susan's verbal agility and her father's sarcasm or withdrawal. One night she got so angry at her older sister that she worked up the courage to say something truly awful. "I hope you get heartburn and die!"

Susan—and Sam and Eve—guffawed.

Susan still considered Lorraine the brave sister. She had athletic ability and remarkable physical strength. Susan thought her little sister was exactly the sort of person you'd want along on an adventure, even though Lorraine had just turned ten a few weeks earlier.

"Let's go," Susan said, patting her cigarettes.

Much less elaborately clad in a skirt and tights, Lorraine fell into place at Susan's side. The Gordon girls strolled out of the house looking nothing at all like a typical junior high student from Harbor Isle and her kid sister. Susan and Lorraine were at large this bright weekend afternoon, bound for no less exotic a place than Brooklyn, New York. They were off to join up with history.

Hail hail rock 'n' roll!

Outside the old Brooklyn Paramount, a movie palace like the ones where Eve had dreamed away so many youthful afternoons, Susan and

Lorraine noticed that most of the other girls were in tight black pants and elephant socks. A few wore toreador or peg pants in various shades of pink. Many of the white boys—about half the crowd looked to be white—huddled in black-leather circles, slicking back their ducktails and carefully composing their James Dean or Elvis faces into sneers.

The kids filed calmly into the huge theater, and after a few minutes an ordinary-looking man bounded on stage. It wasn't until he started to talk that Susan and Lorraine realized they were gazing at the one and only Alan Freed.

Rock 'n' roll and Alan Freed had actually come to Harbor Isle on the radio thanks to the power of television. Trying to sidestep the fate of the Hollywood movie industry, which had by now lost half its audience to TV, certain radio programmers convinced sponsors that by "formatting" their shows to appeal to specific preferences, they could corral identifiable markets of consumers who would stay tuned through the commercials.

A show like *Make-Believe Ballroom*, a Susan and Eve Gordon favorite for many years, began to offer a short musical segment featuring "rhythm and blues," though much of this renamed and updated "race music" Eve had known since the 1930s was banned because of its blatant sexual suggestiveness. The mere mention of the New York City piano player Thomas Waller, known in rhythm-and-blues circles as "Fats," drew titters from white music-lovers who knew about his "dirty" songs. Traditional blues was still widely considered the profane counterpart of gospel music, and R&B was an underground form until Alan Freed.

Freed, the WINS disc jockey whose near-hysterical delivery penetrated the walls of 221 Lincoln, had been calling the driving music he played "rock 'n' roll" since 1950. Susan would sit next to the radio every night, neatly jotting in a notebook the titles and performers of all the songs he played. This cataloging process helped Susan choose 78- and 45-rpm records to add to her collection, but she also took notes because she wanted to understand and remember everything she could about music that could change her mood and make her entire body tingle. A few of her school friends seemed to "feel" the pure emotion of the music too, and Susan wanted to talk to them about it, to be close to others who'd had the same experience.

When Susan found out that Alan Freed was renting some of New York's underutilized movie palaces to present live shows featuring the rock 'n' roll musicians she'd heard on the radio, she and Lorraine began to discuss whether attending would require asking permission, running away from home for the night, or running away for good. By the spring of 1956 there were already reports that a great many decent Americans—in particular the parents of other children who'd begged to be allowed to see Alan Freed's shows—were quite concerned about rock 'n' roll and about the state of the nation's youth in general.

A Sunday night CBS-TV special hosted by Eric Sevareid exposed the dangerous hysteria that swept the audience during these movie palace evenings. Psychiatrists told Sevareid that the shows were symptomatic of some "pathology" in these children's "home life." Witnesses testifying before Senator Estes Kefauver's Juvenile Delinquency Subcommittee made official the often implied connection between rock 'n' roll and the fearsome rise in too many American towns of that sauntering, switchblade-toting threat to the social fabric—the "JD."

In 1956 a number of shootings and sadistic gang rapes involving adolescent boys—for the most part white—generated publicity so unnerving that a considerable portion of the population became more afraid of American teenagers than of the Russians, who were currently engaged in crushing the Hungarian Revolution. Crimes committed by young people made daily headlines in New York and other cities. "Our Vicious Young Hoodlums: Is There Any Hope?" asked *Newsweek*.

Woeful confessions by the parents of delinquents also appeared in the press—none could imagine what had gone wrong. Not since the flapper phenomenon of the 1920s, which was interpreted as a dire assault on the nation's moral underpinnings, had so much fear about family stability been aroused by forces "from within." By the 1940s the term "youth culture" generally connoted, for most parents, oversized letter sweaters, perhaps a certain recalcitrance of mind, and an occasionally exaggerated fascination with glamour. But the JDs now terrifying American parents were not stuffing themselves into phone booths. That most of the children who committed terrible crimes were very poor was hidden by the fact that they looked like those kids on CBS who were "hypnotized" by rock 'n' roll. The Very Reverend Monsignor John P. Carroll, director of the Catholic Youth Organization in Boston, lamented that the forces of order were already too late. The music was so virulent that it had "already left its scar on youth," he said. A Connecticut psychiatrist quoted in the national press called rock 'n' roll a "communicable disease."

Confronted with the onus of distributing such stuff over the airwaves, Alan Freed was defiant. "As long as there are radio stations like this in America," Susan heard him declare on WINS, "*we are going to rock 'n' roll!*"

Eve wanted to tell her daughters that they were most certainly not allowed to go to Brooklyn for the show, but the only justification she could think of was that the idea scared the daylights out of her. As a high school student, Eve had left school early many times to travel by public transport to the old New York Paramount in Times Square. She'd sat in the audience screaming from the moment Frank Sinatra appeared on stage. She remembered the movie palaces in their heyday. How could she be so hypocritical as to forbid adventures of the sort that had marked the happiest days of her own youth?

The bands—Freed had assembled twenty of them—took to the stage at the Brooklyn Paramount and began to play, one after another, each somehow more astounding than the last, and each allowed to play only two or three songs. That, along with the dazzling colors, created a three-ring-circus effect. The groups came on in some of the most amazing clothing Susan and Lorraine had ever seen—shimmering outfits, parodic variations on the blandest of formal attire. The Isley Brothers were Christmasy in bright red tuxedo jackets with shiny green satin lapels.

On came the Cleftones, the G-Clefs, the Platters, and the Moonglows. Ben E. King and the Drifters performed "There Goes My Baby." A fast-picking, glowering singer named Chuck Berry did "Maybelline," kicking one leg in the air and propelling himself magically across the stage while playing his guitar like a man possessed. Screamin' Jay Hawkins, King Curtis, and Clarence "Frogman" Henry offered more traditional rhythm and blues. Susan and Lorraine stood and screamed with all the other kids when the Ink Spots, the Mills Brothers, the Cadillacs, and Bo Diddley strode onto the stage. Jackie Wilson sang sad love songs, and some girls started to cry, and when the Isley Brothers exhorted the crowd to join in on "Shout!" everyone roared right on cue.

Susan and Lorraine felt the show leave the stage and flow like lava into the audience. The music encircled the girls from Harbor Isle as young people danced in the aisles beside them. The show was a purity of sensation that resonated inside them, pulsing, expansive, full of joy.

For Lorraine the enthralling spectacle was enhanced by the presence of black people—the *shvartzes* her grandmother and father talked about. They were all around her. Lorraine's whole life had been something of a serenade because of her mother's penchant for turning dialogue into song ("If you don't be-hay-ave," Eve would croon now and then, "I will break your leh-eggs"), but never before had she seen such passion and overpowering emotion. She watched black girls sway to and fro and tried to move like they did. Within a few months, over radio and television, Lorraine would experience for the first time the oratorical fervor of Martin Luther King, Jr., the young preacher who was leading the bus boycott in Montgomery, Alabama, and she would hear the same revivalist song in his eloquent words.

The Alan Freed rock 'n' roll shows of 1955 and 1956 marked a brief but stirring American moment that the teenagers who saw them would always remember. In Brooklyn, New York, and even in Memphis, Tennessee—a state where National Guard troops in M-41 tanks were called out in the fall of 1956 to protect black schoolchildren from a potentially murderous mob—white people and black people came together to celebrate music powerful enough to break down ancient walls.

America's nearly twenty million black citizens were finally beginning to be heard in 1956. For two years words like "civil rights," "segregation," and "integration" had been turning up in the national discourse more and more frequently. Since the beginning of the year the name of an Alabama seamstress—Rosa Parks—had been mentioned in discussions hundreds of miles away from the bus routes of Montgomery, where she sat down so famously in the "wrong" seat.

The Supreme Court had proclaimed two years ago in *Brown* v. *Board of Education* that public schools must be desegregated "with all deliberate speed," but in many towns under court order to integrate their schools, such as Mansfield, Texas, and Clinton, Tennessee, white citizens battled police and National Guardsmen, burned crosses, and came out to scream threats at local blacks many of them had known all their lives. "I'd rather have my kids grow up stupid like me than go to school with niggers," a white resident of Clinton told the northern reporter David Halberstam.

During the spring, members of the White Citizens Council in Birmingham, Alabama, who had already purged the city of the rock 'n' roll music they associated with outside pressure to change, rushed a stage and beat up the gentle balladeer Nat King Cole. In many ways the vigilantes who attacked the singer and cleaned out Birmingham's jukeboxes were on to something. More than court decisions and boycotts, more than news reports of black students protected by tanks and bayonets, what inoculated millions of the younger generation against the racist assumptions of their parents was the straight shot of humanity administered by the driving power of the new music.

The sounds that obsessed Susan and Lorraine reminded Eve for the first time in ages of the tap-dancing brothers from Harlem she'd met at the Catskills hotels. Along with another black dancer renowned for a manic step he called the "frog dance," the brothers became summer pals of Eve's. They always talked about getting together back in the city, living so close by and all, but somehow they never managed it.

"This music is different. It scares me," Eve admitted to Sam.

"Ah, come on, it's normal," he counseled.

Sam and Eve both approved of the civil rights agitation and legal decisions of the moment. In 1942, when Sam was stationed in Georgia and Eve came down to visit him once, Eve had seen that southern blacks were indeed oppressed. "Hated—just for their color," she would say. "It was a terrible thing to see."

Sam told her about a fellow soldier from the Deep South who boasted to him about "lynching a nigger." "A fourteen-year-old boy," Sam related to Eve in disgust. "The guy was bragging to me that he didn't even get in trouble."

Northern blacks, however, already had "plenty of civil rights," according to Sam, and only lacked the fortitude to use them properly. "They have the right to work hard like everybody else up here in the North. The right to do a good job," he would say.

Sam contended that decent people—"real human beings," as he put it—got up early in the morning, arrived at work on time, and kept working until their eyes rolled back in their heads from the sheer effort of doing things right. If there were "Italian jobs," if there were Irishmen who "rushed from work to a gin mill to weld a can of beer to their hands," if some people didn't make the grade ("and plenty of Jews don't, mind you"), Sam Gordon was the first to say so, and never mind ethnicity.

When challenged about these generalizations—in particular the increasingly untenable stereotype of Negro lethargy—Sam would quote a black Harlem-based business associate, a bookie, numbers runner, owner of a string of Laundromats, and owner/developer of Harlem houses and apartment buildings, several dozen of which were being wired or rewired by the Dynamic Electric duo of Sam Gordon and Louis Bernstein, who had been partners for seven years now.

The Harlem entrepreneur was a tall and strikingly handsome young man with glistening black hair. He ran his empire out of a luncheonette, and it was there, at his regular table, that Sam listened to him hold forth on the distinction between "Negroes" and "niggers." He would not rent apartments or houses to "shiftless niggers"—and this, as Sam would stress, from a Negro, not from him. Except for one major financial setback, when an auto accident on Seventh Avenue left a taxi fully perpendicular to the street and "every single *shvartze* in Harlem played the taxi's plate number that day" at the entrepreneur's expense, Sam considered him a huge success in life. Moreover, Sam liked and respected his regular employer. He *knew* the man—which was more than could be said for some of his "ultraliberal" neighbors or either of his two eldest daughters, who by the end of the year had taken over the playroom stereo to listen to "*shvartzes* singing about Jesus."

By the end of the show in Brooklyn on that memorable evening, the aisles were completely clogged. Everyone was dancing, singing, surging toward the stage. Lorraine was only ten years old, and Susan had just turned thirteen, but inside the Brooklyn Paramount they were truly sisters, bridging the chronological divide that separated them in the suburbs. The rocking, exuberant crowd in the theater was integrated in every way by the music, by how it made them feel.

As the frenzy built, Lorraine and Susan heard low shouts from the back of the auditorium. They turned to see policemen bullying their way through the crowd, flailing their nightsticks at the dancers. A cop passing Susan and Lorraine's row growled, "Cocksuckers! You cocksuckers!" They watched in horror as his nightstick came down on a young man's back.

Within two years Alan Freed's pioneering rock shows—generational badges for those lucky enough to have been in attendance—would end. By then, Freed had been arrested several times for threatening the public order. As the police surged into one of his shows in Boston, he shouted, "Hey, kids, the cops don't want you to have a good time!"

Susan and Lorraine went to several other rock 'n' roll shows together. Much later, after so many things had come between them—differences of geography, ideology, economic station, religion—no matter where they were, the mere thought of the music they'd discovered in 1956 made each think of the other, and of the singular ecstasy of those glorious days and nights they'd shared.

1957

Simon Samberg died on Father's Day, the jug of cheap wine he had guzzled daily for decades blamed for the "complications" his doctors said he suffered a few weeks after the last of his several strokes. "He started his drinking because he was cold," Eve would say. "He stood all day in a vat of ice pulling huge crates of fish onto a table. He drank to keep warm."

"It was retirement that killed him," Sam contended. "He got bored."

The Gordons hadn't seen Simon Samberg as often as they saw the Goldenbergs, though Simon did move in for a time after Rebecca died. Every day Eve or Susan hiked over the bridge to get a gallon jug and enough smelly Pall Mall cigarettes for five average smokers. Simon would withdraw into the boozy haze of his room for the rest of the day, often with a book of Jack London stories in English or a Yiddish translation.

"Dad, there are so many women out there who would love to spend time with you," Eve would say. "You should get out more."

"I can't get married again," Simon would reply. "I smoke too much."

"Such a pessimist," Eve would say to Sam. "So old-fashioned. He's not a lover of life."

The Gordon girls tended to stay away from their gruff, moody grandfather, though after he'd suffered a small stroke two years ago he'd become much more amenable to interaction with the children. Lorraine often combed his hair, over and over again, because he said he loved it. She wondered how she could have been so terrified of her gentle grandfather before.

Lorraine also enjoyed the solitary visits of Papa Joe Goldenberg, who would walk down to the beach with her to watch the horseshoe crabs plod across the sand. But for the most part, Lorraine and her sisters were aware of the complicated tensions between their parents and grandparents.

The children knew that Sam's habit of arriving at Mama Yetta's house on Sunday and immediately taking a nap that would last until it was time to leave was not a coincidence. Susan and Lorraine were beginning to sense that their father's gigantic mood swings might have something to do with his own parents.

Even Sheila had noticed how Mama Yetta would shake her head disapprovingly when Eve's back was turned. Sheila was only seven, but she'd heard Yetta complain to Susan and Lorraine about Eve. "She never lets my Sammy rest. He was a boy with a blueprint mind, he could have been an engineer, but she made him go right to work. She still has him running himself ragged around the house, project after project with no rest."

In the suburbs, and in the books and magazines suburbanites read, these intergenerational conflicts were called "in-law problems." But the tensions between urban parents and their suburban children were so common as to indicate that forces larger than family dynamics were at work. The epidemic "in-law problems" of the 1950s suggested that Alexis de Tocqueville's famous observations in *Democracy in America* were as relevant as when he first made them more than a century ago. According to Tocqueville, families in aristocratic nations remain the same for centuries: "Generations become, as it were, contemporaneous. A man knows his forefathers and respects them; he thinks he already sees his remote descendants and he loves them." In a democratic nation, however, "the woof of time is every instant broken and the track of generations effaced....the interest of man is confined to those in close propinquity to himself."

The doctors at Meadowbrook Hospital in Mineola, Long Island, told Eve that Simon had a strong heart. They said his most recent stroke was slight and that he would surely recover quickly. When one of them called to tell Eve her father had died, he said that they hadn't accounted for the physical effects of Simon's drinking. After Eve received the phone call she went outside to hang the wash. She was loading the *Sputnik*-like limbs of the aluminum drying contraption that adorned most Harbor Isle backyards—reaching down and reaching up, draping and spinning in a deep trance—when Susan rode up on her cherished Schwinn. The new bicycle had fat tires that lifted the rider easily over high curbs. It was burgundy with a great deal of gold trim. The bike was symbolically essential to Susan's ability to bear her own childhood, because for the most part, Susan felt deprived.

Susan looked around Harbor Isle and saw "typical families" so different from her own that the Gordons' life in the suburbs hardly seemed an improvement over the crowded days of sleeping in one room back in the Bronx. She had friends who got five dollars—sometimes ten—for each A or B on their report cards. She could list a dozen Harbor Isle kids who'd gone off on a "family vacation" during the past year (as had half of all American families). She could rattle off the addresses of six or seven *other* homes where the teens in residence were welcome to use the new automatic sewing machines. She even knew the makes and models of the new cars parked in front of certain Harbor Isle dwellings.

Teenagers in America now accounted for the purchase of ten billion dollars' worth of goods over the course of a single year. They carried cash in their pockets; they were suddenly lords and ladies of discretionary spending, a market unto themselves. Neither the conceit of "keeping up with the Joneses," a phrase coined by comic strip artist "Pop" Momand in 1913, nor the "conspicuous consumption" described by Thorstein Veblen in his turn-of-the-century masterwork, *The Theory of the Leisure Class*, quite captured the intensity of the unbridled lust displayed by the children of the postwar suburbanites.

Susan would look back and contend that Sheila and Ricky were brought up in "a different family," a better one because it was a prosperous one. If other kids were paid for good grades, Susan's father ignored her A's, commenting only on the U next to "conduct." In *real* middle-class families the best thing a child could do was bring home an A.

Sam sat in the audience during Susan's junior high graduation ceremony and watched his daughter, wearing a simple yellow summer dress she'd purchased herself, as she returned to the stage several times to collect most of the academic prizes and awards. Sam was terribly proud, but he believed he couldn't afford to tell Susan. He couldn't show his hand.

So Susan thought of herself as a child deprived of both approval and merchandise, the material signs of normal family life and parental love. Susan didn't understand that Sam was waiting for her to accept *him*. She didn't perceive his sarcasm as a protective mask lowered automatically over his pain, and she never guessed that the heat of each of their battles only hardened her father's defensive glaze.

Sometimes Sam and his fourteen-year-old daughter just looked at each other across the table, each little more than a figment in the other's mind.

One night when Sam came home late, Susan hit him with two simple questions: "When is this family finally going on a vacation?" and "When are we going to get a sewing machine?" Susan now made some of her own clothes—outfits as stylish as the ones she believed the family couldn't afford. She wanted a new sewing machine to replace the ancient treadle-driven Singer bequeathed to her by Rebecca Samberg. But her father exploded with rage. He kicked a hole through the basement door, then jumped into his van and drove crazily down the street.

◆━◆

In the face of family discord, Sheila always fled from the line of fire. One evening when her sisters' jousting with her father turned ominous, Sheila sat on the stairs outside her room and started to cry. Her huge green eyes, flecked with the opaline colors of tropical shores—when people looked at Sheila they occasionally commented that all they saw were those eyes—poured tears into small hands pressed hard to her face as if she could keep the tears inside.

Eve heard a choking noise and found Sheila weeping on the stairs.

Sheila was the "easy" Gordon girl. If she misbehaved, the extent of her audacity was to finish all the other children's birthday cake at one of the endless rounds of parties for the neighborhood's many eight-year-olds. If she entertained material desires beyond the family's means, they were private dreams of perhaps someday sleeping under a canopied bed in a room with wallpaper like a garden of pink and white flowers. Sheila never screamed and she never brawled.

"What's wrong, honey?" Eve asked, putting her arms around her youngest daughter. "Why are you crying?"

What was wrong was that Sheila had come to believe there wasn't room for her in the Gordon family. The two powerful combinations—her mother and father on the one hand, her two older sisters on the other—took up the whole house.

Sheila was stuck outside with her little brother, whom she alternately loved and hated. She'd recently dreamed that Ricky was sitting in his high chair and she was playing with him when his neck suddenly started to stretch and his baby head swelled into a monster head. Ricky was eating her alive when Sheila woke up screaming.

Sheila looked up from the steps and tried to tell her mother what was wrong. Her sobs were coming loud and hard now, almost like little screams. "You and Daddy...only care about Susan and Lorraine. And you don't...care about me."

Eve gathered Sheila in. "That's not true, darling," she said. "If I give more attention to Susan and Lorraine, it's only because they *need* more attention right now. You don't give us trouble."

Sheila had heard Sam and Eve commiserating about their warring, willful older girls. Susan and Lorraine were "pains in the neck." They "always wanted more." Encircled by her mother's arms ("She's so sensitive," Eve would say later. "The slightest thing …"), Sheila vowed right there on the stairs to be an even better daughter. She would be more than just the easy one—she would be the wheel that *never* squeaked.

<hr />

As Susan approached Eve at the outdoor drying rack the day Simon died, she noticed tears in her mother's eyes. But Susan desperately needed permission to attend a party that night where there would be some important boys. Susan already had a boyfriend named Bob Morgan. Sheila loved to sneak into the playroom when Bob and Susan were together, but they always caught her peeking at them and asked her to leave. Sheila knew they wanted to start kissing.

"You have to kiss me first," she would say to Bob—an interesting variation on the usual custom of giving the pesky little sister a dime.

Bob would comply, and Sheila would run squealing with pleasure to her bedroom.

Susan thought that a boyfriend like Bob was as essential to her happiness, to her "status," as the party she wanted to attend.

"Ma, can I—"

"Leave me alone." Eve kept looking at the damp clothes in her hands. "Can't you see that I'm grieving?"

Eve went into the city soon after Simon's small estate was divided among his children. Three weeks later, the Gordons finally got new living room furniture.

1958

I want the money. Nobody loves money better than I do. But I'm not the kind of guy who can work evenings and weekends and all the rest of it. I've been through one war. Maybe another one's coming. If one is, I want to be able to look back and figure I spent the time between wars with my family, the way it should have been spent ..."

Yes, but then again, the man speaking, Mr. Tom Rath, had children who didn't impinge upon his precious family feeling with their constant demands for vacations and sewing machines. Had Tom Rath been an acquaintance or colleague of Sam Gordon's instead of the protagonist of *The Man in the Gray Flannel Suit*, the best-selling 1953 book and the popular 1956 movie, Sam would have gone on to point out that at least Tom could get home to his family at night because he took the train.

It took Sam Gordon several hours to get home from work one night in June. It was so late when he finally pulled into the driveway that he figured the girls would be asleep. Lorraine and Susan's verbal skirmishes had lately escalated to gladiatorial combat—scratching and clawing—so at least the traffic had spared him a fight and he could eat his dinner in peace. But when he walked in the door, he heard Susan and Lorraine arguing upstairs. Eve was sitting at the kitchen table with her chin in her hands. "The telephone," she said, in a tone of absolute defeat.

Sam felt himself begin to "boil"; a fierceness he remembered from the "tiger fights" of his youth rose up in him. He bounded up the stairs and into the bedroom Susan and Lorraine shared. Before the girls realized what had happened, Sam was standing beside the desk under the

window. They saw the telephone in one hand; the other hand was gripping a wire no longer connected to the wall.

Susan was in front of the closet door when her father began his
windup. Sam didn't aim, and the fact that Susan ducked ever so slightly
was clearly a matter of chance. The telephone slammed into the closet
door, just to one side of her head, with such force that it splintered the
wood and ricocheted across the room.

Eve didn't sleep at all that night. She'd made it up the stairs in time
to watch in horror from the bedroom doorway. *Dead from a telephone*,
she kept thinking. *If she hadn't ducked, my husband would have killed our
daughter with a phone.*

Eve's voice was shaky when she dialed Bell Telephone the next
morning to report some trouble with one of the monopoly's wires. She
eventually confessed. "The truth is my husband pulled the cord out of
the wall."

"Do you have daughters?" the phone company man asked.

Eve said that they did.

"Jeez. I've thought of it so many times. I only wish I had the nerve."

Though Sam had committed to memory at least one hundred routes
through the mazelike back streets of the outer boroughs of New York
City, he'd begun to find himself trapped and anxious in a traffic jam several times each week. Everyone was traveling by car these days. From a
peak in 1946, usage of urban mass transit had plummeted steadily every
year. According to a Brookings Institution study, 212 local transit companies had gone out of business in the United States in 1956 alone,
leaving 120 American cities without any form of public transportation
at all.

The Long Island Expressway, wide and proud, was only three years
old, but it had been crowded from the start, and radio stations were soon
offering special reports on what they called "rush hour" conditions. The
most ambitious decade of road construction since the Roman Empire—
a forty-one-thousand-mile supernetwork ordained and financed by the
Interstate Highway Act of 1956—was now well under way, but the
"mobile, fluid labor force" so essential to postwar prosperity was spending too much time stuck in traffic to notice. Men now compared notes
on how long it took them to get home, on auto air-conditioning, seat
coverings, and radio reception, as avidly as women swapped recipes and
compared the stoves and refrigerators that represented their own claim
to freedom in the suburbs.

Every few days Sam was stuck on a bridge or in a tunnel. He would take deep breaths, as if the flow of air could keep him from "boiling over" like a car radiator. Sam would sometimes sit for hours pondering the bitter irony of a life composed of rising in the darkness of one night, working long hours in lightless shafts, and going nowhere at all on a highway during the second night of his day, a prisoner trapped inside a vehicle that only a few years earlier he'd considered his ticket to the good life. And when he finally got home, he could look forward to a four-hour-old dinner eaten to a serenade of sibling tiger fights and a wife's sad inventory of another quarrelsome day in heaven on earth.

One evening not long before the flying telephone episode, Sam listened to Eve's report and said, "I'm sick of my job. Look at me. Look what time it is. I don't even have any money to give you, Eve. I gotta make a change. I think I'm gonna leave Louie."

Louis Bernstein was a decent electrician, a conservative man with a bellyful of ulcers. Louie and his wife had no kids and still rented an apartment in the city. Louie didn't understand why Sam couldn't make do with the small weekly draw they both took out of the business, and Sam couldn't understand why Louie didn't want to take the high-paying "panic work" that included Sam's personal guarantee that a factory shut down late on Saturday would be up and running again the next Monday morning. Since Sam would pay a union man to fill in for Louie on Sundays, as often as not he had little to show for his seventh day of labor.

Louie Bernstein was not impressed by Sam's contention that complex factory work was more intellectually compelling than the rote "house work" of wiring a home or apartment building. By now Sam Gordon could stroll into the cellar of any office tower or sprawling factory, take one look at the distribution panels, subservices, and subpanels, and see the entire structure in his mind as a three-dimensional image of wires and essential connections. He could see right through the skin of a building, to the arteries and veins and organs. A few seconds later he would be mentally ticking off the materials and time required to do the job at hand, thinking the whole thing through to the end. Then he would state his fair price and a completion date, and though his customers were often stunned by the absence of paperwork, they would usually shake hands right there. Sam was an inspired practitioner of a craft that didn't require inspiration.

If Sam could forgive his "illustrious partner" for lack of inspiration, he could never forgive Louie's refusal to buy the building at the corner of Forty-fifth Street and Tenth Avenue where they rented work space. The owner of the four-story building had taken Sam and Louie aside and offered to sell the place for five thousand dollars—no money down.

"No, I just don't want to be a landlord," Louie said, hugging his perforated abdomen.

"Louie, the man is *giving* us a building in New York City. The monthly payments won't be much more than our current rent. We'll have seven spaces to rent out! This is property for us. This is ownership. This is the future!"

"Not for me," said Louie.

Yetta was there when Sam formally announced the dissolution of the Dynamic Electric partnership.

"I'm gonna try to find business closer to home," Sam said. "Louie will get all the Manhattan jobs and contracts, and he'll give me a thousand bucks to get started. We have about fifteen hundred dollars in savings on top of that."

"So how do you expect to live?" asked Yetta Goldenberg, her voice rising from low on the "So" to high on the "live."

"It'll be rough sledding," Sam allowed.

"We have faith that it will work," Eve said, staring at Yetta, whose inevitable skepticism only sparked her sense of adventure. "I'm going to learn to do his bookkeeping. We're going to make it just fine."

During the weeks between Sam's business decision and the night he winged the phone, the economic slowdown that began at the end of 1957 was designated a recession—one severe enough, in fact, to "curl your hair," the secretary of the treasury warned reporters. After nearly full employment in 1955, five million Americans (seven percent of the work force) were unemployed by the middle of 1958. The gross national product had ceased growing. The flagging of national fortunes was symbolized in December 1957, in front of a huge national television audience, by the sight of the Vanguard, the mighty rocket that was to reclaim American superiority in the space race, rising a pitiful arm's length from the outer crust of southern Florida before keeling over on its side. (On January 31, 1958, a Jupiter rocket was launched successfully, though Russian superiority in space would persist for several more years.)

Much later President Eisenhower would say that 1958 was the worst year of his life. The problems with the space program were connected to an intensification of the ongoing educational crisis caused by the Russian launch of *Sputnik* in 1957. And the president and the Congress were at a loss as to how to cure the economic recession.

By 1958 it was clear to Sam that many of the accountants, lawyers, and other white-collar Harbor Isle pioneers had either moved to bigger homes or had begun to pay professional builders, renovators, and even—the height of decadence in Sam's estimation—*gardeners* to do work they once did themselves. This, coupled with Sam and Eve's sense that the social scene in Harbor Isle was "cliquing off" into exclusive little groups, indicated that something was happening to the democracy of Harbor Isle. And if Sam had any doubts, all he had to do was ask his kids.

"You know what it means to be middle-class?" Sam would say to friends in town who also felt that life was changing. "It means that your kids look out the front window to keep track of who's got more."

Sam might go on to report that not one but two telephone lines now ran into 221 Lincoln, that there was a phone in every room, and that this was still not enough. In an expansive mood, he would reminisce about the many childhood hours he'd spent standing in a candy store beside the sole telephone in the neighborhood. A call would come through, the store owner would write the message on a slip of paper, and young Sam would sprint off to deliver it in hopes of a two-cent tip.

"*This* was a job," Sam would say, as he watched his friends nod in resignation.

Sometimes Sam would watch Susan or Lorraine talking on the telephone, and he'd see that they'd disappeared. His daughters had escaped to the other end of the line, and it was the sight of them looking so much happier for it that wounded Sam most of all.

Sam was still smarting from the most recent bout of family resentment over the prewar twenty-foot lap strake powerboat he'd bought a year earlier. He had worked every Sunday for a year caulking the bottom of the aged craft and rebuilding its old Dodge engine. He'd even named it the *Evie G.* and had just begun to discover the peace of mind available to a boat owner running the trafficless tides when complaints arose from the shore.

The average American adult now spent sixty-two percent of his or her time with spouse and family, a record high—and a tribute, perhaps, to the stunning success of the "togetherness" and "new father" campaigns. The measure of family involvement would plummet by twenty percent over the next thirty years, but in 1958 Sam's wife and children wanted a dad who stuck around and conformed to the national average.

But Sam was out at sea or stuck in traffic.

———◆◆◆———

Night after night, Sheila had the same two dreams. In the nightmare, she would come home to 221 Lincoln and find it dark and abandoned. Sheila's house was never dark, and her mother seemed to inhabit the bright kitchen perpetually, so the emptiness alone frightened her. She would climb up the stairs to Susan and Lorraine's room, but nobody was there. Then, in Sam and Eve's darkened bedroom, figures would suddenly appear, charging at her on all fours. Sheila recognized her frothing father, her mother, and her two sisters—even though each of the figures wore the ferocious face of a wild animal.

In the other recurrent dream, the good one, Sheila stood in the most beautiful of all green meadows on a perfect summer's day. A pony lolled off to one side, and she felt nothing but the pure joy of being alone and at peace.

Sheila would wake up in the morning and hear her mother's footsteps in the kitchen. Eve didn't walk around the house; she moved in a cross between a trot and a march. The sound made Sheila's stomach ache because she was awake now and there was no telling what strife the day would bring.

Recently Sheila had spent two days in the hospital. She'd begun to complain about her stomachaches so often that Eve and Sam had agreed to the suggestion of Dr. Forrest, the family general practitioner, that she should undergo tests. The day after Sheila drank the chalky barium emulsion and lay very still while X-rays were taken, her mother and father appeared with gifts—a board game and a toy. Sheila was thrilled, and she basked in their obvious relief that the tests were all negative.

When Sheila got back home, a large bottle full of a creamy jade-colored dilution of paregoric, an opium derivative prescribed to calm a jumpy belly, took up residence in her bedroom. The nightmares continued, as did the familial battling and her abiding fear of what each day would bring. And whenever Susan or Lorraine noticed her clutching her stomach, they would intone in a mocking singsong, "Time to get the green medicine for Sheila!"

———◆◆◆———

"Yeah, and where'd you get *that* idea?" Sam would say, no longer assuming that Susan's galling lectures were inspired by teachers paid with his own tax dollars. "What new friend told you that?"

Then Lorraine would chime in with her opinion, lifted from some book Susan had given her, Sam figured. Sheila read Susan's books too— or at least she tried.

When they weren't at war, Sam's two oldest daughters stood shoulder to shoulder "like a gang putting me on trial," he'd say. Not only did they disagree with him and President Eisenhower, not only did they disdain paternal authority and hard work—they mocked all the values Sam cherished. They smirked at normal life like it was a joke.

After dinner—if Sam got home at a reasonable hour—he and Sheila would watch television together. To Sam's great pleasure, the television industry was in the process of dropping the pretense that the medium was designed for families and children. In the mid-fifties nearly forty hours of weekly programming were specifically tailored to children. Television, experts said, would nurture them, build their vocabulary, and even build their "morale."

"Our kids have fathers and mothers again, and our fathers and mothers have their kids back with them," the famed TV cowboy William "Hopalong Cassidy" Boyd once proclaimed. A few killjoys among the experts worried aloud in 1958 about "children who can communicate with the TV screen, but not with their parents," but the television set was generally thought to have lured family members out of their isolation and gathered them around the electronic hearth.

Sam had always considered television westerns like *Hopalong Cassidy* diluted homilies for children, Manichaean conflicts between the men in black and the men in white. But now a new breed of western was stampeding children's programming off the air. Twenty after-dinner dramas were now set on the American frontier, and within two years there would be thirty tales of "real cowboys" acting out diluted homilies for adults.

Sheila's favorite part about her TV evenings with her father was watching him settle into close company with horsemen, gunslingers, and riverboat gamblers. Week after week Sam watched Seth Adams endeavor to get his people safely to the golden land of California on *Wagon Train*. Sam Gordon was right there—assuming he got home in time—when the redwood-tall Chuck Connors, who starred in *The Rifleman*, strapping young son at his side, struggled every Tuesday on ABC to maintain the tiny spread cleared by his own hand in the midst of every evil the New Mexico Territory of 1888 could throw his way.

And like millions of others, Sam loved *Gunsmoke*. For a while this first of the "adult" westerns had been filmed in an old firehouse on Ninth Avenue, down the street from Sam and Louie's shop. The producers of *Gunsmoke* showed up one day and asked Sam if he wanted to be the staff electrician, but when he and Eve discussed the offer they decided a western for grown-ups would never last. Now, every Saturday night, Marshal Matt Dillon of the long shadow and granite face, his feelings buried deep where a man's feelings belonged, kept the peace in Dodge City. Marshal Dillon was unencumbered by family, and the scriptwriters had yet to strand him in a traffic jam. He was a free man save for the austere imperatives of laws that had nothing to do with the dinner-table "bullshit" that aired before the show. The duplicity Matt Dillon faced was the kind you could spot from fifty paces. Fathers in the Old West strung the fences, built the houses, and protected flock and family. In exchange they were accorded a kind of respect that toward the end of most episodes looked a lot like love.

The new westerns confirmed Sam's growing sense that almost everything about the older America was better than what he had now. Lately, every time he took a bite out of a bagel, Sam was transported back to childhood streets, to bakeries where brick ovens warmed the sidewalks from below. "How could you ever tell a kid how a bagel tasted then, Eve?" Sam would say, breaking out of a reverie. Eve knew exactly what he meant.

Sam Gordon spurned certain modern amenities as a matter of principle. Deodorant was one. Eve often inquired whether he couldn't make his stand over a different product.

Sam's favorite reading material these days concerned the Civil War. He was endlessly fascinated by the logistics of a war that required "more horses than men." "A significant part of both armies was tied up just getting hay to the horses," he'd explain. "Thousands of men moving hay. People just don't think about things like that anymore."

Everyone who knew Sam Gordon agreed he would have prospered as a cowboy. If he hadn't been born too late, if he hadn't been hemmed in by poverty, family responsibility, the war, and family responsibility again—the work of being a husband, father, breadwinner, and owner of a parcel of land in the middle of a suburb—it could have been Sam out there on the prairie. But instead, the local quarter sections were baseball diamonds, and there were a few groomed and weedless square feet where the back forty should be. His corral was a bit of weathered rail fence that the kids and their friends sat on so often it was splintered and bowed.

* * *

Over the course of the year, a small coterie of American writers had begun to lay out a generational perspective known as "beat." New poetry and novels like Jack Kerouac's *On the Road* electrified thousands of bright young Americans, particularly those who felt oppressed by the forces of convention. As if on behalf of parents, teachers, and other authority figures, *Time* called these kids "a pack of oddballs." Kerouac said they were harmless, just young Americans "desirous of everything at the same time."

But after two years of national soul-searching prompted by juvenile delinquency and rock 'n' roll, the American suburbs were awash with tales of youthful ruin no less unsettling than the stories of children fallen from the ideal families of Victorian times. Sons and daughters were rejecting their parents and going beat. Apparently the change went deeper than the effects of rock 'n' roll: the kids often left home for places like San Francisco or Greenwich Village, where they yearned to dwell among drug addicts, prostitutes, petty criminals, and the beat artists they celebrated—or so it seemed to many parents. Like Charles Starkweather, the nineteen-year-old "mad dog" killer who had gone on a spree in Nebraska and Wyoming at the beginning of the year and murdered eleven innocent people, and who was found by professional observers to have displayed "belligerent and uncooperative attitudes toward authority" from an early age, the beats demonstrated "no satisfactory anchorage in social life" and were viewed as dire threats.

Jack Kerouac said that the beat aesthetic actually derived from the "old American whoopee." Kerouac's grandfather was a "wild, self-believing" individualist, the kind of fellow, according to his grandson, who took lanterns out into storms and dared the wind to extinguish the light. The beats and the people they wrote about wanted to "prowl the wilderness" once again, to head for the open road in search of all that had been lost to competition, to "the rat race," to traffic jams, suburbs, and cities.

If there was one member of the Gordon family of Harbor Isle who longed to "lone it" across America like the tortured narrator of Allen Ginsberg's landmark beat poem *Howl*, one who yearned to spin out into the open and "burn, burn, burn...exploding like spiders across the sky," in Kerouac's words, it was Sam. Born too late to chase Pancho Villa and too early to quit school and run off to San Francisco or Greenwich Village, Sam sat mesmerized before the RCA when the cowboys appeared, a little girl who worshiped him by his side, watching her father watch TV.

Yosef Goldenberg died of a heart attack in upstate New York in October.

The old cavalryman had been in the VA hospital for a month, and Sam had visited him several times. He was just about to go again when his brother, Freddy, asked him to delay the trip so they could go together. For a while, especially when Freddy sold jewelry in a summer community not far from Harbor Isle, the two brothers had stayed in close touch, but they hadn't seen much of each other since Freddy's wedding a year earlier.

Joe died while Sam was waiting for Freddy. Sam couldn't shake nightmares about him dying all alone "in the kind of place where a man's just a number, like he was just another piece of fish."

"You did what you could," Eve kept saying.

In Sam's dreams Papa Joe died horribly. He was only sixty-two.

Yetta had told Sam ever since he was a boy that one of the causes of the family's poverty was Joe's habit of spending money on himself and, she implied, on other women. But Sam recalled his defeated, occasionally volatile, even violent father coming home without money from the fur markets—the closest a man with a family could get to the lost adventure of the fur trades during those hard times, Sam figured. He thought back on his father's life and felt compassion. As he remembered Papa Joe's romantic stories of his youth and then the days when the adventures were over, a profound sense formed in Sam's mind that the scene of a man's best endeavors was often far from home.

"I should have been there when he died," Sam said, over and over again.

The children were kept away from the funeral, as they had been when Simon died. Afterward, Susan was watching Sam and Freddy pack away some of Papa Joe's old clothes when the reality of what had occurred came to her all at once. She started shaking with sobs and she went up to Sam, but the sight of her tears overwhelmed him with grief.

"Be quiet!" Sam raged, and then his hand rushed out from the past and landed hard against his daughter's cheek.

1959

From Susan's perspective—soon to be sweet sixteen and perched on the couch in the playroom, surrounded by high school boys who'd arrived amid a serenade of squealing tires—it looked like Eve was flirting. In a slinky sequined red evening gown, she was doing Liz Taylor, smiling and saying hello in a tone of voice Susan didn't like, and looking as if she might break into song.

And the boys who had come to see Susan all smiled right back.

My own mother, Susan thought.

For over two years, except when she was dressing for rock 'n' roll, Susan had been refining her personal style in counterpoint to Eve's flamboyance. She favored plain plaid skirts, and she'd collected many angora sweaters in pastel shades, some with angora trim along the collar. Though the general effect of these fuzzy cocoons suggested piles of stuffed animals atop thousands of girlhood bedspreads, Susan knew that as early as seventh grade, boys had been eyeing the Eve Gordonesque contours beneath the fuzz. It was in seventh grade that a boy had looked her over and said, "Hey! Sweater Girl!"

Sweater Girl: rife with implications of bosoms, "bombshells," and "sex goddesses" Susan had no wish to emulate. Susan only wanted to be "cute." She wanted, in fact, to be cute "like Debbie."

Debbie Reynolds was not only cute; she was as "bouncy" as one of the omnipresent Superballs now rebounding off millions of American walls. So ebullient was Debbie Reynolds that the men in her movie life never seemed to mind that she was also quite intelligent. They loved her for the marvelous breath of fresh air she was, on screen and off—or so it had seemed until the recent "tragedy" and the speculation in popular magazines that Debbie Reynolds had "lost the will to live."

Debbie's husband, Eddie Fisher, father of their two young children, had been stolen by another movie star, a voluptuous violet-eyed temptress—that "modern Eve," Elizabeth Taylor.

Liz was Eve Gordon's favorite.

The infamous Debbie-Eddie-Liz love triangle had shaken the confidence of millions of American women who'd been enchanted by the Debbie-Eddie match since their marriage in 1955. Before Liz, "people everywhere had felt a close personal identification with this young couple," lamented one writer in *McCall's*. "Eddie and Debbie were in show business, but they seemed more like a family who lived down the block. Maybe they were going to prove that you could be a star in Hollywood and still stay married."

Debbie, as her fans knew, had never had a "regular guy" until she met Eddie, a teen singing idol, the slight Jewish son of a Philadelphia "vegetable huckster." Eddie had gotten his start at the very Catskills resorts where Eve Gordon used to work. To the considerable distress of his fan clubs and also of a "publicity-relations counselor" at MGM who warned Debbie that she would ruin her virginal allure, the couple was married at Jenny Grossinger's hotel, an event of only slightly less magnitude in the current mythology of romantic love than the rebirth through marriage of actress Grace Kelly the following year, as Her Serene Highness, Princess Grace of Monaco. (Kelly's wedding gifts were front-page news. "Of all the parts she ever played," wrote biographer Gwen Robyns, "her own wedding was her finest performance.")

Two years after the Fisher-Reynolds marriage, their "close friends" Elizabeth Taylor and wealthy producer Mike Todd (born Avrum Goldbogen in Minneapolis) got married—the bride, at twenty-seven, for the third time. But Todd was killed a year later in the crash of his plane, the *Lucky Liz*. As very few Americans did not know by late September of 1958, one of Miss Taylor's very best friends, Eddie Fisher, went to console the widow, a convert to Judaism out of respect for her late husband. A sordid sighting of Eddie and Liz at no less sacrosanct a spot than Grossinger's followed.

Several months later, her marriage in ruins, Debbie was depicted in one article as still unable to throw out the matchbooks emblazoned with THE FISHERS. "Elizabeth has no girlfriends," Debbie declared, apparently delivering her version of a scathing rebuke. She refused to speculate on the prospects for Eddie's new marriage (Liz would dump him for Richard

Burton in two years, and he would check into New York's Payne Whitney clinic to be treated for "mental distress"), but she selflessly stated for
the record, "Eddie is already a very lucky man. How many men ever
have two women who love them?"

"She never would have married Eddie if Mike had lived," Eve
insisted.

Eve Gordon and Liz Taylor had both performed professionally as
children. They both had a "full figure," a beauty mark near their upper
lips, and lower back pain. But what made Eve think of Liz as her sister
and close friend was her sense that they reacted similarly to suffering.
Though a recent convert, "Liz has a Jewish personality," Eve
announced. "She has a *yiddishe kopf*"—by which she meant that the
actress thought like a Jew. "And she has a *strong* personality"—by which
she meant that in the face of adversity, Liz's instinct, like Eve's, was
to act.

But Eve's love of Elizabeth Taylor served to complicate issues of sex
and love for her daughters. That a vixen was accorded such respect by
their mother added to a welter of mixed signals about the mystical
union of women and men. Lorraine's closest friend, Ellen Levy, a straw-
berry blonde who looked like she hailed from the Debbie camp but had
a number of Liz ideas, proclaimed right in front of Lorraine and several
other friends that Sam and Eve Gordon "took the prize as the most red-
hot and madly-in-love parents in Harbor Isle."

Lorraine was too mortified to speak.

"Yeah, her mom and dad *dance* together and kiss like people in the
movies," Ellen enthused to the others. "Lorraine is s-o-o-o lucky."

Meanwhile, the erotic content of the world outside the house was
on the rise. *Playboy* magazine could be found in the drawers—if not on
top—of respectable bedside tables, and Brigitte Bardot had garnered a
wide following with her titillating mix of Debbie's little-girl act and Liz's
heat. Grace Metalious's "scorching" novel of middle-class passion,
Peyton Place, had been read by millions in the three years since it was
published, and because of the infamous Dr. Kinsey and his report—still
controversial years after its publication—a casual reader or listener to
cocktail conversation might have been apprised of the fact that great
numbers of American women slept in the nude, that couples throughout the nation experimented with "unnatural acts," and that nearly
seven of ten women achieved orgasm with their husbands.

In Harbor Isle, there were indications that a few women achieved
orgasm with men who were not their husbands. Adultery—at least in its
publicly acknowledged form—had come to the little island by 1959.

There had been no divorces as yet, but a Harbor Isle wife had recently disappeared with the family gardener—the local Lady Chatterley providing hours of juicy discussion over the mah-jongg tiles. Almost every night one of the Gordons' neighbors walked the family dog over to the home of a close friend for a rendezvous with the close friend's wife. Sam knew of other husbands who conformed to the Victorian stereotypes, behaving as if encounters with women in motels and brothels had nothing to do with the solidity or sanctity of family life.

If the flood of erotic messages delivered by the popular culture confused Eve and Sam's children, more perplexing were Eve's movie-star-slinky evening gowns and the dirty jokes that drew grinning men to her side. The girls pondered their mother's oft-repeated contention that she was not "a woman's woman" (Debbie Reynolds had said precisely the same thing…of Liz), and were left wondering what it meant to be "a man's woman."

It appeared to Susan and Lorraine—and less explicitly to Sheila, who was only nine—that Eve's potent sexuality was essential to the fundamental security of the Gordon family. Eve's observant daughters deduced from her example that men were not necessarily superior but were far more powerful, and that a successful woman was one who understood how to "harness" the power.

Eve believed that her children's sexuality—their "passionate" natures—was a matter of genetics. "What the daughter does, the mother did," as the old Jewish proverb had it. She thought that her daughters had inherited her sex drive and would learn the raw facts of sex outside the house, just as she had. "Everyone learns the basics at some point," said Sam, who was also at a loss for the right words to describe what sex education books for children tended to call "the miracle of life."

Sam and Eve never had "that talk" with any of their children (though Susan would recall one discussion about "the birds and the bees" back in the Bronx). Nor did it cross Eve's mind that the education of her daughters was lacking in other respects. She might have admitted that their schooling in the arts of the kitchen—which at 221 Lincoln was Eve's alone, off limits to everyone else—was more theoretical than practical, but at least they'd watched her cook. Lorraine was "a natural" with needle and thread, and Susan was what Eve described as "enthusiastic." Eve encouraged them in these female skills, but as for herself, "I started knitting the first sweater I ever made for a boyfriend when I was fifteen," she told each of the girls in turn. "I finished it in time to give it to some guy three boyfriends later."

Around the time Susan was born, sociologist Talcott Parsons had written that one reason there was no female analogue to the American "bad boy" was that it was "possible from an early age to initiate girls directly into many important aspects of the adult female roles."

Eve worked hard to convey to her girls that a woman could be creative at tasks that were essential to their success in a world of men. But Lorraine and Susan could see that Eve was so afraid of Sam's temper that she sometimes didn't speak her mind. They knew, as did millions of children their age, that a near-desperate need for security was what animated most of the things their mother did, and they couldn't help but note the toll: they remembered her breaking those plates.

A generation of children born to the Depression-era parents who settled the suburbs had grown up observing this desire for security and had by now replicated it in the form of a popular social institution called "going steady." A 1959 poll found that fifty-seven percent of American teens had gone, or were now going, steady. The ritual was governed by complicated rules (frequently spelled out in short features in magazines for women and girls) specifying dating restrictions, allowable numbers of phone calls per week, and even the proper positioning of "pins" and other elements of display that were as sacred to middle-class teenagers as the American flag was to their parents.

Though it would quickly be overshadowed by far more harrowing parental concerns, the benign practice of going steady was widely perceived as a "national problem" during the late 1950s. Until World War II, courting rituals were based on what one social historian has called "promiscuous popularity." Like Eve Samberg, who filled many a dance card before giving up her stable of boyfriends for Sam, a successful teen during prewar times had lots of dates. Those who excelled at a kind of free-market notion of social success were accorded high status (sociologist William Waller referred to a "campus rating complex"). In contrast to this "competitive dating," in 1959—a year when it looked like the Russians had bigger and better bombs, a year when a generation of bland, conformist, security-conscious teenagers seemed ill-prepared to inherit the most powerful nation on earth—many parents and intellectuals regarded going steady not only as an invitation to sexual experimentation but as downright anti-American. At a White House conference on the family, which was declared "a central force in democracy," a keynote speaker warned that the major obstacle to the national mission was the lack of "imaginative and unorthodox thinking" and the "dull uniformity" evident among American youth.

One of the boys Susan thought she saw leering at her mother's red-sequined form in the playroom that evening was a steady boyfriend who would soon begin to pressure Susan unceasingly to "go all the way." Susan couldn't believe how denigrated his campaign made her feel. When she refused his advances, the boy "dropped" her.

No one in the family knew what had happened, but they all knew how deeply Susan was hurt, because she cried inconsolably for days.

"Just forget about it," Eve said. "Don't be depressed. Forget it, Susan. It doesn't matter. Everything will look better in the morning."

But it did matter. It mattered more than her mother appeared capable of understanding. If Susan Gordon and her ex-boyfriend had ordered embossed matchbooks instead of exchanging jewelry and clothing as symbols of their commitment, Susan would not have been able to throw them away.

———◦◦◦———

The event Ricky Gordon would later recall as his earliest memory occurred when he was three. As he stood in the cement tub his father used for washing brushes and his blackened, work-hardened hands, Ricky's mother bathed him with a soft sponge. There was little more to the memory than that.

Ricky would remember other, even more fragmentary sensations: sister smells; the clickety-clack of mothers together around a table in the afternoon ("One dot! Two bam! Three crack!"); cakes piled high; the smell of coffee everywhere; the colors of the local beach.

Ricky's sisters dressed him up and posed him in dramatic settings like a little doll. They put makeup on him. And they read him poems all the time—especially Lorraine, who sometimes imagined that she was Ricky's real mother. Susan felt that poetry was essential to Ricky's education because it would someday be his salvation from the family, just as books and libraries had become her own means of escape. For several years to come, Ricky only heard the words of the poems as a kind of music his sisters sang to him. The first lines he remembered were the last lines of "Ballad of the Harp-Weaver," by Edna St. Vincent Millay—a favorite of Susan's—where the ragged little boy wakes up to find his mother, her hands still on the harp strings, "frozen dead" beside the new clothes she has woven for him.

But the bath in the cement tub was the first recollection that came back complete. Years later, Ricky could still describe the feeling of a soft sponge and warm water trickling down his body into the tub. And all the while, as his mother washed him, a man he couldn't quite see loomed in the background like a phantom.

<hr />

One day in July, poised over her cutting board, the inevitable sibling battles raging loudly in other rooms, Eve suddenly felt that she would surely suffocate if she didn't get out. At first, the sensation reminded her of her brief panics when the beautician lowered the silver drying helmet over her head, or when Sam draped his heavy leg over her in bed. But then it got worse. Eve felt like she was being strangled. She was gasping for air when her screaming, warring children piled into the kitchen, demanding adjudication. When she spoke, something in her voice silenced them.

"I am leaving," Eve said, her face expressionless. "I am leaving you. I am leaving…here."

Eve strode quickly from the kitchen and out the front door. Susan, Lorraine, and Sheila rushed to the picture window in the living room in time to see her break into a run. In 1959, in Harbor Isle, a mother did not run. The sight, so aberrant and surreal, made the girls, and then Ricky, burst into tears. The four Gordon children stood side by side at the window, sobbing with terror, as their mother sprinted past the towering mulberry tree in the front yard and disappeared into the blackness of a lilac-scented summer's night.

Only a day or two earlier, tension had reached a dramatic pitch in another American kitchen, in Moscow. "The Soviet dictator," as President Eisenhower sometimes referred to Nikita Khrushchev, was escorting the visiting American vice president, Richard Nixon, through a working model of a "typical" American home constructed in the middle of Moscow's Sokoloniki Park. The model home was part of a cultural exchange inspired by a volley of peace overtures between the superpowers that began in late 1958 (the hard-line secretary of state, John Foster Dulles, died in May 1959) and reached a crescendo with Khrushchev's tour of the United States in September 1959. A Soviet science and technology exhibit opened at the New York Coliseum in June, and a corresponding American exhibition—albeit with a much stronger consumerist orientation ("a panorama of U. S. life," as it was described in *Look*)—had now begun in central Moscow.

As Khrushchev and Nixon passed the model American grocery store, a shining example of the great and varied gifts of American capitalism, the American vice president said, "You may be interested to know that my father owned a small general store in California." (Such evocations of early family life had become trusty standards for Richard Nixon ever since the success of his Checkers speech.) "All the Nixon boys worked there while going to school," the vice president continued.

"All shopkeepers are thieves," Khrushchev snorted, apparently unimpressed with Nixon's command of Norman Rockwellesque recollections.

Articles in the Moscow newspapers asserted that the model home at the exhibition was no more representative of a typical American worker's home than the Taj Mahal or Buckingham Palace was typical of dwellings in India or England—and they were right. Though the "typical ranch house" on display in Sokoloniki Park was of a type that would have cost $11,000 back in the United States, its "miracle kitchen" was a $250,000 prototypical wonderland featuring a computer (an "electronic brain") that operated trap doors, as many colored lights as Sam had built into his playroom, a closed-circuit television system, an early microwave oven, and an automatic dishwasher that "walked" along behind a model housewife (played by the Illinois-born daughter of Ukrainian immigrants to America, a Miss Ann Anderson), trained to demonstrate to visiting Russian women that kitchens could be cleaned by a robot like the one she had right there. Robots, the "typical" kitchen display implied, had "freed" the American housewife as Lincoln had freed the slaves.

Nixon was drinking a Pepsi-Cola when he and Khrushchev came to the model kitchen. In what became known around the world as the Kitchen Debate, they stopped their tour to compare the merits of Russian and American washing machines (the Russians produced only a tenth of America's four million models within a year). Nixon argued the case for extreme variety and freedom of choice, while Khrushchev championed what would be known twenty-five years later as "streamlining a product line," since ultimately the purpose of all the machines was to wash clothes.

From there, the debate descended to unveiled threats of mutual military destruction. Khrushchev jabbed Nixon with his thick peasant thumb as his famous "rubberoid" smile (advertised as a selling point of the "Nikita dolls" currently popular in the United States) narrowed into a fierce frown. "We are strong! We can beat you," he barked. Nixon wagged his finger at Khrushchev, chiding him for "playing with the most destructive thing in the world." Before they left the kitchen, Khrushchev said to his translator, "Thank the housewife for letting us use her kitchen for our argument."

In the wake of all the publicity about the Moscow Kitchen Debate, Eve Gordon was not the only American woman who wondered where a man like Richard Nixon had acquired his washing-machine expertise. In *Cosmopolitan* Patricia Nixon was quoted as saying, "I still do all our nice laundry....I always press Dick's suits with a steam iron." Mrs. Nixon allowed that "some people think that's silly, but it's actually easier than sending them out." Like the president, "Dick Nixon fancies himself an outdoor steak chef," *Cosmopolitan* reported, but there was little in the article to suggest that the vice president strayed into the "handsome paneled" kitchen in the family's eleven-room home. Thirteen-year-old Tricia and eleven-year-old Julie ("Tricia has yet to have a date or want one. She never plays jive records, or monopolizes the telephone," Pat reported) considered cooking in the Nixon kitchen an "absorbing interest."

Unlike the Nixon children, the Gordon girls were not welcome in the kitchen. "All electric," chock-full of round-cornered white conveniences, the kitchen was Eve's domain. It was there that she found solace for the deepest wounds of her days.

A kitchen can be a stage for a wife in the right frame of mind. A kitchen can be filled with jokes and songs. In the kitchen Eve showed her stuff. ("If my wife had ten children, she'd take care of them with ease," Sam would boast to their friends. "Is that an insult or a compliment?" Eve would always ask.) In the kitchen Eve performed an intricate ballet of simultaneous but separate tasks. In the kitchen she would conjure urban ghosts to haunt the bland culinary landscape of Harbor Isle. She was famous for her spaghetti and pot roast, and friends commented that her kitchen smelled like their grandmothers' kitchens back in the city.

Eve occasionally had nightmares set in her own kitchen. Some nights she dreamed that she couldn't find the coffee, others that she had the coffee but couldn't get water out of the tap. Sometimes she felt that the kitchen was much too far away from the rest of the family, and this year's advertisements for Formica countertops indicated that in this she was not alone. Pictures showed counters extending out of the kitchen into various other rooms, and the copy touted Formica as part of a "definite trend toward making Mother a member of the family again."

But there were plenty of days when Eve was thankful for the separateness of the kitchen, especially the days when she needed to cry. Good days and bad, the kitchen had always been Eve's sanctum. Lately, though, there'd been a few times when the kitchen didn't help, when

Eve couldn't sing or even cry. Those were the terrible days when the walls closed in and she wanted to run away.

The night she finally did, Eve was already dizzy when the children rushed into the kitchen and pushed her over the edge. She continued to whirl amid the appliances, but she began thinking, *Where is it written that I must be peacemaker to the children, nighttime seductress to Sam, and cook of every single meal?* No answers came, so Eve put down her knife and bolted for the front door. She was still moving double-time when she crossed the camelback bridge.

Sam got home half an hour later. He found the children crying together in the kitchen. Susan broke the news: "Mommy ran away."

Suddenly suburban family life was under fire from all quarters. Academics had been framing a harsh critique of the suburban ethos for most of the decade, and there had been signs of discontent like John Keats's popular 1957 book *The Crack in the Picture Window,* but now the mass media were holding the postwar suburbs up as factories for conformist organization men and security-crazed mothers at best, and cesspools of "social and mental disease" at worst. *New Yorker* cartoons made fun of the suburban family ethic of "togetherness," and *McCall's* dropped the word from the hallowed place it had occupied on the cover since 1954.

Much as the muckrakers of fifty years ago had exposed the "shame of the cities," writers now catalogued the myriad syndromes and deficiencies exhibited by the "cheerful robots" who lived in what sociologist C. Wright Mills called the "illusion" of the suburbs—the parents of the leisure-addicted, faddish, anti-intellectual children who had recently inspired so much worry about national flabbiness and drift. In *The Crack in the Picture Window,* Keats had called the postwar settlements "jails of the soul" brimming with potential "Mongolian idiots." John and Mary Drone, the exemplary suburbanites in his book, go deeply into debt to buy a house from Ronald Suave; they live near the Fecunds, the Spleens, the Amiables, the Faints, and the obnoxious Mrs. Ardis Voter. Mary Drone knows something is not quite right about a life composed of endless discussions of toilet training, but she doesn't know what to do about it.

No citizen of the American suburbs —so recently "paradise," Sam and Eve's "heaven on earth"—was the object of more concern from the revisionists of the moment than the "young suburban wife," source of dull children and ingrained family neuroses. (A pseudopsychoanalytic construct, "momism," had been knotting apron strings into a hangman's noose since Philip Wylie coined the term in 1942, in *Generation of*

Vipers.) The mother and wife now bore daily moral responsibility for everything that was right and wrong about family life. If there was a single observation about families accepted by urban suburb-haters, professional family boosters, large segments of the social science community, and even writers of advertisements, it was that the job of being a good housewife was getting harder all the time.

In coming months CBS would air a special called "The Trapped Housewife," and *Newsweek* would proclaim that the American woman had grown "dissatisfied with a lot that women of other lands can only dream of. Her discontent is deep, pervasive and impervious to the superficial remedies which are offered at every hand." (In a scholarly article published three years earlier in *Psychiatry*, Donald Horton and R. Richard Whol described the sad phenomenon of "parasocial intimacy," a behavior that caused isolated, psychologically deprived women to identify with distant celebrities they read about in magazines or saw on TV.) Women lost sleep, experienced heart palpitations, and found that their spoons were trembling in mid-stir because they suffered from "housewife syndrome," the popular term for one of the many suburban psychological afflictions. By September 1960 *Good Housekeeping* was carrying news of a "strange stirring, a dissatisfied groping, a yearning search that is going on in the minds of women," in a provocative article titled "Women Are People Too!" by a freelance writer named Betty Friedan.

Eve walked her regular route past the Radcliffe Road Elementary School. By the time she reached the little luncheonette where she always stopped for coffee and a piece of cake during her shopping trips, the muscles in her face had started to relax—a sign that she would soon stop crying.

Over her second cup of coffee Eve began to wonder what the hell she was doing. *I'm punishing Sammy,* she thought. *I'm punishing Sammy, who has no dinner, just because the kids made me crazy.* She flipped mentally through some of the simple phrases she often recited to herself, little aphorisms, bits of wisdom she passed along to the girls: *Don't cut on the Formica....Clean while you cook....You have to suffer to be beautiful....Nobody ever said being a parent is easy....A marriage is a compromise....As Scarlett O'Hara found, you survive at the expense of the purity of your early dreams* (she hadn't actually tried this last one out on the girls yet, but she was waiting for her chance).

To be in love is to know what causes other people pain. At this, Eve stood up. Sammy hadn't had his dinner. She would at least go home and feed him. Then maybe she'd run away.

When Eve walked into the house, the girls were still crying. Sam looked scared. They were about to get in the car and search for her. She went directly to the kitchen to finish making dinner. She figured she and Sam—and perhaps she and her daughters—would talk about what had happened after dinner.

They did talk about it, but not after dinner. Not until the summer of 1978.

1960

The boys shuffled grandly down the bleak linoleum Main Street of Oceanside High between classes, chanting in jazzy choral rhythms the opening lines of a strange-sounding poem. *"I saw the best minds of my generation destroyed by madness, starving hysterical naked,/dragging themselves through the negro streets at dawn looking for an angry fix,/angelheaded hipsters burning for the ancient heavenly connection to the starry dynamo in the machinery of night ..."*

Susan knew many of the lines her friends were reciting by heart, and she'd read enough of Allen Ginsberg's *Howl* to understand that the point of view darted airborne across the American scene, at once observant, loving, and repelled. Ginsberg would later say that he'd written the 112 stanzas during a single weekend under the spell of drugs. *Howl* was populated by American characters "who lit cigarettes in boxcars...who loned it through the streets of Idaho...who distributed Supercommunist pamphlets in Union Square...who copulated ecstatic and insatiate...who wept at the romance of the street with their pushcarts full of onions and bad music."

"Basic values," as they were so often called, were mocked openly in *Howl*; cultural certitudes, and even the physical look of "middle-of-the-road" America—Eisenhower's metaphor—were rendered alien and obscene: "Robot apartments! invisible suburbs!...invincible madhouses! granite cocks! monstrous bombs!"

Susan was aware that her association with Oceanside High's less than a dozen would-be beats had diminished her popularity, but only when she lost a close election for class vice president did she realize the extent of the social toll. Susan's close friend and campaign manager, Maris Cakars (author of the catchy election slogan "I'm choosin' Susan"), argued that she was defeated because she was one of the relatively small number of Harbor Isle Jews at the large school. "No," Susan said, "it's because I hang around with you and the other hipsters."

Susan had always been popular ("not cheerleader popular, but popular"), in part because she'd worked hard to obscure her academic prowess and avoid the social Siberia reserved for the "brains." Susan was certainly pretty in her Gypsy-style white blouses, but she never thought so. Though she imagined herself tragically misunderstood, others saw her as a happy, pretty, bright-eyed girl with a lazy, disarming smile.

Some of Susan's friends of long standing—among them girls who could drop the names of department stores as easily as Susan rattled off obscure blues singers and beat novelists, girls who "only want to grow up and be just like their parents," Susan said—had begun to think she was "cool." And that was all Susan wanted to be: *cool*, a beatnik term connoting a stylishly blasé exterior hiding the churning angst of a poet.

But Susan didn't think she was cool, or knew enough, or had enough, and the disparity between her sense of self and others' perceptions was growing larger by the month. It was like the dinner-table dilemma: where her father saw arrogance and animus, she saw a sweet, injured puppy desperately in need of love.

Like Holden Caulfield in J. D. Salinger's *Catcher in the Rye*—a beacon to adolescents since its publication in 1951—Susan saw that a sensitive being could fall sick merely by living in a world of sadness and irony and adult hypocrisy. And she knew the narrator of Jack Kerouac's *On the Road* had taken to the highway to recuperate from an illness brought on in part by the realization that "everything was dead." All this meant that camaraderie with others who shared a sense of the problem was essential, even if it meant trading in the class vice presidency for a bunch of "baby hipsters" plumbing the poetic mysteries of karma in the hallway between algebra and phys ed.

"Mrs. Gordon, I'm calling to see if Susan feels any better today," the high school nurse said, not for the first time.

"Oh, much, much better, thank you," Eve said, ever skilled at improvisation. She knew Susan had cut school again to go to New York City with that troublemaker with the strange foreign name.

Everyone at Oceanside High School knew Maris Cakars, because Maris had been allowed to broadcast a satirical show over the school PA system during morning homeroom, until the day he made a sardonic reference to the principal (incorporating the "Tough luck, Charlie" line from the ubiquitous Star Kist tuna ad) and was suspended from school. Maris was tall and slender, with faintly Asiatic eyes. He had been born in Latvia, and his family had come to the United States in 1949, when he was seven. His father—whom he called "Pop"—reminded everyone regularly that the Cakars' American interlude would end the moment Latvia reclaimed its freedom from the Communists. (The challenges to Soviet hegemony in Poland and Hungary in 1956 had offered brief hope, but then came the television images of tanks in Budapest and the news of some twenty-five thousand Hungarians killed.)

Pop was unimpressed with Maris's arcane literary tastes and his "pacifism," which he considered prime among his boy's "bullshit ideas." When Mr. Cakars came home from long days tending other people's lawns and shrubs (he had trained to be a teacher in Latvia), he often wondered how much in the way of bullshit ideas a man in America was expected to take at his own dinner table.

After dinner Maris would shut himself in his bedroom with his radio and wait for Jean Shepherd to go on the air. Shepherd offered rambling monologues about his small-town American boyhood and about his present life in free-spirited Greenwich Village. The combination was explosive, because it sounded like he'd retained the best of boyhood by spending his evenings in a Greenwich Village bar called the Cock and Bull, along with novelists Norman Mailer and James Baldwin and his buddies Jack Kerouac and Allen Ginsberg. Everyone in the know gathered in the legendary Village, there to toast their liberation from a dying culture.

If Alan Freed had urged teens to get up and dance, Shepherd encouraged them to get up and go. All Maris and Susan wanted to do—like tens of thousands of other suburban teens within range of Jean Shepherd's pleasant voice—was light out for Greenwich Village. In one of his Sunday sermons, the Reverend Norman Vincent Peale called Shepherd "one of the great negative forces in life," and within a few years an article in the New York Times would note that the phenomenon of middle-class children flocking to the world he described each night showed that he was a more pronounced influence on the younger generation in the New York City area than J. D. Salinger.

Shepherd always contended that he never gave a second thought to all the truant teens from Long Island, New Jersey, and Westchester who came looking for him on MacDougal Street in their black T-shirts. "One of the problems with the 1950s was that it was too much about kids,"

Shepherd would later recall. "It was as if kids had suddenly become superior to adults by force of some mystical moral orchestration."

——◆——

For some time Lorraine had been noticing that Susan managed to keep various after-hours social commitments by climbing out of windows. Lorraine had a different idea of sneakiness. Like her older sister, she yearned for freedom and adventure, but she had already developed her own style.

One evening in the late spring, Lorraine tiptoed downstairs in her party dress and walked right out the front door of 221 Lincoln Avenue to meet Jesus, who was waiting three blocks away with Ellen Levy, Lorraine's sidekick, at fifteen a year older than Lorraine. Jesus Ramirez was Lorraine's date for the night, but she and Ellen had decided she ought to skip the traditional parlor introduction to the parents. Lorraine had heard Sam's dismissive metaphor—"A Puerto Rican could do that job"—too often. She had heard her father refer to black people—the best, wisest, most spirited, and noblest of all varieties of Americans, in her opinion—as *shvartzes* and even "Mau-Maus."

As Lorraine approached Ellen and Jesus, a brilliant dancer from nearby Hempstead, she saw how stunningly he was dressed for the evening and immediately imagined Sam's reaction. Beneath a closely tailored sports jacket he wore a skin-tight T-shirt studded with thousands of tiny black sequins shimmering like chain mail. Lorraine reflected sadly that she was a girl with a father who would never understand a boy like Jesus.

Though Ellen sometimes teased Lorraine about being shy and nervous (when Lorraine was baby-sitting, Ellen would knock on the windows and make noises outside), she could think of no better companion with whom to explore the real world than Lorraine Gordon. For more than a year the girls had been venturing to teen hangouts in Long Island communities bordering the city—places both geographically close to and culturally removed from Harbor Isle—where they invariably ended up flirting with exotic boys in leather jackets. They now knew honest-to-God Brooklyn boys with names like Mugsy and Rip, and boys with police records—real-life JDs—and boys who said "dis" instead of "this," which Lorraine found as entrancing as the Bronx candy-store owner's "mine goodness" had been when she and Susan were little girls.

For their chaste, romantic expeditions to the realm of the lower classes, Ellen persuaded Lorraine to clothe her "cute figure"—she was much more sinewy and athletic than Susan or Eve—in tight corduroy skirts and black stockings. Ellen would don one of her recent finds from the racks of the Salvation Army store. "When people all over the world have to wear rags," she announced, "it's just not right to have expensive new clothes."

Ellen's parents, Ralph and Muriel Levy, were "permissive" by Harbor Isle standards ("They're liberals," Ellen explained), but they grounded her for weeks when her urban ramblings brought her and Lorraine home from Brooklyn one night after one o'clock. That was nothing compared to the night the Levys came home to find their ornamental saber covered with blood, stains all over the living room rug, and an open brandy bottle in the den. Some of Ellen's "new friends" had decided to have a duel, and Ellen got in the way. Makeshift tourniquets and movie-inspired applications of brandy failed to stanch the bleeding, so the kids had gone off to the emergency room to get Ellen stitched up. Ralph and Muriel were sure there'd been a murder, and Ellen was grounded for a month.

But the black-jacketed boys, lone cigarettes tucked above their ears, packs rolled up in the sleeves of their T-shirts, lost much of their allure when Lorraine and Ellen discovered that just as close to home—in Rockville Centre, not three miles away—there were "Negroes" and other dark-skinned boys with names like Julio and Jesus, who spoke accented English, wore crosses, were graceful and uninhibited on the dance floor, and seemed to regard Ellen and Lorraine with the same awe the girls had for them.

In addition to rock 'n' roll and blues, Lorraine was now a gospel music fan, and like Susan and Maris Cakars, she refused even to listen to the "cover" versions of songs performed by white musicians and promoted by the record industry in place of the original versions by blacks. Lorraine knew about Blind Lemon Jefferson and Muddy Waters and countless other black musical masters who were said to be poor and unknown because white people preferred the sound and sight of white people singing.

Ellen's parents paid dues to an organization called CORE—the Congress of Racial Equality—which for the last seventeen years, "without malice or hatred," had sought to resist racial discrimination in the United States. CORE had adopted the "sit-in" from the American labor movement, and espoused a philosophy of Gandhian nonviolence. Ellen had heard about "pacifism" at home for many years, and she'd told her parents when she turned thirteen that she wanted to be a Quaker.

Lorraine and Ellen had followed the news of the sit-ins that began in Greensboro, North Carolina, in February, but what was most compelling to Ellen, the child of liberals, was that the four black college freshmen who refused to leave a whites-only Woolworth's lunch counter were kids. Before that, civil rights had been the sober business of adults; the children who were desegregating schoolrooms all over the South always had grown-ups at their sides. When Ezell Blair, Jr., Joseph McNeil, David Richmond, and Franklin McLain sat down on those stools in Woolworth's, it was an older black waitress who reproached them. "Fellows," she said, "you make our race look bad."

Sam Gordon told Lorraine all the time that serious association with people who were not of her faith—let alone her race—was bad for the Jews. The parents of the young blacks Ellen and Lorraine knew had taught them to turn the other cheek and keep to their own kind. This adult advice—identical on both sides—inspired in Lorraine the same sense of solidarity she got from black music and dancing. "I love Negroes," she would say to Ellen without irony. And she really did. This affinity—which her parents would soon perceive as repudiation and rebellion—was only strengthened by Sam and his "Mau-Maus," which sounded painfully similar to the rhetoric of Leander Perez, the terrifying leader of the White Citizens Council of New Orleans, who asked the city's whites if they were going to sit around doing nothing until their daughters were raped by the "Congolese" in town.

During a Goldenberg family visit to Harbor Isle that summer, Cousin Precious asked, "Would you ever kiss a Negro, Lorraine?"

"If I really liked him I would," Lorraine said, not defiantly, just as a matter of fact.

"Eee-yew!" Precious screamed. "With those lips!"

Precious apparently could not keep her disgust to herself, for Lorraine was shortly called into family conference.

"Now we've got two rebels," Sam said to Eve. "This is all Susan's fault. She's training Lorraine. We bring them to a place full of Jewish kids, and they go out to find goyim."

Sam had a saying: "Have assholes for friends, and you'll turn into one." But when Sam tried to advise his girls, this theory of socialization invariably came out as a demand that they associate with other Jews. Sam claimed Jews drank less and worked harder than most Christians. He also believed Jewish men treated women with respect, so he wanted Jewish men for his daughters. Somehow, in making these points—perhaps it was the pressure, the glare of disapproval he always saw in Susan's eyes, and lately in Lorraine's too—Sam tended to offer extreme examples to bolster his argument.

"Ever hear of the Crusades?" he'd bark at the children. "You probably think the Crusades were about the Holy Grail or something? Right? Well, those Crusades were Jew-hunting expeditions. *That's* what they were. You talk about what's happening to…Nee-groes in the South, but what do you know about the synagogues bombed in Georgia and even Illinois?"

Then Sam asked them what was wrong with Jews—why didn't they have more Jewish friends? Sam believed that it was his responsibility as a Jewish father to ask such questions. Since the time of the ancient rabbis it was home and family—what sociologist Albert Gordon called the "miniature sanctuary" in his recent book, *Jews in Suburbia*, and what Sam was not alone in considering the basic institution of his faith—that taught Jewish children the spiritual and moral qualities of God. At home, Sam would add, they also learned the basic techniques of survival in a hostile culture.

The girls would listen, but then one of them—usually Susan, who was even more contentious now that she was a hipster—would immediately throw Frankie Huber in Sam's face. His old Bronx buddy Frankie, the sweetest of all guys, turned into a weapon by his kids. "What about Frankie Huber, your *best friend*, Dad? He's not Jewish."

And what could he say? "Eve, how is it possible that we have two anti-Semites for daughters?" he'd ask later.

It wasn't that Sam hated members of other minorities—not at all. If he had a gripe with the civil rights movement of recent years, it was only that the activists seemed to be contesting the moral preeminence of the Jews. As if the crimes against American Negroes held a candle to the genocide in Europe. Sam's disapproval of the girls' fascination with different races wasn't so much a matter of color—it was that their new friends were not Jewish, and perhaps more important, that most of them were poor. Sam had moved his family to Harbor Isle to get *away* from poverty.

So even as he kept his distance from Judaism's rituals and traditions in his daily life, Sam attempted to raise the banner of this ancient religion brought to the world by a biblical father who was willing to kill his own son, such was his faith in God. But all he got in return was *tsuris*. It was the prophet Micah who said it a long time ago: "The son treats the father with contempt, the daughter rises up against the mother, the daughter-in-law against her mother-in-law. A man's enemies are the men of his own house."

* * *

After Precious's revelation, Sam and Eve summoned Lorraine and reproached her, as usual, for her cultural preferences. As usual, Lorraine did not attempt to tell them about the mystical power of the music, or about the kindness and respect she and Ellen found among new friends like Jesus Ramirez.

"Anyone would want to get out of this place and meet new people. It's all the same. Everyone's rich and boring and Jewish," she said instead.

"Listen, my darling," Eve cut in, trying to keep things calm. "I've lived in Harlem. I've lived next to a Puerto Rican whorehouse in the Bronx. That Harbor Isle is so Jewish is not so terrible; it's just fine with me."

But there was more than rebellion behind Lorraine's and Susan's provocation of Sam. His obvious disappointment in them was as painful as his rage, and they resented his refusal to pick them up at the Island Park train station late at night. It was if they had to conform to their father's prejudices to qualify for his protection. This wounded both of them and inspired retaliation.

"Well, it's not fine with me," Lorraine sneered. "It's not fine with me to live in a *ghetto* like Harbor Isle."

Sam would later describe those words—a ghetto—as "hands reaching out into my belly and ripping out my guts."

"How much farther from a ghetto could we have taken them, Eve?" Sam said after Lorraine had gone off to find Ellen. "It's like they want to kill me."

Lorraine thought that the rules her father tried to impose had lost all meaning because they came from a vanished world nothing like the America of 1960. She and Susan were far from alone in their desire to find beauty and excitement outside the ancient traditions and the new suburbs. It wasn't really that they hated Harbor Isle; they just resisted the false or shallow meanings with which the parental pioneers had invested it.

So what was a girl like Lorraine to do except creep quietly, boldly, out the front door, passing behind parents absorbed in a TV program and in front of the knowing grin of the Negro lawn jockey, to spend precious hours in the company of understanding friends like the sweet spangled boy who could dance a girl into a dream.

———◆———

If Vice President Richard M. Nixon had taken a cue from eleven-year-old Sheila Gordon and spent some time observing how a typical American voter of independent mind—Sam Gordon, for instance—could lose himself completely in the resonant images on TV, he might have altered his performance during the first of his "Great Debates" with Senator John F. Kennedy, on September 26, when Sam, Eve, and some seventy-five million other citizens tuned in and saw Nixon's small eyes darting back and forth like metronomes between his pulsing temples.

The vice president had decided to shun the Machiavellian politicking for which he was so famous, because "sincerity counts above everything else on television," as he noted before the first debate began, perhaps thinking of the success of his Checkers speech eight years ago. Since then, television had arguably changed from a novelty into the single most powerful force in national life, and "sincerity" was no match for the heavy makeup and harsh lighting that made Nixon look haggard and unnatural compared to his handsome, energetic oppponent.

Popular history has buried the fact that radio listeners thought Nixon was the better debater. Kennedy's voice was rather high, and his affect flat—an apparent effort to address intimations that he was "immature" at forty-three, only four years younger than Nixon. The two men actually had a great deal in common, not least the distinction of being young candidates in a nation happy to be guided by a man close to seventy. Kennedy and Nixon had been junior officers, not generals, in World War II, and were now typical young dads of the family decade, vying to inherit the mantle of an older model of the American father.

But for the two-term limitation imposed by the Twenty-second Amendment—posthumous Republican revenge for Franklin Roosevelt's unprecedented four terms—Republican Dwight Eisenhower might have continued to be president of the United States for a long time. Columnist Walter Lippmann had quipped that even propped up stone-dead for campaign appearances, Eisenhower would have triumphed in the election of 1960. Eight years later, when Ike lay ill from his sixth heart attack, twenty Americans formally offered to donate their own hearts for a transplant.

So it was no help when this hugely popular president, asked to name Nixon's most important contribution to his administration over eight years, said he needed a week to think about it. Nor did Kennedy's send-ups of some of Nixon's finest moments further the Republican cause. ("Mr. Nixon may be very experienced in kitchen debates....So are a great many other married men I know.") And in the television debates, viewed by thousands of undecided voters like Sam and Eve, the fact that the two candidates took similar positions on so many issues was over-shadowed by aesthetics—Kennedy's style. Eve decided to vote for him on the spot, though she considered herself "bad at politics." She was uneasy with the language of politics, and election time—which intensi-fied Susan's stormy debates with Sam—made her feel anxious and out of control. Still, she liked what she saw in John F. Kennedy.

Sam had recently become "a registered Republican for local politics and an independent during elections." In the first year after the breakup of Dynamic Electric, Sam had made as much money as he had in five years with Louie Bernstein, and Eve had quickly become a careful, skill-ful bookkeeper. Nassau County, scene of significant Ku Klux Klan activ-ity before World War II, was a conservative Republican stronghold in which Sam's young SGE Electric Company was doing a lot of business, and he'd decided to declare himself a Republican as a matter of protec-tive coloration, an expedient of the sort a businessman had to face. "Besides, I agree with the things Republicans want for business," he would say. "I'm an employer now, not an employee, and I might have to ask for somethin' someday."

Sam watched the debates with an open mind. Both candidates seemed to think that America was "falling behind" while Russia bulged with muscle and will, and Sam agreed. He remained undecided for sev-eral more weeks, but when he was alone in the booth, he cast his ballot for Kennedy. Sam had listened to Kennedy accept his party's nomina-tion, sounding like a man who'd watched plenty of episodes of *Gun-smoke* and *The Rifleman* himself. Addressing "the young at heart…the stout of spirit, regardless of party," he said that the nation was on "the new frontier of the 1960s…a frontier of unknown opportunity and perils."

When John Kennedy rose to take the oath of office on a cold day the following January, he would proclaim, "The torch has been passed to a new generation of Americans, born in this century, tempered by war, disciplined by a hard and bitter peace." He sounded a bit disappointed, even angry, that American life had not fulfilled the promise it seemed to hold immediately after the war. Sam decided Kennedy had been the right choice, the candidate most like him.

❦

Sixth-grader Sheila Gordon trudged through the falling snow after school. She passed a long line of cars, each with a waiting mother in front and a cloud of exhaust billowing out the back. The cars passed her as Sheila walked over the bridge. She was only a block into the deepening snow on Harbor Isle when she noticed that the boy from school with the terrible scar was behind her.

Most of the other kids at school were scared of the boy, whose scar was said to be the result of a large bomb he made in the family garage. The boy tended to respond to his classmates' stares with intimidating remarks and the occasional outburst of violence, but Sheila had always believed he only behaved like that because his feelings were hurt. Sheila was one of the few students who were kind to the boy with the scar, so she was stunned when a large ball of ice flew past her head.

Sheila turned and saw the boy approaching quickly, packing and repacking a wet snowball into a dangerous missile. She was at a corner, and as she looked in all directions through the heavy snowfall, down streets she'd always wandered safe and secure, there was nobody to be seen. She was only a few blocks from home with a murderous kid on her tail. Sheila considered the silent suburban streets, the proximity of home, and the terrible threat of a boy she'd shown only gentle caring, and everything about this apparent moment of reality suddenly seemed unreal. It could have been an episode from *The Twilight Zone*, a favorite of Sheila's and Sam's since it premiered last year.

Then another iceball whizzed past her head, and Sheila broke into a run.

Benjamin De Mott had recently noted in the pages of *Commentary* a "deeply lodged suspicion of the times...that events and individuals are unreal." An anthropologist at Harvard contended that the nearly one-third of all American children growing up in the suburbs were liable to fail the nation not because of their conformity but because they were being raised on "filtered experience." Yet from the relatively sheltered suburban viewpoint of Sheila Gordon, the world was chock full of lurking scarred boys whose actions made no sense at all. The Nazi mass murderer Adolf Eichmann had been tracked down by Israeli agents and was now in jail in Jerusalem, "regretting nothing." "The Ballad of Caryl Chessman" and "The Death Song of Caryl Chessman," odes to a man sent to the gas chamber in May, not for murder but for sexual crimes he either did or did not commit back in 1948, played on the radio. An international celebrity after twelve years on Death Row and nine stays of execution, Chessman told the public at his final press conference, "I have a masochistic pleasure in what I'm doing, I assure you. I intend to walk in and sit and die." And he did just that.

At a conference at Stanford University, the promising young author of *Goodbye, Columbus* complained in a speech that even a fiction writer "has his hands full in trying to understand, describe, and then make *credible* much of American reality. The actuality," said Philip Roth, "is continually outdoing our talents, and the culture tosses up figures almost daily that are the envy of any novelist."

Roth cited the case of the Grimes sisters, Pattie and Babs, Chicago girls who went to see an Elvis Presley movie "for the sixth or seventh time" and never returned. After the Chicago media had bombarded the public with evidence that Pattie and Babs were "good girls," their confessed murderer, one Benny Bedwell, claimed that he'd killed them after several weeks of sex games in local flophouses. At a joint news conference, Benny's mom apologized to Pattie and Babs's mom on behalf of her son, who promptly changed his story and declared his innocence. A local Chicago club hired him to play guitar, and soon "Benny Bedwell Blues" could be heard on the radio. Meanwhile, the victims' grieving mother was deluged with contributions, among them a brand-new kitchen (she was thrilled, the press reported). She used some of the money she received to buy two parakeets, which she named Pattie and Babs. Roth went on to mention the presidential debates, the beats, and the H-bomb as realities no less daunting to the artistic imagination.

Sheila had never heard of Philip Roth, but to a sensitive girl attempting nothing more daring than to walk home from school, the barrage of televised violence and mayhem indicated that irrational acts could penetrate any wall and sneak up behind you on any street, even in the perpetual present of Harbor Isle.

The scarred boy was getting closer, so Sheila ran up a shoveled walkway to the nearest house, knocked on the door, and rang the bell. A woman answered, and Sheila heard herself pleading. "Can I just stay here until that boy goes away?"

The woman let her in and pointed to a telephone. "You should call your mother."

Sheila looked at the phone. She pictured her mother slogging through the snow to save her. At dinner, Eve might tell Sam that she had had to rescue Sheila from a snowball. Sheila thought about the day her friend Nancy Leff's mother picked her up on the way to school. The rain was coming down so hard that Sheila was completely soaked. "I'd just like to know what you were going to do if I hadn't stopped!" Nancy's mom said—which Sheila interpreted to mean, "Your life is not normal, Sheila Gordon. Your mother can't drive."

Sheila knew she couldn't call her mother, and she knew she wouldn't tell anyone what had happened. She'd go home and it would be "get the green medicine for Sheila" time, and her sisters might tease her again about her stomachaches. But nobody would ever know about the terror and shame of the afternoon.

"I'll dial for you," the woman was saying.

"No, thank you."

Sheila watched from the window until the disfigured boy from school got bored and left. Then she went back out into the empty, snow-filled afternoon.

1961

Whenever Mama Yetta Goldenberg came to Harbor Isle for the weekend, five-year-old Ricky would climb up on the green brocade couch beside his amply bosomed grandmother to watch *The Lawrence Welk Show*. The startling couch sat comfortably amid the medley of greens displayed by Eve's many house plants, amid the verdant hues of plentiful throw pillows, beside the bright emerald flashes glinting from tabletops full of *tchotchkes*, and below the Floridian flora that covered two walls in bright paintings and prints.

Mama Yetta's favorite television program was on ABC on Saturday nights, so Ricky was allowed to stay up late, though the rest of the family scattered as soon as Welk's unmistakable "Bubbles in the Wine" theme song was heard at the stroke of nine. Between eight-thirty and nine, on the same channel, the ineffable "It" had once again been left to young Beaver Cleaver, whose character and moral fortitude had been tested weekly since October 1957—but to Ricky Gordon, none of Beaver's trials even began to approach the exquisite, strangely addictive suffering he experienced in the company of Yetta and Lawrence Welk on those Saturday nights.

Mama Yetta never uttered a single word during Welk's show. She would emerge from the kitchen during the theme song with a lump of sugar lodged between her front teeth and a large glass of steaming hot water in her hand, a wedge of lemon bobbing on the misty surface. Puckering her lips, Yetta would plant a kiss on the rim of the glass and begin sucking lemon water through the sugar cube, staring all the while through foggy lenses at a grinning bandleader with a five-thousand-dollar handmade accordion and an accent thicker than Yetta's.

Throughout his long career Welk managed the considerable feat of sounding like an immigrant "just off the boat" despite having been born in North Dakota.

Ricky would begin to hyperventilate as Yetta's sucking persisted, long, loud, and excruciating; the sound was like a hundred yards of material being slowly ripped apart in front of a microphone wired to a public address system in the middle of Ricky's brain. He would writhe on the green couch as the ceaseless slurping made his legs vibrate and an unscratchable itch radiated like a hot sun from beneath both his kneecaps. By the time the Lennon Sisters came on (a famous photograph showed the four of them standing behind their little Lennon Brother, who was kneeling beside his little Lennon bed with his hands clasped in prayer—it looked to Ricky as if he was begging for mercy), Ricky imagined that thousands of tiny ants were loose under his clothes. As his grandmother sucked and sucked and sucked, he'd roll back and forth hugging himself, eventually burying his face in the couch in case he screamed from the perfect ecstatic horror of it all.

Why in the world he submitted himself so obsessively to the torture of Yetta Goldenberg's sugar cube and Lawrence Welk's corny music would remain one of the unsolved mysteries of Ricky Gordon's life.

Susan entered Vassar College in the fall. The stylish and sophisticated First Lady, Jacqueline Bouvier Kennedy, had attended Vassar for several years, as Susan would occasionally shed her nonchalance long enough to mention in passing. Vassar was also the alma mater of the heroic Edna St. Vincent Millay, Class of '17.

Susan was one of Harbor Isle's most honored high school seniors. "Lots of luck Susan!" cheered *the Harbor Isle Beacon*, reporting that Susan was a semifinalist in an American Field Service competition for the "student who best portrays the character, action, and attitude of American youth." The winner would earn a scholarship to study in Europe and display his or her exemplary qualities there.

Susan didn't make the finals of the AFS contest, but she was a runner-up in a National Council of Teachers of English scholarship competition. Asked to describe an individual from "history or life" who best exemplified commitment to "truths of the human heart," she wrote an essay about Sonya Marmeladovna, the God-fearing, long-suffering prostitute heroine of Dostoyevsky's *Crime and Punishment*. Through vivid example, Susan explained, Sonya taught the protagonist, Raskolnikov, the Christian virtues of humility, patience, and sacrifice.

Other 1961 runners-up from the New York area wrote essays about Albert Schweitzer, Gwen Verdon, and Ben-Hur. One confident contestant wrote that the truths in question were best exemplified by "Myself," as he titled his essay, and another wrote lovingly of Dr. William Sherp, apparently a pediatrician in Dix Hills, a suburb not far from Harbor Isle.

In the final months of her junior year, Susan had begun receiving unsolicited letters from small colleges as far away as North Dakota. Their kind words and richly embossed stationery did not prevail over her parents' demand that she attend college in the state of New York. Sam and Eve thought it unnatural for a daughter to move thousands of miles away to go to school. So Susan applied to Barnard College, the women's division of Columbia University, in upper Manhattan; to Cornell University in Ithaca ("Place might as well be in North Dakota," commented Sam, map in hand. "You really want to be cold for four years?"); and to Vassar, in Poughkeepsie, like Barnard one of the elite Seven Sisters, an all-women's college founded a century earlier by a local brewer, Matthew Vassar, whose pastor had convinced him that furthering the education of young women might boost a rich man into heaven.

Some twenty thousand women had earned Vassar degrees since then. Eve Gordon could not abide the idea that her daughter would follow in their footsteps. To Eve, Vassar meant that Susan would waste four of her most eligible years in a place as devoid of Jews and marriageable young men as your average nunnery. Like most American mothers of the time—even those who'd attended college—Eve still subscribed to the mid-century assumption that since men wanted wives "who will bolster their egos rather than detract from them," as one textbook on marriage and family put it, college women were liable never to marry at all.

By 1961, some middle-class mothers had discarded this view, in part because of the popular depiction of American campus life as a nonstop Sadie Hawkins Day, a husband-hunting festival lasting either four years, two years, or until vows were exchanged. With a recent Gallup Poll indicating that virtually every girl between sixteen and twenty-one expected to be married by the time she was twenty-two, observers like sociologist David Riesman lamented this longing for domestic bliss and its effects on the nation's intellectual resources. "The same emphasis on the affective side of life, on the family as the most important element in the good life which has influenced the career decisions of men," he wrote in an essay called "Permissiveness and Sex Roles," "has also led even the most brilliant and energetic college women to decide that they do not want to undertake long preparation for careers which might cut them off from the chances of marriage or in some subtle way defeminize them."

Eve Gordon believed that her eldest daughter was already "you shouldn't want to know how defeminized." Eve had noticed that Susan's capacity to attract boyfriends was matched by a talent for losing them, a pattern she blamed on Susan's compulsive reading, her inability to let a man win an argument or even a board game, her ineptness in the kitchen, her rejection of makeup on her beat—or more recently her "folkie"—outings, and her penchant for political talk of the sort Eve had never heard except from men. By and large, Susan thought and acted in ways more appropriate to a son, Eve believed. When she considered how this might cripple her daughter's future, tears filled her eyes—she couldn't help it. Vassar College might ruin Susan's life.

To Susan, her mother's anxiety was further evidence that the Gordons were not "the typical Jewish family we're supposed to be." Jews were supposed to cherish learning, their traditional route to assimilation, but Sam and Eve seemed to resent her going away to school, perhaps because she would have teachers and friends and experiences that were beyond their control—another example of the hypocrisy typical of suburban life and Gordon life, both of which Susan would soon be leaving far behind.

Sam was anxious at first about Vassar's fifteen-hundred-dollar tuition fee and thirteen-hundred-dollar room and board charges—sums he considered beyond the means of a workingman bringing home under twenty thousand dollars a year. He also feared that a snooty place like Vassar would further estrange him from a daughter who resented him in large part, he believed, because she was "just too goddamned smart." Years later, Sam would steel himself and venture to tell Susan that he was always intimidated by her intelligence: "Ya know, when you were little...we used to say we took the wrong baby out of the hospital. You were so damned smart."

Lorraine and Ellen Levy were a rapt audience at the fall drama of Susan's Exodus (Leon Uris's best-selling book, the movie, and the theme song were everywhere). Ellen Levy loved watching Susan get ready to leave. She loved the very idea of Susan Gordon. She studied the laconic, adenoidal, sort of whiny way Susan talked, and tried to imitate it, just as she copied Susan's audacious application of black eyeliner. Ellen could not copy Susan's big, pretty head or her wonderful teeth, though she certainly would have if she'd known how.

"She's *so* cool," Ellen would say to Lorraine, who agreed completely but didn't want to. "She even makes going to a stuffy college like Vassar seem cool."

Ellen thought Susan was cool because she seemed both to know all things and not to care. The consummate black-clad "folkie" one day, Susan could metamorphose the next into a picture-perfect vision of the campus Golden Girl. Ellen and Lorraine marveled as Susan carefully enhanced the line of her eyebrows, stroked length from her lashes with mascara, and wound a black velvet headband around a flawless flip—the result of one of the Golden Girl requirements Susan loathed. In her opinion, she later told Ellen and Lorraine, "the proper punishment for Eichmann," the Nazi war criminal whose trial began in Israel in September, "would be to force him to wear brush rollers to bed for the rest of his life."

This was the kind of line Ellen Levy adored. She was jealous that Lorraine got to live with such sexy parents and wonderful sisters. Ellen's house, just a few blocks away, had marble on the foyer floor. Her father drove a Thunderbird, and her mother had dozens of pairs of spiked heels in every color lined up in her closet. Muriel Levy regularly cooked sirloin steaks and frozen lobster tails that Ralph got through a business connection (Ralph's Bait Shop, a popular local emporium, was only one of Mr. Levy's business concerns). She served baked potatoes—"premade," Ellen complained—bought at the local delicatessen. Ellen much preferred the meatloaf and casseroles that came from Eve Gordon's kitchen. She coveted the Bonnie Doon knee socks Susan, Lorraine, and Sheila wore.

Ellen thought the Gordons were rich.

Eve was about to embark on a pre-college shopping trip with Susan when Sam took her aside. "She earned herself a scholarship," he said. "Now it's our turn to pitch in. If we go into hock a little bit, that's okay."

The acceptance letter from Barnard College had offered a scholarship that Sam would have to supplement substantially, and Susan would have to live at home and commute to school. At Vassar, the college's own scholarship award to Susan, along with one from the New York State Board of Regents, would cover all but a tiny portion of her tuition, room, and board. Sam had been impressed and relieved.

Eve went forth to shop armed with punch-pressed steel charge cards bristling with serial numbers and looking like wallet-sized dog tags. Some college girls—though not Susan—had their own charge accounts nowadays, "Campus Deb Accounts" that let them finance coed necessities.

Reigning Vassar fashions were like nothing Susan had ever seen in

Manhattan shops or high-fashion magazines, but she could remember each McMullen blouse tucked into the specific plaid of each kilt-style skirt she'd seen on the day of her interview in Poughkeepsie last year. Vassar girls not only had sweaters but *Shetland* sweaters made from thick imported yarn and draped insouciantly around the shoulders. They wore flowered scarves (Susan's research indicated a Vassar preference for Liberty Lawn prints), and their shoes were invariably Pappagallo flats.

Susan wanted down pillows and a comforter "like Aunt Syl's." Of all the relatives, Susan thought that only Sam's sister Sylvia, who worked at a jewelry outlet on Forty-seventh Street in Manhattan, truly understood "luxury." When Susan picked out a thirty-dollar goosedown comforter at Bloomingdale's, Eve had to force one hand to force the other to pull the charge plate out of her purse. The Liberty print blouses Susan wanted were a fortune, but Sam had told her to go ahead and spend.

Ellen Levy and Lorraine were in attendance when the packages were unwrapped. Lorraine was jealous of the preparations, of course, but the thought of her sister's imminent departure made her cry. She couldn't fully resent Susan's privilege and success, because she knew better than anyone else in the family how terribly sad Susan was much of the time. Only Lorraine knew that Susan was lonely, like some tormented genius in a book; only she had seen how deeply Susan's boyfriends had hurt her. Susan needed them to love her completely, and yet—as Eve also perceived—she couldn't help chasing them away.

Susan had told Sam that Vassar "looks like a poem," and once he'd lugged her bags into her dormitory and was wandering around while she and Eve unpacked, he could see it too. Sam strolled along paths bordered by wildflowers and elegant trees. Beside a small lake he found artful wrought-iron benches set back invitingly in the shade, as if someone had considered aspects of color and the angle of the sun before deciding where to place them. Sam sat in a garden named for Shakespeare and contemplated the spire of a chapel named for Rockefeller. The campus was full of stately old buildings, and there was even an observatory.

Sam had begun to regret his truncated education. Nothing made him feel more alive than learning. True, he was more comfortable with hard facts than with ephemeral ideas, but lately he'd been doing business with better-educated men, and he didn't know how to talk to them. If only he'd finished school. The ideas and answers were right there in his head, but as in his skirmishes with Susan, he lacked the confidence to speak his mind. The value of a good education, Sam thought, is knowing how

much you know and being able to say it. As he roamed the cloistered preserve where Susan would spend four years with other girls like her, Sam
was glad that his daughter would have a better chance than he'd had.

Sam walked slowly to a building where plain but dainty food and
refreshments were being served to parents of arriving freshmen. A
woman Sam pegged by her clothes and manner as quite well-to-do took
his hand and shook it firmly. "I've just deposited my second Vassar student," she announced. Sam said he'd delivered his first.

"Well. You certainly are in for a wonderful experience. You and your
wife will be up here all the time…for the events, you know. The Association is very active, and you'll come up on weekends and stay in
Alumni House for the dances. My husband and I just love it here."
Apparently, accommodations in the opulent visitors' quarters could be
had for just a dollar a night.

"A buck a night," Sam said as they pulled onto the scenic Taconic
Parkway and headed home. "Well, I guess I'll just have to rearrange my
work schedule, huh?" Surprised, Eve looked over and saw that Sam was
smiling. "How about that place?" he said. "This is really gonna be such a
time."

———◆———

Toward the end of the first year of the Kennedy era—which would be a
"golden age of poetry and power," Robert Frost predicted, a moment
that would appear in retrospect as perhaps the apogee of American capitalism—Sam and Eve Gordon took a vacation. Business was that good.
Sam always had a few hundred dollars in cash in his pocket, and Eve's
money anxieties were restricted to spring struggles with the Internal
Revenue Service and a certain ingrained sleeplessness over monthly
bills.

The phone often rang in the middle of the night at 221 Lincoln.
Sam finally had a solid list of factory clients he considered "real human
beings," and most of them knew that only he understood the intricacies
and quirks of their electrical systems. They also knew Sam was the kind
of guy they could call at any hour if something he'd worked on had gone
wrong. Sam's customers respected him. He drew strength from his business relationships and pride from the success of an enterprise that now
provided half a dozen SGE employees with "food and clothing for their
families" (that was how Sam saw the wages he paid). But success had
also brought occasional reflection. "Ya know, Eve, some days I'm driving
along, and everything between the war and now is like a blur. It's all
work and kids."

Whence the daring idea of a vacation. Eve made reservations at the old Saxony Hotel in Miami Beach.

Yetta agreed to take a week off from terrorizing the kosher butchers in the borough of Queens, where she'd recently moved, to care for Lorraine, Sheila, and Ricky in Harbor Isle. She welcomed the opportunity to subject her grandchildren to her running lecture on the differences between "nice Jewish girls" and the ones who inhabited 221 Lincoln Avenue. Jewish girls, according to Mama Yetta, did not whistle, eat pork, or play records with lyrics invoking Jesus Christ, and they certainly didn't sing "O Holy Night" (the rabbi at the Island Park Jewish Center had taken Eve to task when he heard that her choral ensemble had performed the carol at a church).

Lorraine and Sheila couldn't stand the sarcasm in Yetta's voice. It reminded them of Sam when he got angry. Lorraine was probably the only girl in the neighborhood who didn't like prime-time television, precisely because so much of it relied on facetious put-downs, and she would simply leave when Yetta shifted into gear. Sheila was often alone at the kitchen table listening to Yetta make Eve sound like a storybook witch. One afternoon Sheila was peeling an apple when it came to her that she could stop the slander if she reached over and plunged the paring knife into her spitting serpent of a grandmother.

Sam and Eve came back to their room at the Saxony from a long evening of joyous dancing. As Eve took off the fancy maternity clothes she was wearing (she was five months pregnant), she noticed she was staining slightly. Sam called the hotel doctor, who came up and gave her an injection. "Don't worry," the doctor said.

Eve woke Sam a few hours later. "Call an ambulance," she whispered.

Eve needed a blood transfusion before she was released. She was told to stay in bed at the hotel. Ricky and Sheila cried on the phone when Eve told them about the miscarriage. She called Susan at college. "I can't believe you, Mom," Susan said. "Don't you know about birth control pills?"

Of course Eve knew about the Pill, everyone did. Women all over Harbor Isle were buying those twenty little Enovids that offered a full month of freedom for eleven dollars. Eve wasn't offended by Susan's assumption that she was ignorant, nor even by her daughter's lack of empathy for a loss Eve couldn't help but regard as a death. What hurt was that Susan seemed to think that the pregnancy must have been a mistake, as if it was no longer appropriate for Eve to have sex and conceive a child because she was forty years old.

Susan would later be shocked at her mother's injured feelings. She'd only meant her rejoinder as a joke, and once again she had been misunderstood.

Two days later, when Eve was still so weak from loss of blood that she could barely walk to the bathroom, Yetta phoned the Saxony to announce that she was going back to Queens. "Come home now," Sam's mother demanded. "I refuse to entertain every single *sheygitz* for miles around!"—a reference to the non-Jewish Island Park boys interspersed among the Harbor Isle boys who frequented the playroom. "Every boy in Long Island is down there lying around. I won't stand for it anymore."

It would later turn out that just as Yetta had "happened upon" a pound of bacon in Eve's refrigerator fifteen years earlier, she had somehow "come across" a letter to Sam from one of Papa Joe's sisters, who wrote that Joe was never a happy man because his wife was mean to him.

Eve was still under doctor's orders to remain in bed to avoid further hemorrhaging, but Sam loaded up the car, and they drove the fourteen hundred miles back home.

Yetta's bags were waiting in the foyer when they opened the front door. Sam took his suitcases out of the car and put hers in. Then he drove his mother home in silence.

It was six months before he spoke to her again.

1962

It was still very early in the morning when Eve glanced up from her second round of sweet rolls and third cup of coffee to see a bearded stranger who looked to be seven feet tall emerge from the playroom and stroll into her kitchen. He wore a faded work shirt, blue jeans, and huge steel-toed boots, the kind capable of protecting a construction worker's toes from steel I-beams. Many suburban mothers might have assumed he was a workingman, but Eve, something of a student of youthful costumes these days, realized that the getup was connected to manual labor only insofar as hard work was often the subject of folk songs.

"Good morning," the man said in a deep voice, his smile more amused than friendly.

"Hi," said Eve, still sipping.

It was not the first time in recent months that Lorraine had invited "new friends from the Village" to camp out on the playroom floor. Most of the young folkies Lorraine met at clubs or in Washington Square Park were urban kids, and they seemed to relish the chance to visit a typical suburban home, almost as anthropologists looked forward to a dig. The giant standing in front of Eve had spent much of the evening inspecting household appliances, comic books, canned goods, Sam's "Gordon's Hacienda" sign, the colored-light panel, the lawn jockey, and any number of other items as if they were artifacts laden with hidden meaning (information of the sort that Canadian critic Marshall McLuhan called a "message" in his new book, *The Gutenberg Galaxy*), or as if they were the stuff of what painter Roy Lichtenstein would soon describe as "pop art."

"Hello," the young man said again.

"Want some coffee?" said Eve.

The man kept staring. "Aren't you shocked?" he asked.

"Why? What happened?"

"You never even saw me before, and here I walk right into your kitchen. Doesn't it shock you?"

"No," Eve sighed. "This I'm beginning to get used to."

Since Lorraine was only fifteen and had yet to obtain a decent fake ID, she often set out for the Village unsure if she'd get past the door of the Dugout, Cafe La Metro, Gaslight, the Fat Black Pussy Cat, or the other clubs and coffeehouses she liked. Though she couldn't do much about her age, Lorraine was determined to look every bit as folkie as Joan Baez, whose every song, outfit, and finger placement on the guitar she now studied late into the night. She and Ellen Levy went barefoot to New York City one day because Joan Baez wore no shoes (they decided later that even Joan must wear shoes when taking public transportation).

For an evening of poetry or folk music in Greenwich Village Lorraine wore a black cotton turtleneck, black tights, and black flats, and carried a tiny black pocketbook. Her thick hair parted in the middle like heavy curtains to reveal a face without makeup. Behind her harlequin glasses, Lorraine's folk singer eyes always seemed on the verge of filling with tears.

Maris Cakars, Susan's close friend, was now a student at Lafayette College in Easton, Pennsylvania, though he was planning to transfer to Columbia College. When he was in town, he often accompanied Lorraine to the city.

One evening Maris and Lorraine went to Gerde's Folk City together. They sat down at one of the few tables in the club, next to a skinny kid wearing a striped cap like a railroad engineer's. The kid had on a blue salt-of-the-earth shirt, and he looked much too young to be hunkering over his glass of wine legally. He was sucking deeply on a cigarette less than an inch long.

Everyone chatted between tables in the folk clubs, and Maris and Lorraine noticed that the skinny kid spoke with a country twang, kind of like Marshal Dillon on *Gunsmoke* or Henry Fonda as Tom Joad in *The Grapes of Wrath*. Lorraine watched him wind some sort of metal harness around his neck and fit it with a battered harmonica that she recognized immediately as one of the reinforced models favored by players who really knew how to make a harmonica cry. When the kid got up on the tiny stage and began to talk the blues, his twang was even stronger.

Back in suburban Minnesota, Abe and Beatrice Zimmerman believed they'd made a fair deal with their son before he left the state. For one year he could go off and do whatever he wanted in the way of personal exploration, but if at the end of that time the Zimmermans were less than pleased with Robert's "progress," he was to return immediately to college. It had now been more than a year, and Bob Dylan—who denied that his name change was inspired by Welsh poet Dylan Thomas—had progressed to the point of singing for Lorraine Gordon at Gerde's Folk City. By then, he had played backup harmonica on a record album; been hooted off the stage by a Village crowd that preferred an odd young singer with a ukulele, pink socks, and the unlikely name Tiny Tim; and cut his own first album, soon to be released.

Lorraine was thrilled by the way Dylan moaned out traditional blues numbers she knew. His original songs were mysterious, and when he played his harmonica, she began to shudder with emotion, because a well-blown harmonica can sound like air rushing out of the soul. When his set was over, Dylan sat down next to Lorraine and Maris and offered to share his wine. Folkies were like that. Lorraine loved the folk scene because there was no separation between performers and audience. Rock 'n' roll had been like that only briefly, before Elvis and the others turned into "distant stars like Frank Sinatra," as Lorraine put it.

Lorraine was not in the least surprised when Bob Dylan became famous in the course of the year. In the late fall he appeared at Carnegie Hall. "Nowhere was there one word of hope or remedy," the *New York Times* reviewer complained of the young singer's work, noting a "lack of discipline and an apparent willingness to settle for the first idea and form that entered the writer's head. Dylan was born the year of Pearl Harbor and his appeal is to a group even younger. Unlike the next older generation, who came back from World War II and Korea seeking only security and happiness, these younger people seem to be in bitter, vocal revolt against the world today."

Near the arch at the northern edge of Washington Square Park folk lovers of all ages and colors gathered regularly. Lorraine, Maris, and Susan, when she could get a ride into town, counted themselves in the camp that disdained the Kingston Trio and considered Peter, Paul, and Mary the artificial creation of a record company.

Lorraine and Maris went to see the Weavers, authenticated as "originals" by the young people who'd launched the current revival of folk music on college campuses back in 1958. To Maris, the political content of this older music distinguished the folk scene from the more arty and nihilistic beat scene; the arcane philosophy of the beats had by now been reduced to the televised image of Maynard G. Krebs, the goateed layabout on *The Dobie Gillis Show*. Lorraine loved the Weavers and Pete Seeger. She understood that their songs were connected to the romance of ancient political dreams that lived on, even in places like Harbor Isle, among people who revered Ethel and Julius Rosenberg as martyrs to an ideology rather than pitying them like Sam and Eve did, as parents who'd made terrible errors but whose children deserved to grow up with a mom and dad.

Lorraine had "outgrown" rock 'n' roll. Wealthy, much older people dressed in tuxedos and polka-dot dresses were "making the scene" at New York Clubs like the Peppermint Lounge, the Dom, Trude Heller's, or the Cheetah. Half the mothers and fathers in Harbor Isle wanted their kids to watch them demonstrate the Twist. Along with Susan, Maris, and Ellen Levy, Lorraine had attended shows at the Apollo Theater on 125th Street in Harlem, stomping and bellowing through James Brown and Sam Cooke concerts. She still played gospel records on the stereo in the playroom when Sam was out of the house ("Jesus Be a Fence All Around Me" was a current favorite), and she dreamed of being "saved" by music like the black women who seemed to fall into a trance, wailing "Sweet Jesus" and swaying from side to side.

Whenever Susan came home for a weekend or a school vacation, there were hootenannies at 221 Lincoln Avenue. Ricky and Sheila would sit on the floor while the older girls played "I'll Fly Away" or Jesse Fuller's "San Francisco Bay Blues." Susan would strum hard and fast on a Goya steel-string she'd picked up at a Lower East Side pawnshop, forming the basic G, C, and D-seventh chords she'd learned from friends. Lorraine's sweet, clear voice—even higher than Joan Baez's soaring soprano—would echo up and down the split levels as she plucked her beautiful steel-string Lady Martin guitar, occasionally breaking into complex chords she'd learned by watching the players in Washington Square.

Eve, who sometimes sang along in her jazzy soprano, had accompanied Lorraine to Silver & Horland, the famous musical instrument shop in midtown Manhattan. Sam, who loved the family harmony created by the hootenannies and often joined Eve, Sheila, and Ricky in the audience (sometimes he asked the girls to play for him at dinnertime), had told Eve to let Lorraine get the guitar she wanted. The Lady Martin had a rich sunburst finish and came with the type of strong case made for trips to the city on the Long Island Rail Road—or for tossing into an open boxcar on the run.

* * *

Eve and Sam Gordon's two older girls had something of a *reputation* in Harbor Isle. Susan's Vassar credentials notwithstanding, the ladies at the local beauty shop had begun to cluck that Eve Gordon was a mother who had "her hands full." And the fact was that Eve *did* worry about the strange men who appeared in her kitchen after a night on the playroom floor. Still, she was reluctant to rein in kids who were so smart and creative and clearly in love with aspects of the larger culture that baffled her more by the day.

"Our parents were in a sad situation," Bob Dylan would later say of this moment when children seemed to be changing in ways for which their elders were completely unprepared. "They were probably just into no down payments and aluminum cans. I don't know what kind of knowledge they could have really passed on." Or as he would put it next year, in direct and resonant form, "Your sons and daughters are beyond your command....Your whole world is rapidly aging."

———◆———

Though nuclear mealtimes could still be a problem, Eve Gordon had spent some of her happiest moments entertaining jabbering family and friends around her table. But there was something about the gaggle of Vassar girls Susan brought home that spring that made Eve jumpy. From the moment the delegation from Poughkeepsie entered 221 Lincoln—stiffly and formally, Eve thought—she felt herself tensing up. It was as if her role was not to enjoy her guests, but to *receive* these representatives of her daughter's new life, a life about which Susan had told Sam and Eve almost nothing, never mind inviting them to see for themselves as visitors to the campus.

As she hung spring coats in the front closet, Eve noted the stylistic influence of Jacqueline Kennedy and Audrey Hepburn as Holly Golightly in last year's *Breakfast at Tiffany's*. When the girls all slipped off their sensible flats, Eve saw the words SAKS FIFTH AVENUE burned into the soft leather interiors of one pair and suddenly heard her own nervous voice exclaim, "Saks!"

The owner of the shoes, the very pretty blond daughter of a New Jersey physician who went to church every Sunday and voted a straight Republican ticket, looked at Susan Gordon's mother in the throes of an epiphany. Susan Kent had never once considered that shoes from Saks were anything more than shoes from Saks, but as she looked at Eve and thought about the brilliant and worldly Susan Gordon's constant talk of being the "scholarship student at Vassar," she added a new insight to an embryonic set of sociological observations. Susan Kent's horizons had already been broadened by Susan Gordon's insistence that she come along to help desegregate a lunch counter in eastern Maryland. Now Susan Gordon and her mother were helping her understand something about class distinctions, or as she put it, that "America is arranged in steps."

Eve set out sweet rolls and cake and poured coffee. Though her lifetime of reading crowds and her innate good timing told her that what this party needed was a good joke, she decided to retire to her kitchen and listen to the Vassar girls in the dining room, who sounded like they were stuffing her pound cake up their noses instead of eating it. *Not even Jackie talks like this,* Eve thought. She had watched the delicate First Lady's television tour of the White House in February (a house so large it was no wonder a woman couldn't keep an eye on her man, Eve would say years later), but Jackie's breathy nasal delivery was nothing to the sounds coming from the Vassar girls, her own daughter included. In general, their upper-class titters and ironic rejoinders made Eve think in anger and sorrow that these young ladies were "slumming it" in Harbor Isle.

Susan Kent, who'd picked up some rhetorical flourishes in drama class, was saying, "Yes, but I still cannot *believe* that so few remained seated! I mean, the speech was utterly absurd."

The speech under discussion—delivered at a compulsory convocation by Vassar's imposing president, Miss Sarah Gibson Blanding—had received national attention. As the *New York Herald Tribune* and *Life* reported, Blanding declared that any Vassar girl who could not abide by the "highest standards" of the college—by which she specifically meant the virtues of chastity and temperance—would be expelled. Officially the harangue was said to have been prompted by a student government request for clarification of these "standards" (imposed by a college rulebook that also required skirts at dinner and men out of the dorms by seven o'clock in the evening) but Eve heard her visitors claim that the "real" reason for Blanding's speech was a scandalous affair between a Vassar girl and *a married man,* conducted in *an apartment* in New York City. Susan Gordon and Susan Kent, who had both departed the ranks of Vassar virgins weeks earlier, remained seated throughout the standing ovation most of their classmates gave Miss Blanding at the close of her speech.

Eve was not displeased that her daughter had resisted moral dictation (the girls hadn't mentioned Susan's loss of virginity), but when she heard them talking about their adventurous efforts to desegregate the northernmost tip of the Old South, the conservative Eastern Shore of Maryland, she could hardly keep from bursting into the room.

A few weeks ago Susan had phoned home on Sunday. "Ma," she'd said casually, as if asking for the car keys, "can I go on a Freedom Ride?" The very words—"Freedom Ride"—terrified Eve. They evoked white kids from Wisconsin with their teeth kicked in, police dogs, iron pipes, smoke pouring out of Greyhound buses.

The Freedom Rides of the spring of 1961, organized by CORE and the new Student Nonviolent Coordinating Committee (SNCC), had been met with more overt violence than any civil rights action before. Southern law enforcement officials like Eugene "Bull" Connor of Birmingham, Alabama, did nothing to protect protesters from savage white mobs, and Attorney General Robert Kennedy called out U.S. marshals and National Guard troops on several occasions. By the spring of 1962 it was quite clear to Eve Gordon that a girl like her Susan, given to defending "downtrodden Negroes" in full voice, and apparently unafraid of authority, could easily get herself killed just about anywhere south of New York City.

"No!" Eve had barked into the phone. "Absolutely not, Susan. You cannot go on a Freedom Ride."

Susan Kent was the one with the car, so she drove. Susan Gordon had already talked her politically naïve friend into driving down to Washington to picket the White House along with five thousand others organized by the Student Peace Union, a three-year-old organization with over seventy campus chapters, formed out of frustration with "older," more ploddingly "liberal" organizations seeking to ban nuclear weapons.

"But how can I go?" Susan Kent had asked. "I don't, you know, *belong* to anything."

Susan Gordon was wearing her Village clothes. Her guitar leaned against the wall, and books by Edna St. Vincent Millay sat on her nightstand. "If you believe they should stop testing nuclear bombs, you can march," she said patiently.

The most penetrating political observation the sophomore Susan Kent could have mustered before she got to know the sophisticated freshman Susan Gordon was that a Republican sounded a lot like a Democrat once you listened to what they were saying. Susan Gordon, on the other hand, was dating a law student who was a member of the daring-sounding Young People's Socialist League (YPSL—everyone called it "Yipsil") and was involved with the Student Peace Union. Susan Gordon spent a lot of time talking politics with Susan Kent, who couldn't help wondering if the attraction had something to do with the fact that she was one of the lucky Vassar girls who had a car.

Now, on the way down to a sit-in near Chesapeake Bay, the two Susans detoured to New Haven, Connecticut, and stopped at the headquarters of the Northern Student Movement, just a few doors away from Yale's secret society of aristocratic undergrads, Skull and Bones. The NSM, an Ivy League offshoot of SNCC, had been participating in Freedom Rides, sit-ins, and voter registration drives in the Deep South for the past two years. More recently, its twelve hundred members (less than half a dozen from Vassar) had turned their energies toward tutoring ghetto children in Philadelphia and staging sit-ins along Maryland's Eastern Shore. Susan Gordon was not an official NSM member, but as one of the most politically knowledgeable girls in Jewett Tower, she had gone through the motions of asking Eve for permission to take part in the sit-ins (there was some talk that those under twenty-one might need a note from parents) and then decided to ignore her mother's flat no in the name of universal civil rights, brotherhood, and freedom.

The two Susans were joined by three NSM Yale boys, and they headed south. Susan Kent was stopped for speeding and had her license confiscated in New Jersey, but they continued to Wilmington, Delaware, where the now infamous Route 40 jogged west toward Washington, D.C. A bill was currently wending its way through the Maryland legislature that would force the desegregation of hotels and restaurants near Route 40. Apparently enough African diplomats traveled the road between Washington and the United Nations in New York to make segregated roadside facilities an embarrassment to President Kennedy, who had personally pressured Maryland authorities. When a writer for the *Nation* asked the owner of a roadside diner what he thought of the bill, the man replied that the ambassador to the United States from Chad looked like "just an ordinary run-of-the-mill nigger."

In a church in Cambridge, Maryland, the girls listened to various speakers explain the legal ramifications of a sit-in. "Civil disobedience has its consequences," said an attorney who warned the gathered protesters that criminal charges might affect the rest of their lives. Susan Kent was relieved that she and Susan Gordon were allowed to be part of the small contingent of black and white students who were dropped off in front of a coffeeshop an hour later.

Old salt Maryland watermen looked on as the band of integrationists lined the counter inside. A waitress approached impassively. One of the black students ordered first. After eating food they didn't want and drinking more coffee than they needed, the Susans waited ambivalently with the others in the parking lot. The organizers who picked them up reported that there had been arrests elsewhere in town, so they assembled in front of the Cambridge jail to sing "We Shall Overcome."

One of the Vassar visitors was talking about the dance that was held after the jailed protesters were released on bail when their hostess emerged from the kitchen and pulled up a chair. Despite her discomfort, Eve noted pleasant, welcoming smiles from all the girls at the table except one. She was positive she was correctly reading a look she'd never seen on Susan's face before. For the first time Eve saw the bull-dozer eyes Sam had been describing for the past seventeen years. Susan's eyes said, *You don't belong here.* They said, *You're not good enough to sit here with us.*

It came to Eve at the table that Susan had never invited them to one of the Vassar weekends they'd heard about because she was embarrassed. Eve thought, *I am her immigrant Rebecca, her Yetta, and Vassar is her Harbor Isle. I am a source of shame.* The turbulence of her emotions prevented her from wondering whether a daughter who was truly embarrassed by her mother and her mother's house would bring her friends to stay overnight. All Eve heard was the artifice of their voices, and all she could see was that look on Susan's face.

"Susan, may I talk to you in the kitchen?" Eve whirled as soon as they were through the door. "I am your mother!" she sputtered. "I know how much smarter than me you think you are, but don't you *ever* treat me like you're better than I am! Vassar or no Vassar!"

Susan staggered back to her friends, feeling guilty but mainly confused. How could Eve fail to realize that *Susan* was the one who was out of place? How could Eve be so blind to the humiliation of working at Waldbaum's supermarket during vacations? Susan saw herself as "the Jewish scholarship girl among the debs." At her very first mixer, she relaxed in the arms of a handsome freshman from Williams College and heard him say, "Wow, if my father only knew I was dancing with a Jew."

There were a few other Jewish girls at school—her friend Debbie, who'd appeared the first day in a society matron's artichoke hairdo, carrying a case loaded with enough makeup to fill the only deep drawer in the standard-issue dorm bureau, and a classmate descended from the Rothschilds of European banking fame—but they were all rich. Susan and the Rothschild heiress played a running game as they watched their fellow students pass under their window: "Which ones would hide you from the Nazis?"

Susan couldn't believe that her own mother didn't understand that she was only passing as a Vassar girl, that her apparent sophistication, knowledge of the larger world, and commitment to social change—all that intermingling of bravado and irony—were the armor she wore around her lack of confidence. How could Eve not see how alike they were?

✦

By the end of the third day of the standoff, Lorraine was convinced that the world was coming to an end. Her fears had grown by leaps and bounds since October 22, when President Kennedy reported the presence of Russian missiles in Cuba. Now a military blockade of the island was in place, and sure to be challenged soon. Lorraine was waiting for the thermonuclear war Nikita Khrushchev described as an "abyss" in a letter he'd just sent to Kennedy.

Around Oceanside High the popular conception of Armageddon had changed significantly since Susan was issued her civil defense dog tags more than a decade earlier. As the bombs grew more and more powerful (a fifty-eight-megaton "super-bomb" had been tested by the Russians in the fall of 1961), the image of The End had condensed in Lorraine's mind from a series of blinding explosions to a single flash of instant doom. Every time the Island Park air raid siren sounded at noon, or the deafening Oceanside High evacuation alarm bleated during a drill, or the TV and radio emitted weird sounds from the technological netherworld during CONELRAD broadcasting system tests, Lorraine prepared to die.

For all the diplomatic brinkmanship and threats of button-pushing played out in the 1950s, it was the young idealist John F. Kennedy who terrified the largest number of American children by far with his talk of bombs. It was Kennedy, among recent American presidents, who most often seemed to be embroiled in situations that could easily lead to falling bombs. And it was Kennedy who said in 1962 that the "prudent" American family would be well advised to have a home bomb shelter. Shortly thereafter a government booklet entitled *Family Fallout Shelter* was mailed by request to twenty-two million American families, over half the households in the country. Five different models were described, ranging from simple cinderblock constructions to fortified steel encasements designed to keep out crazed neighbors who'd failed to heed the president's warning (an index of the declining "sense of community" critics of the suburbs would emphasize throughout the sixties). Norman Cousins, editor of *Saturday Review*, reported that a four-year-old Chicago boy had tried to strangle his two-year-old sister after nightmares in which there were too many siblings to fit into the family shelter.

The Cuban Missile Crisis was as terrifying to Sam Gordon as to the next man, but he refused to apply his abundant know-how to building a bomb shelter. An eyewitness in Liège to a destructive force not a fraction as powerful as one of these new bombs, Sam scoffed at the idea of gravel and steel protecting his family from thermonuclear harm. "I'll tell ya what," Sam said to Lorraine. "When they put parachutes back in commercial airplanes, I'll start worrying about how we're gonna survive the bomb in a family shelter."

※

Perhaps because intimations of destruction were so much in the air toward the end of the year, it suddenly dawned on six-year-old Ricky Gordon as he was watching *The Three Stooges* upstairs in his parents' bedroom that someday he would die. The idea of being dead, "in the ground" or "frozen dead" like the mother in "Ballad of the Harp-Weaver," was bad enough. But the thought of not knowing where he would go when he died was so stunning that Ricky, after several minutes of trying to imagine his death, began to cry so hard that he could barely crawl off the corduroy bedspread to scream for Eve.

A few terrible events had already darkened Ricky's young life, one of them only a few weeks earlier, when he'd somehow caught his penis in the zipper of his trousers after using the bathroom at school. His teacher, Mrs. Caspar, had worked to extricate Ricky from his humiliating predicament in full view of his kindergarten class. But now, as he ran down the stairs in search of his mother, Ricky was sure that dying must be even worse.

Eve was in the kitchen.

"Where! Where will I go when I die?" Ricky sobbed.

Eve sat down and calmly pulled Ricky onto her lap. "When people die, they go to a place with shuffleboard courts. They all go together to a beautiful little beach where the water's always warm and the children are always happy."

Ricky looked up. "It's…it's like the beach…like the Beach Club."

"That's right," Eve said, "only with movie theaters."

"Will you be there?"

"Of course. I'll be sitting at a table playing mah-jongg."

In years to come Ricky would have moments when existence seemed even less hopeful or comprehensible than when he'd fled the sight of Larry, Moe, and Curly whacking each other over the head and run to ask his mother about eternity. He would discover many things more worthy of fear and confusion. But when he recalled that the world also contained mothers so prescient that without missing a beat they could create a vision of heaven from images of a child's favorite spot on earth, Ricky would manage to remember that terrifying as it was, life had its small salvations.

1963

A few weeks shy of his forty-fourth birthday, in February, his widow's peak tapering to a sharper arrowhead by the month, a new fishing boat being readied for the coming season (the original *Evie G.* having been replaced by a craft of more recent provenance)—and yes, as all of Harbor Isle knew, a Cadillac in the driveway, used but in mint condition—Sam Gordon left his work behind and strolled out onto the quarterdeck of the R.M.S. *Mauretania.* He was ecstatic.

As the good ship *Mauretania* steamed away from a nation of plywood and other inferior laminates, Sam admired the heavily polished teak deck. "Eve," he said, his mind whirling with estimates of square footage multiplied by the probable wholesale price of the timber, "do you have any idea what a deck like this would cost today? And these panels—bird's-eye birch, Eve!" Sam announced during their tour of the grand old ship's majestic interior. "Maybe the most expensive wood in the world." Around every corner, crew members in starched naval whites greeted Sam and Eve with almost military obsequiousness. The Gordons just kept grinning.

For two full weeks Sam and Eve would be traveling the West Indies in the company of Sam's new Masonic brothers and their wives. Sam had laid out two thousand dollars for the tickets, rationalizing as best he could the consequences of leaving SGE Electric without a captain. By the time the *Mauretania* had cleared the harbor and was sailing the open seas, Sam knew it was worth it. He already felt renewed.

With dinner-table conversation given over entirely to pitched battles about interpretations of world and domestic events, Lorraine and Sheila seldom heard Sam speak in a normal tone of voice. From Sheila's perspective, it seemed that Lorraine and Sam had stepped up the intensity of their disagreements so as to fill the void left by Susan's departure. Sam still spoke gently to Ricky at times, and the children assumed that he and Eve talked when they were alone behind their bedroom door, but their father's real communication—much of it impenetrable jargon about engines and fish—was reserved for other men. He was a Mason now. Masons were secret fathers, the children assumed. They told secrets and protected a secret world.

"It's not a secret organization," Sam told Eve when she prodded him to answer the children's questions about the fraternal order that was taking up so much of his time. "It's an organization with secrets."

At first Sam had been hesitant about joining the Free and Accepted Order of Masons. His army experience had soured him on uniformed fellowship, and the one stag party he'd attended a few years earlier, thrown by the local Knights of Pythias, had given him the willies. ("Those guys seemed so desperate," he'd reported to Eve.) When he finally agreed to be inducted into a Masonic lodge that accepted Jewish members (many did not), the ponderous initiation ritual struck him as childish. There was a lot of bowing and scraping and talk about the sun, the moon, and "the Grand Architect," by which the Long Beach Masons appeared to mean God.

But Sam couldn't ignore the fact that the lodge drew together doctors, lawyers, professors, local politicians, factory foremen, shop owners, businessmen, and guys who worked with their hands as he did—and that they all seemed strangely comfortable together, as the men of Harbor Isle had in the halcyon days. The Masons talked easily together, man to man, as they didn't feel free to do at home or at work. "Masons get together to be human beings together," Sam explained to friends who asked him about his new interest. Under the old leaded-glass onion dome of the ornate lodge building in Long Beach, social barriers melted away, and you could spend two or three companionable hours among like-minded men who wouldn't challenge your very existence or tell you that times had changed.

Some four million American men were Masons. Harry Truman, Sam learned, was still a member in good standing. So was Ike. Frederick the Great had been a Mason, and so had Mozart and Haydn and many of the Founding Fathers, including George Washington and Ben Franklin. The United States motto, "E Pluribus Unum," was borrowed from the Masons. The origins of the order were ancient and debatable, but it was thought to have arisen among medieval stonemasons and cathedral builders. Its traditions were liberal and democratic, and it had always been banned by totalitarian regimes (Sam dimly recalled Hitler ranting about "Jews and Masons").

Sam began to read Masonic literature, and he was delighted that most of it concerned the craft of building. The texts likened the building of a man's spirit and moral character to the building of his house: "Many, many years ago in Europe," Sam would explain, "the only thing a man could give his son was his house, so he would put his all into the family's house; he made it himself out of stone so it would last beyond him for a thousand years, from generation to generation. A Mason is a builder, a good father, and a man." Sam read that the stonemason's tools—the plumb line, the square, the level—were all symbols of the grand architecture of what the texts referred to as "the secret of what it is to be a man."

For much of the postwar era, popular literature and general cultural messages had suggested that a man rising to middle-class prosperity would find himself and "be himself" within the loving confines of the autonomous, privatized American family. But with the backlash against "togetherness" over the last few years, the role of the "new father" was also being questioned. "Don't Be a Pal to Your Son," a *Reader's Digest* article advised. "What child wants a forty-year-old man for a friend?" scoffed the curmudgeonly Al Capp, creator of the long-running comic strip *Li'l Abner*.

"Sam, you're away too much," Eve complained. "The children need you around."

But Sam observed that Ricky and Sheila had become constant companions and close friends, giggling at private jokes at the dinner table. They had formed an exclusive bond. As for his two older daughters, their abiding lack of interest in him seemed to have turned into overt contempt. His Masonic brothers understood this. They talked about it.

Wearing tuxedos, pulling on fat cigars after retiring from the grand birch-lined dining room of the *Mauretania*, excused from the company of their wives, the Masons would discuss—in so many words—the turbulent times, children who seemed like strangers, and their great good fortune in having a secret place where a man could still be a man.

With fences mended in the aftermath of her last baby-sitting venture in the suburbs, Yetta had agreed to fill in while Sam and Eve were off on their cruise. Mother and son were cordial before they left, but Sam was still smarting from Yetta's parting shot: "You know, Sam, you used to be a nice guy, but then you got a Cadillac."

One of Sam's few worries during the two weeks of the Caribbean cruise was that somebody might steal his car. It was not a particularly ostentatious Cadillac by the lush standards of its year—the 1959 Eldorado Brougham, after all, had a vanity case fitted into the dash, a lipstick holder, and a set of four golden drinking cups. Sam's 1959 model had rocketship fins so big and high that you could spot it in a crowded parking lot at two hundred yards. Its "pinky-beige" top looked like a great tinted pompadour, its vast chromium grille like an old-fashioned mustachio, silvered and elegant. The thing was almost as long as a first down, and Sam couldn't help worrying about it. Somebody had already swiped the tail lights while it was parked right in his driveway.

But all in all, there was precious little to brood about on the R.M.S. *Mauretania*. Now Sam finally understood why people took vacations.

<hr />

When he first met Ricky Gordon, Peter Randsman was a curly-haired eight-year-old whose older sister called him "Seacliff the Seagull" because he hadn't yet "grown into" his nose.

Peter's mom, Bernice, wife of the same Sam Randsman who'd driven up back in 1953 and asked Sam Gordon if Harbor Isle was a good place to live, tried to assure Peter that not only was it possible for a face to grow into harmony with a nose, but that he already looked a lot like Richard Chamberlain. But Peter knew that the actor who played Dr. Kildare on TV was far more handsome than he, just as he knew that it was for reasons beyond his nose—reasons having to do with how he spoke, walked, ran, and threw balls—that so many other boys taunted him.

One early summer afternoon on Casino Beach, known as "the Catholic beach" to the Jewish children from Harbor Isle who crossed over the bridge (Island Park kids often called Harbor Isle "Hebrew Isle"), Peter was encircled by a group of tall, athletic boys. Peter Probst, who was fourteen and perhaps the most handsome of all the Casino Beach regulars, was among them. "Hi, sweet pea," one of the boys said. Another imitated little Peter's girlish way of talking. "Hiya, fairy," said a third.

Then Peter heard his big sister, Nancy, screaming, "Leave him alone!" as she pushed the laughing boys away. Nancy and Peter were both in tears by the time the boys left.

"You shouldn't take them seriously, Peter," Nancy said. "You see that girl over there, Sheila Gordon?"

"Yeah, Sheila," Peter said, glancing at Nancy's pretty friend. Sheila had great big eyes and wore her hair in a stiff arrangement that looked like a space helmet in a science fiction movie and was called a "bubble." Peter thought Sheila looked like Lesley Gore, singer of the spring hit "It's My Party."

"Well, do you know Sheila's little brother, Ricky? The boys all tease him too, but he doesn't even care. They dressed Ricky up like a clown and put makeup on him once, and he's so cool he just laughed. All those guys say Ricky's cool."

The Island Park kids thought Ricky was cool. Peter was stunned. Cool Ricky Gordon.

Peter had seen and heard about Ricky Gordon, but the two boys had never met. The Randsman family had moved in only three blocks from the Gordons, but Peter was a year ahead of Ricky in school.

"Maybe you can meet him," Nancy said, thinking that her brother and Sheila's could perhaps be different together, since being different in places like Harbor Isle and Island Park was so hard.

Sheila was now something of an honorary "over-the-bridge" girl. She was welcomed and accepted by Peter Probst.

To Harbor Isleites, the Probst family of Island Park stood for Island Park Catholics in general. On the Harbor Isle side of the wooden bridge, "Probst" was as evocative as "Snopes" was to readers of Faulkner. Though the politically and socially hidebound prewar WASPs of Long Island disdainfully lumped Nassau County's Irish Catholics in with the late-arriving Jews and the late-arriving Italians, to the Harbor Isle Jewish kids the Probsts were "real Americans."

Probst men were stalwarts of the local volunteer fire department. Probsts excelled at sports. Probsts were large and competent with tools (Mr. Probst was a steamfitter). If Sam Gordon's home featured many well-constructed additions and ingenious refinements, Mr. Probst had built his whole house by himself from scratch.

Susan was friendly with one of the Probst sisters, Kathleen; Lorraine had dated a brother named Gene. But Sheila had recently soared above her sisters on the local social scale by becoming a regular member of the Casino Beach crowd dominated by Peter Probst.

Peter and his brothers (he was the youngest of eleven children) had grown up thinking of the abandoned, overgrown island across the rickety wooden bridge as a great place to play war games. But with the advent of Harbor Isle Estates, their mother told them that they might do well to avoid it. "Just stay away," Mrs. Probst warned vaguely. And from that point on, "the Jewish girls of Harbor Isle" possessed a powerful and dangerous allure for the Probst boys.

Sheila had discovered that she felt more at home on "the other side." The children there were less bookish and serious than her older sisters or many of her Harbor Isle peers. Mothers were less often seen driving their children around Island Park because on the other side of the bridge it was thought that children should fend for themselves. In Island Park there were rarely dinner-table fights, because the fathers didn't speak at all. If Island Park children required punishment, they got smacked instead of being tortured with protestations of "disappointment," which sounded to most of the Jewish kids Sheila knew like a threat of sudden denial of parental love.

In an instant, of course, Sheila would have traded all her good-looking new Island Park friends for any one of Susan's or Lorraine's brilliant and fascinating comrades, but she refused to compete for them. Sheila had decided that she was the dumb and untalented Gordon girl. She'd been a superior student for years, but lately she got 80's on papers and tests without even studying or doing her homework. Caring about grades was not important in Island Park circles. Yet Sheila's efforts to "declass," as a sociologist might have put it, took their toll: she often had nightmares about going to school without her homework, her books, or even her clothes.

Before Nancy Randsman or Sheila Gordon got around to arranging a meeting of their younger brothers, Peter spotted Ricky in a driveway jumping rope with a girl named Debbie. Peter ducked behind some bushes and watched.

Ricky had big ears instead of a big nose, but Peter thought he was handsome. When it was Ricky's turn to jump, Peter noticed that he ceremoniously took off his shoes. Even from a distance, Peter was sure the shoes were loafers. *Penny loafers*, shiny and obviously new, a deep, rich shade of red that Peter had never seen before. Peter Randsman had always, *always*, wanted a pair of penny loafers, shoes his parents considered "stupid and impractical."

Ricky Gordon was a skilled rope jumper; he could handle "double Dutch" techniques in his bare feet. Peter loved the way Ricky jumped, the way he looked, and the giggly, chipmunk-quick way he talked. He realized he must have unconsciously moved closer when he saw Ricky staring at him.

"Peter?" Ricky said, grinning. "You're Peter, aren't you? Come out and jump with us."

Peter was mute with embarrassment at first. Eventually, he forced himself to speak. "Ricky, can I try on your loafers?"

"Ab-so-*lutely*," Ricky said in his chirpy voice.

Not just okay, but absolutely.

Peter stood stock-still in the perfect shoes for ten minutes without moving at all, thinking all the while that he was in the presence of the single greatest seven-year-old—no, the greatest *person*—in the whole world.

"Why don't you come to my house tonight, Peter?" Ricky suggested. "*The Beverly Hillbillies in Marineland* special is on, and we have a new color TV, and I have to rest my foot because of my hangnail, so ask your mom if you can come over after dinner."

Ricky Gordon. "Oxblood" penny loafers (that's what they were called, Ricky said), a color TV, and a hangnail too....Peter couldn't eat his dinner. "Mom," he finally asked, "what's a hangnail?"

Peter could tell his mother was not impressed by his invitation to the Gordon home. Bernice Randsman liked Eve, and she'd gleaned enough information through the mah-jongg grapevine to feel sympathetic about Eve's "full hands." But wild daughters aside, Bernice also considered the Gordons one of the "fast" families in town; they were late-night dancers, and they were flashy, with their Cadillac and new boat. And then there was the little boy, who was not quite...right, Bernice Randsman feared.

As Peter was leaving, he heard his mother say to Nancy, "What are you starting here?"

Peter walked the three short blocks and turned the corner at Sam Gordon's bit of cowboy fence. He passed the longest automobile he'd ever seen, and shuddering with fear, he rang the bell.

Ricky ushered Peter into the living room, sat down, and put his one unsocked foot up on the arm of another chair. Peter stared at the garish colored light streaming from the huge television screen in the corner of the room. He turned and noticed Ricky's mother sitting under the hanging lamp she called her "Tiffany."

Ricky's mother offered a warm greeting as Peter became aware of the strong smell of cooking. The odors made him light-headed. Like Ellen Levy's mom, Bernice Randsman did not cook. She "heated up." Peter would never forget the two cakes she'd baked—both from Betty Crocker mixes. Much of the Randsmans' food came from a local shop called the Happy Hostess. TV dinners were regular fare at Peter's house, and when the Swanson division of Campbell Soup sought to extend its empire to frozen breakfasts in 1963, the Randsmans were the first on their block to own a freezerful.

Peter kept blinking at all the bright colors on display in the Gordon living room. The green couch made his eyes water. Then he thought he heard someone shriek, "Penis! Peter the Penis!" He looked up and saw Sheila Gordon, who said the unsayable word again—in front of her mother. And Ricky.

"Penis." Of all the names Peter had been called, this was surely the worst. The girl who looked like Lesley Gore had said the word, and her little brother and even her *mother* had barely noticed, as if the Gordons' supply of active nouns was different from the rest of Harbor Isle's. Sheila had said *penis*...out loud.

Peter stared at Jed, Granny, Jethro, and Elly May, the whole strange and motherless Ozark family enjoying the leaping whales and dolphins of Marineland in living color. Even the Beverly Hillbillies were entirely too vivid at the Gordon house. Peter thought he might faint.

Later, up in Ricky's bedroom, the two boys began to talk...and talk, faster and faster, their voices rising into a falsetto overdrive powered by a euphoric sense that each had found in the other a friend who was magically the same. That night Peter Randsman and Ricky Gordon made plans and exchanged pledges of loyalty that extended far into a future there was no doubt they would share. They would be best friends forever. By the time Peter went home, both boys knew that they would never feel quite so alone again.

———◆———

On August 28, 250,000 people gathered at the Lincoln Memorial in the steamy Washington heat and strained to hear Martin Luther King, Jr., sing out his dream of freedom and equality. That same week, Sam, Eve, and Susan Gordon found themselves surrounded by a crowd of angry blacks in no mood for brotherhood.

One of the few enthusiasms Sam and Susan shared was Jewish delicatessen food. Susan had a summer job and was living at home, and she'd come along to the tiny museum of ethnic sensations from the past that was the deli in nearby Long Beach. Since the Gordons' move to Long Island, as Sam observed on the way there, the neighborhood around the deli had "changed."

Backing the 1959 Cadillac out of parking lots designed for lesser vehicles was always difficult, and that day a loud metallic clunk was heard. Within seconds a furious black man appeared.

Sam got out of his car, noting that the damage to the other car was slight.

"You in your *Cadillac*," the man yelled. "You think you can just run *our* cars right over! You better pay me now," he said menacingly, reminding Sam of a barroom drunk.

"Look," Sam said, "take this business card over to Bridge Auto in Island Park and tell them Sam Gordon says to fix your car up. They'll send me the bill."

"Pay now," the man said as a crowd of curious onlookers gathered.

"Get in the store," Sam said to Susan and Eve, who were cowering in the car.

The crowd parted as Sam hustled them back into the deli, where they stood at the window and waited until the enraged man got back in his car.

"You know who that is, don't you?" Sam said to Susan, still staring at the parking lot. "That's the guy you're out marching for all the time."

Then Sam turned to his daughter and saw the Look. Sam could not abide the Look. It made him feel like a cornered fighter gasping for air against the ropes. "Sometimes she looks at me like that and I want to kill myself," Sam admitted to Eve. The Look said that Sam was "an idiot," that he was not the father he should have been, that he wasn't man enough.

"All I've ever wanted was a good relationship with my family," Sam would lament to his wife. "But she's an A-number-one bitch. She won't accept me."

Sam had tried to keep his guard up for almost ten years, since he'd first decided that if Susan couldn't accept him, he would not accept her. But then he'd see the Look and realize from the pain that she'd landed another blow.

Sam had seen the Look on other faces, most recently in the eyes of the man who was now driving out of the delicatessen parking lot with a slight dent in his front fender.

In June, Medgar Evers, the thirty-seven-year-old NAACP field secretary in Mississippi, had been cut down by a bullet from a powerful hunting rifle. In September, four little girls would be killed in the bombing of a black Birmingham church. In the course of 1963, many of the younger black civil rights leaders—notably James Farmer of CORE and John Lewis of SNCC—had begun to seed their calls for nonviolent protest with words of outrage.

Last semester, President Blanding had granted an audience to a three-member student delegation including Susan and her friend Sylvia Drew, one of only a few black students on campus. Sylvia's father, the brilliant physician Charles R. Drew, had led a team that developed blood plasma storage techniques responsible for saving many thousands of lives on the battlefields of World War II. As schoolchildren, black and white, would eventually begin to learn in elementary school, Sylvia's father was seriously hurt in an auto accident in North Carolina in 1950, and because of Jim Crow regulations, he died at forty-six in a segregated medical facility with no access to the blood plasma technology he'd pioneered.

When Sylvia Drew arrived at Vassar as a freshman in 1961, she noticed that the black students had been assigned the few single dormitory rooms. Upon inquiry, she was told by a Vassar dean, "We have quite a few girls from the South here, and we don't want anyone to be offended."

"That's called segregation," Sylvia replied. "I'm going to the *New York Times*."

The unwritten single-rooms-for-blacks policy was dropped, but Sylvia Drew never felt comfortable at Vassar, even though as the daughter of a black man who'd made it through Amherst College in the 1920s she'd been steeled all her life to the subtleties of white prejudice. Sylvia liked Susan Gordon, one of the few white girls on campus who was angry and willing to acknowledge in 1963 that life at Vassar was, in a favorite term of the existentialists they studied, "absurd." The two young women felt trapped in an ivory tower in a nation whose commissioner of education, Lawrence Derthick, Ph.D., had recently admitted that he'd never heard of the novels *Brave New World* and *1984*. Susan and Sylvia had classmates at Vassar who'd never heard of the Spanish Civil War.

Susan was deeply impressed by her philosophy professor, Maria Stavrides, who had studied with Martin Heidegger and strolled through the Black Forest with him (revelations about his Nazi sympathies were still years away). Stavrides assigned Jean-Paul Sartre and Albert Camus, and Susan saw in postwar French existentialism far more resonant and thoughtful considerations of anxiety, death, God, and "the genuine self" than were offered either by traditional philosophy or the attitudinizing of the beats. Heidegger said that modern man was "estranged." Man's glorification of reason ("Follow reason" was the Masons' central motto, and therefore Sam's) had obscured real thought and denied primal passions that were part of being human and alive. Sartre wrote about freedom. The most essential of all human freedoms, he claimed, was the freedom to say no. Existentialism appeared to Susan Gordon and tens of thousands of other college students as a significant advance over religion's prohibitions, fulminations, and compendiums of fear.

"Whatever I do, I give up my whole self to it," Vassar graduate Edna St. Vincent Millay once wrote. Visions of hope and fear, ideas old and new, passionate strivings after truth and experience—Susan tried to live authentically in the moment, but the moment felt at once full and empty. She often got depressed, and just as often she wanted to be shocking.

The students were meeting with President Blanding to discuss the fate of Carol Merrit, "a Negro alumna of Vassar College" and staffer for the Student Nonviolent Coordinating Committee, who had been jailed in Canton, Mississippi, on charges of "contributing to the delinquency of a minor"—a Southern tactic for blocking voter registration efforts.

Susan and Sylvia Drew knew they had almost no support from their fellow students for their contention that the college should take action on Merrit's behalf, and so did Sarah Blanding. She listened to Sylvia's plea, and while noting that she was proud of Vassar girls who stood up for their beliefs, she repeated her contention that Miss Merrit would be fine in the end, because "the human frame can take a great deal." Susan left the meeting feeling hopeless, as she had not long ago when only five Vassarites showed up to form a chapter of Students for a Democratic Society.

At first Susan had regarded SDS as an extension of sectarian quarrels within the family of the American left, which for half a century had been as prone to fearsome conflicts and ruptures as the Goldenberg family. Susan got what would be her only A at Vassar for a paper on Leon Trotsky's close associate Max Schactman, whose particular parsing of socialist theory led to the founding of a group called the Schactmanites, who of course loathed all the other kinds of socialists. By 1963 the Young People's Socialist League was dying, and Susan was no longer dating the YPSL law student. The Student Peace Union was a year from dissolution, and lately Susan was becoming too bored by left-wing theorizing to care.

But in the summer of 1962, SDS had held its first convention, in Port Huron, Michigan, and its ringing claim to represent people like Susan Gordon, members of what might be "the last generation in the experiment with living," made SDS sound like a different child of the progressive family. SDS's novel formulation—contained in the seminal Port Huron Statement, which was soon circulating on nearly every American campus—was that a generation of middle-class children had been physically and morally injured by racism, fear of war, and myriad hypocrisies that made them feel "a stranger and afraid in a world I never made," as A. E. Housman put it for an earlier generation. The SDS manifesto proclaimed that "loneliness, estrangement, and isolation" were symptoms of "the vast distance between man and man." Feelings of helplessness and indifference had to be given form, the document continued, "so that people may see the political, social and economic sources of their private troubles and organize to change society."

The author of much of the Port Huron Statement, with its harsh analysis of American society and its rousing call for "participatory democracy," was Tom Hayden, a twenty-three-year-old graduate of the University of Michigan. Hayden had come to a politicized view of the American "doldrums" after hitchhiking around the country, looking for the beats in San Francisco, and reading Camus on the importance of moral struggle against "absurd" odds.

One night at dinner with Sam, Eve, and the rest of the family, when Susan was still new to Marxist thought, she explained that her father, who was listening attentively, was "typical of bourgeois capitalists" in that he lived by exploiting his working-class labor force.

At this, Sam put down his fork. "In what way do I...exploit these people, Susan?" He was calm at first, almost bemused, sure this time he was above reproach.

Eve was already on her feet piling food on every plate and proposing a slew of alternative topics for family discussion.

"Well, you *obviously* exploit Bernie Denodio," Susan said. Bernie was one of the senior men on Sam's crew.

Even Lorraine, whose dinner table bellicosity sometimes surpassed Susan's onslaughts, sat back in awe. Eve, Lorraine, Sheila, and Ricky all turned wide eyes to Sam, like spectators watching a tennis match in slow motion.

"I exploit *Bernie?*" Sam said. (It came out "Boynee"—his Lower East Side accent overtook him in combative moments.) "I *exploit* Bernie Denodio? Bernie, huh? Bernie Denodio, who just bought a sixteen-thousand-dollar house I signed the note for, with a down payment from money he took home from my jobs. Bernie Denodio, who's collected a bigger paycheck than I have one out of every two weeks since I taught him everything he knows about being an electrician?...*That* Bernie? *THAT BERNIE!* Who in the *hell* you been listening to, Susan?" Sam rose from his chair, his eyes wild with images of working through two thousand black mornings beside Bernie Denodio, sharing one White Owl after another. "Did you get that from some pipe-smoking pinko college professor?"

Sam stormed off, his heart shriveling up hard and small, his mind entertaining basic questions, like Job.

At school, Susan sometimes told her friends about her father, a man with a photographic memory, who could look out a car window at any given instant and tell you a hundred things you never knew about the physical world he saw. "He fought his way off the streets of the Lower East Side," she would say.

Still, Vassar's father-daughter weekends would come and go, because Susan couldn't imagine how a father-daughter who couldn't spend five minutes together without going to war could possibly survive two days. Susan knew that she changed around Sam. She really was a bitch, just like he said. And she knew him well enough to get to him where he was least well defended. But a basic instinct told her that only when she convinced him that she was as smart as he was would he forgive whatever terrible things she'd done to push him away when she was small. Only then, Susan believed, would he finally love her.

◆━━◆

America may have had its legendary families before—the Adamses, the Roosevelts (Eleanor, widow of Franklin, niece of Theodore, daughter of an alcoholic society queen, had died just last year)—and they may have trailed clouds of glory in their time, but no American family had ever been so photogenic as the Kennedys. And no family album could possibly compete with the avalanche of happy, loving images of John and Jackie and the kids.

Average fathers never looked quite as thoughtful in photos as JFK did, but then, average fathers didn't bear the weight of the world as he did, day by day, picture after picture. The man's image would remain frozen in the memories of Americans old enough to remember the day he died—the picture-perfect young father with the beautiful family that had replaced all the advertising and television and ladies' magazine families as the nation's mythic model of happiness.

Eve Gordon had yet to recover from the Kennedys' loss of Patrick, the premature baby who was born and died in August. Eve knew that the family had suffered a stillbirth some years earlier, and her well-informed empathy for their personal pain made the First Lady's smile, captured so often and so prominently, all the more poignant, just as it underscored the young president's idealistic rhetoric.

And then came the photographs and the grainy home-movie

footage of the assassination. From then on, almost everything that went wrong in the world—and so much did—would be traced back somehow to that moment, "the end of innocence," as it was often called. For years to come, whenever something went seriously awry, thousands of Americans would summon a vision of the thirty-fifth president and mentally replay the tragic loss. Kennedy's death would always hit close to home.

Eve heard about the shooting while she was having her hair done at Franco Finelli, a beauty shop in Long Beach. She went home and sat by herself in front of the color television set, crying over each new image of a family in ruins.

Susan was crossing the leaf-strewn quad when she noticed the flag being lowered to half-staff. She and eight other girls rented a motel room off campus and sat sobbing in front of the television for three days and nights. The sight of little John-John saluting on the steps of St. Matthew's Cathedral was almost too much to bear. Susan had always expressed disdain for Kennedy's cautious liberalism, but now that he was dead she was overwhelmed with grief.

Lorraine was walking out of history class with Mr. Sobel, her favorite teacher, when a weeping friend told them the news. Immediately she listened for the sirens. She recognized the numbing sensation that descended on her as the same feeling of impending doom she had felt during the Cuban Missile Crisis. Lorraine spent much of the following week expecting the end of the world.

Sheila was in her freshman home economics class at Oceanside High when the announcement was made. She thought about the fatherless children and started to cry.

Ricky's teacher, a Mrs. Clark, was so tough-minded and stern that she reminded Ricky of a man. Mrs. Clark had the sort of stony face that never showed anything, let alone grief. But when somebody came into the room and gave her a note that November day, Ricky was astounded to see her face collapse completely and contort with sobs. The sight made Ricky so nervous that he started to giggle.

Sam was working on a job somewhere at the time. He would later acknowledge that it was odd because of his excellent memory and the magnitude of the event, but for some reason he could never recall exactly where he was when he heard the terrible news.

It was snowing the night Lorraine was cast out of the house.

Sam had been complaining about Lorraine's recent missions of mercy to the non-Jewish poor of East Harlem.

"Just find me a poor Jew, Dad. I'll tutor him!" she'd rejoined.

Sam went on to catalogue Lorraine's other sins: civil disobedience at high school—"And you're proud of it! You're proud of refusing to say the Pledge of Allegiance to our country!"—and her close association with Maris Cakars, "that Communist troublemaker." Sam had a strong suspicion that Lorraine was having sex with Maris.

On her seventeenth birthday Maris had presented Lorraine with an original poem. The poet shows her walking in Harlem and wonders why she isn't more afraid: "You are beautiful and have your ways, already the preciseness of your touch mystifies me/You are like the wind which has laws and perfections of its own."

Lorraine loved to listen to Maris talk about his dreams of "organizing the poor of the Lower East Side." He gave Lorraine Tolstoy's *The Kingdom of Heaven Is Within Us* and books about Gandhi and others who'd championed nonviolent action. But Maris also wanted to "go all the way," and though Lorraine had a visceral fear of the male anatomy—something she couldn't logically explain—she decided it was time to "become a woman," as Maris put it. So Sam was right.

Though they were dating regularly, Maris seldom came to the house on Lincoln Avenue because of Sam's disapproval. During one of their worst fights, Sam had called Lorraine a "tramp," and another time a "whore," but Lorraine suffered the insults because for the first time she was in love. Sex was only the sign of love, and she figured she'd get used to it. Not only did she have an older, idealistic new boyfriend, she had a man who came from the special world inhabited by her big sister.

Lately Lorraine's jealousy of Susan's way with words was more intense than ever. Her attempts to describe her passions or her rage always fell short. At home, she was often reduced to a damn-the-torpedoes approach. Susan stood back in shock the first time she saw and heard the "changed Lorraine" Eve had been telling her about. "I hate you!" Lorraine had screamed at Eve as Susan looked on during a visit. "I wouldn't care if you died of cancer!"

Now, as Sam continued to deliver a stream of ironic gibes, Lorraine yelled, "Why don't you just kill me and get it over with?"

"Get up," Sam said, his voice strangely low. "Get up and get out of this house."

Lorraine ran outside without her coat. She hugged her thin arms to her chest and ran through the snow to Ellen Levy's house, for solace, and perhaps for some lobster tails.

Ellen Levy was suddenly one of Harbor Isle's most famous citizens. Not since *Newsweek* noted that the town was home to the 1932 Olympic gold medalist in speed skating, Irving Jaffe, had one of Harbor Isle's own ascended into the limelight as spectacularly as Lorraine's best friend. A veteran of acting lessons and some summer theater, Ellen now appeared regularly on a new television show starring the "princess of teendom," Patty Duke.

The two main characters on *The Patty Duke Show* were identical cousins, both, of course, played by Patty. Special effects being relatively primitive in those days, this meant that each time zany, all-American, forever-in-a-fix but good-hearted Patty Lane faced the camera to talk to her prim Scottish-born cousin Cathy, someone had to stand with her back to the camera and pretend to be Cathy, and when it was Cathy's turn to show her face, someone had to play Patty. For most of the show's run that someone was a girl named Rita McLaughlin, but briefly, as every kid in Harbor Isle and much of Island Park knew, she was none other than Ellen Levy, whose six-roller flip could be made to arc Patty-like or Cathy-like for the edification of millions every Wednesday night.

Ellen noticed almost every day on the set that Patty, who had recently won an Academy Award for her portrayal of the young Helen Keller in *The Miracle Worker*, was not a happy girl. Sometimes Patty would cry so hard and uncontrollably between takes that they had to stop shooting for the day.

When she was feeling better, Patty liked to ask Ellen questions. "Where do you guys go after school?" "I hear kids are wearing sandals. What kind of store sells sandals?" "Where do cool kids go on dates?" She particularly enjoyed hearing about Ellen's adventures in Harlem. One time she asked, "What does it feel like to kiss a Negro?" Ellen, who had tried it on occasion, described the feeling as best she could.

Every Sunday Ellen and Lorraine went to the American Friends Service Committee "project house" on East 111th Street in East Harlem. From there they were sent out into the community to the homes of children who lived in the sort of harrowing poverty Michael Harrington had documented and brought to shocked national attention in his damning 1962 book, *The Other America*. After tutoring Spanish-speaking children in English, Lorraine and Ellen would return to the Friends project house to hang around with local boys. The walk back to the Lexington Avenue subway meant running a gauntlet of men making clicking noises with their tongues, but as Ellen explained to Patty Duke, "Girls from a place as average as Harbor Isle, New York, have to look for things they don't already know."

Sometimes Patty would keep grilling Ellen between takes. "Is this what it's like, Ellen?" she asked one afternoon, referring to the zany scene they'd just completed. "You know, two girls talking like we just did? Is this what high school's like for you guys?"

"Well," Ellen said, hesitating between being nice and being honest, "it's...no, not at all. It's really not like this at all."

Lorraine was now a member in good standing of a notorious circle of Oceanside High students known as the Pinkos. Shoulder to shoulder with her Pinko friends Steve Press, Marge Cooperman, and four or five others, Lorraine refused as a matter of course to rise and recite the Pledge of Allegiance, and she refused to evacuate the school building during air raid drills (in this, at least, Lorraine agreed with her father, who continued to insist, using one of Susan's favorite words, that hiding in basements bomb shelters was "absurd"). Lorraine and the other Pinkos also refused to attend gym class, an act of civil disobedience meant to protest an "authoritarian environment."

After one air raid drill, when the Pinkos remained resolutely in their seats, they were sentenced to stay after school and calculate complex logarithms under the tutelage of one of the most demanding math teachers of all. Lorraine was crying over the math punishment when she got home, and Eve rushed to the school on her behalf—though not in defense of her Gandhian principles. "She had her period," Eve protested to the exacting math teacher. "I don't care what she's done, it's cruel to punish a girl who has her period."

School administrators noticed that the anarchic defiance of the Pinkos was beginning to affect Oceanside's more "well-adjusted" students. Eventually, the anti-pledge, anti-gym, anti-air-raid contingent was asked to convene in the office of the school's recently hired staff psychologist, Morton Schwartzstein—"just to talk about things," as he put it.

Many public school systems in middle-class communities now had psychologists on staff, but most did little more than administer the batteries of tests that measured IQ. Morton Schwartzstein had been hired as part of a progressive effort to address a noticeable surge in adolescent disputatiousness and nonconformity. Schwartzstein, who had Freudian training, was not the only educational expert in the early 1960s who believed that a spitball propelled at an adolescent girl through an adolescent boy's straw was an act worthy of further interpretation.

The number of clinical practitioners of the psychological sciences had increased sixfold since Sam came home from World War II, yet estimates indicated that four of five school-age Americans in need of psychological treatment were as yet unserved. At the time, inferior academic performance and "antisocial behavior" in school were rarely connected to a child's psychological development or home life.

Morton Schwartzstein considered "the Pinko problem" at Oceanside High in part a function of very bright students internalizing moral imperatives in the context of an extremely restrictive environment. He also thought it had a lot to do with sex. More specifically, it was a matter of largely unconscious and primal instinctual drives (the id) in conflict with the ego, the psyche's management system, according to Freud. "It is in the very nature of man, in Freud's view," readers of the *Atlantic Monthly* were informed in a forty-nine-page article, "The Freudian Revolution," "that he cannot live outside society, while at the same time it is in the very nature of society to require renunciation of instinctual gratification."

Lorraine told Morton Schwartzstein about her resentment of one of the gym teachers, a woman she thought had a sadistic penchant for "armpit checks" designed to search out reprobate hairs and other evidence of insufficient personal hygiene. Schwartstein listened and felt assured that the Pinko gym boycott stemmed from psychosexual adjustment dilemmas spawned by the trauma of having to undress in front of peers.

Lorraine and her friends liked Morton Schwartzstein, and but for his advanced age (twenty-eight), they imagined he might have boycotted gym class and sat out air raid drills too, and even gone to Washington Square or East Harlem with them. Since New York statutes permitted students to be excused from gym for medical reasons, Schwartzstein arranged for the Pinkos to attend regular "talking sessions." Lorraine found the meetings comforting and sometimes strangely exhilarating because of things she heard herself say about how difficult it was to be seventeen, and angry or afraid so often, and always unable to express the feelings in words.

One of the hardest things for Lorraine to understand, she told the others as they exchanged stories of parental rage, was that when she and her father took opposite sides, her mother would never protect her. Eve would rush to school to confront a vengeful math teacher, but she wouldn't say a word to Sam.

* * *

The phone rang as Ralph Levy was pacing back and forth in his living room saying, "I've always had a lot of respect for Sam Gordon, but I can't approve of throwing a girl out in the snow."

"It's your mom," Muriel Levy said to Lorraine.

Eve whispered, "I put your coat out on the back porch."

Lorraine stayed at Ellen's for two days. When she came home, she refused to look at her parents or speak to them for several days.

As Sam was well aware, one thing Eve Gordon could not abide was silent brooding. "If you're going to live in my house, you have to talk, Lorraine," Eve said, stomping into her room. "I don't think you have enough money for Kotex outside this house, so I suggest you start talking right away. I don't give a damn *what* you say, but you have to talk."

"Okay, I'll talk."

"You know what I hope for you, Lorraine?" Eve said before leaving the room. "I hope your children are like you."

⬥

On the nights Sam got home before Ricky was in bed, Ricky would sprint through the house as soon as he heard his father's car. He would wait next to the front door on the bottom step of the stairs and leap into Sam's arms as his father stepped inside. He would wrap his arms around Sam's neck and kiss his cool, stubbled face, squealing "Daddy! Daddy!" while Sam held him close.

Sam couldn't wait until his son and heir was finally old enough to take his rightful place at his side. Ricky would lend some balance to his life. Sam was sure of it. Ricky would mitigate the tribulations of having a family comprised of too many women for its own collective good.

As a kind of trial run, Sam had taken Ricky out fishing twice this year, and both times Ricky had thrown up. Sam took Ricky to Playland, where he threw up on a ride called the Man in the Moon. They went to the zoo twice, and Ricky threw up twice. "You weren't even moving. Why the zoo?" Sam asked. It was the dirty smell, but Ricky was too embarrassed to say so.

The little Christmas-tree-shaped gadget attached to the dashboard of the Cadillac gave off such an overpowering odor of spruce that Ricky thought he would throw up every time he took a ride with Sam. Ricky would concentrate hard on not throwing up inside a car owned by the best of all fathers, who deserved a son who didn't throw up at all.

Sam had also thrown up a lot as a boy. Yetta forced him to eat huge breakfasts in the morning before taking the subway to school, and Sam threw up on the train. But he never told Ricky about the humiliation of those boyhood mornings.

One cold winter night Ricky heard the car door slam and bounded out of his bedroom to the stairs. The front door opened and Ricky hollered, "Daddy!" But when he jumped up, Sam caught him and held him at arm's length. Ricky tried to kiss his father hello, but Sam averted his face.

"We don't do this anymore," Sam said, his voice cold as the night. "You're getting too old." Then he put Ricky down on the floor and turned away.

1964

Sam discovered *a word*; it was carved into the wooden paneling of the playroom. He beheld the desecration of the finest room in Gordon's Hacienda, a room that only a decade earlier had been heralded up and down the streets of Harbor Isle as a paternal achievement of historic significance. He stared at the deeply etched word, wondering if he could survive another year of invasions like this.

In New York City, a stand-up comic named Lenny Bruce was contending from the witness stand in criminal court that words like the one Sam discovered in his converted garage—obscenities previously relegated to subway walls and playgrounds, never uttered aloud except in furtive sexual suggestions or the odd expression of physical pain—were subject to protection under First Amendment guarantees no matter where they appeared, even in a nightclub act for public consumption.

Susan had recently announced that she wanted to transfer to the University of California at Berkeley. (Susan Kent, her political protégé and close friend, had already transferred there in search of "the real world," which was not to be found at Vassar, she said.) In Berkeley, the university had barred civil rights groups from soliciting funds on campus, and by the middle of the year—a year, according to observers of population trends, that marked the end of the "baby boom" just as the oldest of the bulging horde were entering college—the Free Speech Movement had exploded. Hundreds of student demonstrators would be arrested under banners that proclaimed their right of free expression.

It appeared to Sam and Eve that Susan's desire to transfer might have something to do with the fact that she was on the verge of being expelled from Vassar. A woman who said she was "warden" of the college had phoned them to report their daughter's "deliberate falsification of a statement, verbal or written"—a crime according to the "rules for the orderly conduct of the Vassar community." Susan had forged her friend Debbie's name on the dormitory "late signout sheet," and now a committee of students and faculty would decide her fate.

"Your daughter," the warden said grimly at the end of the phone call, "is inherently dishonest."

Home from spring break, sitting in her Shetland sweater with her knees pressed together, Susan did not look like a perpetrator of high crimes. "I want to go to California," she said tearfully.

"California's a loser place," her father said. "California's where people go who can't make it anywhere else."

Though the Vassar committee decided not to expel Susan, she was restricted to freshman social privileges and stripped of her scholarship.

FUCK. Sam kept staring at the word on his wall. *They come right into a man's home*, he thought.

FUCK. The "Kilroy Was Here" of a new generation.

———◆———

Ricky and Peter loved to spy on Sheila and her friends. The boys would marvel secretly at the fourteen- and fifteen-year-old girls shaving their legs, setting each other's hair, applying lipstick, donning white party dresses. After the girls went out, they would play with the collection of beauty equipment Sheila referred to as her "things." Ricky and Peter would dream of being movie stars—exactly the status they accorded Sheila and her beautiful friends.

Ricky's big sister Sheila took him on three-mile hikes to the movie theaters in Long Beach. They'd recently seen a double feature together, a Doris Day matrimonial comedy, *The Thrill of It All*, as well as a strange, grainy movie in French entitled *Huis Clos*, an adaptation of Jean-Paul Sartre's play *No Exit*. Ricky and Sheila would always remember the second part of the double feature as a weirdly stimulating depiction of exotic ideas.

Only Sheila, Ricky believed, could make oatmeal of the consistency he preferred (a fact they both endeavored to keep from the jealous kitchen queen who was their mom). Ricky and Sheila had by now become best friends. Sheila finally had a member of the family who understood her.

Nothing about Sheila was more alluring to Ricky than the sight of her weeping beside her record player, swaying prayerfully to the sound of the Beatles singing "This Boy."

From the moment Sheila first played side one of *Meet the Beatles!*, she knew that the cute boys from across the ocean could never be mean or break a young girl's heart. "This boy would be happy just to love you," they sang to her. All they wanted was to "hold your hand."

The Beatles moved into 221 Lincoln Avenue and remained there as long as there were children at home. The Beatles created moods that pervaded the house, and more important to Sheila, they took the edge off moods that were already in residence. The band so completely filled the gaps in Sheila's defense system that for many years the boys from Liverpool "became my life." The Beatles were everything.

By the time Sheila formally announced that henceforth she wanted to be addressed as "president of the Anti Folk Music in the Gordon Family Club," said family had arrayed itself in front of the TV to watch both Beatles appearances on *The Ed Sullivan Show* in February. ("It's not Frank Sinatra," Sam said with a shrug.) A quarter-million love letters to the boys languished in a Long Island warehouse by the second appearance, and one factory was said to be turning out thirty-five thousand Beatles wigs a day.

"The girls who shriek when they see the Beatles are not very well able to explain why they feel the way they do," wrote a journalist in the *New Republic*. "'They move me,' said one. 'They give me a new feeling of youth,' said another." A February issue of *Science News Letter* reported that the nation's psychologists were "puzzled." Perhaps girls needed an analogue to sports in order to "release sexual energy." Or maybe the deadpan expressions and "suave disdain" the Beatles displayed in performance stood for "alienation" in the minds of the girls. A British reporter, veteran of the earlier Beatles contagion in England, recalled that a doctor back home had explained that "this sort of activity was important for young women because it made the pains of pregnancy easier for them when they grew up and got married."

———◆———

Eve reached out and clutched her little girl, her lucky little Eskimo, her brave one. "You don't have to get married, Lorraine. Just so you know you don't have to."

Lorraine sat cross-legged on her bed, looking down. She realized her pregnancy and plans to be married would cause her mother and father a great deal of pain, but this knowledge was joined by a revelation: that a simple biological condition would enable her to transcend high school and childhood in one nine-month swoop. By virtue of pregnancy, Lorraine would relocate to the golden city of Manhattan, scene of her favorite days. Young and expectant, she would leave behind the war zone of 221 Lincoln and move to a private island of music and adventure and babies and young love.

"You're only seventeen, Lorraine. You're too young to get married," Eve said, her voice gentle and very sad. She ached with guilt. "What can I do?"

"One thing." Lorraine looked up at her mother. "Tell Daddy."

So prudish was Lorraine considered by the other Oceanside High Pinkos that they called her "Pash," short for "Passion Flower." Lorraine's sexual hesitancy didn't track with her sophisticated taste in music, books, and bohemian ideas, nor with her involvement with a college man like Maris Cakars. So her friends teased Pash about being "slow."

Ellen Levy had expended a great deal of energy convincing Lorraine to go out on a blind date with Bobby Shapiro. Ellen knew that Lorraine had been devastated when Maris broke up with her at the turn of the year, and all the more so when he transferred his attentions to Susan Kent, Susan Gordon's lovely blond friend, whom he'd met a year earlier when she was visiting at the Gordons'. (Among the things they had in common, Maris and Susan Kent joked, was that they both believed they numbered among Susan Gordon's closest friends because they had access to a car.)

Ellen was becoming bored by Lorraine's pining over Maris, a man who was "in love with life," a man of "true ideals." From the beginning she had thought that Lorraine's interest in Maris was "one of those family things" having to do with Lorraine's relationship with Susan Gordon, who wouldn't know of her younger sister's love for her close friend Maris for another year.

"Just meet Bobby Shapiro," Ellen Levy persisted. "Or at least take a look at him. I'm telling you, Lorraine, this boy looks exactly like you. You could be brother and sister. You even talk the same way." Ellen told friends that Lorraine and Bobby were sure to fall madly in love. "It'll be like two people looking in a mirror."

Ellen was half right. The moment Bobby Shapiro saw Lorraine Gordon, he fell madly in love. Bobby must have known a hundred beatnik and folkie girls, but not one of them was as fresh and pure and poetic as Lorraine Gordon. She was beautiful and innocent. She was smart and passionate. She knew music, and she could sing. Bobby was entranced.

Bobby Shapiro was two years older than Lorraine and about to enter Boston University in the fall. The son of two schoolteachers, he'd grown up on the Upper West Side of Manhattan and attended the elite Hunter College Elementary School and then Bronx Science, a public high school for children with special academic gifts, like Stuyvesant, where Sam had gone briefly.

Bobby told Lorraine stories about a former girlfriend who was a heroin addict. City kids were closer to the Village, to Harlem, to art and adventure. Lorraine regarded Bobby's encyclopedic command of rhythm and blues, folk, and even jazz as a badge of his privileged urban youth.

Lorraine told Bobby stories about life on Lincoln Avenue. She said her mother sang and her father threw telephones. Bobby heard about a brilliant older sister who could read when she was two, and about the sweet younger sister and cute little brother whom Lorraine seemed to believe she was protecting by her presence. Now she was the one who drew the family fire.

Not long after they began dating, Bobby met the older sister. Susan picked Bobby and Lorraine up at the Island Park train station one Sunday when she was in town. She couldn't help noticing how alike they looked—similarly tousled hair, skinny and ragged in matching mouton jackets, his-and-hers runny noses. They reminded Susan of Hansel and Gretel, two slightly woebegone siblings lost in the forest.

Bobby spent the day with the Gordons. He thought Susan had a lot of style, and he was impressed by her guitar and vocal duets with Lorraine, particularly their countrified version of "I'll Fly Away." Sheila seemed hurt and angry when she caught Bobby and Lorraine making out in the playroom. Eve was warm and funny, and Sam seemed so lost in brooding thought, so unresponsive when Lorraine tried to talk to him, that Bobby figured something bad had just happened to him.

Bobby could never quite understand what aspect of her home life Lorraine kept saying she wanted to flee. "It's the dishonesty. It's the pain. It's feeling like I'm supposed to make everyone happy and better," she'd try to explain. Bobby only wanted Lorraine Gordon to love him completely and truly and forever. They didn't exactly sit down and plan to have a baby, but they did talk about how adults would try to stop them from living in the city on their own if they did.

Bobby always considered what came next a "conscious mistake." Lorraine missed two periods. Then another. Bobby could tell that Lorraine was euphoric too. They were like two people parachuting from an airplane for the first time.

"I *want* to get married," Lorraine said, trying to comfort Eve. "I really want to."

The news spread quickly through Oceanside High. One of the Pinkos was leaving school to get married. She *had to*. "Oh God, Lorraine," Ellen Levy moaned. "Why did I open my big mouth? You were just supposed to fall in love, not…this."

The number of teenage pregnancies in the United States had risen by 150 percent since Pearl Harbor, and though the phenomenon wasn't rare anymore (two of Sheila's close friends would soon confide that they were pregnant), it still caused a considerable stir.

In the odd calculus of high school social life, since Lorraine was a Harbor Isle girl and not a "greaser," since she was a seasoned folkie and very smart (she scored a 98 on her New York State Math Regents Exam and 99 in English), the news of her pregnancy boosted her prestige exponentially. Just at the moment when she'd finally become "cool" by suburban standards, Lorraine was informed that Oceanside administrators expected her to leave school, even though she would only be at the beginning of her fifth month at graduation time. It began to dawn on Lorraine that there might be unforeseen consequences to her radical decision to become a mother.

"Come with me, Bobby," Sam Gordon said after returning from a fishing trip on a Saturday afternoon. "I'm gonna buy you a suit."

Sam had remained silent throughout the trauma of Lorraine's decision and the subsequent preparations for the small wedding. Eve did tell Lorraine that when he heard the news her father had asked, "Doesn't she know about birth control?"—which Lorraine found ironic since his discovery of a rolled, foil-wrapped Trojan condom under a chair in the playroom had caused a huge fight last year.

Sam spent a lot of time in consultation with himself, reflecting often that things could be worse. Bobby Shapiro had been hired by a Manhattan international currency exchange. "This, at least, is good," Sam would tell himself. "He's Jewish, after all."

Eve begged Lorraine to wear a girdle to flatten her belly. In the acquiescent spirit of the occasion, Lorraine duly wriggled into something borrowed and tight for her wedding day.

Bobby's mother, Sylvia, who had been divorced from his father since Bobby was little, arrived at the postnuptial celebration at the Gordons' house in the company of a light-skinned black man, her constant companion of recent years, a reserved Harlem school principal who would soon marry her. Lorraine thought Sylvia's interracial relationship was one of the most promising indications about her future mother-in-law.

Public awareness of an increase in "Negro-white marriages" (recently confirmed by New York's city clerk, Herman Katz) had led to much conjecture about the meaning of the trend. Some observers said that such marriages were forms of rebellion or public demonstrations of a lack of prejudice. A Columbia University professor of psychiatry, Nathan Ackerman, who since 1937 had been busy breaking ground in the study of the psychology of the family (as opposed to the psychology of the individuals who comprised the family), found in interracial marriages "evidence of a sick resolve" directed against family or society, or an "emotional living out, in action, of certain genuine but uncontrolled feelings of identification with the other race." At this stage in our cultural progress, Dr. Ackerman was quoted as saying in *Christian Century,* any interracial experience was "abnormal."

Mama Yetta Goldenberg was in high spirits after the rabbi concluded the short marriage ceremony. After years of entertaining one *sheygitz* after another in the playroom, Lorraine was at least marrying a Jew. Next to Bobby, Yetta was probably the happiest person in the room. She chatted at length with Bobby's "charming stepfather."

"Such a nice man, such a learned man," Yetta said to Lorraine. "With that handsome dark skin, he's Sephardic, I'll bet."

Lorraine looked at her grandmother and briefly considered whether on such a special day Yetta's smug conjecture might be allowed to pass. Maybe just this once. But then Lorraine thought of Yetta's snarling references to "the element" and of the deep prejudices she thought her father had learned as a boy. Lorraine kept looking at Yetta, who'd lost so much of her family to murderous racial hatred. She really wanted to let this one slide, but then again …

"Oh no, Mama Yetta," Lorraine said brightly. "He's not Jewish at all. In fact, the man you were talking to is a Negro."

Yetta clapped her hands to her soft cheeks, as if she'd sprung a leak. Lorraine watched her stagger backward, one hand fluttering to her heart as she groaned, "Oy, oy, oy." The new Mrs. Shapiro felt a twinge of remorse, but she reminded herself that nobody ever said it was easy to be honest in a society predicated on hypocrisy.

The mah-jongg girls noticed that there were tears in Eve's eyes when she described Lorraine's wedding.

Several of the regulars considered Eve their scout. So many things kept happening to her in the course of being a suburban wife and mother of four that to her mah-jongg partners it was as if she were up on a ridge gazing into the future, on a dangerous reconnaissance mission on behalf of them all. They were happy, for Eve as well as for themselves, when she managed to turn her *tsuris* into a good joke, and they all hated it when she cried.

She'd smiled at first when she talked about the little wedding she'd "made" for Lorraine, but she started to cry when she thought of herself at twenty-two, a "child without sense," pregnant with Susan. Lorraine was only seventeen.

As Eve reconstructed the course of events, Susan got bored because she'd had to spend a night at home in Harbor Isle. She'd called Maris, who came over and met the pretty blonde with the fancy-shmancy shoes and promptly dumped Lorraine, who took up with Bobby Shapiro on the rebound. And now—when it had taken Liz Taylor's lawyers more than two years to unravel the finances of her marriage to Eddie so she could finally marry Richard—Lorraine had been transformed in a matter of weeks from an angry child into a wife and expectant mother who was at that very moment wandering the streets of Manhattan in search of a place to live.

Eve had read enough thick novels to know that a century earlier news of troubled or injured or "errant" or "ungrateful" children caused mothers and even fathers to take to their beds and occasionally die from grief. Times were different, of course, but Eve still found herself looking in the mirror and asking, "How much can a person be expected to see?"

"She's not happy," said one of the mah-jongg players, Esther, when Eve went to the kitchen to get more coffee.

"She's happy," Rose said assuringly. "She's as happy as she can be."

The players could hear words being exchanged in the kitchen. Eve was talking to her last and only compliant daughter. "*I'm* not the one who got pregnant! I am too old for a curfew!" they heard Sheila say.

Guests on the radio shows that purveyed expert advice to listeners began to speculate that an overly "child-centered" postwar ethos might be behind the apparent obstreperousness of American youth, who had been the object of ceaseless concern since the juvenile delinquency crisis of the mid-fifties. Betty Friedan, in her groundbreaking *The Feminine Mystique*, belonged to the school of thought that described suburban children (whose mothers were the main focus of her book) as "apathetic, dependent, infantile, purposeless." But others warned that children were out of control and crying out for discipline.

A few days before Eve's mah-jongg game, she had attempted to assert her authority over her eight-year-old son by phoning the Island Park Library. "This is Eve Gordon," she'd said as Ricky, Sheila, and Susan—home for a weekend visit—looked on. "I am the mother of Ricky Gordon—Ricky Ian Gordon of 221 Lincoln Avenue in Harbor Isle—who has *four* overdue library books that he is *too irresponsible to return!*" Eve demanded that Ricky's library card be revoked, and that he "never be allowed to enter the library again!"

Eve looked bewildered when she hung up the phone. She turned to see Ricky and Susan sitting at the kitchen counter, convulsed from the effort of trying not to laugh.

The girls at the card table fell silent when they heard Sheila challenge Eve in the kitchen. They waited for a punchy rejoinder. Eve would take off the gloves about now and let loose with a zinger, an appropriate bit of stage business that would put her teenage daughter in her proper place. But Eve didn't say a thing. She returned to the table with more coffee, and the girls again saw her tears.

Finally she rallied. "Well, it's like Sam says. Anyone who has daughters should get a free supply of tranquilizers."

The girls smiled and nodded as they returned to the game.

———◆———

Ricky sat atop the shoulders of his new brother, Bobby Shapiro. He gazed over Bobby's curls at Michelangelo's *Pietà*, a marble image of a loving mother and her dead child that made Ricky shiver, not because the sculpture was sad but because it was so beautiful. The *Pietà* had come to the 1964 New York World's Fair from Rome, packed in a crate designed to stay afloat even if the ship sank.

Bobby carried Ricky all over the hundreds of acres of Progesslands and Futuramas laid out in Flushing Meadow, Queens, not far from Shea Stadium, new home of the Mets and Jets. They looked at a giant whitewall tire and ate sweet Belgian waffles, but toward the end of the day, Ricky asked if they could go back to stand in the long line in front of the pavilion with the beautiful statue. Though he was only eight, Ricky drew more pleasure from art and culture than most adults. He could already pick out the right keys on the family piano after hearing a melody only one time. Eve had allowed Ricky to go to the movie ver-

sion of *West Side Story* with Peter Randsman, and they had cried
through the entire film. Ever since, Eve and Sam had noticed that
Ricky spent a great deal of time in the playroom pretending to be Anita
and singing "A Boy Like That" at top voice. Peter and Ricky also went
to see *My Fair Lady* at the nearby Laurel Theater, and they could both
do a mean imitation of Audrey Hepburn as Eliza Doolittle.

Ricky loved to listen to Bobby Shapiro play his mandolin. Bobby
would take Ricky on his lap and help him stretch his fingers to play
chords on the mandolin or the piano. Bobby enjoyed spending time
with his little brother-in-law, though it made him uncomfortable when
Sheila treated Ricky like a little doll. Once he saw Sheila and her
friends giggling hysterically as Ricky touched their breasts. "I know
they're just playing around," Bobby said to Lorraine, "but it still makes
me nervous."

Despite the *Pietà*, movie musicals, his deep friendship with Peter Randsman, and the addition of the gentle and caring Bobby Shapiro to his
family, Ricky didn't have the best of summers. He'd managed to keep
from throwing up on a fishing trip with Sam and Uncle Freddy, but
visions of gut-encrusted hooks and the terrible lidless stare of dying fish
came back to him in nightmares for weeks.

Apparently because of the way he walked and ran, the children who
lived in the house across the street—Raymond, Roseanne, Robin, Rene,
Roberta, Regina, Ronald, and Rhonda (sons and daughters of Ray and
Rose, owners of the snarling, smelly, unalliterative German shepherd
guard dog Duke)—had begun to taunt Ricky every time he went out to
play. "Your mother's a sexpot!" they'd say, and they'd tease him about
Sam's Cadillac, a rarity in the little town. The Gordons had always been
on good terms with the huge family across the street, fellow Harbor Isle
pioneers. But now they'd turned on Ricky like a horde. When Ricky
ran, they'd make flapping motions with their arms and yell "Sic, Duke!"
if the dog was outside. Roseanne pulled Ricky's pants down in the middle of Lincoln Avenue, and when Island Park's little electrified mail van
knocked him off his bike, his tormentors stood on their lawn and
laughed. They'd throw firecrackers at him when he wasn't looking,
making him fly through the air like a diver doing a layout, and there the
gang of brothers and sisters would be, howling from across the street.

Ricky told Peter Randsman about each new incident (Peter had his
own across-the-street bullies to contend with), and he told Eve, but
since he sensed that these trials were of the sort a boy had to deal with

on his own, he didn't tell Sam. So Ricky was surprised and hopeful when his father came into his room during the early summer to "have a talk" about Ricky's social interactions in the neighborhood.

"Ricky," Sam said formally, man to man, "I want you to stop playing with little girls."

Ricky sucked in his confusion and stared at his father. "Okay," he said.

Ricky was positive that washing Susan's new boyfriend's new cherry-red Ford Mustang, Model 2 + 2, was just the sort of boyish endeavor that would impress grown men like Sam and the new boyfriend. By the time Ricky realized he'd forgotten to roll up the windows, it was too late. He decided to make the best of the error and began to suds up the Mustang's sporty bucket seats.

The boyfriend looked like the intense and intellectually serious young man he was. His name was Michael Lydon, and he had dark eyes, a long jawline, and brown hair that fell over his forehead in the style of Robert Kennedy, brother of his late hero.

Michael's Ford Mustang was a long-term loan, courtesy of the Ford Motor Company. As star columnist on the Yale Daily News, he was one of seventy student journalists from around the country invited to visit Ford's River Rouge plant in Dearborn, Michigan, where a young executive named Lee Iacocca gave a rousing speech about a brand-new car that would mean nothing less than a new way of life for young Americans. With its long hood—and a back seat that only a hardy short-term passenger could love—the Mustang was Ford's answer to the projection that by 1966 half of all Americans would be under twenty-five. Priced below $2,500, with easy monthly payment plans available, the Mustang was targeted to youthful car buyers as specifically as Harbor Isle's tract houses had been designed for men who came home from the war to raise families.

Michael and the other student journalists were escorted to a test track where seventy red Mustang convertibles were lined up side by side. They would have to return the cars eventually, but such was American automotive achievement and profitability in 1964 that the dream car could be theirs for quite a while.

Of course the gift in no way softened Michael's acerbic reference to Lee Iacocca, "our latest champion knight bound to defend the holy grail of free enterprise," as he put it in his popular "In a Mellotone" column in the Daily. Michael Lydon—Yale man and JFK man of long standing, still reeling from the president's assassination—was first and foremost a serious liberal journalist. He was well aware that the Mustang was a bribe.

Peter Randsman looked at the bubbly mess Ricky had made in Michael's Mustang. "My dad always closes the windows," Peter said.

Michael, tall and florid, lumbered out of the house. Peter and Ricky looked up as he started bellowing, "No-o-o-o-o!"

Clearly out of control, Michael drew his long arm back and slapped Ricky in the face. Ricky ran into the house, Michael jogging behind him. "Are you okay? Are you okay? I'm sorry," he kept saying.

Ricky didn't want Michael to see him crying, but when he finally turned around he saw that Michael Lydon, a grown man in Ricky's esti-mation, had put his hands over his eyes and was crying himself.

Susan was still embroiled in the charges stemming from her Vassar forgery when she got a phone call from a Yalie, a junior, who had a low voice and an accent very much like John Kennedy's.

"I'll go out with you," Susan said, "but I might be getting kicked out of school soon."

Michael was clearly out to impress the troublemaker from Vassar on their first date. They journeyed south to Harlem, to 125th Street and the grand old Apollo Theater, for a performance by James Brown, the screaming, bounding master of "soul music"—a term that would begin to supplant "rhythm and blues" this year. Susan could tell that Michael knew his music. His range extended from Duke Ellington (whom he worshiped) to Hank Ballard and the Midnighters.

Susan pegged Michael Lydon for one of those Irish Catholic kids who dreamed of being the kind of bad boy he could never really be. Like Susan, Michael was a scholarship student among the rich kids. Michael came from a big family, five sons and a daughter. Now that Jack Kennedy was dead, his heroes were almost all blacks and Jews. He loved the writings of S. J. Perelman and the poetic folk songs of Leonard Cohen.

Susan and Michael began to see a lot of each other. One night she dipped into her supply of colorful amphetamine study aids and wrote him a twelve-page letter on their long debate about whether main-stream American society was "worth the trouble" of adjusting to or not.

Michael telephoned her. "You're a really, really good writer," said one of Yale's finest journalists. Susan was thrilled.

Still, with his New Frontier politics and talk of "working within the system," Michael was an unlikely boyfriend for Susan, who considered herself far to the left of anyone who believed the Peace Corps was politically progressive. In the *Yale Daily*, Michael had written a ringing eulogy to JFK: "New words and feelings must now be found to fit a new era when we turn back to work without the man." Michael's comments on foreign affairs were precocious and sometimes curmudgeonly. He wrote about Castro's Cuba and the brushfire skirmishes along the border of China. "In a Mellotone" took up issues of Communist containment in Southeast Asia: "The hope that Vietnamese neutralism is viable is false for the same reason that hope of total victory is false. China cannot be allowed to spread unchecked into Southeast Asia....we are not going to win this war in Vietnam. We need not lose it." "Can anyone really imagine John Glenn in the Senate?" he wrote in another column. "John Glenn, a balding former test pilot, the man who followed some monkeys into space?...the Sagging Sixties' pathetic answer to Charles Lindbergh? Why doesn't he just write a book and fade away?"

In February Michael had written a withering piece about the Beatles. "Whenever the first strains of 'I Want to Hold Your Hand' begin to twitch my stirrup bones, I send out silent screams for help to Gene Vincent, Chuck Berry, Elvis...those other greats who have long defended the American way of rock....I weep for you, America." Michael was disgusted by the hyperventilating girls who flung themselves at the Beatles. Like Lorraine Shapiro and other young purists, he resented the hysterical welcome for this bunch of half-talented British invaders who were robbing superior black American musicians of their art, their heritage, and their livelihood. It was disgraceful that black bandleader Cab Calloway had been given a back seat to the Beatles during *The Ed Sullivan Show*, he said. Calloway was "a real pro" by comparison to the Fab Four and would "be back with Sullivan when the Beatles won't be able to buy their way into the studio."

Sheila, the chief Beatles partisan in the family, once tried to get a rise out of Susan's stiff new boyfriend by calling his preferences "ten years behind the times." "I cannot *believe* you don't know who Herman's Hermits are!" she crowed. Sheila spoke in a way Michael found entertaining and of journalistic interest. Michael heard Sheila describe an unregenerate local Harbor Isle "hitter," still sporting a black leather jacket and a greasy ducktail, as "a fifty-four." After ascertaining from Sheila that "fifty-four" referred to 1954, he went back to New Haven and wrote a column about the style and lexicon of American teens.

Sam and Eve seemed impressed that Michael was about to leave for several weeks in the Deep South. He would write articles for the *Boston Globe* about efforts to register black voters in a state that had come to represent to many Americans (even those who hadn't seen it for themselves, as Sam and Eve had during the war) all that was most evil and unjust about their country. Martin Luther King, Jr., said that Mississippi was "sweltering with the people's injustice, sweltering with the heat of oppression." Michael was on his way there to cover what would soon be known as Freedom Summer, and while Sam and Eve admired his courage, they were glad his girlfriend wasn't going along.

Susan was about to begin working as a waitress. She would have gone south as a volunteer for the Council of Federated Organizations (a coalition of NAACP, CORE, and Southern Christian Leadership Conference organizers), but she couldn't afford the more than one thousand dollars it cost. Seven hundred northern college students who were able to pay their way were headed down to a region so resistant to change that after two full years of concerted organizing efforts, the percentage of eligible minority voters registered in Mississippi had risen from 5.3 to 6.7. Michael went down as a reporter, though that didn't stop local editorialists from raging about "sarcastic, martini-sipping pseudo-intellectuals" in their state and accusing him by name of being a paid agitator for the Council of Federated Organizations.

Only days after Ricky flooded the Mustang Lee Iacocca had loaned him, Michael would be in Philadelphia, Mississippi, notebook in hand, watching Rita Schwerner walk around a charred Ford station wagon. Rita's husband, a twenty-four-year-old New Yorker also named Michael, had been missing for eleven days. Witnesses said that Mickey Schwerner and two other civil rights workers—Andrew Goodman and James Chaney—had last been seen in the Ford.

Michael reported that Rita "almost broke down," then strode over to a police car occupied by Sheriff Lawrence Rainey, who seemed "embarrassed" to make Mrs. Schwerner's acquaintance and had trouble recalling her name. "If there is anyone who wants to stop me asking questions," Rita said as she left the sheriff's car, "they'll have to kill me."

Michael would travel the state of Mississippi until the end of the summer. He watched Martin Luther King in action. He interviewed student organizers just out of jail. He talked to a black mother whose nineteen-year-old son had been murdered in the town of Meadville. He watched people stand in a registration line for an entire day, waiting to mark an X on a form and join the twelve hundred others registered in the state during all of Freedom Summer. In August, a few weeks after Congress passed a sweeping Civil Rights Act, Michael was covering the integration of the public schools in Biloxi when a bulldozer uncovered the remains of Mickey Schwerner, Andrew Goodman, and James Chaney. He would be back in class in New Haven that October, when

Sheriff Rainey was charged with civil rights violations. Three years later, seven local members of the Ku Klux Klan—one of them Rainey's deputy, Cecil Price—were convicted of their murders, and Rainey was cleared of the charges against him.

⎯⎯◆⎯⎯

Bobby and Lorraine got an apartment on the Lower East Side in a tenement building no more than fifty yards from the railroad flat where six-year-old Sam Goldenberg got so cold at night that he later decided he'd work himself to death before he'd ever live in such a place again. The apartment was just north of Tompkins Square Park, and a few blocks east of the old "Jewish Rialto" on Second Avenue, where Yiddish theater and Jewish restaurants had once flourished.

Each time Sam came to visit, he noticed that the sounds of East Eleventh Street between Avenues A and B were much different now. The buildings looked the same—every bit as old as they'd looked back in the 1920s—but Sam couldn't identify the music flooding the noisy street. The air had changed too. Eleventh Street now reeked, Sam thought, of "people who don't care."

The north side of the block was the sovereign turf of a Puerto Rican street gang led by a man known as Bananas; the south side was controlled by a motorcycle gang run by an equally forbidding fellow. The block was full of hard faces like the ones Sam often saw these days on the evening news.

Bobby and Lorraine were paying forty-five dollars a month for an airless, lightless fifth-floor walkup. "You know, I've seen some pretty damned sorry old apartments in my time," Sam told Eve after their first visit, "but that one is right up there. The kitchen floor must have a fifteen-inch rake. The place makes you seasick."

A few weeks before the baby was due, Sam showed up at the apartment with Bernie Denodio and some of his other men. Bobby had decided to begin fixing the place up himself by ripping out the original kitchen cabinets. Thick, choking clouds of century-old black dust had billowed into the apartment from the open walls, providing ample cover for the primordial horde of cockroaches that followed. The slightest movement called forth another burst of black soot, and Sam and his men were coughing like miners until they got the new plywood paneling up. Sam asked Bobby to stand clear, but Bobby couldn't help coming over now and then to show his father-in-law the Indian-head pennies he'd found inside the open walls. Bobby had cleaned and classified his finds like some happy archeologist.

In Sam's opinion, Bobby was a decent enough guy with some plenty kooky ideas. He talked incessantly about building a "geodesic dome," which sounded like an impractical structure to Sam, though he considered it a good sign that a kid "in this day and age" wanted to build *something*.

And then Bobby broke the news that he'd left the currency exchange for a new job.

"So you're a baby-sitter now," Sam said. "And you call this a career? This is a married man's job? Baby-sitting?"

"It's a day-care center, Sam," Bobby replied. "It's not baby-sitting."

In response to a seventy-three-percent rise in the number of working mothers over the past ten years, a new government program, Head Start, was due to open experimental facilities in New York City in October. President Lyndon B. Johnson had called for "total victory" in a "national war on poverty" and outlined a social welfare program so ambitious that it would be compared to the New Deal, as Johnson would be compared to Sam's hero, Franklin Roosevelt. For a hopeful instant, young Americans like Bobby and Lorraine loooked at Lyndon Johnson—with his Texas hill country accent, his tall frame, his constant display of old-fashioned manly pride, his empathy for the poor and disenfranchised (he only wanted for all Americans what his beloved mother had wanted for him, he said: "a decent job"), and his vision of the Great Society—and wondered if he might not turn out to be a great man.

Bobby Shapiro also wanted to "help people." Over six thousand children were enrolled in eighty-five day-care programs in Manhattan, but the names of five thousand more were on various waiting lists. New programs like the one that had hired Bobby were opening by the week.

"Come on. That's not a job, Bobby," Sam Gordon said. Then his voice got lower and uncharacteristically tentative. "Why don't you...instead...how about comin' to work for me?"

"No thanks," Bobby said quickly. "I want to work with kids."

"You're gonna have your own kid. And you have a wife. What man leaves a decent job to be a baby-sitter?"

Sam was quiet on the drive home. Then he said, "They *want* it, Eve. That's what I can't get over. Lorraine wants poverty...like it's something good."

Each time the cool, wet tenement breeze hit Sam at the bottom of the stairwell on East Eleventh Street, it hurt. He felt like the butt of some vicious joke. How could his daughter possibly want the very streets he'd worked so hard to leave behind? Sam had led his family away from hunger and cold beds and city fear, and now his child wanted to go back. He'd stood by and watched Lorraine leave his house like some immigrant child bride, off to the Lower East Side and a way of life that seemed like a ghostly X-ray of the good life of his dreams.

It took Sam years to realize that the extent and depth of the rage he felt—and sometimes couldn't help but show—had something to do with Lorraine's departure. At the time, when he thought of his pregnant and married daughter, all he knew was that certain mistakes must have been made, mistakes that had something to do with the true nature of "girls."

Girls, Sam believed, were "natural rebels," one and all. They were born with feelings of entitlement and were capable of duplicities most men couldn't imagine. Mothers were basically girls, and therein lay the source of some of the family problems that kept him awake at night. Because "a mother naturally casts a father as the bad guy," the father was reduced to little more than a scary mask, a "thing" to be pulled from a closet shelf around dinnertime to instill fear and exert control. "Put away the mask and there's a mother's smile," Sam had come to see.

Later in life, when Sam felt moved to offer advice to a young father, he would tell him to "bribe your kids." He often lamented not having gone along the day Lorraine picked out her cherished guitar or Susan bought her down comforter for college, because he was sure the girls thought these things that he'd ordained came from Eve. He wished he'd bought Valentines for all the Gordon women every year, because he'd loved the sight of their pleasure the two or three times he did.

"Kids love their mother and see their father as the tiger. A mother is a fairy godmother; a father is the one who beats them up and denies them things."

The way Sam saw it, Eve got the children and he got his power and his cold pride.

It was quiet at 221 Lincoln now that Susan was back at school and Lorraine was gone. Ricky and Sheila sensed that the family had begun anew the day Lorraine left. The four remaining Gordons came to the table as if from hiding places to relish the peace and quiet. Despite their skill at inflicting pain from in close, in a strange way Sam missed his girls and felt remorse. So after ten hours of work, or instead of going fishing on Sundays, he showed up to turn an apartment no more inviting than a jail cell into a decent place for his little girl and her family.

⬤

Magdalena Shapiro was born on October 11. That same day, on the campaign trail, a seventeen-year-old boy hit Lyndon Johnson on the head with his Goldwater-Miller placard and crushed his hat. An eighteen-year-old in the same crowd was arrested for carrying a concealed revolver. Only two weeks earlier the Warren Commission had issued its report on the assassination of John Kennedy and had recommended that Johnson start watching his back. The president—"the biggest faker in the U.S." and "the phoniest individual who ever came around," according to Richard Nixon, who had announced his retirement from politics two years ago after losing the California gubernatorial race—made it clear that he had no intention of not mixing with the crowds.

Despite Sam's local Republicanism and the fact that Barry Goldwater owned palomino ponies and wore cowboy hats, Sam—and Eve—would vote for LBJ. Goldwater's televised suggestion that "low yield" atomic weapons might be employed on behalf of the South Vietnamese forces and the more than ten thousand American advisers fighting the good fight in Vietnam didn't sit well with Sam the former foot soldier. Though he was partly Jewish, Goldwater didn't have anything to offer the Gordons to overcome the fact that he was so bellicose and frightening.

When the contractions began coming one after another, wave upon wave, Lorraine felt as if she was being torn apart from within. She screamed as loud as she could, as much out of terror as pain. Bobby and Lorraine had studied the controversial "natural childbirth" methods described thirty years earlier by a British doctor, Grantly Dick-Read, and Lorraine had decided to forgo anesthesia. As magazines like McCall's and some progressive doctors had begun to tell pregnant women, in light of the psychiatric view that childbirth represented "the culmination of a woman's psychosexual development," it might be best to stay awake. "Natural childbirth" was beginning to come into vogue, but just as Eve had lacked basic information the first time around, no Read Method text and no one at the hospital clinic had ever told Lorraine how much labor hurts.

"Stop screaming," snapped a busy doctor. "You'll scare the others."

"Mom!" Lorraine screamed. Eve squeezed her hand until the nurses made her go out and wait with Bobby.

The nice Puerto Rican lady from the apartment downstairs couldn't resist commenting on Lorraine and Bobby's choice of names. "You have named your little baby after a whore!" she said. "Change it."

Lorraine was less surprised when Yetta Goldenberg announced that the name of her first great-granddaughter—inspired by Lorraine's recent reading of Nikos Kazantzakis's *Last Temptation of Christ*—would never cross her lips. If Lorraine would not reconsider, Yetta would henceforth refer to Magdalena Shapiro as "Magda."

Until the cold weather came, Lorraine often put Magdalena in a buggy and sat on the front stoop playing her guitar. Local children would always gather around, joined by the ganglord Bananas, who wore a cross dangling from one ear. Lorraine's Spanish was getting better. Oceanside High hadn't let Lorraine finish school, but nearby Washington Irving High was happy to have her, and she was valedictorian of her graduating class. She wanted to go on to Barnard College, though she knew she would have to get a scholarship. But unlike Susan she didn't get in. Lorraine planned to register at City College in January. New York City residents could study for free there.

Eve came to visit Lorraine and Maggie often. She walked to the LIRR station in Island Park, changed trains in Queens, and took two subways from Penn Station to the Lower East Side. Lorraine looked forward to the days her mother came, and every time Eve put her coat on to leave, she would fight down a powerful instinct to go home with her. The sight of baby Maggie waking so warm and perfect from her sleep, or the thought of sweet Ricky or of her empty bed in Harbor Isle, sometimes made Lorraine cry. But there was no longer "a direction home," as the now famous Bob Dylan put it.

Lorraine held back her panic and tended conscientiously to her little girl while Bobby was at work, but she couldn't stop brooding over her sudden transition from daughter to lonely mother and wife. As she sat with Maggie in Tompkins Square Park, both of them bundled against the cold, she realized the loss of her childhood felt just like she'd always imagined it would feel if someone you loved passed away.

❦

Just before Christmas, a few days after Martin Luther King, Jr., accepted the Nobel Peace Prize and restated his belief that only nonviolent methods could create a world in which "none shall be afraid," a marauding gang composed of Roseanne, Robin, Rene, and Roberta (or maybe it was Raymond, Roseanne, Roberta, and Ronald—Ricky was never certain) chased Ricky down on their front lawn, hoisted him high in the air, and tossed him into the middle of the life-sized Nativity scene their father assembled each year on their front lawn. Ricky landed hard on his back beside the colorful plastic Jesus.

Ricky decided the best strategy available to him under the circumstances was to play dead, so he lay there in an ornate manger set on a frozen suburban lawn for a long time, until the neighbor children got bored and went inside.

1965

Eve didn't find it unusual that a girl soon to complete her education would want to announce her plans to be married; nor did she think moving the wedding date back into the school year because of an accidental pregnancy was a cause for concern. But she did have her doubts about Michael Lydon. She was convinced that beneath the patina of fine New Haven eating-club manners and all that solicitous regard, Susan's fiancé was often mocking her and Sam, laughing at them from a pedestal of elite education and youth. Eve consoled herself with the thought that at least Susan's marriage would mark the end of a stormy adolescence. At least there was that.

Sam was less resigned: "I will! I will!" he raged. "I promise you I will disown her. We won't have a thing to do with her. For a thousand years not one member of my immediate family has ever married outside the religion. I refuse to accept this. I will disown her."

Eve's jaw muscles twitched, and her nervous tic—the legacy, she always said, of brothers who bellowed and punched their little sister in the shoulder too often—was making her squint. Yet her eyes were steady as they locked into Sam's. "No, Sam, you won't," she said softly.

News of Michael and Susan's wedding plans traveled up and down the Eastern Seaboard. In the leathery lounges of Yale's libraries and clubs, gossip about the displeasure of Michael's mother—"Mother Lydon"—competed with a spate of rumors: that Susan got pregnant to snare her Yalie, that she was not pregnant at all but said she was, that she had Lydon under a spell.

Susan was indeed pregnant, and if she'd pressed Michael to marry her before she found out, it was only because she was in the grips of a traditional Seven Sisters panic about what she would do with her future. Michael was the kind of boy who could help a girl have a normal life.

"You'll never find a man," Eve had often told her. "Who wants to marry a woman who doesn't cook or clean up? Look at your room," Eve would say. "You're more like a man."

For her part, in light of her impending marriage, Susan had been scrutinizing her mother's life. She saw Eve as powerless, afraid, and trapped.

In her widely discussed book *The Feminine Mystique*, Betty Friedan, a Smith grad and mother of three, wrote that the source of the "trapped housewife" syndrome of recent years was also the source of problems "which have been torturing women and their husbands and children, and puzzling their doctors and educators for years"—namely, "that voice within women that says: 'I want something more than my husband and my children and my home.'" Friedan described a "new breed" of postwar all-American suburban wives—women hungry for "sanctuary" and "perfectly willing to fill their days with the trivia of housewifery."

Betty Friedan grew up in Peoria, Illinois, as something of an outcast. She was bookish, not perky or cute, and because she was Jewish she was not welcomed into the high school sororities and other social cliques formed by the "successful" girls in town. Friedan studied psychology and social science in college, and freelanced for magazines after she graduated and was raising a family. In researching *The Feminine Mystique*, she came across a 1956 study indicating that settled Vassar alums twenty-five years out of Poughkeepsie had "regressed" to a level below that of the current senior class according to a "development scale" designed to measure mental and emotional growth.

Susan agreed with Friedan that too many "immature self-seeking" young women were pursuing early marriage. She'd been disgusted by a classroom discussion of Simone de Beauvoir's contention, in *The Second Sex*, that motherhood was not the acme of female existence but a role best assumed by women fulfilled and "whole" because they had the same opportunities in life as men. Most of the girls in Susan's class were scandalized by the idea.

One Vassar teacher, economics professor Margaret Meyers, argued to her class that the generation of cowed suburban mothers was a product of the Depression and the war, which Susan had always thought had far more impact on her father. "The Depression turned women back from their access to work and so from self-respect," Professor Meyers lectured. "During World War II all the women rushed to get married before the men were killed off."

What would appear in retrospect as the beginning of a fundamental reassessment of what it really meant to be a woman seemed to many college seniors in 1965 to be a critique of the postwar suburban family that had produced the great majority of them. As Susan's panic about what to do with the rest of her life intensified, marriage to a young man who wanted the most cosmopolitan, intellectually compelling, and adventurous of lives looked like a surefire way to avoid the trap of "the feminine mystique."

Susan and Michael would launch their marriage into what Martin Luther King called a "sea of affluence," at a time when half of each dollar spent in America went for "luxury goods." Making money almost seemed beside the point. The young couple were at the forefront of "the twenty-five-and-under Generation," which so dominated the news over the next two years that *Time* broke from tradition in 1967 and named the entire generation "Man of the Year." In something like a parody of the traditional Boy Scout virtues, the publisher of *Time*, Bernhard Auer, described the magazine's honorees as "well-educated, affluent, rebellious, responsible, pragmatic, idealistic, brave, 'alienated,' and hopeful."

Susan and Michael would marry, and Susan would leave the prison of Vassar to complete her last semester of study at Yale. After that, she and Michael were talking of going abroad, out into the world.

Like Bob Dylan—who'd lately turned away from protest activities—and many others who'd made it their business to inveigh against the status quo, Susan was willing to trade in a certain amount of moral and political outrage for a new adventure of family that was free of the ties of the past. In the spring, when many American campuses were embroiled in "teach-ins" and furious demonstrations against American escalation of a faraway war in Vietnam, Michael Lydon, "a student of government who has covered big events in the South for the *Boston Globe*," as a biographical note in the *Globe* described him, went south for the Boston paper again to report on the effect of voter registration campaigns in eleven southern states. This time his reports were "objective" and analytical, the work of an aspiring professional journalist—a far cry from the impassioned dispatches he had filed during Freedom Summer.

By then the Lydons knew they would soon be leaving for London, where Susan would become a young mother. Much to his own mother's consternation, Michael had been denied a fellowship to Cambridge University, which proscribed wives and children, and would be working as a journalist trainee for *Newsweek* magazine. So the great adventure would commence in London, a place that was swirling with new cultural energies. But to an Irish Catholic scholarship student and a Jewish scholarship student, London beckoned like some transatlantic extension of Yale's snobby high-WASP Fence Club.

Susan and Michael's friends at Yale, and the tiny coterie of political activists at Vassar, wondered what had possessed two gifted campus stars to do something as conventional as get married, but they were sure that a couple with so much aplomb and style knew what they were doing.

It galled Susan that after all she'd read and experienced, she still had no idea at all what she wanted to do. One of the best things about Michael Lydon was that he knew exactly where he was going. Michael managed to be normal without being tedious.

Michael lay awake at night or fell into uneasy dreams. He had no idea where he was going. Whatever he did had to be accomplished with "Kennedyesque" grandeur. Should he be a liberal journalist? A reform politician? A professor? A bohemian? He didn't have a clue beyond his *Newsweek* job. Thank God for Susan's worldly sophistication and cool, sexy self-possession.

"I *will* disown her," Sam insisted again, hurt in ways he couldn't quite explain by Susan's plans to marry outside the religious fold.

"Sam," Eve said calmly. "If you ever disown one of our children, you also disown me. Cut off my arm if you have to, but if you disown one of our kids that will be it."

Sam went to work on the January day when a group of Gordons, along with some of Michael Lydon's family who came down from Boston, accompanied Susan and Michael to a judge's chambers. Yetta sat shiva in her apartment in Queens.

But Sam did agree to attend the small celebration the Lydons held in Boston later that month. Sam chatted with Mrs. Lydon, a teacher, and with Michael's father, who worked for the phone company. Sam later muttered about "always leaving a goyish party hungry," though he conceded that Michael's family did not seem to be "the drinking type of Irish."

Two weeks later, Sam drove to New Haven. The visit was short and uncomfortable. "I'm getting A's here, Dad," Susan said. "Yale's so much easier than Vassar it's a joke."

Sam rose to put on his windbreaker. He pressed something into Susan's hand, said good-bye, and walked out the door. When Susan unrolled the bit of paper, she saw that it was a hundred-dollar bill.

During the late spring Susan and Michael graduated. Susan didn't bother to attend the ceremony. "Not even that," Sam said when he heard she would not "commence." "Not even the simple courtesy of let-ting me feel proud."

***

"The man *nev*-er, *nev*-er rests," Aunt Sylvia was always saying. "It's like he is *day*-ting her, already. *Ev*-ery single night! Do you think she ever says, 'Go to sleep early, Sammy. You work so hard, Sammy'? No. Not her. Comes the night and my brother Sam has to take his wife out danc-ing *all night long!*"

The Gordons usually went "clubbing" on Saturday nights. Sam would return from work between five and eight o'clock and go straight to bed without eating supper. He was up again at ten to get dressed. Eve shim-mied into something sexy but with enough give to let her mambo, tango, samba, and generally cut the proverbial rug until sunup the next morning.

Sam and Eve often didn't decide which club to patronize until they were driving along the Lido Beach "strip," a stretch of Long Island shoreline dotted with bustling latter-day Xanadus such as the Sands, the Capri, the Malibu, the Coral Reef (home of "the first steel swimming pool in the Eastern U.S."), and of course El Patio. Sam loved El Patio. "Beyond vast parking lots designed to accommodate as many as 2,700 Cadillacs," wrote a reporter for the Long Island paper *Newsday*, "lie pas-tel-tinted dining rooms, gleaming dance floors, mural-covered cocktail lounges, Olympic-sized swimming pools, modish cabanas, and well-groomed beaches." A wall of sweat-soaked humanity no less than twenty feet thick might separate the huge bar at El Patio from anyone out on the dance floor in desperate need of a drink, but Sam and Eve didn't drink much these days, so who cared?

As "the beach club movement" grew, Sam and Eve began to take several lessons a week to make sure they were on top of the latest Latin American dances. Out on the dance floor at one of the clubs, they wouldn't stop to eat for fear of missing a single Tito Puente or Tito Rodriguez number.

If Trinidad "Trini" Lopez was at El Patio, Sam and Eve always tried to be there too. King of the "surf" sound since 1963, Trini was a great favorite at the clubs, singing "If I Had a Hammer" and "Sinner Man" over and over by special request. If he tried to take a break, the crowd went crazy—truly crazy, Sam and Eve both thought. "No!" they'd scream, like something terrible would happen if they stopped dancing. One night Trini kept trying to take a break, but the crowd demanded

"Sinner Man" again and again. Sam and Eve were pressed to the front of the stage when Lopez—a humble man who often talked about his immigrant father plowing fields back in Texas, and his mother slapping laundry against rocks by the river—thanked the crowd and tried to leave the stage for the third or fourth time. But an angry uproar began once again. "No! No!" the people chanted "More!" Trini Lopez's dark eyes flashed and though he leaned away from the microphone, Sam still heard him say quite clearly, "Ah, fuck you all."

Sam and Eve danced madly into the morning to the pounding Latin beat. They danced until their hearts raced. The floor was so packed that you could close your eyes and lose your balance and you still wouldn't fall. Everyone looked like they'd jumped in the swimming pool. Sometimes a dancer would flash a goofy little smile and break into the Monkey, the Frug, the Watusi, or a dance named the Jerk—aptly, in the estimation of the beach club fanatics.

"If you have a dull life and spend too much time sitting at home, it's hard to be happy," Sam counseled a Masonic brother who said his wife complained all the time. "Let a woman get dressed up in her finest and put on her jewelry, and it's like a shot in the arm. One night out might last her a week."

And the same was true of a man, Sam believed.

A psychoanalyst named Dr. Elliott Jacques was now at work on a suitable term for a widespread "condition" afflicting adults as they became aware of their "relative powerlessness to stall or control the passage of time." Jacques would soon call the condition a "mid-life crisis."

Sam was forty-six now, and Eve was approaching forty-five. Sam was the first to acknowledge that a life could be thrown off course—"especially by kids"—but beneath a spinning ball of mirrors, dancing to Tito or Trini with skill, flourish, and complete abandon, it was possible to let go of time altogether, just back away and let it slide. By two or three in the morning, on the best of the beach club nights, a man could imagine himself ageless, anywhere or nowhere, lost in the sensual joys of music and movement and the touch of a sexy woman who smelled of sweet perfume.

A few years later, the clubs began to close down, but Sam and Eve would always look back on their Lido Beach days in much the same way they would remember their first years in Harbor Isle. Both were experiences you were sad to see end, but the fact that moments so perfect could be part of life at all made the rest easier to bear.

Ricky was struggling to find the secret of being a happy camper. Camp Lenape rolled elegantly over eighty heavily wooded acres along Lake Fairview in Pennsylvania's Pocono Mountains. A man Sam knew from his brief stint with the Knights of Pythias had recently purchased the camp and had recruited a number of boys from the South Shore of Long Island. Ricky Gordon was one of the few who never once received a 10 during bunk inspection.

Ricky also seemed to have an almost biological need to talk, at all times, under any circumstances. Almost every night after lights-out, the patrolling counselor would order him out of his bunk in boot camp tones, march him outside, and ceremoniously mark a spot on a two-hundred-year-old pine tree at a point level with Ricky's hairline. Ricky was commanded to press his nose to the spot until he "learned to shut up"—which he never did.

Ricky's early difficulties at camp were compounded by a cabinmate who convinced him that the bats seen swooping about Camp Lenape at dusk had killed their share of nine-year-olds in summers past. Ricky was sure he could feel the creatures landing on Sam's old army blanket while he was sleeping, and the thought sent him screaming into the night. Shortly thereafter, he'd be standing on tiptoe sniffing another evergreen.

Even worse was the terrible trouble Ricky had going to the bathroom without his mother. Eve knew that Dr. Spock wouldn't have approved, but she'd achieved dramatic toilet-training results by standing at the bathroom door saying, "Come on, baby. Come on, Ricky. Do it for Mommy!" The upshot was that Eve had virtually become part of Ricky's metabolism. Holding out through a day at school was easy enough, but a summer at Lenape was impossible. After a week the counselors noticed that instead of talking all the time Ricky was running in little circles.

Eve had always counted herself among the small group of Harbor Isle mothers who didn't believe in the ritual rustication of their children each summer. Five hundred bucks for eight weeks at camp was real money to Sam and Eve. But by the end of spring, it looked like a summer out of town was essential to Ricky's continued health. His constant torment at the hands of the R children had gone completely out of control. Every time Eve looked out the window, it seemed that Ricky was in swift flight before the neighbor children and their dog.

One day Eve got so upset that she ran outside, grabbed Roseanne (Roberta?), and poured a handful of pebbles down the back of her

T-shirt. Later Ricky heard his mother weeping as she described her retaliation to one of her mah-jongg friends on the phone.

"Sam," Eve said that night. "This has gotten out of hand. It's time for you to go over and have a man-to-man with Ray."

Sam refused.

"They're torturing our son!"

But Sam, child pugilist who never ran away from kids who called him kike on the city streets of his youth, never went across the street to talk to Ray.

Eve was already upset because Sam had stopped going bowling. Eve loved their bowling nights together. She had trophies commemorating the several occasions when she'd bowled over two hundred in league competition. Everybody in America was bowling these days. Twenty-three million citizens bowled regularly. Thirty thousand new lanes would be laid out during 1965 alone to accommodate all the action. But Sam Gordon had decided that bowling was "too much like business." "I compete all day, I don't need it at night," he'd said.

It never crossed Eve's mind to continue without Sam, because she believed bowling was for couples, unlike mah-jongg and, apparently, protecting the kids.

It was Eve who decided that Harbor Isle, like the South Bronx in the early 1950s, was no longer safe for children. It was Eve who sent Ricky away for the summer. He would be the first Gordon to go to camp, an evacuee from the neighborhood war zone.

Ricky's fortunes at Camp Lenape underwent a radical change the day he auditioned for the camp musical production. Lenape's owner had told Eve he'd designed the summer program for "creative children" who might be intimidated by the athleticism and military atmosphere of so many summer camps. Lenape would be perfect for a child as sensitive and musical as Ricky, he said.

Ever since Eve saw seven-year-old Ricky sit down at the living room piano and play the first movement of the "Moonlight" Sonata from start to finish after only hearing it once, Ricky had been taking piano lessons with a local teacher, Mrs. Fox. Peter Randsman took lessons with Mrs. Fox too, and they went together after school, though Peter found it frustrating to sit through Ricky's lesson because playing the piano came so much more easily to his best friend. Mrs. Fox had a skin condition, so the boys had something to giggle about for hours after leaving her house. One day during Peter's lesson, not long before Ricky went to camp, he spotted a weathered volume on Mrs. Fox's bookshelf. He pulled down the *The Victor Book of the Opera* and began to study the photographs of exotic scenes. Singers in gorgeous, outlandish costumes—sometimes hundreds of them—were depicted on huge stages. *La Forza del Destino*, *L'Elisir d'Amore*, *Götterdämmerung*—the words in the book and the people's names were wonderfully strange and musical.

"Yuck, opera," Peter said when Ricky showed him the book.

"No, you have to *look*."

Ricky and Peter sat on the couch turning the pages, and within weeks they were both applying their allowances to their new passion.

"What's that?" Sam said, listening at the door of the playroom.

"Opera," said Eve with a shrug.

The big camp musical production of the summer was *The King and I*. Ricky waited impatiently for his turn at the audition. Finally at center stage, he threw his head back like a wolf preparing to bay at the moon, and let fly—a cappella—with "Look at *me*! I'm as helpless as a kitten up a *tre-e-e*!" Ricky sang out each word of "Misty," compensating for his lack of tone with volume and enthusiasm. He was rewarded with the part of Lewis, son of the civilizing influence Anna. (Ricky's favorite line was, "Mother! The natives are half naked!") He was mesmerized by the Rodgers and Hammerstein songs, and throughout rehearsals he couldn't wait for opening night.

By that time Ricky had developed a severe crush on a girl named Leslie Gold. Leslie attended Camp Blue Sky, Lenape's sister camp across the lake, and the sight of her sitting in the audience on opening night made Ricky sing "I Whistle a Happy Tune" even louder than he had during rehearsals. Between breaths, he looked out at Leslie, and then at all the other campers and counselors grinning up at the stage, ready to explode into applause. When the clapping began, Ricky felt such a rush of elation that forever after, when he looked out at a crowd made happy by his talent, he would think back to the stage at Camp Lenape, to his summer as a refugee from Harbor Isle, and he'd mark the moment once again as the beginning of his life.

⊰⊱

Just before they left for England in the early fall, Susan and Michael Lydon drove into New York City to rescue Lorraine. She was so hysterical on the phone that Susan couldn't quite make out what she said, except for a plaintive "I need you, Susan."

"I'm coming," Susan said.

Susan was saddened by the irony of Lorraine's call so close to her departure. She had often daydreamed about walking the narrow streets south of Washington Square Park with Lorraine and Maggie, of telling family stories with her little sister as veterans told war stories. Now that both of them had moved on to "new lives," Susan wanted to be close to Lorraine, but she couldn't quite bring herself to confide her dreams of afternoon talks in Greenwich Village cafés, and Lorraine never phoned until the day she called in distress.

Lorraine looked like she'd been crying for a long time when Michael and Susan arrived at her apartment. A young man in Buddy Holly eyeglasses was sitting in a chair cradling Maggie, who looked happy as always, gazing out with clear, calm eyes at the drama at hand. "This is Joel," Lorraine said. "My friend from City College."

Bobby Shapiro, Lorraine reported, had stomped off in search of a bar—even though he rarely took a drink. "It's not just Bobby, it's everybody," Lorraine sobbed. "Everybody is so *mad* at me!"

Bobby Shapiro was angry about most aspects of his marriage, Lorraine's distance from him and the presence of Joel among them. Recently Bobby had gotten so angry that Lorraine feared he might hurt her. Ellen Levy's new husband, Marty, rushed over from their nearby apartment to protect Lorraine and Maggie that night, but there was really no need.

Lorraine sensed similarities between the anger and resentment that suffused her brief marriage and the abiding rage she felt when she went to protests against Lyndon Johnson's foreign war. Since February, when Vietcong guerrillas had attacked American support installations near Pleiku air base, killing eight Americans, many citizens had come to realize that the nation was at war. President Johnson had ordered bombing runs against North Vietnam after the attack on Pleiku, and the guerrillas had escalated their attacks on American outposts, which grew more numerous as the 35,000 American troops in Vietnam in early spring grew to 125,000 by early summer.

The first teach-ins about the conflict were held in March. At City College Lorraine heard speakers claim that the escalation was illegal under the Geneva Accords of 1954. Some of them also said the fighting was immoral. In April, Students for a Democratic Society sponsored a national protest in Washington from which the most notable "adult" left-wing groups hastened to dissociate themselves. As the civil rights movement now had a division between young and old, so the New Left was at odds with the Old Left.

During October protest marches were organized in thirty American cities. One hundred thousand college and university students attended antiwar teach-ins as a national network of coordinated dissent—a movement—quickly took form. At one teach-in at Rutgers University in New Jersey, a student called a Coast Guard officer a "drip" for serving in an immoral military and was slapped by the officer's mother. The incident made the *New York Times* because the student, Allen Marain, hit the woman back ("Student Punches Mother," read the headline).

At marches in New York and other cities, protesters chanted and held aloft enlarged photographs of a Vietnamese mother with her maimed child, and some young men burned their draft cards. A thousand hecklers taunted Lorraine and more than ten thousand others during a march and rally on the East Side in early October. Attorney General Nicholas Katzenbach announced that a federal investigation into the groups "behind the protest" would soon begin. General Eisenhower said he "deplored" the protests, and a New York City mayoral candidate, journalist William F. Buckley, castigated "mincing young slobs strutting their epicene resentment."

Protesters against a war in a place most Americans still couldn't locate on a map actually dressed quite conservatively in 1965, especially by standards to come. Lorraine's old friend from high school, her fellow Pinko Steve Press, came down from Columbia University to visit Lorraine and Maggie and found himself embroiled in a heated debate over proper attire for opponents of a corrupt and moribund political system.

"If we're going to make them listen, we have to look like them," Steve Press contended. "We have to stop looking like beatniks."

"So in other words," Lorraine replied, "you want to cloak our disapproval of a fascist president and an illegal military action in a respectable outfit. Is that it, Steve?"

Press went back to Columbia thinking that he'd never seen the avowed pacifist among their high school gang so intense or angry.

The marches and protests seemed to gather more rage by the month. Many Americans Susan's age displayed a political sensibility formed by the civil rights movement, but for others Lorraine's age and younger, the seminal event was the new war in Vietnam, an official betrayal of basic American ideals, a cynical sacrifice of innocents masterminded by the briefly beloved and suddenly worst of all possible father figures, Lyndon Johnson. A man who had truly seemed to care for the poor and downtrodden was now seen as arrogant, hypocritical, falsely pious, and vengeful. With his Last Frontiersman routine ("Come home with that coonskin on the wall," he would say to American soldiers at Cam Ranh Bay), LBJ was willing to let children die in defense of little more than his own misbegotten pride, his harshest critics believed. The president sought, as he put it, to unite "the dream of a Great Society at home and the inescapable demands of our obligations halfway around the world" (or, "The Nigras had their civil rights and the rednecks could be killing gooks," as Norman Mailer caricatured Johnson's strategy at a teach-in in Berkeley), but instead he united the antiwar movement.

Lorraine found herself resisting the pure and complete hatred of Johnson she saw in many of her peers. Whatever Eve and Sam might think of her dramatic change a few years before she left home, Lorraine was not a hater. "I hate you," she'd tell them sometimes, but she never really took the emotion to heart. Lorraine couldn't completely hate the president because she wanted to believe that even the most distant of fathers could reclaim that early burst of love.

Michael and Susan found Bobby Shapiro hunkered at a bar not far from the apartment, trying to look like a heartbroken tough guy in a movie, looking instead like a heartbroken little boy at a bar. All Bobby wanted was to be the one who got to love Lorraine. His dream for the future was a little geodesic dome surrounded by a white picket fence, Lorraine playing her sweet guitar, he his mandolin, and Maggie growing into the harmonies over time.

"Let's just have a good time, Lorraine," Bobby would plead. "You can be whatever you want to be. Anything. Let's just be together."

But now he understood that Lorraine couldn't really love him, and after the worst of his pain subsided, he would look back and realize that while Lorraine had seen him as her destination for a time, he was only her ticket to leave. "Maybe someone who acted tougher, more like an adult, would have made her happy," Bobby told friends when the divorce was official.

Lorraine had packed her guitar, her suitcase, Maggie, and Maggie's paraphernalia by the time Susan and Michael got back to the apartment. Michael loaded up the car, and the newlyweds drove Lorraine and her daughter away.

——◦•◦——

By the end of her junior year of high school, Sheila was completely in love with the local Adonis, Peter Probst—and he was in love with her. Still, to the constant Beatles serenade in the background, Sheila wondered why she wasn't getting the parental attention she'd always hoped would be hers when Lorraine and Susan left. True, there were the beach club evenings, Sam's boats, and the bowling league, but that wasn't why Sheila never got "her turn" with Sam and Eve. It was because the only way to get their attention was to get in trouble. Sheila opted instead for Peter Probst and the Beatles.

"Why can't you have a Jewish boyfriend?" Sam asked Sheila one night, mechanically by now.

"Because all the Jewish boys in Harbor Isle smoke pot, Daddy," Sheila replied.

Sam nodded and walked slowly away from his "easy child," muttering to himself.

Eve spoke up from across the room when Sam was gone. "Sheila, you girls are gonna put me in the loony bin. And it won't be long."

1966

Susan and Michael Lydon had no more planned to be right in the middle of kinky, emancipated, Swinging London in the glory year, 1966, than Sam Gordon was present at the Battle of the Bulge out of a predilection for historical moments. In two or three years, when jealous peers expressed awe at the Lydons' uncanny instincts—to have known that London was the place to be that year, to have up and gone where *it* was *at*—Susan and Michael tried not to gloat. "Who knew?" Susan would say.

Michael's *Newsweek* credentials gained them entrée to the sorts of genteel functions they'd expected: diplomatic receptions, sherry parties in university common rooms. These, along with the occasional high tea, had been their image of England. Little wonder that they found themselves completely unprepared for the startling, vibrant, "switched-on" London scene.

An American abroad in white Courrèges boots and a bell-bottom pants suit—or perhaps a skirt a demure inch or so above the knee—Susan wandered through an old stone city in the throes of a costume change. Polyvinyl chloride outerwear glistened in checkerboard yellows and blacks, men sported suits of gaudily dyed velvet and satin, women wore ironic granny shoes, Beatle boots, earrings that would never fit in a jewelry box, and stockings patterned wildly all the way up to the thigh. The fashion queen of 221 Lincoln Avenue considered dresses with geometric Saint Laurent prints in the spirit of Mondrian. She visited Mary Quant's boutique in the King's Road, and Biba's on Kensington High Street. She strolled down a short alley that was on the brink of world fame, but she didn't buy much on Carnaby Street.

During their first spring in London, *Time* magazine beat *Newsweek* to the stands with a cover story comparing "The London Scene" of 1966 to *fin de siècle* Vienna, or Paris in the 1920s. "Seized by change...liberated by affluence," London was consecrated in *Time* as "the city of the decade." The burst of hyperbolic American reporting on the most commercial aspects of London's popular culture in the early months of 1966 was only the latest development in a venerable history of transatlantic comparison, bickering, disputes, reconciliation, defensiveness, chronic international Oedipal ambivalence, and separation anxiety between Great Britain and the United States.

Swinging London was depicted in *Time* (and then in *Look, Newsweek, Life,* and the *Saturday Evening Post*) as a phenomenon created, sustained, and "dominated by youth." The Londoners in American magazines and television reports were a hybrid of the comically stereotyped Brit, ineffectual, quaint, and slightly befuddled, and the cuddliness projected by John, Paul, George, and Ringo from 1964 to early 1967. The subtle effect of such publicity in the United States was to trivialize the unsettling behavior of young people, to acknowledge the hegemony of youth while reducing it to a "fad," a matter of style instead of substance, with its epicenter, happily, an ocean away—where a similar process was under way.

In England, the trumpeting of Carnaby Street, the photographic leering at miniskirts, the whole Swinging London mystique, served to allay anxiety over the dramatic ascension of so many northern working-class kids with guitars and bone-thin models who sounded like garbage haulers (*Time* called the scene a "Swinging Meritocracy"). The recasting of social change as a revolution in style obscured the fact that even middle-class British children had begun to mock the "superior" classes unmercifully.

Authority figures in England, from parents to politicians, had spent much of the past five years in what British sociologist Stanley Cohen called a "moral panic" over what was happening to the kids. Just as American JDs had been perceived as a modern plague not so long ago, English youth and their strange tribal battles on seaside piers and beaches were now the object of worried adult scrutiny. After the famous Battle of Margate between gangs of Mods in Edwardian gear and leather-jacketed Rockers (analogous to the Hoods and Rocks of Island Park and Harbor Isle), a local editorialist declared the fighting "without parallel in English history." Dr. George Simpson, the Margate magistrate, decried "long-haired, mentally unstable, petty little hoodlums, these sawdust Caesars who can only find courage like rats hunting in packs."

And fueling all the action was a driving beat. There were all-night dances in London's Shepherds Bush. The kids went wild in the dance clubs to the music of sneering, leather-clad rock bands. For a time during 1966 the prominence of the Beatles and the preponderance of ironic media coverage made the music appear harmless. The most dangerous kids in England were simply "fab." Though there had been occasional disturbing signs—like the presence of Mods and Rockers alongside college students and leading intellectuals at some of the "Ban the Bomb" rallies in London —it was generally understood throughout the English-speaking world that British "youth," as Mick Jagger, lead singer of the Rolling Stones, told *Time*, had "become emancipated" in a colorful and essentially nonthreatening way.

Friends of the attractive and brilliant twenty-two-year-old Lydons, who lived on Sydney Street in fashionable Chelsea, occasionally observed that Susan and Michael's emancipation was particularly stylish. They were making the Swinging London scene almost exactly as magazine articles prescribed—that is, in the context of upward mobility.

Kevin Buckley, an acquaintance of Michael's from Yale and now his colleague at *Newsweek*, arrived for dinner at the Lydons' flat one evening dressed in the same innocuous tie, button-down shirt, and rumpled suit he'd worn throughout his college years. Michael greeted Kevin in a knit turtleneck, and Kevin couldn't help noticing that his hair was approaching Beatles length. The Who, a West London club rock band, was playing at low volume in the sitting room on a very good stereo ("Talkin' 'bout my my...g-g-g-generation"), and Kevin stared at startling Marimekko textiles framed on the walls and covering large pillows arrayed casually around the room. Susan was in the kitchen being creative with a casserole.

At dinner, Michael and Susan talked easily about the virtues of Chinese pig bristles used in the manufacture of fine Kent hair brushes. They spoke of the problems of the British Labour Party, the outlandish theories of Wilhelm Reich, the accuracy of the Swinging London movie *Blow-Up*.

Kevin Buckley went home thinking that while he had come to the world of professional journalism from Yale with the assumption that his success would largely depend on his capacity to act and look like his elders, Michael Lydon and his witty, pretty wife seemed to have found an alternative route to the top. Michael had apparently figured out how to be a "professionalist" (a coinage by a young Yale psychologist, Kenneth Keniston, who traced the estimable quest for merit among recent American college graduates to the fact that since "no young man can hope simply to repeat the life pattern of his father, talent must be continually improved"), but he and Susan were also stylish, vital, smart—and almost English.

"They've kind of gone native," Buckley reported to other *Yale Daily* and *Harvard Crimson* vets working as journalists in London and various European cities.

On a trip to Paris, Susan shopped the Right Bank and purchased a tasteful Hermès scarf and an expensive leather handbag. A young ex-*Yale Daily* man named Peter Osnos, who was working in France for *Time*, was impressed by Susan's bluntness and breadth of intellect, which seemed to complement Michael and his budding career quite nicely. Her views were rather idealistic and opinionated by the standards of these foreign postings, but Osnos thought the combination worked.

As Eve Gordon had already observed to her displeasure, Susan had a good ear for accents, and by now her speech betrayed not a single audible connection to the South Shore of Long Island or the home of an electrician born on the Lower East Side. When Eve hung up the phone after transatlantic reports of weekends in Paris, new furniture, a car, and dinner out at "posh" restaurants, she would feel lost because her daughter was much too far away. Sam would listen too. "I'm pullin' down fifteen a year," he'd say. "Sounds like Michael's makin' twice what I bring home."

Because Susan was so many miles from home when her labor pains began, Eve didn't think for a moment about going to London. To Eve, Susan was almost as far away and inaccessible as Sam had been when Susan was born.

Susan's baby was stillborn. An X-ray showed that the baby was dead when she arrived at the hospital after her water broke.

When Susan called Eve with the news, Eve closed up as she had when her parents died and when Sam left her to go to war—a reaction that was out of her control. The absence of emotion in her mother's voice reminded Susan of the way Eve had spoken the day Cleo, the family dog, was killed on Lincoln Avenue. Susan got the same message now—that there were times when her mother could not afford to feel.

But Susan was in a strange, damp, distant place where the entire population seemed to display less palpable emotion than the Gordon family in Harbor Isle on an average Sunday afternoon. Susan came home from the hospital to find that Michael hadn't changed the stained bed sheets from the night she went into labor. The sight of the sheets, the memory of the unbelievable pain of childbirth ending in death instead of life, the flat sound of a mother's voice—a mother who *should have come*—all of it would return to Susan in dreams and stupors for many years.

Around the *Newsweek* office Michael Lydon became known as "the fifth Beatle." While most of the other staffers were interested in politics, Michael began to lecture his colleagues at length on aspects of Chuck Berry's guitar-playing technique evident in Rolling Stone Keith Richards' rhythms. Though Michael had previously believed that white people had no right or moral claim to the blues at all, he now went to hear the Bluesbreakers, Cream, the Kinks, and the Yardbirds, and decided that maybe British "blue-eyed" blues wasn't so bad after all.

"You know, even back at the *Daily*," Michael told Susan, "I always got more comments from readers when I wrote about music."

The Lydons sat in special press seats at the Hammersmith Odeon— a London movie palace not unlike the Paramount theaters in New York—for what turned out to be the Beatles' last British tour. Michael managed to wangle an interview with Paul McCartney and John Lennon for *Newsweek*, and though two years earlier he hadn't been able even to look at the screen when the Beatles appeared on *The Ed Sullivan Show*, he was entranced by John and Paul. During the interview, he realized that he had a lot in common with them. John and Paul were about the same age as Michael, they all had a certain tough-kid-made-good flair, and they easily shared many reference points: Bob Dylan, Chuck Berry, folk music, even the Bomb. Three of the Beatles, like Michael, were married.

Michael came away from his talk with John and Paul thinking that the salient difference between him and the two pleasant, wisecracking Englishmen was that they were doing what they wanted to do. They'd figured it all out, and they didn't care who noticed. John would soon make his famous statement about the relative fame of the Beatles and Jesus Christ. John was living as he saw fit.

From that point on, Michael Lydon was wildly in love with the Beatles. He worked hard at imitating their cocksure insouciance and what he saw as their refreshing way of not worrying what people thought of them while remaining alert and available to the pull of the times. As he strolled past the house where Paul McCartney was living with a girlfriend named Jane Asher, he'd sing old Shirelles songs in hopes that

Paul, a known Shirelles fan, might hear him and invite him inside. He went to watch "the boys" play soccer in Hyde Park, and he pored over their lyrics, especially the more serious and enigmatic lines on their 1965 album, *Rubber Soul*, which included the haunting "In My Life" and several other songs indicating that there was more to the Beatles than was first thought. When they released *Revolver* in 1966, armies of youthful Beatlemaniacs "Beatle hopping" to three-chord melodies were suddenly eclipsed by serious students of popular music like Michael and Susan. *Revolver* was full of exotic rhythms and harmonic flourishes never attempted before on a pop music record. Michael also pondered Bob Dylan's lyrics as he'd recently pondered the essential tomes of Western civilization at Yale. If one was not "busy being born," Dylan taught, one was "busy dying."

The former JFK man was now a Beatles man, a Dylan man, a Who and Yardbirds man loyal and true. By the middle of 1966, Michael had discovered in the Beatles four young men his own age whom he would still identify as his "role models" twenty-five years later.

Lorraine expected to see Mick Jagger waiting on the corner of Sydney Street when she climbed out of the sputtering, high-roofed black taxi. She also expected to see her ever-cool big sister, but she discovered to her horror that the idealistic and acerbic Susan she'd grown up with had been transformed into a perky young housewife. "But leave it to Susan," Lorraine would admit when she returned home from London. "She still managed to make being a wife look interesting."

"Miss Gourmet," Lorraine teased as Susan whipped up a new creation in the tiny cube the Brits called a kitchen, with its spartan "cooker" and "fridge." "Eve won't believe it, Susan."

Miss Bourgeois, Lorraine thought to herself. *What is going on here?*

Lorraine listened carefully to the witty dialogue between Susan and Michael, trying to place it. Then it came to her—*The Million Dollar Movie*, those old films Eve considered no less essential to a daughter's education than geography or math, Fred and Ginger's lessons in style. "Even their fights were genteel," Lorraine reported to Gina Schick, her new sidekick back in New York. "I could feel the two of them trying so hard to be normal. It was truly bizarre. Susan screamed at me like a madwoman for eating some gourmet soup she was saving. They only fixed me up with one date, and the whole time I missed Maggie and was chilled to the bone."

Susan noticed that Lorraine was always shivering during her visit, and there was something about her complexion that wasn't right. And Susan was sure that Lorraine...smelled. "Even after a bath she smelled," Susan said to Michael after her sister went home. "I think there's something wrong with Lorraine."

Gina Schick loved Lorraine's detailed stories about the Gordon family. Aside from being a Barnard College graduate (major in anthropology, minor in Oriental studies, good knowledge of Sanskrit), an independent student of macrobiotic food and Japanese art, and an employee of a small print and poster business run by an Englishman named Ralph Metzner, one of the leaders of the quasi-religious "movement" surrounding hallucinogenic drugs, Gina had been raised to consider family stories far less trivial than most postwar children were given to believe. Gina's maternal grandfather had been a practicing psychoanalyst in Austria during Freud's time. Her mother was a clinical psychologist in northern California, and Gina had first experienced psychotherapy as a young teen.

When Bobby Shapiro, who came regularly to take Maggie for a day, first met Lorraine's friend Gina, he couldn't stop gawking. "She looks exactly like your sister Susan," Bobby said. "They even talk the same way."

Lorraine hadn't noticed.

When it was Gina's turn to describe her childhood in Palo Alto, she told Lorraine that "everything was in order at home, everything always clean." Gina Schick's mother, born Jewish and raised Catholic in Paris, was divorced from her father, an engineer and man of the left who'd spent time in Cuba since Castro's revolution. Gina and Lorraine not only shared apparently neat suburban childhoods but early and ill-advised marriages (Gina's to a City College student who had lately begun to date Lorraine). Gina and Lorraine also shared the firm belief that on the whole, they'd be happier and more at peace with the world if they were Japanese. Both of them had "discovered Japan."

Gina, student of the Orient, brought home more and more reading material. Lorraine, in order to spend a portion of each day surrounded by graceful items made in Japan, took a part-time job at Azuma, a store on Eighth Street in the Village that retailed ashtrays, paper lamps, and other Eastern artifacts. Gina dated an expatriate Japanese poet, and Lorraine went out with his friend, a Japanese painter. On double dates, the girls would sit in the Cafe Figaro, attentively listening to vociferous arguments about life and art in Japanese, a language neither of them understood. They studied Japanese cooking, and one evening made a huge batch of sukiyaki for some Japanese artist friends and the poet Allen Ginsberg, now so famous that he'd hired Bob Dylan's manager to arrange his appearances. Ginsberg, a practicing Buddhist (Buddhism was one of Gina and Lorraine's main interests), hosted the party along with his friend, Peter Orlovsky, whom he introduced as "my wife," just as he had to a television audience on a recent show.

Gina and Lorraine were ecstatic over the success of the evening. Lorraine was nineteen years old and only a dozen miles from the cultural wasteland of Harbor Isle, yet she was surrounded each day by offerings from the best of other cultures and other times. She had a new and sophisticated best friend, and they were hip to a Greenwich Village scene that encompassed Buddhism, folk music, gospel, Sanskrit, psychoanalysis, sweet little Maggie, and even the daydream that but for some cosmic error they would have been born Japanese. By any measure, Lorraine decided after her visit to Susan in London, Greenwich Village was where it was at, and *she* was in the right place to be.

The minute Sam and Eve left for one of their evenings out, Ricky and Peter Randsman would gather the essentials from Eve's and Sheila's drawers and take up their positions before the long mirror in the upstairs bathroom. By mutual consent, Ricky was "the best at hair," so Peter would bow down to be "brushed out," back to front, just like Sheila and Peter's sister, Nancy, did with their gorgeous friends.

Though Sam and Eve went out more often than the Randsmans, the boys loved to have Peter's house to themselves because they could make finger drawings on the new faux-velvet jet-black wallpaper. Then they would sprint up to Nancy's bedroom to try on her incredible fall, a light brown switch of perfectly straight hair stored atop a sphere of white polystyrene in a cylindrical case covered in go-go-boot black vinyl and ringed by the fattest of silver zippers. The unzipping of the black case alone was a matter of serious ceremony for the boys.

One evening during the late spring Peter and Ricky were at the bathroom mirror at Ricky's house in full regalia. Ricky had just completed Peter's brush-out and fitted them both with bright Patty Duke–style headbands. Peter, "the best at makeup" by virtue of watching his mother transform herself into Harbor Isle's answer to Lana Turner a thousand times, had applied their lipstick, rouge, and mascara. He'd just managed a wide tarring of black eyeliner that more or less followed the shape of their eyes when they heard Sam and Eve downstairs, only an hour after they'd gone out.

The boys looked at each other in horror. They both stared into the mirror, and in that instant—for the first time—Peter and Ricky understood that their nocturnal efforts to be just like their beloved sisters might not be something a parent would understand. Ricky leaped over to slam the bathroom door. He locked it, panting noisily as he ran back and forth across the small bathroom.

"What are we gonna do?" Peter moaned.

The boys fell upon a bath towel and tried to wipe the heavy makeup off, smearing it across their faces. As they ripped off their headbands, they heard a high-pitched cackling sound pierce the bathroom: "Open this door!"

Except for one or two terrifying occasions, Peter had never seen Eve Gordon enraged, but he'd heard stories. Eve's furious "I'll cripple you!" was not considered an idle threat at the Gordons' house, and "Eat it or I'll shove it down your throat" had become a reality the night Eve took a serving of veal—the only thing she cooked that Ricky couldn't abide because of its "gooshiness"—put it in his mouth, and shoved it down his throat. Sam and Eve left Ricky with a babysitter that night, and while they were out Ricky threw up—which meant that at least he didn't have to eat veal anymore. Eve told any guests at the table on veal nights that Ricky was "allergic."

Now Ricky was cowering in the far corner of the upstairs bathroom, curled up in a fetal pose Gina Schick's Freudian grandfather might have observed with a knowing "Ah-hah!" Eve was pounding away on the door.

When his mother got this angry, Ricky imagined her rage as something separate from her, alive inside her and in control. Since Eve had read in a magazine that "the change of life could ruin a woman," as she paraphrased the article, "ruin her as a person," she had been warning Sam to brace himself for her menopause. "If I get excited, flushed, fatigued, or suddenly begin to cry over nothing, don't you start getting excited too." But Eve never mentioned the exigencies of menopause to the kids.

When "the change" began, Eve had found that if the house was completely in order, everything at a right angle to the nearest surface, dustless and secure, she could quell the anxiety and remorse that came over her by lying down on the living room couch and staring at a painting she'd won at a PTA luncheon. It was a stormy picture of waves breaking on a rock-strewn shore. If she stared at it long enough, Eve felt like she was inside the scene.

Not long before Eve and Sam surprised Peter and Ricky in the bathroom, Sheila had decided to surprise her beleaguered mother with a gift: Van Gogh's *The Bridge* and another print, a Marc Chagall rabbi, both purchased during a jaunt to one of her favorite places, the Metropolitan Museum of Art in Manhattan. As part of the surprise, Sheila had thoughtfully rearranged the paintings and prints on the living room wall.

"What have you done! What have you done!" Eve had screamed. Sheila stood by as her mother seized several throw pillows and flung them at the wall. Then she picked up a glass ashtray, and Sheila ran for the front door. Ricky was sitting on the stoop when she flew out of the house, just as a tremendous crash was heard from inside.

"She could have killed me," Sheila had said.

Covered with makeup, Ricky reconsidered Sheila's observation as Sam's deep voice joined Eve's soprano on the other side of the locked bathroom door.

"Open it now!" they yelled in unison.

On his good days, Ricky Gordon walked around Harbor Isle wearing a gigantic orange-slice grin. Ricky had a rooster-comb cowlick, large ears, and cheeks that puffed up and glowed with enthusiasm, especially for his several abiding passions.

One of these was music. From Italian opera to the strange Gregorian chants and Japanese melodies Lorraine and her friend Gina played for him in the city, from his brother-in-law Michael's "best friends," the Beatles, to Peter Randsman's hearty rendition of "My Lord and Master" from *The King and I,* Ricky loved it all.

Girls were another passion: Donna Rutigliano, Lisa Virzi, Lori Cohen, and Jody Pilchik—especially Jody, who had the blackest, most beautiful hair he'd ever seen and a slightly scratchy voice that made his eyes go blurry. Ricky rode his bike past Jody's house every chance he got. When the two lines formed for square dancing at school—boys in one and girls in the other—Ricky would feel physically ill if he didn't get one of the pretty girls as a partner.

A third passion was an eleven-inch-tall companion named GI Joe, who'd replaced his former companion, Barbie, two years earlier, shortly after Sam summoned Ricky for "a little talk about dolls." GI Joe had a scar on his right cheek and a battle-hardened face. Ricky's Joe owned every one of the available "action outfits," including the coveted frog-man getup. In general, Ricky had innumerable passions and almost no complaints at all. He believed that his life was full—except that it was so often at risk.

"I think you should unlock the door," Peter said.

Ricky turned the knob, and Eve was upon him so quickly that Peter thought she must have been about to batter down the door when Ricky pulled it open. A noticeable bulging of both eyes was her only immediate reaction to the boys' ghoulish faces, but then she swept Peter to one side and began slapping Ricky back into the corner where he'd just been cowering. Ricky pulled a bath towel down and covered himself like a dying Caesar. "What…are…you…doing?" Eve screamed, slapping away. "It's *my* makeup! Not yours. It's *mine*."

Peter was wondering if purloined makeup was actually the issue at hand when Eve spun and glared at him. "Go home, Peter. Go on. Get out of here!"

"But I'm supposed to sleep over," Peter heard himself protest.

Eve stopped slapping Ricky and turned more slowly to his friend. "I said…go *home*."

Peter ran, stopping downstairs to wash his face, though he knew he still didn't look altogether normal when he got home. His mother was in the den knitting.

"Why are you home?" Bernice said, glancing up.

"Ricky didn't feel good. He got sick all of a sudden," Peter said.

"Oh well, it's good you didn't stay over then," Bernice said sweetly. "If you're around people who are sick, you can get sick too."

Lorraine, bravest of all the Gordon children, ingested a significant dose of pharmaceutically pure, honest-to-God Sandoz Corporation lysergic acid diethylamide—or such were the claims of the local purveyor about the above-ground origins of his LSD. She sat down and waited for the better part of an hour to find out what all the hoopla was about. "Tune-in—Be reborn. Drop-back-in to express it. Start a new sequence of behavior that reflects your vision," in the words of Timothy Leary, late of the Harvard University faculty (fired in 1963), and author of *The Psychedelic Reader* and other literary amalgams of acadamese, rhetoric, shards of automatic writing, and lines from the Tibetan *Book of the Dead*. Ever since Professor Leary had chewed some peyote buttons in Mexico at the beginning of the decade, he'd claimed over and over that the key to Understanding was as accessible as the nearest hallucinogen.

Leary preached that even if mankind "got together" in the "one big family" often mentioned by civil rights workers, antiwar protesters, and the like, society would remain as chaotic as an "anthill" unless people learned to open themselves up to experience through LSD. Once enlightened, society would reconstitute itself according to the animating principles of an ancient social unit, the clan, "a small group of human beings organized around a religious goal." Leary, and the running reportage carried in local New York papers like the *East Village Other*, implied that LSD would be the source of a new religion—though a good trip also meant that a woman would "inevitably have several hundred orgasms." The phenomenon known as a "bad trip," to Timothy Leary, was the result of a "spiritual voyager's" failure of will and lack of faith.

A very bad trip was what Lorraine feared was in store for her when an hour or so after taking the acid that allegedly came from the Sandoz labs in Switzerland, where LSD was first synthesized in 1938, she felt herself hurtling through a deep, dark, attenuating tunnel that she realized, with a jolt of terror, was the inside of her mind.

Lorraine had first smoked marijuana during the summer of 1962, on the way to the first annual Philadelphia Folk Festival in a crowded car with her sister Susan, Maris Cakars, and some kids she didn't know. Lorraine suddenly started to cry and pant and beg to be taken to a hospital because she was having a heart attack. Some of the kids had laughed at her and joked about dumping her at the side of the road. But Lorraine forgot her unhappy introduction to drugs when she fell in love with amphetamines—speed—which she was taking so regularly by 1966 that a fetid patina often formed like a glaze on her skin. Susan had clearly noticed the smell in London, and Eve sometimes remarked that Lorraine might think about a new deodorant, sounding just like a mother in a television commercial.

Soon, in the company of Gina Schick and dozens of bright and well-read middle-class students and artists, many of whom she had met through Maris Cakars, brave Lorraine began to shoot heroin—the drug of drugs, junk, shit, smack (this last a street term derived from the Yiddish word for a sniff or pinch, *shmeck*). Columbia and Barnard junkies (and junkies at other Ivy League schools) would do their homework, ace their exams, and then head downtown to join other privileged adventurers on a hunt for heroin among much less privileged urbanites who tended to carry sharp knives and have nicknames like Bad Bobby and Spanish Eddie. The heroin hunts were the ultimate in "slumming it." One of Lorraine and Gina's heroin connections offered to teach the girls to shoplift; another asked if they'd like to learn to turn tricks to raise some extra cash.

At first, Lorraine wouldn't let herself disappear into the powerful drug until Maggie was safely deposited with Eve for one of her many weekend visits. But soon she was only waiting until Maggie was asleep to shoot up. When heroin was coursing through her body, Lorraine felt capable of intellectually sidling up to the very core of pain caused by family troubles and by an immoral, hateful war. The drug—this glorious drug—protected her from the pain and allowed her to think in peace. Junk let her look into the awful face of truth, and there Lorraine could see how much she missed Sam and Eve. She could luxuriate in her longing cushioned by heroin, secret of poets and jazzmen.

Only thoughts of Maggie—her sweet, calm little Maggie, who said words to her now and took obvious pleasure in so many things—could penetrate the blinkered, pleasant sadness of her high. *Maggie lives*, Lorraine would think from behind the barricade of junk, and then, with a morbid twist on Descartes, *therefore I don't*. Then the high would fade and Lorraine would wonder if this was what it was like to be dead.

By the end of the summer hippies from California were appearing on the streets of the Lower East Side—the "East Village," as the newcomers preferred to call it. Back when Lorraine and Susan first began to explore the Village, "hippie" was a pejorative diminutive of "hipster" applied by the original beats to the green kids who were drawn to the city by Jean Shepherd's radio show, Kerouac's books, and Ginsberg's poetry.

Gina and Lorraine were at first no less skeptical of the new wave of hippies. Many of them wore stovepipe hats or what appeared to be biblical garb, and spoke as if they thought it was cool to be inarticulate. Or perhaps, as Gina surmised, they were "just dumb." The migrants' fixed smiles, wide eyes, and perpetually awestricken utterances in some cases indicated that they were tripping on LSD, though they seemed bent on appearing to be high and in the throes of a mystical experience even when they were not. The epiphany-faces often told tales of others who'd glimpsed ultimate truth, "white light," while high on the drug—notably, British novelist and essayist Aldous Huxley, who'd written that the "doors of perception" could indeed be chemically unlatched. Most hippies seemed to believe (with variations, depending on the storyteller) that in 1963 Huxley had taken a massive dose of some hallucinogen, assumed a squatting position, and exclaimed, his eyes wide open with joy, "I thought so!" before falling back dead.

"I don't think it's that they're dumb," Lorraine would say.

"Well, then it's a good act," Gina would reply.

Gina's experience with Ralph Metzner and his Day-Glo poster business made her skeptical of the spiritual aspects of LSD. Gina had experimented with another hallucinogen, mescaline, back in 1961, and she could recall no divine sightings at the time. And besides, the fade to basic beatnik black promised by heroin—the thinking girl's high, Gina and Lorraine believed—would be awfully hard to beat.

But then Gina began to hear from friends back home in California that her old guitar-playing buddy from Palo Alto High, Jerry Garcia, was making quite a name for himself with his band, the Grateful Dead, which had appeared at a glorious mass LSD party thrown by Ken Kesey and his Merry Pranksters this past January, the "San Francisco Trips Festival." By the fall many novice trippers were assuring Lorraine and Gina that neither the West Coast version of the acid gospel nor Leary's rigid spiritual directives were required for a good high, and some friends suggested to Lorraine that she could bypass the psychotherapy Sam and Eve had finally allowed her to begin with a much cheaper and less time-consuming tab of LSD.

So the dose of purported Sandoz was shortly obtained and stored in Lorraine and Gina's refrigerator—a sacrilege, Eve would have cried—in their apartment at 1 Willett Street. Lorraine had taken the drug twice in the company of experienced trippers, as was advised, but she'd felt nothing either time. The afternoon she skeptically wolfed down some more LSD and fell into a black tubular hole she was sure was the interior of her life, Lorraine was alone.

Or *was* she alone? Still inside the lightless drainpipe of the trip, totally unaware by now that this was a drug experience and not a state of forever, Lorraine suddenly thought Maggie was with her. Then she thought Maggie wasn't with her. Then she thought Maggie was lost. Lorraine started to cry.

All corners and angles in the room seemed hinged and every wall hung with whirling wheels of color. Lorraine was getting younger, careening into her past, her terror intensifying as she became a little girl again. She reached up to hold her spinning head, but her fingers went right through her skull! "The ghost of 'lec-trici-ty howls in the bones of her face," a line from a Dylan song she played over and over—*this* was why it had always haunted her so. Lorraine wheeled into the blackness of outer space, younger than a baby. Out she flew, full of terror and sadness.

Gina found her later, rocking back and forth on the floor, gripping her head. Maggie was with Eve. Gina administered a powerful Thorazine tablet, and Lorraine eventually began to feel better. She kept muttering something about realizing there was "an edge" after all.

*   *   *

Lorraine had never been completely comfortable with her new therapist, but she tried to describe her LSD experience during the next session. She told her young psychologist that seeing the distant border of
all things—the edge at the precipice of "the void inside you"—made her
understand what desperation felt like. High on marijuana at a recent
party with Maggie, she'd become so panicked while searching for the
way out that she'd realized why people jump out windows, she said.

Though he regretted his contravention of patient confidentiality
within minutes of making the call (he even wrote Lorraine a long letter,
begging her to forgive him and come back), the therapist phoned Eve
after Lorraine left his office. He reported that her little girl had taken
LSD and had contemplated a plunge from an upper story while under
the influence of drugs.

The phone call was not Eve's first warning about Lorraine taking drugs.
Not a month earlier, a family friend named Lou Calderon had followed
Eve into the kitchen during a big Sunday gathering. "Lorraine's *on*
something, Eve," Lou had said.

"What the hell does that mean?" Eve snapped.

"I'm a volunteer fireman," Lou replied with authority. "I see a lot."

Then Ellen Levy had phoned 221 Lincoln Avenue. "Mrs. Gordon,
Lorraine's in big trouble," Ellen said. "She's…taking drugs."

Eve was infuriated. How could these people—just because Lorraine
looked kind of shabby and brought cockroaches home in her laundry
bag on occasion—accuse her of being on drugs? Eve was quite sure that
Lorraine couldn't stand drugs. Eve couldn't even take cough medicine
without becoming violently ill, so she assumed the same was true of all
her children.

Just to be safe, Eve took Lorraine to the family doctor for a
"checkup."

"She's not taking drugs," Eve said indignantly to Ellen Levy the
next time she called. "I took her for a checkup and she's fine."

"Well, she's not. She's a heroin addict," Ellen blurted. "She's a
junkie. I was just at her apar—"

"She's not!" Eve yelled into the phone.

But Eve did subsequently urge Lorraine to bring Maggie to Harbor
Isle more often, and she convinced Sam that it was wise for them to
relent and finance the latest of their children's rich-kid desires—psychotherapy.

If Sam had less to say about Lorraine all the time, he had plenty to
say about "headshrinkers": "Since kids don't want their fathers and

mothers to teach them anymore, somebody with a fancy degree gets paid big money for telling them things. These headshrinkers, they just took what parents used to do and made it a business." Sam was stunned by Eve's insistence that they come up with fifty dollars for each of Lorraine's three sessions a week, but he could tell from her tone that something was seriously wrong.

Eve began trying to learn as much as a suburban parent could about the world of drugs. Performers she remembered from the old days had taken drugs, but that was in their background, that was what they knew. Now "dope," according to several magazines, was "invading the suburbs." One article in Look asserted that children in search of "kicks" took drugs as the "ultimate defiance of adult authority." Newsweek reported on a twelve-year-old boy who sniffed glue and threatened to stab his father to death. A partygoer in a suburb near Boston had overdosed on "goofballs" and died, Eve read (the corpse was tossed in a closet, the closet was nailed shut, and "the party went on"). A Reader's Digest condensation of a longer article in Life described the gruesome existence of heroin addicts in New York City. "You could hear about your mother dying," said a young habitué of "Needle Park" on Manhattan's Upper West Side, "and you wouldn't even shed a tear."

Mothers. Fathers. Adults. The implication was always there. Children left home and hurt themselves with drugs because of what happened in their families.

After the call from Lorraine's therapist, Eve tried to learn about LSD. If magazines made urban youth on heroin sound as remote from a middle-class mother as the plight of the very poor, if goofballs in the suburbs were reported in a tone of sober concern, daily conversation and the popular literature on LSD expressed the same kind of moral panic that had made British observers liken teenage rumbles on the beach to the worst days of the Blitz. A New York boy, Stephen Kessler, claimed not to remember that he'd killed his mother after taking LSD. Life put the drug on its cover in March, and Time compared the "psychedelic smorgasbord" to a spreading "disease." The Senate Subcommittee on Juvenile Delinquency convened hearings to look into this new threat to public health and safety and the nation's youth. Allen Ginsberg, one of the witnesses, told the subcommittee that drugs were a "refuge for a person in a plastic world."

After pondering the therapist's disclosure that suicide had crossed her daughter's drug-addled mind, Eve phoned Lorraine to discuss the matter. "What do you think you're doing! I...I'll take your daughter away!" Eve sputtered. "I'll have you put...in jail!"

Lorraine was very calm and extremely rational in the face of her mother's cultural ignorance of drug experimentation—even though the bad trip had shattered her. Within a few days, it became clear to Eve that she had been irrational on the phone, and that the therapist's call was so unprofessional as to border on malpractice.

"But who knew?" Eve said at mah-jongg. "Who knew going to a psychiatrist is like confession or something?"

From their faces, Eve could tell that the girls thought everybody knew that.

"Such a big secret. Heaven forbid a doctor should call a mother and say her daughter wants to jump out a goddamn window!"

The day Maggie came to spend a few weeks in Harbor Isle, Sheila was scheduled to have her tonsils out. Only Sheila remembered the appointment, and though she didn't say anything to Sam or Eve, she never forgot that she was forgotten that day.

Sheila eventually reminded Eve about her tonsils.

"We'll get to it," Eve said, "but not now."

Sheila had her tonsils removed in 1973, when she was twenty-three.

———————

Susan came off the plane from London pushing Michael in a wheelchair. Michael wore dark glasses to hide his bright yellow face. Susan had slipped the glasses on back at Heathrow, thinking the airlines might stop a passenger with jaundice from getting on the flight.

Lorraine bounded up and hugged them both. Before she even asked Michael how he was feeling, she pulled up her sleeve to reveal tiny black needle tracks. "Don't tell Mommy," Lorraine said. "Promise me you won't tell."

Susan had come home fearing her husband might die from a serious case of hepatitis that had not responded to treatment in England, but in Harbor Isle Eve plied him with storied Jewish nostrums like chicken soup and "rescued Michael from the dead," as Sam always put it. When he was stronger, he and Susan went to visit Lorraine in the city, where they took turns administering a stern lecture on the evils of hard drugs. Susan was particularly concerned about LSD. Since Vassar was right down the road from Timothy Leary's headquarters, an estate in Millbrook, New York, where he had launched many of his LSD incursions into the human personality, Susan felt she knew all about LSD. Maris Cakars had once advised her that anyone who took LSD and was in the least "unbalanced mentally" would probably "go over the edge" and never come back. Susan smoked pot and took amphetamines, but heroin and LSD were playing with fire. She conveyed this to her little sister in no uncertain terms.

Michael and Susan were shortly due to return to Europe and tour the Loire Valley for a month in their Peugeot. In what Gina Schick considered a haughty, offhand tone, Susan also reported that she was writing articles now. The *Times* of London had published her "on the arts," as had the *International Herald Tribune* and a magazine called *London Life*.

"Boy," Gina said when Susan and Michael left, "is your sister ever stuck-up."

◦—◆—◦

As he regularly did when family dramas reached a crescendo, Ricky eavesdropped on an upstairs phone extension while his mother told his sister she might take her daughter away and throw Lorraine in jail. A week later, Ricky pushed Magdalena Shapiro's stroller over to Peter's house to share the latest sister news. "Guess what," Ricky said, helping Maggie out of the stroller. "Lorraine's a heroin addict."

Ricky gazed at Peter hopefully, but Peter had to admit he didn't know if being a heroin addict was good or bad either. The boys decided to go inside and ask Peter's mother.

Sister news arrived at 221 Lincoln daily. From Ricky's perspective, his sister Sheila had become Harbor Isle's very own Juliet—girlfriend to the coolest, nicest, handsomest Probst in the known world. The vicissitudes of their passionate romance, conducted on both sides without parental approbation, were as compelling to Ricky's imagination as his confident assumption that his sister Susan was a dear personal friend of the Beatles. His sister Lorraine, who'd always treated him like a grown-up and a close friend, was passionate about folk songs, Bob Dylan, Negro spirituals, and injustice, exotic Southeast Asian strains of rice and heroin from the same general vicinity, Viennese psychoanalysis and its American revisions, and an array of boyfriends so diverse that an afternoon in her apartment on the Lower East Side sometimes reminded him of his class field trip to the United Nations.

Phone calls at odd hours, heated family gatherings around the dinner table, low intense talk of his sisters when Sam and Eve thought they were alone, letters from abroad—all of it made Ricky think that there was more drama in his middle-class suburban family than in anything on television. Though being the ten-year-old little brother of these brilliant, beautiful explorer-queens was exciting and had vividly colored Ricky's daydreams, his house often seemed to vibrate with the anxieties his older sisters caused, as if by remote control. Still, Ricky considered a night at home with his parents in turmoil—at the very end of the year over Susan's plans to relocate to California, the "loser state" Sam so mistrusted—preferable to a night when they went out and left him all alone, beside himself with terror.

Maggie had gone home with Lorraine shortly before Ricky's fear of the night surged to new levels at the Lido Theater in Island Park. He and Peter had gone to see *The Swinger*, a "wicked comedy" starring Ann-Margret and Tony Franciosa. Ricky and Peter adored Ann-Margret. Peter liked to pull his sweatshirt up over his head inside-out so it hung down his back just like Ann-Margret's hair. For a boy who would soon turn eleven, he could do an extremely convincing rendition of her sexy opening number from *Bye Bye Birdie*.

But *The Swinger* was on a double bill that night with *Psycho*, and though Ricky screamed out loud several times at Alfred Hitchcock's first shocks to the system, for most of the movie he sat pressed into his chair with his mouth agape, like a test pilot in an old film clip demonstrating the human effect of extreme G-force.

Peter's mother picked the boys up at the Lido and took them to a deli after the show. Peter noticed that Ricky could neither talk nor eat—a sure sign that something was very wrong.

Something was. In Chicago, a man named Richard Speck made eight student nurses lie on their dormitory floor and killed them one after another like cattle in a slaughterhouse. A Texas kid who looked from his pictures like one of those clean-cut types Ricky wouldn't have thought to fear—a boy who hated his father and loved his mother ("with all my heart," Charles Whitman, Jr., said after he shot her in the head and stabbed her in the chest)—had told the University of Texas school psychiatrist he kept "thinking about going up on the tower with a deer rifle and start shooting people," and four months later did just that, shooting forty-five people in ninety-four minutes, killing more than a dozen of them before he killed himself.

There were now so many intimidating young men living and roaming near Harbor Isle that Ricky considered his hometown a sinister, ominous place. Greasers in roaring cars with squealing tires cruised the same streets his sisters had found far too placid and secure. Tough kids hung out in front of Pop's Bar over the bridge in Island Park with a contemptuous "What's it to ya?" air that seemed to have bled from the city along the southern shore of Long Island, out past the towns where Lorraine and Ellen Levy used to scout for working-class boys.

Sam saw the change too, from a different angle. It was as if some restless hunting tribe had been pacified, as LBJ was promising to do for the villagers of Vietnam, and had settled in Harbor Isle, their former warlike ways turned inward until the violence reemerged in their kids.

Ricky had been called names and beaten up. Among the many reasons he loved to visit Lorraine was that he felt safe playing with children who couldn't speak English in the vacant lot opposite her apartment building, much safer than he did going to the candy store where he lived.

But then Ricky saw *Psycho*.

Norman Bates loved his dead mother—and he *was* his dead mother. Norman Bates and Richard Speck and Charles Whitman and the bad kids in front of the candy store were all lurking in the night when Ricky got home from the movies. He was sure of it.

Sam and Eve had gone dancing, so Ricky checked and rechecked the doors, as he always did when they were out late. He got a big knife from the kitchen and a large hammer from the tool box. He turned on every light in the house and waited.

Ricky didn't know where Kelly Street or Hunt's Point Avenue was. His knowledge of World War II came entirely from television and the GI Joe games he contrived on his bedroom rug. If you asked Ricky who Sam and Eve Goldenberg were, he would have paused to think. He lived in a place called Harbor Isle, where nothing of the past was reflected at all. There was only the moment, and the moment was too often fraught with fear.

So when his parents went out and Peter couldn't sleep over, a boy who was old enough to stay at home without a baby-sitter closed up like a clamshell and sat in a brightly lit suburban living room, clutching his father's hammer in one hand and his mother's knife in the other.

1967

As if impelled by an unerring instinct, Susan and Michael Lydon—
something of a "golden couple," according to advance notice on the
Newsweek grapevine—left London and arrived in San Francisco in time
to witness from an appropriate journalistic distance the "First Human
Be-In" on January 14. The Be-In was to be held in Golden Gate Park,
not far from where the city kept a rescued herd of American Buffalo,
and only a mile from the Haight-Ashbury district, a hippie stronghold
from which two or three thousand personal affronts to the dominant
culture were due to emerge for what the hippie organizers called a
"Gathering of the Tribes."

The press releases announcing the Be-In portrayed the event as
something of a ceremonial peace conference designed to fuse the
increasingly radical political rebels from Berkeley with the cultural
rebels—the ever-loving hippies of the Haight—on the other side of San
Francisco Bay. To hostile observers of the local youth scene, however,
there was little apparent difference between the radicals and the hippies
who responded to the call to "celebrate and prophesy the epoch of liberation, love, peace, compassion, and unity of mankind" on that bright
January day in Golden Gate Park. California's governor, Ronald Reagan, had already dismissed all long-haired college students as "bums,"
reporting with some authority that they engaged in "sexual orgies so vile
I cannot describe them to you." But then, Governor Reagan was known
for his rather broad statements, the declaration that the solution to the
war in Vietnam was to bomb the nation flat and pave it over as a parking lot being only one of his bold proposals.

Susan selected a culturally neutral pair of amber "wheat jeans" and a simple black turtleneck for the Be-In. Michael also chose a turtleneck, a garment that had lately cropped up as formal evening wear, its double-thick collar sometimes supporting ponderous peace medallions that dangled on the chests of corporate executives and fathers who wished their children would finally grow up.

Susan and Michael—notebook in hand—zigzagged through the crowd at the Be-In. Susan thought that the gathering of ten to twenty thousand seemed to be dominated by kids from the outlying suburbs, and that she could have been one of them if she hadn't married and become so much more mature. The young hippie girls wore thrift-store lingerie as dresses and sported flowered, stocking-tight body suits. Men and boys wore robes and flowers and grand plumes in their long hair. Kids wore swastikas and Iron Crosses, Mexican *chalecos*, Indian saris, and Kit Carson fringe, turbans, top hats, berets, coonskins, and World War I flying ace helmets. Gigantic bearded men in leather jackets with "Hell's Angels" emblazoned on the back wandered around with walkie-talkies and drug-widened smiles. Members of the motorcycle club had beaten up antiwar marchers in Berkeley not long ago, but in the spirit of the Be-In the Angels seemed just that. Hundreds of tabs of LSD passed from hand to hand. The air was heavy with pot and with the tinkling of hundreds of little bells. The music was supplied by the Grateful Dead, and the audience in Golden Gate Park got up and danced while members of the press helped each other identify radical and countercultural celebrities. Antiwar activist Jerry Rubin, who usually appeared in costume, was there in a New Left work shirt. Allen Ginsberg was in white, and Timothy Leary managed to look like a former faculty member even with a sort of tropical flower arrangement around his neck and in his hair.

Shortly after the Be-In, *Newsweek* published a groundbreaking report from "the hub of the hippie world" by Hendrik Hertzberg, the journalist Michael had replaced at the San Francisco bureau, a former *Harvard Crimson* man and fellow recipient of a 1964 red Ford Mustang. The article launched a full year of national publicity for the San Francisco hippies. "They want to change the United States from within—by means of a vague regimen of all-embracing love," Hertzberg wrote. "They are nonviolent, mystical, bizarre."

By late spring tour buses were clogging the streets of Haight-Ashbury. ("We are now entering the largest hippie colony in the world and the very heart and fountainhead of the hippie subculture.") CBS ran an hour-long documentary about the Haight, and by June, the beginning of the Summer of Love, perhaps one hundred thousand young Americans had left their families behind and come to San Francisco to join the freedom-loving new tribes.

One of the most troubling things about the hippies, in the estimation of many adults, was their apparent antipathy toward the postwar all-American family. The "Betty Crocker–Miss Clairol family institution" was little more than "a death form," according to a Digger quoted in one magazine. (The Diggers, a band of latter-day Robin Hoods, worked to feed the penniless flower children of Haight-Ashbury.) Rick Hertzberg reported in his *Newsweek* article that hippies were "experimenting with new kinds of family systems." In the Haight, "it is not unusual to find two dozen people living together as an extended family unit. The community itself is organized almost as a tribe composed of a series of clans."

"We want to get Western man out of the cities and back into the tribes and villages," Timothy Leary told the crowd at the January Be-In. Allen Ginsberg called for a redefinition of the American family along the lines of an extended matrilineal social unit with all the children raised together. The poet was also a fan of communal orgies, which he referred to by the vastly overused term "sacrament."

Hippies were contemptuous of the very foundations of the traditional American family: hard work and money. And they celebrated unrestricted sexuality. "There are no hippies who believe in chastity, or look askance at marital infidelity, or see even marriage itself as a virtue. Physical love is a delight—to be chewed upon as often and freely as a handful of sesame seeds," Hertzberg wrote. "If this hippie life-style continues to grow at its present rate," warned one student of the family, Professor Richard Fairfield, "marriage and the family will be obsolete by the twenty-first century." The power of the hippies was experienced in American families as the sudden disappearance to the West or East Coast of their sons and daughters. The hippies became a symbol of what family historian Edward Shorter called a "massive uninterest" in parental values.

The Lydon family—Susan and Michael—hung their stylishly framed textiles throughout a sunny railroad apartment on Chestnut Street, atop Telegraph Hill. It was an apartment fit for a golden couple, both of them twenty-four years old and newly arrived from the British front of the changing culture.

"I'm too old to be a flower child," Susan said without regret after the Be-In.

Michael nodded, but as he would later admit in an essay, he had in fact seen the future at the Human Be-In. From then on, he was no longer content to explore life and lifestyles only as a professional witness, and he began to look for an escape hatch and a way to be free. Michael suspected that the transition from upstanding family man and *Newsweek* star to hippie would require "nearly as much unbecoming as becoming, pain as pleasure, forgetting as learning." Until he figured out how to do it, Michael decided to settle down, to continue to be a good husband and a good reporter, to watch and wait.

———◆———

Sheila took the train into the city to spend the night with Lorraine, her urbane, adventurous sister, whom Sheila considered "the goddess of the Lower East Side." Sheila baby-sat for Maggie while Lorraine was working at Azuma. Gina Schick was in the hospital having a baby.

Last year Gina and a fairly long-term boyfriend had decided to have a child, agreeing that their "daring and free" relationship, their private social experiment, would not require marriage. But during her pregnancy, Gina's boyfriend had given her ample reason to doubt his future capacities as a father, married or not. For one thing, he hit her, usually when he was tripping. For another, he was constantly telling her to make her occasional LSD trips daily excursions so that they would have a cool child. Then he summarily disposed of a kitten because it made noise. "What will you do if the baby cries? Get rid of it?" Gina asked. "If you're a good mother, the baby won't cry," the young man replied—ominously, Gina thought.

Shortly thereafter, Gina had kicked her boyfriend out of her six-room, fifty-dollar-a-month apartment and asked her friend Lorraine to be her roommate.

Since then Lorraine and Gina had taken very good care of each other. They made great vats of spaghetti and meatballs. They went to protest marches together and came home to pore over books like *Seduction of the Minotaur*, by Anaïs Nin. Gina helped Lorraine take care of Maggie, a quiet child of two and a half, not so much withdrawn and shy as observant, even thoughtful, if thoughtfulness could be ascribed to one so young. And for hours on end, Gina and Lorraine relived their childhoods together, intent on demystifying the past to break free of it.

Gina had heard all about flying telephones and crawl-space afternoons on Lincoln Avenue, so she was surprised to see such a warm smile on Sam Gordon's handsome face when she finally met him during Lorraine's move to Willett Street. Sam was sitting at the kitchen table in a T-shirt and open windbreaker. Gina was nervous because of Lorraine's stories, and also because she felt generally uncomfortable around "older men," a legacy, she speculated analytically, of her own father's absence.

"Say, um, did you know Willett Street used to run all the way through to Grand?" Sam said shyly. Lorraine's father described the Lower East Side of old, and Gina presented him with some cigars from Cuba. Sam invited her to his sister Sylvia's house for a family dinner. Eve came into the kitchen and began cleaning and cooking as if it was her own apartment. Maggie climbed up on Sam's lap, and he tickled her until she screeched with glee. All the Gordons were laughing and smiling and singing. Gina looked on with envy. Lorraine clearly had "a normal American family." Later Gina told Lorraine, "You come from the family I've always dreamed about."

Lorraine nursed Gina through her morning sickness and spent hours in consultation as Gina agonized over what to do about her pregnancy now that she knew her original plan was a mistake. She could always have an illegal abortion, but even sophisticated women feared the consequences of such a step in 1967.

Whenever Maggie, Lorraine, and Gina went to the kind of event where the police were pelted with flowers when they arrived, like the New York variation on the Be-In held in Central Park on Easter Sunday, pairs of young men would come up and ask them for dates. It seemed there was something exotic and alluring about a pretty, pregnant girl in the company of a mother who looked too young to have a toddler.

Lorraine had promised Eve she'd stay clean when she moved in with Gina, and except for pot, the girls avoided drugs. Lorraine suffered terrible tremors when she stopped using heroin. She felt like a cataclysmic upheaval was happening inside her.

Bobby Shapiro came by often to pick Maggie up, and though she seemed overjoyed when her father arrived, she seemed equally overjoyed when he brought her back. The apartment on Willett Street was the kind of place a little girl, her mother, and a pregnant friend could be happy together. It was the home of a little family.

But everything began to change in the spring. Urban renewal—the slum dweller's most palpable connection to President Johnson's Great Society—came to Willett Street in the form of documents announcing that the city had acquired the building where the girls lived and would soon tear it down to make way for a new structure. As the leaseholder, Gina was offered a preferred position on public housing waiting lists or—if she was willing to move her highly educated but low-income self out of the five boroughs of New York City—a cash payment of over one thousand dollars. Gina had often mentioned her desire to return to California, and later, when she decided to give her baby up for adoption, Lorraine knew she was preparing to leave town and start anew.

Shortly before Gina went into labor, her mother descended from California. It seemed to Lorraine that Mrs. Schick thought she hadn't taken proper care of Gina at all.

Sheila was lying awake in her sleeping bag when Lorraine returned to the apartment with a security guard from Azuma. She was disappointed that her big sister hadn't come home alone so they could stay up late talking. It was always good to talk to Lorraine about life and love. But beyond that Sheila didn't give the security guard a second thought. Lorraine was a divorcée, a woman of the world.

After the man left, Lorraine was overcome with guilt. Ever since her bad LSD trip "shattered" her, she had noticed that waking feelings of remorse and shame translated into dreams of doom, so she'd started taking Mellaril, a pill that blotted dreams away. Now, on her way back to her bedroom after showing the security guard out, she stopped and looked down at her little sister in her sleeping bag, and it came to her that she was failing Sheila and Gina and Maggie and everyone else too. All she wanted to do was sleep. She reached for the bottle of Mellaril.

In the morning Sheila phoned home. Her voice sounded odd. "Mommy…I can't wake up Lorraine. And there's an empty bottle of pills, Mommy," she said, starting to cry. "She won't open her eyes."

"Is Maggie there?" Eve asked quickly.

"Of course," Sheila said.

"Make Lorraine stand up. Call her doctor. I'll be there soon."

Sam had been gone since dawn, so Eve grabbed her coat and sprinted across Harbor Isle in the direction of the train station. She gasped for air all the way to New York. Bursting off the train, she ran to the taxi waiting line, butted in front, and stole the first cab. The Willett Street walkup reminded Eve of the stairs the mother had to climb in *Barefoot in the Park*. Maggie would always stand at the top, impatiently urging her grandmother to hurry, but this time Eve ran up the stairs without stopping.

Lorraine was leaning against a wall with Sheila at her side. Her eyes were half shut though she seemed to be trying to lift her lids by raising her eyebrows. "Wanted to sleep," Lorraine said.

"Yeah, sure," panted her mother.

"All she needs is to be walked around the room for a time," said a woman with a European accent and an attitude that Eve didn't much like.

"What are you, a doctor?" Eve asked Gina's mother. "Screw walking around! I don't have time to walk her around. She's gonna go get her stomach pumped!"

Eve gave Sheila some money and told her to take Maggie back to Harbor Isle. Lorraine went limp when Eve tried to pull her to the door, so Eve half dragged and half carried her daughter down the five long flights of stairs.

"Bellevue Hospital," Eve said to the taxi driver.

Lorraine perked up. "No. No. No. Not Bellevue," she mumbled. "Beth Israel." The doctor who'd prescribed her sedatives was affiliated with Beth Israel, which was a private hospital, unlike Bellevue, a massive public facility.

"Bellevue," Eve told the cabbie again. "That's where you take people to get their stomachs pumped."

At the hospital, an intern came into Lorraine's curtained cubicle. "Do you know what day it is?"

Lorraine squinted up without her glasses, full of contempt. "Yes, I do," she snarled.

"Who's the president of the United States?"

"Some fascist pig by the name of Johnson," Lorraine said.

They pumped her stomach twice. Lorraine was always convinced that the second time was the idea of the patriotic doctor, pumping for the President.

Drug cases at Bellevue were sent from the emergency room to the psychiatric wing, whose director had lately been quoted widely in articles about the stunning surge in drug-related admissions. Lorraine was wheeled into a huge ward where everyone was crying or cursing or laughing and some patients' arms were lashed to the sides of their beds. Eve came in and was immediately reminded of the war-crazed veterans she'd tried to entertain back in the Bronx.

"Get me out of here," Lorraine demanded, squinting at Eve.

"No," Eve said. "They want to keep you till tomorrow."

On the way home, Eve kept worrying about Sam. *How far can a man be dragged down? How much is a father expected to see? Sam won't be able to take this. Sam is a man with family pride.*

The next day, Lorraine was sitting up in her bed when she saw her father standing at the door of the ward in his windbreaker. He was looking from bed to bed, trying to pick his daughter out in the grim, noisy

room. Lorraine stared at Sam and realized for the first time in her life
that he was scared. He stood there blinking, as if to chase the scene
away with his eyelashes. The sight of her father's face, pathetically rearranged, made Lorraine cry.

"Why?" Sam had asked when Eve told him where Lorraine was.
"Why would anybody take a drug?"

Sam had once asked his father the same thing. They'd gone to the
movies and seen a short feature about opium dens. Papa Joe had served
in the Far East with the army. "Opium is one of those things a low-grade
person can do to go even lower," Sam's father said.

"But *why* do they do that?"

"Because some people are just nutty," Papa Joe said.

As poor and hopeless as he'd been at times, Sam could understand
the desire to grab the only kick you might ever hope to have. But this
was his Lorraine. This "episode," as it would always be known inside the
family, meant that his daughter had somehow descended below the level
of misery where he'd started, which in turn meant that he had failed.

Sam finally spotted Lorraine amid the psychos. He lowered his head
and walked slowly to her bedside.

It was Eve who finally checked Lorraine out of Bellevue. As soon as
they got back to the Willett Street apartment, Eve threw her coat aside,
went into the bathroom, got down on her hands and knees, and started
to clean. She scrubbed back and forth over the ancient stains marking
the juncture of toilet and tile.

"Ma, please come out," Lorraine called. "Don't clean anymore."

"I'll take your kid away for good!" Eve yelled, her brush in overdrive. "You're not responsible enough to be a mother! You don't deserve
to be a mother!" The harangue continued to the syncopation of Eve's
scrubbing for half an hour. She finally emerged with nothing more to
say, though she'd decided down on the bathroom floor that she had to
reestablish a sense of personal control.

As soon as she got home she phoned Lou Calderon, the patient
family friend. "Louie, you once offered to teach me to drive," Eve said.
"Is the offer still open?"

Lou said yes.

One of Magdalena Shapiro's earliest memories was a dream. Her mother
was crying hard in the bathroom of their apartment on Willett Street.
Maggie was banging on the door, screaming, "Mommy! Mommy!" But

there was no answer. She was cold and clammy and screaming away when she woke up with Nanny Eve sitting beside her in Harbor Isle.

◆━◆

As Ricky and Peter Randsman were returning on the bus from the arcades along the boardwalk in nearby Long Beach, an older boy got up and walked back to their seat. "You're a little fairy," he said to Ricky. Then he unzipped his fly and urinated all over Ricky's shirt.

A friend of Bernice Randsman's reported that she'd seen Peter and Ricky gallivanting among the young toughs in Long Beach that day. Peter had told his mother he was going out to "play ball with the boys." At dinner, Bernice told him she didn't want him to play with Ricky anymore.

"But why?" Peter asked, his stomach beginning to burn.

"Because he's a fairy," Bernice said. "And I don't like the way he's rubbing off on you."

Perhaps in reaction to his realization that he "couldn't cope" with Lorraine's "refusal to be normal," Sam dedicated a portion of his summer to "making a man out of Ricky." Sam insisted that Ricky join a Little League team.

Little League baseball had been around since 1939, when a lumber executive in a small town in Pennsylvania reasoned that without adult supervision young boys would never stop arguing long enough to play nine innings. The boom years of Little League coincided with the postwar American boom years. At eleven, Ricky was a latecomer to the national pastime. ("One thing Ricky's not," Susan commented to Eve on the phone when she heard the news, "is a Little Leaguer.") Most of the other boys on his team had been playing since they were eight.

Peter Randsman was in his second Little League season. He would run out and stand in the farthest reach of right field, sweat pouring from under his cap, more from anxiety than from the heat. He prayed fervently to the baseball in the pitcher's glove: "Please oh please don't come...please." Every time Peter went to the on-deck circle, one teammate or another invariably came up to whisper, "Don't swing," so he never did.

Ricky had every intention of swinging away and hitting a home run on his first trip to the plate, but the very first pitch hit him square in the eye and knocked him flat, ending his Little League career within seconds of its inception.

Sam took Ricky several miles out to sea in his latest powerboat, the *Evie G. III*. The sea breeze cooled Ricky's blackened eye, but whenever a trough exposed the raw and relentless roar of the engine, Ricky quivered with fear, though he refused to cry. He was determined to make his father proud. He would plunge hooks into the bait now; he would force himself to touch the cold, pearly skin of the fish. Sam finally cut the engine ("Too far away from shore to ever get back alive if something goes wrong," as he told Ricky to no small traumatic effect), and father and son began to fish. Sam reeled in a big one, and Ricky turned and threw up over the gunwale.

On Saturday mornings, the campaign continued with Sam pounding on Ricky's bedroom door at 6:30 a.m., barking, "Let's get to work!"

"Okay now, go get the small adjustable wrench," Sam would say.

Ricky was afraid to ask the obvious question, so he would stand in the garage counting off seconds and consoling himself with the fact that at least he hadn't been ordered into the dreaded crawl space under the house. After a while, Ricky would take a deep breath and go back to Sam. "I couldn't find it, Daddy."

Sam would shake his head and mutter. "Go look again."

Ricky would return shortly. "I've looked and looked."

Sam would get the adjustable wrench himself, and Ricky would stare at it and try to remember its special name.

"He hates me," Ricky would tell Eve at the end of the weekend.

"Nah. Don't say silly things," Eve would reply.

Ricky believed that his father arose most mornings of the week to labor all day long inside deep, dark holes, places no less terrifying and airless than the crawl space. He often wondered how anyone could survive such a life.

Ricky would walk alongside his father on the way to the docks, through Harbor Isle air heavily perfumed with lilac or honeysuckle, and listen to Sam describe the whys and wherefores of the physical world. Like Susan before him, Ricky would sit next to Sam in the car or the truck as Sam explained everything they passed—the power lines, the trees, the factories, the roadbeds, the bridges, the cloud formations, the precise nature of the work being done by anybody they saw in a uniform (assuming the anybody "cared enough to do the job right")—and he would feel more desolate by the minute and the mile. Not only could he not do any of the things his father did; he couldn't even care about the tens of thousands of things his father knew. Ricky wondered if there was anything sadder than that.

* * *

The annual "Summer Rendezvous" from which Ricky floated out to sea one day began with Sam herding Eve, Ricky, and the latest family dog, Marquis de Maximilian III, into the *Evie G. III*. Then they motored out just beyond Long Beach, where they pulled alongside boats occupied by Sam's brother Masons and their wives, children, and assorted pets. The men lashed all the boats together, food and drink appeared in lavish profusion, and the offshore picnic commenced.

As always, Maximilian III whimpered after an hour, indicating his need of a patch of dry land. It was Ricky's job to get into the little dinghy attached to the *Evie G. III* and row Max to shore. Max had become a Gordon by default shortly after Sam's brother, Freddy, presented him as a gift to Mama Yetta, complete with pedigree papers and his august name. But Yetta kept hitting Maximilian with a broom, so Sam, ever a friend to animals, rescued him. Ricky liked the yappy little Corgi.

Ricky was actually a decent rower, with his Camp Lenape training and a strong back, but for some reason the winds or the tide propelled the boat away from shore. Ricky grunted and flailed away with the oars, but if he pulled too hard the boat went in circles, still moving out to sea. Every time the boat turned around, Ricky saw Sam glaring at him.

Sam mounted the bow of the *Evie G. III* and bellowed loud, angry instructions at Ricky. By now all the other Rendezvous celebrants were gathered on the decks of their own boats to observe Ricky's folly. Everything he did seemed to make the boat move toward the horizon. Sam kept screaming, louder and louder, so incapacitating Ricky that he stopped rowing and watched the flotilla of American leisure grow smaller in the distance. Max's little tail stopped wagging, and Ricky gathered the dog in close as Sam's voice boomed across the waters.

Eve joined Sam on the bow. "Get him back," she said.

Sam continued to stare at the dot on the horizon, at his son, his only son, who played with dolls, couldn't find a wrench to save his life, and loved *opera*. "How does a thing like this happen?" Sam would ask Eve. "I mean, I don't want to criticize, but just tell me how a little kid can love opera." Sam wondered if fate had relegated Ricky to a houseful of women for too long. (As a third-grader, Ricky had tried to convince his teacher that he couldn't attend gym class because he had his period.) Sam figured a man launched his children into the flow and then they drifted away on their own, perhaps remembering the few things you taught them about navigation while you had the chance, and perhaps—

as was apparently the case with his children—ignoring you entirely. Sam was beginning to see that the father-and-son summer was not turning out as he'd planned.

"Don't panic," he told Eve. "He knows how to swim."

But Eve had just read a story—or maybe she'd heard it over mahjongg—about a boy who committed suicide because his father tried to make a man out him. "You have to get him back!" she yelled.

Sam sighed and dove off the front of the boat.

Ricky sat hunched up, watching his father swim. When Sam draped one of his big arms across the side of the dinghy, Ricky jumped over him and swam hard in the direction of the *Evie G. III*.

By the middle of the summer Susan and Michael had managed to weigh anchor safely just at the edge of the magnificent countercultural gyre. They could reach out from their elite golden life (journalism, marriage, affluence, post–Ivy League intellectual distance) and still touch and be touched by the currents around them, much as they'd both left the suburbs behind even before they had the nerve to sneak away into the whirl. Again, the secret was the music.

The Lydons were among the more than one thousand accredited journalists crowded into the front seats of an arena set on a bit of coastal plain near Monterey, California. A few feet above Susan's head, at the microphone—*on* the microphone, over and around the microphone, almost as if she could suck it inside while she wailed high and rough— was a girl exactly Susan's age singing the heart out of Big Mama Willie Mae Thornton's blues classic, "Ball and Chain."

"Janis," the singer's mother would often say, "why do you scream like that when you've got such a pretty voice?"

Like Lorraine and Susan years ago, Janis Joplin could never understand why anyone with access to recordings by the likes of Bessie Smith and Big Mama Thornton would ever want to listen to a white girl sing. Still, in 1961, Joplin hitchhiked from Texas to California to be a beatnik and a singer. Now, with the press and an unprecedented audience of fifty thousand in front of her, under a banner that read, "Love, Flowers, and Music," with a band called Big Brother and the Holding Company behind her, she was appearing at the first annual Monterey International Pop Festival.

Joplin sang "like a demonic angel," according to Michael Lydon's "Pop Powwow," as his report was titled back at *Newsweek* headquarters in New York. By the end of "Ball and Chain" her ribbed-knit pants suit was completely soaked with sweat, and her left nipple looked "hard enough to put out your eye," wrote Robert Christgau in *Esquire*. People who saw Janis Joplin live were struck by her physical presence and the sensuality of her performances, which evoked vivid fantasies of fevered sex. "Do it," Janis would grunt and groan in a manner no mother could possibly approve of. *Let go!* she seemed to say with every song.

For three days Susan and Michael ventured out to the music from the little motel room they were sharing, hippie-style, with "crashers" down from San Francisco: poet Michael McClure and two hysterically funny guys from Los Angeles, cartoonist Terry Gilliam (later of Monty Python fame) and comedian Harry Shearer. Twenty-two hours of music were packed into the three days and nights of the Monterey festival. Local Bay Area bands like Jefferson Airplane, the Grateful Dead, and Buffalo Springfield were joined by Simon and Garfunkel and the Indian musician Ravi Shankar. The hippies in the audience—the great majority of them high on doses of LSD that were being passed around like candy—went crazy when Otis Redding, dressed in an electric-green suit right out of the old Alan Freed shows of ten years earlier, crooned "I've Been Loving You Too Long." The Who appeared, direct from London. They performed "My Generation" ("a violent demand for the supremacy of youth," Michael wrote in *Newsweek*) and smashed their instruments to bits at the end of the set. A self-taught guitarist who used to play the Greenwich Village clubs Lorraine frequented came on next. Jimi Hendrix did blues riffs with his teeth, or with the neck of his guitar projecting between his legs. In his orange frock coat, he approached the microphone. "Last night, whew...but...today I think everything is all right. You know, I'm not losing my mind." Hendrix set his guitar on fire, and the crowd roared.

In San Francisco the Lydons had begun to attend rock concerts held in huge dance halls like the Fillmore and the Avalon Ballroom—Sam and Eve's Lido Beach clubs gone hip and wild. Rigged with massive speakers and blinding, pulsating colored lights, the auditoriums were dark caverns meant to be filled with the force of rock music. "Rock palaces," they were called, and after reports about Monterey spread, "rock festivals" were organized all across the nation. The festivals, Susan later wrote, were stages for the new "play of consciousness" generated by rock 'n' roll, and the music, as Michael wrote, was designed to welcome a "nation of fifth Beatles" to a world of pure sensation.

Around the time Michael's boss at *Newsweek* suggested that a haircut might be a condition of further employment, staff star though he was, Michael decided that what he really wanted to be was a "rock critic." Few of the swarm of journalists at Monterey would have been so precious as to describe their fascination with rock as criticism. In 1966, when a Columbia graduate named Richard Goldstein told the editor of the *Village Voice* he wanted to be a "rock 'n' roll critic," the editor asked, "What's that?" But by the time *Sgt. Pepper's Lonely Hearts Club Band* was released that summer, Goldstein's courageous—or foolhardy—review of the nation's number-one album ("busy, hippy, and cluttered" were among his indictments) ran not far from the classical and opera coverage in no less a publication than the *New York Times*. Suddenly it seemed as if the world of rock was an appropriate arena for intellectual and professional pursuit, though not in the opinion of Michael's editors at *Newsweek*, who were much more concerned about the length of their reporter's hair. There were suspicions back in New York that the young Lydons might be in the process of "going native" among the hippies.

If some of Michael and Susan's new acquaintances in San Francisco were hippies in East Coast eyes, they were certainly elite and successful variations on the Haight-Ashbury national media stereotype. By virtue of Michael's *Newsweek* connection, the Lydons' circle included actors, playwrights, artists, rock musicians, rock "impresarios" like transplanted New Yorker Bill Graham, radical lawyers, Pacific Heights socialites, and any number of others who popped up in Herb Caen's famous gossip column in the *San Francisco Examiner*.

Several new friends were associated with the radical national magazine *Ramparts*, which went from monthly to bimonthly publication in June in an effort to become financially solvent. Begun six years earlier as a liberal Catholic journal carrying Conrad Aiken and Allen Ginsberg poems, *Ramparts* had gone on to publish some of the most vivid and controversial investigative journalism since the early years of the century. For many politically active Americans, the thoroughly documented reports in *Ramparts* were in large part responsible for the now widely shared assumption that institutions such as the federal government and its agencies, major American universities, corporations, and student associations were not above wholesale premeditated corruption.

Susan and Michael got to know *Ramparts* writer and editor Robert Scheer, a Bronx boy who had twice been to Vietnam as a journalist and had recently run unsuccessfully for Congress in Berkeley. Susan became friendly with Bob Scheer's wife, Anne, a beautiful Californian who was pregnant with their first child. Soon Susan discovered, much to her delight, that she was pregnant again too.

Bob Scheer wasn't so sure about serious rock writing, but he gave

Michael several freelance assignments, as did Seymour Peck, a respected editor of the Sunday "Arts and Leisure" section of the *New York Times*. "Michael Lydon writes frequently about pop music," read the biographical squib for his *Times* article about soul star Wilson Pickett. He also wrote a long piece for the annual college edition of *Esquire* on the proliferation of underground journals and newspapers.

The prose in many of these underground papers—some personally peddled by their editors and writers to young people standing in line at rock concerts or stalled in foot traffic during protest marches—was often rough and formless, but Michael and Susan were both impressed by the way some of it replicated the rough and formless cultural moment. For several years Norman Mailer and a few other writers had been pioneering a genre of impressionistic, heated, eyewitness journalism that relayed the who-what-when-where of mainstream journalism while also offering the reader a sense of how it felt to be inside an event—the Republican National Convention of 1964, say, as in Mailer's *Esquire* reportage.

To Susan in particular, it seemed that in terms of journalistic truth there was but a tiny leap from describing how *it* felt to describing how *I* felt. The first person was rapidly becoming popular with some of the nascent rock critics, many of whom were unashamedly partisan. Susan's plan upon relocating to San Francisco was to become a writer, not a reporter, yet it now appeared that the new culture had opened a new avenue of journalistic expression.

At Monterey, Michael had met a twenty-one-year-old rock writer named Jann Wenner, who called him at the *Newsweek* office during the late summer. Over drinks, Michael listened to Wenner's enthusiastic plans to start up a new national magazine dedicated to the fact and larger meaning of rock music. He went home and told Susan that Wenner wanted him to leave *Newsweek* to be managing editor of what he intended to call *Rolling Stone*. "How many issues of a magazine can you do about rock bands breaking up?" Susan wondered, but Michael liked Wenner's idea of locating a generation of readers through the music. He began to make phone calls for the new magazine from his desk at *Newsweek*. Susan joined Wenner and a few others in a small office to type mailing labels, answer the phone, and brainstorm together at impromptu meetings.

By fall, Susan was moving around the office with difficulty. Eve had always said it was tough to be pregnant when it was hot. Jann Wenner and some of the other men would tease her in a whining falsetto, mocking her groans and complaints. If Michael was in the office, Susan would wait for him to come to her defense. She always thought it was strange that he never did.

Susan wrote a movie review for the second issue of *Rolling Stone* (the first sold only six or seven thousand copies, though forty thousand were printed). Wenner made her rewrite it because, he told her sternly, "the first person is not reporting." Her second *Rolling Stone* article was a review of another movie, *The Graduate*, "obviously about the generation gap," Susan observed of Mike Nichols's vision of a well-educated young man adrift off upper-middle-class shores until he finds love, both passing and true. "The characters of the grown-ups in the movie, his parents and particularly Mrs. Robinson, his evil, corrupt mistress, are purposely kept hazy." The adults, Susan complained, were "comic caricatures half-perceived."

Michael put the day off as long he possibly could, but rather than lose his job at *Newsweek* he finally cut his hair.

———◆———

Toward the end of the year, flower children began turning up dead in Greenwich Village. Public attention focused on the case of Linda Rae Fitzpatrick, an eighteen-year-old girl from a well-off family who was raped and murdered in an East Village boiler room. Her parents alarmed many other suburban parents when they told reporters that the whole time Linda was running around the Village, barefoot and high on LSD, in the company of a young man known as Groovy (he was found murdered beside her), they had believed what their daughter had told them—that she was "studying art" in New York. Under the headline "Trouble in Hippieland," *Newsweek* quoted a "nineteen-year-old New York hippie": "Linda and Groovy were sacrifices, the movement's first real martyrs. But they showed us something, man. They showed us you can't find God and love in Sodom and Gomorrah. So it's time to split." The article also quoted "a Washington mother": "I wonder if I'm really getting through to my daughter. How can anyone be certain? For all I know she could be leading a double life too. I die a little every day."

Sheila worked after school and on weekends at a local ice cream parlor called Jan's. She was saving up for her move to New York City, a postgraduate experience she was quite sure would be as educational as college and far more exhilarating. Sheila, Peter Probst, and often Ricky went to Manhattan whenever she had time off. On the rare occasions when she wasn't out with Peter, she would retire to her bedroom with the Beatles.

Eve was used to hearing "She's Leaving Home" playing in Sheila's bedroom. "We gave them everything," they sang. It seemed to Eve that they were mocking the fact that parents wanted to understand, as if it were hypocrisy.

Lately, in dribs and drabs—from remarks of Lorraine's that sounded like they came straight from her psychotherapy with a new head-shrinker, from discussions with other parents, from reports in magazines—Eve was beginning to accumulate evidence that the experts concurred with her own gut feelings of guilt and remorse about the family. The problem with "the kids," some of them seemed to be saying, stemmed from secret injuries done to them by their families.

Articles with titles like "The Familial Genesis of Psychoses"—sounding significantly more accusatory than the earlier suggestion that a family might *have* a neurosis—were still restricted to professional publications during the early 1960s. Even the dramatic 1962 claim by psychoanalytically attuned anthropologist Jules Henry—that psychoses were burgeoning because the modern American family transmitted "cultural ills" to children and created a "foundation of insanity"—did not filter far from the psychiatric literature. But now a clinical vision of the family as a complex "unity of interacting personalities" was beginning to emerge through the work of a small but articulate band of "family therapists." In 1960 *Look* magazine had reported on Dr. Murray Bowen and a number of family specialists whose theory and treatment methodology were roiling the psychoanalytic establishment. Dr. Bowen said that after ten thousand hours of therapy with entire families he could no longer see an individual patient without picturing all the patients' family members sitting close by "like phantoms."

The fewer than four hundred practicing family therapists in the country in the late 1960s (Bowen, Virginia Satir, Nathan Ackerman, Donald Jackson, and several others were conducting the most original research in the field) believed that the family was something more than a collection of discrete psyches or the sum of the "object relations" that often accounted for the nature of human interactions, according to Freud. Bowen taught that the "emotional field" of the nuclear family was the source of the self. The family, he and the other maverick researchers contended, was an organic whole, an intricate and delicate system comprised of connections more powerful than any individual force within it.

Lyman Wynne, a schizophrenia specialist, believed that the culturally reinforced "togetherness" so central to the "normal all-American family" of the 1950s had served to mask true feelings and ambivalences. Since families needed to maintain the appearance of cohesion and stability at all costs, rigid "rules" began to govern family interactions. When the rules became too rigid, according to a recent report by a research group working under Margaret Mead's former husband, anthropologist Gregory Bateson, then each communication became at once an assault on the family's symmetry and an attempt to gain control.

In "family system" theory, the family structure remains inscribed in the mind alongside a strict sense of the geometric relationships among family members. Each new message—telling your father to go away when you are two and he suddenly appears, getting pregnant out of wedlock, telling your mother that your father hates you because you're the wrong sort of boy—powerfully affects the equilibrium of the system. So strong are the warring instinctual drives to be an independent individual on the one hand, and to remain dependent and connected on the other—all within the context of a single family—that psychological problems can be passed along from generation to generation, Bowen and his colleagues believed. An individual never leaves the family; it is only possible, he claimed, to "disengage" from the past, to "grow away" from the family web with a certain amount of grace.

Lorraine's new therapist, Lloyd Delaney, was a tall, mustachioed black man, a poet, and a peace and civil rights activist who'd led sit-ins as early as 1963. He told Lorraine and the other patients he gathered for group therapy under the trees of Central Park to call him Lloyd. He wore Nehru jackets and a teardrop-shaped peace symbol around his neck.

Lloyd was a Sullivanian, practicing in the tradition of the late Harry Stack Sullivan, an American revisionist of Freud, who broke with the master's orthodoxy over issues of biological determinism versus the role of culture and society in the formation of personality. Freud described an encapsulated, "intrapersonal," instinctually driven, and invariably conflicted self; Sullivan, who died in 1949, contended that psychological problems derived from attractions and repulsions between human beings. He believed that people needed love, ripened from early maternal tenderness, and that troubled psyches were a function of something going wrong in this delicate process. Sullivan's theories of "interpersonal relations" had inspired Murray Bowen and many of the family therapists, as well as a more traditional practitioner (and believer in bucolic group therapy sessions) like Lloyd Delaney.

Lorraine told Lloyd about the complications of love and anger at 221 Lincoln Avenue. She talked about her father's—and her own—desire to be normal, to be part of a normal family.

The concept of the "normal"—the family's *raison d'être* for so much of the postwar era—was the core of the problem, in the view of R. D. Laing, another of the increasingly outspoken commentators on what appeared to be a psychological and intergenerational malaise. "Normal men have killed perhaps one hundred million of their fellow normal men in the last fifty years," the British psychiatrist wrote in his new book, *The Politics of Experience*. In pursuit of the "normal," families made their children "lose themselves" and become "absurd."

Dr. Laing's reliance on the existentialist concept of the absurd made sense to Lorraine as she observed and participated in the political progression "from protest to resistance" that autumn. The normal men—heirs of the "hardheaded" pragmatism of John Kennedy and his aides—seemed bent on expanding the war in Vietnam, and Lorraine knew many people her age who were determined to stop them. She went to a march in Washington with a man who was packing a gun. She spent time with friends who were active members of the highly disciplined, far-left Progressive Labor Party. As the crowds at marches and meetings became more and more clean-cut by the month, Lorraine's PL friends went on romantic jaunts through housing projects like Masaryk Towers, where she and Maggie had lived since 1 Willett Street was torn down, in search of true soldiers of the working class to come join the cause. The PL people would stop residents in the hallways and ask if they'd heard of Mao. Lorraine listened to them and envied their assuredness. Even Sam Gordon never sounded quite so sure he was right.

Lorraine was also helping Maris Cakars and his wife, Susan Kent Cakars, put out their magazine, *WIN*, a publication of the pacifist Workshop in Nonviolence. Lorraine had recently run into Maris after an antiwar march in Philadelphia. He had just been released from jail, where an angry policeman had shaved off his hair. Lorraine told her first boyfriend about getting pregnant, married, and divorced, about shooting drugs and taking too many pills. "Things got so much more confusing than when we were young," she said. Maris hung his butchered head and looked like he was going to cry. It was true. They had been young together back in 1964, and only three years had passed since then.

Lorraine listened to radicals who told her it was time to resist the immoral forces of order actively, and in some ways the argument made sense. She listened to David Dellinger and other advocates of nonviolence promote a pacifist line at the *WIN* office, and that made sense too. Hippies she knew said that hatred and war could be defeated with weapons of beauty and universal love, and most of all Lorraine wanted to believe they were right.

During a group therapy session, Lloyd Delaney asked if members wanted to experience a mescaline trip together. Lloyd, as the group knew, was an acquaintance of Timothy Leary's. Though some people expressed their eagerness to participate, Lorraine admitted that she was too scared. "Then what you have to learn today," Delaney told her, "is that there's nothing wrong with saying no."

After the session Lorraine rushed home because she missed Maggie. Maggie was her touchstone these days. Sometimes it seemed like the world was disappearing into confusion, but Maggie remained rooted and immovable like a tree.

On the way to her apartment, Lorraine always stopped to cover sleeping Bowery Bums with their jackets. Nineteen sixty-seven was a tough year for many Americans, and she just wanted the bums to wake up and be okay.

1968

Through the caffeinated vapors rising from a cup pressed hard to her lips, Eve watched Sam stroll into the kitchen. "I have to go to the city, Sam," she said in a strangely spiritless voice. "I have to identify the body."

Sam filled his chest and stood at attention. A child of some friends of theirs, a girl of twenty, had recently jumped out of a window and died. Something to do with drugs and various crises of mind and home. It was already clear to Sam and Eve that her parents would never be the same.

"It's my brother Sid," Eve said. "He was hit by a subway train in Brooklyn."

Sid Samberg, who'd helped create the Gordon family of Harbor Isle by pinning a photograph of his own glamorous sister to his army foot-locker instead of Betty Grable, had grown into something of a "with it" middle-aged man, still actively trying to "find himself" at fifty-one. He was working nights for the New York City Transit Authority and taking courses by day in pursuit of his dream of becoming a writer.

According to the family account of Sid's death on February 16, he had an ocular disorder that occasionally gave him double vision. When he looked up at the oncoming train that night as he was working on the track, happy-go-lucky Uncle Sid saw two trains coming at him and stepped out of the way of the one that wasn't there. Sam suffered this illogical analysis of the cause of the tragedy without comment. "Sid, you've got no business working in the subways," he had told his dreamy brother-in-law. He was sure that Sid had failed to follow proper safety procedures, but he decided to allow the apocryphal double-vision story to stand. Sam figured that families could bear only so much reality.

* * *

Something of a pall had settled over Eve's mah-jongg game. The players assumed it was the wildness of the times, the loss of so many subjects of conversation—children—to alienation, family civil war, even death. Harbor Isle's middle-class children were not dying in Vietnam (though children from surrounding working-class communities certainly were— nearly six of ten eligible young men received exemptions or deferments during the Vietnam War, and almost all of them came from families that understood how the system worked), but they were disappearing from the purview of the mah-jongg game nonetheless, out open windows or out into ways of life no more imaginable to their parents than life on another planet.

"I guess I'm not smart enough to figure out what's going on," Eve told the girls after her brother died. "Who can find reasons for things anymore? Who has the time? I don't want to know the answers, and I don't want to know the goddamn questions either."

By the end of February, before the apocalyptic events of spring led into the apocalyptic events of summer, Eve had a sorrowful hunch that the coming year would be one for dying.

———◆·◆———

"I've got a present for you," Sam said.

Ricky gasped with joy. He watched his father slowly unsheathe a thirty-two-inch-long plum-colored glass cylinder fitted into a ceramic electrical fixture. Sam plugged the "black light" in, and suddenly Ricky's Jefferson Airplane poster was hovering weirdly bright and alive several inches from his recently repainted deep-green bedroom wall. Another poster, of a Day-Glo Hasidic rabbi, seemed to vibrate in space. Ricky and Sam exchanged skeletal psychedelic grins.

"Thanks, Daddy," Ricky said.

Ricky's dreams were back-lit in Day-Glo hues. He was the only sixth-grader in Harbor Isle whose bedroom reeked of incense. When the black light wasn't on, he went in for flickering candles. Once Ricky decided to create the largest of all "hippie candles" by melting down dozens of ordinary orange candles in one of Eve's spaghetti pots. When it came time to pour the brew into a gallon milk carton, the hot paraffin broke through and filled each and every crevice of Eve's kitchen floor. She was not amused.

Ricky hammered constantly on the piano these days. From any room in the house Eve could hear him singing his original songs in a loud, earnest voice that occasionally cracked and elevated to a screech (he'd just turned twelve). One of his new tunes, "The Evil Devil," told of an encounter with a dead body on a crowded city street. "It did not seem to matter much to them," Ricky bleated, "but it did to me-e-e-e!" Another of his compositions was entitled "Black Thorn to Hell."

> I saw a black thorn wrapped around an apple tree
> To Mr. Black Thorn I'm singing
> Don't sting me with your evil poison
> But he snapped her up and sucked blood from her thigh
> And he wrapped his venomous fangs around her bones. ...

The refrain went simply, "To hell, to hell, to hell, to hell."

Like his sisters, Ricky said he was "antiwar," though he avoided specifying what this meant because he wasn't sure. Still, he did write an "antiwar ballad" during the height of the ferocious Vietcong and North Vietnamese assault in South Vietnam in January, later known as the Tet offensive. "War brings bloodshed, says you'll die, but it duz-unt say when," Ricky sang out to visitors to Lincoln Avenue. "I say, peace on earth, goodwill to meh-hen....Oh, I wish I was a dove."

Sam saw that Ricky worked at his music like a little trouper, and though he never mentioned it, he was proud of his son's diligence. But Sam was still unsettled by Ricky's adoration of opera. He just couldn't understand that at all.

The very word "opera" gave Ricky a profound physical sensation matched, he said, only when he heard the word "penis." Ricky presented a report to his sixth-grade class on an opera he called "Dee Walker," about "a guy named Sigmund who goes into the wrong house and pulls a magic sword out of a tree." The piece had been written long ago, Ricky told his classmates, by a man named Richard *Wagner*.

"That's wonderful, Ricky," said his gentle, protective teacher, Mr. Sears. "In Germany, where the composer lived, they say '*Vahgner*.'"

Before his terrible accident, Uncle Sid had presented Ricky with an ornate score of George Gershwin's *Porgy and Bess* that he said he'd found in an empty subway car. Ricky placed the score beside an album by a local Greenwich Village band called the Fugs, a recent loan from Lorraine.

One Saturday in early spring, Ricky took the train to the city to see Sheila, who was now "living with" Peter Probst in the same apartment, sleeping in the same bed. At first Ricky wondered if Sheila's scandalous cohabitation with the handsomest of all the Probsts would confirm the local image of "the scandal-ridden Gordon family," which must have been what made Bernice Randsman tell Peter to steer clear of him (though the ban had been lifted in less than two weeks). But after a while Sheila's passionate relationship with Peter became a source of pride and excitement. Before her graduation from Oceanside High last year, Sheila had become embroiled in what Ricky knew to be "a love triangle" involving Peter and his best friend, the captain of the football team. During Peter's first semester away at college, the football player had made a play for Sheila, who dated him briefly. Sheila had missed her prom because of the entanglement, but now she and Peter were living in an apartment on East Seventh Street near the famous McSorley's bar, an institution currently enjoying the last two of its more than one hundred years as a male bastion (the tavern would be "liberated" by local women on August 10, 1970).

Sheila was taking courses at night and working by day at a Wienerwald restaurant, part of a European-owned chain whose decor looked like American Provincial gone Bavarian. She was still wearing her green Wienerwald uniform the Saturday afternoon she took Ricky to her "favorite movie," Luis Buñuel's Los Olvidados. Ricky watched with his mouth hanging open as the tale of a sweet little boy's utter poverty and consequent corruption unfolded. The critic who called Buñuel's film "the single most depressing movie ever made" was not alone in his assessment, but Ricky forced his gaze back up to the screen through the entire gruesome experience, even when the boy's corpse was tossed onto a pile of rubble, because Los Olvidados was his sister's favorite. Sheila also took Ricky to see a French movie called Pierrot le Fou. Susan had told Ricky on the phone that the movie "changed my entire life," and the idea thrilled him—just the thought of living at a time when a single movie could change a life.

Lorraine took Ricky to a movie in which twelfth-century Japanese warriors slaughtered each other unceasingly for a full ninety minutes. Lorraine said Kinugasa's Gate of Hell was her favorite. "Japanese art," she told her little brother, "allows you to feel your spirit." Lorraine and Ricky also went to see a brooding trumpeter named Miles Davis and blues master B. B. King, who smiled as he made a guitar he called Lucille cry like an injured little girl. Peter Probst and Sheila took him to a Laura Nyro concert. The next weekend Sheila took Ricky and Peter Randsman to see the small Amato Opera Company on the Bowery perform Il Trovatore.

Lorraine held Ricky's hand at an antiwar demonstration. A man twisted tubular balloons into the shape of a hat and handed it to Ricky while people behind him waved red flags and yelled "Ho, Ho, Ho Chi Minh!" Ricky knew that all his sisters loathed President Johnson, but he wasn't quite sure why. He could barely recognize the president on television. After the march, realizing that Ricky was bored by all the speeches, Lorraine took him down to the Electric Lotus store on East Sixth Street to see the latest hippie gear. Ricky loved the East Village. It looked like the storybooks in the children's section of the library had opened up and poured their princesses and jesters into the city streets.

Back in Lorraine's poster-lined apartment, Ricky would play with Maggie and examine his sister's reading material: Oriental texts, *East Village Other*, *Avant Garde*, and his favorite, *Fuck You: A Magazine of the Arts*. He loved to read the "Village Bulletin Board" section on the back page of the *Village Voice*: "Become Friends with Your Body; Sensuous Ear Piercing; A New Humanist Dating Service; Theater of Psychodrama; Narcotics Addiction Can Be Cured; Gay Power; Charts by Benida; Eugene McCarthy for President; Ed: Call Home, Worried Sick. Mom, Dad, Andy; Debbie Jane Call Home; Robin—We Miss You— Please Call & Come Home—Daddy."

When Ricky got to the bottom of the page, he'd go back to the top and read it all again.

——— ❖ ———

Shuna Lydon, Sam and Eve's second grandchild, was born on March 20. Susan and Michael appropriated their baby daughter's unusual name from Shuna Harwood, a London fashion editor they'd known. Mocking the recent Bay Area penchant for naming babies after flowers and stars, Michael suggested during the late months of Susan's pregnancy that they call their child "Fireplug" or "Garage Door" Lydon.

Susan wanted to experience natural childbirth. She and Michael joined a class to study the Lamaze method, a variation on the older British techniques Lorraine had tried when Maggie was born. Lamaze was the current preference of local hippies, whose childbirth and other maternal protocols Susan considered above reproach, despite their disdain for traditional family forms. As her contractions grew stronger and the astounding pain became more than she thought she could bear—at the very point when her definition of physical pain was permanently recast—Susan pushed Shuna into the world and immediately experienced a rushing, surging, expansive wave of pleasure unlike anything she'd ever felt. Susan would always remember the euphoria associated with the start of Shuna's life as a "cosmic" sensation, a cosmic childbirth in a cosmic time.

Susan and Michael's friends came to visit, and it was clear to them that the sunny apartment on Telegraph Hill was full of joy. Susan and Michael would hug each other with the calm, pale-skinned infant between them and say they were making a "Shuna fish sandwich." Eve was due to arrive the first week of April, and meanwhile Susan called often and listened to her mother's advice. A paperback edition of Benjamin Spock's famous book remained unopened on her shelf.

By the spring of 1968 it appeared that there were actually two Spocks (three counting the emotionless alien on *Star Trek*): the Dr. Spock who wrote the acknowledged bible of child-rearing, and the radical antiwar activist Dr. Spock. Two days after Lyndon Johnson won the presidential election of 1964, he had phoned the nation's best-known pediatrician. "Dr. Spock," said the president, "I hope I will be worthy of your trust." Now Dr. Spock was facing a jail sentence (along with another member of the establishment, former CIA man and current Yale University chaplain William Sloane Coffin) for "conspiracy to aid and abet" some of the thousands of men who'd burned or turned in their draft cards. In April, a month after Shuna's birth, Columbia students took over the campus to protest war-related research and the university's plans to build a gym on land used by the neighboring Harlem community; Columbia's president, Grayson Kirk, who invited the New York City Police to storm student strongholds, blamed the uprising on "the permissive doctrines of Dr. Spock." A few months later, Republican vice-presidential candidate Spiro T. Agnew singled out Spock and his "permissivist" theories as the cause of the youth rebellion.

Just before Eve arrived, Susan put Shuna in a Moses basket and traveled across the bay to Berkeley for a meeting at her friend Anne Weills Scheer's house. Susan had asked to be included in the regular talking sessions Anne and half a dozen of her friends had recently begun. The Berkeley "women's group," as they were soon known, also included Susan's friend Nancy Bardacke, whose husband, Frank, a.k.a. F.J., was one of the rare Bay Area characters considered both a hippie and a serious radical in good standing. Several of the other women in the group were the wives or girlfriends of various political "heavies," leaders of the local and national antiwar movement.

The women got together for "consciousness raising," an innovation that was just beginning to take hold in the Bay Area, in Greenwich Village, and in university communities among progressive women who were tired of the way they were treated by otherwise politically sensitive men. The current role of women in the hip Bay Area community was indicated by a recent communication circulated around Haight-Ashbury and by San Francisco Diggers seeking to rally local hippies to protest police actions, and published in British journalist David Caute's *The Year of the Barricades*: "Our men are tough. They have style, guile, balls, imagination and autonomy. Our women are soft, skilled, fuck like angels; radiate children, scent and colors like the crazy bells that mark our time."

At the meetings in Berkeley, Susan heard women who were far more involved in politics than she express their frustration over baking brownies and operating mimeograph machines while their husbands and boyfriends mounted the barricades and spouted revolution. Susan spoke up, mentioning that she had been relegated to secretarial duties during her stint at *Rolling Stone*. She listened closely as some of the other women talked about their fathers.

Eve flew into San Francisco and immediately began cooking, cleaning, and refusing to relinquish Shuna, even for a nap. After Susan put Shuna to bed, she and Eve sat together in the spring sunshine on a little terrace overlooking San Francisco Bay. They drank coffee and talked about children.

"Oh, here," Eve said at one point, pulling out a lustrous string of pearls. "This is from your father."

Susan clutched the necklace firmly, with both hands.

Michael Lydon quit his job at *Newsweek* two weeks after Shuna was born. Michael would not, he announced, take another full-time job with a venture as commercial as *Rolling Stone* magazine. He would be a freelance writer. He would be free. "I want Shuna to be proud of me," Michael explained to stunned friends. "I'm not even proud of myself, so I have to make a change."

Michael wanted to "drop out" and so "get in." He wanted to get busy with the job of "being born," as Dylan put it. The counterculture—the music and the hippies and the Be-In—had shown him how important that was. Michael never stopped to question the viability of his plan to live well by his wits, and he never considered the singular economic and historical circumstances that made his easy attitude possible. He simply felt that he had missed too much by "covering the story" of his, the best and most courageous of all generations. Now Michael wanted to be one with his day and drop out. He was a father, after all, and he wanted to make his beautiful little Shuna proud.

Sheila, Peter, Lorraine, Maggie, and various city friends trekked regularly to Harbor Isle for Eve's Sunday meals. At many of the gatherings, Sam would infuriate his children and their guests. "I don't care what they do," he would proclaim. "No kids are ever gonna change a nation."

But on March 31, Lyndon Johnson appeared on television and gave a speech that made Sam wonder if he was wrong. The president sat with a large three-ring notebook open before him, looking like a mourner in his black suit and tie. For half an hour Johnson described his plans to curtail the war effort in Vietnam, largely by restricting bombing to the southern areas of North Vietnam. He called for peace talks with the enemy, and then he glanced somberly off camera toward his wife. "This country's ultimate strength lies in the unity of our people," Johnson said, and then employed a metaphor evoking Lincoln and the Civil War: "There is division in the American house now." He implied that he would work to heal the nation's rift instead of concentrating on the "partisan causes" that had been the daily stuff of Lyndon Johnson's entire political life. Then, with no change of tone, he said, "Accordingly, I shall not seek and will not accept the nomination of my party for another term as your president."

Lyndon Johnson would later recall that by the time he made his dramatic announcement, his life had become a "continuous nightmare." He had dreams of being tied down while thousands of screaming people ran toward him. At night he was haunted by dead children ("The killing!" he railed to his staff one evening), and by day he was haunted by children who hated him. And all he'd ever wanted, like so many tragic fathers too proud to bend, was to be loved.

Across the nation, thousands of "brothers" and "sisters" of the movement congratulated one another after the speech. So crude and Machiavellian had Johnson's maneuvering become that millions of Americans now thought the antiwar "kids" had a point. A Gallup Poll indicated that six of ten citizens disapproved of Johnson's handling of his job. Establishment newspaper editorial writers and even some of LBJ's own advisers were turning against the war because of various pragmatic analyses of the military and political ramifications, but for a time it appeared to the antiwar regulars that they had been heard.

The president had been brought down, Robert Kennedy had joined Eugene McCarthy in the race for the Democratic presidential nomination, and the elated young people who celebrated Johnson's fall were positive they would soon go on to stop a war. By next year, many of them would admit that they almost missed LBJ. At least you could tell what he was up to.

* * *

Four days after Johnson's speech, Martin Luther King, Jr., was assassi-
nated at the age of thirty-nine, shot through the neck less than two
weeks after a group of "seemingly normal guys," as one of their friends in
Charlie Company, First Battalion, 20th Infantry, would call them,
gunned down hundreds of Vietnamese peasants in the village of My Lai.
The American boys at My Lai herded women and children into ditches
and lobbed in grenades. They cut up bodies and tossed the limbs
around.

"People are often surprised to learn that I am an optimist," Martin
Luther King wrote just before he died. He was optimistic because "man
has the capacity to do right as well as wrong, and his history is a path
upward not downward."

King's death dealt the final blow to the warm universalism of the
early civil rights movement, the concept of brotherhood, of the
"beloved community," that had drawn so many young whites to the
cause so passionately. Before the assassination, King had become
increasingly outspoken in his opposition to the Vietnam War, and various antiwar leaders had asked him to declare for the presidency, perhaps
with Dr. Spock as his running mate. He declined, but after he was
killed, many of his mourners realized that Martin Luther King was probably one of the few Americans of his time who had the presence, intelligence, and moral authority to be president of the United States in the
way of the "heroes and patriots" Sam Gordon admired. Even Sam
admitted that great Americans were nowhere to be found anymore.

To some Americans, it was Bobby Kennedy who picked up Martin
Luther King's standard. He too had come to believe that the Vietnam
War was immoral, and a tragic waste of resources that should be used to
address poverty and discrimination. Everywhere he went girls screamed
and crowds surged forward to touch the slender, handsome candidate,
cynosure of hope for millions. Kennedy seemed to float to victory in the
California Democratic primary on June 5. Press reports often mentioned
the "glow" that surrounded him at the Ambassador Hotel in Los Angeles, his wife, pregnant with their eleventh child, at his side.

Then a man rushed forward from the crowd and shot Bobby
Kennedy in the head.

Sam and Eve tuned in the Vietnam War every evening at the appointed
hour, almost as they used to gather for *Father Knows Best*. American
families watched a Saigon policeman fire a bullet into the head of a
young man in a plaid sport shirt—a Vietcong officer, according to

reports—and as the image was reprinted and replayed, the look on the young man's face entered public consciousness alongside Lee Harvey Oswald's grimace when the bullet hit his belly in Dallas. On CBS, American soldiers were shown cutting off the ears of dead Vietcong.

"I'm a patriot," Sam heard himself say when he was challenged by one of the kids. "This is my country, right or wrong." At these words, Susan, Michael, Lorraine, Sheila, Peter, Ricky, and their friends would roll their eyes and relegate Sam to the realm of hopeless cliché epitomized in their minds by the Republican candidate for vice president, Spiro Agnew.

In fact, Sam had never approved of the Vietnam War. He considered the conflict yet another instance of the French finding that they were unable to take care of themselves and contriving to draw other nations in to "shed blood for them." Sending American troops to replace French troops in Vietnam, "an Oriental country where corruption is normal," was ill-advised from the start, Sam said. He also found it impossible to believe General William Westmoreland, and out of earshot of his children he could be heard railing against the use of "body counts" to measure progress against a guerrilla army that hid in the countryside just like the early American revolutionaries.

"This is no war," the family's war veteran would rage at the television screen. "We should just quit it. These wogs have taken guerrilla warfare and turned it around on us." But then the news would switch to the home front, or Lorraine or Sheila would come to Harbor Isle for dinner. "You can't have people rioting in the streets of Chicago!" Sam proclaimed in August when Mayor Richard J. Daley's police clubbed antiwar protesters at the Democratic National Convention. "What kid can tell a president what to do?"

The protesters were not only close to home. They were everywhere: in England, France, Germany, Yugoslavia, and Mexico, where the Olympics Games were shortly due to commence. In China, young members of the Red Guard were literally forcing teachers, bosses, and their own parents to their knees, putting dunce caps on them, parading them through the streets.

Sam and Eve were bewildered by the spectacle of American youth of the postwar middle class rising up against the bedrock conceptions of middle-class society. A congressional committee was investigating "mixed Communist and black nationalist elements" planning "guerrilla-type operations" in the United States. To Sam and Eve and millions of other Americans, the divided house seemed to grow more divided by the day.

Even at work Sam saw it. He was shocked by some of the young men he met on job sites. "Ah, come on, Sam," they'd say, "why don't you loosen up and try some pot?"

"They said it like there's nothing wrong with it," Sam reported to Eve.

"What did you say?"

"I said, 'I don't need your pot because I've always known where my life's goin'.'"

The rampaging students at Columbia took over the university president's office and drank up his liquor, just as Sam's kids and their friends used to drink up his stock in the playroom before he put in a lock. "I know of no time in our history when the gap between generations has been wider or more potentially dangerous," said President Kirk. Marshall McLuhan said the "generation gap" was a clash between a generation raised in front of a glowing television that magnified and glorified all things, and a generation that grew up before TV. The eminent psychologist Erik Erikson claimed that dissenting American youth were only playing out the secret desires of their parents in ways the parents could not bear to see.

"Fuck," "motherfucker," or permutations thereof were now visible on classroom and barracks walls, as well as in Sam's playroom. "Fighting for peace is like fucking for chastity" went the popular campus slogan.

The grinning midwesterner, Humphrey, was closing in on the resurrected Californian by the closing days of the presidential campaign. "I don't think either of 'em are any good," Sam sighed in early November. "I'm sitting on the fence until the last minute."

Then, at the last minute, he and Eve both voted for Nixon.

<hr />

Peter Randsman was at his friend Connie's house twisting the blond mane of her new Tressie doll into a French braid when Ricky ran in, gasping for breath. "I think I just burned down the haunted house," Ricky said. "I think I did."

Peter was concerned about his best friend. Ricky had only avoided suspension from school a few weeks earlier because of his mother's eleventh-hour intervention.

"Let me ask you something," Eve said, storming into the principal's office. "Do you smoke cigarettes?"

"Yes, I do," the principal said, "but I don't—"

"Well, you are not going to suspend my son from school for smoking until you quit yourself. And that's that."

Then Eve took Ricky to the family doctor, who had once worked in a prison, Gordon gossip had it. "If you continue to smoke," Dr. Forrest said, "you will die, Ricky. Your body and your heart are trying to grow, but your smoking is killing the process. If you want to grow up at all, you must quit."

"I just can't do it. I can't quit," Ricky lamented to Peter. "I love smoking too much."

Ricky phoned Dr. Forrest himself. "Are you *sure* you're not exaggerating? Other people say I won't really die."

"You will. You may reach thirteen, but I assure you, if you continue to smoke, you will die. It's as simple as that," Forrest said.

Ricky began sneaking out of the house in the middle of the night to forage the streets of Harbor Isle for what he called "juicy butts," which he would smoke with the neighborhood "hitters." The hitters were tough kids who smoked banana peels and sniffed gasoline fumes looking for a high. Peter Randsman didn't understand why Ricky sought the late-night company of the hitters, and Ricky didn't tell him it was because he was doubtful about making it out of seventh grade alive.

At an assembly, Ricky had performed "Oh, I Wish I Was a Dove" and several other original tunes to an uproarious ovation and subsequent hallway compliments that went on for weeks. And yet in gym class, the teacher called him a "fag" in front of the other boys, just because of the way he dribbled a basketball. Then there was the humiliation of the "slam books." The first slam book—a spiral notebook passed from desk to desk so that each student could write frank comments about others in the class—had appeared among schoolgirls in New Orleans in 1949, the year Sheila was born. After nearly two decades of liberating candor, slam books read like precursors of the brutal truth-telling sessions favored by the "human potential movement" that would flourish in the 1970s.

When the slam books came to Ricky, he saw words like "fag," "sissy," "homo," "girl," and "fem" beside his name. The list grew longer all the time, and Ricky began to see each slam book as a new edition of his death warrant.

Ricky often met Eve for lunch at Jackie's Doughnuts, a little place that was close to his school and to the new building Sam had just built on Austin Boulevard in Island Park as headquarters of the growth industry that was SGE Electric. Eve was now the office manager as well as the bookkeeper.

Ricky tried to tell his mother he was scared at school.

"Don't worry, honey," she'd say. "Everybody has things like this happen at school."

So Ricky turned to the hitters, hoping they would protect him. Not long before he rushed into Connie's house looking for Peter Randsman, he went to a party with some of them. When everyone else had gone home, Ricky was talking to Gil, an older boy who wasn't particularly tough himself but was friends with the truly tough kids. Gil asked Ricky if he wanted to play a game. Then Gil took out his penis. "See if you can make your mouth touch it," he said.

Ricky thought this was a stupid excuse for a game, but in his fervid desire to please, he brushed his lips against Gil's penis.

"Ee-yew," Ricky said.

Then Gil did the same to Ricky.

The second time they played the stupid game, in an old house by the water that kids in Harbor Isle thought was haunted, Ricky and Gil accidentally set fire to a mattress. They thought the fire was out when they left. An hour later, volunteer firemen backed away from the flames and let the ramshackle structure burn to the ground.

During the following week, it seemed to Ricky that every remnant of the masculinity he'd been trying to understand and display for so many years—for his manly father, for his mother, who seemed to love and defer to his father's manliness, even for his three sisters, who cried over their guitars and beside their record players for all their men—was stripped away. Older, bigger boys began to knock Ricky down, to bully him into corners and punch him, to beat him up at every opportunity. It turned out that Gil told the hitters that Ricky had given him "a blow job." After several days of taunts and physical abuse, Ricky still didn't know what a blow job was.

"You-oo blew Gi-il."

"Hey, blown Gil lately?"

Ricky didn't even know who some of the boys were. All he knew was that they would probably kill him soon.

Eve was driving in the direction of Green Acres Mall with Ricky when a carful of boys pulled alongside. They were gesticulating at Ricky as if they wanted him to roll down the window.

He did.

"How's Gil?" they all began to chant.

Ricky quickly rolled the window up. He glanced over at his mother, who was staring more than intently over the dash, her eyes unnaturally wide. Ricky had noticed that behind the wheel, Eve looked like someone who'd just spotted an oncoming tractor-trailer moving head-on into her lane. The thing that most terrified Eve was the idea of hurting someone. Ever since she got her driver's license, she'd had regular nightmares of hurting a child with a car.

Ricky looked over at the boys, who were pointing at him and howling with laughter. Then he turned back to Eve.

Not then—not ever—would Ricky tell his mother that every kid in town wanted to kill her son because they believed he'd administered something called a blow job to a boy named Gil. He settled back into his seat next to Eve, staring just as hard as she was out the front window of the car, four eyes jacked wide open by fear.

<hr />

Of all the children of Sam and Eve Gordon, Sheila experienced by far the most graceful entry into the broad orbit of the counterculture. She was weighed down by only the tiniest of claims to political outrage (the sense of futurelessness she shared with so many peers after the murders of 1968, a feeling that underscored her childhood observation that those who stood up and spoke out would be hated and shot down), and she had a willing and equally enthusiastic traveling companion in Peter Probst. Most important, Sheila loved the launching compound called LSD—which an estimated one million Americans had tried by 1968.

Inside the perfect bright rainbow of her first LSD trip, Sheila powered weightless and true through the most breathtaking scenery. A turn of the head caused flowers to bloom; a kiss unleashed a tornado of sweet sensations that curled up and around her entire body. Feelings of euphoria were laid out as if on a buffet, and insights flamed up like shooting stars, dissolving the edges of doubt and fear. Like Aldous Huxley in his legendary last epiphany, Sheila seized the cosmic chance to say, "Of course." She tripped again and wondered how a miraculous drug that unlocked such sweet glory could ever be associated with desperation or despair.

"Tell me you didn't feel full of love and happiness," she'd say to Lorraine.

"I didn't feel full of love or happiness," Lorraine would snap. "I fell into a black tunnel. I thought the world was doomed, and for the record, I haven't begun to recover to this day."

But Sheila floated on LSD clouds. High together, she and Peter Probst would discuss their plans. First they would go on their own Magical Mystery Tour. They would simply take off toward the setting sun, touring the Arcadian republic like vagabonds or Beatles in Peter's recently acquired Volkswagen van, the counterculture's Model T. They would play music in the car. They would follow their well-lighted dreams.

"And I want a farm," Peter would say. "In California. Out on...the land."

Former high school jocks and handsome regular guys like Peter had by now embraced the "drug culture" previously associated with bookish, less coordinated, and more political types. A countercultural pose offered the camaraderie of the high and a general relaxation (of work ethic, sexual taboos, dress restrictions, upper limits on stereo volume) that fit in like a puzzle piece where the old team spirit had been. Tickets to the counterculture were widely available during 1968, even as the shooting and street fighting raged. *Hair*, the "Tribal Love-Rock Musical," brought a carefully packaged rendition of the Age of Aquarius to Broadway.

To a nineteen-year-old girl who didn't want to replicate her parents' life, who didn't feel the need to change the whole world, and who was in love with a boy who felt the same, the counterculture looked like a new way of life designed by God.

◆

By the end of the year there was tension in the Lydon family.

Michael stopped in regularly at the *Ramparts* office, site of Susan's first full-time job. He would arrive with Shuna in his arms, and Susan would take the baby into an empty office for her midday feeding. Susan emerged one afternoon with Shuna and heard one of the *Ramparts* senior editors discussing a feature assignment with Michael. *Ramparts* was willing to send him on the road in Texas with country singer Johnny Cash.

"He doesn't know shit about country music!" Susan fumed to the sympathetic members of her women's group. "Michael knows I've been a Johnny Cash freak for years. My sister and I played Johnny Cash songs on our guitars. I can still imitate Johnny Cash. And *I'm* on the staff of the magazine, not him. This is just the same old shit. Not one female rock writer has been sent out on the road with a band." She went on to tell them how Michael's *Harvard Crimson* and *Yale Daily* buddies were welcomed to *Newsweek* as trainees and shortly as full reporters while a brilliant Vassar classmate like her friend Lyn Povich was given a secretarial job in the Paris bureau. "Lyn had to call the correspondents 'mister.'"

At home, Susan told Michael that she deeply resented his incursion onto her musical and professional turf. "You know I should write about Johnny Cash," she said.

"I can't understand where you're coming from, Susan. I don't think you should be so upset," he replied. "Let's face facts. You're my competition now. When bad things happen to my competition, I'm kind of glad."

Susan's women's group had lately been discussing love, sex, and work. For several months, they concentrated on the specific issue of competition with your man. Only a year ago, in a widely used sociology text, Louis Wirth had reiterated the dominant view that in modern urban American life, intimate personal relations had been replaced by "impersonal and rational" obsessions with money, things, and the self. This was true of every single one of society's institutions, Wirth's thesis ran, except for the special haven of the nuclear family.

"I was speechless," Susan told Anne, Nancy, Suzy, Consie, and the other women in Berkeley. "I mean, how can a husband want his own wife to fail?"

As much as she resented Michael's travels with Johnny Cash, Susan was uneasy about flying to Chicago to cover a women's convention at Thanksgiving. The trip would mean weaning Shuna, though Susan would not have dreamed of discussing her dilemma with her superiors at *Ramparts*. The wives and girlfriends of senior *Ramparts* editors had lobbied hard to get Susan hired as a "woman writer," a campaign they framed as a matter of civil rights, an effort to end what some of the newer feminist texts coming out of New York City would call "six thousand years of male oppression." "Okay, Susan, I'll hire you," Bob Scheer had said. "But you have to promise that you won't cry in the office."

Susan stood underdressed and damp in the slush at a Chicago forest preserve, her breasts aching and full of milk, as some two hundred radical women from all over North America discussed ways to distinguish the concept of "women's liberation" from the reformist and seemingly middle-class goals of the National Organization for Women, founded by *Feminine Mystique* author Betty Friedan in 1966. The "liberation" of women had first been discussed in SDS circles that same year, and four or five consciousness-raising groups had begun to meet in late 1967 and early 1968. Now, from one such group in New York, emerged the Women's International Terrorist Conspiracy from Hell. The women of WITCH railed against the "Imperialist Phallic Society" on the floor of the New York Stock Exchange and at the Miss America Pageant in

Atlantic City. A small constituency was beginning to form around an ideology more radical than the ideas of Betty Friedan.

A contingent of women at the Chicago meeting wanted to bar a member of the "mainstream" press like Susan from the proceedings, so she had to wait while one of her friends from the Berkeley women's group argued her case and eventually got her invited inside.

It was true that Susan was mainstream. She was writing about the counterculture, but her articles ran in the *New York Times*. She contributed a regular column to *Eye* magazine, the Hearst Corporation's attempt to cover the psychedelic scene. The *Eye* logo appeared in the sort of Day-Glo rainbow shades observable on the packaging of supermarket products by the end of 1968, and the magazine carried articles like "Almost Instant Flamboyant Fluorescent Decal-Decorated Car." Each issue of *Eye* contained a free "Big Fat Wall Poster in Psychedelic Color," and the advice columnist prefaced her insights about boyfriend problems or parent problems with lines like "Heloise digs your attitude."

In the "Electric Last Minute" section of *Eye*, Susan reported hip San Francisco news. Country Joe McDonald, leader of Country Joe and the Fish, "took a wife," she related on one occasion, and she wrote a brief note about "an Oakland militant Negro group" called the Black Panthers. Susan explained to the readers of *Eye* that the Panthers (several of whom, including Eldridge Cleaver, she'd talked with at length at the *Ramparts* office) believed in cooperating with "sympathetic whites" and bearing arms in case unsympathetic whites tried to attack them.

Susan was not a "movement woman" like many of the others in her women's group, and Michael was not, for that matter, a "movement heavy." He was even willing to do house chores while Susan went off to *Ramparts* to work.

When she returned to San Francisco, Michael told Susan about the "groovy" Thanksgiving dinner he and Shuna had attended. Their undiapered daughter had urinated all over the lap of movie star Shirley MacLaine.

Michael was fond of the kind of Bay Area hippie-speak that made Susan want to punch certain locals in the nose: "into your head," "your own thing," and the catchall adjective "groovy." Susan couldn't stand it. He talked incessantly about needing to "get closer to the youth scene." Susan desperately desired to do the same thing—she wanted to trip away on LSD every single day, she wanted to sate her sensual longings with intense erotic experiences—but she didn't think she could become one with her times within the numbing confines of monogamy. Michael seemed as idealistic and naïve about the counterculture as he had about JFK. He was one of those men who hung back from the forefront taking notes, like a race car driver "drafting" in the vacuum created by the lead cars speeding through the air.

Susan wanted to touch the glow, to feel the sparks raining hot on her skin.

Most of their friends, radical and not, still considered Michael and Susan Lydon a "golden couple." Still, some of them did wonder if perhaps something was wrong when Michael and Susan left a year-end holiday party separately, both of them forgetting that Shuna was still asleep in one of the bedrooms near the coats.

"You know what, Michael," Susan said when they were back home together. "Everything is not groovy."

1969

Ricky became a bar mitzvah—a son of duty, a man—in the late spring of the year Dwight Eisenhower died, the year Neil Armstrong walked on the moon and Richard Burton consecrated his love for Liz Taylor with a million-dollar diamond nearly as big as a cueball. The bar mitzvah boy's parents had told him to buy any suit he desired for his special Saturday. As he rose from his chair and stood poised before the large crowd at the Island Park Jewish Center, most of the celebrants judged the result one of Sam and Eve Gordon's mistakes.

Ricky appeared to be wearing orange shoes. Not the dull orange of the leather boots he'd purchased a year earlier, but a particularly bright shade. Over a white Nehru-style shirt adorned by a single black stud, Ricky wore a luminous tuxedo jacket in a deep, dreamy blue favored by the lounge singers for whom the rented jacket was designed. The tuxedo was bordered with rich black piping velvety as the Randsmans' wallpaper, the whole effect suggesting a Day-Glo poster under black light.

Ricky didn't know what the Hebrew words he was reading from the Torah actually meant, but for five years he'd spent two afternoons a week and every Sunday morning learning to master the pronunciation. With the same enthusiasm he put into his performance of "Black Thorn from Hell," Ricky threw himself full force into his lines, reaching for the little grace-note yodels like an aspiring cantor, albeit one who had passed through a religious education and a modern Jewish boyhood without understanding very much about his religion at all.

For Ricky, Peter Randsman, and most of their Harbor Isle friends, being Jewish meant being able to parade their freedom in front of the Christian kids outside the classroom window during the fall High Holidays. What Ricky knew of the Judaism of his Mama Yetta he'd derived entirely from a trip to New York City to see *Fiddler on the Roof* and from his observation that her faith seemed to be largely compounded of superstition and fear. The Holocaust still inhabited the Gordon household as it had when Susan and Lorraine were small. Sheila had pored over Sam's corpse-laden "war books" as Lorraine had before her; Ricky dreamed of the blaring Gestapo sirens in *The Diary of Anne Frank* as Susan had listened to the sound of the Nuremberg Trials through her Bronx bedroom wall. The Judaism of loss and terror Ricky associated with Europe and his grandmother. He knew enough about what Yetta called "the murders" of twenty-five years ago to surmise that for his grandmother being Jewish was like being haunted.

Asked to name the sacred institution that commanded Sam Gordon's fealty and faith, Ricky did not hesitate: "The Masons." Ricky knew that Sam had once been a bar mitzvah boy himself, but he understood from his father's stories of his childhood that Sam became a man when he was forced to lug buttons through the garment district for a handful of change. As for his mother, she was Jewish in the style of Milton Berle or Danny Kaye. The most Jewish thing about life at 221 Lincoln at all times except the two High Holidays was the food that came from Eve's kitchen. Ricky often heard his sisters decry the hypocritical, ornamental Judaism observable in "materialistic" suburbs like Harbor Isle. "We rarely had Sabbath candles on Friday nights," Susan would say. "It's like they left being Jewish back in the Bronx."

In 1966 *Time* had run a cover story about an apparent mass falling away from organized religion. Provocatively called "Is God Dead?," the article quoted Simone de Beauvoir as saying that it was easier for people to "think of a world without a creator than of a creator loaded with all the contradictions of the world." Three years later, many Jewish children of secularized postwar families were actively repudiating the faith of their forefathers.

This was cause for concern among the rabbinate. An epidemic of marriages to non-Jews, and what Dr. Judah Nadich of the Park Avenue Synagogue in Manhattan called "the growing ignorance of the Jewish heritage," were worrisome enough, but both trends paled before "the open hostility" of young Jews who'd moved into the public spotlight in ways that embarrassed their parents. Jewish children seasoned at the dinner table were now in the streets, still talking loudly of racism and exploitation on the part of their elders. By some estimates over one-third of all New Left activists were Jewish, and by the spring of 1969 there was hardly a suburb with a Jewish population where the local gossip wasn't full of sons and daughters whose pictures had appeared in the paper "for the wrong reasons."

In the fall, two Jewish men named Hoffman faced off in a federal courtroom in Chicago. Judge Julius Hoffman, seventy-four, of German Jewish extraction, was a distinguished representative of the establishment; defendant Abbie Hoffman, Yippie leader, of Eastern European stock, was apparently bent on making the establishment look at once foolish and murderous. To many American Jews, the confrontation was like an airing of dirty family laundry in front of the whole world. "You're a disgrace to the Jews, runt!" Abbie Hoffman screamed at the judge before the conspiracy trial of the Chicago Seven was finally over. "You should have served Hitler better!" When Allen Ginsberg testified at the famous trial, he was asked to recite *Howl*. At one point the poet addressed Judge Hoffman thus: "Moloch the stunned governments! Moloch whose ear is a smoking tomb! Moloch whose blood is running money!"

Sam and Eve were not among the great number of American Jews who now searched the newspapers, shaking their heads over certain resonant last names as Jews had done back in the days of the Rosenbergs. The younger generation's rejection of the faith actually enabled Sam and Eve to overlook the extent to which they had both fallen away from theology, ritual, and formal prayer. Most feasts and fasts observed during their childhoods now passed unacknowledged, as also seemed to be the case in the majority of Harbor Isle homes.

Eve Gordon kept the faith by tossing Yiddish words into jokes and conversation, though she found herself asked to translate more and more often. Sam Gordon still had a knee-jerk reaction whenever talk turned to his children's paucity of Jewish friends. Less than a year earlier Sheila had abruptly exited Sam's car at a stoplight several miles from home, after he'd demanded a census of her Jewish acquaintances. Sam still mourned his oldest daughter's intermarriage, and he feared that Sheila would soon follow in Susan's footsteps. Sam believed that his running commentary and, more than that, his pain were signs of his lasting loyalty to the Judaism of his forefathers.

And of course there was Ricky's study of Hebrew—a mitzvah culminating that fine spring day as Sam and Eve's only son stood alone before the community, sealing his Jewish-American postwar boyhood by reading a solemn pledge always to live according to the highest ideals of his faith and to dedicate himself to the Torah. Ricky recited the words clearly in the language he did not understand.

* * *

After the ceremony, Ricky stood at the reception beside a huge turquoise cake, grinning from ear to ear as his mother—resplendent for the occasion in a shocking-pink minidress, a big pink hat with a turned-up brim, and an extremely *now* pair of white stockings—went to the microphone and began to sing an old Al Jolson favorite, "Rock-a-Bye Your Baby," segueing into a stylish rendition of the Judy Garland hit "You Made Me Love You."

Ricky was overjoyed. He adored the sound of his mother singing. After working on his latest composition at the piano or practicing a classical piece for his next lesson, Ricky liked to bang out the opening flourish of one of the hundreds of show tunes his mother knew. He would play the introduction to "If He Walked into My Life Today" or "As Long as He Needs Me," and if the Broadway melodies didn't immediately depress her—as they still did sometimes—Eve would appear in the kitchen doorway, wiping her hands on a dish towel. She'd stride majestically to the piano and place her hands on Ricky's shoulders, chiming in at the appropriate moment in the artless, almost casually clear voice that once won Evie Samberg a prize in Central Park: "Did he need a stronger hand?" she would croon. "Did he need a lighter touch? Was I soft or was I tough? Did I give too much?"

Eve occasionally cried at the end of a song. Ricky would cry too, and if Peter Randsman was there—enraptured as always by the very idea of a mother who could sing so beautifully—he would join them.

When Eve finished singing and the bar mitzvah celebrants stopped applauding and whistling for the mother of the day (the band broke into "Get Back," the Beatles hit), Ricky grinned his way through a room packed tight with Gordons, Goldenbergs, Sambergs, and dozens of other relatives and friends. He came upon his beaming father, who was posing for pictures. Sam was wearing a brown suit and a fedora, its brim cocked down toward one eye.

Susan, who had flown in for the occasion, was dressed in one of her Swinging London outfits, a white mini crosshatched by a barely discernible geometric print. With her glimmering stockings, pale Mary Quant Chelsea-girl makeup, and simple haircut, Shuna in her arms, she looked like the perfect with-it mom. Sheila also looked stylish on Peter Probst's long arm in an outfit from Paraphernalia, one of Ricky's favorite Greenwich Village shops. Lorraine, Ricky thought, was looking rather prim in a chiffon pants suit she'd made herself. Her gold shoes matched the gold lamé purse she was clutching, and her hair was parted in the center and pulled tightly away from her oval glasses. Maggie, now four and a half, stood close by her mother's side, taking it all in.

My Jewish sisters, Ricky thought. *An Anglo-Saxon, an Island Park Catholic girl, and an Oriental.*

Ricky continued to shake hands with people who were clearly staring at his shoes. He wove through the crowd bravely, gathering *mazel tovs* and wet kisses, though all he really wanted to do was locate the magnificent Jody Pilchik.

When Jody had accepted the invitation to his bar mitzvah, Ricky felt for the first time that his years of Hebrew school were worth the effort. Ricky was in love with several girls, but he was so completely in love with Jody Pilchik that he would walk up and down in front of her house for hours. Ricky wrote poems for Jody. He'd discovered from her friends what her favorite songs were, and he sat in the living room at home and played them over and over.

Since Jody Pilchik inhabited a seventh-grade social plane a bit loftier than Ricky's own, other girls had filled in as surrogates. Ricky and Peter Randsman tended to court and break up with girls as a team. They'd recently broken up with two Harbor Isle girls, and Ricky's girlfriend had been so crushed that she'd thrown his silver ID bracelet down a sewer and made "phony phone calls" to the Gordon house for more than a week. Sometimes Peter felt like "a dork" with his girlfriends because Ricky was so self-possessed, and much more adept at "getting stuff off of girls," by which Peter meant petting and kissing deeply during Spin the Bottle. One seventh-grade girl who'd gone with both Ricky and Peter had said to Peter, "You know, Ricky is so much better at playing with my tits," and Peter was so mortified he almost started to cry.

Peter's mother had been furious at her husband when he recently promoted the idea that Peter and Ricky should "see Times Square" instead of going to the Metropolitan Opera House, their usual destination on the day trips they were now allowed to take alone. In February, Ricky had "run away from home" to see the great soprano Roberta Peters in *Lucia di Lammermoor.* Sixteen inches of snow had fallen on the New York metropolitan area; six thousand travelers were stranded at Kennedy Airport (three people were found dead in the parking lot). The Long Island Rail Road was shut down for much of the day of the performance, but Ricky still defied Eve's orders and went to the Met.

"Sa-a-a-m!" Bernice Randsman yelled. "What are you doing? Times Square is disgusting."

Much later, Sam Randsman would admit to Peter that at the time he thought a day in Times Square might be just the thing to make

Peter's "natural sex drive" kick in and overpower the unsettling effeminacy his father thought he exhibited sometimes.

Ricky wore a pair of new Lancelubber "elephant bell" trousers to Times Square. The pants had a fly no more than three inches long, and the material down at the ankle flared out like a tuba. He also had on the handmade leather sandals he'd purchased during a recent journey through the Village with Lorraine. The sandals had woven thongs that crisscrossed above Ricky's ankles like a centurion's footwear.

The boys were strolling up Broadway when Ricky was drawn to a dilapidated shop. A small sign said, "SEXUAL PARTS COVERED," and Ricky saw a scattering of books and magazines with photographs of hard-muscled men and soft-looking women, all of them grimacing and undressed. Ricky instantly felt like he was on fire.

One of the Catholic boys from over the bridge had shown Ricky and Peter pornography three years earlier. Ricky still kept one of the boy's magazines, wrinkled and dog-eared, under his bed at home. Inside the magazine were pictures of a man named Roland and some woman. Ricky liked to look at Roland's penis. But it was Peter who had their first orgasm. He showed Ricky how to do it when they were taking a shower together one day, and once or twice afterward they soaped each other up and down, but their interest soon waned. Every so often, as Dr. Kinsey had discovered so many all-American boys did, they had jerking-off contests in the playroom when Sam and Eve were out.

But at the sight of near nudity in the window of a *store*—with uniformed policemen and little old ladies strolling right behind them—Ricky and Peter squealed with excitement. Ricky charged the door of the shop, but a man stopped him. "Get outta here," he said.

"I'm much older than I look!" Ricky said, which at least made the man laugh.

They returned to the window, moving up and down the tiny stretch of Broadway like caged tigers in a zoo. At one point Ricky glanced up from a photograph of a naked man and found Peter staring back at him. Though they would not speak of it at the time, or for several years to come, neither Ricky nor Peter would ever forget the silent moment they shared in front of the window in Times Square, because they both realized within the duration of the glance that as Ricky would later put it, "something was brewing."

On the ride back home, Ricky tried to imagine the male organs hidden by the black electrician's tape someone had placed over the photographs in the shopwindow, and Peter daydreamed about a janitor at school. Every day Peter waited for the dark-haired, mustachioed janitor to pass by his open classroom door, and then he entered a vivid fantasy of following him into the boys' room and pulling down his pants. The fantasy always ended there.

Peter never told Ricky about the janitor, and Ricky never told Peter that he dreamed about tearing the electrical tape off the pictures behind the smudged window for weeks on end.

During his search for Jody Pilchik, Ricky spotted the yarmulked heads of Michael Lydon and Peter Probst towering above the crowd. The brother-in-law and the brother-in-law-to-be (Sheila had revealed their secret plans to Ricky) both looked comical because of the way the skull-caps floated tenuously atop their long hair. Peter Probst had come to the event in a bright purple shirt and a suit jacket he'd purchased the previous weekend under Sam Gordon's watchful eye.

Peter and Michael were convulsed with laughter. They were staring at Aunt Sylvia, her husband, Harry—whom she and everyone else in the family called "Chummy Doll"—and her daughter, Precious. Presh was abundantly layered in makeup, and Ricky wondered if her gigantic hairdo had been designed around one of those cone-shaped rubber markers used at highway construction sites. Seconds earlier, Michael had approached Sylvia and her family. Shaking Harry's hand, he'd said, "Hello there, *Chummy Doll*"—at which he'd reeled away in hysterics. Now Peter and Michael were doubled up in the middle of the room as Michael kept wrapping his Boston accent around the phrase "Hello, Chummy Doll."

For her part, Aunt Sylvia harbored strong opinions about Susan's Yale boy. "Brilliant. Brilliant. *Brill*-iant," she would grant. "But *ul*-timately, the boy's like a dead lox."

Continuing through the crowd, Ricky heard his grandmother's voice. Yetta was complaining about "certain senior citizens" with whom she played cards in Queens. "I don't just mean afraid to lose. I mean quarter-point types. People who waste a woman's time ..." Then he saw Susan approach Yetta with Shuna in her arms and hold the sleeping baby under her great-grandmother's gaze.

"Do you want to see, Mama Yetta?" Susan asked.

Yetta didn't move her head. Her eyes descended briefly. "Well, Susan, she certainly doesn't look Jewish."

Ricky thought Susan was going to cry. He watched her turn and rush away, and then he followed her through the crowd toward Eve.

As all of Ricky's friends knew by now, Susan was in the process of becoming famous. She had recently written a *Ramparts* article contrasting the Beatles and the Rolling Stones (she found the Beatles essentially "bourgeois"), and another about a movie starring Vanessa Redgrave as the great dancer Isadora Duncan. Susan declared that the commercial intent of the movie had obscured Isadora Duncan's truly revolutionary womanhood because "our culture is still not ready to accept any woman as a hero....she had to be debased....Isadora opposed the degradation and dependence imposed on women by the marriage contract and maintained the right of women to love and bear children freely as they chose."

If her published prose was any indication, Susan had suddenly recovered the intense political commitment of her Vassar days. Her return to ideology had been inspired by the increasingly frank sharing of intimate information in her consciousness-raising group, where the women began to perceive their personal relationships as predicated on power, not unlike politics.

Susan had not only returned to politics. She had also embarked on an extramarital affair with a hippie who worked in the *Ramparts* mailroom, and she had finally taken LSD. The sparks were flying, and as far as the mother of a one-year-old child was able, Susan was "getting free."

Most of the women in Susan's consciousness-raising group had recently shed or replaced their men. Anne Weills and Bob Scheer had split up, and Anne was now living with Chicago Seven defendant Tom Hayden, main author of the SDS Port Huron Statement and arguably the consummate movement heavy. Susan's friend Consie Miller had broken up with *Ramparts* editor Sol Stern.

Michael found out about Susan's affair not long before Ricky's bar mitzvah. He was crushed. He immediately started looking for a new place to live, away from circles of women who gathered secretly and plotted. He would soon move out of the house to Mendocino County. So as not to ruin Ricky's day, Susan and Michael had decided to keep their marital news to themselves.

Several people came up to Susan to brave a comment on another of her *Ramparts* articles, which Eve had been passing around Harbor Isle. A polemic called "The Politics of Orgasm," it had made quite a splash in vanguard circles where more and more women were beginning to call themselves "feminists." The article was in part the result of the no-holds-barred discussions of sex in her women's group. It turned out that many of the women had miserable sex lives, that several of them rarely experienced orgasm, and that all of them fantasized about a much richer erotic life.

"The Politics of Orgasm" opened with a succinct review of Freud's contention that as a developmentally healthy girl grows to womanhood, sexual feeling is transferred from the clitoris to the vagina. Freudian revisionists had challenged the thesis as early as the 1920s, but Susan drew upon more recent research into the physiology of sex, arguing that the findings of Dr. William Masters and Virginia Johnson, as reported in their 1966 book *Human Sexual Response,* obliterated the Freudian doctrine that women who could not "progress" from clitoral to vaginal orgasm (i.e., to dependence on a man) were neurotic, immature, and masculine. Susan went on to decry the fact that Masters and Johnson's research, which showed conclusively that all female orgasms, however achieved, are centered in the clitoris, had as yet had no impact on other psychoanalytic orthodoxies such as "penis envy." The reason, according to Susan's powerful essay, was that the outmoded analysis served to render women "sexually, as well as economically, socially, and politically subservient."

When Susan arrived in town for the bar mitzvah, Sam took her aside. "I read that article," he said.

Susan braced.

"I'm no kinda literary genius or anything, but that article was entirely clear to me. Some Puerto Rican could pick it up and understand it—unlike one of your illustrious husband's articles," Sam added. "I don't know what it is, but Michael writes things you need a dictionary and a Philadelphia lawyer to figure out. But your articles are clear. It sounds like you really knew what you were talkin' about too."

Then he strolled away, leaving Susan too happy to speak.

Lorraine stood listening to her brother-in-law hold forth to one of Eve's cousins about the absurdity of Nixon's decision, as the American death toll in Vietnam passed thirty-four thousand, to step up bombing raids to historic levels of intensity while the peace talks continued in Paris. When he finished, Lorraine said, "You know what, Michael? You sound so…I don't know, so detached. It makes me wonder, if somebody was about to jump out the window, would you grab them or just keep talking at them?"

Michael knew he was detached, and all he wanted to be was more detached, and reconnected to what really mattered. Back in the Bay Area shortly after Ricky's bar mitzvah, many young people his age who'd retreated from apparently futile protest into the easier "lifestyle" of the counterculture would be shocked back into action by the sheer brutality the Berkeley police unleashed against demonstrators protesting the University of California's plans to close off a vacant lot the local street people called People's Park. But as police shotguns wounded nearly fifty Berkeleyites and killed one, Michael had already moved to Mendocino County, where his rent in Elk, a tiny coastal town, was all of sixty dollars a month. Michael wouldn't even have to do much work for pay, except to go off on an occasional tour with a band he liked. In 1968 some sixty-nine percent of Americans told pollsters from the Yankelovich organization that yes, "hard work always pays off." By 1969 only thirty-nine percent agreed that this was true.

Michael would chop firewood in Elk, gaze out at the sea, and "get high with a little help from my friends," as he put it. Michael wanted simply to *be* what he was doing at the moment—a "cook when I cooked, a writer when I wrote, a dreamer when dreaming." Of his marriage he would say, "It was a thing of another time."

Lorraine realized that she resented Michael's cool political dissection because she feared that her own political passions lacked sophistication. She felt the same way when she read "The Politics of Orgasm."

When Lorraine wasn't taking courses at City College or working part-time for the Dell Publishing Company (she'd just proofread the paperback edition of Eldridge Cleaver's *Soul on Ice*), she was pursuing her own brand of feminist consciousness by playing and singing with a three-woman band called Goldflower, after the heroine of a popular contemporary Chinese tale. In the course of the story, Goldflower is sold into slavery by her husband's family and learns to fight back with the help of the people's revolution.

Goldflower's other members were Laura Lieben, a gifted guitarist with a knack for complex vocal harmonies, and Beverly Grant, who had one of the most wonderfully bluesy voices Lorraine had ever heard. Bev could make her voice go all gravelly and powerful, like a man's. She was also much more serious about women's liberation than anyone else Lorraine knew. Back in 1967, she had joined the first women's consciousness-raising group in New York (there were several claimants to the distinction "first women's group in the country," including Susan's Berkeley group). The next year, as members of WITCH, Bev and her CR group friend Robin Morgan, a poet and increasingly prominent feminist activist, had made the papers after they set off a stink bomb at the Miss America Pageant during the evening-gown competition.

Bev was four years older than Lorraine. She grew up in Portland, Oregon, where her father never had much luck keeping a job and her mother worked long hours to support a family of eight. One of the songs Bev wrote for Goldflower was about her family gathering around the television set when she was young, wishing they could be like the families on the screen. Lorraine got choked up every time they practiced the number. Bev made some money singing in a trio with her two older sisters until she graduated from high school. She moved to New York, met and married a black jazz musician, worked for years as a secretary to support him, and eventually got divorced. "You can't begin to really understand political oppression unless you understand the oppression of being a woman," Bev would say.

With Sam's financial assistance, Lorraine had become the proud owner of a Gibson SG electric guitar, which she'd fitted with a set of Super-Slinky strings so supple she could make the instrument moan and weep, almost like B. B. King with Lucille. Lorraine's sweet, clear voice was so different from Bev's husky wail that Goldflower's sound was startling, and if the reaction of their earliest audiences was any indication, damn good.

Bev and Lorraine both wrote songs about getting over men—specific men and men in general. One of Lorraine's Goldflower numbers went:

> I think that I became a woman today
> I got to do things my own way
> Can't play the love game any longer
> But you know each day I'm getting so much stronger.

She wrote another called "Make That Journey":

> Our lives have been full of illusions
> and it's time we make peace with our souls
> There really is a way out of all this confusion
> I found a way to be whole.
> Helping each other we can make the goal
> Come on and make that journey home.

Bev said it was uncool for Goldflower to accept assistance from men while lugging their huge amplifiers on stage, so Lorraine was often suffering from muscle spasms by the time the new "girl band," which was gaining notoriety in lower Manhattan, finally began to play. Goldflower had appeared at several political rallies and at an event billed as a "women's dance," where no men were allowed.

Lorraine had stopped shaving her legs and armpits, which bothered some of the men she knew so much that she'd begun to see body hair as a handy way of smoking out sexist men. But Lorraine was covered up for Ricky's bar mitzvah, because she was sure that the extended family would expect to be scandalized by their divorced, dope-fiend (she assumed that word of the "episode" of April 1967 had spread), hippie-radical-rock relative. As she clutched the gold lamé purse she'd borrowed from Eve, Lorraine was determined to look and act the part—in every antiquated sense of the term—of a "good girl."

Ricky knew that the stylish dress Sheila was wearing at the reception was one of the sole survivors of a closet purge that had winnowed her wardrobe down to several embroidered peasant blouses, two pairs of brightly patched blue jeans, and a Mexican wool poncho. He had seen the closet empty during his cherished visits to the communal home in nearby Rockville Centre that Sheila and Peter now shared with a young couple named Kenny and Sue; their two-year-old son, "little Kenny"; another young man; a one-hundred-pound reticular python named Jenny; an ever-changing population of rabbits and mice that ebbed and flowed according to Jenny's appetite; various smaller reptiles; and a veritable pack of dogs, several sporting red bandanna collars (both a current canine fashion statement and a political statement about "oppressive" leather collars that impinged on a dog's freedom).

Sheila and Peter had decided to leave Greenwich Village for this quilt-filled suburban ménage. Peter was now an apprentice steamfitter, following, at least during working hours, in his father's footsteps. ("Because of the union, the kid's bringing home—if you can call it that—five hundred bucks a week," Sam said disgustedly.) Sheila had decided to stop taking college courses. She was working at a photographic processing lab, though she would have preferred to be a photographer. Her teachers at the Art Students League on Fifty-seventh Street in Manhattan had encouraged her to develop her obvious knack for photography and drawing, but just as she'd refused to continue piano lessons in a family full of accomplished musicians, she restricted her picture-taking to hundreds of shots of Peter Probst. By fiddling with lighting, camera angles, and lenses, Sheila made Peter taller, tougher, cooler, and even more handsome than he really was.

"He's got no culture, and she thinks she's gonna change him," Eve would worry over mah-jongg. "What if she marries Peter because she thinks she can change him? You can't change a man. You can temper him a little, but they just don't change."

If Susan was now drawing the sort of sustenance traditionally provided by the family from a tight-knit group of like-minded liberated women, and if Lorraine now identified herself first and foremost as a member of Goldflower, then Sheila had become a kind of mother to the crowded, colorful family in the house in Rockville Centre. Bearded, long-haired Kenny and his wife, Sue, were college graduates and had been something of a charismatic couple back at school, it was said, always at the front of the protest marches with their baby on their shoulders. Dozens of their friends mingled easily with the construction workers and steamfitters Peter brought home. Many of the girls were Jewish and upper-middle-class; many of the boys were not. Religious differences and the apparent divide between the higher and lower echelons of the middle class—the same "otherness" that had been so titillating and bothersome to Peter and Sheila and their friends on either side of the Harbor Isle bridge—now seemed to be erased by a countercultural ethos that made a family member out of anyone willing to stir the soup in the common kitchen.

Experiments in progressive, joyful, harmonious communal life now ranged from the daring coed dormitories that had been established at many universities to "alternate societies" like the Morning Star Ranch north of San Francisco, founded four years earlier by Bay Area musician Lou Gottlieb, who invited anyone interested to come live with him in "a place called Morning Star." Popular San Francisco rock bands like the Grateful Dead and Jefferson Airplane shared houses and regarded themselves as family. In contrast to the cage of blood families, the communes that were springing up most prominently in New York, Boston, and San Francisco were to be "postbiological," with roles defined by mutual support and the democratic, utilitarian allocation of authority, instead of the luck of the genetic draw. "The White House," prophesied Yippie leader Jerry Rubin, "will become one big commune."

Some of the new communes were ideologically based, and some, like Sheila and Peter's, were more easygoing and haphazard, but all of them shared the conviction that the traditional family was oppressive. Still, "family" remained the essential metaphor for these intentional communal associations, which some 3.5 million Americans would soon claim to have tried. Even the horrifying crimes of the non-nuclear Manson Family in August tarnished the word only briefly.

Sheila was the responsible one at the group house, more den mother than earth mother. The family dogs were under no circumstances allowed in Sheila and Peter's bedroom, and she often skipped the parties and bar-hopping the others enjoyed after big dinners and long discussions topped off by drugs. "Really, I want to stay. You guys go ahead," she'd insist. She liked to straighten up and put little Kenny to bed.

On weekends Sheila and Peter went camping in upstate New York. They'd build a fire and talk about California and the piece of land they would buy. Peter's job allowed him to work and save money for a few months, then take off for another few. Besides, they didn't need much money. All their belongings now fit in a knapsack. "I want to raise crops when we get the farm," Peter would repeat as they huddled beside the campfire. Then, on Sunday night, they would drive back to the suburbs, to a house loosely organized around some new ideas about doing "the family thing" right.

Sam Gordon wore the biggest grin at Ricky's reception. "This is what a family lives for," he kept saying to relatives and friends.

Lately Sam was given to remarking, "You just don't see happy families anymore. Go to a store and watch them shop. Go to a park....Where are they? Families are breaking down."

It was certainly true that the divorce rate was higher than at any time since World War II. Magazines carried articles about "runaway wives" who placed their own happiness above family loyalty. One historian of the family detected growing "indifference to family identity," a new "instability in the life of the couple," and a wholesale demolition of the "nest notion" of the nuclear family—alarming news if ethologist Konrad Lorenz, author of *On Aggression*, was correct in asserting that an individual could not "evolve all his inherent faculties unless it's done within the frame of the normal family."

Sam loved Ricky's bar mitzvah because it was heavy with family feeling. It was a joyous day. "Show me a normal, happy family," Sam would say most other days. "Just look into any backyard—even an Italian backyard. You just don't see happy families together anymore." He would sometimes turn to Eve while they were watching television or driving. "What happened?" he would ask.

Eve could fill in the rest of the question, but she didn't know what had happened to normal, happy families either.

Ricky despaired that Jody Pilchik must have had enough of his bar mitzvah during the ceremony and gone home, but then he spotted her standing with some other girls just outside the reception hall. He took one long look at Jody and tried hard to be a man and not to cry.

"It's her mother. Her mother did it to her!" Ricky told Peter Randsman as they trudged through Harbor Isle together later in the day. Ricky kept shaking his head. "She looked so *terrible*." Jody Pilchik's gorgeous hair had been done up for the bar mitzvah in outlandish fat curls. Her mother had taken her to Arlene's Beauty Salon in Island Park, and Arlene, as Ricky put it, had given her "sixty-year-old hair!" He couldn't believe it.

Peter had spent much of the long day being jealous of Ricky's bar mitzvah. So many people had come. So many gifts had been given. And that electric-blue jacket Ricky had been allowed to rent! Bernice and Sam Randsman had called the little party they'd given Peter an "unofficial bar mitzvah," but Peter knew his mother associated religious observance with hypocrisy and that was why he hadn't had a bar mitzvah of his own.

But now Peter didn't feel jealous anymore. Now it was just Ricky and him again, side by side.

<hr>

By the middle of the summer it seemed that the largest of all American generations had been cleft in two, with those who attended the Woodstock Music and Art Fair or claimed they had in one camp, and those who missed it in the other. Two Gordons represented the family in the mud at Bethel, New York. One had a good time.

By the time Lorraine got to Woodstock, the toilet paper was already gone. She was early enough to penetrate the dense perimeter of the crowd. As she waded toward the music, she felt the escape routes closing behind her with each step. She couldn't stop wondering if she would ever get out. Meanwhile, Sheila and Peter pulled out their camp stove, lanterns, tent, and portable tape player, and decided to make the best of being stuck more than a mile from the stage.

Susan's friend Country Joe McDonald (*of course*, thought Lorraine) was up on stage with the Fish doing a rousing rendition of his 1965 antiwar song, "I Feel Like I'm Fixin' to Die Rag." Country Joe led the crowd in a responsive spelling of the word that was chiseled into Sam's playroom wall and would still have brought dinner to a halt in the middleclass homes from which most of the happy half-million chanters hailed.

Gina Schick and her new husband, Hal, a ranking SDS member, were visiting Lorraine in New York in early August and had planned to accompany her to the music festival. But Hal said he had better things to do than lie around with a bunch of stoned-out suburban hippies and make some promoter rich, so Lorraine had traveled upstate with a friend from her therapy group. Just when she thought a drink of water might help her stop feeling so short of breath, rumors passed through the crowd about "bad acid" in the water supply. Enterprising concertgoers were soon selling cups of water they claimed they'd collected from the falling rain, but Lorraine decided it was safer to drink and eat nothing at all.

By nightfall, she was parched, starving, her muscles cramped from panic. Lorraine felt the loud music pounding her down into the mud, like a hailstorm beating crops into the wet earth. The laughing, smoking, rocking crowd was sucking away her air, and the weird, blasting light from the stage turned all the faces around her into the cackling green witch in *The Wizard of Oz*. Lorraine tried to concentrate on the music, but she felt like she was back in the crawl space, a brick in each hand, the beat urging her to hurry up.

An Indian guru arrived by helicopter to bless the festival. A handsome man with a huge, flowing beard, Swami Satchidananda sat crosslegged on a white corduroy bedspread. "The future of the whole world is in your hands," he said. "You can make it or break it....The entire world is going to know what American youth can do for humanity." The swami went on to observe that music is the celestial sound, something Lorraine had known for a long time, though it was calming to hear it from this gentle-voiced man.

From helicopters bearing gurus and photographers, Woodstock looked like a new culture spontaneously generated over six hundred rolling acres, a teeming instant sixties subdivision. For many Americans this same aerial view of Woodstock would become the defining image of the generation of kids who loved rock and drugs and didn't want to die in Vietnam.

"Where do you live?" Judge Julius Hoffman asked Abbie Hoffman from the bench.

"I live in Woodstock Nation," Abbie said.

But right in the middle of it, Lorraine did not feel at home on the hallowed ground. Woodstock was closing in on her, as Eve's kitchen sometimes did on a bad day. Lorraine put her head down like a fullback and charged out in search of air. She finally broke free and began to walk as fast as she could until she found a bus stop four miles away in a town called Liberty. The last song she heard before she left was Jimi Hendrix's rendition of "The Star-spangled Banner," technically so precise, she thought, his guitar turning the anthem into a screeching wall of plaintive sound.

❦

Though Ricky continued to wonder for many years how a person actually went about "becoming a man," he was sure that his childhood had

ended three months after his bar mitzvah, in the middle of his first experience with LSD.

Allen Ginsberg said that everyone over fourteen should try LSD at
least once, but Ricky and some of his friends believed that thirteen-
year-olds were getting older all the time. Within a ten-yard span of Long
Beach boardwalk, retailers pushed a wide variety of popular recreational
drugs. One evening at dusk a young man offered Ricky "the safe trip,"
displaying several huge capsules bigger than the Darvons every mother
in Harbor Isle seemed to take for headaches. Each capsule was packed
with white powder. "It's all natural," said the man. Enough tales of LSD
babies born with wings and gills and suction cups had circulated to
make dealers and trippers alike entertain the conceit that their LSD was
"organic mescaline." The first reports of the potential genetic damage
some scientists said LSD would cause had been carried in the *East Village Other* under the bold disclaimer "Don't read this if you're tripping."

Ricky had first smoked pot a year earlier with Sheila and Peter
Probst when Sam and Eve went away for a weekend. Peter had drawn a
"far-out, trippy" portrait of Bob Dylan, and though Ricky hadn't felt
much at all, he was convinced Peter's artistry was connected to the
drug. He also noticed that taking "a toke" with Sheila and the gang at
the communal house in Rockville Centre was a ticket into their incredible world. Pot meant he wasn't the irritating little brother anymore. But
when it came to LSD, Sheila played down the delirious, sun-filled glory
of her own experiences. She and Peter admitted that it was pretty damn
great and all, but Sheila stopped short of saying that it was the source of
perhaps the most pleasurable moments of her life. "It's a lot different
than pot, and you're only thirteen," she'd caution. "Don't even think
about it."

From his general cultural knowledge Ricky deduced that an LSD
trip felt like a Day-Glo poster looked. How bad could that be? He knew
Lorraine "had a bummer" on LSD, but he wasn't sure of the details of an
event two years old, a historical expanse that by mid-1969 seemed to
many Americans, not only a boy of thirteen, like a very long time.

"Take a half," said the guy on the Long Beach boardwalk.

Ricky took a whole and went off to see his Harbor Isle friend April,
who lived with her family in an apartment above Chuck's Marina, a
working boatyard at the edge of town. April was known at school for
her love of black. Her clothes were black, her bedroom walls were black,
her sheets were black, even her window shades were black. Ricky
respected her consistency, if not her taste.

At April's house, an hour or so after leaving the boardwalk, Ricky began to laugh so hard that he was gasping, harder and harder, until he barely had time to empty his lungs of air and inhale. Then he got scared and stopped laughing abruptly. He looked around April's black bedroom and noticed that it was a bit smaller than when he'd come in. He stood up and went to a much larger room that opened onto a terrace overlooking the water. An empyrean acid light blasted through the picture window, and Ricky was so dazzled he couldn't see. When his vision cleared, even the big room was much too small. Then he realized that it was *the world* that was too small. *Bummer,* he kept trying to think. *I know what this is. I'm freaking out....I've flipped.*

"April," he yelled, "you have to get me to...THE HOSPITAL!"

April, who'd seen a few movies in her time, stood toe-to-toe with Ricky and slapped him across the face. "Calm down," she commanded. "Snap out of it."

Ricky walked home. He looked up at the moon, where men would soon walk on the Ocean of Storms, and he saw a churning, leaping ring of angry color curling around it like the last rush of smoke before an explosion of flame. "I'm gonna die," Ricky said out loud.

Eve was asleep, but Max came down wagging his tail. Ricky fell to his knees and hugged the annoying little dog, the only being who could save his life. Ricky sat on his bed holding Maxie's face in his hands and stared into his eyes, cold nose to hot, until he decided that what he really needed was for his mommy to tuck him in. He was halfway up the stairs when he heard Sam come through the front door. Ricky bolted back to his room and threw up all over everything.

Sam stuck his head in and crinkled his nose. "I drank too much," Ricky managed. "I'll clean it up."

A few minutes later, Eve came into Ricky's room and sat down on his bed. She talked quietly to him for hours while Ricky wept.

Just before sunrise Ricky got to sleep. When he awoke on a windy morning, he went outside and looked at the green grass and the swaying trees. He gave thanks for every shrub in the yard, tears filling his eyes.

A week later, before his piano lesson, Ricky smoked some pot with a friend and felt a crackling above his ears. "I'm thinking so hard that my hair is burning off my head!" he said, though his friend tried to assure him he wasn't really on fire. Ricky rushed to the bathroom after his lesson, filled the basin with water, and plunged his head in over and over. The room was closing in again, only this time there was a door. The looming portal before him was the single most terrifying thing Ricky had ever seen. He watched the door open, and all of his worst fears—the sidewalk humiliations, the name-calling, Norman Bates, the Anne Frank sirens of doom...all of it—entered him. "This will be me forever," Ricky thought. "I am tragic."

Ricky's piano teacher heard him crying uncontrollably and phoned Eve.

"I'm going crazy, Mom," Ricky said when she came to pick him up.

As soon as he got home, Ricky called Lorraine, and within minutes the sound of her calm voice began to "bring him down." She talked in a loving whisper, drawing on a body of wisdom only someone of her experience could understand. Like everyone she knew, Lorraine kept a spare Thorazine in her medicine cabinet.

Eve held Ricky's hand until he went to sleep. "It'll be okay in the morning. Everything looks better in the sunshine," she said, quoting Al Jolson in a voice almost as soft and full of knowledge as Lorraine's.

The next day Eve took Ricky to see Dr. Forrest. "There's no telling how many times the symptoms will reappear," the family doctor said with his usual authority after Ricky admitted taking what he thought was mescaline. "These visions might come back for years." And sure enough, every time Ricky felt a bit strange at night, he'd remember what Dr. Forrest said, and the visions would return. Then Eve would leave her bed and come to him. She'd hold his hand and talk until the horror went away.

Nearly eighty years ago, William James had introduced his landmark *Principles of Psychology* by declaring that "there is one main, everyday notion of reality to which we always return from outside spheres of reality like art, religion, mysticism, dreams, drugged states, sex, play, and ritual." Back in the old days, when Ricky was twelve, he would have agreed, but now he knew that people could return to reality changed by a visit to "outside spheres." By the end of the year Ricky had stopped eating in restaurants or accepting offers of chewing gum from friends. He feared that everything he ate or drank might be laced with LSD. He carried a Thorazine tablet in his pocket at all times. He tried to make sure he was always near a telephone so he could call his mother or Lorraine to say he was once again paralyzed by the thought that he would never feel happy or safe again. Ricky said he felt "broken" now, not so much by the drug itself, but by the thought that the door to his worst fears would never close again.

———◆———

On December 3, the family's flower child got married. Peter Probst and Sheila Gordon went to a local justice of the peace and exchanged vows in the presence of their immediate families. Only Susan was missing. She had deadlines to meet. The Rolling Stones were coming to town. "And besides, you shouldn't be getting married, Sheila," Susan said on the phone. "You're a kid."

Sheila never allowed it to cross her mind that her parents, in Long Island parlance, should have "made" her a big wedding. Members of her family had been married without fanfare since the days of the Goldenbergs. The celebration was thrown by the communal household in Rockville Centre. Eve and Mrs. Probst both contributed to a feast the housemates had been preparing for days.

Sam and Eve were still dazed by Susan's recent revelation that she and Michael were no longer living together. "Should I be shocked? The man had to cook his own food and clean his own house. Should I be surprised?" Eve said when Susan called, but this was armor, like her jokes. In fact she was more than shocked.

"She's in love with him," Eve said to Sam. "I'm positive of it."

Two of their three daughters had hurtled out from Sam and Eve's family circle into combinations that hadn't held. And now Sheila was marrying her Probst. But theirs would be a new sort of marriage, they said. It would be a marriage dedicated to following their dreams.

Sam stood by and watched his least angry and "oppressed" daughter marry "her *sheygitz* union steamfitter." *This is what passes for a happy family*, Sam thought, looking around the hippie commune camouflaged among the suburban homes. *This is the future*.

Michael Lydon spent the last months of the decade in the company of the infamous Rolling Stones.

"We used to be like a pack," the band's drummer, Charlie Watts, complained to Michael one night before a show, "like...a family, in a way."

Guitarist Keith Richards came offstage, away from the thrumming hysteria of another crowd, and said to Michael, "I wonder what these kids are *like* now."

Herman Kahn, a conservative student of social trends, claimed that all the worry (usually from quarters other than the Rolling Stones) about what young Americans were "really like" was entirely unnecessary. "Mainstream society can handle having thirty percent of its people reducing life to a child's game," Kahn said. At decade's end, many observers were noting that at least since the time of Aristotle young people had appeared to their parents as a volatile and threatening class but had always been slapped into reality by the inherent demands of growing up.

Others were less sure. "These kids will never fit back into the machine. They've been bent," said Timothy Leary, who was right there on the stage on December 6 when the Rolling Stones began to play at the Altamont Speedway outside San Francisco—a name that to the huge audience gathered there seemed destined to join Woodstock, Carnaby Street, Telegraph Avenue in Berkeley, the Village, the Haight, Grant Park, and all the other shrines of the world lit by the special glow of a new dawn.

Susan and Shuna had moved into a little house in Berkeley. Susan painted each of the rooms in bright colors: one was red, one green, and one a very bright purple. Sometimes when Susan was aloft on LSD, she liked to get down on the floor in one of the colorful rooms and observe Shuna at play, marveling at the little life she'd help make. There were few things that didn't hold the possibility of epiphany for Susan these days.

She was collecting unemployment compensation, for which she qualified because *Ramparts* had been going in and out of bankruptcy protection since February, and she'd recently written several freelance articles, one about the takeover of Alcatraz Island by radical American Indians, and another, for the *New York Times Magazine*, about actress Ruth Gordon and her husband, writer Garson Kanin. The Kanins had managed to stay married for twenty-seven years—just like Sam and Eve. "In all successful marriages, I've observed," Garson Kanin told Susan, "a delicate balance has been found."

When Susan wasn't writing or playing with Shuna or contemplating her daughter from a chemical peak, she liked to knit or sew. Outside the oppressive nuclear family, she found these activities soothing and even creative. Susan often thought she was well on the way to finding a balance that would protect her when she felt overwhelmed by regret.

Michael loaned his official Rolling Stones concert tour button to the occupants of a huge white van ferrying eighteen Stones fans from Berkeley to Altamont. The button allowed Susan and the others in the van to park backstage at three in the morning.

Michael had spent much of the evening wandering through the eerie floodlight that shone on an even eerier crowd. This was not the typical mix of college students and postsuburban flower children, but "weirdos,…speed freaks with hollow eyes and missing teeth, dead-faced acid heads burned out by countless flashes, old beatniks clutching gallons of red wine," as Michael would later write. By morning three to four hundred thousand people were straining against a four-foot-high stage guarded by Hell's Angels. By the time Santana had finished their set, it was clear to Susan and Michael (who strolled the stands together to catch up after a long while apart) that the Angels, who'd gently tended lost children at the Be-In only three years earlier, had resurfaced at Altamont as motorcycle thugs. They looked ugly and hungry, like the Morlocks in H. G. Wells's *Time Machine*, up from the underworld to prey on the weak.

Susan watched in horror as Angels wielding pool cues beat a naked fat boy. Jefferson Airplane performed, and the Angels beat up one of the band members. When Crosby, Stills, Nash and Young came on (Susan had written about them earlier that year), she settled back as the LSD she'd taken kicked in. Later, there was a long wait. It was dark when Mick Jagger and the Rolling Stones finally began to play, just before some of the Angels opened a gaping hole in a young man's head and jumped up and down on him until he was dead.

Susan descended quickly into a very bad trip, along with thousands of others in the audience. A rock festival—the consummate representation of countercultural tranquillity—had suddenly been invaded by the kind of violence usually associated with faraway rice paddies or police raids against Black Panthers in Chicago.

The white van headed back to San Francisco. Two concert-goers were run over and killed during the mass exodus. Ten miles past a gas station, someone in the van realized they'd left one of their number behind in the bathroom. They turned around and went back.

"One third of a million postwar boom babies gather in a Demolition Derby junkyard by a California freeway to get stoned and listen to rock 'n' roll—is that what it has all been about?" Michael Lydon would soon ask in print.

"So fucking detached," Susan said when she read his piece. "Distant and removed from the worst day of my whole life."

"You know what the trouble with Michael is?" Susan told Greil Marcus, a *Rolling Stone* writer they both knew. "He doesn't realize there's a void."

During a Sunday telephone update, Eve told Susan about Sheila's wedding, and Susan tried to tell Eve about Altamont. "Everyone in Berkeley thinks the end is coming," Susan said. "I looked out my kitchen window and saw blood flowing down the streets."

Flashbacks. Eve Gordon knew what this meant. Susan had them now, and Lorraine. Even Ricky, whose flashbacks were the worst of all. Eve wondered why it was that her children had to be dog soldiers, all four of them right up there in the front lines. Each appeared capable of packing an eternity of experience into a single year. They began the decade as a bunch of smart, if smart-assed, kids and ended it as a feminist writer, ex-wife, LSD victim, and single mother; a feminist revolutionary rock musician, ex-junkie, ex-wife, and single mother; a suburban flower child, communard, and wife; and a bar mitzvah boy who composed depressing songs and called out for his mommy at night because he was having terrible visions.

None of this, Eve thought, seemed entirely normal.

"All of them are different, my kids," Eve told the mah-jongg girls. "My children are like separate moons."

Ricky came home from a pre–New Year's jaunt to the Village and scurried up to his room. Eve followed him after a while and found him staring proudly at a new poster he'd tacked up on his bedroom wall, which he'd recently painted a shade of pale peach. The poster was an enlarged photograph of a little Vietnamese girl screaming and running naked down a dusty road. It was understood that the girl had just been badly burned by napalm—the stuff American pilots had dropped during the World War II battle for Peleliu Island, where Sam had lost so many of his friends.

"Unh-unh," said Eve when she saw the poster. "Too much. Absolutely not. Take it down right now. Take it *down!*"

Later Sam stalked silently into Ricky's room, a cardboard box under his long arm. He began to toss all Ricky's candles, his exotic incense holders, and his entire collection of variously shaped and scented incense into the box.

Sam turned and looked at Ricky when he finished. "These things are fire hazards," he said. "I don't want the house to burn down."

1970

The men of the Long Beach Masonic Lodge received an elegant engraved invitation a few days into the new year: "Brethren," it began. "There are but few 'Great Days' that happen to a man in his lifetime. Among these are usually his marriage, the birth of his children, and sharing the wonderful happenings in life with members of his family. You, my brothers, are my Masonic family, and I share with you the honor you have bestowed upon me by electing me Master of Long Beach Lodge."

It was signed, "Samuel Gordon, Master Elect."

Sam lingered over the ceremony of donning his tuxedo. Everything about it—the symmetry of collar and tie, the clarifying contrast of black and white, the gleaming studs in the heavily starched fabric, the stately top hat—the whole reflected the settled nobility of a fraternity that had never repudiated, and never would, the elegant, manly celebration of humanity through the idea of order. A Mason was simply not willing to forgo certain older simplicities: that the metaphor of brotherhood represented the best and most honorable feelings among men; that this brotherhood was powerful; and that the best thing a man could do, as the order's motto instructed, was to "follow reason."

Sam worried that governing a family and a business was scant preparation for becoming a Worshipful Master of the Long Beach lodge. "An absolute dictator, a monarch," was how Sam described the power he would wield for the coming year. The word of the Master was never challenged. He could simply banish a brother Mason, if only from a meeting, like an ancient king. The sole check on the Master's authority inside the lodge was the possibility that the brethren would stay away from meetings if the love of power turned him into a "pain in the ass." Sam had seen such boycotts before.

When his year was over, Sam hoped to be remembered as "not a dictator but a Solomon. Solomon got the job as king of the Jews because God thought David had shed too much blood." Solomon, Sam said, was "a very fair type of person."

Women were not allowed to attend the installation of a new Masonic Master, so Eve could only brush proudly at Sam's shoulders and watch him walk out the door. Pausing on the front stoop, Sam adjusted his top hat to an angle just a few degrees off plumb. Then he strode off, past the grinning, white-faced lawn jockey—the paint job a gift from the appearance-conscious wife of a fellow Mason—out into an evening of men and secrets.

By 1970, Sam Gordon had "tossed all his marbles in" with the Masons, as he put it. Aside from all the time he spent at lodge meetings or memorizing Masonic texts at home, Sam had personally restored the lodge's huge leaded-glass dome, which took up much of the ceiling of the old Zion Temple building and had Masonic symbols inscribed on each of nearly forty glass panels. Sam could no longer abide the single bare light bulb dangling ignobly from something so beautiful and lovingly crafted, and he'd brought in his crew to fit the dome with twelve carefully concealed fixtures. Cost and time were no object.

As a veteran Mason, Sam now claimed at least casual acquaintance with "twenty percent of the residents of Long Island." It wasn't that he cashed in his Masonic chips often, but it was reassuring and occasionally expedient that a man could cut through local red tape and "get things done" via the Masonic network. In places like Italy and France, the Masons were often accused of being a clandestine fraternal order that wielded shadowy influence within the central government. On Long Island—where local governments were trying to rein in the galloping real estate development of the past twenty years, where newspaper stories about zoning and other regulatory scandals were clogging editors' desks—it was good to know that a lot of the guys at the water company and the Long Island Lighting Company, and many building inspectors, judges, and local politicians, were brother Masons. "And no more than fifteen or twenty percent of them Jews," Sam would add.

Yet Sam knew that during his tenure as Master his business would certainly suffer. He would never be able to reclaim some of the accounts he'd lose because he had less time for SGE. Even his current fascination with real estate would have to be put aside during the year. Ever since his "illustrious partner" had refused to allow Dynamic Electric to purchase that five-thousand-dollar building on the West Side of Manhattan—that five-thousand-dollar building the owner wanted to give away, the one a parking lot developer bought for no less than $125,000 only a few years later—Sam had dreamed of getting into real estate. It took him several years to figure out the game, but recently he'd managed to put up an office building on a vacant lot on Austin Boulevard in Island Park. And he did it without borrowing a nickel from the bank.

With Nixon's men tightening the money supply, the cost of a bank loan was at a historic high, and there was even talk of a world recession. Yet for some reason prices kept rising. Recession, austerity, and increased joblessness (the latter phenomenon thought by economists to bear an inverse relationship to inflation) were all over the news, but still prices rose. It was apparent to Sam that if you held your real estate free and clear, as he did with his Austin Boulevard lot, and if you developed it without a loan, you could just ride the values skyward.

These novel economic permutations (a new term, "stagflation," would soon be coined to describe them) prompted Richard Nixon to invoke a new array of controls. By next year the President would go so far as to pronounce himself a Keynesian, an ideological reversal no less stunning than if he'd announced that henceforth he would be a Democrat. But for all the fiddling—price freezes, wage freezes, interest-rate adjustments—prices went on rising along with unemployment, and in two years angry consumers would be boycotting meat.

Sam got on the inflation rocket by paying the construction teams that built his three-story Austin Boulevard place only as he could. When he had cash he paid them, bit by bit, just as customers had paid him for a quarter of a century. The entire Austin Boulevard deal had required only thirteen thousand dollars in cash, and the place was worth three times that figure already, free and clear.

Sam observed that being rich in America meant understanding the fluidity of a business commitment, and even more profoundly, being able to envisage parking lots in place of factory walk-ups and new factories in place of vacant lots. Sam had returned home with dirty hands at the end of thousands of days only to watch the skills he'd mastered being superseded by what seemed to him the far lesser knack for salesmanship or "managing" the real work of others. Now it was evident that significant fortunes could be amassed by not working at all. It was clearly more profitable to own than to work, and Sam sometimes found it hard not to be bitter about having entered the property game so late even though he'd sensed this truth all along.

On the evening of his great day, the Master-elect rose from a huge wooden throne cushioned in thick red felt and stood before his Masonic brethren at a wooden lectern fitted with a plaque bearing an image of a carpenter's square—*norma* in Latin, the etymological root of "normal," modifier of so many of Sam Gordon's dreams. Behind him was a Masonic altar. Taught as a boy that Jews simply do not kneel, Sam had approached the altar with echoes of "Better to die on your feet" in his head, and had knelt on the old parquet floor because that was what Masons had always done. Around his neck hung another *norma* on a thick satin ribbon, and around his waist was a tasseled satin and white-lamb's-wool apron embossed with a *norma* and a watchful "third eye." The white of the wool represented purity, innocence, honor, and distinction. A Mason often requested burial in his apron, a garment that the family members mourning his loss would never have seen before.

Some years ago, when Sam had given his first speech at the lodge, a thirty-five-minute lecture on Masonic symbols, he'd had diarrhea all day. What had terrified him most was the thought of trying to sound as well educated and controlled as the other speakers he'd heard. But as soon as he began, Sam felt himself steer into a groove. In the silence between his sentences, Sam sensed respect. Ever since then the podium at the lodge had been one of his favorite places.

"Life is like a house," Sam began at his installation. "It is something built. And a successful life is created by pouring your love and energy into building the house right."

Sam felt warmth and approbation from his audience. He felt himself sailing into a new decade as a Masonic captain, a king like Solomon. His year of leadership would be indeed be recalled as superior for a long time to come. Men would seek him out for Masonic "intercourse" or just to ask his advice. Sam's mastery of his lodge and the respect he got made him feel like the father in a family of old.

In many ways, 1970 would be the best of all Sam's years.

⟨◦⟩

Twenty-year-old Jeff Miller of Plainview, Long Island, sixteen miles from Harbor Isle, was lying in a parking lot just beyond the end zone of a nearby football field, a girl wailing skyward beside him.

Five days earlier, on April 30, in a televised address, President

Nixon had announced that he'd ordered some thirty thousand U.S. troops into Cambodia to destroy North Vietnamese sanctuaries there, and his speech had triggered widespread student protests. Across the national "chasm of misunderstanding" he had acknowledged the previous summer, Nixon called the enraged students "bums." "Imagine they are wearing brown shirts or white sheets," added Vice President Agnew.

Now some of the bums lay dead, and none of them were wearing brown shirts or white sheets, or the gas masks and helmets favored by European antiwar protesters and the more hardened American street fighters of last fall's Days of Rage. "When the firing stopped," wrote a *New York Times* reporter who'd been standing among the demonstrating students at Kent State University in Ohio, "a slim girl, wearing a cowboy shirt and faded jeans, was lying face down on the road at the edge of the parking lot, blood pouring out onto the macadam."

The girl's name was Allison Krause. She had been killed, along with Jeff Miller and two other students, when Ohio National Guardsmen opened fire on the demonstrators. "Four dead," as the haunting Neil Young song would put it, "in Ohio."

It would emerge that Richard Nixon had screened and rescreened the movie *Patton* before he appeared on television on April 30, looking pumped up and determined to seek military victory in Southeast Asia instead of the "honorable" settlement to which he'd pledged himself so often. "America has never been defeated in the proud one-hundred-ninety-year history of this country," Nixon proclaimed, sitting before a large map, "and we shall not be defeated in Vietnam."

Nixon took pains to portray the U.S. action as an "incursion," not an invasion, a brief but necessary contravention of the "neutrality of the Cambodian people," which the administration had previously been scrupulous in its efforts to respect, he said. Secret military actions had actually been taking place in Cambodia for a long time. These earlier "incursions" were kept secret in hopes of building a national consensus in support of a Patton-like lunge for victory. Now the secret had become a lie.

Nixon was apparently so taken up with his spring military venture that when antiwar protests began in the wake of his speech, he told his glowering assistant, John Ehrlichman, to "take care" of the problem so he could concentrate on the offensive. At Kent State a group of students burned down the ROTC building on May 2. The shootings occurred two days later, and by the next day, the nation's campuses were exploding.

Lorraine happened to be in Ann Arbor that week, at the University of Michigan, where students had already taken over the ROTC building, located a large cache of weapons, and were looking for ammunition. The walls of Ann Arbor bristled with slogans like "Seize the Time," "Serve the People," and "Off the Pig," divergent commands representing distinct political sensibilities—until the shootings brought them all into the same circle of rage.

Lorraine, a pacifist, had come to Ann Arbor to help out an old Oceanside High friend, a young woman who was not a pacifist at all. She'd agreed to sing at a fund-raiser for a small group of radicals called the White Panther Party. A leader of the local Ann Arbor chapter, one Lawrence "Pun" Plamondon, was now living "underground." Ever since his indictment on charges stemming from a 1968 explosion in a building students believed was the scene of CIA activity, Plamondon had been staying at one of the many "safe houses" established in upper Michigan by the growing ranks of underground political radicals. A radicalized onetime greaser from Belleville, Michigan, Pun was typical of the harder breed of kids now prominent at protests. His messages from hiding were often read at rallies or printed in the *Ann Arbor Argus,* an underground newspaper. Just before Lorraine arrived, he had published an open letter to his high school principal: "You were watching Ed Sullivan ten years ago, and you're still watching Ed Sullivan. You think nothing has changed."

Unlike Pun and hundreds of other activists who were dropping out of day-to-day life that spring to lose themselves in "the belly of the whale," Lorraine remained a pacifist, though she was beginning to lose her grasp of the logic of nonviolence. Eight weeks earlier Bev Grant, her fellow Goldflower, just back from cutting sugarcane in Cuba, had joined a group of committed radicals for revolutionary study sessions, her new militance kindled by an explosion that rocked Greenwich Village and killed three members of the Weather Underground who were making bombs in a townhouse on West Eleventh Street. Bev often argued the case for violence between songs at Goldflower rehearsals these days.

Like tens of thousands of other veterans of the years of hopefulness, veterans of teenage visits to the ghetto, of five years of relentless protest against the war, of dinner table battles that had torn so many families apart by now, Lorraine heard Nixon's late April speech as a bitter revelation that she had little to show for all her years of activism but anger and shame. Many old movement people were calling demonstrations "actions" now. In New York protesters jumped turnstiles en masse— "subway actions"—and "trashed" store windows on the way to meeting points in Central Park or Times Square.

Before the Kent State killings, half of all American students said they would apply the word "imperialism" to the war in Vietnam. After the shootings, three of five college students came out to demonstrate in a climate of greater potential for violent official reprisal than at any time since the labor demonstrations of a half century earlier. Three of four students now called for "basic changes in the system." For them, the rhetoric of liberal consensus and nonviolent civil disobedience, the lessons of Gandhi and Martin Luther King, were supplanted by the will to violence. In the name of revolution some young people now drove out to the country on weekends for target practice and self-defense training. Just before the Ann Arbor rally where Lorraine was supposed to sing, the formerly nonviolent undergraduates in the ROTC building found rifle ammunition in the basement.

Lorraine was a pacifist who believed that genocide was rooted in the American psyche. She believed that nothing "official" could be believed and that nothing would ever be forgiven on either side of the popular divide. On her way to a morning class at Hunter College, she'd recently felt compelled to stop a Vietnamese woman. "I want you to know...I'm ashamed to be an American," she'd blurted. Now she realized that shame didn't change anything. The most honest and angry people Lorraine knew were seriously considering violence this spring—every conversation seemed to include at least one high-adrenaline advocate of "armed struggle"—and she felt it was incumbent upon her to decide what kind of child of the sixties she was going to be.

Lorraine knew she was the Gordon to act. She was the brave one. She was the one who'd launched a gale-force "I hate you" at her parents. Lorraine had been revolutionary for a long time, but this decision to harden her stance would involve letting go of important parts of her life for what could easily be forever. It would mean no Sunday meals in Harbor Isle or phone calls back home. It would mean Maggie growing up without her.

"The issue of violence is to this generation what the issue of sex was to the Victorian world," Yale psychologist Kenneth Keniston had written in his 1968 book, *Young Radicals*. Another academic drawn to the culture and politics of protest, Philip E. Slater, argued in his new book, *The Pursuit of Loneliness*, that the violence was the result of fathers unable to deal with the contradictions between machines and morality, between love and fear. A presidential commission on campus unrest would warn later in the year that "a nation that has lost the allegiance of part of its youth, is a nation that has lost part of its future." But Vice President Agnew, speaking on behalf of Americans who deplored the wave of protests (six of ten adults said the Kent State students were at fault), called the commission's dire findings nothing more than "pablum for the permissivists."

From behind the microphone the Ann Arbor rally seemed to stretch to the horizon. Lorraine clutched her Gibson too close, and her fingers felt stiff on the frets as she began a rendition of Bob Dylan's "Masters of War," a furious address to the builders of "death planes" who "hide behind desks" and "fasten the triggers for the others to fire."

"You've thrown the worst fear that can ever be hurled," she sang out over the landscape of sad and furious faces, "to bring children into the world ..." By the time she came to the final verse of the song ("And I hope that you die and your death will come soon .../And I'll stand o'er your grave/'Til I'm sure that you're dead"), Lorraine was singing a dirge instead of an anthem. With fists pounding the air as far as she could see, she decided not to sing the last lines at all. Lorraine's "Masters of War" would be a memorial to fallen children, not a call to arms. Sweet-voiced Lorraine, who couldn't recall more than a few moments in all of her nearly twenty-four years when she hadn't felt betrayed by authority, was prevented from taking the ultimate step into opposition by the thought of a little girl.

Over at the ROTC building, after a long and vehement debate, the ammunition boxes remained unopened.

<hr />

At the time of the Kent State shootings, Susan and Shuna were guests in the Greenwich Village apartment of John Simon, an editor at Random House who'd recently advanced Susan ten thousand dollars—a magnificent sum in those days—to write a book that he hoped would make her "the next Simone de Beauvoir."

Susan had received much flattering response to her *Ramparts* piece on the psychology, physiology, and politics of the female orgasm. A few women even telephoned to say that her article had changed their lives. Two callers told her they'd read it out loud to their husbands as a kind of manifesto. In the underground and feminist press, and in formal and informal discussions among women, the terms "orgasm" and "clitoris" were now as ubiquitous as they had once been unspoken.

John Simon had called Susan to ask, in effect, if she wanted to be a rich and famous feminist. He said that the new dialogue about women and sex was sure to surface as a hot topic. "If you can write the first readable feminist analysis of sex in America, it's sure to be a classic," Simon said. In 1968 a New York teacher and sculptor had turned part of her doctoral dissertation into a controversial *New American Review* article attacking the sexism of Norman Mailer and Henry Miller. Doubleday would be publishing the rewritten dissertation in book form later this year, but Kate Millett's *Sexual Politics* would undoubtedly be much too pedantic to interest the general reader, Simon thought.

Writer Susan Brownmiller had recently described her personal experience in a women's consciousness-raising group for the *New York Times Magazine*. ("One Village group to which these girls belong," read a photo caption, "believes that lib will liberate men, too—though they may not like it.") Angry women demonstrated at the offices of *Ladies' Home Journal* to protest the magazine's "demeaning" portrayal of women, and nearly fifty female employees of *Newsweek* filed a complaint with the Equal Employment Opportunity Commission detailing the kind of blatant discrimination Susan had seen back when Michael and other Ivy League males got jobs as reporters while Ivy League women became researchers and secretaries. The commencement speaker at Vassar this year would be a writer named Gloria Steinem. A movement was coming into the national spotlight, and feminism was making inroads into the mainstream world of publishing.

Susan had used a spare ID of Sheila's to fly to New York on the cheap. Youth fares had created a whole new interstate transportation system, an essential if unsung element in the dissemination of the alternative culture, accounting for the omnipresence of certain political activists and facilitating a profitable recreational drug trade. Sheila's frayed image on the card didn't look much like Susan, but these days looks changed easily and often.

In New York Susan met with John Simon at Random House and went to a literary agency on Sixth Avenue, where she was told by Lynn Nesbit, an agent Simon had recommended, "You'll be on *Johnny Carson*." Susan didn't know if she wanted to be on *Johnny Carson*. She wasn't so sure about being rich, famous, and accepted by "the establishment." Such were the times.

Outside the sisterly confines of Susan's own Berkeley CR group, the women's movement ranged from the entirely middle-class National Organization for Women to antiwar feminists who were now so radicalized that their loathing for white men often surpassed their hatred of the war. Susan didn't identify with a particular feminist camp, and the internecine hairsplitting turned her off. On top of that, the author of "The Politics of Orgasm" didn't consider herself much of an expert on sex. "And if I made a list of all the things I would never want to do in life, I think maybe talking about orgasms on *Johnny Carson* might be right up there," she told Bardacke, who happened to be in New York at the time of the book offer.

"Oh, come on," F.J. said. "Ten grand, Susan. Just take it. I'll help you out with the fieldwork."

Susan gave part of the money to Eve before she left town. Eve had recently acquired a stockbroker and an interest in the flagging securities market. Eve said stocks were bound to go up in the long run and promised to invest Susan's money so it would grow.

Back in Berkeley, several of Susan's political friends were less than impressed with the new book project. "Shuna's gonna go off to school someday," Tom Hayden said, "and kids are gonna point her out: 'There's Shuna. Her mom's the orgasm lady.'"

Articulate and apparently unflappable, Hayden had testified forcefully before the House Un-American Activities Committee in the early sixties and the National Commission on the Causes and Prevention of Violence in 1968. He'd come away from his famous trial in Chicago last year more radicalized than ever before and had seriously considered going underground to avoid a possible jail term while his conviction was under appeal. He could easily have joined many former SDS comrades in the underground, but—as he would write of the moment years later—while "the lure of violence and martyrdom were powerful subterranean forces" in his makeup, he decided instead to follow the "lure of family."

Tom Hayden hadn't been in contact with his parents for several years, and he had a young sister who was growing up completely unaware of her famous brother. He had often thought that perhaps a life of sincere political commitment was so precarious that it should be "empty of family," but in the Berkeley of 1970 he found an alternative in a local collective known as the Red Family. The three Red Family houses were havens dedicated to promoting feminism, defending harassed Black Panthers, activists, and drug users from the Berkeley authorities, and transcending the traditional terrible nuclear family. As one Red Family member, a friend of Susan's from her women's group, would later sum up the impulse behind the rush to communal living, "We hated families. It was as simple as that." These new associations would be far better—rational, meritocratic, democratic, and loving too.

By the middle of 1970 it seemed that at least one address on every tree-lined street in Berkeley was a commune. Communal decor was so predictable that a "typical model commune" could easily have been replicated in a Soviet park: aged Oriental carpets, dusty bottle-glass window arrangements, macrame planters bursting with greenery, peacock feathers reflected in smoky antique mirrors. Lavender and patchouli mingled with the scent of marijuana, whose nation of origin residents could often identify from a single whiff. Drying herbs hung in cluttered Edenic kitchens full of huge jars and great wooden bowls. Bedrooms with mattresses on the floor were "spaces," though wanting your "own space" was apt to be construed as an antisocial inability to share. Yet just as the identical houses of Harbor Isle were customized within a very short time, most of these intentional communities soon acquired distinct characteristics. Bay Area experiments of 1970 included religious communes, doctors' and nurses' communes, group marriage communes, and even a commune called Morehouse, where relatively well-to-do residents collectively dedicated themselves to exploring the pinnacles of sexual possibility.

When Michael Lydon came to Berkeley to see Shuna, or when Susan and Shuna were in the mood to go visiting, they often went over to the Fisherman collective, whose symbol, the "clenched fish"—a raised fist strangling a confused-looking ichthyoid—could be spotted on T-shirts in downtown Berkeley. The Fisherman motto was "You don't need a fisherman to know when something's fishy." Susan also enjoyed hanging out at the Wolsey Street Commune (most urban communes from Berkeley to Boston were named for their street), where the artistic residents spent their days making muslin clothing with seashell appliqués or decorating the paneling with "trippy" frescoes. Susan would clomp around Wolsey Street in knee-high forest-green boots with three-inch heels, getting high on pot and chatting for hours with Susie Angel-Cloud and the others.

Susan and Shuna had had a chance to move into a commune earlier in the year, when Susan decided she could no longer afford the hundred-and-seventy-five-dollar rent on her house. But since Susan believed she needed the experience of truly "being alone"—the scariest thing she could think of—she and Shuna moved instead to a tiny house on Stuart Street where the rent was just eighty-five dollars a month.

Susan and Shuna often went around the house naked because nobody could see in from the street. There was a little front yard full of roses and fig trees where they whiled away many a fragrant Berkeley day. Rock writer Bob Christgau, who "crashed" with Susan for a while, reported in the *Village Voice* that he'd stayed "with Susan Lydon, who used to make her living writing about rock and roll and women's liberation and now just makes her living." Christgau was impressed that Susan could make what money she needed by bartering at local flea markets so alive with colorful, exotic garb that they resembled the grand bazaars of Central Asia. Susan now collected and traded various native and pseudo-native crafts that reflected a hippie aesthetic she'd described memorably last year in the "Arts and Leisure" section of the *New York Times* by itemizing the furnishings in singer Joni Mitchell's home: "... votive candles, blooming azaleas, a turkey made of pine cones, dried flowers, old dolls, Victorian shadow boxes, colored glass...art nouveau lamp in the shape of a frog holding a lily pad, a collection of cloisonné boxes, bowls and ashtrays, patchwork quilts ..."

Susan's own house was such a clutter of scraps and dust that a scraggly local dope dealer who came to the door one day said, "You know what, Susan? You oughta hire one of those little hippie chicks to come clean this place up." Another time, Tom Hayden told Susan that her laid-back, unproductive days were a symptom of her "bourgeois individualist ways." Susan still wrote a few articles—the one about Joni, another about Bob Dylan's former backup group, the Band—and she interviewed F. J. Bardacke, Susie Angel-Cloud, and other friends about their sex lives for her new book. But Susan wasn't really "into" work. She was into quilts. She liked the idea that collecting and trading quilts was what she "did."

Susan was also deeply into drinking *cafe latte*. She spent mornings, afternoons, entire days nursing cups of the strong Italian coffee at the Mediterranean, a Berkeley hangout on Telegraph Avenue that everyone called the Med. "It's like you think we're going to make the revolution at the Med," Tom Hayden scoffed. "But I love the Med," Susan replied. She loved the coffee and the atmosphere. She loved to look out onto Telegraph Avenue and watch Shuna toddle past drug dealers, hippies, and leafleters. Some of Susan's friends thought she shouldn't let Shuna loose on the street like that and told her she wasn't being a good mother. Anne Weills warned that a mother "shouldn't become so lost inside herself."

One day Susan sauntered down Telegraph Avenue with her beautiful Hermès purse from Paris under her arm. She strode up to a Goodwill Industries bin and threw the purse inside. Soon thereafter *Time* and *Newsweek* both ran long cover stories on the women's movement. Books and articles on all facets of the feminist critique of the status quo were suddenly appearing by the week. The personal was becoming more political all the time, as Susan and her female friends often told Tom

Hayden, who was soon accused of being an oppressive male chauvinist and summarily purged from his Red Family.

——◆——

Ricky wore a black armband in the halls of Lincoln-Orens Junior High School, but he wasn't sure why. Ever since his stirring seventh-grade performance of "Oh, I Wish I Was a Dove," it had been widely assumed that the school's best anthem writer, whose three sisters were all cool and famously in the know, must also be politically advanced and brimming with the latest moral passions. Ricky had even attended a massive antiwar demonstration in Washington, D.C., along with Peter Probst and Sheila.

But Ricky secretly considered his armband a style statement, like his hair—now several inches below his ears—and his huge construction worker's boots, and his frayed bell-bottom jeans shingled with brightly colored patches. He'd really gone to that march in Washington only because he'd heard Joni Mitchell might be there. When Joni didn't show, Ricky was alternately bored and guilt-ridden because the sea of passion and anger surrounding him didn't move him. He just didn't understand. Back in May, something terrible had happened at Kent State, but the shootings meant little to Ricky until Crosby, Stills, and Nash came out with "Find the Cost of Freedom." Without music as an anchor, Ricky felt perpetually at sea in the counterculture. Even though he of all the Gordon children was closest to the demographic epicenter of the baby boom (the fourteen- to twenty-four-year-old population had almost doubled in the last ten years), he still needed the music to ground him.

Ricky's patched jeans, featuring bits of ribbon and quilting Susan had exported to Harbor Isle, were modeled after the blue jeans on the back cover of Neil Young's *After the Gold Rush* album. Young (lately of Crosby, Stills, Nash and Young) was Ricky's favorite popular singer and songwriter next to fellow Canadian Joni, with whom Ricky had fallen deeply in love during *Alice's Restaurant*. A young speed freak fell off his motorcycle and died in the 1969 film, and at his funeral a waiflike blonde sang one of the most haunting melodies Ricky had ever heard. He owned all of Joni Mitchell's records and had written her heartfelt letters in wartime volume: "I just think you are the greatest single thing in the whole wide world, Joni." When Susan had dinner with Joni while working on her *Times* article, she somehow forgot to mention her connection to the Ricky Ian Gordon who wrote those letters.

Lorraine took Ricky to see the Who perform their rock opera,

Tommy, that spring, but the music hurt his ears. He preferred dark, intense songs like Joni's, or ballads like Crosby, Stills and Nash's "Guenevere," or powerful evocations of reality like Neil Young's "The Needle and the Damage Done."

In the living room of 221 Lincoln, toward the end of the year, Eve introduced Ricky to a middle-aged couple who'd come to look at the house. "Play them something," Eve said with a huge, slightly unnatural do-it-or-else smile.

Eve had been talking about selling the house for over a year. She'd say that Sam dreamed of being closer to the water or that she was weary of negotiating four separate levels, but Ricky knew that his mother hadn't felt the same about Lincoln Avenue since the tortures that had driven him to Camp Lenape five years ago. She thought the house had brought the family bad luck. The same house that had once embodied Eve's oldest dreams of happiness was now full of screams and silences, nightmares and flashbacks. Every so often Sam and Eve would put 221 Lincoln on the market to see what happened.

"Play the nice people a song, Ricky," Eve said again, beckoning the extremely uncomfortable-looking prospective buyers to take a seat.

Ricky chose one of his own compositions, a recent piece based on a poem he'd come across in an *Avant Garde* magazine Susan had left behind. The opening lyrics were about a junkie's corpse lying somewhere on the streets of the Lower East Side, needles protruding from a lifeless arm. As the chorus reiterated, a great deal of bloodshed had preceded his terrible end. Most of the song chronicled similar deaths amid even larger pools of blood, though the last verse lightened up to describe junkie prostitutes plying their trade.

When Ricky finished, he looked at Eve, who was sitting on the edge of one of her comfortable chairs wearing the oh-so-proud smile he loved. Ricky turned to the house-hunting couple and saw the husband helping his wife up as if she were sick. He led her straight to the door without saying a word, and they were never heard from again.

1971

Lorraine, Bev Grant, and Laura Lieben opened their concert before the assembled inmates of the Niantic Correctional Facility, a Connecticut prison for women, with the tune so many audiences—from the huge crowd at the star-studded Randall's Island Rock Festival the previous summer to the smaller groups at Greenwich Village political events—had come to associate with Goldflower. Their signature number was one of Bev's creations, a driving rocker called "Tired of Bastards Fuckin' Over Me."

Bev marched up to the microphone and splayed her heavy combat boots Amazon-wide. She sneered into the bright light filling the small prison gymnasium and began.

> I'm walkin' down the street,
> And every man I meet says,
> "Baby ain't you sweet,"
> I could scream,
> "Those guys are sick!
> And think only of their pricks."
> It ain't sweet ...

Goldflower concerts were dominated by Bev, who often talked her lines or growled them out with determined fury. Bev refused to speak between songs because she was just too pissed off for frivolous stage patter.

Before the concert, a lawyer for one of the Black Panther Party members in the audience asked the band to "be cool," but Bev couldn't help snarling at the guards. Niantic, a deceptively bucolic arrangement of cottagelike buildings, was where the state had remanded Erica Huggins and Joan Brown, two Black Panthers who were being tried in New Haven along with fellow Panther Bobby Seale for the alleged kidnapping and murder of another Panther thought to be an informant. Opposing attorneys had grilled 618 potential jurors to find twelve who were not already convinced of the radicals' guilt or innocence.

Black Panther men and women in New York, Illinois, Connecticut, Michigan, Missouri, California, Louisiana, and several other states had lately been streaming into American courtrooms and prisons. The Panther 21 trial in New York and the Panther 13 trial in New Haven were followed avidly for their raucous outbursts and constant assertions by defendants, attorneys, activists, and a few journalists that the trials were part of a coordinated government campaign to destroy the Black Panthers once and for all. Not long before the Goldflower concert, conductor Leonard Bernstein hosted a fund-raiser for jailed black activists in New York. Students and faculty at Union Theological Seminary voted to use a portion of the institution's endowment to finance bail for Black Panther defendants.

Later revelations would confirm that the Black Panthers had been targeted under the FBI's KBE ("Key Black Extremist") program and a general government-directed effort to "get them," as the head of the Justice Department's civil rights division put it. The mayor of Seattle refused to allow what he called these "Gestapo-type" anti-Panther tactics, but in other cities—like Chicago, where Fred Hampton and Mark Clark, two key Black Panther leaders, were killed during a predawn police raid in 1969—the program was carried out enthusiastically. In Connecticut a mistrial would end proceedings involving Huggins and Brown, but meanwhile they sat with the other inmates as Lorraine, Bev, and Laura serenaded them with "Tired of Bastards Fuckin' Over Me."

During a brief retuning, Lorraine noticed that several inmates in the front rows were staring at her. In fact, they were *leering*. At first she told herself they were just being friendly, but then one puckered her lips and another winked. Lorraine heard suggestive catcalls that were far more unnerving than anything she'd endured near a construction site.

Goldflower played so regularly at the women's dances held almost every weekend in Manhattan that the band was now closely identified with flourishing communities of feminist separatists and radical lesbians, two militant offshoots of the women's movement. Lorraine found herself entertaining audiences dominated by women she was positive would drag her out back and beat her to a pulp if they realized that she not only didn't hate men but actually enjoyed them. Men would be "divested of cocks" in a perfect world, said Robin Morgan, Bev's old women's group buddy, and the anthologizer of Susan's famous orgasm article in the popular *Sisterhood Is Powerful* reader. Recently Robin Morgan had been assailed by one of the "wild voices keening" she'd summoned in her manifesto "Good Bye to All That"; while she was breastfeeding her infant son in an underground newspaper office, a feminist sister had suggested that she toss her "pig male baby" into the garbage.

The separatist feminist clarion call ("Seize reproduction, create artificial wombs") was less threatening to Lorraine than the rise of political lesbianism. Lorraine had had a very close friend who impulsively expressed her physical attraction, but Lorraine had said no and now the friend was lost. Even Bev felt the pressure to give up men, though she would never let her confusion show.

The release of "latent homosexual needs is the pivot upon which their liberation as women would occur," argued lesbian writer Jill Johnston, referring to straight feminists like Lorraine and Bev. Radicalized men and women all over the country were breaking traditional heterosexual boundaries, taking the next logical step toward liberation as a "sign of mental health," as one feminist put it. The political statement often transcended sexual orientation.

"It makes me feel so guilty," Lorraine told Bev. "I just couldn't do it with women. And I hate playing for people who would call me a traitor if they knew what I'm really like."

Bev considered Lorraine the true musical talent in the Goldflower family, and she could see that Lorraine was beginning to back away from the band just as they were becoming well known. Because of Maggie, Lorraine often refused to hit the road for out-of-town gigs, and Lorraine's best and least nerve-racking sets were sometimes shored up by Valium resolve. Once in a while when the band did a show, Maggie would come on stage and shyly tap a tambourine. Sometimes the players would fall into synch with her, and their three strong, unique voices would propel a song at the audience in a way that made the crowd beam back, full of emotion. You could see the faces change from the stage and feel the power.

Bev realized that Lorraine was feeling out of step with the vanguard feminism of Goldflower's fans. Lorraine had a little girl, and to many of the women Goldflower entertained, being a mother was at best a curiosity. They denounced the nuclear family as a moral dungeon that nurtured men and wrapped women in chains, and many feminists also rejected progressive efforts to create consensual families. The communes and collectives were "sham families" according to the feminist critics, full of role-ridden "Betty Crocker–style" oppression masquerading as something hip. The very word "family," they pointed out, derived from the Latin *famulus*, which meant servant, slave, or possession.

At the end of the Niantic set, Bev led the band in "Babylon," which she'd co-written with her friend Lynne Phillips in honor of all the Black Panther women in jail in New York. "Women who have listened to my song will understand we must prepare to fight," the lyrics went toward the end. "Our history of servitude is long. The time has come to seize our timeless right....In fear and pain, our rage regain. ..."

"Girls," said Sam Gordon. "They've all gone wild!"

And it wasn't just his girls. Every young woman past puberty was either "running around with a mattress on her back, just because she's so afraid she's gonna miss something," or endeavoring to assure a "long life alone" by agitating for the liberation Sam believed most of them already had. Teaching a girl to go out and have herself a career might be a perfectly good thing, but to Sam's ear the rhetoric of women's liberation sounded like a call for half the human race to sacrifice their fundamental self-respect. Women were "knocking down a pedestal" men had worked hard to build for them, and Sam was sure they'd eventually be good and sorry.

"You don't think your mother's had a good life being a woman?" he'd ask his girls. "Do you hear her complaining?"

Sometime during the past year each of Sam Gordon's daughters—first Lorraine, then Susan, and then, amazingly, Sheila—had looked into his face and called him a "male chauvinist pig." To his face. A *pig*.

"I've never mistreated a woman in my life," Sam would reply stiffly, deeply offended. Sam was proud that he'd never once considered belonging to any synagogue where Eve wasn't allowed to pray at his side. He'd grown up surrounded by immigrant men who treated their wives like slaves, and he'd vowed as a very young man never to do that to his own wife. It was a vow he'd made without the assistance of women "on parade" in the streets, and one he believed he'd kept with no prodding from keening voices.

But nowadays all it took was "Say, Eve, gimme an apple" and Sam's girls went ape. Sam knew many other men in the same boat, mostly other fathers, but even some sons. They'd all nod vigorously when Sam unknowingly echoed Sigmund Freud's famous query. "It makes you wonder," he would say, "what women really want." Thank goodness his Eve "wasn't the type" to go off in search of further liberation. Sam believed Eve was happy to be the woman she was.

On the whole, he was right. Eve listened closely to what her daughters had to say about the women's movement, and she read articles on the subject when she could. While the feminist analysis made her aware of how very much she "catered" to Sam, as Eve put it, she refused to believe she'd ever "lost her personality," as the "libbers" claimed was invariably the case in marriages of her vintage. According to a survey conducted by pollster Daniel Yankelovich, by May 1971 the number of American college students who believed marriage was obsolete had risen from twenty-four to thirty-four percent within the course of a single year. But according to Eve, all these new complaints about marriage stemmed from a failure of insight. In her own marriage, Eve got what she needed: she got her way. She was liberated, even if she didn't show it directly, by virtue of her carefully orchestrated program of planning and execution.

Recently Eve had made the mistake of losing her temper with Sam. She got mad and said, "Fuck you." This was not planned.

For seven days—*seven days*—Sam refused to say a word to her. Eve thought the strain of it would kill her. Women had to be smart, and "Fuck you" just wasn't smart.

When Lorraine and the other girls spoke to Eve of liberation, all she heard was a demand that she change Sam. That was the biggest fallacy of women's liberation. Feminists thought men could change; Eve was sure they could not. Women were better at changing than men.

"It's about an entire society changing its consciousness, Ma," Susan would try to explain during her many visits east. "The whole idea of being a woman has to change."

"That's not how it sounds to me," Eve would say. "You think you can change men. Men don't change."

<hr />

Sam came home one night and discovered Peter Probst halfway up the iron staircase, his frame apparently affixed to the side of Sam and Eve's new house. Sam's son-in-law was barely conscious, but somehow his fingers gripped the wall sufficiently to keep him there, splayed out like a spider.

Sam could smell the liquor from the bottom of the stairs. He thought about Peter and Sheila's land-based houseboat of a hippie van, a vehicle they dropped off regularly with Sam for repairs, the first time with a headlight hanging out of its socket, the next with a badly twisted fender. Once Sam had asked a buddy at the local body shop to do a major job on the van, and the guy only wanted three hundred bucks for a lot of work. Sheila said they were too strapped to pay, so Sam popped for the repair bill only to find the van back in front of the new SGE Marina three weeks later with its side caved in.

Now Sam looked up at Sheila's vertically comatose husband and understood. *My sweet daughter married an asshole.*

Sam moved up to the step just below Peter, who moaned softly. Sam leaned close. "Go back to the gin mill," he said. "Get the hell out of here."

Sam and Eve had sold the house on Lincoln Avenue not long after Sam found out that the rundown old boatyard a few blocks away was for sale. The marina and the apartment above the dock were owned by Chuck Bloom, father of April of the black bedroom.

Though Sam and Eve's move involved a migration of less than a quarter of a mile, it was like abandoning a suburban ideal now too weighted with former dreams. Out at the old marina Sam could see oil tankers moving across the open sea, and if he squinted he could make out the Verrazano Narrows Bridge. On late summer evenings, shortly after the move, Sam and Eve stood on their new balcony above the boat slips and saw the spire of the Empire State Building skewer the falling sun. At the edge of Harbor Isle, right up against the sea lanes, Sam watched clouds of birds rising endlessly above the marshy islands in the distance, as though they were being hurled up from inside the earth. He watched, and it felt like the surface of the world was falling away. It felt like he was ascending and Harbor Isle's streets and houses and the sad memories of children and parents all dancing and all the same were so far away that they no longer mattered.

The move also meant that Sam would add a small portion of the three-and-a-half-billion-dollar recreational boating industry to his electrical contracting and real estate ventures. It never crossed his mind simply to let the marina go, to make the boatyard just a picturesque place to live. Because of the way Sam Gordon tore into his hobbies, he already understood the secret recesses of a motorboat as well as he knew what was under the skin of an intricately wired factory. There was work to be done in a boat.

Sam had learned that boats were basically unwieldy, unpredictable, and imperfect things forced to exist in a hostile and corrosive environment. He had seen boat engines with all their seams and nuts fused and melted away, as if they'd been soaking in battery acid. Moving parts became so brittle inside a boat that the metal often broke when you tried to work with it. Fixing an "I/O"—a powerboat with the engine inside the hold and the drive train protruding from the hull—meant twisting into dark, cramped interiors. It meant that the wake from a passing boat made your head bang back and forth against a bulkhead like a bell clapper while spark plugs stabbed your chest. And it was risky work too. A boat with just a teacup's worth of entrapped and vaporized gasoline was like a floating time bomb.

Only minutes after Sam first heard that Chuck's Marina was going up for sale, SGE Marine Corporation's structure (single proprietorship, a labor force of one) and market niche (the most difficult and dangerous boats on the water, the I/Os) were fully alive in his mind. Being nose to nose with possible tragedy was already a daily thing for Sam, and working like a worm in the dark was second nature.

The first time Eve came to see the shabby boatyard apartment, she counted the iron stairs. Seventeen without risers, like a fire escape against a tenement wall. An ugly apartment opening out onto winches, boating paraphernalia, and floating pools of oil.

"We can make this beautiful," Sam said.

"Then we'll buy it," said Eve.

Eve soon heard through the grapevine that the mah-jongg players of Harbor Isle were universally appalled. Such a beautiful house on a corner lot on Lincoln—a palace of a house—traded for a hovel, a shack that harked back to the island's uninhabited past.

Sam and Eve painted the living room bright yellow and bought a dazzling green shag rug. Sam fitted the entire wall that faced the water with floor-to-ceiling sliding glass doors. Eve covered every surface with colorful knickknacks and padded the room with her embroidered pillow collection.

The kitchen was the best. Not only did it open directly into the sunshine of the living room, but if you looked up at the stove while you were cooking dinner, it reflected the sunset. Eve was sure this would be her best kitchen yet. Here she would never feel cut off, as she occasionally had in her other kitchens. "A woman needs an open kitchen," she told her friends.

The kitchen and the living room were perfect for gatherings. Everyone would come to this new home, Eve thought, like ships seeking harbor. They'd come and feel as she felt, renewed by the light.

1972

Ricky stood outside Carnegie Hall at four in the morning. An icy winter rain soaked him thoroughly during the first hour of his vigil, but Ricky didn't care. All that mattered was that he was first in line, and that he would be right there in the front row when his beloved Joni Mitchell began to play.

The mixture of obsessive planning and pure stubbornness that preceded the Joni Mitchell ticket pilgrimage was reminiscent of Ricky's excursion to the Met to see Roberta Peters during the historic sixteen-inch snowfall of 1969. (Twenty years later Sam Gordon was still wondering if any other American boy had ever run away from home to see an opera, if any other father had ever been tested by such a son.) In preparation for his first Joni Mitchell concert, Ricky spent several months embroidering a long denim dress with butterflies, birds in flight, and a variety of sunsets. Employing the satin stitch he'd recently mastered, he had committed entire spring forest scenes to the gift by the time of the concert, all to the accompaniment of Joni Mitchell songs playing over and over on his stereo.

While browsing in a head shop in Greenwich Village, Ricky had found a record about the characteristics of Scorpios—Joni's astrological sign—and sent it to her in California. One of his most prized possessions was a single piece of heavy plain stationery, folded twice.

December 11, 1970

Hello Ricky,

Thank you for all your letters and drawings and thoughtful things. I love things you make yourself. I haven't played the record yet because thieves ripped off my record player.

I'm on my way to San Francisco to sing on a friend's record and to get out of the L.A. air.

Goodbye.

At the bottom of the page, in a childlike hand, was the signature of Joni Mitchell, born Roberta Joan Anderson in Saskatoon, Saskatchewan, where she began what she once described as "a constant war to liberate myself from values not applicable to the period in which I live."

Of all the writers and singers of introspective ballads who'd risen to an AM radio level of mass popularity—James Taylor, Carole King, Elton John—Joni Mitchell was perhaps the most complex and sensitive. Her lyrical considerations of romantic love were delivered with a sophistication that transcended the soppy truisms of most "singer/songwriters." Ricky had heard that as a teenager Joni had married and quickly divorced, like Lorraine. Seemingly wounded, fragile as blown glass, Joni gave Ricky the musical score for the emotional dissonance he experienced so often these days. "I don't know who I am," she wrote in her famous ode to the Woodstock festival, "but life is for learning."

By the time the box office opened at ten, Ricky could barely force his frozen, clawlike right hand into his jeans pocket. He managed to withdraw the check and push it into the booth. A ticket representing nothing less than first-row center slid back toward him along with a gust of warm air.

"Hey there. Wait just a minute. What's this?" said the man inside the booth as Ricky was turning away. Back went the ticket and out came the check, which had no signature. Eve had forgotten to sign it.

Ricky began to cry piteously. The ticket seller and the people behind him stared as he collapsed against the glass enclosure like a prisoner falling hopelessly against the bars of his cell. Eventually he was able to right himself and trudge numbly past the hundreds of other Joni Mitchell fans now waiting in line.

At an earlier time Ricky would have tried to explain to his mother why he would probably never forgive her. If not for recent family dramas occasioned by Ricky's desire for professional psychological guidance, he might have felt more inclined to tell Eve about his unimaginable joy when he clutched that ticket and his crushing despair when it was taken away. But lately Ricky was endeavoring to keep his own counsel when it came to matters of emotional turmoil. He was even beginning to fear that this might be a requirement of growing up.

High school was turning out to be a trying experience, but Ricky was far more concerned about the content of his daydreams. He knew he spent too much time dwelling on the thought of losing his mind. He often felt brittle, like the brother in *The Glass Menagerie* or a character in J. D. Salinger—unshielded from the world, tormented by sex, yearning for the prepubescent idyll of a mother washing you in a tub and sisters reading you stories about harps spinning gold.

Lately, Ricky got frazzled in unfamiliar surroundings. He was sure that he'd begun to grind his teeth at night. He had one recurrent daydream about falling off a motorcycle at high speed like the kid in *Alice's Restaurant*, and he relived his harrowing sexual encounter with Gil far too often, he thought. Once in a while, Ricky even wondered what it would be like to kill himself. He decided it would be no fun.

Luckily, the terrors were mitigated by Ricky's certainty that one or more of his sisters had at one time or another felt or pondered similar things. Usually it was Lorraine who knew best what he was talking about. It seemed to Ricky that Lorraine, who had apparently experienced every single drug reaction and unhealthy fantasy imaginable, had also discovered various means of defusing the panic they engendered. Lorraine could talk about paralyzing sensations or thoughts in a way that often made fear fall away. She had been a serious student of psychology at Hunter College, and she was tuned in to the inexorable cultural dissemination of psychotherapeutic ideas from the shrink's couch to the living room couch in the most average of American homes.

You could now see people on any subway or bus reading *Psychology Today*, a magazine that popularized the psychological sciences. In 1970 the *New York Times Magazine* ran a long article about the family therapy movement by Sara Davidson, who explained the rudiments of the "family system" theories of Murray Bowen and his colleagues. Part of the article focused on the problems of a suburban Boston family named Gordon—among them a teenage son, Jimmy, who mainlined speed and was convinced that his mind was being tape-recorded for broadcast on a local radio station. The Gordons were being treated by a psychologist named Ross Speck, who invited their friends, neighbors, and relatives to form "networks" and "committees" to help not only Jimmy but his dad, Paul Gordon, who likened his marriage to his car dealership ("If you last for twenty-four years, you must be doing something right"), and his mom, Audrey Gordon, who was timid about the entire therapeutic exercise ("I grew up in a generation where you didn't talk about your private life"). During the intense encounters Davidson described, one neighbor exclaimed, "Parents are being put on the spot today because of crummy kids," then broke down in tears and admitted that his own teenage daughter had just run away to become "a hippie."

But family therapy was only one of many proposed solutions for the widely acknowledged family malaise that sent worried parents to magazine racks and psychology sections of bookstores. There were almost as many new theories and approaches as there were troubled families. Humanists, behaviorists, traditionalists, feminist psychiatrists, and proponents of other radical alternatives all sought to put clinical information before the public. R. D. Laing said he agreed with the family system theorists that children were indeed "programmed" by their families— but they were programmed to achieve a neurotic conformity with the status quo. The result was either pathology or rebellion—both realistic reactions to the dark absurdity of modern life, said Laing, who was often accused of portraying schizophrenics as heroes because he thought their behavior was a legitimate response to the way things were.

After the publication of his book *The Politics of the Family*, Dr. Laing, the father of seven, was upset that so many readers saw his work as an attack on the sanctity of family. "Some of my most fulfilled experiences have been in my own family," he said. "It's marvelous when it works, and as everyone knows, it's absolute hell when it doesn't." And because it was hell in so many American households in 1972, the search for a firm science of family would become a central preoccupation for the next twenty years.

Bits and pieces of popular psychology cropped up now and again when Sam discussed "the kids" with his brother Masons, or when Eve and the girls talked about family and the disconcerting times. But among the Gordons, only Lorraine and Ricky were eager to seek help from students of the mind.

For all her reading and consciousness-raising, Susan shied away from the recent literature of the personal. Though she would sometimes fall into sadness and call her family "a ball of pain," she found it hard not to scoff at Lorraine's contention that serious psychotherapy was an essential step along the road to self-discovery.

Lorraine told Susan she'd experienced breakthroughs. She was now positive that there was a way to unravel the Gordian knot of the Gordons, and other families too.

Sheila had ruled out therapy as a means of addressing her general unhappiness and the specific problems she and Peter were having, a decision she'd made several years ago after hearing her parents air their views on the subject.

To Ricky, Lorraine was the family trailblazer, and maybe because he'd learned to tell her all his deepest fears, he found it easy to talk to the school psychologist about the errant thoughts that came into his head.

William Fetzer had a nineteenth-century prizefighter's handlebar mustache and a chin-strap beard. Unlike Morton Schwartzstein, who made a novel effort back when Lorraine was in high school to speak with troubled students instead of just testing them, Fetzer managed a staff of eight professionals working out of the "psychologist's office" at West Hempstead High. (The teens of Harbor Isle were no longer welcome at Oceanside High because of a nasty dispute over tax revenues that arose soon after the new Long Island Lighting Company power plant was constructed just offshore.) After listening quietly to what Ricky had to say, Mr. Fetzer insisted he see a psychiatrist.

Eve drove him to his appointment, looking no less terrorized by the challenge of navigating an automobile than she had five years earlier when she finally got her license. They didn't talk much on the way.

Ricky missed his junior high lunches with his mother at Jackie's Doughnuts. He couldn't tell her everything anymore, but Eve still came to his room in the middle of bad nights—Our Lady of the Boatyard, he teasingly called her—and sat beside him quoting wise men to help ease his pain. "No matter how bad it seems at night, everything looks better in the sunshine of a morning," she'd say.

"Into the cauldron of morning," Ricky would think. *Sylvia Plath.*

After he saw Ricky, the psychiatrist called Eve into his small office. Ricky went to the waiting room. "I think it would be beneficial if your son entered treatment," the doctor said. "I would recommend that he come in three times each week. After a while, I'd like you and your husband to come in too."

"How much is this gonna cost?" Eve asked.

"My fee is seventy-five dollars per session," he said.

Eve smiled and thanked the psychiatrist for his time and consideration. She said she'd get back to him soon.

The minute Ricky closed the car door, Eve shifted into high gear. "Do you know we took out a loan to pay our taxes for last year! Do you think in your wildest dreams that we can afford this? We struggle! Don't you understand that?" The car was soon weaving all over the road.

"You need a psychiatrist? Talk to me!" Eve sputtered, her face bright red. "I'll talk to you all fucking night if you want, but don't you dare go trying to wreck my marriage. You're gonna put me in a loony bin!"

* * *

Eve firmly believed that if you knew how to talk to yourself in the mirror, you could cope with almost anything. When it came to high-priced psychiatry, Eve allowed herself the thought that if a person of her own background and experience could survive with the aid of nothing more than a mirror, cleaning the house, and quoting philosophical song lyrics, then other people should be able to manage too.

Sam basically agreed. He also talked to himself, not face to face in a mirror, but in his head. By now he felt he'd had sufficient experience with "the psychology industry" to have figured out its operative scam. "The whole thing is based on getting people to hate their mothers," he said. "Then—if there's enough money left—they get you out of the mother-hating, over a period of years, of course. And meanwhile, you pay and pay."

Sam admitted that there were certain situations—Eve in the pit of a mood, for instance—when a good psychiatrist might be some help. Still, he couldn't abide what he saw as the moral shortcomings of the therapy business. Having saturated their primary market, wealthy people with problems, the shrinks were now setting their sights on humbler homes. "I grew up when a sick kid just lay there and died," Sam said. "Now everybody has a psychiatrist just because people get sad."

Not long after the unsuccessful visit to the shrink, Ricky went to his mother with an alternative plan. "I think I'd be happier at a private school in Manhattan. I've checked into two—Walden and Dalton— and the whole thing will only cost around three thousand dollars."

Eve started to scream again. It was then that she'd given him the unsigned check.

Ricky entered the ornate vastness of Carnegie Hall and paused at the back, trying to take it in. Three weeks earlier, an hour after the tragedy at the head of the ticket line, he'd managed to locate a branch of Eve's bank and convert the check into a money order, but by the time he returned to the box office, the tickets for all but the most distant seats were sold. Ricky's friends Jodi and Julie Siegel were sitting in the first row, and Sheila was in the eleventh row with some classmates he recognized. Ricky couldn't help himself. As soon as the lights went down, he ran through the orchestra section past Sheila right up to Jodi and Julie, who were under the very lip of the stage.

"I'm sitting with you," Ricky announced.

Jodi shrugged and moved over. Ricky wedged in and looked slowly to his left. There, two seats away, was Mary Travers of Peter, Paul and

Mary! And there, to his right, just one seat away, was…Neil Young! Ricky felt light-headed. He cradled the colorfully decorated package bearing the embroidered dress.

Joni Mitchell came out on the huge stage from the wings and floated across to a microphone just above Ricky's head, sylphlike, gorgeous as a song. She was carrying the guitar he knew she'd tuned in her special Joni way. She opened with several songs performed so perfectly that Ricky had tears in his eyes. She was tuning her dulcimer, telling a story clearly meant to lead into "Carrie," one of his favorites, when Ricky suddenly felt himself stand up and push his package toward the singer's feet. "Joni…I'm Ricky," he said.

Joni Mitchell stopped talking and looked down at the package, which had clearly been assembled with great care. She broke into a grin. "Ricky? Ricky Gordon? Ricky Gordon my pen pal?" She was staring at him, still speaking into the microphone. "Hi, Ricky." She picked up the package. "I just love things people make themselves," she said. "Thanks, Ricky. Thanks."

Ricky just stood there staring back. When he finally sat down, Sheila and her friends and Jodi and Julie and Ricky's classmates and many others in the huge crowd cheered.

The next day Ricky was mobbed several times in the hallways at school. Everyone knew. Everyone had heard a variation on the story. Ricky was a celebrity, a hero, because of his bold connection to the larger culture that really mattered. For a long time the experience made him feel that he could rise above the darkness of his passing thoughts after all.

"*We are stardust,*" Joni sang. "*We are golden.*"

<hr />

Harry Hughes, Lorraine's new boyfriend, warned her that her introductory dinner with his folks might be marred by his father, a longtime railroad employee who was known to his friends and family as "the Duke" and liked to crack the odd "Jewish lawyer" joke.

"What's he like, your father?" Lorraine asked the young man with whom she'd fallen madly in love.

Though it was difficult for someone of Harry's age and experience to acknowledge that the mainstream culture had actually provided a useful reference point, the comparison sprang to his lips. "Well," he said, "he's like Archie Bunker."

How many millions of fathers previously excoriated in a hundred colorful ways were now condemned succinctly as Archie Bunkers?

Though Sam Gordon and others like him still clung to the eternal verities of *Gunsmoke*, by the middle of 1972 more than fifty million Americans preferred to tune in on Saturday evening and watch Archie browbeat his wife, Edith, or call blacks "jungle bunnies" and Jews "Hebes."

If the Duke was indeed like Archie, then by inexact analogy Harry Hughes was like Mike Stivic, *All in the Family*'s liberal sociology student. Harry was a liberal-minded graduate student (psychology) at Hunter College, but unlike Archie's son-in-law, he bore the scars of a young veteran of the war in Vietnam.

Vietnam vets had yet to be turned into prime-time clichés. Soldiers still appeared on television during the news hour, but they were mainly POWs, concentration-camp-thin and ravaged, or they were long-haired combat vets in weathered fatigue jackets, like Harry—though Harry never broke from one of the many antiwar marches he attended to handcuff himself to the gates in front of the White House, and he never stormed the Statue of Liberty as a group of former soldiers had done last December, so he had never been on the news.

When Harry Hughes was just seventeen, he began to ponder day and night how he might flee the tedium of hanging out in front of the candy store in Hempstead, his Long Island birthplace, a few miles from Harbor Isle. It was 1965, and Harry could only imagine three escape routes: a blue-collar job and the early marriage that appeared to go with it, the vague and expensive option of "going off to college," and the opportunity to "see the world" in a military uniform.

Though Harry was extremely intelligent, he was an "underachiever" in school. Too sensitive and smart to be a tough, and too tough to be mainstream-bright, he hung around with a small group of teen nomads he would later describe as "anti-intellectuals." His record in school, and his fear of ending up like the Duke, planning and replanning his retirement from a boring job, led Harry to enlist in the United States Marine Corps. Wars and the fact that the marines fought them did not figure in his analysis.

Harry would never be able to pinpoint whether the magnitude of the flaw in his thinking came to him within seconds or hours of delivering the papers his parents had to sign because he was under age. But sometime during the first half of his first day in the service, while men screamed commands all around him, he wondered if the marines had been the best of choices for a boy who'd had trouble with authority since he was small.

At boot camp on Parris Island, South Carolina—scene of so much rapid resocialization—Harry experienced basic training as unremitting

sadism practiced by men who demanded instant obedience with a feroc-
ity that suggested they would happily kill you at the least sign that you
didn't much like being told what to do. The torture of stateside training
continued until the early weeks of 1967, when Harry found himself
wading through the muck of rice paddies and "pacifying" hamlets in
South Vietnam. Harry noticed that constant rumors about what might
happen to overzealous officers now that the men had live ammunition
tended to tone down the spit-and-polish routine. Working the deadly
trails between Loc Ninh and Na Trang, he actually found himself able
to relax for the first time since leaving Hempstead.

During his five months "in country," Harry survived six extended
combat operations, more than some men, fewer than many others. He
was part of the huge marine-led Operation Union, in which unit after
unit was wiped out in firefights with North Vietnamese regulars hiding
in caves and fields of sugarcane. Many of Harry's friends were killed by
the accidental rocketing of their positions by American pilots. He saw
much of the war by the light of fires rising from villages or by the weird
glow of arc lights and flares. During rest stops, guys on patrol would stick
cigarettes in the mouths of severed heads and get high on killer grass.

Harry stayed in the marines for two years after being shipped home
from Vietnam. By the time he was discharged, he believed that many of
the worst things about the Vietnam War were indistinguishable from
the worst things about the U.S. Marines. He'd unwittingly allowed himself to become part of an organization that demanded much more than
he thought anyone should ever be asked to relinquish. Finally out of the
marines, in his gentle, almost halting way, Harry vowed that he would
never again be a part of any group that required him to sacrifice essential aspects of himself. So while he marched and carried signs along with
other antiwar vets to protest the May 1972 mining of Haiphong harbor,
he never joined Vietnam Veterans Against the War.

When Harry first met Lorraine that spring and she asked about his
long hair, he joked, "I can't look at a barber without seeing the drill
instructor standing over my shoulder." But it wasn't really a joke. His
mane of hair parted down the middle and the little Rasputin goatee he
sported were in part an homage to his musical hero, the leaping flutist
Ian Anderson, leader of a band called Jethro Tull. But Harry's hair was
also civilian camouflage. Long hair was one way many of the three million who went to war tried to melt into the ranks of the twenty-five or
thirty million eligible men their age who had stayed home like Mike
Stivic on All in the Family.

* * *

Harry Hughes didn't just fall in love with Lorraine Gordon Shapiro. He was lifted and transported by love. The first time he chatted with her outside a psychology class at Hunter, after a lecture on learning theory, Harry felt a towering wave of infatuation break over him. Lorraine's fresh, sparkling spirit made him tingle. With her glasses and sharp features, she conformed to none of Harry's centerfold images of desirable girls, but he shared Eve's view that she was radiant in a way that was hard to define, glowing with an inner energy or inner light. He was inspired by her ideals, by her feminism, by her musicianship...by just looking at her.

Harry learned that Lorraine had once been much angrier than she was now, once more political, and once into dangerous drugs. Like everyone else, she had plenty of residual problems rooted in family entanglements. Harry heard about a rough relationship with her father, but Lorraine felt therapy was helping her repair the bridges to her family.

Rather than carrying scars from her short marriage, Lorraine had Maggie, a gift, the brightest and most engaging little girl Harry knew—not that he knew many. "She's like a veteran kid," Harry would tell Lorraine. "It's like she knows all sorts of things even though she's small." Lorraine often thought that there was something "gyroscopic" about almost eight-year-old Magdalena Shapiro. It was as if she possessed an internal mechanism that gave her a balance and perspective Lorraine wondered if she would ever achieve herself.

Maggie took to Harry immediately, and he began to love her too. He stayed up late at night drawing her skillful cartoons and greeting cards. And he wrote long, impassioned love letters to Maggie's mother. They went on outings to city parks, just like the little family Goldenberg during Sam's first years home. Sitting under the trees in their similar buckskin jackets, Harry and Lorraine would play Bob Dylan songs on their similar guitars.

Harry decided 1972 was his golden year. Everywhere he looked he saw people who seemed lost and full of despair, but he and Lorraine and Maggie were together and happy. Despite all the dire warnings about family dissolution, the vast majority of 350,000 readers polled by *Better Homes and Gardens* said they did not long for the "good old days of family life" because family life was just fine as it was. Harry agreed. He felt at home with Maggie and Lorraine. And as tradition required, he wanted Lorraine to meet his folks.

Lorraine had never seen so much blood coming out of a single slab of meat as when the Duke addressed the roast. She had lately declared herself a vegetarian. Susan, Sheila, and Ricky loved to joke about the demarcation line that defined Lorraine's new diet. "I will no longer," she declared, "eat anything with mucus."

Harry's father was much taller and handsomer than Archie Bunker. His wife was also tall and had beautiful red hair not in the least like Edith's. Their house was simple but still far grander than the Bunkers' row house in Queens.

The first thing Harry did upon entering the living room was to turn all the framed pictures of himself in crew cut and uniform toward the wall.

"Does he still like to get up on his soapbox?" the Duke asked Lorraine. Harry hung his head.

It was clear within minutes that Harry's father was a member in good standing of "the silent majority." He subscribed to the "square virtues" President Nixon had been trumpeting in the name of the millions of ordinary Americans he claimed supported his policies and must now speak up. Mr. Hughes was one of the "honest and patriotic" Americans Nixon had called to the domestic barricades as irregulars at the end of 1969. The following spring, just a few days after the shootings at Kent State, a group of "hard-hats" had bloodied peace marchers in Lower Manhattan with vise-grips, claw hammers, and other objects of the sort Lorraine used to ferry between her father's toolbox and his waiting hand.

Since the beginning of the 1970s, a new archetype had arisen to confront the nation's hippie-radical "bums": the father in a shirt with his name inscribed in an oval over the pocket. The workingman—as caricatured in Archie Bunker, so beloved for the epithets that were humorously ironic to some and the simple truth to others—had joined the drill sergeant and the charging policeman. The old left-wing romance of working people shoulder to shoulder with youth was all but forgotten.

Lorraine was polite enough at dinner, but she did speak her mind when the denigration of George McGovern began. The Democratic presidential nominee was certainly old-fashioned in Lorraine's estimation, but she would soon vote for the well-meaning senator from South Dakota, her hatred of liberals having been tempered by time. Like so many others, Lorraine believed in 1972 that the movement had been subverted, or at least subsumed by elements of the establishment. Still, she ventured to differ with Harry's father about the Equal Rights Amendment, racial issues, and what she belittled as "the so-called peace talks" in Paris.

Harry suspected that his folks were probably not disposed to like Lorraine because of her religion, but now he could tell that they were utterly appalled by his choice of a young woman with such outlandish views. This was not an episode of *All in the Family*. It was real and tinged with pain. But then, parental approval was of little consequence to Harry Hughes, because Harry was in love.

As soon as Harry and his new girlfriend left the house, his quiet, pretty mother carefully turned back the photographs of her son the marine.

❧

One of Shuna Lydon's earliest memories was of an afternoon at her friend Sunlight's house. They were on their way upstairs to play when Shuna saw Sunlight's mom sitting on the floor of the living room, dressed in a long white robe. Other grown-ups, also in white, were on the floor too. They weren't talking, just sitting.

"Come on, Shuna," Sunlight said. "Let's play."

Shuna kept staring into the living room.

"Come on, Shuna."

"But what are they doing?"

Sunlight sighed, exasperated by having to state the obvious. "They're getting high and meditating. Now come on. Let's *play*."

The girls ran upstairs.

Shuna was only four, but she and Sunlight and Seven Anne MacDonald and some of the other Blue Fairyland kids thought of themselves as much, much older. Since their parents were always going to meetings, they talked about going to meetings too, though they often fell asleep when they did. Shuna's friend Christopher Scheer, son of Bob Scheer and Anne Weills, called his divorced mother and father "Bob" and "Anne." Blue Fairyland kids were kind of like short grown-ups.

Blue Fairyland, which some called a "day-care center," others a "nursery" or an "experiment in nurturing," was two years old now. The members of the Red Family collective who founded the program believed that two-year-olds would thrive together outside traditional family structures. At one point, the Blue Fairyland house behind the Red Family house on Hilegus Street was even fitted with little bunks, but the full-time kibbutzlike experiment never got going. Another early idea was that political men could "get in touch with their nurturing sides" while children established identities and internalized values in a progressive and democratic environment. In the spirit of participatory democracy, the children were asked to name the program. Thus, Blue Fairyland.

A year earlier, when President Nixon vetoed the Child Development Act that would have provided federal funds for day-care programs, he said he didn't approve of "communal approaches to child-rearing" because they undermined "family-centered traditions." American life was already far too "child-centered," according to Nixon.

In later years Blue Fairyland teachers, parents, and students would look back fondly but often critically at the experiment. A lot of candles were cast in sand, a lot of leaves pressed and Tarot cards laid out in the attempt to connect child care to a larger public and political purpose, but many of the parents were really using Blue Fairyland to back away from the emotionally demanding and time-consuming responsibilities of having children at a historical moment when there seemed to be so many other important things to do. Some would remember Blue Fairyland as a "dumping ground."

Susan had already watched one of her favorite boyfriends sail under the Golden Gate Bridge into the sunset and out of her life for good. The guy wanted her to go off around the world in his big sloop, but Susan had a child. She stood with Shuna in her arms, watching the boat and its skipper sail away. Now Susan was in love with another man, so Shuna was spending a lot of time at Blue Fairyland, where some of the teachers and other parents noted that she was looking more waiflike all the time. She'd always been the kind of kid who had a perpetual runny nose, but lately she seemed to be wearing soiled clothes.

Shuna would remember her Blue Fairyland days happily, and as she came back into contact with some of her classmates as adults, she thought that many of them indeed "shared good values" of the sort the founders intended. But she'd remember too that Blue Fairyland confused her. It was the first place in Shuna's experience where "children could act like adults and adults could act just like kids."

"Guess what, Ma," Susan said when she called Eve one Sunday. "You won't believe it, but I finally have a Jewish boyfriend."

"*Mazel tov*," said Eve. She could hear the excitement in Susan's voice, but she'd heard it before. "What does he do?"

"Well, he's...well, a drummer. He's kind of a famous rock star, really."

"A rock star?" Eve said. "That means the Jewish part doesn't count."

* * *

A curly-haired Brooklyn boy who had always wanted to be an artist when he grew up, David Getz won a Fulbright scholarship to study art in Poland and then taught painting at the California School of Fine Arts in San Francisco. In 1966 David decided to supplement his income with the same sort of part-time employment he'd had since his days playing in bar mitzvah bands and on weekends at Catskills hotels. Even in Poland David had played the drums to keep himself in canvas and oil paint.

David had grown up on Alan Freed and fifties rock 'n' roll concerts at the Brooklyn movie palaces, though at sixteen he'd cast them aside in favor of Dixieland jazz. But in the middle of 1966 David took a job as drummer for a local band called Big Brother and the Holding Company. He joined the group three weeks before the arrival of a new lead singer, a hard-drinking Texas girl named Janis Joplin who sang like an injured angel. Janis was a girl with problems, but oh, could she sing the blues.

David Getz emerged from his five years with the famous band (Janis left Big Brother in 1969 and died from a drug overdose in 1970) with only partial hearing in one ear, with much more money than he could ever have made from a long life of teaching art, and with automatic entrée to any gathering or happening in the Bay Area.

The trendy San Francisco scene Susan and Michael Lydon had first experienced as a relatively tiny network of area artists, lefties new and old, ex–New Yorkers, and hippies with good jobs was now a fully stratified "hipoisie" spread out around San Francisco, a class of local elites ranging from rockers to hip entrepreneurs who'd prospered from both legal and illegal trades. The scene had its particular material preferences (old cars, antiques, Oriental rugs, cocaine, marijuana genetically refined and nurtured like the finest wine) and its own pattern of urban exodus from the dark and threatening remnants of the counterculture out to the woody suburbs of Sonoma and Marin counties.

When David Getz met Susan Lydon at a party, he was still playing the drums and writing songs, but like many other San Francisco rock personages, he spent a lot of his time puttering around a big house in Fairfax, a Marin County town where he lived with his daughter by a former marriage, Alzara, who was a year younger than Shuna. The house was a sprawling redwood-lined labyrinth set so high on a steep, wooded hill that alongside the hundreds of stairs leading up from the road David had installed an elevator to transport his drums. Not long after they started "seeing" each other, in the euphemism of the moment, Susan began to help David collect antiques and wall hangings for the big house. She spent hours stringing colorful glass beads in front of the windows.

Susan and David loved to act like smart New York Jews adrift in the land of the Californians. They'd sit around the house in Marin having ironic conversations about organic gardening. They'd boom out, "Have a nice day!" to the locals and grin slyly at each other. Susan delighted David Getz, but he was often struck by how much his smart new girlfriend reminded him of Janis Joplin in a way. Janis was one of those women who made men nervous because of her cloying need to be loved. David said Janis needed to be every man's "goddess." Susan was so much in need of being loved that David sometimes wanted to run away.

But David knew he needed a woman like Susan. Though his rock star credentials got him past the door and into the right social circles, he wasn't really comfortable around people the way Susan was. Susan knew everyone in San Francisco; she could manage the rare crossover between the culture people and the political types in Berkeley, and she wasn't afraid to call any of them on the phone. One night as Susan's date, David ended up on a couch beside Francis Ford Coppola at the director's house in San Francisco. David and Francis agreed that *The Thief of Baghdad* was probably the best movie ever made.

Susan could make things like this happen, and she appreciated David's jokes. But Susan was also, he thought, "extremely white." For all she'd done and seen, he found it strange that Susan was so lacking in cool. It was as if the things she knew came from books. She knew music, for instance, but jazz would never really run in her veins. David couldn't quite put his finger on why it was so, but Susan was not at all cool.

Feminist writer Sally Kempton had recently contended in *Esquire* that it was hard for women to be cool because men had stolen cool and turned it into a private male preserve. And there were those who believed, as had been argued since the 1950s, that only black people could be truly cool. But everyone agreed that in the post-sixties Thermidor it was harder to be cool all the time, no matter what you did or what you had or what color you were—and particularly hard for Susan, David Getz observed, because in so many ways cool was all she had ever wanted to be.

By the early days of his junior year in high school, Ricky could barely discern the boundary between life and art, both of which stretched before him as a single golden continuum. Asked to name his favorite movie, he'd say that his favorite *film* was Ingmar Bergman's *The Silence*, in which women masturbated and small boys urinated meaningfully in dark hallways. Another favorite was Bergman's *Winter Light,* considered by many viewers one of the most austere and incomprehensible films of all time. Ricky had recently been mesmerized by Visconti's film version of Mann's *Death in Venice,* and he was sure that its profundity was deepened rather than diminished by the incongruous presence of his father snoring noisily beside him through the whole thing. "With a title like that, it's gotta be one of those spaghetti westerns," Sam had said when he saw the marquee on the way home from Sunday lunch at Yetta's. "Let's go."

It was a rare week in which Ricky didn't phone one or all of his sisters to report that yet another European film had "completely changed" his life. Ricky borrowed or pilfered every film book in the Island Park library, and late into most nights he pored over the most complex discussion of film aesthetics he could find.

He also read Camus. He said *The Plague* changed his life because it opened his eyes to "the power of metaphor." The piano pieces Ricky chose to learn and his preferences in twentieth-century opera were becoming more highbrow by the week. He regularly foraged New York City for advanced cultural experiences—a nude ballet in Brooklyn on a Friday night, an Antonioni festival at the Elgin Theater in Manhattan the next afternoon. He took a course in film criticism at the New School for Social Research in the Village. He took a dance class at the Alvin Ailey School in which all the other students were female and black.

Ricky was able to pursue art so doggedly these days because shortly after Eve told him that therapy bills might ruin her marriage and that changing schools was out of the question, he had transferred to the new "free school" program recently begun at West Hempstead High. The alternative school was called SAFE, for Students and Faculty Education, though to most of the students the name meant sanctuary or safe harbor. Beyond not having to worry about grades, the SAFE program meant that Ricky would often arrive at school before eight o'clock in the morning, say hello to his SAFE adviser, Art Sherin—a young man with thick dark hair and an aggressive beard—and be hard at work broadening his cultural horizons in Manhattan two hours later.

So many "free" and "alternative" schools had sprung up in American cities and towns by the fall of 1972 that their proponents considered themselves part of a movement. In Berkeley an advocate of progressive education predicted that by 1975 there would be twenty-five thousand to thirty thousand such school experiments serving two million American students. The entire Berkeley public school system (which would soon adopt Blue Fairyland as a model for its preschool program) was already based on twenty-four alternative schools, each designed to liberate the learning process by making it "relevant" to the "outside world." All free schools incorporated aspects of participatory decision-making, community involvement, a minimal reliance on grades (which were seen as part of a corporate model of achievement), self-motivated programs of study, and sedulous efforts to preclude the pervasive racism and sexism of mainstream educational institutions. But educators and parents who saw the free schools as "training grounds for liberation" deplored the recent vogue for setting up free-form alternative programs *inside* existing public schools—"schools within the schools"—as an example of the establishment's considerable powers of cooptation.

The free-school movement had come to the public schools via a new generation of reformist young teachers and administrators who had gone to college in the rebellious, questioning atmosphere of the sixties. A faculty like West Hempstead's was now as starkly divided along lines of appearance as the "freaks" and the "jocks" in the student body. There were female teachers who looked like classic schoolmarms and male teachers who looked like Vince Lombardi or Mayor Daley. The other thirty or forty percent of the faculty would have been right at home at a Grateful Dead concert. Art Sherin of the SAFE program was a graduate of Antioch College, a veteran of the Peace Corps, and a teacher in Harlem until his worried mother submitted an application under his name at West Hempstead.

Three factions within the West Hempstead High faculty constantly debated the purpose of the year-old SAFE program. One loathed the innovation as little more than camouflage for student and faculty shirkers (whom they called "the radicals"); another saw it as an internal gulag for troubled, disaffected, and underachieving students; and the third believed SAFE could indeed nurture the exceptional gifts and special interests of students not sufficiently challenged by the mainstream curriculum.

Ricky Ian Gordon, a charter member of all three student categories, was one of the first SAFE transferees. Sam and Eve never thought to stand in the way of the change because it was all official and on the up-and-up.

Ricky immediately began to absorb a dozen foreign films a month. After a day taking courses at the school of life, he would rendezvous at the fountain in front of Lincoln Center with Peter Randsman and their new, equally opera-obsessed buddy Arthur Levy. The boys would adjourn for a stimulating Left Bank exchange of ideas—about the similarities between a Bergman film like *Summer Interlude* and a piece of musical theater like Brecht and Weill's *Threepenny Opera,* for instance—and Ricky would return to SAFE the next morning to rehash his insights with Art, as the SAFE students called Mr. Sherin. Like some athlete in training, Ricky felt himself becoming stronger and more self-assured because of SAFE. He stopped having nightmares about being tortured by the gym teacher just because of the way he dribbled in for a layup.

In earlier years Ricky's teachers might have read his precocity as obstreperousness, as Susan's had. They might have interpreted his anti-authoritarian impulses as psychological problems, as Lorraine's had. And they might have ignored his underachievement altogether, as Sheila's had. Like Harry Hughes, he might have seen his options narrowed down to little more than a choice between colors of uniform.

So Ricky would always consider himself saved by SAFE. The program made a home for him, even as it made him see his home with Sam and Eve as a cultural wasteland he would eventually have to transcend. Ricky now realized that he wanted a great deal from the future. He wanted nothing less than "an enduring prominence," as he jotted in his journal. He wanted art, fame, and the same heady life he was now experiencing as a gift of this brief antistructural moment in American secondary education.

The SAFE program would end at West Hempstead and at thousands of other schools within five years. But few of the students or teachers who experienced the best of the experiment would ever learn or teach in quite the same way again.

1973

Sheila watched the counterculture deliquesce in the living room of her communal household. She watched from a distance, through the door of her quilt-covered bedroom sanctuary. She saw the experiment in sharing day-to-day family life outside ties of blood and tradition descend into near-violent disputation and a kind of sloppy degeneracy. The snake cages in the Rockville Centre house were no longer cleaned regularly, and visitors often commented that the place smelled like a zoo. The golden couple that anchored the household, Kenny and Sue, screamed at each other all the time. There were fights about child-care responsibilities and money. Group cooking was a rarity, as were the turgid after-dinner conclaves that Ricky and his friends had found so romantic and emblematic of the great gift of being Sheila's age instead of their own.

The counterculture grapevine was carrying ominous news of communes turning authoritarian or dangerous, of political groups turning into street gangs. And Sheila's commune was not the only one where relations between upper-middle-class college graduates and lower-middle-class kids who'd gone straight into punching a time clock were fraying badly.

One powerful new catalyst altering the look and feel of many houses like the one Peter and Sheila shared was an insidious pill usually known by one of its several trade names, among them Soper and Quaalude (lude for short). The generic sedative-hypnotic methaqualone, a pill that cost four cents to make and had been retailed 185 million times by prescription at forty cents a pop, was billed as the "nonaddictive downer." In the realm of recreational drugs, ludes were not far from what rubbing alcohol and Sterno were to the Bowery.

The crisp synaptic expansiveness of psychedelics was nowhere to be found in the vaunted Quaalude trip. Gone were the Day-Glo visions, and the awful nightmares too. Even marijuana offered the occasional insight, however fleeting and narrow. Ludes turned you into porridge. All of a sudden the feat of pronouncing every word in a sentence correctly was cause for celebration, and remaining upright a great victory. Driving a car on a quick errand without sideswiping anything or anyone was nothing short of miraculous.

Eve Gordon always maintained that the true purpose of all the drug-taking was sex without guilt. "It's just my opinion," she'd say, "but it's not much different from the way men used to loosen up women with liquor." Quaalude sex was indeed described by those who'd tried it as glandular imperative unimpeded by inhibition. *The Joy of Sex*, a best-selling text now on display on millions of coffee tables, argued diagrammatically that good sex was like gourmet cuisine. Quaalude sex was more like chewing so many pieces of gum at once that it was hard to name the flavor. Sometimes Sheila came home to find several people high on ludes having sex together on her bed. The invasion made her feel sick.

Piled in candy dishes at frat parties and in the rec rooms of respectable homes, this new drug enshrouded the countercultural color wheel by the beginning of 1973, hiding the bright hues of former glory.

Peter Probst sometimes went out for the evening and came home the next day. Sheila would dial number after number, unashamedly looking for her husband, and on occasion a woman she didn't know would answer and hand Peter the phone. One night when Susan was in town from California, Peter chased her around Sam and Eve's living room and wrestled her down on the couch. It might have been a joke, but Susan and Sheila knew that he was out of control. Still, there were times when Peter and Sheila were like high school sweethearts again. Peter would talk constantly about California and the open road. "San Francisco first," he'd say. "San Francisco and the whole trip. Then we'll head out of town and find a piece of land."

The vision of a piece of land now animated a steady stream of young families and groups of friends. Local farmers from Oregon to the Ozarks stood back with bemused interest as immigrant hippies tried to learn how to grow food and keep warm by reading manuals and books. Taking to the highway and finding some land were popular alternatives at the beginning of 1973. But then, roaming the country and moving on in search of happiness was not an invention of the current generation.

Peter and Sheila took cross-country practice runs in the van, Sheila with her wardrobe winnowed to one pair of bell-bottom jeans, two peasant blouses, and a simple bandanna, and Peter looking like some hippie Greek god, Sheila thought. They played road music on the tape deck at high volume.

As soon as Peter finished his apprenticeship as a steamfitter and was fully licensed, they would go. They'd leave the communal sleaziness behind and find a better place.

Just before the planned move west, Sheila left Peter at a messy party and went for a quiet drink with two close girlfriends. "He gets so crazy. Sometimes I don't know how long I can take it," Sheila confided. Jokingly she added, "He's probably gone to bed with every single woman I know. I wouldn't be surprised if he's slept with you guys."

"Well, I certainly haven't," said one of the close friends.

"Well…" said the other. There was a long pause.

Sheila went to find a phone. She called one of Peter's best friends and suggested they get together. She downed two brightly colored Tuinals and marched off into the night to get with the moment. Peter was enraged when he heard what Sheila had done and immediately left for California without her.

Sheila lost more than twenty pounds in a matter of weeks. She began to stay away from the boatyard and its lovely view of the water because there was something about family sympathy she found impossible to bear.

———◆———

Ricky was out when Peter Randsman dropped by the boatyard to visit Eve, as he had done often since his family moved to Long Beach two years earlier. Peter introduced Eve to Charlie, his close friend at the local college they both attended. Charlie had heard more than a few Eve Gordon stories. He knew you could call her by her first name, and that she still wore a two-piece bathing suit to the beach at nearly *fifty-two*, and that she had an outrageous needlepoint pillow collection, which he was now studying with pleasure (in particular, the Elizabeth Taylor pillow, and another of a woman with huge bare breasts).

Most of Ricky's newer friends—performers or musicians or artists of one sort or another—loved to come to the boatyard to eat and listen to Ricky's mother talk or sing. One of them, Richie, was already steeped in

Gordon lore and knew all about Eve's singing career. It was Richie who'd made the likeness of Liz Taylor on Eve's pillow, in the style of those velveteen portraits of wide-eyed children sold at sidewalk fairs. To Richie and the others, Eve was in the same league with Liz and Streisand and Judy Garland, and her Catskill past was the very definition of adorable kitsch.

Peter loved to visit Eve for less stylish reasons. He had never fully recovered from the Gordons' move away from 221 Lincoln, the site of so many of his best memories, but at least he could still have coffee with Eve, who never changed and always made him feel close to his past.

Not long after Peter and Charlie finished their cake and left, Ricky came home.

"Guess who was just here," Eve said. "Peter and his fiancé."

Ricky wasn't sure he'd heard.

"Charlie was here—Peter's fiancé," she said again. "Peter's...gay, isn't he, Ricky?"

Ricky walked purposefully to the refrigerator and pretended to stare idly inside as his mother named several of his other friends. "All of them—gay. Am I right?" Eve's tone was less accusatory than urgent. "And...you too, Ricky," he heard her say over the steady hum of the fridge. "What about it? Are you gay?"

Last year Ricky had been madly and passionately in love with a girl named Gloria, no less than a future Miss Hempstead, the most stunning young woman at West Hempstead High and arguably in Nassau County. Ricky got to know her while playing Perchik in the school production of *Fiddler on the Roof*. Gloria sang in the chorus.

Ricky and Gloria went out on a dinner date to Enrique and Palieri's, the boisterous Italian place at the edge of Green Acres Mall. They drank wine, and later Gloria put her slender arms around him, cocked her head to the side, and started making out. Ricky would always remember exactly how her deep kisses tasted, because there was something about it that just wasn't right. They went to a production of *Brigadoon* at Long Beach High, starring the graduating senior Peter Randsman. ("Such a baritone—and on my little Peter," Eve would say. "Like Gordon MacRae or something.") During "Come to Me, Bend to Me," Ricky stared at the actor who was singing the moving number and felt a profound urgency that for the first time in his life came to him in words: *I want him.*

It had taken him a week to get up the nerve to dump Gloria, an act that defied all social and sexual logic Ricky could imagine. Still, he took her aside between classes. "I just can't seem to give myself to you," was the unfortunate line that came out, but at least it was done.

Less than a year later, without any help from foreign movies, Ricky's life had "completely changed." By now he'd had sex with several members of the West Hempstead High School football team, and with boys and men he'd met at the wild Quaalude parties he went to with Peter and Sheila and their freewheeling friends. For some of his partners, the sex was nothing more than a passing notion, a chance to experiment, or an impulse launched by some recently ingested drug, but to Ricky it was part of becoming "gay." All his life Ricky had borne the stigma of a "differentness" that made growing up in a postwar suburb like Harbor Isle harrowing and even dangerous. But suddenly, in a matter of a few years, "being gay" had begun to emerge as just another way to live. In New York and San Francisco gay people "came out" in droves to toast the latest victory and plan the next assault on convention. A gay rights bill was now before the New York City Council, and Gay Pride Day would be celebrated in the streets in July. By the end of the year three hundred gay Princeton students would attend an all-gay dance. NBC executives would seek the advice of gay men in an effort to make their shows less offensive to homosexuals.

The American Psychiatric Association, another heterosexual bastion, was stormed by gay activists at a convention in May. The diagnostic bible used by psychiatrists still classified homosexuality as a "deviation," on the same list with sadomasochism. Members of the gay liberation movement lobbied for a nonpejorative definition—"lifestyle," for instance. Speaking for the establishment, a New York psychiatrist, Charles Socarides, assured the APA conclave in Honolulu that society did not cause homosexuality, childhoods did (specifically, "a domineering mother who will not let her children achieve autonomy, and an absent, weak, or rejecting father"). The APA voted to support full civil rights for homosexuals, and the committee on nomenclature was charged with the task of deciding whether to move homosexuality out of the "sexual deviance" pages of the official manual.

In 1974 homosexuality was removed from the APA's list of psychiatric afflictions altogether. By then estimates indicated that twenty to thirty million citizens—by inference, the children of forty to sixty million parents—were homosexual. The movement formed in the wake of a relatively small incident in the summer of 1969, when policemen from the New York City morals squad raided the Stonewall Inn, a Greenwich Village bar, and were beaten back by gay patrons, had made enormous strides. Now being socially gay in public, dancing or holding hands, or having sex in private or quasi-private settings was an act of militance, rife with political implications. Gay sex was a form of celebrating a great victory.

Several months before Peter Randsman brought Charlie to the boatyard, Peter and Ricky's opera buddy, Arthur Levy, told them about a place called the Firehouse, where a Manhattan gay organization sponsored tea dances on Sunday nights. The next Sunday the three boys went to the city.

Most of the men at the Firehouse were much older, but Ricky didn't care. Peter and Arthur stood back jealously and watched Ricky allow himself to be picked up and taken home by a guy from Far Rockaway, a Long Island town where Ricky had never been. The sex part of the evening scared Ricky even more than it hurt. On the way home in the man's car, he had to try hard not to cry.

"Well," Eve said. "Are you?"

Ricky leaned closer to the leftovers in the refrigerator. The big door bumped against his back as he tried to escape his mother's question.

Just a few months earlier Sam Randsman had said, "Your mother can't take what I'm about to ask you, Peter—"

After a short pause, Peter looked up at his beloved father and said, "Yes."

"I can accept Ricky and Arthur being like that, but…I love you," Bernice said, more able to take it than her husband had guessed.

The Randsmans asked Peter to see a psychiatrist. He did, and the psychiatrist reported that Peter was a well-adjusted young man who was homosexual.

Ricky stared at the glassy surfaces of Saran-wrapped bowls. Eve loved him. Eve was his kindred spirit. He could lie to her, but she'd know. He remembered the time he lied when she asked if he'd stolen fifteen dollars from her purse. He thought he'd hidden the money safely in his tape recorder, but then he found a note on his bed: "I'm so disappointed. I thought I gave you enough."

Ricky closed the refrigerator door and went back to the table. "Yeah, Ma, me too. I guess I'm gay."

"I don't really understand this, Ricky," Eve said gently. "But if it's what you are I accept it. I'm sad for you because life is hard and lonely enough already. I think gay people choose a lonely life."

"I don't feel like I chose this," Ricky said. "It sort of chose me."

"I don't think Daddy should know," said Eve.

* * *

Ricky finally met Charlie a few hours later. If Charlie, who resembled the singer John Denver, wasn't quite Peter's fiancé, he was at least his true love of the moment. Charlie let Ricky drive his car for a while before Peter got a terrible headache and asked to go home. "Feel better," Charlie said, kissing Peter good-bye when they dropped him off in Long Beach.

During the ride back to Ricky's, Charlie said, "We should get to know each other better." Sam and Eve were out for the afternoon, so Ricky invited Charlie back to the boatyard, where they had sex.

"While I was lying there with a migraine!" Peter raged when Ricky came over later and confessed his transgressions with Charlie.

"I'm really, really sorry," Ricky said. "It's just been a weird day."

<hr />

Sam drove Eve, Sylvia, and Yetta out to visit Papa Joe's grave. Each time they made the trip, someone mentioned Joe's self-sacrificing purchase of the expensive cubic footage at the cemetery. Everybody agreed that buying a family plot was among the best things a man could do for his loved ones.

"Sammy," Sylvia said on the way, "your Sheila tells me she has an *in*-ter-est in nursing. You should do something for her. Maybe she'd meet a nice Jewish *doc*-tor and get rid of that Irish bum."

"They're still married," Eve snapped.

"Does this mean a Jewish doctor from a *hos*-pital wouldn't be better?"

"They're still in love," Eve said.

Sam looked over at Eve when he stopped at a red light. He spoke quietly, but the family in back could hear. "You know what, Eve, sometimes I wonder if your ears hear what comes out of your mouth."

Not long after that, an acquaintance came up to Eve at the Harbor Isle Beach Club. The woman was weeping over the news of a daughter's divorce. "How do you take it? You have this in your family. How can you stand it?" the woman blubbered.

"You just do," Eve said.

"But how, Eve? How?"

"By reminding yourself it's not your own divorce," Eve said.

Then, as Eve was standing in the shallow end of the pool, another woman she knew began to cry beside her.

"What's the matter?"

"My son...is gay," the woman managed.

"Ah, so what," Eve said.

"Wh-what? He's *gay*. I sent him to a psychiatrist who says there's nothing that can be done."

"Do you love him?" Eve asked.

"Of course, he's my son."

"Then forget the whole thing and accept it. He is what he is. He's healthy. Maybe he's even happy. It's his life, and once you learn to accept him you'll feel a lot better. Besides, this way he won't be dropping off any children for you to take care of."

Two weeks later, the woman from the pool phoned Eve. "I'm calling to say that what you said to me has changed my life, Eve. Thank you."

Everybody had family problems. And now everybody had family problems they wanted to discuss. The shift in the vocabulary of family trouble from "*the* American family" to "*my* family" was indelibly marked and undoubtedly promoted by a 1973 television documentary about the Loud family of California. For thirteen weeks, millions of parents and children sat down in front of the TV like football fans and watched the Loud family falling apart. The Louds of *An American Family* were to the family struggles of 1973 what the Joads of *The Grapes of Wrath* were to the family struggles of the years preceding the publication of John Steinbeck's novel in 1939, but now the yoke of prewar poverty had been replaced by the yoke of postwar affluence, by generational schism, and by ennui.

Since the end of World War II—with the chorus of "expert" family watchers commenting from the sidelines—real families had retreated further and further into privacy and dissociation while self-contained TV families and the occasional book family took over as cultural paradigms, replacing the model of entwined generations dwelling in a single house, or the small societies of tenements and Main Streets where there was nothing much to do but compare family intimacies. Households and houses grew more and more separate as the extended family declined. The postwar American suburbs were the apotheosis of privatization. Keeping family business private was thought to be one of the hallmarks of ascent and privilege.

Now the family was opening up again. In coming years the near-fetishistic sharing of intimate matters would completely reverse earlier privacy trends, and the public revelation of family truth would become a path to personal enlightenment and mental health. Watching the Louds week after week, Americans saw real parents and children hurting one another. The family sanctum was on full display at its very worst. There was extramarital sex, homosexuality, and the divorce of Bill and Pat

Loud, stars of the show. There were fires and car accidents and business reversals, and during every episode, the tortured effort to "communicate."

Millions of Americans entering the second half of their lives could look at Bill Loud trying to engage his directionless teenage son in a "What are you gonna make of yourself?" discussion and feel assured that they weren't the only parents who'd faced such blank aggression. Meanwhile, millions of younger Americans, witnessing the same scene, saw drugs in the boy's eyes and found it humorous or sad but in any case typical that a father could sit there uttering platitudes while his son's mind was so far away.

The Loud moment arrived at the Gordons' at the same time as the Sheila moment and a flood of new empirical evidence of family trouble. Sheila and Peter were separated now, and though Sheila talked about moving to California, the family assumed her marriage was over, soon to be included in a national divorce rate that had doubled over ten years. Newspapers reported that divorcing couples now went to court to fight over the privilege of *not* keeping the children. A California psychologist quoted in the *New York Times* claimed that the American family, however powerful it might be as an icon of popular culture, was no longer "the basic unit of our society." Harvard professor Carle Zimmerman, tireless prophet of the disintegration of the American family since World War II, compared the "extinction of faith in the familistic system" in the early 1970s to the antifamily ethos of ancient Greece and Rome in decline. According to Alvin Toffler's best-selling *Future Shock*, average families would soon be predicated upon temporary relationships. Even Margaret Mead—who for years had been pointing to unusual family arrangements throughout history as evidence of the institution's elasticity and essential toughness—admitted that the rebelliousness of youth, the rise of communes, and the practice of living together called into question "the very meaning and structure of the stable family unit as our society has known it."

Confronted with expert opinion, Eve liked to relate the story of poor Dr. Forrest, the Gordon family GP, who'd refused to believe that Lorraine had whooping cough when she most certainly did, and who assured Ricky that LSD would stay in his system for a year. During her stressful spring Eve had gone to see Dr. Forrest. She told him she felt so sick she thought she was going to die. "People don't die so quickly," Forrest said. "I wouldn't worry." Shortly thereafter, while watching the Academy Awards on TV, the doctor died in his easy chair.

"Need I say more?" Eve would ask at the end of her parable.

In truth, Eve would very much have liked to blame experts or teachers or music or *something* for the things that were happening to her family. For all her mah-jongg and poolside bravado and the solid advice she dispensed, Eve was confused. She wondered why all three of her girls' marriages had gone wrong. She couldn't stop wondering why Ricky was gay. When she closed her eyes, Eve saw trouble hovering over her family "like a swarm."

Three days before Peter Randsman brought Charlie to the house, Eve had discovered a letter in Ricky's room—a love letter to a boy. She read it twice and then sat on Ricky's bed and cried. Later, she called Lorraine. "Of course, I've known for a long time," Lorraine said. "But I haven't ever talked to Ricky about it." Susan said she'd known Ricky was gay since her college days. The sisters all knew, but none of them knew why.

Eve had no intention of consulting Aunt Sylvia on the matter, but when Sylvia heard about Ricky's admission some time later, she said she'd realized Ricky was "funny like that" when he was only six and kept criticizing her for wearing the same bathing suit every time she came out to go to the beach. "Is that bathing suit stuck to you, Aunt Syl?" she recalled Ricky saying—hardly, she thought, the normal observation of a normal boy.

After Eve reread the love letter and cried again, she had a talk with herself. She remembered the first time she was confronted with young men "like that" in her show business days. She decided then that they weren't meant to be understood. They just were. The recollection helped a bit.

Eve wished she could hold fate or luck or her children's friendships with "assholes" responsible for her family troubles. She wanted someone to blame, but she was too busy blaming herself. She "had" guilt. She had it like you had the flu. It was in her system, screwing everything up. She wondered what she could have taught Susan about husbands that would have helped her keep Michael. She ached with guilt over Sheila and she ached for Ricky. She could still remember every detail of Lorraine's "episode" at Bellevue as if it had occurred last week, in part because she'd never decided how much of it was her fault.

As far as Eve could tell, Sam wasn't haunted by guilt. He was always pointing to universals outside the family core: California was a "loser state" where bad things happened to people stupid enough to live there (Susan); take a child out of poverty, and it's to poverty the child seeks to return (Lorraine); Jewish girls were asking for trouble unless they married Jewish boys who didn't drink (Sheila); girls were too goddamn smart for their own good (all three, along with their entire sex). The list went on. But then, Sam shouldn't have to feel like it was his fault, Eve would tell herself, since he was hardly ever around.

It amazed Eve that even as the children grew older and moved away, their capacity to inflict pain never seemed to diminish at all. It often felt like they were still inside her. But at least you could talk about it and feel a little better. You could talk to yourself, or you could talk to your friends. This Eve Gordon had known long before the Louds and the retreat from family privacy, and long before Susan's excited reports about her women's group—as if Eve hadn't been talking in women's groups all her life.

"You know what I think?" Eve said one afternoon, wiping away the last of her tears over Sheila's troubles. "I think women should just marry women."

The mah-jongg girls all burst out laughing.

"Whose turn?" somebody asked.

On the way to his wedding, stopped at a traffic light, Harry Hughes stared out of Eve's car and considered running away. He could throw open the door and disappear. Maybe it was typical, he thought, this desire to just disappear.

Sam said he'd join the entourage later, at the reception. Lorraine said her father stayed away from the little ceremony before a local justice of the peace out of habit. Harry's parents were in attendance, looking quite glum, but none of the rest of his horde of close relations were there. Harry had invited his pal Rat and another old friend, Billy, who wore a huge beach ball of an Afro, several strings of beads, and an embroidered collarless shirt. Billy read some religious poetry during the short ceremony.

Sheila stood up front, looking very skinny, and Ricky stood near the back of the room. He still thought of Lorraine's latest man as a potentially crazed Vietnam veteran, the sort you occasionally heard about on the news. Susan didn't come to town for the wedding because it had not been described to her as "a family event" like Ricky's bar mitzvah.

Only a small wedge of Harry's handsome face was visible through his slightly parted curtain of hair. He wore a velvet jacket over a white cowboy shirt that was studded with pearl snaps and had twin embroidered pocket slits shaped like smiles.

The bride wore a floral peasant dress Harry had picked out and a string of pearls borrowed from Eve. A garland of flowers crowned a modified shag haircut that was similar to the one Jane Fonda sported in *Klute*, though somewhat less severe.

Maggie also wore a peasant dress. Throughout the ceremony she fiddled with the curly threads hanging from her stuffed lamb.

Back at the Gordons' a larger group hovered around a table laden with Eve's best cooking. Harry was talking to a half-circle of well-wishers, elaborating a point with a sweeping motion of his left hand, when his new wedding ring, as yet unsized, flew into the air and landed with a loud clang that brought conversation to a halt. Everyone in the room silently watched the wedding ring whirl like a top. Just as it was about to fall over, Harry bent down and picked it up.

❖

Ricky and Peter Randsman were due to spend the summer at the Chautauqua Institution, a 750-acre complex in southwestern New York State where musically gifted young people were invited to study dance, theater, or a specific instrument. Ricky hated Chautauqua immediately. He hated its elegantly porched buildings, gingerbread cottages, and bell towers, its gatehouse and fenced-in forest. He resented its quietude and long lists of rules, and he couldn't stand the traditionalist piano instructors.

"It's so…oh, I don't know, so *goyishe*," Ricky said.

"And who are you, Sam Gordon?" Peter said.

Ricky cried on the telephone to Eve.

Sheila was waiting for him at the train station only a few days later. "Ricky, brace yourself," she said. "You're spending the rest of the summer working for Daddy."

The next morning Ricky left a letter for Eve on his bed before setting off with his father. It said that since he wasn't sure he would survive the summer, he wanted his mother to know that he loved her and appreciated everything that she'd done for him in the past.

Ricky's first assignment was to scrape the paint off an ancient metal machine with a steel brush. When he finished, Sam glanced at the machine and said, "Now I'm going to teach you how to repaint it." This part went surprisingly well until Ricky climbed a scaffold to get at the top. Sam found him there some time later, paralyzed with fear, drenched with sweat, hoarsely whispering, "Daddy, help me." Sam had to climb up and talk Ricky back to the ground.

Ricky would take a deep breath and follow Sam into what looked like tiny blowholes in walls and ceilings, inching along through ducts that reverberated in the blackness every time he banged his head. The crawl space beneath 221 Lincoln seemed light and airy in remembered comparison. Wedged shoulder to shoulder or back to back with his son, Sam would explain how and why the wires came together while Ricky tried for all he was worth not to panic or scream.

"He's a disaster," Sam would report to Eve at the end of every work-day. "I can't imagine a kid less suited to being an electrician. He can't concentrate; he disappears all the time; he's scared of everything. I mean, you'd have to see it to believe it, Eve. My kid." But no matter what Sam said, he persisted in entertaining dreams of Ricky treading in his footsteps. Illogical though it may have been, Sam Gordon was still waiting for Ricky to grow up and "come into the business." His full love of his son would certainly flourish if he could only teach him a trade they could share.

Given the state of the economy and rising unemployment, Sam couldn't complain about business. There was never much spare cash around because his assets were either tied up in equity or poured into overhead, but SGE Electric always had work. SGE Marine Corporation was also booming. Word of the guy who had a way with troubled engines had spread along the coastline, and the owners of huge, opulent boats vied for a place on Sam Gordon's waiting list. But Sam could still feel himself bumping up against economic limitations and limitations of his own. He needed a son to come in and take his businesses into the next generation.

Sam wanted to teach Ricky the trade and then retire to Florida. "You know, I'd come back up to help him out with the tough jobs," he'd tell Eve while she wondered what in the world to say to a man so far gone in fantasy

Sam could see himself watching with pride from Miami while Ricky built a glorious future upon his life's work. One of Sam's best clients had a dynamo of a son who'd taken over his father's window glazing business and turned it into one of the biggest aluminum operations in the coun-try. The young man had a beautiful, rambling home in Kings Point where Ricky and Sam went one morning on a job.

"Here, Ricky," Sam said realistically. "Stand right here and dig a hole."

An hour later, when Sam returned, Ricky was gone and the hole was undug. Sam circled the big house. Thinking he heard music, he cupped his hands against the living room window and looked inside. There was Ricky, his wild hair halfway down his T-shirt, his heavy boots working the pedals of a huge grand piano. The aluminum magnate's wife stood beside him.

Sam stormed into the living room. "*This* is what I brought you here for?"

"You have some nerve making this boy dig ditches, Sam Gordon," the lady of the house interrupted, taking him aside. "When Ricky is applying to college, I want you to call me," she said. "We have an association with the Juilliard School. Really, Sam," she reiterated before he and Ricky went back outside, "a musical genius should not be digging ditches."

Ricky simply could not understand why a man gifted with such a powerful mind had chosen to work all day in black holes most people were scared even to enter. Ricky always said Sam's decision had something to do with the Great Depression, though he was never quite sure what that meant.

Ricky marveled at the body of knowledge so easily at his father's command. He believed that Sam's "shamanistic mastery" (as Susan would later describe it in a poem) of the world of things, organic and inorganic, extended to every known realm save children and families. At the end of their workdays together, Ricky would be struck anew by the fact that nothing in all Sam's vast understanding remotely overlapped any of his only son's interests.

Ricky agonized for his father. Doomed to live in a time when people measured success in terms of their kids, he'd been dealt an array of intense, intelligent daughters who challenged him at every turn, and saddled with a son, a man's man of an entirely different kind, who daydreamed every single note of Hindemith's Third Piano Sonata while his father, in all his immeasurable good faith, explained the whys and wherefores of circuitry and electrical resistance. The role of hardworking American husband and father had never before been the object of so little respect and so much doubt, and though Sam didn't know it yet, he was and would remain the only Gordon to fill it.

Ricky was devastated for Sam when the marina blew up late that summer.

Sam had been looking forward to the change of seasons. He loved the way autumn transformed the view. Sam and Eve took long turns sitting in the antique barber's chair his longtime clients at Little Sisters of the Poor had given him. Sam, Ricky, and Harry Hughes had lugged the huge chair up the slender staircase. Visitors liked to settle down in it, and Eve would have to raise her voice to get them over to the table for dinner.

Sam thrilled to the sight of flock after flock of ducks, geese, and even swans flying by every fall, so thick some days that they obscured the ocean beyond the marshy inlets. At every glance there was so much life gliding over the water that if you kept staring long enough you'd lose yourself in it. This, Sam said, was the best moment of all.

Ricky was shaving one morning when the bathroom floor shook and a muffled boom rose over the sound of water running into the sink. Ricky looked into the living room and saw his friend Skip DeMar coming through the front door. Skip raced to the phone. "Fire department," he yelled as he dialed. "Look!"

Outside the big window, the entire marina was exploding into towering flames. Hundreds of gallons of burning gasoline boomed to life. All the boats along the entire length of the dock were lost in a wall of fire. Bits of deck and hull swirled in the inferno. Then the water seemed to catch fire too, a strange sizzling sound jumping from the surface. Sam was off on an errand, but Ricky spotted Eve running from one end of the dock to the other, her arms pumping up and down in the air, her small form darkened by the intensity of the fire. He was immobilized by the sight of her, circled in a glowing nimbus, running back and forth shaking her fists at the sky, screaming and screaming at the flames.

Of course they were insured. Sam even bought a badly damaged Chris Craft Coho back from the insurance company (it was a leak in the Coho's gas line that had caused the fire) and began to fix it up. But for a long time after the summer of Ricky's partnership with his father, the glorious view that could stop Eve's puttering and make Sam relax like a sleepy lion was cluttered and befouled by the charred remains of work undone.

◆━◆━◆

Sheila's long-awaited move to northern California differed in every way from the song-filled dream she'd entertained for so many years. Flowerless and manless, she arrived in Berkeley looking half-starved, though her enthusiastic exploration of the wonderful new whole-grain organic baked goods available in the Bay Area soon began to fill out her small frame.

Peter Probst was also in the San Francisco area, "shacked up" with his new "tall blond" girlfriend. Peter's rebound was a Gordon girl's nightmare starring the perfect man-burglar, a woman who looked serene and superior and had a nose "like a model." David Getz's girlfriend before Susan had been just such a woman ("Like right out of a Philip Roth novel," David would moonily recall), and Susan imagined herself engaged in constant battle with the ex's tall blond ghost.

Susan's time was now so much in demand, between her relationship with David and her recent prominence as a feature writer, that Sheila barely saw her eldest sister after she arrived. "How about this," Susan had said. "Since I'm away so often, maybe you can move into my house in Berkeley and just kind of be there when Shuna's at home."

Sheila agreed.

During 1973, a long article by Susan Lydon appeared in a widely read newspaper or magazine every six or eight weeks. If journalists and free-lance writers had always been something of an elite because of their access to the public eye, their free passes, and their proximity to the stars of politics and popular culture, lately certain of the more successful writers of short nonfiction had become stars themselves, even figuring in the stories they told.

Susan had never worked so hard as she did on a long profile of Randy Newman for the Sunday *New York Times Magazine*. Despite an addiction to daytime television, Newman wrote smart songs about sexual insecurity and relationships between parents and children. Susan struggled for weeks to surpass mere description and render a complex portrait of the young songwriter. She also wrote articles for the much discussed new magazine Ms., which was described by Gloria Steinem, one of its founders, as a "how-to" publication launched to help women "seize control" of their lives. The first time Susan went to the Ms. office in New York, several staffers applauded when she was introduced. Though Random House had rejected the pages she submitted about sex and politics, Susan's essay on orgasm was still regarded as prescient literary inspiration to the cause.

Susan did a piece for Ms. about singer-songwriter Helen Reddy, whose "I Am Woman" had recently managed to win the commercial distinction of a Grammy Award while being adopted as a feminist anthem. In Reddy's estimation, she told Susan, the women's movement had "become less of a radical movement and more of a grass-roots movement." The singer was about to do a series of shows in a Las Vegas nightclub as comedian Flip Wilson's replacement, and an all-woman construction crew had recently added to her luxurious Los Angeles home. Susan presented the singer as somewhat less heroic than the revolutionary feminist Isadora Duncan, whom she'd written about four years earlier. She showed Helen Reddy and her song ("I am strong, I am invincible, I am woman") as successes in a feminist niche in the American marketplace—like Ms. and Susan herself.

Susan wrote a *Times Magazine* profile of the former cop Joseph

Wambaugh, now a best-selling author, and another of Mark Spitz, the American swimmer who'd won seven gold medals at the 1972 summer Olympics in Munich and had since become a kind of poster boy for a return to wholesome all-American youth. Spitz had always said he wanted to retire from competitive swimming, settle down with his wife, and become a small-town dentist, but then, Susan reported, representatives of the dairy industry approached him about doing commercials. The ensuing marketing of Mark Spitz—"the most blatant exploitation of a human body since Marilyn Monroe's celebrated nude calendar"— was the focus of Susan's controversial article.

Asked how he felt about "playing the conquering Jew in Munich," Spitz said he liked Germany "even though this lamp shade is probably made out of one of my aunts." Susan portrayed the swimmer as a young man programmed for success by his father from the age of eight. "The well-paid operations manager for Schnitzer Steel Products, a large Oakland scrap metal firm that specializes in grinding up cars," Arnold Spitz told Susan that he was indeed the greatest motivating factor in his son's life. "Because of what I've given of myself, this is what I created....I've got my life tied up in this kid."

The *Times* printed some of the many angry letters readers sent in after Susan's demolition of Mark Spitz appeared. One reader compared her to the members of Black September, the terrorist group responsible for massacring eleven Israeli athletes in Munich; another likened her to Hitler.

Sam Gordon was appalled. "How could you have done such a thing to a Jewish boy, a national hero?"

"A Jew who makes a joke about lamp shades," Susan said.

Ricky's teachers read Susan's articles and considered her a famous writer, and Eve's mah-jongg friends saw the size of her name in print and nodded their heads.

By the end of the year, it seemed that Susan had cast aside her hippie lassitude and rehitched her career to journalism—specifically to a burgeoning literary genre dubbed "New Journalism" in a recent essay by one of its best-known practitioners, Tom Wolfe. Wolfe described the maturation of a decade-old "higher," more "emotionally involving" journalism that sought to create a sense of character and place "like a novel." He disassociated the genre from New Left reportage, though many of the best New Journalists were in fact veterans of the slogan-laden, polemical underground papers who'd decided to lighten up on ideology and heat up their prose.

When Susan and Michael Lydon first learned the proper components of good sober journalism, the notion that the writer belonged in the story was considered absurd (as when *Rolling Stone* editor Jann Wenner criticized the first-person movie review Susan submitted for the premiere issue). Now it was all the rage in feature-writing circles to weave information about yourself into a piece. As the family had emerged from the privacy of the home, the self had emerged from the privacy of the psyche. The popular fascination with self—a self, the self, myself—led writers to interject personal information, insights, and even feelings as a means of getting at the truth. The myth of journalistic objectivity would be replaced by the fact of a subjective presence.

For all her rock star profiles and fascination with the new culture, Susan's prose was still closer to the clean sentences found in the *New York Times* (or in the dignified English newspapers, or for that matter in the *Yale Daily*) than to the pyrotechnics of Tom Wolfe or Hunter Thompson. But toward the end of the year, Susan employed the first-person narrative form in a deeply personal story about her lifelong hero Fred Astaire. Published in *Rolling Stone,* another alternative creation that was now firmly ensconced in a market niche, the article opened with an ode to Eve Gordon, a mother who let her daughter cut school to watch Fred Astaire dance.

Susan went on to describe her meeting with Astaire, now seventy-four, "a few months older than the century." The night before, she'd dreamed about him, she said. In the dream they went to a restaurant where the tables were so close together that Susan tripped and couldn't keep her balance, but Astaire glided among the chair legs "as freely as if he had been on an empty dance floor." At the end of the long article, Susan revealed that the reality of meeting Fred Astaire did not give her "the pure rush of pleasure" induced by the sound of his voice and the tapping of his feet when she was a child. Only later did the experience take on the aspects of fantasy she cherished, Susan wrote, only "after some time had passed, and it felt like a dream."

Sheila saw Peter Probst every so often in Berkeley, and they'd even talked about trying to get back together. But one night Peter discovered another man in the house and stomped off in a rage. Sheila thought the right to be angry was all hers, so she refused to seek Peter out and explain that she had no romantic attachment to the man.

Sheila occasionally went up to Fairfax with Shuna to visit Susan and David, but she often didn't see Susan for days on end. Susan did attempt to help Sheila with her photography by getting her an assignment from the *New York Times* to photograph blues musician Taj Mahal, the subject of one of Susan's articles. Taj was a college-educated black man from the North who specialized in re-creating the southern musical heritage his mother had hoped he'd leave behind. He charmed and flattered Sheila, and her picture of him ran prominently in the *Times*, but she was convinced the paper wouldn't have given her photography a second look if her brilliant sister hadn't pulled strings. Her sister, whose life was all the more glittering because of Sheila's assistance.

In the morning, Sheila would drop Shuna at Blue Fairyland, a place that did not impress her in the least. She watched the wives of hippies and famous rock stars dumping their children at Blue Fairyland and going off to shop. Everywhere Sheila looked in Berkeley she saw women who acted like it wasn't cool to be a mother—women she was sure wouldn't care about or understand a heartbroken child weeping on the stairs.

Sheila looked forward to Shuna's return later in the day, and her time alone with her buoyant, runny-nosed niece became more and more precious to her. Sheila had dreamed of being a good mother since she was a little girl, and by the end of the year her relationship with Shuna so closely resembled her fantasy that she began to resent Susan being around the house at all. Sheila and the Blue Fairyland teachers were mothers to Shuna for six days out of seven, and then Susan would suddenly reappear to erase a week of feelings.

One day Sheila blurted out, "I don't want to take care of Shuna anymore unless she can really be my daughter."

Susan stared at her. "What do you mean by that?"

"I mean...I want to adopt her. It hurts too much otherwise."

"Oh, Sheila, don't be so silly," Susan scoffed.

Susan made sure Sheila didn't see how upset she was. Back in Fairfax, she called Eve to report that Sheila was acting really weird.

Eve told Ricky he was going to spend the Christmas holidays in California. "Sheila sounds terrible," she said. "I want you to go out and cheer her up."

Ricky had heard descriptions of the new 747s from friends, but nobody had ever mentioned the piano lounge! He played Stephen Sondheim all the way to San Francisco. He'd learned dozens of the young composer's songs since Peter Randsman played him the album of *Company*, and though he was not about to raise musical comedy to the realm of high art, he'd recently seen Sondheim's *Follies*, a brilliant cloaking of images of decay and hopelessness in the bright frock of a Broadway musical, and he'd seen *A Little Night Music* too. Ricky judged

Sondheim brilliant, and special in a way that made him feel strangely jealous.

Sheila had gained weight. In a Gordon woman, Ricky knew, this was a sure indication of sadness. He watched Sheila trudge across Susan's little kitchen and carve her fifth and sixth slices of organic oatmeal bread. Sheila spread a thick coating of butter over each piece, ate them quickly, and then phoned in an order for some "soul food from a takeout joint."

Watching Sheila eat like this made Ricky nervous. He pondered once again the Job-like trials connected to having three older sisters, not one of whom was what you'd call light or easygoing. All of them suffered biblically when things went awry.

By the time the soul food arrived, Ricky realized his stomach was beginning to convulse. It felt hot, and he had sharp pains.

There was a noise from another room, and Sheila got up to look. Ricky heard Peter Probst's voice, unusually high-pitched and obviously upset. "Not…leaving…without …" Ricky moved to the doorway. Peter was leaving for New York, he said, to follow his recently departed tall blonde, but not without his stereo and various other consumer goods he claimed were his.

"Well, it's not your stereo!" Sheila yelled. "We have two major possessions as far as I know. A car and a stereo. The keys to the car are in your hand. Now get in your car and drive away!"

"The stereo's mine!" Peter screamed.

Suddenly Sheila's voice became calm. Ricky peered into the living room and heard her say, "Oh, all right, Peter. I'll help you get it in the car."

Sheila disconnected one of the big wooden speakers and hoisted it onto her shoulder. Ricky followed at a distance as she lugged it outside. Just short of the car, she raised the speaker high over her head like some apoplectic Atlas and threw it to the pavement with all her might. Wheeling around, she rushed past Peter back into the house, reappeared with the other speaker, and slammed it down on top of the car, driving a dent so far into the roof that the metal protruded into the interior like a little stalactite.

Ricky fled inside, but all of a sudden Sheila and Peter were there too, slapping and hitting, throwing each other back and forth across the living room. Ricky put his hands up and stepped into the fray with fraternal resolve, only to be thrown hard against the brick fireplace. He toppled to the floor in a fetal ball and started to wail.

Peter and Sheila stopped.

"Hospital!" Ricky cried, clutching his stomach.

Ricky was discharged after several hours of observation. A doctor told him he had a pre-ulcerative condition. He was to take Mylanta, stick to a bland diet, and yes, the doctor agreed when Ricky returned to the hospital for the third time in two days, he might recuperate faster at home.

Ricky left town the following morning.

1974

If only the Jews had made a homeland in the Bronx," Sam opined to Harry Hughes, "then none of this would be happening"—"this" being the desert war the Israelis had almost lost last fall, the edgy military alerts and superpower muscle-flexing evident in response, and above and beyond the rest, these endless, anxious lines, these idling automobiles waiting for gas.

"They could have done somethin' with the Bronx," said Harry's father-in-law and new boss.

"Umm-huh," said Harry.

It was said that some metropolitan area gas stations would pump you only three bucks' worth and then shoo you away. Out in the Far West, gas station attendants were packing sidearms. In Manhattan there had been several fistfights and a few knife fights between motorists and attendants. Two tanker trucks carrying three thousand gallons of fuel each had been hijacked in broad daylight and never recovered.

Because of the fuel crisis, the three of four Americans who drove to work were now required to go no faster than fifty-five miles per hour, but that sounded like a considerable clip to Sam's new apprentice all those mornings and evenings he found himself stuck in heavy traffic or long gas lines, absently agreeing with each and every point his father-in-law saw fit to make. "Nixon! The shmuck. This was a good president before he started playin' George Washington and the cherry tree," Sam said. "You gotta know he had every chance in the world to get rid of the tapes. This is what we call a shmuck. Know what I mean by shmuck?"

"Umm-huh," Harry said.

"I mean, there musta been something in the guy's makeup that just wouldn't let him go and do it. It's not like Agnew, a real crook. Nixon's like a mystery. The man could have just burned the things up. This is a shmuck."

"Umm-huh."

"What's a president?" Sam would ask.

Harry knew it was not within the bounds of his job description to provide an answer.

"He's just a guy who sets policy—policy ruined by people working for him, people, by the way, who have no real loyalty to the organization."

This loathing of large organizations was one Sam truth Harry had to respect. Harry noticed that Sam was always looking to avoid intermediaries, to cut out the middleman. He shunned institutions and went out of his way to deal with people one to one. Sam dodged programmatic dictates like a skier working a line of slalom poles. He and Harry had learned a similar mistrust of large organizations from their experience of two very different wars.

Often, during a long commute to or from a job site, or while they were waiting in line, Sam would talk about his difficulties with the bureaucratic culture in terms of his own career. He told Harry that for all his expertise, the electric game, as he was willing to play it, was not a road to riches. "Big money in contracting means you have to play politics. The way I do it you can at least make a few bucks and steer clear of the bullshit, but there's no pot of gold."

Harry observed that delegating even the most inconsequential of tasks that Sam Gordon could execute more efficiently himself caused his new boss almost physical distress. "I figure a man doing business on his own is maybe ninety, ninety-five percent efficient if he knows what he's doing," Sam would say. "He takes on one man, now he's fifty percent efficient. Ten men, maybe things work five percent of the time."

Since Harry Hughes was the most obvious source of the arithmetic dilution of the potential efficiency of SGE Electric, he was never quite sure what to make of this particular line of thought. Sam's utility theories often flowed directly into his lengthy running commentaries on the utter stupidity displayed by people who'd attended college. Since Harry had recently graduated from City College, this too caused him to wonder what he was supposed to think or say during these long rides through the first or second darkness of the day.

Sam paid Harry three dollars and fifty cents an hour—a sum, he noted often, that was more than generous in light of the low productivity of a newcomer and the many skilled workers currently jobless in an economic downturn people were learning to call a recession.

Each night Harry returned home to Lorraine and Maggie feeling bloodless and utterly spent, with nothing left but his abiding awe of Sam. Each homecoming concluded the previously unimagined tortures that were a typical day for Sam Gordon. Harry thought that what Sam did for a living gave a whole new meaning to "grueling." The work was backbreaking, dangerous, dehumanizing, desiccating, demoralizing. Harry could go on with words beginning with "d" until bedtime, which occurred shortly after he got back to the little suburban apartment he and Lorraine were renting, and shortly before he had to get up and hit the road again with Sam.

Harry wrote a letter to Susan and another to Ricky, who'd left home for Pittsburgh early in January to enter Carnegie Mellon University a semester early. "As you probably have heard," Harry told both of them, "I am now working for your father—the Taras Bulba of the electrical industry."

Around the time newspapers began to run articles like "Can the Suburbs Survive the Lines at the Pump?" Harry, Lorraine, and Maggie had abandoned New York City for a Long Island suburb called Selden, in Suffolk County, some thirty miles from Harbor Isle. Not long before, Lorraine had been caught in an ugly battle on Houston Street. She was sitting in a taxi near her apartment when a gang of men with knives and machetes came flying from Avenue D toward another gang armed with huge clubs and long knives. As the men slashed and stabbed each other on all sides of the taxi, Lorraine kept screaming at the terrified cabbie until he pulled partway up on the sidewalk and drove off.

"I just can't deal with it anymore," Lorraine told Harry. "It's like the city's changing." Manhattan looked and felt completely different than in the days when Lorraine wandered through East Harlem trying to lend a hand, and much changed since she and Bobby Shapiro first moved into the confusion of languages and gang loyalties on the Lower East Side and lived there without the slightest fear. The city was full of anger now. Lorraine thought she could feel it all around her, closing in.

She was also having a lot of trouble breathing lately, and the *New York Times* reported that the city air she managed to suck in was more polluted all the time. Some days Lorraine felt her throat constricting. "If you're breathing freely you're not likely to be terribly frightened," radical psychiatrist R. D. Laing said during a visit to New York. "How many

can sigh a heartfelt sigh? How many can laugh calmly? If people learned
to breathe freely a lot of the mental dust and disturbed mental hardware
would settle down."

Lorraine wanted to move her own creaking mental hardware out of
town to a relatively undeveloped part of Long Island close to a campus
of the State University of New York. Selden fit the bill. Lorraine could
attend the university at Stony Brook, where she could finish her B.A.
and then work toward the master's degree that would enable her to
become a psychotherapist. Harry didn't want to move back to Long
Island at all, but he agreed to rent a railroad flat in Selden anyway.

Within a week of the move, Lorraine had acquired several new
allergies, and her ailments got worse. She often said it felt like her brain
was Jell-O. Her chest hurt terribly, and sometimes she felt as if the baro-
metric pressure alone would push all the air out of her lungs and make
her implode like one of those deep-sea divers they used to bury in their
steel helmets after an accident.

Susan and Gina Schick, Lorraine's old roommate from the sixties,
both made trips east and went out to visit Lorraine and Harry in their
new exurban home. Both were shocked at how Lorraine's sinewy sturdi-
ness had dissipated in a welter of afflictions. All she talked about was
her health and her textbook's worth of new phobias. Now that Lorraine
had traded the profound yearnings of her politics and art for the simpler
traditions of the nuclear family, for the visible borders of a quiet little
town, and for the venerable dogmas of the classical science of the mind,
it struck her friends and family as wholly ironic that she seemed so with-
ered and afraid. She now refused to take a train or a subway at all (thus
the taxi experience at Houston and Avenue D), and she would no
longer be enclosed in the modern coffin of an elevator. Lorraine had
dreams in which a train (Sam, according to the student of psychology
Harry Hughes) was speeding past so quickly that she couldn't get on.

From Harry's perspective, Lorraine's clear admiration for her father
was strange to behold, considering what she'd described to him both
analytically and anecdotally as their snarled past. But he could see that
Lorraine was thrilled when Sam and his men descended on their new
place in Selden to help renovate it. It was then that Sam had suggested
Harry come to work for him—just until he decided what to do with his
psychology degree. Harry observed with perplexity Lorraine's obvious
pleasure when he decided to ignore his college training for a while and
work for the screaming night train of his wife's unconscious.

Now Harry Hughes spent many more of his waking hours with Sam
Gordon than Lorraine ever had, even when she was his weekend assis-

tant during the pioneer days in Harbor Isle. Sideburn to sideburn, the two war veterans sat in traffic or gas lines for hours on end, and over and over Harry said, "Umm-huh."

———◆———

Ricky returned to his dorm room very late on the night of his triumphant tryst with a campus heartthrob, a man who looked quite a lot like the young Tyrone Power. Ricky hoped that Richie, his roommate at Carnegie Mellon—a close friend from back home, creator of Eve's famous needlepoint Liz Taylor throw pillow—would be asleep when he got back. Richie had been boisterously obsessed with the same Tyrone Power lookalike for some time. But when Ricky approached their room, he could hear Streisand inside. Barbra was belting out her number-one single, "The Way We Were," at extreme volume. Ricky pushed open the door, and by the light of many flickering candles he saw Richie sitting in the middle of the floor glaring up at him, the razor-sharp blade of an X-acto knife dramatically poised a few inches from his wrist.

Richie had always been given to stagy gestures. Back in high school he'd completed a huge pile of pen-and-ink drawings and retired to his bedroom for three days, refusing all nourishment, until his mother and father agreed to take him to Las Vegas so he could deliver the drawings to Barbra Streisand personally. Barbra sent a brief but gracious note of thanks to Richie's table from her dressing room.

Richie fit right in at Carnegie Mellon's renowned College of Fine Arts, alma mater of Andy Warhol, a place where teenage students of the dramatic arts considered themselves mature actors with rich, multifaceted offstage personae. Architecture students were architects at Carnegie Mellon. Writers of poetry were poets. Serious painters, sculptors, designers, and composers stayed up all night over their work. Students gathered to analyze obscure films and poems every night; in the cafeteria arguments raged over interpretations of Thomas Mann's novels or the more baffling passages in Gertrude Stein. Any number of people wandered around campus singing in full voice, like nobody Ricky had ever known except his own mother. The most casual discussions of life and art coruscated with intensity and passion. It was as if this college in Pittsburgh was an anteroom of the great concert halls and salons of New York and the capitals of Europe. The same "artiness" that had always made Ricky feel so much the outsider was now all but compulsory.

Ricky had been consumed with jealousy when Richie went off to Carnegie Mellon. Richie was what Ricky thought of as the *other* kind of Jewish boy from Long Island. He drove around in the family Mercedes-

Benz; he lived in a huge house and carried his mother's Bloomingdale's charge card in his wallet. Richie had friends like the astonishing Jill Silverstein, who bought her entire fall wardrobe for her senior year of high school in the single color olive. Ricky and Peter Randsman coveted and attempted to copy any number of things Richie had or did. When Richie got a nose job, Peter—Seacliff the Seagull no longer—got one too.

Not long after Richie abandoned Ricky for Pittsburgh, he began to send back descriptions of an ivied sanctum where young Tyrone Powers walked hand in hand down school hallways. Being gay at Carnegie was apparently indistinguishable from being talented; being gay, to hear Richie tell it, was better than normal. It was cool.

Sam and Eve soon began to hear a great deal about Carnegie Mellon. Ricky said he was planning to graduate from high school a semester in advance and go to Carnegie through the early-admissions program.

"Ricky, listen," Sam said gently. "I don't think you should get your hopes up."

"He's dreaming," Sam told Eve when they were alone. "I've never even seen him do homework. Not once. He'll be lucky if he graduates from high school at all. With this crazy free-school bit, he doesn't even have a record to show."

Still, Sam and Eve let Ricky go to Carnegie for an audition and paid for his plane ticket. And when he was quickly accepted, Eve wrote out his tuition checks.

Richie told his Carnegie circle that his "gorgeous and talented friend Ricky Gordon" would soon join them. Ricky's ferocious program of calisthenics since he'd decided he wanted to be "brave-looking" when he went to college had already produced a noticeable effect. Though a day rarely passed when he didn't still see himself fleeing the neighborhood bullies with his pants around his knees, his fear was now girded in muscle.

As soon as Ricky arrived at Carnegie, some of the most intelligent and attractive people he'd ever encountered began to seek him out, apparently just for the chance to meet him and to look at him. As word of his musical talent got around campus, students came by to ask if he would play them some songs. He set several Sylvia Plath poems to music, and he worked on settings for poems by Anne Sexton, another suicidal young mother with whom Ricky felt a strange affinity. He played the Plath pieces for several sophisticated listeners, who exclaimed, "Wow, you wrote that?" He stayed up all one night to score twelve pages of assorted sonnets by a young woman at Carnegie who admired his work.

Though accepted as a piano major, Ricky soon realized that his fellow majors generally practiced six or seven hours a day. Since he had never been able to practice for more than half an hour or so without getting antsy, he sat down and in three weeks wrote all the material required for a transfer to the composition department. Writing music was easy.

By the middle of his second semester, in part thanks to thousands of push-ups and a simple geographical relocation, Ricky Gordon was a new man. A prodigy to some, he was suddenly the good-looking kid who roomed with Richie, the guy who told long, hysterical stories about his sister in California who'd done a hundred cool things and sent him exotic quilts and grew rosary vines and his sister in Long Island who'd been in a rock 'n' roll band and was once a junkie and was now into vegetarianism and yoga. Many of Ricky's friends could already do their own Eve Gordon imitation. Everyone wanted to meet Eve, and everyone wanted to know Ricky. In a way he had never experienced before, Ricky finally felt at home.

———◆———

One of Shuna's favorite things was to roll up and down the pink and aqua hills of San Francisco in a car, singing as loud as she could. Shuna and her mother sang to the radio. They were best at the Beach Boys.

Singing with her mom on a sunny day, Shuna would imagine that they were really best friends, even though she was only six. Some mornings her mother would say, "You're not going to school today. Let's go do something"—just like friends. The next day Shuna would go to school with a note stating that she'd been sick, even though it wasn't true.

Once Shuna protested, "But I *want* to go to school, Mom."

"No," her mother said. "Today you're hanging out with me."

Shuna knew that meant her mom didn't want to get up and leave all the people who were at the house right then to drive her to school.

But usually Shuna would say, "I don't want to go to school, I want to take a nap and spend today with you," and usually her mother would say, "Cool."

Shuna liked Alzara Getz okay, though sometimes she thought she was spoiled. She really liked the big house in Fairfax, and she liked David. What she didn't like was watching her mom treat David's daughter like a real daughter, especially since David—and her mom too—treated Shuna more like a friend. Shuna thought this was weird. It *annoyed* her. Sometimes you wanted to be more than everyone's friend.

Different women came to see David when her mother wasn't there, and men with long hair came to see her mom when David wasn't there. Shuna accompanied her mother to one guy's house a lot that spring. She enjoyed wandering around, and she was particularly drawn to the room that had a table like in a doctor's office, and all kinds of glass tubes, and very long needles to give shots with, and lots of cotton balls.

Eve climbed out of the car in Fairfax to look for David Getz's house. She finally spotted it through a stand of second-growth timber, at the top of a very steep hill and what appeared to be several hundred wooden steps.

"Do you have any idea what a guy'd charge to get a couch up there?" Sam said as he mounted the staircase. "Five hundred bucks minimum. Bringing in groceries has gotta be a major operation. This is a heart attack place."

Sam was incapable of uttering the word "California" without the modifying tag "a loser place." He'd agreed to brave modern America's densest concentration of losers and a possible coronary only because he and Eve had decided Sheila was in need of rescue. But Sheila, it turned out, didn't want to be rescued. She didn't even want to visit her older sister, so Sam and Eve drove alone to Marin County and the house on the hill.

Sheila was convinced that Susan and David only invited her to the house to witness their interminable efforts to be cool. A cool, happy, rich hippie family surrounded by redwood—the whole scene in Fairfax gave Sheila the willies. Meanwhile, Susan figured Sheila didn't come up much because she was lost without a man and dreaded the thought of being a third wheel, like all the Gordon women.

Shuna was spending most of her time with David and Susan now, so Sheila had rented a room in a house in Berkeley. That was where Sam and Eve had gone first. "Sheila, we've come to take you back to civilization," Sam said, and Sheila said, "No."

Sam waited patiently beside Eve through all three of her rest stops on the way up the hill. When they finally reached the top, Sam walked around the house, bending down often to inspect footings and supports. "What a piece-of-shit place," he announced. "The back isn't even on the ground. There's just a pole holding it up maybe sixty feet in the air. I don't know if I can take this, Eve." Sam still equated structural solidity with the moral soundness of the people who lived inside. Always had.

Susan greeted them without fanfare. It was difficult for her to muster emotion during family reunions. Always had been. Same for Sam.

David Getz welcomed Susan's parents. His stylishly long curly side-burns were just like Sam's. In 1974 half the guys on the average construction crew looked like former drummers for Big Brother and the Holding Company.

"Hi," Sam said. "Listen, why doncha fix the tires on that Volkswagen at the bottom of the hill?"

Susan showed them from room to room, pointing out the huge collection of antiques, quilts, old toys, wooden boxes, and assorted amulets she and David had amassed. She was sure Sam would notice the superior workmanship of the objects she'd lovingly acquired. (Back home, Eve put Sam on the telephone to critique Susan's artifacts for Ricky. "You wouldn't of believed it," Sam said. "The whole damned house was covered in rhinestone crucifixes.") Susan watched her father approach an end table and squint at a framed photograph in which she was standing unashamedly and almost defiantly naked beside Shuna.

"A whole house filled with old things, beautiful things," Susan said to Eve after Sam reeled out of the room. "A whole house, and all Daddy can see is one picture."

For some reason Sam returned home from California believing that Susan was intimately acquainted through her journalistic connections with the kidnappers of Patricia Hearst. ("It's terrible! Sixty days ago, she was a lovely child," Patty's father lamented to the press.) Susan didn't know any of the members of the Symbionese Liberation Army (Sam called it the "Symbolese Liberation Army") who had been killed in the recent firestorm attack in Los Angeles, and she didn't know the rogue child of privilege now called Tanya. Even if she had, with the way she'd been feeling lately, the Patty Hearst story wouldn't have offered her much of a buzz.

Writing wasn't much of a buzz these days period. Young people in colleges all over the country wanted to be hip freelance feature writers like Susan Lydon (the trend would soon be curtailed when the publication of *All the President's Men*, Woodward and Bernstein's Watergate exposé, shifted the glamour to investigative journalism), but Susan had come to think that her articles, however prominently they appeared, almost immediately "fell down a well." Nobody ever said much about them, and if they did, they never said enough. Hanging out with the stars was no big kick anymore, and politics—including feminist politics, with all its schisms and sisterly warfare—was becoming a drag. *Roe* v.

Wade had made abortion legal the previous year, and state legislatures were ratifying the Equal Rights Amendment by the month, but the movement that had once touched Susan more profoundly than any other no longer moved her.

Susan was thirty years old. She'd ridden her myriad ambitions a long way. From any number of angles, she seemed to be thriving—so pretty and talented and successful in so many things. But Susan was sure that something was missing, and whatever it was was the key to everything else.

Not long after Sam stomped down the long staircase, muttering about not even being offered a cup of coffee, Susan was back in Harbor Isle for a brief visit. On a warm early summer Sunday, she left Shuna with Maggie and Eve in the elevated living room and boarded a boat full of Goldenbergs and Gordons headed out to sea.

As soon as Sam cleared the reconstructed dock, his brother, Susan's uncle Freddy, moved up to join him in front. Susan sat down next to Mama Yetta in back. As the wind picked up, Susan huddled close to Yetta, who with age had come to resemble the perfect Jewish grandmother of memory and Broadway myth.

"So. When are you going to do something normal, Susan?" Yetta asked from the side of her mouth. "When are you going to do something decent?"

Susan started to cry.

"Look at yourself. Maybe if you got married to a nice boy, but...ach, who'd want you now? Look at yourself, Susan. No decent man would want you."

Susan looked at her father standing windward at the helm. She was sure that if he knew about Mama Yetta's cruel attack he'd make her stop, or at least he'd say, "Forget it, Susan. You know how she is." But when she tearfully went up front to tell him, Sam just stared at her. "Don't be disrespectful to your grandmother," he said.

By the standards of the ages, by Yetta's standards, Susan believed her life was a shambles. It was true. "I do love you," David Getz had said the last time they cried together, "but you just don't turn me on." David was always trying to be "open and honest" about his feelings. The effect was very similar to Yetta's.

Eve was livid when Susan recounted what Yetta had said on the boat ride. She was having trouble discerning Susan's old confidence lately.

Her girls appeared to be losing their bravado all at once. Something was happening, even to Susan, who dazzled strangers with her chutzpah and panache and served up gold medal winners for all to see.

Eve put her arms around her sobbing daughter. Yetta appeared in the living room, breathless from the steps. Eve drew her mother-in-law into the back hallway, which was lined with family photographs on both walls.

"How could you? Can't you tell she needs her self-esteem built up? She comes home and you knock her into the toilet."

Yetta waved her hand dismissively and went back to the living room and her favorite chair.

<hr />

Around the time Sheila agreed to attend the Arica Institute's forty-day training regimen in hopes of achieving enlightenment or at least a modicum of spiritual release, she was feeling more lonely, ugly, overweight, unloved, uptight, and generally miserable than ever before. But Arica could "save your life," Susan, David Getz, and Gina Schick all assured her.

Sheila had moved from Berkeley to Gina's big house overlooking the colorful rooftops of San Francisco and the beautiful bay beyond. Gina's ex-husband, Hal, upon hearing the news, told friends that "the least crazy of the Gordon sisters" was living with Gina and the two kids.

Gina and Susan were now good friends. Gina often recalled her negative impression of the bourgeois Ivy League Susan she'd met less than a decade ago in New York, and she still remembered vividly Susan's offputting practice of telling the occasional insensitive joke when Gina first began to see the Lydons in San Francisco, but she believed that their current closeness was possible because the women's movement had taught women to be friends. Betty Friedan said that women in the movement had over time become "family."

Gina was actually enthralled by Susan. She found herself pondering everything Susan said, just as Ellen Levy used to study and adore Lorraine's big sister back in Harbor Isle. Susan gave Gina clothes. Gina gave Susan a car she didn't need. When Susan hitched up with Arica, the Cadillac of spiritual vehicles this season, Gina joined too.

From Sheila's perspective, the arrayed force of Susan, Gina (whom she'd always respected), and David Getz (on whom she had something of a crush) all pushing her to try Arica was too much to resist. She sold her camera and photographic accessories and borrowed the balance required to pay for her spiritual track-clearing from Eve.

The rigidity of the Arica experience seemed a bit much to Sheila from the start: forty ten-hour days of special chanting, breathing exercises, meditation, dancing, massages, and encounter sessions. Saturdays were free, but participants were expected to observe an "objective silence," which meant that you weren't supposed to speak about much more than your basic biological needs. There were severe dietary restrictions to be honored for the duration; smoking was allowed only during short breaks; and, most unsettling to Sheila, you had to submit to before-and-after photographs.

Arica and its disciplines, Sheila had been told, would clear away the "unessential" thoughts responsible for her current misery. Arica would launch nothing short of a full-scale mental and physical battle between the obfuscatory forces of ego and the far more natural forces of "essence." According to her new "trainers," Sheila would learn the techniques of "self-realization and the clarification of consciousness." She would soon reexamine the negative experiences in her life in a way that would render her pain-free.

The change would be so great you'd be able to see it in a Polaroid.

The lightning bolt of "spiritual renaissance" and "consciousness revolution" now lit stages all across the Republic. The Reverend Sun Myung Moon, a Korean businessman, had recently been inspired by a personal conversation with Jesus to come to America and spread the word that the Messiah was here and that by the way, Jesus said He's Korean. Moon's acolytes submitted to group sex initiations designed to "cleanse" their blood. At a large rally, the reverend called Watergate-embattled Richard Nixon an "archangel" as Tricia, the president's daughter, applauded at his side. Not two months earlier, Rennie Davis, a former New Left polemicist and one of the Chicago Seven, had helped organize the rental of the Houston Astrodome for a mass celebration on behalf of the Divine Light Mission and its fifteen-year-old guru, Mahara-ji. The "divine light," the pubescent master taught, could be glimpsed at home simply by pressing a thumb or finger into your eye socket until you saw flashes. Throughout the country, stadiums and auditoriums previously monopolized by football teams, local theater groups, and PTA committees were being invaded by the teachers of enlightenment.

The San Francisco Bay Area was now a fairground for spiritual conventions, festivals, temples, and schools. American practitioners of meditation techniques, rebirthing systems, Rolfing, encounter therapy, Scientology, the occult, and variations on Zen Buddhism and the yogic disciplines of Hinduism could be found with ease. By the fall of 1974, the more dubious subdisciplines of the new spiritualism were on display in San Francisco alongside intellectually complex hybrids like Arica, with its mix of religion, philosophy, and psychology. This profusion of spiritual designs had clearly arisen in counterpoint to diminished hopes for fundamental political and social change, and during the nadir of popular faith in the scientific method. Scholarly journals were filled with articles attempting to address the declining respect for American science and defend objective methods of seeking truth.

Meanwhile, more and more people with good educations and successful careers were entering programs like Arica's forty-day training (for a more rigorous three-month version you had to go to New York) in hopes of achieving the blissful epiphany that science, drugs, lifestyle alterations, and rebellion had failed to offer. Though Arica could be described in metaphysical terms or as a scientific alternative to neo-Freudian therapy, most novices paid out the three thousand dollars for the three-month session or the five hundred for the forty-day mini-course because the word on the street was that Arica was a surefire path to the full glory of a good acid trip without the acid.

Susan knew some of the Bay Area seekers who'd begun to interrupt political discussions or drug trips around five years ago with increasingly urgent reports from places like Nepal or the Esalen Institute down the coast in Big Sur. These early consciousness explorers were considered a "spiritual fringe element" in the Berkeley circles Susan frequented. She'd always figured "the spiritual path" was yet another detour. The central argument pitched to more earthbound sorts was that if you changed yourself the world would also change. This struck Susan as absurd, and no less ineffectual than the antiquated, corrupt, and spiritually empty religiosity of her childhood.

In 1970 Susan had attended a going-away party for a group of spiritual types who were leaving on a pilgrimage to Arica, a tiny village in northern Chile. Their goal was to find a thirty-nine-year-old former Bolivian civil servant who was beginning to make a name for himself as a gifted mystic. Some Berkeley friends wanted Susan to write an article for the *New York Times* about what the pilgrims learned in Chile, but at the time she said she had better things to do.

That was before writing lost its buzz, before David's affection for her became mired in "I love you like a sister," and before the images of global doom that assailed her during her bad LSD trip at Altamont began coming back so often that a vision of a dying planet now formed the backdrop for most of Susan's days.

* * *

Oscar Ichazo, son of a soldier and self-made man who never understood him at all, began to experience strange seizures when he was six years old. His heart would pound and his mind would race out of control. He saw images of heaven and hell so vivid and terrifying that each time he came back to consciousness, he was both amazed to be alive and determined to master a mind that could harbor so much fear. Oscar later studied varieties of religious experience, Hindu philosophy, alchemy, and other "wisdom traditions" ranging from witchcraft to the martial arts. As a young man he wandered through India and the Orient until he fell into a coma in 1964 and awoke with the conviction that he'd "reached the totality" and was finally prepared to teach others what he'd learned.

Oscar Ichazo told the spiritual tourists who sought him out in Arica that from his own distillations of modern and ancient thought he'd developed an entirely new and scientific means of analyzing the human psyche. The disciplines and philosophies he'd discovered would not only clarify individual consciousness; they would form the basis of the institutions of the future "meta-society" Ichazo foresaw. Human beings, he declared, are born fearless, loving, and in every way perfect, but they quickly descend into the darkness of the "I"—into personality and ego. The ego perceives the world as alien and dangerous because it constantly fails to satisfy the deeper needs of the self and hides behind veils of illusion. Personality is a kind of defensive layer blocking the superior clarity of essence. The individualism so prized in Western culture is nothing more than the shoring up of internal walls built by desire and fear.

Ichazo's Arican disciplines were designed to open up energy channels that would bypass the ego. Learning to "breathe into the kath," a "vital energy center" located four inches below the navel, for instance, would open a path for clear energy and experience. Strenuous exercises called "psychocalisthenics," as well as breathing techniques and African dances, led to concentration on twelve sections of the body and mind that each represented a discrete array of physiological and psychological functions.

If you were having trouble with your kidneys, extensive Arica training would allow you to figure out what unneeded ideas and experiences you ought to dispense with to ease the pain. A many-layered technique called "protoanalaysis" furthered Arican enlightenment by identifying the characteristics of an individual ego so that it could be controlled and eventually neutralized. Ichazo made "enneagons"—diagrams of the nine basic styles or points of "ego fixation"—to assist in the "reading" of a personality. The tensions and fixations of the psyche were interrelated by a "logic of unity" he called "trialectics."

As expensive and demanding as Arica was, it attracted many thousands of followers from a postwar generation raised on the lasting significance of having a "good"—or at least "well-adjusted"—personality. Arica was only one of a very long list of new recipes for dissolving the ego-ridden personalities young people had acquired growing up.

There were now Arica Institutes in nine American cities. Oscar Ichazo lived in New York City and had become one of the carriage trade's "spiritual dignitaries." Through his senior assistants, the trainers (he himself was rarely seen), he claimed that the school he had founded was a product of the times. Four specific events had caused America to "grow up" over the last forty of its nearly two hundred years: the Depression, World War II, and the wars in Korea and Vietnam. Ichazo allowed that several other phenomena, such as LSD and the recent oil crisis, had also altered the American "mentality," but Arica represented nothing less than the next big change. Trained Aricans would transform the whole world. Arica had arrived in America just in time to help the awakening happen fast enough to "save Western culture from the death toward which it is speeding." If there was no substantive elevation in the current level of general consciousness, Ichazo said, if men and women could not achieve complete equality, then the forecast was not rosy.

It was the Arica mix of politics and apocalypse—and the less lofty promise of a drug-free high—that broke through Susan's long-cherished skepticism about psychotherapy and so much of the mumbo-jumbo she'd heard over the years. Ever alert to design and fashion, she was also drawn to the Arica style. Arica had a "look." The San Francisco facility on Market Street was a series of very clean empty rooms adorned with just a few bright rugs. Yantras—diagrammatic depictions of spoken mantras, "images that followed laws of form and color in a way that transmitted precise energies to the inner being"—hung on the bright white walls.

Susan and David were invited to the homes of some of the "original forty" pioneers who'd sought Oscar out in Latin America, and they were guests of various trainers in wealthy neighborhoods like San Francisco's Pacific Heights. In Arican homes, objects were never displayed on the gleaming counters or tabletops. The furniture was made of glass or chrome. Almost every serious Arican they met, of either sex, had the same short haircut, and the men always looked like they'd just had a close shave. Aricans were extremely lean and fit and androgynous-looking in the jumpsuits and body stockings they all wore. Trainers and other advanced Aricans were "in essence." They were clear channels, open circuits between Oscar Ichazo and the world.

Many Aricans were rich and didn't have to work. More than a million dollars of the movement's budget was supplied through donations over and above the considerable fees. Ex-Yippie Jerry Rubin would soon write that the Aricans he studied with were like "spiritual Spartans," but the look was really far more defenseless and narcissistic than that.

Susan thought she looked so run-down that she avoided mirrors or friends who might notice. She knew she looked like what she had so quickly and so very insidiously become: a weekend junkie who would have preferred to use heroin every single day.

To veterans of the hip and new like Susan Lydon and David Getz, the alleged danger of getting hooked on drugs was in the same league as Nixon's slogan "Peace with honor"—an entirely conventional piece of propaganda comprised of more lies than truths. Snorting up a couple of lines of coke or heroin, or even the odd subcutaneous "skin pop" or daring full puncture of a vein, was not only considered relatively harmless in the world of successful writers and well-to-do rock drummers with redwood homes; it was pretty damn cool. The marijuana Susan and David and their friends smoked was so potent it made your head spin in a second. Heroin was viewed as something of an elegant corruption—a drug for "with-it" reverse snobs—even as junkie soldiers came home from Vietnam and the junkie poor went to jail and died. But then, drugs had always caused problems for people of the class that got drafted and put in jail.

Beyond its jazzy status, heroin gave you an incredible high, Susan thought. It made you feel lovingly buffered and protected, like someone peering at the world through a private one-way mirror. Heroin laid down a sensuous sound track under a vision of a world melting into peace. Heroin was different from other drugs because it was alive. Susan had taken a lot of speed when she was struggling with her Randy Newman profile. There had been times when she was so wired on amphetamines that she was sure Randy was right there on the desk beside her IBM Selectric, talking her through the task. But a heroin high came with its own voice. The heroin voice whispered in a way that made your eyes roll back: "Everything will be fine." High with David,

Susan heard him say he loved her. They would weep together and tell each other everything would be fine.

Susan and David co-authored an article about Janis Joplin for Ms. In the course of reviewing two recently published books about the singer's short life, they posited that recent history had "created and consumed heroes with hysterical speed and a cruel and frightening hunger." Janis Joplin had found herself "torn between extreme and unresolvable poles," and so she turned "logically to junk. The junkie avoids having to make choices, distilling all possibilities into one....Janis was a born junkie, with a jones for love."

Susan's attachment to heroin made David Getz nervous. Getting high was only cool, he thought, if you kept it in control. David knew that their "open" relationship led Susan to men who were full-timers on the stuff and definitely not cool.

Susan and Gina Schick had "done up" together occasionally, but by the time Susan convinced her to try Arica training, Gina had awakened once or twice with a feeling she recognized from her Lower East Side days as dope sickness. She'd immediately backed away from heroin. By then, with her income from writing dwindling because of her erratic work habits, Susan had begun selling off her belongings to help finance her highs.

When Susan first went to Arica, she admitted with the openness required of trainees that she'd been feeling her love of heroin around her like a death grip. She said she was afraid. Arica, Susan hoped, would be the key to trading these precious highs for a less corrosive buzz. Near the pinnacle of Arica's calibrated measurement of spiritual liberation, she learned, was "The Permanent 24," a "basic satori" experience, a "place of inner and outer peace, joy and harmony" that would feel like the best recollections from childhood. In 24 you could sink back into the lost, loving circle of extended family back in the Bronx. In 24 the Fred Astaire movies never ended, and your highs would be nothing but the best essence of your self.

One morning Susan took Shuna to Devil's Slide, a nude beach north of San Francisco. The Arican penchant for nakedness was usually traced to the Esalen experience of many early Aricans. (On a recent visit to New York, Susan had exposed the upper half of her slender form to the sun at a beach not far from Harbor Isle, but she eventually put her top back on after several threats of violence.) At Devil's Slide, a small group of Aricans began to do some of the basic psychocalisthenics and headstands. Susan hadn't been notably diligent in her practice of the physical disciplines, and she shied away from meditative headstands because she considered them beyond her. She was never strong and good in gym like Lorraine.

But this time, while Shuna dug holes in the sand, Susan undressed and decided to stand on her head. As she stabilized upside down, she felt her legs assume what she imagined was a perfect lotus position above her. They folded almost by themselves, and within seconds—for the first time—Susan felt herself relax into the posture. The relaxation exceeded anything she'd ever felt, even a heroin buzz. A powerful sensation began to flow through her body, and Susan recognized it instantly: utter bliss, an overpowering, numinous contentment she'd known only once before, in the immediate afterglow of Shuna's birth. Weightless and aloft, in complete control, euphoric but not giddy, Susan stood on her head in the sun and allowed her mind to shuffle through a thick album of previous sensory journeys.

Until now Arica had provided an intellectual framework that suited Susan's tastes. It was perfect for a cerebral skeptic fearful of psychoanalysis, anxious to make a change, yet determined to stay cool. Until now the allure had been the aesthetics and the extremely cool new friends, the instant community, the decent politics, the open understanding of sexuality and drug experimentation. But suddenly, upside down, Susan could see the connection so many old acidheads made between the current spiritual trip and the former chemical trip.

As Shuna dug in the sand and the waves rolled in hard a few yards away, Susan decided she could get hooked on this feeling. She would come out with her hands up, lotus-palmed and empty of all things. She would surrender herself once and for all and become an Arican.

Sheila was often bored by the repetitive exercises, and she genuinely feared the encounter sessions when Arica students sat facing each other in "lines" and were instructed to provide first an objective description and then a subjective description of the person opposite them.

"Well, I certainly don't like your accent one bit," said the man across from Sheila subjectively. "Like, I just hate the way you say 'cawling' instead of calling and 'foynd out' instead of 'find out.'" Other people in other lines told her she was cute, not so cute, pretty, ugly, and a little overweight.

Sheila thought it was bad enough to be a single woman without a boyfriend who had sold her camera equipment to spend forty days with a roomful of women and gay men, but having those women and gay men sit across from you and pronounce you overweight was just...meanness, pure and simple.

When the training was almost over, Sheila was told that she would soon be free enough of her ego to face all her problems and shortcomings. At the very end of the program, she and the other students would test their new access to clarity by getting up on stage alone to answer any and all questions.

On the appointed day Sheila stood before the large audience as calmly as she could. The first questioner was a woman she knew to be a respected and progressive psychologist. If anyone in the room should know that even after forty days Sheila was still an overweight girl who'd never felt more insecure and unhappy than she did right now, it was surely this smiling middle-aged therapist.

"Sheila," the woman said, "what I would like you to tell all of us is this. Exactly how much do you weigh?"

Sam didn't have much to say about Gerald Ford, the man who replaced the first American president ever to resign from office. Nobody did. Next fall, a woman named Sarah Jane Moore would take a potshot at the president and proclaim him a "nebbish," an opinion shared by many Americans who would never have dreamed of expressing it with a gun.

By the end of the year, inflation would soar close to fourteen percent, and unemployment would exceed seven percent. When Gerald Ford appeared with a goofy red-and-white button on his lapel that said WIN—for "Whip Inflation Now"—the effect was so generally dumbfounding that it was hard to find anyone who knew what to say.

So Sam had little to say about Ford. Nor did he offer a comment on the retirement of Wilt Chamberlain or the death of Ed Sullivan. He noted only in passing the massive layoffs of auto workers and the sex scandal surrounding Congressman Wilbur Mills. As the year drew to a close, Harry noticed that Sam's hobbyhorses were becoming less timely. He talked more of the past.

As far as the work went, Harry sometimes came home thinking he'd had it easier trying to stay alive in Vietnam. His best days were the ones when the legendary Bernie Denodio, exploited proletarian, attempted to supplement Sam's cursory explanations of procedure and technique. Harry knew that Sam Gordon was a truly brilliant electrician. He knew it as sure as he knew that no matter how hard he tried, he would never make the grade. Sometimes Harry felt sorry for Sam. He'd started with nothing, inherited nothing, and spent all his life building an enterprise he could pass along. He had three daughters, a son with no interest in his business, and now a son-in-law who was so clearly unfit even for the simplest electrical work that it was laughable.

Harry couldn't wait for it to end, but he couldn't bring himself to leave.

Whenever Sam forced himself to watch Harry work, he'd try to remember the specific historical forces that led to his own handiness. Grow up without money, Sam believed, and you learned how to manipulate the material world yourself. It was that simple.

Lately, with two labor-intensive businesses and a small real estate portfolio to manage, Sam found himself putting in longer hours than ever. Ever since a guy named Dr. Wayne Oates had come out with all that stuff about "workaholism" back in 1971, Sam had tried to be more aware of his John Henry ways. All of a sudden, even some of his friends regarded his habit of working until he couldn't see straight as unhealthy, and hardly a visit passed when one of his kids didn't feel moved to say that Sam should have spent more time with them when they were growing up.

"So you would have wanted me to just hang around instead of working? How would we have lived?" he'd retort.

Whether he was a workaholic or just a working Joe trying to make a decent living, Sam had to admit there were more and more days—no two ways around it—when he didn't feel much like himself. He figured this was a sign of age. Sam would soon be fifty-six, and he thought often about a future less consumed by work. But Ricky was out of the picture as far as the business was concerned (Sam had finally acknowledged this truth), and that left Harry Hughes. When Sam tried to imagine Harry as heir to his electrical contracting business, he found himself unconsciously shaking his head. Since Harry had an education, Sam thought maybe he'd "get it" if he saw how things were supposed to be done in a book. He gave Harry all sorts of books about electricity, but it was hard to tell if his quiet, long-haired son-in-law even glanced at them. Harry squandered a lot of time watching the clock, and sometimes Sam could swear he went off and hid behind doors and walls, just standing there in the dark so he wouldn't have to work. Sam wondered if Harry had learned to shirk like this in the marines.

That winter Sam decided something had to be done. Harry needed an incentive, so Sam would give him a shot in the arm.

* * *

One cold evening Sam was unusually silent on the way home. Not a word about the recession or the gas lines crossed his lips. When Sam finally did speak, there was a generous, almost misty tone in his voice that Harry had never heard. "I guess you know Ricky has no interest in this business," he said. "So I think you should know something. What I'm really doing here is grooming you. Harry, someday the business can be yours."

1975

Yetta Goldenberg lay ill in bed watching people who'd been dead for many years wander through her Queens apartment. She recognized all of them and called out to each by name. Eve was asleep in the living room at Yetta's place when the roll call began. She got up and went to her mother-in-law's bedside. Sylvia came in too. "They're all our people. Family, dead since the Holocaust," Sylvia said.

Ever since she was a little girl, Eve had wondered about the destination of souls after their owners died. Long before Lorraine's recent talk of reincarnation, she considered it entirely reasonable that people might come back again and again, born out of some depthless sea of souls. Being Eve, she tended to snap herself out of such reveries with a punchline ("Then again, who gives a shit?"), but as she held Yetta's hand now, she was certain that Sam's mother was seeing ancestors beside her bed. So Eve Gordon, daughter of Rebecca, who had vivid dreams that came true, said, "I see them too, Mom. We should say hello."

Yetta had insisted for so long, with typical vehemence, that her debilitation was due to a case of shingles that Sam, Sylvia, Blanche, and Freddy felt free not to tell their mother the truth about her illness. As public knowledge grew and debate about cancer intensified, the very word had acquired terrible resonance. Even healthy Americans could now name a dozen permutations of a disease that ten years earlier had been the province of specialists. Symptoms and warning signs were the stuff of casual conversation, and speculation about the genesis of cancer was no longer confined to research laboratories. There was mounting evidence that many cancers were not "natural," that causes could be located in various man-made alterations and degradations of the "ecology," another omnipresent word by the middle of the decade, a lexical descendant of the Greek for "house."

Eve had been with Yetta in her hospital room just before the doctors decided nothing more could be done and sent her home to die.

"Eve, I think you'll tell me the truth," Yetta said. "They're all lying to me, aren't they? I really have cancer."

"Yeah," Eve said. "You do."

Yetta's expression didn't change. "Just stay with me, Havale," she said. "Just until I take my medicine." *Hava* was Hebrew for "Eve," the first female name in the Bible, and -*le* the Yiddish diminutive that imbued a name with love.

The active circle of Yetta Goldenberg's extended family was quite small, almost as much the result of unforgiven slights as of genocide and attrition. At all times Mama Yetta appeared ready and willing to enumerate the sins of her historical clan. She carried a mental record of familial crime that read like a police blotter, devoid of extenuating circumstances, previous kindnesses exhibited by the perpetrators, and references to past moments of closeness and good cheer that might have lightened the load.

When Eve watched Sam—her Sammy, as she still thought of him but rarely called him anymore—attempting to field the family life thrown at him over the years by the kids and the work and the times, she often pictured Mama Yetta and told herself once again that she was married to "a miracle man." Sam had survived a mother who wouldn't budge, and in Eve's estimation budging was the first thing you had to learn to do in a family.

Eve still ached over things Yetta had said to her in the forties, about how her mother was dirty and the Sambergs weren't much like Jews. She often wondered if Yetta had armored herself in such an immovable and harsh presence in order to protect a part of her that was too sensitive and hurt to be exposed. Whatever it was, nobody Eve had ever known could wield the saber of sarcasm more adeptly than the old woman now confined to her bed. Just recently, though, Eve had seen another side.

Not long before Yetta got sick, a Goldenberg cousin had come over from Israel to visit. It turned out that the woman could speak only Spanish, Hebrew, and Yiddish, so Eve interpreted for Yetta, whose command of Yiddish had disappeared over time, leaving only an accent behind. At one point Eve interrupted her fluent relay of family gossip to remark, "This is really something, huh, Mom? Your shiksa daughter-in-law—the only one who can speak to the Israeli." For over thirty years Eve had dreamed of saying something like this, but she was sure Yetta would stomp out of the house, perhaps for good. She was astonished when Yetta looked up with a twinkle in her eye and flashed a little smile.

After the ancestors had come and gone from Yetta's bedroom, Sylvia went back to bed in the other room. Eve pulled up a chair, still holding Yetta's hand. She watched the old woman slowly turn her head. "Havale," Yetta said. "You're my friend."

❯❯◆❮❮

A thin, bird-filled light seeped into Sam and Eve's living room. Dawn edged across the rug to reveal what appeared to be a vertical human form, dead still, completely naked, and upside down.

Sam Gordon was often heard to say, "Nothin' surprises me anymore," or "You can't shock me now," and there really wasn't too much he came across these days that elicited the dumbstruck disbelief that used to mark his ordinary experience of home life before the kids left. But the sight of his son-in-law—heir-apparent to SGE Electric, a man to whom Sam had recently considered offering a personalized invitation to become a Mason—standing on his head stark naked with his long legs folded into a nautical knot, apparently sound asleep at five in the morning...this, Sam found himself thinking, *this* was something different.

Sam moved closer to Harry Hughes and cleared his throat. He bent down and stared into Harry's face. Sure enough, out like a goddamn light. But for propriety, Sam would have hustled Eve out of bed to have a look.

Harry's grasp of electrical work might have been improving lately, but if so his progress was extremely subtle. Another employee of Sam's had just brought his own son into SGE to learn the business, so Sam now had not one but two young men on his payroll with no interest in the work at hand. He entertained a hunch that Harry and the new kid disappeared so often because they were sneaking off to smoke pot, like the young steelworkers and auto workers managers blamed for problems when confronted with bad statistics or consumer complaints.

"I get no return on my investment," Sam told Eve, borrowing from the financial vocabulary that was infiltrating everyday speech. "I just gotta let him go."

Eve sighed.

"I'll let him down easy. Don't worry about that."

"Harry," Sam said at the end of the next day, "you're not suited to electrical work. So Harry, you're fired."

Not long after Harry joined the more than eight percent of the work force now unemployed ("The State of the Union," President Ford had said in January, "is not good"), Sam began to notice him out on the dock trying to tie himself in knots. A small tape player sat droning nearby, something about "the center of the univer-er-er-erse." Harry got up at 4 a.m. to do his yoga exercises, and Lorraine had become far more adamant about the immorality of eating anything that had mucous membranes.

"Think about it, Mom. Look at the chickens next time you're in a store and tell me, just tell me they don't remind you of babies."

"Sure thing, Lorraine," Eve would say. "I'll do just that tomorrow."

Harry, Lorraine, and Maggie had moved into a new house much closer to Sam and Eve, less than ten minutes away in Long Beach. It was painted pink and shaped like a miniature Dutch farmhouse. Sam and his men did a good job cleaning it up, though Lorraine got a bit tense when she heard her father swearing about the "Italian wiring" he found above the kitchen ceiling. But Sam's passing irritation was soon overshadowed by his much stronger reaction to the sign Harry put up on the door of what he and Lorraine called the "yoga room."

"'Please remove shoes before entering,'" Sam read aloud. He looked inside the best room in the house. The rugs were gone and there were strange pictures of people with six arms coming out of them up on the walls.

"I'm sick," Sam said when he got home. "I got instant indigestion in that room. I don't know if I can hack this one, Eve."

"What do they do, pray to those things?" Eve asked.

"God knows," said Sam.

Sam knew that the world was full of pious charlatans. "They come back every day and in every age," he said, trying to settle his stomach. "In my day it was Father Divine. All kinds of wealthy Jewish ladies gave him their fortunes. He was the Messiah in a limousine, and the women all flocked to the guy."

Now they were back, the child stealers and hucksters, but this time they were South American weirdos and Indians with rags on their heads. First they'd teach kids how to sleep on their heads without any clothes on and tell them to turn a perfectly good living room into a shrine, but then, Sam was sure, they'd start asking for more.

* * *

The previous summer, bored on a local beach, Harry began to leaf idly through a book about yoga. A pragmatist (as a student, he'd been drawn to the biochemical aspects of the psychological sciences), Harry had always scoffed at the exotic spirituality so many of his contemporaries were espousing. But the hatha yoga postures depicted in the little book intrigued him, if only because he considered himself unusually limber.

The book offered a step-by-step method of understanding the yogic traditions. "Integral Yoga," it said, was a relatively recent system of physical and philosophical teachings formulated by the esteemed Indian-born, New York-based yoga master Swami Satchidananda, who had attracted a large and far-flung following since he was airlifted in to bless the Woodstock festival back in 1969. He was widely considered one of the "class acts" among the many Indian and Asian yoga teachers now instructing an estimated two or three million American students.

Harry went to one of Satchidananda's weekly lectures in New York City. A man with a gigantic white beard and flowing black-and-white-hair longer than Harry's sat on a stage in a thronelike chair. His long fingers curled gently over the arms of the huge chair as he spoke in heavily accented English with a lilting meter that seemed strangely ancient to Harry and soothed him. Harry listened, and he had the feeling that the evening's talk, on various conceptions of human happiness, was directed right at him. It was as if this Indian guy somehow knew that there was something sorely lacking in the life of Harry Hughes.

Yogiraj Sri Swami Satchidananda was born in southern India in 1914 to privileged and observant Hindu parents who named their son Ramaswamy. Like other children from religious families, young Ramaswamy loved to play Guru and Disciple with his friends. When he grew up, he was anything but a holy man. A strikingly handsome, chain-smoking manager at India's National Electric Works, he fell in love, married, and settled down to raise a family. But as with so many other worldly things, he would say that he never felt wholly "attached" during his five years as a "householder," or as the father of two sons by the time his wife died a few years later.

After his wife's death, Ramaswamy left his children with his mother and went off on a spiritual quest that took him to mountaintops and deep into jungles and forests. For years Ramaswamy searched out men revered as sages and saints, and spiritual masters said to be 160 years old. His mother despaired over her son's apparent love of poverty. "Is this the type of life I conceived and brought you up for?" she'd ask during his short visits home.

In 1949, having finally found his own spiritual master in the Himalayas, Satchidananda (meaning "Existence-Knowledge-Bliss Absolute") was initiated as a swami. Within a few years he was well known in Indian yoga circles, though he didn't achieve an international reputation until young spiritual prospectors from the United States discovered his teachings in the mid-1960s. At the time, the Beatles and other celebrities had begun to travel to India, looking to jettison the barbarian taint of the West in favor of Eastern serenity. Wealthy patrons in New York and Paris were soon importing spiritual tutors by the month.

The Americans who went to study with Satchidananda abroad warned him that he wouldn't like the United States, a "crazy place," but the guru planned a two-day visit to see for himself. He came to New York in 1966 as a guest of the artist Peter Max, who'd made a fortune creating images drawn from the psychedelic experience, just as Leroy Neiman got rich painting sports events.

Satchidananda said he was intrigued by America and Americans, rude and disrespectful though he found them, and he decided to stay a while. By 1967 he had distinguished himself from the many other swamis in New York City by serving the unruly and often heavily medicated flower children who'd offended him when he first arrived. Satchidananda argued to less tolerant spiritual masters that "the kids" were simply frustrated because their homes and religions and schools had failed them. "Where do you go if your institutions don't offer you anything?" he'd ask. "To a tepee in Vermont, that's where....They are all searching for the necklace that's around their necks. Eventually they'll look in the mirror and see it." Satchidananda claimed that Integral Yoga was a way to exit the drug culture. "The problem with drugs is that while they elevate you, they immediately drop you back down again. Yoga," he said memorably, gave you a "natural high."

Word circulated on the nascent spiritual grapevine that Satchidananda had cured a disciple's kidney ailment by blessing a glass of water. He performed a marriage ceremony for two followers and attended the big Jewish gala the newlyweds' parents threw in a restaurant in the Bronx (more than half his serious students were Jewish). Seven months before he went to Woodstock, Satchidananda sold out an evening at Carnegie Hall. By the beginning of the 1970s, there were thousands of Integral Yoga devotees—doctors and stockbrokers among them—studying at fifteen centers around the country. As Satchidananda told a writer for the *Wall Street Journal,* yoga had come to America and "gone public."

* * *

The natural human state, Harry heard Swami Satchidananda explain, was in essence peaceful and happy, but we tended to seek happiness outside ourselves. "Look at the people who run entire countries and have garnered great wealth," Satchidananda suggested. Had they found happiness in power and possessions? "Just as a scale has to register zero in order to accurately do its work, judgment must derive from a neutral vision of all things. This is the gift of yoga," a science of the mind, a "grandsire of Western approaches to the mind." All you had to lose by practicing yoga was the ego that tormented you. "Suffering," Satchidananda said, "is nothing more than the burning up of your ego." Harry was enthralled.

The idea of reincarnation used to amuse Harry when it didn't threaten him, but after he heard about it from the swami he found it reassuring. Karma—lessons you'd failed to learn returning in the form of experience (what some people might call good luck or bad)—encompassed a vision of a morally resonant past in which you'd played a role. Karma was truth stored like seeds "in the granary of your mind," as Satchidananda put it. Even the late Lyndon Johnson had believed in karma. LBJ, Harry knew, had once said it was "God's marks" that visited John Kennedy for his part in the deaths of Diem and Trujillo. Tragedy was systematized by karma. History fell into line.

If Eastern religion existed only to explain away evil, Harry was sure he wouldn't have been so interested, but yoga addressed issues of health and seemed to offer an avenue to understanding and controlling your actions. Through yoga, joining the marines and getting married too soon would become demystified past experiences. Eventually, Harry would learn to control his mind. What Sam saw in his living room at dawn was the manifestation of Harry's decision to strip away the layers of illusion and get at the truth. Harry was determined to become what the swami called in his books and lectures a "realized self."

One of the central tenets of Integral Yoga was contained in the statement "Truth is one, paths are many." To Lorraine, it sounded like a succinct version of her own guiding philosophy. It was the same liberal sentiment that had inspired her earliest questioning of the rules according to Mama Yetta and Sam and convention. Yoga's promise of better health also appealed to her, since her long list of allergies and fears was endless now and calm eluded her every day.

Lorraine went to the city with Harry to see the beautiful man who sat on a throne with his legs tucked up under white flowing robes. She thought his speaking voice was like a warm breeze, like music, sensuous and soothing. It made her eyes blur. Satchidananda would break into a little song during his lecture, then quote from Hindu scripture, then from a Christian text. Sometimes he'd offer an aphorism in his native Tamil. He ended many sentences with a parental, slightly mocking "Hmm?" that always drew an appreciative laugh from the crowd.

The guru clearly enjoyed playing word games with his second language: "You might be after a diamond—you are mad after it, dying for it. That is why it's called a die-amond."

"More wants, less pleasure, less joy," he'd chant like a beat poet reading from his works.

Lorraine was well aware that both Freud and Jung had considered the possibility of something more primordial than the unconscious. She'd always been attracted to the idea of a superconscious layered with reincarnated psyches from the past. Lorraine Gordon Shapiro Hughes had spent much of her life trying to harden her ego against the harsh vagaries of her times. She'd believed for as long as she could remember that living the good life would be rewarded with psychic peace. Romantic that she was, she'd always thought that a passionate love between two people could break down the walls of ego and form a union exponentially stronger, however much the evidence seemed to contradict her when she considered the state of most relationships. Now, feeling more afraid and battered than ever before, she found the idea of simply reducing the power of ego, of turning down the volume, utterly compelling. Freud said that yoga killed off the instincts, but Freud and his epigones had yet to offer a road to true calm.

Lorraine watched the guru unfold one of his long fingers. "Yoga means taking it easy," he said, smiling as if he'd told a joke. "It means leaving dis-ease for ease." The elegant man on the stage was nothing less than a living embodiment of the peace she'd always desired. "The purpose of yoga is to be everywhere at home," he said, "to go anywhere at all and still be at home." Lorraine kept staring at the swami, this lean Santa with his musical accent and his sack of thoughts. She began to feel agitated, almost aroused. When he was done, she joined the long line of people waiting to meet him, though when she was finally alone in front of him, she couldn't think of anything to say. She just gazed into his eyes. "They were the kind of eyes that could swallow you up," she said to Harry on the way home. "You could go into those eyes and completely disappear."

Lorraine couldn't sleep that night. She felt hot and jumpy. Lorraine knew the symptoms. She'd fallen in love.

Ricky came home for summer vacation determined to return to Carnegie Mellon as the handsomest man on campus. He had a picture in his mind that was a cross between Charles Atlas and a *Vogue* model. At all costs Ricky would lose the last remnant of what he considered the feminine softness that still clung to his frame, dangerously pliant. Each day after he got back to the boatyard from his summer job as a waiter in an Italian restaurant in Manhattan (until cocktail hour, when he turned into the pianist), Ricky would eat dinner and go out to run three or four miles. He owned the special shoes now mandatory for anyone interested in state-of-the-art jogging, and he was fully prepared to experience the superior psychological state running promised as an adjunct to a superior physique.

The long jog was followed by at least half an hour of calisthenics and then a full body inspection before the mirror. A henna preparation had turned Ricky's hair an iridescent shade of black, though he couldn't avoid the stunning realization that it was beginning to recede at a glacial but still noticeable pace, just as Sam's hairline had begun to retreat when he was nineteen.

Ricky invited his friends to the boatyard to continue the evenings of music and talent he'd hosted back at school. They would gather to play instruments and sing, and later to take up the evening's "theme." Ricky always chose the theme. Once it was hair and makeup: Ricky ushered everybody into the bathroom to "re-do" them. Another time it was clothes. There were poetry weekends when Ricky would recite and discuss and analyze poems with complete authority. During spiritual discussion weekends he elucidated the ideas and practices of Arica and Integral Yoga, as he understood the basic components of his sisters' new trips.

For years now, people had had their "things." They "got into" things, "did" their own things. If you were with it, you no longer merely lived and worked and tried to get by, you had an aesthetic of action flexible enough to encompass the next *thing* that came along. During what Ricky called "the health-and-beauty summer" of 1975, he managed to compress an impressively long list of *things* into a brief span. One day he was a psychoanalyst, the next a swami.

He went to see *A Chorus Line* on Broadway and was so completely "blown away" that he learned all the music and lines. Parts of the show, like the famous monologue delivered by Paul, a gay dancer, were so brilliant that Ricky decided to be an actor instead of a pianist or a composer. He memorized the Sammy Goldenbaum monologue from William Inge's *Dark at the Top of the Stairs* and delivered it to anyone who seemed in the least interested.

Susan came to town and took Ricky to a Randy Newman show at the Cafe Carlyle. He wore a new musk scent he'd discovered at Kiehl's, the old-fashioned but trendy pharmacy. He sat next to designer Betsy Johnson, who was wearing a blue-black velvet dress with little rhinestones on it. They chatted away, with Ricky doing most of the talking.

Ricky went to an opera and saw Ned Rorem. Full of courage and excitement, he approached the brilliant, handsome composer during intermission to tell him how much his musical settings of Sylvia Plath had meant to him. But when they began to talk, Ricky noticed that the great composer had a speech impediment. Afterward, he couldn't stop thinking about the irony of someone so gifted and beautiful—as Rorem had described himself in his *Paris Diary*, which Ricky had read—having a flaw. Perfection, after all, was the watchword of the summer.

Exercising, singing, traveling, holding forth, Ricky was off and running that summer, his pace set for him each morning in significant part by the diet drops he took with his coffee.

The drops the doctor had given Eve were the least diluted, most effective speed Ricky had ever tried. He badgered every *zaftig* woman he knew into going to one of the many diet doctors who prescribed the stuff to get him more. Max Jacobson, notorious amphetamine supplier to the stars, who'd pumped up John Kennedy so he could be on top of events like his 1961 summit with Khrushchev in Vienna, was currently the subject of an investigation that would cost him his medical license. The Drug Enforcement Administration and various members of Congress were calling for a ban on the prescription sale of amphetamines for weight reduction because of widespread abuse, but there were hundreds of doctors—well-meaning and not—who were willing to dispense these wonder drugs, first concocted in Germany in the 1930s and used during World War II by exhausted soldiers.

Eve got the diet drops because she was getting—well, frankly, though she didn't like to admit it, "kind of chunky." She was also getting to be...*fifty-five*. Just turning fifty had made her cry all morning until a bank teller asked what was wrong. The teller said Eve looked like Elizabeth Taylor, which certainly helped. But fifty-five! Though nobody was quite sure, her daughter's namesake, Susan Hayward, was thought to be fifty-five when she died only a few months ago. "A brassy charm," said the *Times* obit. "A throaty defiance when she met tragedy."

"She had an unhappy family life, a bad marriage, custody battles over her son, an attempted suicide, and then finally a happy marriage to a man who suddenly up and dies," Eve told her friends. Eve had to wonder if through it all Susan Hayward had managed to remain "brassy." Whatever else might be said of Liz Taylor, she would be brassy until she died.

All sorts of women told Eve that there was a doctor in Long Beach who would give her drops to make her thin again. Metrecal, the Mead Johnson Company's "miracle formula" of 1959, was now a tame over-the-counter remedy like aspirin. You needed a doctor to prescribe speed.

All the years she'd been shaped like the proverbial hourglass, the truth was that Eve had never thought she looked good enough, no matter what she wore, but now she felt that the throaty defiance and brassy charm that had always covered her self-doubt were faltering and in need of a supplement, so she went for the diet drops. Of the triumvirate mentioned so often as evidence of suburban decline—neurosis, alienation, and obesity—obesity was the only one you could deal with at breakfast. The doctor told her to put eight drops in her morning beverage, but since Eve had a history of reacting to drugs, she took only four. Ricky would secretly take ten drops every morning and replace the purloined Methedrine with water—and Eve still lost weight. She also found that more than ever, she wanted to gab.

Ricky and Eve sat before their light nothing of a breakfast talking about Ricky's cultural or material passion of the moment and half-moment. They rehashed family matters and discovered new things they never knew they shared. They found, for instance, that they both had a recurrent dream about living in one of those huge marble bathrooms in the homes of the rich (literary critic Edmund Wilson once said he'd had more sublime thoughts in an American bathroom than in any cathedral in Europe). With a bathroom like the one they both dreamed about, Ricky and Eve agreed, who would ever want to leave?

When Ricky's friends came and the music started up, Eve would ply them with cakes from Entenmann's bakery, and sometimes she'd join in and sing. One of Ricky's friends described her as "a typical mother, with a twist."

Eve was always a hit during the summer of 1975.

A Carnegie Mellon friend of Ricky's stopped by the restaurant where he worked to ask if by any chance he was free to accompany her to a party at Stephen Sondheim's East Side brownstone four days from now. Ricky spent the better part of the following ninety-six hours (he wasn't sleeping much anyway) doing push-ups, listening to or playing Stephen Sondheim songs, looking in the mirror, and agitating himself to the edge of seizure over what he was going to wear.

Ricky had come to regard Sondheim as a living, youthful incarna-
tion of the classical masters of the past. He had now seen *A Little Night
Music* six times. Sondheim adorned his musicals with enormous intelligence and emotional complexity, with a sense of movement and rich
empathetic characters, and never resorted to hackneyed plot lines or
caricature. Ricky wanted to be just like him. And now he was going to a
party at Stephen Sondheim's house.

Atop the stone steps leading up from East Forty-ninth Street, Ricky
and his friend Kim rang the bell beside the great man's door. Ricky was
wearing a pair of tight jeans and a very tight black turtleneck that
accentuated his bulky shoulders. The door swung open, and there stood
Stephen Sondheim, smiling, introducing himself, and beckoning Ricky
inside. Ricky fought off a powerful impulse to fall to his knees and pro-
fess his devotion. "I think your work is so brilliant," he said instead,
pretty cool.

Ricky ordered a Scotch on the rocks at a small bar. He'd never had
Scotch, but he'd always thought it sounded like a manly drink.

"Let me take you on a tour," Stephen Sondheim said. They strolled
side by side past producer Harold Prince and actor Joel Grey. Stephen
stopped to say hello to Anthony Perkins and then took Ricky to see his
collection of antique pinball machines and other old games. There were
games and puzzles everywhere, which seemed perfect in light of the
intricacy and inventiveness of Sondheim's work.

I am the luckiest teenager in the world. I am the happiest boy alive, Ricky
was thinking when he felt his stomach heave. He was sure that in the
next few seconds he would vomit right in front of Stephen Sondheim,
so he excused himself abruptly. Maybe it was the Scotch, or maybe the
Scotch in combination with the diet drops, but Ricky could barely make
it out of the bathroom to find Kim. Within minutes he was in a cab
headed for Penn Station.

Ricky and Eve spent most of the following day sitting out on the
balcony above the boat slips. No matter what happened, a sunny day at
the boatyard made Ricky feel better. This home of Sam and Eve's had
become a naturally happy place, and sometimes it awed Ricky to
see how content his parents seemed against the changing colors and
the sea.

By the end of the morning, Ricky felt stronger, and his tragic
retelling of the evening's events gave way to humor. "But he talked to
me," he kept saying to Eve. "Stephen Sondheim talked to me like I was
a real person."

Eve smiled, sipped her coffee, and stared out into the distance, seeing her own moments up close to the stars and hearing old songs in the waves.

——◆——

Lorraine looked in through the doorway at Harry, who remained appropriately grim-faced as Susan gazed up at the ceiling, working her mouth like a penguin downing a fish. Lorraine leaned into the room and heard her sister talking playfully to her husband about sexual technique.

Anyone who knew Lorraine could attest that she was a confirmed nonjudgmental person—truth is one, paths are many—but from a specifically yogic point of view, she didn't understand Susan's need to describe her bedroom habits to Harry. She knew Susan had already told Ricky all about her new skills during this same visit.

Lorraine also had trouble grasping the spiritual purpose of Aricans running around naked half the time, jumping into saunas together, and in general pursuing their liberation of consciousness in a manner that closely resembled an extended orgy. Normal middle-class people had been standing in movie lines to watch pornography ever since the success of *Deep Throat* in 1972, and it wasn't at all odd to find *The Joy of Sex* and other uninhibited "how-to" texts on family book shelves. Advocates of "open" marriages that would help couples "kick the togetherness habit" counseled the pursuit of sexual pleasure as a means of liberation. Popular entertainment was full of sex. Conversations were full of sex. But Lorraine refused to believe that it was suddenly cool to discuss blow jobs in your sister and brother-in-law's living room. She resented the hedonism of Arica, which offered nothing penitential or heartfelt. Where yoga held out the chance to be spiritually reborn, Arica seemed like a jumble of intellectual equivocations designed to foster guilt-free self-indulgence.

"All your rules are unnecessary," Susan said when Lorraine described the changes she and Harry were making in their day-to-day life. According to Oscar Ichazo, the old spiritual traditions, with their moral strictures and piety, had spawned sexual violence, incest, and other modern plagues. Just do the Arica exercises, Susan said, study the complex "manifestations," "domains," maps, and other guides to various locales of the psyche, and you would simply *know* what you were doing at all times.

One day around the time the American embassy was evacuated in Saigon, marking the weirdly anticlimatic conclusion of the foreign war that would forever mar Harry Hughes's memories of the past, Harry had stopped in at one of the big "Arica houses" where Susan was staying during a visit to New York. He was greeted warmly at the door of the large apartment by a lovely young woman who was completely naked except for a pair of velvet slippers. Inside there were more naked Aricans sitting on thick carpets with other Aricans dressed in velvet pajama suits "designed to improve charisma," Harry was told. He found the scene fascinating and extremely erotic, but out of respect for his and Lorraine's newly enhanced spiritual devotion, he never told her how much his hour at the Arica apartment turned him on. He also decided not to tell Lorraine how much he'd enjoyed Gina Schick's recent visit to their house in Long Beach, when in true Arican style she'd walked around wearing only bedroom slippers much of the time.

The fact was that the nudity and Susan's suggestive talk inspired crackling, vivid fantasies in Harry. He had often perceived a kind of electrical aura encircling the three Gordon girls, as if they shared some collective sexual charge. Something about "the sisters" turned him on. But with Satchidananda's help, Harry hoped to distance himself from his lurid daydreams. He and Lorraine often spoke of becoming true followers of Integral Yoga, perhaps teachers. Lately they'd even discussed the idea of trying to live like swamis by abjuring sex. A true yogi was able to draw energy up from the lower and lesser *chakra* of the loins and achieve cosmic orgasms of the mind, releases so complete and perfect that the flawed atavism of sexual intercourse—an act Lorraine was now realizing had served since her teens as a desperate measure of love and of her standing in comparison to her older sister—would simply stop mattering so much.

"No, Harry, really. Your charisma is total," Susan was saying as Lorraine continued to look into the room. Lorraine knew that special flirtatious voice.

"Susan!" she screamed, storming in. She couldn't help it; she wasn't calm. She stalked up to her sister. "If you can't stop being disgusting, you can just get out of here!"

Susan hardly reacted. She had already "read" Lorraine earlier in the day and assigned her psyche to an appropriate location within one of the Arica domains. "Oh, Lorraine," Susan sighed, shooting a grin at Harry. "You're so...so *Puritan.*"

Which in any numbers of ways, as Lorraine was just beginning to see, was quite true.

David Getz spotted Susan against the other side of a crowded elevator rising through Arica's fancy New York City headquarters, a complex Aricans called "24"—a reference both to one of the higher levels of Arican spiritual attainment and to the sleek glass-walled skyscraper's address on West Fifty-seventh Street, just off Fifth Avenue, which led Oscar Ichazo to choose it as his American base. Susan stood surrounded in the elevator by ranking Arican teachers and fellow students registered for the three-thousand-dollar advanced training program David had known she would also be "doing" in New York. (People *did* a course in Arica.)

For some time David had been jealous of Susan's apparently effortless ascent in Arica. With the same combination of charm, instinct, and Olympian aspiration that had propelled her to the forefront of so many other generational experiences, she had already penetrated the Arican inner circle. David was still attracted to Susan's animal propensity to make the scene. People like him—people like him and Sam Gordon, so much better with their hands, better at what they did than at telegraphing what they were—needed a conduit, a legate who could help complete their connection to the social sphere. From the moment David met Sam, he could see how much Sam needed an Eve.

David stared across the elevator car as people jostled to get on and off, thinking of the tension and pain that separated him from Susan now. All of a sudden she was staring back at him. He saw her mouth fall open. He lost sight of her for a second as the elevator filled, but then, through the murmuring irritation of the people between them, thin and red-faced, head down like a halfback's, there was Susan. David barely saw the punch coming. It landed with a noise that reminded him of a cowboy movie, and it would have knocked him flat if the elevator hadn't been so jammed. Susan punched him again.

A man yelled, "Somebody separate those two!"

Susan was pulled away snarling and snorting like she'd lost her mind.

Before she'd finally moved out of the house in Fairfax, David noticed that when they did up together, Susan always did more. David had a girlfriend who got high on heroin, but Susan had a full-fledged junkie boyfriend. Some nights the boyfriend and the girlfriend slept over, the two couples just a wall apart.

"You have to leave. You have to move out of here," David kept saying.

"Shuna and I have nowhere to go," Susan would cry.

Susan and David sold the carefully chosen objects they'd accumulated. They unloaded it all—antiques, quilts, toys—for nickels and dimes.

Eve was concerned when Susan told her she was moving back to the New York City epicenter of Arican life because "the world was ending." Susan said she and Shuna needed a place where there was "no murder and no anger, a place where there isn't any trouble"—a line Eve recognized as Dorothy's wish just before her journey to Oz.

One late summer afternoon, not long after Susan and Shuna suddenly appeared in the New York area and Susan announced to Sam and Eve that they were back for good, Harry, Lorraine, and Maggie joined Susan and Shuna on a jaunt to a relatively unpopulated stretch of beach. The plan was for the grown-ups to meditate while seven-year-old Shuna played with Maggie, almost eleven now.

Harry watched Susan strike a meditative pose. Then she closed her eyes and pitched over onto her back, mouth agape.

Harry went to her. "She's out cold," he said.

Lorraine rushed over, and together they righted Susan. Her eyelids opened slightly, but you couldn't see her eyes. "Meditation," she said.

"Yeah, sure thing, honey," Lorraine said.

"She's totally ripped," Harry said. "Gotta be ludes or something."

Lorraine and Harry laid Susan out on the warm sand.

It was difficult for Lorraine to face the possibility that Susan's life of glamour and achievement and being hip to so many scenes could have worn her down. All these years Lorraine had imagined Susan traveling above the fray, at altitudes where there was much less resistance, less friction, less worry or doubt. Even Susan's choice of spiritual path conformed to the "superior Susan" thesis welded so permanently to Lorraine's sense of self.

Harry would say later that Susan feared success, but Lorraine was beginning to see that behind the pulleys and mirrors, Susan was a lonely girl in terrible pain—still the "blue lady" she'd once written a poem about back when they were kids.

Swami Satchidananda said that once people turned to drugs, they would only turn away from them when they caused dissatisfactions. Yoga would be the last thing on the list of exploratory experiences a seeker discovered, the guru said.

Susan said she was on her way "out the door" of drugs.

Arica had no specific dogma about drugs—to forbid any worldly act would contradict Oscar Ichazo's focus on the limitlessness of human possibility. Yet Susan often portrayed the Arican disciplines as alternatives to getting high.

"Nobody meditates on a handful of Quaaludes," Lorraine said when Susan woke up.

Susan snorted and shook her head.

"You should think about going to therapy," Lorraine said.

"I know what I need," Susan shot back.

On the day of their initiation, Lorraine and Harry fasted. They drove to the Integral Yoga ashram in rural Pomfret, Connecticut, where they donned white initiate's robes. Others were there wearing saffron-colored garments. These were the *sannyasin*, disciples willing to renounce family, worldly goods, and a long list of physical and sensory experiences in order to be swamis. The light reddish color of their robes represented the fire to which they symbolically consigned body, mind, and "all that could be called one's own" in order to become true "instruments of the Divine."

"Gurudev," as only Satchidananda's disciples and "devotees" (who usually retained a role in the external world) were supposed to call him, said that the new yoga names and private mantras he would bestow upon the initiates were like yogurt. His new followers would be the culture from which much would grow. Satchidananda seemed to glide slowly among the initiates, leaning down and whispering. Harry was given the yoga name Hara and his own mantra to repeat over and over again. Gurudev came to Lorraine and spoke the lines of her mantra in her ear. Then he put his long, slender hands on her head. Lorraine thought his finger was inside her skull, pushing the mantra into the middle of her brain.

"You are Leela," Satchidananda said. Leela—a light and joyous name, the Hindi word for "divine play."

≈•◆•≈

Sam covered the mirrors at the boatyard in the traditional way. Mama Yetta was buried next to Papa Joe in the big ten-grave plot. Yetta and Joe shared one large headstone in peace.

Once again Sam praised what his father had done by purchasing the plot. "This way the family won't be scattered to the four winds," he said. "This way everyone can be together—which is a beautiful thing."

Eve put a few mementos from Yetta's apartment in the box that held Sam's love letters from the front. One of the objects was an old-fashioned locket Yetta often wore. It was hard to open, but when it finally gave, Eve saw a small photograph of three figures. The young Freddy and Sylvia were easily recognizable, but the third face was missing. Someone had cut it away in the unmistakable shape of a tiny heart.

For almost two years Eve's Sunday and early evening views out the big picture window had included her husband's efforts to restore the Chris Craft that had burned during the dock explosion. She could barely get Sam inside for a meal, so obsessed was he with returning the twin-engine boat to its pristine state.

Sam had bought the hulk from the insurance company for twenty-five hundred dollars. He traveled all the way to Tennessee to make sure the new flying bridge was made right. Occasionally he appeared topside to grab a few tools, but then he'd snake back down inside the boat and stay there for hours. The electric business was humming along so well lately that Sam figured the boatyard would be paid off in a few years. The marina business was humming along too, but Sam's thoughts were completely concentrated on the big white boat he was bringing back from the dead.

Lorraine sometimes watched from the window along with Eve. "He's meditating," she would say. "This is how he looks for inner peace."

Though Sam felt that with their latest set of abiding truths Susan and Lorraine were pointing the finger at him once again, shortly after his mother died he admitted that he yearned for the chance to step back from his life and take stock. But until he could spare an entire Saturday for himself or knock off for a few days in a row, there were at least the evening rituals of the Masons and the Sunday ceremony of spark plugs poking you in the ribs. There was still the momentary redemption of hearing an engine run clean, and the self-forgetting purity that came from rebuilding something with your own hands.

Theodore Roszak, a student of American culture, explained the popular fascination with new consciousness and experiments in spirituality as a reaction not only to the "waning authority of science," but also to the disappearance of "industrial necessity"—the all-American primacy of work. For millions of people work had lost its meaning. Eager though he was for a change, Sam Gordon was not about to repudiate the crucible of almost all his days. Even Lorraine agreed that Sam already had a mantra pressed deep into his brain: "Work, work, work ..."

Not long after Yetta died, Sam finally finished the big Chris Craft. He and Eve took a long run up the Hudson River, and Eve swam and washed her hair in the clear water ten miles north of the city. On the way back, one of the engines blew, and Sam didn't talk much at home until it was repaired.

"Now it's perfect," he announced. "It's exactly the way I want it." Eve had never heard Sam say anything was perfect.

A few days later Eve was relaxing after some of the canasta girls had gone home (she also played canasta now, though the apparent status leap over mah-jongg was of much less interest to her than the diversion of a new game). She was having one last cup of coffee before joining Sam in bed when someone began to knock hard on the door. "There's smoke pouring out of that big boat with the flying bridge," a neighbor from down the street yelled.

Eve woke Sam, and they went to the picture window. There was smoke and a hint of flame coming out of the Chris Craft's hold. "Get away from the window," he hollered. "Come on!"

Flames suddenly rushed from the hold with a huge animal roar. They roared again and again, rising to the level of the living room. Then there was a much louder sound, a thunderous explosion, and immediately the fire was obscured by one of the heaviest downpours Sam and Eve had ever seen. The rain kept the fire from spreading to the gas tanks, but the boat was ruined.

Ricky was out with Peter Randsman that evening. They'd gone to catch a much ballyhooed new movie called *Jaws*, which Ricky expected would be low-brow but fun. He found that he was actually impressed by the opening shots of a young girl swimming, the peaceful light of life up on the surface of the water juxtaposed with the gruesome shark attack taking place underneath. But as the underwater dismemberment continued, Ricky felt his terror mounting. All these years swimming in the ocean, and this gnashing horror had lurked beneath him the whole time. Within an hour, *Jaws* had all but incapacitated him. Ricky had a brand-new fear, and on the way home he vowed to Peter—as so many other viewers of the film vowed—that he would never swim in the ocean again.

Sam woke Ricky up very early the next morning and told him to meet him down at the dock. Ricky surveyed the damage and tried to think of something to say to his father. Sam was wearing his "let's get to work" face.

"There must be a bunch of holes in the hull," he said. "Get your mask and fins and find the propeller on the bottom. Then take these rags and stuff up the biggest holes."

Ricky was dizzy with terror, and yet he dove under the charred hull again and again, rising through the suspended soot, the blackened oil, and all the splintered detritus floating on the surface, coming up into the light each time more amazed that he still had arms and legs.

In the next few weeks Sam learned that the fire was an act of arson, the result of a misunderstanding between a mechanic who worked for him and a Harbor Isle kid who as a youngster was known in the neighborhood for his practice of shooting cats. He'd gone on to become one of the drug-dealing motorcycle hoodlums so numerous in Nassau County. A few years after the fire, Sam would hear that the kid had disappeared over the Bermuda Triangle on a transcontinental drug run in the company of another man's wife.

An insurance agent called Sam and told him that this time he could buy the boat back for just fifteen hundred dollars. "I wouldn't rebuild or even own another boat if I lived to be seven thousand years old," Sam said. "Thanks for calling, but I'm through with boats forever."

Eve thought that the moral of the Chris Craft fiasco was "Never say anything's perfect," but she didn't mention her insight to Sam for several years.

1976

Harry Hughes's vow to ingest only the simplest of foods—and those in radical moderation—had by now taken him far beyond the lanky ideal of the most observant Arican to the skeletal frame of a true hatha yogi. If Maggie or Shuna begged him, Harry might occasionally suck in his diminished well of organs until the skin above his navel was almost pressing against his spine. He could hold it there for quite a while, looking like a true Indian holy man at the end of a lean winter, while the girls giggled and exclaimed, "Ee-yew!"

For Lorraine, who was almost as skinny as her husband from all the low-fat, calorie-spare vegetable pastiches she prepared, the task of finding pure, untainted food was becoming easier all the time. Alongside the mainstream American food, health care, recreation, and cosmetic industries, new industries had sprung to life. There were now so many alternative retail outlets amid the malls and Miracle Miles and red, white, and blue Bicentennial fireplugs of the New York metropolitan area that it looked like the counterculture was back in business.

Lorraine would shop on the way to her Indian music lessons at the local Institute for Self-Development, a strip complex that also housed a holistic health center and offered course work in dynamic healing, advanced yoga, Korean martial arts, and exotic natural cooking. The institute also served as a clearinghouse for freelance astrologers and psychics who gave more personalized, off-site paranormal consultations, but the sale of information and items connected to corporeal well-being already dwarfed the competition in servicing the spirit or the mind.

The new marketplace and its hip merchants now included Sheila Gordon (she had never changed her named to Probst, in 1969 a controversial decision that now seemed a distinct convenience), back from northern California as the novice proprietor of Higher Grounds, an herb, spice, coffee, and loose tea concession in the back of a thriving health food store not far from Harry and Lorraine's house in Long Beach. Sales of "health food" were in the process of increasing more than elevenfold, to $1.6 billion by the end of the decade. Sales of breakfast cereals containing unprocessed, unhusked grain (or better yet, the husk itself, the suddenly ubiquitous substance called bran) had increased by twenty percent in the last year by the time Sheila opened for business, and "high-fiber" bread sales were up by a third.

The alternative markets benefited from a general skepticism about the safety of processed foods. Carcinogenic cyclamates could have slipped by despite the recent federal ban; baby-deforming DES was known to have been pumped into beef; nitrosamine laced the family bacon; DDT clung to fruits and vegetables; and countless other mutagens and by-products were widely believed to be lying in ambush under the brightly colored packaging of many supermarket staples.

The once simple act of buying groceries now required extensive training. A sharp cultural shift had quickly made any lingering affinity for the white bread that nurtured an entire postwar generation seem as foolish and antiquated as using leeches to treat disease. Status now attached to the knowledgeable purchase of items marked "pure" or "natural," even if some of them tasted rather dry and chalky and others smelled like a recently mowed lawn. An aficionado of the exotic teas Sheila sold had become the cultural equivalent of a wine connoisseur.

Always a hit on the television talk show circuit, Swami Satchidananda—as of the Bicentennial February a naturalized citizen of the "crazy country" his acolytes assured him he'd loathe—now occupied time slots usually reserved for more secular gurus of diet and beauty. The swami sat in on shows such as "Midday Live" in New York City, replacing naturalist Euell Gibbons, who before his recent death at the age of sixty-four had convinced millions of Americans not only to find that verdant picnic spot in the woods but to eat it too. Satchidananda was asked to consult with corporations and speak to medical groups about nutrition, not unlike Dr. Carleton Fredericks, who claimed that psychological states ranging from mild melancholia to uncontrolled mania were the result of a pancreatic overreaction to refined sugar. All over America it was now understood that millions suffered from the clinical condition hypoglycemia.

By 1976, true adherents of an alternative lifestyle like Lorraine and Harry were becoming increasingly marginal to the social and economic mainstream while buttressing a new megamarket through their religious consumption of swamplike food.

Sheila began Higher Grounds shortly after her return from California. She formed a partnership with an old friend, a former body builder named Bobby Binder who'd lately turned vegetarian, seeker, and extremely skinny guy. Bobby was convinced that there were by now sufficient numbers of locals desirous of Celestial Seasonings products, ginseng root, and imported Maracaibo coffee beans to support a small business in the back of his health food store. Sheila borrowed twenty-four hundred dollars from Sam to pay for the big automatic coffee grinder, the quality scale, some old barrels, and the start-up inventory. She found a joyous Peter Max–style print for the front of the counter.

Customers and visiting friends often noted how perfectly Higher Grounds seemed to reflect Sheila's warm and nurturing spirit. Her big welcoming smile was appropriate to the little shop. Between transactions, Sheila would sit on a stool reading about herbs. At first she had a lot of time to read. She waited patiently for business to pick up, content amid the feast of rich odors, alone on an olfactory island of purity and hominess surrounded by a wasteland of frozen suburban fare. Sheila liked being an entrepreneur. Entrepreneurs created their own environment, and they could still lord it over their small empires the way robber barons once ruled their corporations and parents once reigned over families.

When she first came home from California, Sheila sought refuge with Sam and Eve. She decided she would briefly forswear her childhood oath always to maintain a self-reliant distance from the dangers of the family core until she felt healed and safe. For the first time, in her twenty-seventh year, Sheila had her mother and father to herself.

Sam regarded Sheila's return as a rescue operation, one of his most successful ventures as a father. Not only had she agreed to come live at the boatyard—where she was neat and clean and didn't smoke the place up like her eldest sister during her frequent visits—but she welcomed his help in setting up the new business, and more than that, she seemed to appreciate it. Sam didn't like to dwell on the decided dearth of thankyous he'd received over a lifetime of efforts to feed the whirlpool of need that had sucked at him since he was a boy. But he did allow himself to enjoy Sheila's presence and bask in her gratitude.

"You know, I like you so much better like this," Sheila said to her mother after work one afternoon. "You're so much less nervous here."

Eve laughed and agreed.

Sheila would sit out on the balcony with her father and mother and think that if there was something necessarily tenuous and even contrived about this convergence of her childlike moment of need and Sam and Eve's stunning ability to respond to it, then perhaps that was just the way life really was—tenuous and contrived and enormously heartwarming when it all fell into place. So until the family winds shifted again—for she knew they would—Sheila decided to relish her days as sole proprietor of a store that smelled like a dream of paradise and to savor her nights and Sundays with her mom and dad.

In the middle of a clearing in Central Park, Eve and Ricky came upon a huddle of Aricans smoking what Eve assumed to be pot. Susan, clad in jeans and a T-shirt, waved at her mother and brother. Shuna sprinted over immediately from a separate circle of children milling off to one side. "Hi, Nanny! Hi, Ricky!"

"Happy birthday," her grandmother and uncle both said, though Shuna could see that something was amiss from the way Eve was frowning and clutching her purse as if she was afraid somebody would take it away.

Susan had decided Shuna's eighth birthday party should be held in the park because she didn't want a crowd in the new three-bedroom apartment on East Sixty-eighth Street, a fancy place where singer Tony Bennett once lived. Four Aricans split the twelve-hundred-dollar-a-month rent on this, the third New York dwelling for Susan and Shuna since their return last summer. For a short time they'd lived in an Arica apartment on the West Side of Manhattan, in a building called Orwell House ("So appropriate," noted more than one of the old journalism and college friends Susan subjected to glowing descriptions of Arica). They'd also lived in a beautiful brownstone owned by one of the many Arican heirs to a family fortune, its centerpiece a huge communal bathtub on the ground floor.

Aricans moved more often than corporate middle managers, in part as a general testament to their lack of attachment to worldly things. But often the relocations were ordained from above. Aricans were regularly "circulated out" of one set of living quarters or one job in the Arica hierarchy into another. The summary evictions, promotions, and demotions were considered necessary to keep energy flowing in spiritually productive ways.

When she first arrived in New York, Susan had unilaterally circulated Shuna out to Long Beach, where she was to live with Lorraine,

Harry, and Maggie and be a second-grader at the local public school—just until Susan "got settled." Shuna went off to school in her long print dresses and the colorful Telegraph Avenue scarves Aunt Lorraine tied over her straight hair, looking like a pioneer child fresh off a wagon train. She sat in class among girls in tight pigtails, plastic barrettes, and argyle knee socks, as far from the suburban norm of the moment as her rock 'n' roll mother and aunt had been back in the 1950s.

Shuna was placed in an "open classroom" with a "no-walls" curriculum recently designed by the Long Beach school board to allow students to "do their own thing," but she didn't like the Magnolia School. She also didn't like the weird food at Lorraine's house. She did like watching Harry draw pictures and make his belly go away, and she loved spending time with her calm, grown-up cousin. Maggie was eleven now, and in many ways Shuna considered her the most mature member of the family.

After two months Susan came to retrieve Shuna and bring her back to the New York apartment she was sharing with several other Aricans. At first Shuna attended Walden, an elite Manhattan private school (one of the wealthy Aricans paid the bill) that Shuna loathed because her teacher was mean. By the time of her birthday party, Shuna was attending P.S. 158, a public school on the East Side.

Susan often dropped Shuna at her mother's or sister's for long weekends. "Shuna's turning into such a handful," Eve would complain to Sheila and Lorraine. Shuna did tend to argue about everything. She asked for what she wanted in a demanding tone, as if she were owed. Eve reasoned that her granddaughter's behavior had to do with being constantly yanked from place to place or left behind altogether. Every time Shuna said, "I have a lot of mommies," referring to the Arican women, Eve felt her stomach tighten.

"Are you suggesting that family life in Harbor Isle is the best way to raise happy, well-adjusted kids?" Susan scoffed when Eve tried to introduce a discussion of Susan's child-rearing style.

Eve remained calm.

One day she came upon Susan and one of her female Arican friends holding hands. "Susan," Eve asked later, "have you ever *been* with a woman?"

"Occasionally," Susan said.

Again Eve remained composed, though her stomach was churning like the newfangled Cuisinart she would soon give away because a machine "shouldn't do such things" to innocent food. "Well," she managed to say, "sometimes I think you might have had a happier life with just women. Men seem to cause a lot of your problems."

* * *

Eve and Ricky continued to watch Shuna's birthday party from what might as well have been an interplanetary distance. The Aricans kept falling into spasmodic giggling fits inspired by nothing Eve could discern. Pot smoke rose fragrantly over the crowd in little clouds.

"Well, this is what I call one big bunch of shit," Eve observed.

Susan was now a full-time Arican. She had her own office at Arica headquarters on West Fifty-seventh Street and had lately begun to have occasional access to Oscar Ichazo. Her job entailed producing Arican promotional literature and editing instructional texts, but she also took notes on Oscar's lectures and assisted him with his English.

At forty-five, Oscar Ichazo was a handsome man with exotic hooded eyes. He wore his hair cropped close, and his carefully sculpted beard made him look like a jazz musician. In his dazzling if slightly idiosyncratic English, he held forth upon almost any aspect of history or mathematics in a way that made Susan's mind race. She felt as if her "circuits would become overloaded and burn out," as she later put it. Susan's return to the "normal life" available to a single mother of one, after sitting with pad and pen to record the breathtaking cogitations of Oscar Ichazo, was like a sheer drop from the mountaintop. The descent made her feel completely lost.

It was Arica and nothing else, Susan believed, that had successfully weaned her from her overpowering desire for heroin, just as she'd hoped it would when she began her first training. She still downed a handful of Percodans every so often, and she would sit around talking about life and smoking pot with fellow Aricans until she was too stoned to get up from her chair. She still took Quaaludes if they were around, and she smoked cigarettes laced with "angel dust," the weirdly ironic vernacular for PCP, a chemical that made people unnaturally strong, crazy, and incapable of recalling much at all for a long time after they came down. But Susan no longer injected heroin into her slender arms, and in this she felt delivered from certain death. Arica, she said, had saved her life.

Many of Susan's old friends who'd spent time with her since she returned from the West would have been more comfortable with her as a sleepy-eyed junkie than as a wild-eyed Arican. The secularists and skeptics who knew her from her days as a Vassar iconoclast, as Mrs. Michael Lydon, as a hot rock writer, feminist thinker, and New Journalist, didn't want to have anything to do with Susan after hearing her Arica diatribes. Like most of the successful spiritual disciplines, Arica had its share of celebrity participants: actress Lindsay Wagner, who played the Bionic Woman on TV, was a dedicated Arican, as was Sally Kempton, a well-known journalist and the daughter of New York columnist Murray Kempton. Their friends also thought they were lost at sea.

Robert Christgau, Susan's *Village Voice* buddy and onetime lover, now avoided her. Ray Sokolov, a freelance writer and former *Newsweek* correspondent Susan had met in Paris, was appalled by Susan's description of the hedonistic Arica scene in California. At one point Sokolov was sure he heard her boast that all the West Coast Aricans had "tanned assholes." Susan sat in on a poker game with Rick Hertzberg, who nine years earlier had taken her to the Human Be-In in Golden Gate Park. Hertzberg had recently left a writing job at the *New Yorker* to become a speechwriter for New York governor Hugh Carey. Over cards, Susan mentioned that she'd glimpsed the end of the world drawing nigh. "Arica," she said, "is the world's only hope."

After she left, the other poker players spoke of her in funereal tones. "She was so talented," someone said.

"How could someone so sophisticated buy into such a totalitarianism?" Rick Hertzberg wondered aloud.

Back in San Francisco, Gina Schick became disillusioned with Arica and moved on to other spiritual disciplines she found less consuming and contrived. Gina was particularly scandalized by her discovery that Arican mothers were abandoning their children to non-Arican spouses or friends in order to concentrate fully on achieving enlightenment.

But like so many others, Gina would not give up her quest for a spiritual framework on which to prop her battered "self." The obsessive desire to discover one's sense of self—that determinate, confident, trusting, and trusted self once thought to be the end result of a good family life—was now so prevalent that it would soon demarcate a "me generation" and an insidious "culture of narcissism." For every new synthesis of ancient mysticism and philosophy offered like so much tofu or yogurt, there were now two or three homegrown popularizations of humanistic psychology designed to deliver, even more quickly and rationally, intimacy, wholeness, community, and peace—*the answer*—if not once, then most certainly for all.

Ricky, who had for so long romanticized any and all of his oldest sister's intellectual and artistic pursuits, had lately taken to calling Susan "Cultarella." He was baffled by her esoteric argot, and he was "willing to take responsibility," as he put it, for his decision to "share" with Susan his belief that Arica was nothing short of "grotesque."

The word "cult" would not acquire its darkest connotations until late 1978, with the mass suicides in Guyana of nearly a thousand American followers of Jim Jones and his People's Temple. But by 1976 the term had become a popular pejorative used to describe various groups from which some American parents felt compelled to retrieve their children by methods that included kidnapping. "Deprogrammers" who specialized in reclaiming "brainwashed" youths (brainwashing was as much in the news lately as it had been during the Korean War and the earliest days of rock 'n' roll, in part because in early spring it had been the pillar of Patricia Hearst's much publicized courtroom defense of her revolutionary activities) were under indictment in several cities for violating the rights of children past their majority. "I've never seen one of these young people who didn't have some kind of serious failure in family life," said Dr. Herbert Hendin, a Columbia University psychiatrist quoted by *U.S. News and World Report* on the large numbers of children slipping away into the spiritual underground.

Just as Ricky took responsibility for his strong pronouncements on Arica, he now endeavored to "pay attention" to his true feelings and to share those feelings openly, unmodified by the weighty obfuscations and guilt in which he'd previously been mired. Ricky was trying hard to be the "architect of everything he did." He wanted to stop "playing himself" and start "being himself." He would always try to "be there," he said, instead of "living in the pictures in his head." He was dedicated to these goals because Ricky—and perhaps fifty thousand others who currently deployed a similar vocabulary with a similar stridency of emotional resolve—was a recent graduate of an Erhard Seminars Training course, a phenomenon known from campus to cocktail party by its lower case acronym, est.

Ricky's est session—a straight four-day shot of enlightenment—was held at a hotel across the street from Madison Square Garden, storied site of emotion-laden entertainments. He paid his $250 and was ushered to a folding chair. Est trainer Ted Long walked up and down in front of the group of several hundred people and then began to bellow at them like a drill sergeant. Every person in the room, Ted said, was an "asshole." Too many people (assholes) lived lives that "didn't work." Entire lives were being wasted trying to cover up the fact that most people were first and foremost a bunch of assholes.

After five of the fourteen hours of the first of four days in Ted's company, Ricky ached from sitting in a chair for such a long time. The absence of bathroom breaks, for which est was already famous, bothered other students much more than Ricky, who'd been uncomfortable in public restrooms ever since Eve's unfortunate "do it for Mommy" toilet training. But Ricky did not like to be screamed at.

At one point Ted made everyone lie down on the floor. "Now. I want you to imagine that the person on either side of you hates you and is threatening you. Then I want you to respond." As if by second nature, Ricky looked from side to side and immediately imagined a Dantean ring of Renes, Reginas, Roseannes, and the others from across the street on Lincoln Avenue—as well as Yetta's Cossacks—poised and ready to do their worst. When Ted said, "Go ahead, scream! Scream!" Ricky bayed toward the ceiling as loud as he could, like a wild animal in pain.

Werner Erhard, est's founder, garnered a following by consolidating, translating, and packaging standard metaphysical conceptions tailored to the American experience and attention span. Since 1971, Erhard had offered concentrated instruction on how to separate illusion and reality surgically so as to pacify the mind. If this goal differed little from those of dozens of other spiritual systems new and old—Zen Buddhism, for instance—the idea of setting off on the path to transcendence by being called an asshole was certainly novel. Erhard taught students to acknowledge that while they might labor under the illusion that God or fate or karma or parents had caused their abiding pain, the fact was that they'd caused it themselves. All trouble—headaches, cancer, the death of loved ones, being beaten up, robbed, even raped (as Erhard explained to a weeping young woman who shared her recent victimization at an est session he led himself)—all of it could be explained by the all-American individualist refrain, "It's nobody's fault but your own."

But that was *okay*. Forget about the gnawing guilt that Gina Schick's grandpa and his Freudian colleagues had claimed was a necessary consequence of growing up. Attack that ego and you'd be free. By learning to acknowledge that you were not at all okay, by recognizing that the effort to be okay was only a sop for the illusion-filled mind, by no longer working to prove you were okay, you would see that it was okay just to be okay.

Ricky was relatively okay-feeling before he went to est, but there were still things he wished he could control. In particular, he wanted to stop having the fainting spells that came upon him occasionally at school. The most glamorous and sophisticated men and women at Carnegie Mellon sought Ricky out, but he often felt nervous in their presence. Sometimes he'd pass out. One night at dinner with a group of drama students Ricky's forehead bounced right off the tabletop, and when he came to, he burst into helpless tears.

Ricky thought the problem was that he didn't feel worthy of being in the company of these gifted and handsome people. They were the kind of people he'd only dreamed of having as friends before. But a thought like that, he now understood, was the thought of an asshole.

Susan was outraged by Ricky's willingness to hand "a charlatan like Werner Erhard" so much of Sam and Eve's money. "Did you know his name was, like, Jack Rosenberg or something before he took off and left his wife and, like, four kids in Philadelphia? Did you know he got enlightened while driving on a *freeway*? I mean, if it's so easy, Ricky, tell me why people spend thirteen years in dark caves in Tibet trying to get...it."

"Thank you for sharing that," Ricky would reply with that strange, immobile smile visible on so many yellow buttons on so many American lapels.

Well into the 1980s, long after the fall of est and the decline of the smile button, the emotionally "out there" est vocabulary would be employed in the foot-in-the-door sales pitches favored by promoters of pyramid schemes. In 1991 Werner Erhard's second wife would accuse him of beating her. But back in 1976 Erhard was becoming ever more famous and revered. Through an understanding of his "anatomy of the mind," he said, by practicing his "psychokinesis" and "psychocybernetic" exercises, a person could *create* his or her own universe—a decidedly American spiritual conception, and one that appalled masters and teachers of almost every other tradition.

"Susan," Ricky would say to his sister, "you just don't get it."

"Thank you for sharing that, Ricky."

For a while, Ricky believed he really did "get it." When his trainer stopped screaming like an enraged father, Ricky sensed in Ted's sudden change of tone a flood of paternal love. Enclosed in the community of shared angst stirred up during the est sessions, Ricky suddenly felt able to trust strangers with secrets he'd stopped confiding to his own mother years earlier for fear she would scream at him like Ted did.

And it was all so quick. Est didn't take much longer than certain Wagner operas.

As was subtly suggested to all est graduates, Ricky badgered Arthur Levy and Peter Randsman until they both attended an est seminar. Afterward, Peter looked stricken. "Ricky, I...I didn't get it," he admitted, close to tears.

Sam had agreed to drive Ricky back to Pittsburgh after the end of the summer break, but when Ricky came home late on the Sunday morning they were supposed to leave, Eve reported that Sam had stormed out of the house in a rage. Ricky took a cab to the airport to catch a plane.

At school, Ricky sat down and wrote Sam a letter. He recalled the many Sundays when the fully dressed Gordon family had waited for Sam to complete some project before they could leave for an afternoon at Yetta's. "Sometimes three hours, Dad," Ricky said. All for a visit to *his* mother—a visit, Ricky hastened to add (as long as he was sharing), during which Sam usually napped until it was time to leave.

As soon as Ricky dropped the letter into the mail chute he began to reassess his estian analysis of the situation. If everything was indeed his responsibility, then maybe he should have been on time.

Sam, much more open than ever before to reconsiderations of his actions and his life, got on the phone when Eve called Ricky at school. Ricky quickly "acknowledged" that perhaps he'd missed the essential point.

Sam read the letter again after hanging up. "What's got into him?" he asked Eve.

"What's got into all of them?" his wife replied. "I'd ignore the whole thing."

Sam decided to take her advice.

<hr />

"Sometimes people understand and think yoga advocates no sex," Satchidananda said. "This is not so. Yoga teaches the middle path. Yoga is not for the person who never sleeps or always sleeps, nor for the one who always fasts or always feasts."

From a single well-planned swoop toward the middle, just one evening's suspension of celibacy, Lorraine got pregnant. Since she could still recall in vivid detail the terror and humiliation of Maggie's clinic delivery in New York, she was determined to seize as much control as possible this time. Harry and Lorraine attended classes in the Bradley Method, one of several popular natural childbirth techniques. They interviewed a large number of local obstetricians and presented their long list of demands, a hands-off delivery being paramount among them. Several of the doctors politely refused to treat Lorraine; two told her to get out. It was weeks before they finally found a doctor at Mercy Hospital who agreed to their terms.

Sometime during Lorraine's second trimester, Harry stopped feeling constantly afraid. He kept telling himself that nobody was ever truly *ready* to become a parent. As with going to war and getting married it was one of those things in life that defied preparation.

Harry's guru said that having a child was a fateful thing: "A mango seed becomes only a mango tree, not an apple tree." Parents were little more than gardeners, Satchidananda taught. The idea that parenthood meant a mother and father bequeathed something of *themselves* to a child like Gabriel Ram Hughes, born naturally and without incident on June 18, was an illusion, a dangerous myth perpetuated by vanity and ego. The child came with "past memory" and a physical form that Satchidananda likened to a horse, just a powerful frame ridden hard by spirits from the cosmos.

———◆———

Gerald Ford had declared that he would not preside over the "decline and fall of the United States of America," and whether or not that imperial-sounding downfall would ever occur, he had at least been prescient about his role. The new president, southerner Jimmy Carter, had won Sam's and Eve's vote this go-round, though he occasionally sounded like he'd recently been discussing life with Susan, Lorraine, or Ricky.

Carter said America was "sick at heart" and needed "faith." He said moodiness and drift were dragging down the national spirit because of a "lack of roots" and an absence of "anything that lasts in people's lives."

By the close of the Bicentennial summer of 1976, Sam Gordon was galloping regularly into a meaningful past. He finally had a horse.

As a boy, Sam had imagined himself on horseback every day, but his mother kept him away from horses because they frightened her. Then the army mothballed the cavalry the moment Sam joined up. In the suburbs his precious corner of corral was little more than a memorial to the ranch that in a perfect world would have been Sam's home. For almost twenty-five years, since the exodus to the seaside suburbs, thousands of men had looked for escape or light on the water. Like the kids who slept on the inland ponds called waterbeds, Sam had bobbed and floated through his dreams for years. But now, soured on boats and sea adventures since the loss of his lovingly restored Chris Craft Coho, Sam turned back to horses.

He rode every weekend through dense forests not a dozen miles from Harbor Isle, on trails snaking through the elite equestrian wonderland called Old Westbury, still known as "Millionaire Village" when Long Island's manic postwar development arrived at its elegant doorstep and the residents used their clout to force it underground: near Glen Cove

Road the Long Island Expressway actually disappears into a deep trench that serves to muffle the sound of traffic passing the old estates of Whitneys, Phippses, Graces, and Vanderbilts, then reemerges near the Jericho Turnpike and the housing developments beyond. Instead of subdividing their land into squares, many Old Westburians decided to cede transitory property rights to middle-class arrivistes who knew how to handle a horse. Those residents who did sell off their properties were required by local ordinance to leave a ten-foot easement aside for riders. Consequently Sam found himself riding along trails that suddenly opened onto the great lawns of old stone houses. He loped past polo players, antique buggy collectors, and hunt club regulars dressed in royal red.

Sam and his horse would travel deep into the solitude of the forest, far beyond the range of another human voice. The awesome silence was broken only by the roar of a new Concorde streaking toward Paris or London overhead. The jet would pass, and Sam would once again feel so alone that he imagined himself not a cowboy or a cavalryman but a "Comanche scout."

Some days Sheila came along to ride. Sam made a big tack box to hold the equine paraphernalia he was collecting now. Filigree adorned the bottom of the box, and SAM AND SHEILA was stenciled in big letters on top.

Toward the end of the year, Sam shocked his family by musing aloud that he was thinking of taking time off from work to go explore the American West. After seeing Paul Newman in *The Sting* two years earlier, Sam had asked Ricky if he knew any piano rags. From then on, whenever Ricky came to the boatyard, Sam would sit in a chair—just sit there, not fidgeting or jumping around—while Ricky played Scott Joplin rags and other honkytonk songs. Ricky would glance over and see his father's face relax, almost the way Harry's face lost its furrows and clefts when he played his Indian music and fell back into a trance.

"It's the horses," Ricky would say to Lorraine. "Do you think it's possible that Daddy's having one of those past-life experiences?"

"You never know," said Lorraine.

For too much of his life, Sam thought—not unlike so many other men born into the Depression and out of the Second World War—he'd felt stuck, sandwiched between the romantic tales of his wandering, errant horseman father and the romantic wanderings of his errant children, who'd galloped off at the front of their generation. But now, on days when he would have been working at any other time during most of his nearly fifty-eight years, Sam Gordon—armchair picaro and would-be roughrider from way back—roamed his forest primeval. And he finally had a horse fit to bear his somewhat cramped spirit, a horse that might not have come to him from the purity of the cosmos but was at least willing and able to help him reassemble bits and pieces of old dreams from the powerful ebb and flow of his life and times.

1977

Susan was late and Eve was beginning to worry. She'd said she needed to have three inches of mink sewed to the bottom of her old jacket, and Susan had agreed to meet her mother at a mid-Manhattan furrier and shop onward from there. But now Susan was over an hour late, and those violent maternal fantasies of injured children were becoming difficult to suppress.

Like so many suburban mothers and their urban daughters, Eve and Susan liked to hold movable family reunions in the aisles of stores. Beyond the simple expediency of shopping and shmoozing at the same time, a well-stocked retail environment offered turf so distracting that the most formidable emotional barriers of the moment tended to yield to good feelings from the best of the acquisitive past. As an afternoon's baseball game could magically reconnect the most disappointed of fathers and prodigal of sons, the tiny nuances of the Gordon family shopping liturgy—the musical scraping of hangers along aluminum rods, the constant breaks for coffee and cake Eve demanded between each store and most departments, the "little something" she always bought the girls at the very end—all of it represented the most innocent all-American celebration of simple pleasures shared by a daughter and her mom.

On a more serious plane, Eve considered the fact that all of her kids knew how to shop to be among her indisputable accomplishments as a parent. To Eve, a store was the culture's tribal proving ground. Like the American women who seized the reins of family consumption and gave rise to the wonderful urban emporiums of a hundred years earlier, she believed that a store was an arena of human emancipation, a place where a child might come of age. That each of her children had a distinct purchasing style she held up as evidence of her successful nurturing of their creativity at critical junctures: Susan, former couturier to the best-dressed doll in the Bronx, relied on copious magazine research and a stunning level of endurance that allowed her to try on garment after garment until Eve's eyes glazed over; Lorraine was quick, specific, and not in the least amenable to maternal suggestion; Sheila was careful and welcomed commentary; Ricky was an orgiastic, wide-eyed shopper with an appreciation for all good things and the material appetites of an oil sheik.

When Susan finally appeared in the fur salon, Eve couldn't restrain a gasp. It had been only three weeks since she last saw Susan, but she was certain her daughter had lost fifteen or twenty pounds in the interim. Her cheeks were the color of old newspapers, and with her boyish haircut, Eve couldn't help thinking, she looked like a concentration camp victim or a prisoner of war.

Susan barely offered a hello. Eve watched her throw off what appeared to be a full-length leather coat, kid-glove-soft and clearly designer-made. Then Eve's shock over Susan's physical state turned to revulsion, because right there—right in front of her own mother, in a Manhattan shop, looking for all the world like a POW finally back from Hanoi—Susan began to act like...a JAP! Eve thought she would keel over and die.

A JAP! How many times had Eve said to friends over mah-jongg, "At least none of them is a JAP. Not one. With all the other *tsuris*, at least I can say that." While the unflattering associations conjured up by the acronym for "Jewish American Princess" were numerous and variously intended, in Eve's estimation the definitive characteristics of a JAP were physical, libidinal, sartorial, and most of all behavioral. To Eve, a JAP was an adult daughter who could recreate the astonishingly self-involved demands and precise vocal frequencies of early childhood and uncork them publicly and exorbitantly, in front of her father or even complete strangers, at the drop of an overpriced hat.

A loaded rack at an up-market Long Island apparel outlet was a veritable duck blind for spotting JAPs in flight. Every time Eve shopped she thanked God that at least her family had been spared that. JAPs were bad for the Jews (a shameful example of assimilation gone awry), bad for the image of mothers, and bad for shoppers who were serious about the calling.

But here was Susan, waltzing about the shop in full view, whining out orders at an auctioneer's clip. She tried on mink coat after mink coat, haggling with the furrier (a distant cousin of Sam's, no less) as if she were serious about buying. She sent one poor clerk scurrying off to the back several times to see if there were any coats people had ordered and failed to pick up. "Just go look again," she said, staring the woman down until she did what she was told. Eve heard Susan inquire as to payment plans and which credit cards—or combination of credit cards—the store was willing to accept. "And let's talk custom," she said. "How much to have one made up to order?"

Eve staggered to a chair. She had to sit down. She couldn't speak, but she also couldn't stop watching—watching this sallow camp victim swaddled in ranch mink, talking like a character out of Eve's worst nightmares.

Susan reeled over to a rack of furs as Eve approached her gingerly. She took hold of Susan's arm, her fingers circling a shriveled bicep with room to spare. The arm quivered like a dog's hind leg when you touch that certain spot. "I want you to come home with me," she said firmly. "We'll get Shuna and you'll just come."

Susan glared at her. "I have to go to the bathroom," she sniffed; and she sniffed again.

Eve waited in the fitting room for almost fifteen minutes, forcing herself to imagine something more terrifying than Susan suddenly turning into a JAP at the age of thirty-three....*Drugs*, she thought with a start. *Again with the drugs.*

Why did they? And how? How could any of Eve Gordon's children take drugs? Weren't they flesh and blood of a mother who had once taken a colorful Contac time-release cold capsule and fainted in the middle of the A&P, who not two months before this shopping rendezvous, upon opening an American Express bill containing a massive overcharge, had taken a mild tranquilizer and proceeded to pass out while driving? Eve smashed into two parked cars near the Harbor Isle bridge and woke up thinking she'd killed several schoolchildren during the blackout—her worst fear. She vowed never to drive a car again and never to take another pill. So how could she have children who took drugs?

It was becoming clear from increasingly open conversation among parents that almost all the children of Harbor Isle, the pigtailed and crew-cut innocents of the treeless years, had grown up to "experiment" with drugs. Eve still clung to her long-held belief that drugs must give you better orgasms—or at least less guilty ones—but the night-of-passion theory no longer held up against evidence that drug use was becoming a casual, daily, and "acceptable social behavior" in the America of the 1970s, as an intensive sociological study would reveal in a few years. The U.S. Public Health Service had recently reported that the use of marijuana was so widespread among adolescents that they would soon consume more pot than tobacco.

Severed from their connection with rebellion, drugs had joined jogging in the realm of normal middle-class recreation. Lorraine's onetime diet combination of Methedrine and the earliest of macrobiotic cuisines now seemed like the wave of the future. When it was announced later in the year that a new perfume fragrance would be named Opium, only a handful of Asian-Americans bothered to point out that opium was also a substance with a long history of pain.

Eve stood up and strode angrily toward the bathroom. Perhaps she wasn't "with it," but Susan was the mother of a nine-year-old girl. She had responsibilities. This shopping trip had turned into a nightmare.

The bathroom was empty. Eve went back to a hassock in the other room and waited for a long time, but Susan never returned.

Susan and her New York City friends now spent a lot of time sitting around tables covered with white dust. They'd snort and talk, and talk, and talk, and the superior quality of the cocaine would make them brilliant, eloquent, and so strong that they would have leapt over the nearest apartment building if only the perfection of the talk hadn't rooted them to their chairs.

Whereas the cultural associations of heroin harked back to hipster poetry and the coolest jazz—to the discordant, lazy cadences of the underground—coke was about disco and fast tracks and jackpots. Cocaine was the drug of million-buck ideas, of stunning perspicacity and talent that would lead beyond success to domination. By 1977 the pricy powder was being discussed in terms that might have sprung straight from an upscale marketing campaign. Coke was a luxury item, the "champagne" of drugs, the "limousine" of highs. In coming years, heirs to auto fortunes, entertainers, and professional athletes—even Hamilton Jordan, the White House chief of staff—would underscore the status kick offered by cocaine when they either admitted to or were accused of using it.

For Susan, coke had the secondary effect of fully unleashing her breathtaking capacity to shop. Her true shopping self, it turned out, had been repressed since the London years of Biba's and Right Bank Hermès scarves; the social stigma of consumerism, the uniform requirements of faded blue jeans and granny dresses, and a decided lack of capital had stifled her. But now, inspired by a snootful of coke and an American financial industry dedicated to the extension of easy credit, Susan collected designer outfits at record pace. Just a quick pop across the street from Arica headquarters to Bergdorf Goodman, and—using credit cards she'd obtained as an Arica staff member—she could charge a cashmere dress or a shearling coat. At the Arica house where Susan and Shuna now lived, a beautiful antique mews dwelling on Patchin Place in Greenwich Village, people had taken to calling her "Miss Scarsdale."

Cocaine made Susan believe that the more money she spent on clothes, the more would appear from other sources to fill the gap. The money would naturally *circulate* and eventually come back her way. Funds would flow, as in a high school chemistry experiment demonstrating osmosis, from a region of higher concentration to a region of lower concentration through a permeable economic membrane much healthier than the battered ones in Susan's nose.

By the time Susan was circulated out of the Arica house on Patchin Place, not long after the incident at the furrier's, she had run up six thousand dollars in unpaid credit card bills and become generally obnoxious in every way.

Trying to explain her dire credit situation to her mother, Susan hinted that she would accept parental rescue and "pushed" one of Eve's "buttons," as the popular, decidedly computer-age saying went. Eve had been purchasing "little somethings" for her kids and slipping them twenties for many years, but that Susan couldn't see the essential difference between giving gifts and paying off debts made Eve crazy. "Hold it right there, honey. You racked up the bills! You got yourself into it. You figure out how to get yourself out of it." But then came the guilt. "Just don't tell your father about the bills," she said.

At first, only Susan was banished from the mews house. Shuna was to stay behind in the care of the other Aricans while Susan took refuge in an uptown apartment with her boyfriend, Max. But shortly thereafter the occupants of the house decided that Shuna could also do with a bit of circulation, and she was told to leave too. Shuna was not invited to join her mother at Max's apartment, since Max was already fed up with nursing Susan through one cocaine crisis after another. Shuna's father was now living in New York City with his wife, Ellen Mandel, a New York–born photographer he had met before leaving the Bay Area a year earlier. After publishing two excellent books about rock music, *Rock Folk* and *Boogie Lightning*, Michael had been doing less reporting from the sidelines. He and Ellen were performers now, "a duo specializing in pop tunes," as a reviewer in the *New York Times* described their March show at Gerde's Folk City. ("They purvey a...homemade variety of music, with Mr. Lydon's wheezing harmonica and cartoon-character vocals providing a foil for Miss Mandel's more polished piano and singing.")

Michael had a new act and a "new life" with Ellen. The roles of journalist and father were now incidental aspects of discontentments past. Shuna saw her father every so often at the tiny East Village apartment he shared with Ellen, but no one suggested that Shuna should join Michael now. After a flurry of phone calls instigated by Eve, it was decided that she would go back to live with Lorraine, Harry, Maggie, and baby Gabe for a time. Just until Susan felt better.

Eve also decided Susan would move to the boatyard to "get off" cocaine. Sam would be told only that the obvious health problem that prompted the homecoming would respond to a regimen of food and rest. Eve reasoned that a person could "dry out" from drugs as she imagined drinkers "took the cure." In all good faith, she considered cocaine addiction tantamount to a nagging viral infection that could be cured with steaming poultry-based concoctions and a mother's care.

—◆—

From Ricky's perspective the overheated New York City of mid-1977 could just as easily have been the Paris of 1923, Greenwich Village in 1961, or San Francisco during the raucous summer of 1967. The *Washington Post* was reporting the U.S military's imminent production of a "neutron bomb" that "cuts down" on the destruction of buildings and battle tanks while releasing "great quantities of neutrons" that "kill people," and revelations of cash gifts to American congressmen by a man named Tongsun Park were escalating into a scandal of international proportions known as "Koreagate," but Ricky was too dazzled to notice. He saw New York City as a veritable citadel of cultural glories instead of a financially strapped metropolis, scene of a blackout and subsequent looting in July.

The summer actually opened rather inauspiciously in the provinces. Ricky was a member of a small summer stock company at Lake Erie College for Girls in Painesville, Ohio, where the actors were invited to sleep on mattresses spread out backstage, a suitably romantic and nobly bohemian arrangement. The first show was Jean Anouilh's *Waltz of the Toreadors*, in which Ricky played the priest who appears on stage at the very end, a *deus ex machina*, and delivers a lengthy monologue that Ricky understood as central to the meaning of the play, and by extension, to the subsequent worldview of his audience. But on opening night, with some of his close friends from Carnegie Mellon in town for

the performance, Ricky bounded out on the stage, struck an appropriately grave pose opposite his friend Brian Frank, caught sight of the
audience out of the corner of his eye, and forgot his lines.

"Brian, what should I do?" he whispered. Brian shrugged.

Ricky turned to face a huge theater occupied by an opening night
crowd of less than fifteen, and offered ad lib the gist of his lines.

After the Painesville season ended, Ricky decided to follow several
other Carnegie friends who were leaving college without degrees to
become actors, dancers, novelists, and downtown painters in New York
City. The nation's two hundred most prominent performing arts organizations were now in worse fiscal shape than at any time since the Great
Depression, their collective debt load having ballooned to $125 million,
and Ricky's beloved Metropolitan Opera was $15 million in the red. But
he still decided to bypass the tedium of further academic training and
seek art and celebrity in the city. Like a college football star with the
cheers of the crowd fueling his daydreams, Ricky was ready to go pro.
Carnegie offered its talented students little specific advice about
résumés, professional photographs, making connections with agents, or
audition strategies, but the campus ethos and the well-known track
record of recent graduates and nongraduates in New York still gave students reason to believe the big time was theirs for the taking.

Ricky's friend Kit Grover was already showing his paintings in Soho,
a flourishing gallery- and boutique-laden district in Lower Manhattan,
until recently dominated by penurious young artists and adventurous
counterculture entrepreneurs. A trendy gallery owner named Holly
Solomon was planning to make Kit a star. Diane Fratantoni, one of
Ricky's closest friends and a fine singer of his challenging compositions,
a tiny, voluptuous soprano who reminded Eve Gordon of her younger
self, was a member of the national company of A Chorus Line.

Ricky found an apartment on West Seventieth Street. It was a big
place with two bedrooms and lots of windows, just a few steps from the
new boutiques and bars on Columbus Avenue. When Ricky went to his
first operas at Lincoln Center less than ten years earlier, the area a few
blocks to the north where he was now living was considered quite
treacherous for pedestrians. The tiny triangle formed by Broadway crossing in front of the West Seventy-second Street IRT subway station was
then the famous danger zone Needle Park (the official name was Verdi
Square). But by now a process of transformation that city planners and
preservationists called "gentrification" had changed much of that. The
poorer inhabitants were being effectively herded north into little pockets of ethnicity on certain side streets. The immigrants were beginning

to be called "urban pioneers." With its adventurous gay bars, stylish restaurants, and offbeat shops, many of them owned by gay business-men, Ricky's neighborhood would soon be christened by *New York* mag-azine the city's "Left Bank."

The new apartment rented for $485 a month, a sum Ricky would split three ways with his Painesville costar, Brian Frank, and an aspiring novelist named Tom Piechowsky. Tom had grown up in Parma, Ohio, and had an older brother who was a priest. His peers often compared him with the beautiful young men who suffered so intelligently in Eve-lyn Waugh novels. He wore silk-backed vests over dress shirts buttoned all the way to the neck, and he had a languorous way of raising a cigarette to his lips that his admirers found bewitching. Brian was a much less studied, warm-hearted, six-foot-four-inch wise guy. Even when Ricky was on speed, Brian seemed to have more available energy.

During the parties the boys threw regularly, there invariably came a point when Brian and Ricky were asked to do the identical cousins Patty and Cathy Lane singing the theme song from *The Patty Duke Show.* Then Ricky would play the piano or tell stories in character. "Tell the rowboat story," someone would call out. "No, the crawl space." Ricky could instantly become the effeminate son of an absurdly macho father. He could dance across the room, once again the skinny victim fleeing his oppressors from across the street on Lincoln Avenue. With a brilliant sense of timing inherited from Eve and a hundred Borscht Belt *tummlers*, Ricky called on a strain of American humor that took the sting out of remembered differentness and cracked up the crowd.

Peter Randsman was also in New York now, living in an apartment down in the Village on West Fourth Street. Though he was working in a local bar, he had come to the city to be an opera star. He'd worked hard on his huge voice, and his encyclopedic command of the repertory was such that he could identify opera, composer, singer, and conductor from the opening notes of a recording and provide an intelligent critique of each. Peter was also in the process of becoming a muscle man. The sim-ple act of bringing a glass to his lips made his biceps bulge beneath his shirt.

Peter went to the parties at Ricky's place, where everybody was in some way offbeat or special. People took turns being clever or outra-geous, as if from a script. Ricky would play his latest compositions and bring tears to his friend's eyes. The women were good-looking, and the men were gorgeous and gay. Peter felt shy around them. They all seemed so unaware of limits. Overhead was low, the subway was cheap, and standing-room tickets were plentiful. Sebastian Flytes and Oscar Wildes and the New York of a thousand café nights awaited. There was art in the fetid air this summer, and though Ricky's cocksure crowd intimidated Peter, it was still good to be sharing the town with Ricky. Ricky Gordon was like Peter's war buddy; they would be friends forever.

———◆◆◆———

Every weekday morning the yogi Hara Hughes donned the full camouflage regalia of suit and tie and went off once again to serve his country, this time as a twenty-three-thousand-dollar-a-year claims representative for the Social Security Administration.

The landmark federal program Franklin Roosevelt called the "beginning of a new era" was now in bureaucratic and political trouble. Harry spent much of his day filling out forms that facilitated the transfer of indigent, elderly, or disabled citizens from one of several state and federal welfare lists onto the Social Security rosters. He helped adjudicate the claims of poor people who would eventually receive an annual income of less than two thousand dollars after decades of work and regular contribution to an account held somewhere inside the vast system— this at a time when the official poverty line was twenty-four hundred dollars per annum. He also helped many rich people who didn't need Social Security qualify for payments of several thousand dollars a year more than the poor people got. Social Security, after all—as conservative politicians argued in addressing the sudden crises created when the system spent more than it took in—was never intended to be a welfare program. But it now seemed that the macroeconomic measures thought necessary to stop inflation caused unemployment, which in turn caused payroll contributions to the Social Security system to diminish at a time when the number of elderly pensioners was escalating. The shortfall was made up from special old age and disability trust funds collected during the days when the system worked, but the funds could only be raided so many times before general tax revenues would have to be tapped.

Harry felt as insulated from the social purpose of this enormous bureaucracy as he did from the day-to-day reality of people in need. A central tenet of his yoga beliefs was that there was nothing more noble than to serve others—the guru said it over and over, like a mantra, Serve, serve, serve—but at the office, with files surrounding him and no time to stop, Harry couldn't feel a thing. He couldn't really hear what people said. Nothing he saw or learned at the Social Security Administration office in Jamaica, Queens, seemed to have any application at all in the outside world. Social Security was like a separate universe.

Harry's boss and colleagues all knew about his affiliation with Integral Yoga. To all but a number of young female colleagues, the office yogi was a pariah.

Shuna thought the way Harry and Lorraine talked to each other when Harry got home from work was the second-worst thing about living at their house in Long Beach. The worst thing was the healthy meals. She lived for "Shuna's pig-out day," when Lorraine allowed her to eat candy.

Harry always seemed to enjoy Lorraine's "mushed-up" tofu dinners, but one night, as Shuna and Maggie marveled while he kept saying, "Mmm, this is good," after every bite, Lorraine said, "It's fine if you don't like it, Harry, but I expect you to say so."

"No, it's really good," Harry said, taking another bite. "I like it."

"You don't have to pretend."

Maggie and Shuna looked at each other in confusion, as they often had since Shuna's mother went to "get off coke," whatever that meant.

"Just say it!" Lorraine began to scream at Harry. "Just say it. Just say it! I'll help you, just say 'I…don't…like it!'"

Then Lorraine threw something and Harry threw something too.

Finally Harry said, "Okay! Okay, I don't like it!"

But he did like it. Shuna was sure he did.

Maggie told Shuna that Lorraine's soft, whispery way of talking was "fake." Maggie said all the yoga people were fake.

Maggie was Shuna's idol. She was twelve and a half, and as far as Shuna could tell, she knew all things. Maggie understood, for instance, that by the standards of the surrounding community, many aspects of her current life were downright weird. But compared to Shuna, she still considered herself lucky. Even though much of her mother's energy was devoted to her swami and Maggie's new half-brother, she believed Lorraine still thought about her often.

Lorraine, Harry, Maggie, Shuna, and Gabe went to the airport several times to say good-bye or hello to the guru. Maggie would watch the grown-ups hovering around the old man and giggling like children. A bunch of yoga people came to the house and covered the living room floor with flower petals, which Maggie considered "childish." Swami Satchidananda approached Maggie at the ashram in Connecticut one day. "You will come to me when the time is right," he said.

Shuna loved the flower petals all over the living room ("Arica's better," she would say loyally when she and Maggie discussed their parents), but the girls agreed that the worst thing about yoga was that it didn't make Lorraine and Harry stop fighting. Lorraine would criticize the way Harry changed Gabe's diapers or how he failed at his Mr. Fixit chores in front of the whole family at the boatyard—and in front of Sheila's new boyfriend, who had a fancy motorcycle, a fancy car, and a great big fancy boat.

While Harry certainly didn't enjoy what he saw as his public reduction to the hapless, generally inferior, henpecked *sheygitz* caricatured in so many jokes, the sight of Sheila apparently in love was more bothersome by far. From his first reaction to the new guy at the family table—a young man of a generation and state of mind so far removed from Harry's experience that he might as well have been from Mars—he realized that ever since Sheila returned from California he'd imagined her on a pedestal, waiting as in a fairy tale for the perfect man.

Harry had a crush on Sheila (his lust, like Jimmy Carter's, carefully confined to his heart), and as a mostly celibate husband, he didn't much appreciate having his fantasies invaded by a kid five years younger than Sheila whose most fervid belief seemed to be that 1977 was the year to buy municipal bonds. This Martian, this boy named Jon, talked about money for its own sake.

Sheila met Jon during a visit east to see the family when she was still living in California. After she moved home, Sheila dated a friend of Jon's. When the friend moved out of town, Jon asked Sheila out and paid to dock his big boat at SGE Marina for four months in a row so he would have an excuse to see Sam Gordon's daughter. Jon noticed that Sheila was less than impressed by his boat. She thought his BMW 3.0 CS—a fifteen-thousand-dollar automobile when he bought it in 1974 (a year when a new Cadillac Calais could be had for six thousand dollars)—was a Volkswagen. Jon found this charming. He couldn't believe that Sheila had started working as a waitress to support her little business. "You're running negative balances because you're drawing against inventory," he would try to explain to her. "Let's see your last bank rec."

"What's that?" Sheila asked.

Around the time Sheila moved in with Jon, ten months after they began dating, the fragrant enterprise Higher Grounds was interred with full honors in the pantheon of experience past. Jon wasn't surprised, because Sheila "didn't get money at all." He hailed from a hardworking family that was almost indistinguishable from their lucrative midtown Manhattan business, which had purveyed bridal accessories, exotic feathers, ribbons, wedding gown baubles, and extremely intricate imported paper flowers since his mother and father founded it in 1931. Jon's well-to-do father had been lucky enough to have a partner who kept his business going for him while he went off to World War II. Now Jon worked for the business too.

Jon had attended a Palm Beach private boarding school with children named Dodge, as in the automobile, and Fisher, as in "Body by Fisher." Jon always "had more" than most other children. He grew up hearing his parents say things like, "We sent you everywhere. We gave you everything. How can you do this?" "It was thrown in my face," he'd say in his disarming way, "but at least I never wanted for anything."

After several months of observing the Gordons, Jon decided that the emotional intensity of the family was the result of money problems. All the Gordons "knew zero" about money, but all of them lived under its spell. Sam had "busted his ass for a lifetime" only to end up with less than men who'd worked half as hard. The mother—Eve—managed the family finances. She took the kids shopping, a ritual of maternal control. She slipped the youngest and the oldest money all the time behind Sam's back. One day Jon noticed that only Eve's name was on the family checking account. "How come you don't have a joint account?" he asked.

Eve's eyes flashed destruction his way, and he knew that it was money that held the family power structure in place. It was a weird family—one sister went off to meditate before sitting down to a meal, had "a couple thousand dollars' worth of carpets at home" that she didn't want people to walk on, and had served him dinner on paper plates so as not to contaminate the macrobiotic dishes—but as in most families Jon had known, the secret thing between them was money.

Sam clearly admired the scion of a family business that had produced enough expendable income for the kid to own a boat. What with Harry going to work in a tie and well on the way to becoming a *mensch*, and Sheila hooked up with a guy who was wealthy and employed—and *Jewish*—Sam thought things were finally looking up for his daughters.

Sam grilled Jon about business and finance over dinner while Harry, Lorraine, Susan, and Ricky exchanged "Can you believe this guy?" looks that Sheila always noticed. The Gordon children—Sheila included—were hurt by Sam's fascination with this new man at the table. Sam seemed far more interested in Jon than he did in them—just because he had money, they all believed.

"And he's so young. Where is he coming from?" Lorraine wondered after one meal.

An almost surreal subgenre of popular nonfiction had recently appeared. Unlike all those books promising to teach readers "how to make a million," these new works were about personal power in the economic and social arena, about achieving *Success*, about pure *Power and How to Use It* (the title of Michael Korda's popular how-to book). To the generation formed by the middle-class baby boom experience, such books seemed like so many ahistorical blips on the cultural screen. From the same standpoint, most of the younger Gordons thought that the anachronism at the table was young Jon.

<hr />

Sam was now known within the five- or ten-mile radius of wherever he and his heavily customized motor home happened to be as "Covered Wagon." This was Sam's "handle," his technology-inspired entrée into what the *New York Times* called a "nationwide secret society." Some twenty-five million Americans were members of a populist anonymous association of citizens' band radio users. CB civilization had grown with astonishing speed out of a new form of civil disobedience that arose in the early 1970s, when cross-country truckers already enraged by fuel shortages and price rises decided to protest the lowering of the speed limit by circumventing police surveillance and organizing road demonstrations over their two-way radios. By 1976 a significant portion of the motorists on any highway were picking up the "ole radidio" to speak a brand-new language over the squeal of static in an accent that, no matter where they were born, made it sound like home was a hilltop somewhere in eastern Tennessee.

Covered Wagon broadcast the word to this short-lived democracy of cars and trucks from the big, boxy International motor home he'd bought in 1976. As soon as Sam pulled the green-and-white vehicle up to his workshop, he ripped out the inferior couch that opened into a bed and replaced it with a four-inch foam cushion. By the time Sam and Eve rolled out of town onto the "superslab," as the interstate highway system was known in CB land, he'd lowered the floor bed so you could stand up straight, added a four-burner electric stove with an oven (Sam and Eve didn't really like to eat out "after all these years of eating in"), and built in a decent refrigerator, a heater, and a full bathroom with shower. Eve put white curtains on the tiny windows.

Sam rigged a Volvo station wagon to the back so they could take short jaunts once the big house on wheels was hooked up to water and electricity. He figured they'd be seventy feet long, more than twice the length of the old Cadillac that once seemed the biggest noncommercial vehicle on the road.

"Everybody talks about these three-day weekends now," Sam observed not long before he and Eve lit out on the highway. "But I haven't had a *two*-day weekend since I left school. Sunday isn't really enough when you're so washed out that you spend it in a daze." The businesses were just going to have to lie fallow for a few months, he said.

Though Susan was temporarily in residence at the boatyard, still working on "getting back to normal," Sam and Eve planned their big trip around America as if in celebration of an empty nest. For many years, the emotional and psychological nosedive thought to occur after children grew up and left their parents behind had been a staple of magazine and television coverage, but several recent studies—including a quite extensive one by University of Michigan social psychologist Angus Campbell—indicated that "general feelings of happiness and satisfaction" actually dropped away after a couple first had children, and didn't return until the children were gone.

However belatedly, Sam and Eve decided to embark on their own journey of self-discovery. With the road atlas as their sacred text, they headed south into the warm weather, stopping long enough in sparsely developed areas along the western coast of Florida for Sam to articulate his dream of owning land and keeping a blooded horse out back, of "really getting away." They even looked at a small ranch on five acres not far from Sarasota—seventy-five thousand dollars and the use of a pool—but Sam didn't have the down payment on him, and somehow the time didn't seem completely right.

They picked up Interstate 10 near the Georgia border and headed west through Alabama, Mississippi, Louisiana, and from there onto the straight, empty roads of Texas. As dusk fell, the International would join one of the little communities of mobile homes pulled off the highways for a night. People were always friendly in the camps and trailer parks. By the eerie outdoor glow of television sets and the occasional open fire, drivers and shotgun riders traded tips and advice over road atlases and beer.

Sam pointed the cruiser toward Mexico. They explored the border towns of Nogales, Arizona, and El Paso, Texas, which was a stone's throw from the spot near Juàrez where Papa Joe took off after Pancho Villa. In Las Cruces, New Mexico, Sam had to pull the International off the road because of a sandstorm. In Arizona, Sam's favorite state, he and Eve bought big black cowboy hats, wide belts with big buckles, and real cowboy shirts. Sam's shirt was purple with decorative flowers and those pearly white snaps. Family photographs of Sam and Eve during the trip show them grinning like crazy in their cowboy outfits, more fashionable those days on certain streets in San Francisco and Greenwich Village than in Tucson or Santa Fe.

Covered Wagon forged on day after day. Every so often Sam would turn to his wife to report his location. "Eve," he'd say, "I'm in heaven."

1978

Tom Piechowsky sat up on a pullout bed and squinted into the brilliant light of a Harbor Isle morning. Still muddled with sleep, he was positive he'd heard a middle-class American mother of four discussing with her gay son the particularities—mostly the deficiencies—of his sex life. "So," Tom thought or dreamed the mother's voice had intoned, "why don't you go cruising?"

Tom squinted across the living room again. Sure enough, Ricky was sitting at the kitchen counter sipping coffee and regaling his mother with tales of evenings at the Wildwood, a popular gay bar near their apartment with a rough-hewn, manly decor reminiscent of a bunkhouse or a barn. The Wildwood, like so many of the gay cruising grounds of the moment, actually looked like rookie cowpoke Sam Gordon's kind of place.

"And it's not like I even *do* much when I finally meet somebody," Ricky complained. "I get so uncomfortable and shy that nothing much happens. Every gay man in New York is having such a ball, Ma, and I'm lonely…and *so* horny."

"So go do something about it," his mother replied. "Go cruising."

"Excuse me," Tom broke in from across the room. "I hate to employ a cliché, but what's wrong with this picture?"

During his first year in New York, Ricky found that he was often forced to hold art in abeyance out of economic necessity. One of his first part-time jobs was cleaning apartments, a calling he'd mastered as a young boy upon noting the salutary effect a good housecleaning had on Eve. He found his cleaning jobs through an agency called Lend-A-Hand, a popular source of part-time employment for many young New York City artists waiting for a break.

Ricky was sent to clean the apartment of a middle-aged man who immediately informed him that a full day's wages would be his if he would only take off his shoes and socks and allow the man to suck his toes. Ricky tried hard to think about how much extra time he'd have to work on his latest composition as his employer sucked away, masturbating with his free hand.

Ricky got a job at a small publishing house where he was supposed to take telephone orders, but he spent so much time writing lyrics and poetry on company stationery, gabbing on the phone, and teasing the gigantic hairdo of a fellow employee named Anita that when he returned to the office obviously drunk after a St. Patrick's Day lunch, he was dismissed on the spot. He went back to cleaning houses, his goal being to save enough money for a lengthy *Wanderjahr* to Europe in the fall. While cleaning a townhouse owned by a wealthy family in Greenwich Village, Ricky discovered a hoard of gold fillings in a box of family memorabilia relegated to the trash. Though he felt somewhat uncomfortable about it—having been one of 120 million Americans who'd watched the controversial miniseries *Holocaust* not long ago on TV, and what with Lorraine going on incessantly about the lasting consequences of a worldly act according to the doctrines of karmic reaction—Ricky took the fillings to a jewelry store on Forty-seventh Street and walked away with a pocketful of cash.

The extra money came in handy because Ricky had become obsessed with assembling the proper wardrobe of the well-outfitted European traveler, even one carrying a knapsack, as Ricky's friends insisted etiquette required. Ricky often dragged Mary O'Connor, his tall, red-haired, Cleveland-born friend from his Carnegie Mellon days, all over the city in search of clothes, shopping with Susan-like stamina though his journey was still six months away.

Some of the energy burned on these manic shopping jaunts was generated by amphetamines. Ricky got speed from a doctor down the street who seemed much more interested in touching Ricky's genitals during office visits than in getting paid for the pills he dispensed. The doctor was found beaten to death in front of his office less than a year later.

Ricky would take speed during the day, and sometimes he'd take Quaaludes and drink liquor at night before going over to the Wildwood. At most earlier points in history, a simple description of Ricky's activities since he'd arrived so eager and hopeful in New York would have sounded like a story of the moral ruination of a good-hearted, talented boy. But such was the young and adventurous life in New York and many other American cities in 1978 that Ricky thought he was leading a tame existence while the true culture of fun passed him by—especially when it came to sex.

Public life in New York brimmed with sex to an extent undreamed of during early days of the "sexual revolution." In 1963 eighty percent of American women thought that something as relatively tame as premarital sex was "wrong"; only thirty percent thought so by 1975. Pornography had seeped off Times Square screens and shelves and out onto every street corner. Just three blocks from Ricky's apartment was the peppermint-striped entrance to a basement club called Plato's Retreat, where husbands and wives and couples and singles would come every night to take off all their clothes, eat bad hors d'oeuvres, have random or group sex, or stare at strangers having random or group sex, usually in the "mattress room." Asked to describe the scene at Plato's, the club's owner thought for a moment before choosing to call it "mellow."

But even the most vigorous heterosexual swinger believed that any out-of-the-closet American homosexual had far greater access to endless days and nights of serial concupiscence. A new Kinsey Institute study reported that while on one hand many gay couples appeared better adjusted and happier than their straight counterparts, some forty percent of fifteen hundred San Francisco Bay Area homosexuals "cruised" for sexual partners, and nearly three of ten said that they'd had more than one thousand different sexual partners, most of them strangers.

Back at Carnegie Mellon Ricky had felt rather advanced in his comfortable acceptance of his sexual preference. One of his teachers who was more than ten years his senior once approached him and asked, "How do you do it? I'm so envious of how secure you are about being gay. I still feel like I'm supposed to lie and hide." Ricky figured the difference had to do with the times in which they'd grown up.

But sometimes the orgiastic scenes he witnessed in New York made Ricky yearn for a closet to hide in. He was terrified by the back-of-the-bar, back-of-the-bookstore, middle-of-the-bathhouse sexuality that crowned so many evenings and mornings and afternoons for so many of his peers. Ricky guessed he was something of a prude when it came down to it, and he was beginning to wonder if he was in the least bit cool.

His roommate Brian Frank had drawn a bead on being cool by whiling away the hours just before sunrise in discos like Studio 54, a midtown site of sybaritic social activities that had opened during the spring of 1977. Brian had always been more outgoing than Ricky or

Tom, and he seemed to have a natural flair for fashion statements, even back at college. On television now, Brian could be seen singing "Brush your breath, brush your breath, brush your breath with Dentyne" in one commercial, and having his face Xeroxed in another. Tina Turner acted like she'd known Brian Frank for years, hugging him amid the tick-tock cocking and recocking of hips at Studio 54. Brian talked to Liza and Halston and Diana Ross. Brian had style, a bit of new money, decent conversational skills, and career-inspired confidence. Since Ricky lacked all these things, the Studio 54 bouncer would surely know him for the cultural failure he was and turn him away, so he always refused to go. Ricky and Tom would listen to Brian shamble into the apartment early in the morning and not alone, and by midafternoon there were often leather cuffs and articles of Italian clothing strewn around the living room floor.

Ricky occasionally made out with virtual strangers in the Wildwood or in one of the other West Side bars—he did have this one moment on a pool table that his friends teased him about for years—but for the most part sex made him nervous. Being scared of sex as a gay man in New York City in 1978 was very much like being scared of curve balls as a gay Little Leaguer on Long Island in 1964, minus the black eye. Instead of becoming a famous composer, Ricky felt himself becoming a famous prude. Even his own mother thought he should pull himself together and go out cruising. Ricky was twenty-two years old, and he was still trying to be more like the other boys.

❦

Shuna's rescue from the devout home of her Hindu aunt came not a bit too soon. She wanted to eat fast food. She wanted to live with her mom.

Every so often, particularly at the beginning of their separation, Susan appeared at Harry and Lorraine's house. After her mother was gone, Shuna would awaken during the night thinking she was still there. But she wasn't, so Shuna would cry. It was worse when Susan said she was coming by but didn't make it. Then Shuna would have a tantrum, and only Maggie could comfort her.

But now it would be just the two of them again. No extended circle of rich Aricans, just Shuna and her mom—for the first time since they'd left the little house with the roses and fig trees in Berkeley. They would live together in a tall building at the corner of Seventy-first Street and Second Avenue, in an apartment with colorful pillows scattered everywhere and bright Arican symbols on the walls. Susan had a large forest-green bedroom and sheets in the same salubrious hue. Shuna had a blue-and-white room with big windows. The first day at home, Shuna noticed that all of her clothing was carefully folded and organized into drawers. Her mother was neat again, as in the old days, and she'd stopped saying things that didn't sound like her—scary things that came out in someone else's voice. Shuna was sure her mother wouldn't get so sad or angry anymore.

Though Lorraine and Sheila often laughed at their mother's contention that simply by sitting in the antique dentist chair in the living room and looking at the sea, Susan would magically lose her craving for drugs—"dry out" or "get calm," as Eve referred to the rehabilitation process—she indeed appeared to be her old self again. During her respite in Harbor Isle she'd sewed and quilted, read books by the armload, and practiced an advanced Arica meditation called "the Alfa Heat," which was designed to strengthen the "magnetic field," as Oscar Ichazo put it, that lies between the sexual and spiritual "poles" and supports the psyche. Susan occasionally strolled through Harbor Isle, an attractive upper-middle-class suburb shaded by huge sycamore trees. Each house was completely different now, and it made Susan a little sad to recall the stark square prototype replicated 250 times while the families sat watching from the rubble piles.

Not long after Susan and Shuna became a family again, Susan was named editor-in-chief of the *No Time Times*, a slender broadsheet offering news and cultural commentary from a trialectical, protoanalytical, and generally Arican perspective. The paper carried advertisements for the many businesses either owned, run by, or serving members of the Arica community. Underneath the logo of the *No Time Times* was the tag "The Family Newspaper," and Shuna was soon listed on the masthead as "Kids' Editor."

In an article published in the *Vassar Quarterly*, Susan argued that the *No Time Times* was a conduit to true freedom. "Ever since I can remember," Susan wrote to her alumnae sisters, "I've been looking for freedom....At Vassar I had distinct flashes of freedom, brilliant moments when the college seemed like a monastery, and I believed that the truth we learned would set us free." But her subsequent exposure to the journalistic version of "objective" truth, Susan went on, led only to disillusionment and a level of frustration that made it impossible to write anymore. "The pain of my blocked creativity gradually permeated the rest of my life and soon all I really wanted to do was deaden the pain with drugs." Only Arica, Susan wrote, was able to stop the slide. Arica was a means of "transmuting karma into wisdom," and the *No Time Times* was "a product of the seventies, a decade in which the human potential movement has shown, if nothing else, that the capability of a human being is far greater than what was once imagined."

Like others circulated out of the Arican fold, Susan was now back in the good graces of the organization's senior cadres. She began to work day and night on the paper, seven days a week. When she came home, she'd immediately begin to write, edit, or work on her ongoing interviews with Oscar Ichazo. Susan sensed that the combination of constant work and lack of sleep emptied her of the ability to do anything else but continue to work, and she worried about all the time she spent away from Shuna, off "making a living" for the family—and then, of course, she would think about Sam. All those years she'd been so sure that her father had a choice. Never once had she understood his absence as a requirement of doing a job right and supporting a family.

By one Census Bureau estimate, forty percent of all children born during the 1970s would at some point live in a single-parent household, and ninety percent of these households would be headed by a woman. More than fifty-five percent of mothers with children Shuna's age now worked, and according to two economists, Isabel Sawhill and Heather Ross, maintaining a basic standard of living was becoming "virtually impossible" in a single-income household.

Susan tried to tell Eve how enervating it was to be a good editor, a breadwinner, and a mother alone.

"Yeah, sure. Just try four kids," said Eve. "We had nothing. We came from nothing. Your father always says I could have raised ten kids."

Eve's words made Susan feel neutralized, negated, but she slogged on. She worked around the clock because she had responsibilities, a daughter to feed. When she thought she might collapse from exhaustion, she told herself that she was pushing herself to the limit on behalf of a spiritual movement that would soon benefit the whole world.

⸻

There was music at all of the many large gatherings of the clan at the boatyard that summer. "Sing 'Take Me in Your Arms,' Ma," someone would invariably demand.

"Oy, so schmaltzy," Eve would demur, moving toward the piano.

"Schmaltz! Give us schmaltz."

Eve would sing several songs, and then Ricky would play show tunes and perhaps some Joni Mitchell or Judy Collins songs. He'd run through a couple of piano rags for Sam, and if Susan was able to get away, she and Lorraine would play folk songs on their guitars.

Susan tried as hard as everyone else to get back to Harbor Isle for the regular get-togethers that became a mainstay of life at the boatyard in the summer of '78. Gordon children, grandchildren, and even a wide circle of strangers were touched by the powerful centripetal force of home that summer. Sam stopped working on weekends and even adjusted his riding schedule to attend. Sometimes he would take Shuna and Maggie on long walks by the water in the early morning, his heavy arms draped around their shoulders as he told them about the animals they'd see, but by mid-morning he was back in the living room listening quietly to the music and the oral histories, to the "oldies" and the memories that drew sanded-smooth bits and pieces of the past into the boatyard here and now.

Everyone giggled over the cataloging of old boyfriends and raucous nights in the playroom. Lorraine and Susan reminisced about their rock 'n' roll excursions to the Brooklyn Paramount and about Greenwich Village back when it was "great," when drinking wine with Bob Dylan was a matter of course and beats still talked poems and jazz in the cafés. If Sam stepped out of the room, Susan would describe the night she came home from London and lectured Lorraine about the evils of drugs, and Lorraine would follow with an equally ironic account of Susan's "Quaalude meditation" on the beach. Sheila was able to recall in laser-clean detail the fantasia of colors that decorated her perfect acid trips.

Eve never stopped smiling as the story of the night she briefly ran away from home in 1959 was offered up. Ricky recollected the night Sheila smashed the stereo speakers and slugged Peter Probst, and everyone took a turn evoking the subterranean terror of the crawl space under 221 Lincoln, which by the end of a round of telling was no wider than a drainpipe and as dark and airless as outer space.

When Lorraine talked of the past, her devotional whisper often gave way to the enthusiastic, resounding voice of the fearless fighter her sisters and brother now thought of as "the old Lorraine." She told stories about the movement, about marching and resisting, about friends who readied guns for the revolution. Susan said she had friends who'd been ready to fight it out too. Speaking at a time when political extremism was understood within the context of an aberrant personality, convicted bomber Jane Alpert—a Weatherperson who'd surrendered late in 1974 after more than four years underground—reduced her own radical days to "the craziness that came over me." But the barricade tales returned to the boatyard as fragments of a golden age.

There were always outsiders present at these tuneful, retrospective seaside Sundays at Sam and Eve's. Friends of Sheila's often came, and Ricky's friends were forever jockeying for invitations to the boatyard.

His roommates, Tom and Brian, were frequent guests, as was his near-constant companion of recent months, Mary O'Connor. The friends came to listen to these ancient mariners—thirty-four, thirty-one, twenty-nine, and twenty-two—as they told and retold stories of their voyages across the heaving cultural seas, from the early days of folk, rock, protest, the counterculture, drugs, feminism, and gay liberation to the new spirituality.

Mary O'Connor had grown up in a suburb outside Cleveland, the youngest of five children. She remembered clearly the day her brother left for Vietnam, because that same week an FBI agent came to the door looking for another brother, a student at Kent State, who had apparently pocketed a spent shell in the aftermath of an antiwar protest at the college. But Mary never heard anyone in her family describe how those times felt. Nothing was discussed or given a context in her family—not sex or drugs or politics or the mysterious war from which her brother returned with a Bronze Star and a deep reluctance to talk about any of his experiences there at all.

Mary had always felt that she'd been formed as much by experiences she'd missed as by what she'd done and seen. Recent history seemed to carry a taunt—that you'd arrived on the scene just a bit late or a bit early, or perhaps turned your back at the wrong moment while others seized the true meaning of the times. But here at the Gordons' Mary was able to connect with an era at once chronologically brief and lasting in its complicated effect.

Yet the emotional diplomacy that allowed the Gordons and so many other families and friends to remember the recent past in peace also muted the do-or-die urgency of events and issues. Injuries were carefully wrapped in clean, soft gauze. The music set a sweet and placid tone. It would be almost two years before John Sayles deftly depicted a wistful house party for American baby boomers in his film *Return of the Secaucus 7*, and five years before his idea was slickly repackaged and perfectly sound-tracked as a Hollywood movie called *The Big Chill*. But for the last four or five years, a sugary icing sculpted from the remembered past had been spreading over the cultural cake. Big bands were heard on radio and in elevators almost as frequently as during their Depression heyday. Harry Truman was making such a big comeback that a magazine coined the term "Trumania." Elvis Presley was fondly remembered dozens of times and in dozens of ways each day. The Beatles had become a Broadway musical revue, *Beatlemania*. Richard Nixon had recently come out with a surprisingly benign memoir. Such were the elements of a central strain of popular expression, of a vogue that went hand in hand with political drift and a diffuse apathy. Such was the cover story of the moment: nostalgia.

The year's most popular television shows, located just a click or two away from unintentional satires like *Family Feud*, were set in the nostalgic 1950s. The number-one TV show this summer was *Laverne and Shirley*, in which two gum-smacking working-class early-fifties Midwestern girls exchanged one-liners for a bit over twenty minutes in an exercise NBC executive Fred Silverman likened to the seventeenth-century social satires of Molière. *Laverne and Shirley* was a spinoff of the beloved prime-time sitcom *Happy Days*, a weekly fixation of millions for four years running that had already generated its own internal nostalgia in the form of several "classic" episodes. One featured the Fonz—an antisocial character abandoned by his father at three, and therefore affecting a toughness that was in reality eggshell-thin because of his basic goodness of heart—being coaxed out of his life of lonely cool and into the embracing warmth of the Cunningham family, to partake of Christmas in a real American home. The Fonz, who bore no relationship to the occasionally murderous delinquents of the 1950s save his leather jacket, was clearly moved by his inclusion in this tiny community whose members looked so grateful for what they had. One of the most widely discussed books of 1978 was Mary Jo Bane's *Here to Stay*, which argued that all the talk of family decline was a "fantasy" and that stability, tradition, and the American family were as strong as ever before.

This summer the Gordons were mirroring a process of change that the large functionalist school of family social scientists had been describing for some time. Displaced from its "instrumental" role as society's trainer and sustainer, the American family was becoming an institution that served the "expressive" needs of its members. At least for the summer of 1978, the family Gordon looked to those who gathered at the boatyard like a "haven in a heartless world," historian Christopher Lasch's phrase for what the family once was in America before it was "besieged," not only by the coming of the machine age, as had been argued for many years, but also by the family "experts" with their tyranny of insinuations that made parents feel so helpless and unable to "keep up with the kids." Even on the most nostalgic shows, TV kids now seemed brighter and more in control than their moms and dads.

President Carter had worried aloud during his campaign about the American "lack of roots," and as if in response, the television miniseries *Roots*, based on Alex Haley's best-selling novel, engendered a flurry of genealogical research and a renascent pride in family histories. Millions of Americans whose ancestors' immigration experience bore little relationship to Kunta Kinte's in *Roots* went looking for their own roots in places like rural Ireland, where so many Yanks were suddenly traipsing through the bogs in search of headstones that Irish locals dubbed the phenomenon "Boots."

The contagion of American nostalgia in 1978 was just one facet of a massive cultural about-face. Package-tour excursions into ancestry and commercialized doses of "the good old days" were mainstream analogues to all the flourishing programs of self-discovery and spiritual exploration. Incorrigible nostalgia buffs were no less avid in their pursuit than religious enthusiasts or partisans of more secular, psychologically based approaches—a long list of the latter being represented at the boatyard on Sunday afternoons. A vast democracy of styles and methods spread before millions who yearned to locate something in the past that would unlock the secret of being reborn into the future.

Touched by the reflective aura of the moment, Sam was sure that he loved all his children. He could tell he loved them from the way the stories of their adventures made him ache. As much as he enjoyed the music and the sense of family, he actually took as little pleasure in these stories as he did in most of the current nostalgia for the days when postwar dads brought home the bacon for full-time moms to cook and serve to respectful, clean-cut kids. Sam's own packaged recollection of fatherhood back then was more like a movie rendition of Custer's Last Stand than an episode of *Happy Days*. It was war. Sam thought of himself as a war veteran three times over: he'd survived the battle for subsistence during the Depression, the military battle in Europe, and the battle of raising children—and this last campaign had been the longest and hardest of all.

"I would have been a better father if I'd been around the house a little more," Sam said. He now thought he'd made a huge mistake in acceding to the mid-century custom of leaving the child-raising to his wife. In the preface to the most recent edition of *Baby and Child Care*, Benjamin Spock had included a similar *mea culpa:* "Now I recognize that the father's responsibility is as great as the mother's." Sam's newfound determination to take time off for himself and explore had also led him to conclude that he had not only missed the chance to be a better father, but "because I was too busy working all the time, I missed my life."

This summer Sam Gordon was retracing his steps—and a few missteps—by reading the Old Testament, a book, once you stopped to take a close look, that was a combination of historical narrative, poetry, and a lot more family stories than theological dictates. Sam attended regular adult education classes at the Island Park Jewish Center and even went to Friday night services, like many other Americans whose return to synagogue and church had now reversed a twenty-year decline. Shay Kane, the new rabbi at the Jewish center, a man Susan's age, was curious about Sam's sudden appearance there. He knew that Sam Gordon was a member of the Harbor Isle "old guard," but he'd always found him rather distant. Eve Gordon was an "out there" wife who seemed to be an unregenerate personification of the *Yiddishkeit* that most Harbor Isle residents had long ago discarded, and Rabbi Kane approved. But Sam kept to himself.

The rabbi was surprised when Sam took him aside after a service. "I'd like to come talk to you," he said. "I want to tell you about my family." Sam described his Jewish daughters who'd "fallen in love with gurus," and at first it was hard for Rabbi Kane to tell if this disturbed him, because he grinned the whole time he was talking about Lorraine's houseful of graven images. "She's even got a new name. She doesn't even like to go by her name." As the young rabbi listened to Sam's account of his Depression childhood, he thought again, as he had many times, that there was nothing in either his experience or his black bag of spiritual salves that could address the scars of poverty or family troubles.

Sam began to drop in on Rabbi Kane often. The two men discussed secular problems of Judaism—the anti-Semitism Sam said he'd lived with all his working life, the Israelis recently slain on a Haifa bus, Jewish children who turned their backs on their heritage—but Sam was more and more interested in matters biblical and religious. One day he said, "Rabbi, I've forgotten how to pray. I think I vaguely remember sometimes, all those prayers I knew so well, but I can't quite get them back."

<hr />

Sheila was determined to have an "honest marriage" with Jon. This time around she would be married in the here and now—no deferred fantasies, no illusions. Jon underscored her desire by insisting they sign a binding prenuptial agreement. He said the document was meant to assure him that Sheila was marrying "for me and not for any other reason." Marriage contracts like Jon and Sheila's were all the latest. Most were designed to override the usual alimony settlements in case of divorce, but some specified the schools the children must attend, called for mutual agreement on where the family would live, or stipulated frequency of sexual intercourse. A book called *Open Marriage*, by husband-and-wife anthropologists George and Nena O'Neill, recommended that privacy guidelines, definitions of equality and trust, and the right to "open companionship" with others be written into marriage contracts. In *Oh Promise Me but Put It in Writing*, Seattle attorney Paul Ashley wrote that the proliferation of unconventional familylike arrangements argued for the inclusion of all voluntary relationships in the realm of contract law.

Formerly radical "alternatives to the nuclear family" now surfaced in the pages of *Life*, which ran a lengthy special report on the institution of marriage. The article described some of the novel family formations of the moment and suggested that marriage was once again changing in America "because people are demanding new quality from it....Within this cherished framework they are searching as never before for the kinds of honest human relationships that so much of our synthetic society denies them." The number of American couples cohabiting had more than doubled since the communal days of 1970, and many of those who did opt for marriage sought "nonbinding commitments" in keeping with the unbridled sexual adventurism of the times. There were "collective marriages," such as the household of seven adults and four children featured in the *Life* article, and there were marriages in which each spouse was allowed to disappear for a quarter of the year.

Meanwhile, according to a new mental health survey, sixty-two percent of couples in old-fashioned marriages had problems, compared with forty-eight percent when the survey was taken in 1957. Still, it was a testament to the hold of traditional marriage that four of every five people who'd been divorced wanted to remarry, and that three of every ten marriages involved Americans for whom the first try hadn't worked.

Sheila wanted to live in a house inhabited by one wife, one husband, no snakes, and eventually a couple of kids. She didn't want the world, or even the land in California this time. She wanted a normal family. In light of all that had happened, it seemed a simple request.

An Orthodox rabbi performed the first Gordon wedding in living memory not conducted on the fly. It was also the first wedding of one of Sam's children that he attended. One hundred twenty-five guests gathered in a beautiful Long Island yard on a picturesque, boat-strewn inlet. When the rabbi said, "You may kiss the bride," Jon swept Sheila into the air like Rhett Butler, but he lost his balance and Sheila fell to the ground.

* * *

Ricky told many people at the wedding reception about his forthcoming grand tour of the Continent. After much agitation, and against Mary O'Connor's best advice, he'd purchased some extremely expensive leather boots for the trip, as well as a huge, heavy suitcase. Ricky just wasn't the knapsack sort. He'd read Hemingway and Paul Bowles, and he was taking along *Brideshead Revisited*, which he'd already read twice and planned to read again in various picturesque cafes. He left in search of his artistic roots in October.

Toward the end of the month, Mary O'Connor received a letter.

mary, mary, mary, mary, mary

I love you so much, and since at this moment, I love you more than anything in the whole world, I'll tell you the truth about everything, because I need to purge myself. I am looking out the window. The Ionian Sea is the bluest water I've ever seen. I'm on my way to Greece, and I feel as empty as when I left. I really want to cry.

In London, I was still excited because everything was so new and ahead of me. We (I'm traveling with Sean, who will be discussed later) took a train to Milan. The trip lasted all night while it rained through England, France, Germany, Switzerland. Then it rained harder in Italy. We were pressed for a place to stay so we ended up paying $50 for one night.

In Venice, it rained so hard that the canals overflowed and ruined my boots, which you'll be happy to know have since ruined my feet and have proved to be the poorest choice of what to bring thus far. After Venice, we went to Florence, where I managed to feel spiritually dead in front of Michelangelo's David and the Botticellis of the Uffizi.

Then to Brindisi, the most horrible place I've seen since Miami Beach. Now I'm on the boat to Greece with about 500 Americans with knapsacks, and as you have probably already guessed, I'm less than happy.

Sean is really something. I've never been so irritated by someone's presence in my life. He is the kind who has to brush his hair every half hour or so. I find myself so resentful of not being alone, but it's only till November. In November I will do a month alone, and then I will come home—because that's probably all I'll be able to take.

You're the only one I can tell this to, and please, don't read it to anyone. It's too embarrassing…Mary, you better miss me because I think about you all the time and sometimes (all the time), I think about marrying you. It's this sexual thing! But what the fuck—how many people do you really have fun with? You, always. I have fun with you. Oh Mary, if I was only traveling with you.

Please don't worry. It's possible this will all blow over and I'll start having a great time. Most of all, don't you dare think I'm a baby.

I Love You,
Ricky

P.S. I know this is a weird letter.

Three weeks later Ricky cut short his trip. He came home to a strangely pristine nostalgia that would soon fade away, to sex-filled bars and streets that would begin to change too. He came back with his front teeth stained an unhealthy gray by three packs of smelly Gauloise cigarettes a day. He came back to Mary and never mentioned the idea of marriage again.

Ricky said it was good to be home.

1979

Sri Swami Satchidananda shuttled from airport to airport, an inner peacemaker never in greater demand: out to a holistic health conference in San Diego; back to New York for his annual "Swami and the Rabbi" dialogue with Joseph Gelberman, a hip, yoga-practicing Manhattan rabbi; off immediately to speak at Rutgers University before leaving for Los Angeles. Logging first-class air miles like a CEO or a rock star, the swami jetted off on a spiritual tour of Hawaii, Fiji, and New Zealand, where a large crowd of upstanding Wellington Anglicans came to listen to him speak of universal consciousness. Back home, executives of the Pillsbury Corporation heard Satchidananda's views on nutrition. "Food not only makes the body," he explained to the dehydrators of Hungry Jack potato flakes. "It makes the mind....Restlessness of the mind is caused by the diet." Everywhere people were searching for answers, so the "Apostle of Peace," as he was called, was always on the road.

One of the drivers who had the honor of transporting Satchidananda to and from New York area airports was the veteran Integral Yoga disciple Hara Hughes. Swamiji knew that Harry had once driven a cab. "Faster!" Satchidananda would roar from the back seat of the air-conditioned car Harry often borrowed from Sam. "Go faster! Now!" One time he "busted" Harry—the term for the guru's tongue-lashings in Integral Yoga circles—because Harry arrived at the airport in a T-shirt. "*This* is the way you'd go to see your girl!" said Satchidananda, clearly outraged. As a former student of psychology, Harry couldn't help pondering the gender implications of the remark. But he'd been busted nonetheless, and he figured he must have deserved it on some karmic level he hadn't yet discovered.

Most of the high-profile gurus were now classified as either "maternal" or "paternal." A maternal teacher was someone like Baba Ram Dass—the yogic name of former Harvard professor Richard Alpert, who'd been fired for LSD experimentation along with Tim Leary and Gina Schick's old employer Ralph Metzner. Ram Dass had since become a popular spiritual master. He seemed to grin constantly, and his demeanor was all-loving and all-forgiving. The maternal babas were easily identifiable from their official photographs, which always showed them in full chortle, as if someone had just cracked a very good joke.

Satchidananda smiled in his photographs and in person, but unless he was playing with children, his was the half smile of a radiant and knowing inner peace. And the smile was far from constant, for as the most prominent of all the "paternal" yoga masters, Swamiji expected a great deal of his devotees and even more of his full-time disciples. This guru called them as he saw them, so almost every follower of Integral Yoga had been busted at one time or another, an experience they all described as if such extreme disapproval were a great honor.

In private, Swami Satchidananda said he was well aware that many members of his flock sought his love and approbation with all the urgency of very young children. He encouraged his followers to call him "Father" or "Papa" ("though others," he noted, "consider me more like a mother or even a child"). He regarded these familial forms of address and the feelings they represented as somewhat akin to the psychoanalytic doctrine of transference. "If fear of losing my love helps these young people change their lives for the better, then I will allow it." Satchidananda would never really stop loving any of them, he said—no matter what they did—but he was prepared to wield the doubt and fear engendered by the possibility as tools of his trade. The swami was a "God-realized" being. He resided in the world in human form only to serve the spiritual needs of others. His anger, followers believed, was "fake," simply one of several pedagogical styles. Besides, as he often pointed out, nobody ever said becoming enlightened was easy.

On one occasion Harry and Lorraine took their diminutive eighty-one-year-old Indian music teacher, Swami Nadabrahmananda, up to Satchidananda's ashram in Connecticut. Lorraine and Harry loved their lessons with the learned musician. By now they'd completely forsworn rock and blues in favor of the exotic Indian rhythms and motifs he taught them to chant and play on the harmonium and the tabla, an

Indian drum. At the ashram, Lorraine, Harry, and Nadabrahmananda gave an impromptu concert. As soon as they finished, one of Satchidananda's retinue of assistants informed Lorraine and Harry that the guru was livid. They'd presumed to bring another teacher to his ashram without permission, and they were expected to apologize.

After hours of sitting in traffic jams observing his spiritual master in the rearview mirror, Harry had decided that Sri Swami Satchidananda was not only far from serene, he was a bilious and unforgivingly cranky old man. Not once had Harry felt his spiritual bond with Satchidananda enhanced by all the carping, however edifyingly paternal it was meant to be. Worse yet, Harry was sure that his guru didn't really care for him, especially lately. It was almost as if Satchidananda somehow knew that Harry's devotion was failing. But Harry continued to suffer his bustings, riddled with the guilty feelings of a naughty child.

Lorraine—Leela, as she now introduced herself—felt her love for her stern spiritual father growing deeper by the week. She felt entirely unworthy before her master, and she still wasn't quite sure exactly how she was supposed to navigate the specific spiritual path that would win her this great man's respect, but from the moment she woke up she dedicated each day to trying. Lorraine avowed to Harry and her brother and sisters that she stood ready "to die for his love."

For all her devotion and rigid adherence to the purest yogic habits and diet, Lorraine now wheezed heavily with every breath. She'd become terrified of leaving her house; at a distance of no more than one hundred paces from her front door, she wanted to curl up and die. One night Harry convinced her to go to a revival of 2001: A Space Odyssey, and Lorraine experienced a terrifying acid flashback right in the middle of the scene where the astronaut returns to an embryonic state. The mere thought of going out in public, even to shop for food, made Lorraine panic and lose her foothold on the path to peace.

Lorraine was deemed to be suffering from "the biggest problem in phobias today," according to psychiatrist Arthur B. Hardy of Menlo Park, California, as quoted in a recent issue of People, the five-year-old magazine of the culture of celebrity. Hardy, "probably the only doctor in the U.S. who specializes in treating" the "strange ailment" of "agoraphobia," estimated that one in fifty Americans, mostly women, now had this previously obscure disease, which caused severe panic in public places. An article about the new affliction in Ms. suggested that its prevalence among women reflected "the political reality of isolation, powerlessness, and poor self-image that affect women in general....

Female agoraphobics may feel trapped in a bad marriage."

Lorraine consulted the Integral Yoga Institute's doctors and healers about her agoraphobia, and eventually she wrote to Gurudev asking what she should do. He replied immediately. "Know that these are just thought waves, aspects of the mind....through the regular practice of pranayoga and meditation, this will fall away, little by little. Don't hate yourself for having fears, just recognizing them is the first step toward getting them to go away."

Shortly before the onset of her fear of the *agora*—ancient Greek for "marketplace," a setting that seemed to offer spiritual solace to so many other Americans—and not long after Lorraine played the Virgin Mary to Ram's (she now called Gabe by his yogic middle name) baby Jesus in the big Integral Yoga Christmas pageant of 1978 (Satchidananda came as Santa Claus), she began to sense that something was seriously wrong with Harry. She was certain he was betraying her, a conviction that might have had something to do with Harry's torrid affair with one of the secretaries at the Social Security Administration, a wholesale violation of their somewhat contradictory vows of celibacy and marriage.

Devastated, but remembering Satchidananda's quick response to her agoraphobia, Lorraine steeled what remained of her nerve and called her guru on the phone. Through his personal secretary, she communicated the tragic marital news. Satchidananda came to the phone and listened patiently. Lorraine waited for his wise advice.

"Well," he said, sounding irritated, "I don't know what you expect? After all, you weren't giving him any at home."

Lorraine gasped. "But...Gurudev. He's...he's not interested in me."

"I'm sure you know how to make him interested. Good-bye."

By the time two hundred thousand Americans fled the area around the Three Mile Island nuclear plant near Harrisburg, Pennsylvania, in the wake of a reactor accident that spring, Lorraine was beginning to wonder if her panics were caused less by agoraphobia than by the rampant degeneration of the environment. She now talked of going "back to the land" in the spirit of the counterculture pioneers who had been rejecting technology and urban living to varying degrees since the days of the mud bath at Woodstock.

Armed with copies of *Silent Spring*, Rachel Carson's landmark 1962 book about the systematic poisoning of the environment, with E. F. Schumacher's *Small Is Beautiful*, which argued that the fetishistic pursuit of large-scale economic growth was inimical to human values, and perhaps with a subscription to the *Mother Earth News*, thousands of people Lorraine's age had been heading out of town in search of "voluntary simplicity" for several years now. For much of that time, Swami Satchidananda had mused openly about his dream of finding a spot in the countryside to build a model community based on yogic principles. The place would be dominated architecturally by a gigantic flower-shaped "Light of Truth Universal Shrine," or LOTUS, an ecumenical temple for people of all religious backgrounds. Swamiji imagined a room inside with a single central light that would shine on the ceiling and divide there into rays illuminating a symbol of each of the world's great religions. Where to build the shrine was the only remaining question.

In late 1978 Satchidananda's devotee Karuna King—well known outside yoga ranks as pop singer and composer Carole King—had presented her guru with three hundred acres of prime real estate in western Connecticut. A small Integral Yoga community immediately assembled on the hilltop Carole King called Music Mountain, but Satchidananda and his advisers preferred another property, a hundred-acre wooded tract in Dayville, much closer to the current ashram in Pomfret. Early in 1979, the clearing of a site for LOTUS began in Dayville, but by then the swami could be heard expressing doubts about the wisdom of gathering his followers in a place that got as cold as northern Connecticut had during the winter of 1978–79. The cost of heating the Pomfret buildings was almost six thousand dollars a month, and price hikes in the energy sector indicated that winter fuel bills would rise higher. So, like thousands of discouraged back-to-the-landers before him, Satchidananda announced his preference for a warmer locale with a longer growing season for the organic garden and a climate a bit more like…India's, for instance. Carole King's Music Mountain estate was sold in a booming exurban real estate market, and the profits were applied to the purchase of 650 beautiful acres bordering the James River in a primitive reach of Buckingham County in central Virginia. Those acolytes who were "ready" could now move south to build a community on which the guru had bestowed the all-American name Yogaville.

On April Fool's Day, 1979, so disabled by guilt and confusion that he thought he could no longer be a husband, a father, or a disciple, Harry Hughes moved out of the house in Long Beach and away from the world of the harsh father from Chettipalayam.

"In Yogaville," Lorraine told her mother, "love is unwavering and for sure." In Yogaville, far from Harbor Isle and cheating husbands and radioactive waste, Lorraine would sparkle again, just as she had when Harry Hughes fell so deeply in love with her.

⫸⫷

Susan often talked to her aunt Sylvia on the telephone. "Aunt Syl," she said one day after mentioning that she was sick, "I just can't stop thinking about your mushroom and barley soup."

"*Su*-san," Sylvia replied, "if you're feeling low and soup is what you need, then soup, my love, is what you will have."

Susan implored her not to make the long drive from deepest Queens to Manhattan, but Sylvia turned to her husband after hanging up. "It's not such a big deal," she said. "So we'll drive into the city." Sylvia was positive she'd go "kah-*razy*" looking for a place to park, so she sent Chummy Doll to buzz Susan's apartment and ask her to come down.

As soon as she saw Susan stagger out to the street, Sylvia knew something was amiss. From a distance she could see that Susan was shaking. When her niece leaned down to the car window for a kiss, Sylvia cupped her cheeks and felt like she was holding one of those toy dolls sold at circuses and sporting events, their wobbly heads connected to their bodies by little springs. Susan's hands were trembling so violently that Sylvia thought she was having a fit. Her skin was sallow, and her eyes sank into their sockets like a zombie's.

"Susan! Come here! You come here right now!" Sylvia said, pulling Susan's forehead to her lips through the car window. She placed a heavily jeweled hand on Susan's neck, sizing up the situation with maternal precision. "You take this soup and get right back upstairs to bed," Sylvia ordered. "Susan, you have the grippe!"

When she got as dope-sick as she was the day Sylvia and Chummy stopped by, when the stinking poison oozed from her pores, Susan would think back to Lorraine's visit to London. She'd been so naïve then, so intent on being a good upwardly mobile wife, that she'd made Lorraine take a bath—as if a bath could ever wash away the smell of a junkie in need.

Still, Susan considered her recent return to serious drugs nothing more than a casual spur-of-the-moment affair. Sniffing a bit of heroin was a long way from shooting it into your veins, after all. Her nasal highs allowed her to maintain her once-hooked-since-saved story, at the same time transforming a lonely editor of a failing spiritual newspaper and a struggling single mother into a vibrant, youthful woman suddenly hip, much less white, and cool again.

Everyone in New York City, from aging hippies and disc jockeys to public officials and business executives so straight they'd never even tried drugs, now seemed to be "into" cocaine. Everyone wanted a dealer, preferably one who was not physically threatening and operated out of premises where it was safe to go shopping in a business suit. The successful dealer of the moment was serious-minded, articulate, and knowledgeable enough about operating margins and product to offer good value. The powdered commodity that induced a brief, intense euphoria now provided Susan with part-time work. Coke enabled her to feed Shuna and her incredibly hungry little sister, heroin.

Shuna's closest friend among the "regular" non-Arican kids at her current school, P.S. 183, was Sarah. After school one afternoon, Shuna and Sarah got into a big fight near the concrete baseball field in St. Catherine's Park. They said mean things to each other, and they both started to cry. As Shuna was leaving the crowded park, she heard Sarah screaming, "Go ahead, Shuna! Go on home where your mom has big bags of Quaaludes!" Kids stopped playing and stared.

There were already "rumors" about Shuna at school, possibly because she was so thin and pale and ate so much when she went to her friends' houses. It was said that her mother was never home and that Shuna took care of herself like Pippi Longstocking. It was true that Shuna didn't have much to show and tell about her mom. Susan never turned up for parents' day or made Shuna's lunch.

Shuna noticed that drugs sometimes made her mother happier and more energetic than she'd been before. They would go out and do things together for hours on end. They'd sing as they had traveling up and down the San Francisco hills. In the early spring, Shuna accompanied Susan on a trip to the Caribbean island of St. Croix. She was dazzled by their opulent quarters in a hotel near the beach. One morning Susan taught Shuna how to dive, and Shuna would always remember her mother executing artful swan dives, breaking the water with scarcely a splash, like a sleek and graceful fish. Shuna spent a lot of time on her own during the two-week vacation, and when mother and daughter were together, they acted more like old friends. Shuna knew they sometimes looked like a normal eleven-year-old and her mom, though she still had to do some of the basic things for Susan, like saying thank you to people and closing doors behind her.

Shuna did most of the shopping now and all the laundry. Her chores also included going down to the corner deli every morning to buy her mother cigarettes and coffee. Susan paid Ricky to clean the apartment once a week, but Shuna cleaned too. Until recently Shuna had always been the family slob. She tried to avoid taking showers, and her room was often full of moldering food and a wrinkled history of the clothing she'd worn that week. During the "clean period" after Shuna's rescue from life at Lorraine's house, her mother used to yell at her and threaten to give her clothes away if she didn't put them in their proper place. But now Shuna was the clean one, and her mother had become—well, though she would never tell a soul, not Sarah or even Maggie—really, really gross. Her mom's bedroom smelled.

So Shuna cleaned for hours. She'd scrub the same surfaces over and over again, almost like Nanny Eve. She'd clean each tiny room in the dollhouse her mother had made for her back in Berkeley. She'd try to make her mother's bedroom stop smelling.

Shuna believed her mother was still the most tasteful and sophisticated dresser in the world. She loved to stand outside Susan's door while she dressed. Her mother would go out for a long time. Shuna wondered who said thank you for her and closed the doors.

The funny part about apparently telling details like forgetting to close the door was that outsiders—everyone outside the little family of the two of them—never seemed to notice what was going on. Nobody would ever know the truth of their lives, Shuna believed, because her mother was brilliant and witty and gorgeous and everyone loved her so much that they would simply never see.

<hr />

Ricky had to concentrate to be a good housecleaner. His mind would wander to his latest musical setting of a complicated poem. And he couldn't stop thinking about his recent stint as piano accompanist to singer and comedian Phyllis Newman, the wife of lyricist Adolph Green.

At one point Ricky was at their home rehearsing for a show with Newman, Green, his longtime partner Betty Comden, and composer Cy Coleman. It had been a long day, and Ricky went to take a quick shower while the others continued rehearsing. Catching his image in the bathroom mirror, he was visited by one of those epiphanic juxtapositions that yielded what literary critic Kenneth Burke called "perspective by incongruity": *I am standing here naked, looking at the hairs on my ass, and in the next room Betty Comden and Adolph Green are going through their musical life together.*

There was a phone in the bathroom, and Ricky dialed Eve. "Listen,

Ma!" He held the receiver to the bathroom door. "That's the guys who wrote *Singin' in the Rain!*"

One day Ricky was cleaning Susan's apartment—a strange place, he thought, in that no matter how much he cleaned, it was still dingy and kind of musty—when Shuna came home from school and went directly to the kitchen. Ricky watched her pull half a head of red cabbage from the fluorescent void of an otherwise empty refrigerator. Shuna was lately given to food kicks. She had been buying herself red cabbage—and only red cabbage—for weeks. She cut it into several pieces, poured some vinegar on top, and sat down to eat.

"Shunie, is that, like, your dinner?"

"Yeah."

Ricky interpreted the raw cabbage dinner and the utterly depressing atmosphere of the apartment—to say nothing of the eviction notices occasionally taped to the door—as signs of deprivation. He felt ashamed that he'd envied Susan's easy access to the reigning luminaries of the cultural scene and that he'd coveted the huge piles of presents Shuna would tear into on Christmas morning, most of them sent by all those filthy-rich Aricans. He'd also envied the time that Shuna—and Maggie and Gabe and now Sheila's new baby daughter, Danielle—got to spend with his mother and father. Eve was always so caring and good to them, and Sam could love them completely because they were only little kids. But Eve and Sam were *his* mom and dad. They were his.

Only recently, upon seeing what passed for Shuna's supper and hearing the vitriolic things that often came out of her mother's mouth, had Ricky begun to reflect on the irrational depth of his jealousy. Susan was acting like such a bitch, even during boatyard Sundays, that Ricky and several of his friends now called her "the reptile," "the viper," or "the snake." Other times she grew tediously maudlin and would offer sentimental memories she claimed to have of the two years before Sam came back from the war. Ricky was well aware of what Eve called Susan's tendency to feel "oppressed," but now she went off on lengthy tirades about Sam, who "never so much as changed a light bulb in any place *I* ever lived, but how many places has he done over for Sheila and Lorraine?"

"He bought Lorraine that house, you know. Bought it!" Lorraine, in Susan's analysis, got most of the attention by having a corner on problems, and Sheila got the rest by being the family brown-nose.

Susan would attempt to pull her diatribes up just short of Ricky, though the truth was that she deeply resented him too. Ricky appeared to care so much more for his multitude of friends than he did for his oldest sister—who'd introduced him to the poetry she could now hear in his music, shepherded him through some rough times, and protected him from their parents. Nobody had done that for her. Nobody. Of course she mocked Ricky's roommate, that Tom Piechowsky, with those pretentious lyrics for the musical he and Ricky were working on, with that *Beautiful and the Damned* face and that cocky expectation of imminent fame.

If Susan had been born into a different family, she would have been encouraged to attend medical school or law school. Her parents would have been proud of her, because she was every American mom and dad's little dreamgirl. But Ricky was the Gordon who'd been "programmed for success." Ricky was the favorite, the family star. Ricky was her father's only boy and the true child of her mother's heart.

"I could be dying," Susan told Ricky, "dying right in front of them, and they would say, 'Well, Lorraine has problems. Lorraine needs us.'"

"Mommy," Susan blurted during one of her increasingly erratic and emotional boatyard afternoons, "why doesn't Daddy love me?"

"He does love you," Eve said.

So typical, Susan thought. Eve would never just come out and say it—"Yes, there are problems." Couldn't Sam, for that matter, simply have said, "Yes, my mother is hard to take," that day of the boat ride with Mama Yetta, the grandmother Susan still couldn't mourn?

Susan was jealous of them all: of Ricky and Lorraine and Sheila, with her rich-kid husband, her new house, and her gorgeous baby girl; of Eve, perpetual-motion Eve, who'd never had to worry financially, never had to support a child, never had to go out and fight in the world and come home to a place empty of a man.

The taste of family venom came back constantly to Susan, like the taste of Sylvia's soup in her dreams. As she lost hold of so many external attachments, the personal and the internal hypertrophied like an overexercised muscle. The personal is political, her feminist sisters in consciousness had preached, but now all of politics—all of culture and life—seemed personal. Everything was personal and nothing was overlooked. Nothing was forgotten and nothing—nothing—was forgiven.

All of it made Susan yearn to get high, higher than the last time, higher than the pain.

———◈———

Each time Eve briefly exited her normal life and traveled alone to Atlantic City, she'd return to Harbor Isle a brand-new woman. A single day of anonymous gambling made her feel rearmed and refreshed. "Gambling is my therapy," Eve explained to Sam.

"Yeah, sure," said Sam—son of a card shark and once a decent crap-shooter himself—disapprovingly.

It's better than throwing plates, Eve thought. She didn't always tell Sam when she'd been away for the day at the gaming tables, just as she didn't always mention purchasing money orders destined for one of the kids. "Truth," she said, "is not always the best policy."

Eve could name ten neighborhood women who made the long bus trip to Atlantic City at least once a week. On any given day some sixteen thousand gamblers would pass through the timeless, ringing expanse of the Resorts International Casino, which had opened in May 1978 to a first-day crowd so avid that they ignored the fire alarms that went off. A single trip could polish Eve's armor for maybe four weeks, sometimes six. The time she won three hundred dollars playing combinations of the family's various addresses back in the Bronx had restored her for two full months.

Sometimes, behind her stack of chips, Eve would pause to salute the unalloyed bliss inspired by a day at the Atlantic City casinos. It was the same otherworldly feeling she used to get at the old movie palaces before the movies stopped transporting her, before her children turned the simple process of growing up into a drama any mother made of flesh and blood would occasionally need to leave behind in hopes of being, if not reborn, then at least revitalized and ready to go on.

Not long after John Wayne died in June, the president of the United States came forward to begin a riveting if depressing exercise in public introspection that would last through November, when Iranian revolutionaries seized the American embassy in Teheran and held fifty-two hostages. Sounding more like a preacher than the distant, empirically minded manager he'd been so far, Jimmy Carter said he'd decided to speak out in order to reawaken the animating moral purpose citizens of his generation had always considered part of the national bedrock. America was suffering a "spiritual crisis, a malaise," he said. The "misery index," a Carter campaign conceit that measured human tribulation as the sum of inflation and unemployment rates, was now almost eight percentage points higher than when he took office, but through contemplation and reading he'd concluded that economic and social problems such as gas lines and unemployment were only symptoms of a far more profound moral and psychological "crisis of confidence."

"We've always had a faith that the days of our children would be better than our own. Now people are losing that faith," the president lamented. He believed the malaise had begun with the death of John Kennedy and had been intensified by the war in Vietnam, Watergate, and economic decline. Cloistered at Camp David during the summer, Carter discussed the crisis with groups of intellectuals and clergymen while his wife, Rosalynn, scribbled notes. He expressed his dismay at the number of unmarried people living in sin, and he said that his daughter, Amy, was not allowed to watch new movies because of all the four-letter words.

Carter (like Sheila) had read and been impressed by Christopher Lasch's excoriation of American society in his recent best-seller, *The Culture of Narcissism*. Lasch also pointed to the air of sadness and defeat that had lately settled over the most optimistic of all nations: "American confidence has fallen to a low ebb. Those who recently dreamed of world power now despair of governing the city of New York. Defeat in Vietnam, economic stagnation and the impending exhaustion of natural resources have produced a mood of pessimism in higher circles, which spreads through the rest of society as people lose faith in their leaders." The most prominent of those leaders took note of Lasch's argument that a decadent "logic of individualism" had led to a "war of all against all." "The pursuit of happiness" had come to a "dead end," to "a narcissistic preoccupation with the self."

During one of Carter's Camp David variations on a Harbor Isle Sunday conclave, he asked ten assembled clergymen if the American people were "ready to hear the words we have been using tonight? Are they willing to grapple with problems that go deeper than energy shortages— problems as deep as the value systems that dominate our society?" The religious leaders all said yes, but by that time the hostage crisis in Iran seemed to obviate the luxury of brooding over the state of the nation's psyche, and Americans disapproved of the job their ruminative president was doing by nearly two to one.

Jimmy Carter governed into the last days of a soft, woozy nostalgia for bygone American verities that for the most part had never existed. But the same willingness to talk of values that had helped him become president was deeply resented by the end of his term. Americans wanted the hostages back. Americans wanted a "moral" America back. Americans were plenty troubled, and they wanted somebody to tell them from on high that he would bring back the good old days and make them feel better, not worse. Carter was just as nostalgic as the next American, but he seemed ineffectual. It was all very well to mourn the "loss" of the sacred American family, for example, but few citizens believed that wishing people would get married before they shared an address was going to help.

Christopher Lasch thought that narcissism had already transformed the family and in turn had altered the underlying structure of the individual personalities families had once been trusted to shape. Various neo-Freudian psychotherapists were now identifying many of their toughest and most intractable patients as "borderline personalities." Uneasily straddling the boundary between psychological and social experience, these patients—representing by some estimates seven to ten percent of the total population—were highly manipulative and self-destructive. They seemed to love too hard and hate without limit. Borderline personalities were no less fragmented and incomprehensible than the modern society their illness reflected. They rarely got any better.

Up in his pulpit, President Carter was still ransacking the traditional vocabulary of family decline for the source of the psychic distress he perceived. "The breakdown of the American family," he warned, "has reached extremely dangerous proportions." Jimmy Carter—father of four, son of a plain-talking, irascible southern mom who joined the Peace Corps and left for India at the age of sixty-eight, brother of a Bible-thumping, faith-healing, motorcycle-riding sister and a beer-guzzling bantam of a man who was always in some kind of trouble—once surveyed his own family and observed that he was "the only sane one." His mother, Miss Lillian, admitted that on contemplating her colorful clan she sometimes said to herself, "Lillian, you should have stayed a virgin."

Another White House conference on the family was due to convene after the turn of the decade, and it already looked like conservatives who wanted the good family written into some laws and out of others would arrive in force. On the statistical front, family problems were underscored by the fact that young people between the ages of fifteen and nineteen were now killing themselves at triple the rate of twenty years earlier. While the divorce rate had leveled off, family violence and incest were on the rise.

Urie Bronfenbrenner, a prominent child psychologist, claimed that the American family was falling apart because fewer and fewer parents were doing their jobs. Parental duties were being ceded to a "peer-group culture" that often as not was the "essence of anomie." Bronfenbrenner found no more telling indication of social and emotional disintegration than the relatively low priority placed on family responsibility by Americans obsessed with little beyond themselves. Each child, he said, needs "at least one person who has an irrational involvement...someone who thinks that this kid is more important than other people's kids, someone who's in love with him and whom he loves in return."

A highly publicized study by the Carnegie Council on Children, headed by psychologist Kenneth Keniston, concluded that what was new about the American family at the end of the decade was the "intensity of the malaise, the sense of having no guidelines or supports for raising children, the feeling of not being in control as parents, and the widespread sense of personal guilt for what seems to be going awry." The Carnegie report likened the modern parent to a maestro trying to conduct an orchestra playing from different scores in a notation he couldn't read. Parents labored under a "myth of self-sufficiency" though families "are not, nor were they ever, the self-sufficient building blocks of society, exclusively responsible, praiseworthy, and blamable for their own destiny. They are deeply influenced by broad social and economic forces over which they have little control."

This was precisely Sam Gordon's point. Whenever Eve got sad or nervous or acted like she had "a guilt complex" about the family, he'd state his argument again. "People are made by the times, Eve. Just look at us—look at me, workin' with my hands, workin' like an animal all my life. You think it'd be like this for me if there hadn't been a Depression? You saw *Roots*. Look at the average colored family. Women run the families because of what happened during slave days. They sold the men off. It's history, Eve."

If kids were taught bad behavior by asshole friends, weirdo politics by pinko professors, and even weirder religion by fake gurus, of course they'd change. "Lorraine wouldn't have been rebellious unless there was rebellion in the times," Sam would tell his wife. "And Susan, well, Susan wouldn't have taken over twenty years to get used to me if it hadn't been for the war. We're not alone in all this. Look around the neighborhood. Look at everybody else's kids. You see it in every house."

"Eve, it has nothing to do with anything," Rose Brown would say over mah-jongg. "Things just happen in a family."

"Yeah," Eve would say. "Maybe."

Eve tried hard to see Sam's point, but she couldn't blame rock 'n' roll and Hitler for all the incidents she kept reliving, all the family moments that should have come out differently. Family history came back to her as a tale of who had done what to whom, who would never forgive or forget, and what she should have done that she didn't do.

Eve was as adept as the next mother at simply refusing to acknowledge certain things that she feared would topple the family altogether. Asked why Sam didn't love Susan, she'd say he did. Asked for advice, she was nothing if not practical. Susan called up one day miserable and in tears. "I want you to get up off your ass and do something. Clean up that filthy hovel I hear you're living in. Believe me, Susan, you'll feel good. Your mind will be active and you won't be so depressed." Susan called back a few hours later. "Guess what, Ma. You were right."

This, Eve would have told Dr. Urie Bronfenbrenner of Cornell University, was a mother doing her job; this was the "irrational involvement" of a mother who indeed thought her kid was more important than other people's kids, who loved that kid, but who also knew that there were certain pits from which even a day in Atlantic City could not hoist her.

Truth was, Eve didn't trust all the nostalgic, peaceful, and seemingly magical Harbor Isle Sundays of the past year or two. She couldn't buy the idea that so many formerly despotic egos had subsided into a dreamy calm. Having these fiery, self-righteous iconoclasts back at her table in the guise of self-satisfied disciples talking of their Yogavilles and Woodstocks, their Swamijis, Oscars, and Fred Astaires—this Eve could not accept. They could say that sated spiritual hunger was the source of their good cheer, but Eve knew that all her kids were emotional bounty hunters. They told their stories of the family ripped open and exposed to a wild stretch of time for the same reasons the vaudevillians of the lean years told their jokes—because the telling made it easier to go on.

Any other time, a tableful of laughing family members might have looked to Eve like an image of order and control. On TV, a popular character named Mary Hartman, a well-meaning suburban soul, administered solace from her kitchen week after week just like Eve, but in one famous episode someone drowned in one of her lovingly made soups. You would have thought a twist like that could only happen on television, but lately Eve was wondering what dark surprise those happy family gatherings might hold.

"Aaah," she'd say disingenuously when the mah-jongg girls marveled at the prodigal progeny who now came back to her every weekend, "they just like my cooking."

———

Susan and Shuna surprised everyone by arriving at the Thanksgiving feast at Sheila and Jon's new home in time to sit down with the rest of the family. Susan brought the boyfriend who'd thrown up all over Jon's boat, but Jon welcomed him in the spirit of holiday cheer. Everyone cooed over six-month-old Dani, born in May.

The table was piled high with food, and Eve was battling Sheila for a clear flight path for her swoops around the table. As she circled, serving away, conversation ceased long enough for each seated family member to urge her to sit down and eat, just as they always had, just as Eve had done with her mother and Yetta, just as had been done before her for generation upon generation.

Eve finally agreed to sit just as Susan began to announce something in a booming voice that silenced the room. But her words were so lacking in articulation that everyone kept looking at her, expecting her to rephrase whatever important point she wanted to make. Susan snapped to attention in her chair and drew in a large breath, apparently ready to clarify the strange sound she'd just made. She opened her mouth as the irises in her wide-open eyes lolled up and out of sight somewhere near the top of her skull. Then her eyelids snapped shut, her face lost all expression, and her arms fell limp at her sides. Slowly at first, like a tree after the final stroke of the ax, floating for a moment and then hurtling downward, Susan pitched nose-first smack into the center of her plate, where a pile of zucchini pancakes met some of the delicious turkey stuffing she was known to love and a mound of Eve's famous mashed potatoes.

After a few seconds Eve reached over and turned her face so she could breathe.

All eyes, for some reason, focused on Eve. "She's been very tired," Susan's mother said in all sincerity. "She's very, very tired."

The 1970s were like that for a lot of people. It was one of those decades you could start on the brink of celebrity, assured by a New York literary agent that you'd be a guest of Johnny Carson's, and finish out cold at the family table, higher than heaven with your ear in your dinner.

1980

Not long into the new decade, just past his sixty-first birthday, Sam Gordon glanced up from his work and looked around. Some Polish electrician, union man though he was, was making a pretty big stir in his stolid nation. Sam beheld endless television replays of blindfolded men in dress shirts and skewed neckties being herded along by bearded kids in blue jeans as a large crowd jeered the hostage diplomats and cheered the young Iranian revolutionaries. Sam saw that the slow-talking guy from *Death Valley Days* was running for president of the United States. The former governor of the loser state of California kept telling everyone who'd listen that America wasn't over the hill, that with a little pride and moral fortitude skeptics would see that America was still a great place to live.

When he turned from the world to the wiring job at hand, Sam occasionally noticed that the thinner filaments looked blurry, even with his glasses on. He'd always understood that his success was predicated on the effective insinuation of himself—his body, his knowing eyes, his hands—into the gap between power and light, between electron-loaded "juice" and an idle machine. For the first time in his life Sam was beginning to feel slightly less agile. He even found himself wondering now and again if he was getting old.

Meanwhile, right before his clouding eyes, the electric business was being dwarfed by the flourishing electronics business. Many of the manual adjustments Sam was paid to make were now performed by little computers that had no wires or resistors. "And switches," Sam would say, shaking his head. "You can forget switches." Until recently, Sam could recognize and repair any switch you handed him, but now circuits were inscribed on the shiny side of a shard of silicon the size of a tie tack. Semi-conductor chips currently on the market could handle a flow of electricity that not long ago would have required fifty thousand transistors. The chips were hidden in digital clocks and watches, microwave ovens, calculators that fit in your palm, stereo systems, television sets, and countless new or newly transformed appliances, and they had generated some forty thousand unfilled jobs open to anyone trained as an "electronics technologist" or "electronics technician." Sam had always considered himself a technician, but all of a sudden an electrician was like a cavalryman in a world of Sherman tanks.

"If I was only younger," he said to Eve, "I'd go back to school."

Sam found it ironic that the terrifying part about foreseeing a time when the work would dry up wasn't about money. The portfolio of Long Island Lighting Company stock Sam and Eve had been building methodically for thirty years was now worth almost $100,000, and the boatyard would bring nearly twice the $140,000 they'd paid for it. The terror wasn't even in not being able to work, for by now Sam was willing to admit that work was not, in the end, the key to freedom.

The problem was what to do if you didn't work. Sam would never forget the men in the old-folks' homes where he used to do electrical jobs. Some of them had been dying for twenty years, ever since the day they retired. Look at Eve's father. Retirement, boredom, death. Just like that. It was clear that the trick was not to confuse a structural economic transformation that made your job obsolete with the end of your purpose in life, and to refuse, with all your still considerable strength, to equate the physical fact of aging with getting old.

Ronald Reagan was seven years older than Sam, and whatever else you might say about the man, he exuded so much energy and never-say-die fortitude that you really could picture him leaping off his horse and blowing the malaise away. Carter made American sadness and power-lessness sound complicated. Reagan turned everything into a simple case of good guys and bad guys and a lot of bad rules that made it hard for the good guys to get what they deserved. Like Sam, Reagan loved Roosevelt but had grown to resent bureaucracies.

Along with fourteen percent of the male voters who supported Jimmy Carter in 1976, Sam would vote for Reagan. But he didn't actually feel comfortable with the new president—especially after the tawdry inaugural, with the reported $25,000 outfit for Nancy and the donated $200,000 china place settings the First Family would use—until the following summer, when Reagan busted the air traffic controllers' union but good. "Some junior PATCO guy pulling down fifty grand says he's got stress!" Sam raged during the strike. "So he should get a job hauling garbage if he wants to avoid stress." The teachers were suddenly suffering from stress. Everybody was now a victim of the "burn-out" syndrome. Sam and Reagan didn't buy it. It was just a bunch of 1980s-style featherbedding. On this they clearly agreed.

Ronald Reagan called them as he saw them. He tried to be the man he really was, Sam thought. Reagan probably would have worn the same blank and helpless expression as Sam if one of his kids sat down during a lunch break and told him that a ghost had recently joined him in his dreams.

Ricky was doing some part-time work for Sam, painting and helping lay electrical lines. By now, the idea of spending a day with his father caused Ricky much less anxiety than in the past. Besides, painting was one of the few tasks father and son agreed Ricky could do.

"You remember Mitchell Ajï, Dad?" he asked one day. "We called him Peanuts. Remember? He was famous for putting cream cheese and ketchup on his macaroni."

Sam said he did remember Peanuts.

Ricky said his boyhood friend had been much on his mind of late, ever since he heard Peanuts had been killed in a car crash on the first night of Passover. Peanuts always came in first or third in the cruel popularity contests conducted by the fifth-grade teacher who liked to pull on boys' sideburns when they misbehaved. Ricky invariably came in second, fifth grade being a golden year. Ricky couldn't stop thinking about Peanuts's face and how it looked when he giggled or felt embarrassed or cried or momentarily hated his pretty mom. Peanuts had terrible handwriting, mumbled like a drunk, and copied more than a few school reports out of the *World Book* encyclopedia during his early academic career. Ricky could see him in a slow-motion replay of perfect clarity ladling all that cream cheese and ketchup over his macaroni.

"Last night I had a dream about him," Ricky told Sam. "I was at his house having lunch, and nobody at the table—including Peanuts—mentioned that he was dead. I was suddenly overwhelmed by it all, by what a kind friend he was and how sad real life could be. I excused myself and started crying in the other room. Peanuts's mother was silent through the whole dream. She just stared at me.

"In the next scene," Ricky continued with all the intense introspection of the Truffaut characters he revered, "Peanuts and I were riding our bikes down the street. I told him how sad I was when he died, and he told me he knew. We went into a store, and Peanuts told me to cause a ruckus because he was invisible since he was a ghost."

All Sam could do was stare. Not a single word came into his head.

Sometimes when Sam watched Ricky work, he was sure that his son's mind had lofted off and away, and he would think about how much Ricky reminded him of his own father, a poetic dreamer who couldn't fix anything with his hands and wrote with an artist's rounded script. Sam couldn't help but notice that Ricky's hair was thinning. When Sam was little, he used to stare at the back of his father's bare skull and wonder how much time his own hair had left. Now he wondered the same thing on behalf of his son, who was only twenty-four. It made him feel guilty that of all the traits they might have had in common, this strong-backed, likable, strange-talking boy he loved had inherited his own lack of hair. "You can drive the devil out of your garden," somebody once said, "but you will find him again in the garden of your son."

If Ricky, because of what Sam imagined to be a lonely life, needed to tell his father about specters that visited him in dreams, that was fine. But for all his strong feelings about his boy, he could not be expected to know what to say. A man can't be expected to be something other than who he is.

Not long after Ricky started seeing a psychotherapist, Eve was sitting across from her son in the Schrafft's on Forty-second Street when he suddenly burst into woeful sobs that turned heads in all corners of the restaurant. Eve hadn't seen Ricky cry in years, and she doubted she'd ever seen him look so grief-stricken. She immediately blamed the new headshrinker, who scared her more than the gurus. When Eve thought back on Lorraine's experience of therapy, it was hard to dispute Sam's contention that mother hatred was the primary product of the psychological trades. If there was one thing she couldn't abide, it was the idea of being hated again by one of her children.

The incident at Schrafft's occurred not twenty minutes after Eve and Ricky had seen *Ordinary People,* a much discussed movie featuring a less than happy family that lived in a big white house in a big white suburb. The family had lost one son to a boating accident and had almost lost the other, a survivor of the same accident, who was so guilt-ridden and felt so rejected by his mother that he'd attempted suicide. Donald Sutherland played the essentially good if utterly befuddled father, and the perfect ice sculpture of a controlling mom was played by Mary Tyler

Moore, who after years of dominating several laugh-a-minute TV sit-coms had recently turned up on screen and stage as a cancer victim and a quadriplegic. In *Ordinary People*, Moore portrayed a woman so tightly guarded that it looked as if her face might shatter at any moment like a hurled plate.

Though Ricky had seen his share of family situation tragedies—last year's *Kramer vs. Kramer* and Bergman's less recent but far darker and more exhausting *Scenes from a Marriage* among them—something about *Ordinary People*, which would be declared Best Picture at the next Academy Awards ceremony, set him on edge. But it was not the movie alone that made him cry so hard he silenced a busy restaurant.

After they'd ordered coffee, Ricky told Eve that he'd finally finished setting a Sylvia Plath poem for a young singer at Juilliard. The poem ended with the lines "Daddy, you can lie back now / There's a stake in your fat, black heart. / And the villagers never liked you. / They're danc-ing and stomping on you / Daddy, Daddy, you bastard, I'm through." Admittedly, it was not a buoyant lyric, and Ricky had written an extremely difficult piece of music ending on a high D natural, far beyond the range of most singers. He'd sent the carefully wrought piece to the Juilliard student weeks ago and had yet to hear a thing. He said he was tired of coaching singers and supplementing his art with menial labor only to have his real work ignored.

"Just remember," Eve said, "even if you haul shit, that doesn't make you any less worthy as an artist." Then, after a pause, she added, "You know, Daddy was just saying that he understands why you need therapy. He knows your life is…hard."

That was when Ricky burst into tears. After several minutes he was still weeping, unable to catch his breath. He could see that he was scar-ing his mother, which of course scared him too. Ricky hadn't cried in ages, but now he was bawling like a little boy at the thought of Sam tak-ing note of his feelings.

Eve just sat there, unable to speak. It took her several minutes to ask Ricky what was wrong, because in many ways she thought it was unfair that she always had to know. The thing that was so different about these times, she believed, was that everything was noticed. Nothing was just allowed to pass. And nothing was enough. This was true in a lot of fami-lies, but especially, it seemed, for her kids, and especially when it came to aspects of love and their constant search for so many elusive answers.

The more Eve thought about it, the more she felt like her heart was bursting into flames.

* * *

The following Saturday morning the fire in her heart was so intense that Eve decided she was dying. Two of her mah-jongg partners spotted her striding hard down the sidewalk, clutching her chest. Eve had finally agreed to drive a little Chevette Sam bought her, but only to Sheila's or Lorraine's, and only to see her grandchildren. The hospital was not on her motoring itinerary.

Eve's face was bloodless from the intensity of the pain when her friends stopped her. "It's just this burning in my heart," she explained.

"Whaddaya crazy?" said Lorraine Miller. "You could be having a heart attack. Get in the car."

"To tell you the truth, Lorraine," Eve said, resuming her short, fast strides, "if I'm going to die, I'd rather it happen out in the air."

The girls called her a moron as they hustled her into the car and over to the emergency room. It was a peptic ulcer. Now Eve had family troubles and an ulcer too.

Twenty years earlier these sizzling intestinal sores were suffered almost exclusively by men. For every American woman who had an ulcerous erosion back then, there were twenty men. Now women owned a third of the nation's twenty million acid-soured bellies, often treated with a four-year-old wonder drug called cimetidine that was visible on desktops everywhere under the brand name Tagamet.

As a matter of course, doctors now told their ulcer patients that one of the best things they could do was to get to the bottom of the career or family conflicts that might be contributing to their condition. Since the 1930s, when Chicago psychoanalyst Franz Alexander first argued that at least seven maladies—ulcers among them—were caused by emotional conflict, researchers and practitioners propounding the psychosomatic origin of illnesses had been variously invited in and out of the medical mainstream. In 1980, the psychosomatic school was decidedly in. Brain chemistry studies and investigations of meditation and biofeedback abounded. A group of New York researchers had just reported that people mourning a deceased spouse experienced marked changes in the chemistry of their lymph cells, as if their bodies had decided to lower their immunity to a quick reunification with the departed.

The wealth of new medical research into the psychogenic origins of disease was matched by the profitable marketing of diets and books that promised to make you "Fit for Life," or even better, guaranteed "Life Extension." One popular culinary text was called *The Never Say Die Cookbook.* Adjust your lifestyle, calm your mind, and better living would be yours. A placebo in every pot.

* * *

If quieting her churning mind would indeed translate into a settled stomach, if a span of serenity was what the doctor ordered, then Eve was all for it, but somebody would have to talk to her beloved children. The sight of a weeping son in a Schrafft's did not make a mother calm.

Eve's recent rendezvous with Susan at Macy's was another case in point. They'd taken their usual break for coffee, and Susan, less robust and more of a nag by the day, started in again with her spiel. "Why can't Daddy love me?"

"He loves you, already," Eve said.

He loved her. He did. What he didn't do, Eve thought—though she would never say so to her long-suffering daughter—was compliment her. Maybe he should have said nicer things, but in the end, Eve wondered, who ever really got praise she could believe?

"Why don't you order me some coffee," Susan said. "I'll be right back."

Eve waited and ate. She liked the Macy's coffee shop because of the tiny cakes they served, interesting and French. After a few more petits fours, ulcer be damned, she ordered coffee. Glancing at her watch and her train schedule, she remembered all the things she'd promised to help Sheila and Lorraine with this week, thinking that these dates with Susan were more painful all the time.

Eve waited and waited. Once again, Susan never returned from the bathroom.

Somebody was also going to have to speak to Lorraine if Eve was ever to achieve any peace.

Lorraine had broken out in terrible welts all over her neck and stomach and had stopped eating altogether when it became clear that reconciliation with Harry was a lost cause. Swami Satchidananda, who was as critical of marital separation as Jimmy Carter, went so far as to claim that only the children born of a marriage should be allowed to sanction its dissolution, his theory being that once they were old enough to render such a judgment, they would also be able to absorb the shock of divorce to less damaging effect.

Harry and Lorraine had made feeble attempts to reconcile, but by now Harry had reeled away from Lorraine, from the Gordon family, from Maggie, even from four-year-old Gabe. He'd signed over his share in the house and left Lorraine the car, only asking for a few records. But the split still got nasty soon after the lawyers were called in. One day Harry and Lorraine came to blows in a parking lot minutes after a child-support hearing in which Lorraine said she'd had to apply for public assistance.

Soon thereafter, "in a daze," as she later described her state, Lorraine went out on a date with a gentle young public school teacher. In part to settle the psychic and sexual score with Harry, the date turned into a one-night stand that left Lorraine pregnant. The young man, who said he'd fallen in love with her, suggested an abortion. Lorraine drove five hours to see her guru, who was still in Pomfret at the time. When she finally arrived, she told Satchidananda's secretary that she was pregnant and unable to decide what to do. The vision of a guiding intelligence sending souls to earth as children according to a cosmic plan placed a considerable onus on a woman who didn't want to be pregnant.

"He won't see you," the secretary said when she returned. "He says you know what to do."

At subsequent *satsangs* (the free-form lectures and question-and-answer sessions the guru conducted in Pomfret and New York City), Lorraine thought Satchidananda was avoiding her plaintive gaze. When he moved into the crowd, he'd bow to speak softly to others, hug them with the hug she craved, and offer them bits of food, but he wouldn't even look at Lorraine. "What should I do? What does he want of me?" she'd plead to members of his inner circle.

"Gurudev says you already know."

Eve tried hard to understand Lorraine's decision to become a mother again. Lorraine felt that she, and much more so Harry, had betrayed the guru and his teachings already. Satchidananda believed a little spirit was bubbling up toward life within Lorraine, or so she surmised from his Delphic response to her. The father-to-be was now out of the picture, which for Eve made the new pregnancy a madness, but she contained herself out of fear of severing what she considered the last thin tendril still connecting her to Lorraine. Sometimes Eve thought Lorraine was just going to float away.

As the pregnancy progressed, Eve met some colorful new characters. One of Lorraine's soft-spoken yoga friends had a son no more than twelve, with dark hair down to the backs of his thighs. Eve instinctively tried to give the boy a hug when they met, but he jumped away. "I am not allowed to touch women," he said. Not touching at appropriate times was a big part of Lorraine's problem, Eve thought. A husband needed a lot of touching.

Eve had named her children for Hollywood goddesses. In June, Lorraine named her third child after a Hindu god. That Shiva (literally, "auspiciousness" or "destroyer of illusion") Jeremy Hughes would not be circumcised, another tradition of "thousands and thousands of years" broken by a member of the original house of Sam, made Eve's ulcer burn. But it was the name that nearly killed her. "Magdalena Shapiro" might have had something of a cross-ethnic gaudiness, and God knew "Shuna" wasn't in the books of baby names, but at least it didn't mean anything. Shiva. It was like naming a kid Jesus, "for Christ's sake." This name was the stuff of gastric earthquakes.

With his careful beard and serious glasses, Richard Trachtman looked like the young Freud, Ricky thought. Trachtman was a practitioner of "ego psychology," one of the many Freudian offshoots. He believed that a clinical focus on the structure of internal psychological systems developed in response to the process of growing up would help his patients adjust to a world much less amenable than they were to treatment or change.

Since Ricky was determined to open wide a psychotherapeutic "window into the secret places of the soul," he lost no time bringing his therapist up to speed. He told Richard right away that lately he'd been consuming huge meals and then either throwing up on purpose or jogging for miles in hopes of burning the food away.

Shortly after Halloween, Ricky took a break from cleaning Susan's apartment and ate all the candy Shuna had collected from trick-or-treating. "At least twelve pounds of it!" Ricky cried to Richard Trachtman during an emergency therapy session a few hours after the binge. Like "up to twenty percent of women on college campuses," according to one Chicago specialist in eating disorders, Ricky had become a bulimic.

Ricky told Richard he'd grown up believing his two older sisters had drained away the best of his parents "like vampires." He thought of his mother as a "skittery pigeon" who required so much love and approval that he now wondered if he'd tried to provide it at the expense of his own masculinity. Eve was married to Sam, Ricky said, and her name used to be Samberg—"which has to mean something." He reported that whenever he talked to his parents he ended up feeling angry, sad, or guilty. He'd taken an LSD trip once that scared him badly, and when he felt the fear of it come back to him he wanted to die. More often than not, he had been the target of the cruelest children in his suburban hometown.

As the emotional chiaroscuro of his childhood came back to him, Ricky realized how weary he was of playing the feminized jester in a court full of warriors, of turning real family pain into pratfalls and shtick.

From the moment the window of therapy opened onto what Sigmund Freud called the "royal road to the unconscious," which he said was traversable through dreams, Ricky began keeping a journal. Twice a week he wrote about dreams peopled by black men. A black man framed by a bright blue light was tortured to death in front of a crowd. A black man ripped apart by a macabre device. A black man in the middle of a desert was burned alive as he desperately tried to get out of a locked car.

Ricky dreamed he went home to the house on Lincoln Avenue but somebody he didn't know was there. He dreamed that Eve had a new baby but when he went to hold it Sam yelled at him for storming into the room so brusquely, exactly as Sam used to storm in to rouse him in the mornings. He dreamed that Eve's heart was pounding so hard she realized she was dying. She grabbed Ricky and held him tight, begging him never to leave her. They cried together (he was amazed at how easily he cried in his dreams), and she asked him to play something soothing on the piano. He was playing the piano in another dream when he suddenly found himself struggling to swim upstream against a swift river current. His father and his uncle Freddy approached, and though Sam looked down at him like he was an idiot, he saved Ricky anyway.

Then there was the night Ricky dreamed that he and Sam were having a drink together in a gay bar.

"You never *wanted* me to be at home with you," his father said. "That's why I stayed away all those years."

"But when I was little, I was so…uncomfortable around you, Daddy."

"Still," said Sam. "It hurt me. It made me jealous."

Ricky read Sam a poem he'd written, and Sam gave him a nudge, the kind an old buddy dispenses to a barroom sidekick on the next stool. From that point on, Ricky knew in his dream that he and Sam had a world of things in common.

Such dreams! Ricky felt his unconscious bursting with tales. He remembered the background noise, the music, the dreamworld decors. He couldn't resist telling Eve the one in which she called a kind of family meeting. Ricky, Susan, and Sheila were present. "I want to know if all of you are independent and secure," she said, "because I'm leaving your father." Ricky turned to watch a television newscast about a millionairess, a mother of four who'd been arrested for killing her husband and the kids. He moved closer to the screen to get a good look as the woman was taken away. It was Eve.

Ricky heard through the sister grapevine that Sam and Eve had a big fight the night she relayed this dream to his father, but that didn't stop him from telling Sam about Mitchell "Peanuts" Adgi, who'd crossed the line and joined him in a vivid dream. Ricky told Sam about Peanuts because therapy was teaching him how liberating such revelations could be. But when he finished describing Peanuts's visit and looked at his father's face, he instantly knew he was going to have to mourn his childhood under professional auspices or alone.

One night Ricky dreamed he staged a production of *Catcher in the Rye*. He'd just finished reading Salinger's book, having come to it much later than most boys his age. He told Richard Trachtman that while he related profoundly to Holden Caulfield's isolation and loneliness, it was the book's title, coming back to him over and over again like a refrain, that really blew him away. "Catcher in the rye"—Holden's choice of metaphor for himself moved Ricky and made him wonder if his own problem was that he was still like a little child, like "all these little kids" Holden wanted to protect from harm "in this big field of rye."

❧

Mark David Chapman read *Catcher in the Rye* when he was eighteen, and the experience changed his life. Over the next few years he began to believe he was a real-life Holden, a secret-agent Holden wandering a phony world with a gun. By the fall of 1980, Chapman was an overweight twenty-five-year-old, married and employed as a security guard in Hawaii. An ex-druggie and a "pathological narcissist," as the doctors would later conclude, he'd had a personal visit from Jesus Christ and had come to see the world as a Manichean war zone. His brain was a listening post so sophisticated it could hone in on the radio frequencies used by God and the Devil.

In October, the self-described "Holden Caulfield of his generation" reportedly read an article in *Esquire* about former Beatle John Lennon. Once the "conscience of his generation," Lennon had changed into a man of property, the article implied, a hip steward of the bottom line. By the end of the first week of December, Chapman was in New York, walking through Central Park like Holden in the book, summoning a prostitute to his room like Holden, just for a chat.

Abandoned by his own parents, a son of poverty and deprivation, John Lennon had withdrawn into a cocoon of family in recent years. He baked bread, took care of the children, and wrote songs about sadness and love while his wife, Yoko Ono, did most of the wheeling and dealing described in the article his assassin read. Like other residents of his

West Side neighborhood, Ricky would often see the brilliant ex-Beatle strolling along Columbus Avenue, holding his son's hand and looking in windows. Locals tended to pass him by without stopping. Ricky thought he lived in a wonderful part of town because John Lennon could take a walk without being harassed.

On December 8 Ricky attended a workshop sponsored by ASCAP. Charles Strouse, the composer of *Annie*, was on the workshop panel, as was Estelle Parsons, who railed emotionally throughout the session. He'd just come home when the phone rang. It was Tom Piechowsky, who'd recently moved to a new apartment across from Roosevelt Hospital. Tom said he'd just watched some cops carry John Lennon into the emergency room.

Susan cried hard when she heard, and she cried again when she realized she was just too squirrelly and strung out to go to the memorial in Central Park.

The killing made Sheila, the Gordon family's chief Beatles fan, ponder the sense of hopelessness that had marked pivotal public events for so much of her life. John had never been her favorite Beatle, but for days after the murder she hovered near the radio, traveling sadly back to various nearly forgotten moments with each song that was played in his memory.

A member of the swami's flock asked him to say something about John Lennon the night after the shooting. Satchidananda assured Lorraine and the others that Lennon's obvious desire to give something of himself to the world, his wish to see the world at peace, would remain a powerful force, albeit one emanating from another address in the cosmos.

The public impact of the killing of John Lennon has occasionally been likened to the national outpouring in the wake of John Kennedy's assassination. But the mass experience of intense emotional concentration that occurred the day Kennedy was shot—when the memories of so many millions were branded forever with the color of the rug they were standing on or the words their teacher had just uttered—engendered a much more stunning and wounding sadness. Kennedy was supposed to lead the way into the best of all new eras. Nothing like this had happened in recent memory. The context was missing.

By 1980, John Lennon had come to be seen as a well-meaning, emotional, occasionally screwed-up man who still represented the hopefulness of the raucous years when he'd made his name but who was now trying to handle family life and maintain a bit of integrity in a much different time. In one of the last photographs taken of Lennon, he is curled up next to Yoko, naked, fetal, and needy—an innocent. His death was met with a sadness less acute and horrified than the grief over JFK, a powerful but diffuse sense that nothing worked out as planned. A kid who'd misread a book had killed a man who was still trying to grow up.

By the end of 1980, Sam Gordon wasn't the only American who felt older.

1981

Lorraine sent Eve a letter from Charlottesville, Virginia, the lovely old university town she now called her temporary home. She reported that Maggie, Ram, and Shiva were all well, and that Maggie had just appeared in a high school production of *The Me Nobody Knows* (clipping enclosed). Lorraine's job in the records department of a local hospital was keeping her kids in food and the car in enough gas for the regular hour's drive through the Blue Ridge Mountains to Yogaville.

"I'm aware that you and everyone else in the family think I've gotten weird," Lorraine wrote. "But I must continue to explore. I must continue to look for my real Self."

As far as Lorraine could tell, all questing traditions pointed out and away from the family core. Lonely as she often felt after her recent relocation, she remembered that Swamiji had wandered far from home, like Buddha and Mohammed and so many other spiritual seekers. Abraham heard the voice of God say, "Go from your country and your kindred and your father's house to the land that I will show you."

Many Integral Yoga followers had by now moved south to be close to the long-promised Satchidananda Ashram. Often they settled first in Charlottesville or Richmond, because the rural isolation of Yogaville offered few employment opportunities. But everyone came out on weekends to pitch in, raising barns and watching bulldozers mark out the future position of ashram buildings, just as dozens of Bronx and Brooklyn families had once watched similar machines break ground for another kind of retreat called Harbor Isle.

A few months earlier the guru had stood on a rise above the James River and smashed a coconut representing the hard shell of human ego on the bucket of an earthmover. "*Satguru Maharaj Ki!*" he yelled. Victory to the Divine! Then Satchidananda gathered up his robes, climbed into the driver's seat, and expertly began to dig a man-made lake that would eventually reflect his LOTUS shrine.

Maggie liked seeing her mother come home with a smile on her face after a day's work at the hospital, but that was about the extent of her appreciation for Virginia. She'd never wanted to make the pilgrimage. At sixteen, Maggie considered herself a New Yorker and imagined that life in Charlottesville was like being knocked unconscious. She told Ricky and Shuna that she was afraid Virginia would suck the spirit out of her until she spoke as slowly as a southerner or a yogi. All she wanted was to graduate from Long Beach High and go directly to Manhattan. "I've eaten your brown rice too long. I've been through too many diets and too many cures, Mom. Besides, you only want me to come along to baby-sit!"

In part through Eve's intervention, Maggie was allowed to move in with her father and his wife in New York City until she finished high school. But it soon became clear that Bobby Shapiro was in the throes of his own family troubles, so during her senior year Maggie joined her mother and brothers in an apartment in Charlottesville that got so hot on sunny days you could bake bread on the floor, according to Sam.

Maggie largely confined her feelings to her poetry, a body of work that reflected her immersion in Anne Sexton and Sylvia Plath, whose books Ricky had been feeding his quietly angry niece for several years. Lorraine noted as much herself when she discovered one of Maggie's journals, but she believed the instability that had characterized her daughter's life would finally end when Yogaville was ready. Families with a great deal in common would settle together there in peace. Yogaville would be a perfect home. Children would be protected in Yogaville, nurtured like the delicate "young plants" the guru always said they were. Yogaville would be pure. No one would ever smoke cigarettes or drink or take drugs or act or even speak in an immoral way. "Yogaville," Lorraine wrote Eve, would be "a little piece of heaven."

Not thirty miles from where the bulldozers were carving out Yogaville, a man named Jerry Falwell worried regularly and publicly that a "vast outbreak of moral perversion" was plunging the Republic and the God-consecrated American family into a moral abyss. Millions now watched the rotund, colorfully vested Reverend Falwell take to a television pulpit in a studio in Lynchburg, Virginia, a small city in the Blue Ridge foothills.

It was in Lynchburg that Falwell—a forty-eight-year-old, teetotaling, "confessed workaholic" father of three—had begun preaching a fundamentalist strain of Christianity based on a strictly literal reading of the Holy Scriptures (according to which the Flood of Noah's time was what killed the dinosaurs). He also wove into each of his popular sermons a far more secular and politicized gospel of the good and decent life, constantly reiterating that America's Founding Fathers would not be pleased with the moral condition of the nation. At one time the congregation that heard Falwell's jeremiads was so small that his Thomas Road Baptist Church fit into a corner of an old warehouse owned by Lynchburg's Donald Duck Bottling Company. But from the day he began the *Old-Time Gospel Hour* and became a television star, Jerry Falwell had been showing up in newspaper photographs, lately in the company of the former movie star who was now president of the United States.

Swami Satchidananda's travels would soon require a Yogaville airstrip and a twin-engine plane. Jerry Falwell's flock had become so indistinguishable from a powerful grass-roots movement that the shepherd kept an Israeli-built corporate jet waiting for him down at the Lynchburg airport when he was in town. Whereas his robed and bearded neighbor in Yogaville believed people would see the moral path only when they were "ready" (no grinning acolytes promoted Integral Yoga in airports), Falwell was convinced they needed a great deal of help if the nation was to be saved. He claimed that the only salvation from the demonic hedonism of American society lay in being "born again" through the miracle of later-life baptism by the Holy Spirit.

But Falwell and many other less famous evangelical clergymen also preached that reborn Christians had moral obligations extending far beyond the bounds of church and self. They must participate, he said, in a latter-day crusade, a moral incursion deep into the secular realms of culture and politics, all in the name of God and the Founding Fathers, and as Falwell never tired of repeating, in the name of saving "God's first institution," the American family.

"The sanctity of traditional family values" was under attack, Falwell claimed, because Americans who were not "pro-family" sanctioned abortion, homosexuality, feminism, materialism, drugs, liquor, sex education, pornography, and "anti-family" magazines, books, and television shows. *Knots Landing*, a comparatively benign prime-time soap opera, so offended Reverend Falwell that he personally took up a picket sign until advertisers like Procter & Gamble backed away from the program in a panic reminiscent of the blacklist and its effect on the American entertainment industry in the 1950s.

Falwell's Moral Majority, Inc., a political organization founded in 1979, promoted prayer in the public schools, censorship of textbooks, and various other policy changes that would foster the revival of the "traditional family"—by which the leaders of the "New Religious Right" seemed to mean the seventeen percent of households the 1980 census indicated were comprised of a wage-earning father, an at-home mother, and one or more kids. Conservative fundamentalists worked hard to close what they called a "loophole" in the census forms, demanding that the word "heterosexual" be inserted before the word "marriage." They lobbied to bar from the 1980 White House Conference on the Family any delegate not dedicated to stopping the "assault" on the family. "Anti-family" senators with well-known names—Church, McGovern, Bayh, Nelson, Culver, and Magnuson (Falwell would later claim a hand in "throwing out" twelve U.S. senators)—were all removed from public life after a pre-election onslaught that gave them poor "moral report cards." In the early summer of 1981 the Family Protection Act was introduced in the Senate by Roger Jepsen of Idaho. The proposed legislation changed the legal definition of child abuse to allow corporal punishment, barred the Supreme Court from hearing cases involving prayer in public buildings, and contained nearly forty other provisions meant to "strengthen the American family and to remove those Federal government policies which inhibit its strength and prosperity," in the language of the bill.

Jerry Falwell called the election of Ronald Reagan "the best thing to happen in America in twenty years," and though the "Reagan Revolution" was just getting under way, the damaged American family was a powerful justification for radical change. "Work and family," Reagan proclaimed upon accepting his party's nomination in 1980, "are at the center of our lives, the foundation of our dignity as a free people."

The "pro-family" president, beside whom Jerry Falwell took up the honorary moral post held for so long by Billy Graham, was the first president to have been divorced. Ronald Reagan, son of an occasionally employable drinking man, had some guitar-strumming, ballet-dancing children who would not describe their own childhoods in any of the terms he or Jerry Falwell used to extol the American family. The First Lady, Nancy Reagan, whom the president called "Mommy," had been abandoned by her own father. Her maternal style would later be criticized in public by her unhappy daughter.

Reagan, whose television delivery (and work schedule) recalled the paternal sages who presided over exemplary "Golden Age" television families like the Nelsons and the Andersons, welcomed his role as secular spokesman for the family cause of Jerry Falwell and his followers. He said the families of America needed to keep more of the money they were currently sacrificing to taxes. He said the children of America needed better protection. When he claimed that America needed a new nuclear missile, the MX, even that was for the children. He called the missile "the Peacemaker"—which retired admiral Eugene Carroll noted was "like calling a guillotine a headache remedy"—and said it was vital because "our children should not grow up frightened."

Not since the height of the antiwar movement had Americans joined together so powerfully to demand change. The evangelical pro-family forces had no centralized religious hierarchy, yet their national focus seemed political and programmatic. But if you took a look at the largely provincial grass roots of the Christian fundamentalist renewal of the early 1980s—if you turned off Route 60, the road that runs out of Lynchburg toward Yogaville, and drove along a bit of narrow blacktop until you found one of the thousands of little churches full of Americans who'd been born again—what you saw and heard were people scared to death by what had happened to their families. Jerry Falwell often pointed to research conducted by pollster Daniel Yankelovich indicating that some sixty-seven million Americans were hoping, however secretly, that his crusade would be victorious, because they believed his vision of America would be "better for the children."

If you sat in church or turned on one of the several dozen evangelical TV shows featuring average citizens explaining how bad luck and trouble had finally made them ready to be reborn, you would actually hear very little about what the Founding Fathers intended. Instead, these people told harrowing stories of their descent to gambling and drugs and drink and violence and betrayal, almost always at the expense of their families. Failures as children, parents, husbands, and wives, sinners one and all, they had at last decided to be "saved" from the fires of hell and the searing fires of earthly guilt over being part of a family that had not worked.

Pounding on his Bible just as hard as Satchidandana had pounded his coconut on the earthmover, Reverend Falwell warned that these days of 1981 were among "the last of the last days." Hedonism was rampant. Everyone was out for himself. Moral decline was "greater now than ever before in the history of the nation." Every Christian was called upon to "swim against the tide, to walk against the wind, to move upstream." The amens were fervently said and the voting machine levers duly turned, and for the six years these televangelists and politicized preachers would remain in the national spotlight, the checks were surely written. But all along, this counterculture of reborn Christians had been powered by an emotional contagion affecting millions of Americans who'd known more family pain than their consciences could bear. Being reborn into the new Christianity of the moment meant that family chaos could be blamed on external cultural forces and that guilt could be assuaged by sharing it with others and surrendering to a higher power.

In any dusty church parking lot around Yogaville or Lynchburg, you could always find a pickup truck displaying one of the year's most popular bumper stickers: "Christians Aren't Perfect, Just Forgiven."

———❖———

One Sunday Ricky's friend Daniel, who worked for fashion designer Perry Ellis, invited him to an opulent brunch in a converted loft near Penn Station. Beautifully clothed young men with faces and physiques made ageless by constant care chatted above a hollow Plexiglas coffee table that housed a tropical turtle in an appropriate little turtle habitat. On top of the table there were piles of cocaine and delicate hors d'oeuvres carefully dyed by an assiduous caterer to match the thematic colors of the loft, which was done up in stark pinks, lavenders, and cheery yellows over a decor that was actually super hi-tech, with industrial carpeting and shades of gray. (The renascent belle époque preference for chintz and subtler shades had only just begun to take hold over on the East Side.)

Ricky, who was wearing his luminous new Perry Ellis shirt with French cuffs, looked at walls that blazed with modern art. He gazed around a room filled exclusively with successful gay men who held lucrative jobs like Daniel's and represented an "attractive segment of the consumer population," according to recent marketing studies of the habits of "white, single, well-educated, well-paid men who happen to be homosexual." The Advocate, a New York gay newspaper, reported that the gay consumer, blessed with "high earning power and low financial obligations," probably drank a lot of diet soda and owned cowboy boots, a pair of Bass Weejuns, and Levi 501 straight-leg blue jeans. Almost half of gay Manhattan men surveyed by the Advocate had expensive videocassette recording machines, and a fifth said they planned to buy one of the new personal computers now on the market.

All along the streets of the West Side, Ricky saw old brownstones that were being renovated by gay men—often couples—for whom money didn't seem to be an issue. The economy had fallen into a recessionary trough deep enough to bring business bankruptcies to levels not seen since the Depression. What economists called "real wages" had been falling since 1973, and they would continue to fall more quickly over the coming decade. But by the end of 1981 the gay gentry of New York City appeared to be at an economic apogee comparable to the peak reached by American capitalism as a whole twenty years earlier.

The scene at this elegant brunch was entirely different from the tea dance Ricky, Peter, and Arthur had attended at the Firehouse nearly a decade ago. These fashionable men had broken out of all that early politicized posturing. They'd transcended the mainstream and become immune to economic downturns. They were an elite. There was talk among them of friends of friends who'd lunched with Nancy Reagan. If there was anything left of the old phase of hard-won liberation in circles like Daniel's, it was the open, tenacious, and occasionally daring display of sexuality.

Daniel was a sophisticated and strikingly handsome blue-eyed blond. Ricky had been strongly attracted to him and to many of his friends for some time, but—"as usual"—nothing had happened between them.

"Listen, Rick," Daniel said after the brunch, "I'm not feeling so well. Would you mind if we stop in at my apartment for a minute?" On the way Daniel turned to Ricky and said, "You know, I really admire you. When I saw you perform the other night, all I could think about was how lucky you are to really know what you're supposed to do in life. I've never once known what I'm really supposed to do."

Ricky didn't say that in fact he coveted Daniel's looks, his job, his clothes, and most of all, the ease with which he attracted men.

When they got to the apartment, Daniel immediately disappeared into the bathroom. When he came back out, Ricky was assailed by a powerful and terrible odor. Over the next few weeks, Daniel began to beg out of plans with Ricky. He said his back hurt. He mentioned that his mother was upset because every time she called he was taking a nap. Daniel finally went to a doctor, who diagnosed the back pain as the result of an extremely serious case of pneumonia.

"I have to get a new therapist," Daniel said one day.

Ricky asked why.

"Because I need somebody equipped to deal with the fact that I'm dying."

"Oh, *please*," Ricky said. "Daniel, you're so dramatic."

"No, I'm sure I'm not going to get better," Daniel said.

And he didn't, nor did dozens of other successful, popular gay men Ricky envied and desired. By the end of the year, the strange affliction that had descended on Daniel was being called "the gay cancer."

1982

Susan's junkie courage was the envy of her friends. "Sue," her copping friend Laurie would often say, "I wanna hold your hand when the end of the world finally comes. Somehow you'll know just what to do."

Three in the morning on the killing streets of Spanish Harlem or the streets of the Lower East Side, and there she would be, the daughter of parents proud of their ascent out of both neighborhoods, now favorite dope-dealing haunts, a Vassar girl from the suburbs without a bit of makeup on, foraging for her fix with the best of them, exchanging those philosophical junkie apothegms on the lightless landings of abandoned tenements, huddled up in the cold like dogfaces in muddy foxholes, speaking lines suffused with the black humor of those who are ready to die.

"This habit o' mine, it *never* takes a rest," somebody would always say.

"No snow days for the junkies." This was Susan's own and one of her favorites, a certain atavistic pride of authorship glimmering briefly through the craven armor of irony known on the streets as junkie pride.

Though she was now a full-fledged addict, Susan still stood apart from most of her street comrades and new business associates in that she didn't shoot up. She knew stone junkies whose circulatory systems were so inaccessible through their desiccated arms and legs that they plunged needles into their penises and the corners of their eyes. All Susan did was sniff her heroin. And sniff. This simple act now required her to spend many hours on the late-night streets, dressed in her leather jacket, navigating territory alive with scuttling rats. Ever the cunning junkie, Susan discovered that all you had to do was tell yourself that you were a rat too. Then the real ones couldn't scare you anymore.

Susan was writing her autobiography. David Rieff, an editor at Far-
rar, Straus and Giroux, had extended Susan a small advance for a book.
Rieff explained to his colleagues at an editorial meeting that the fragile
but talented writer would describe San Francisco and Berkeley during
their countercultural Golden Age. But when Susan was sufficiently high
to write at all, the elusive beginning of her tale kept receding into history. Her mind would wind back to the most ancient and heroic family
sufferings. She struggled to reconstruct the childhoods of Yetta and
Rebecca, grandmothers who had been uprooted from a rich and embracing culture and had spent the rest of their days looking for the vanished
way of life they had been meant for. Too often Susan would feel the
weight of the imagined past forcing her head down onto her Selectric.
All she could do then was cry.

A lighter strain of Susan's prose appeared on occasion in the *Village
Voice*, where an old and loyal Vassar friend named Mary Peacock
worked as an editor. Susan contributed to Mary's "Getting and Spending" section of the weekly paper. Since she spent more hours on the
streets now than most full-time paupers, she was never far from a store.
She still couldn't pass an interesting-looking shop without going in.
"Harriet Royce's cashmere and nylon blends, $13 to $17, are sybaritic
favorites, and her cotton lisle anklets ($3.75) and knee socks ($4.25)
are extremely high quality and long-wearing....I've been buying my
makeup from Bond Chemists at 61st and Madison ever since the day six
years ago when my friend Carolyn came home from there with a brand
new face." A triptych of photographs accompanying the article showed
Susan's face changing from very hard to very soft.

Susan wrote a lengthy and trenchant review of designer Ralph Lauren's "Americana" collection, featuring thirteen-hundred-dollar patch-
work-quilt skirts. According to Susan, the collection was yet another
example of Lauren "raiding the old hippie mama uniform, one item at a
time....He simply manufactures all your favorite thrift shop classics,"
she contended in the *Voice*, "and sells them back to you at designer
prices." Susan noted that Lauren never really claimed to be a designer
("he doesn't know how to pin a dress"). "While his personal aesthetic
cannot be faulted," she concluded, "his methods have a sleazy distinc-
tive flavor that leaves a bad taste in the mouth."

She wrote about cosmetics, about the faddish layering of preppy
clothing, and occasionally about books. When the *Voice* cut its already
meager fees for articles in half, Susan wrote, "I don't want to sound
immodest or anything, but years of providing food, shelter and clothing
for me and my kid on the low, slow and downright uncertain monies an

educated gal can make as a writer in this town have really honed my wits as sharp as Cuisinart blades. So what I did is...I became a bag writer." The editors ran the piece along with a picture of Shuna sleeping on a park bench beside Susan and a shopping bag full of clothes. It was published at the last possible moment—in all probability for the rest of the century—when an urban bag lady could be presented to progressive middle-class readers as a humorous eccentric. Soon the bag people and the junkies would be joined by entire families, and streets in New York and other American cities would look like streets in the Third World, but for now a Vassar-educated bag lady was still funny.

Most of Susan's shorter articles relied on ironic humor for effect, and many of them were essentially about herself. Even the hippest magazines were moving away from the overt first-person style of the New Journalism, but Susan and aspects of her past adorned the most utilitarian of subjects. A fashion piece recalled her dolls, her knitting books, the contents of her closet at various times, things Eve had said to her, her days at Vassar.

For a time Susan had worked for the *Daily News*. Clay Felker, a former editor of the *Voice*, of *New York* magazine, and then of *Esquire*, had been assigned the task of attracting upscale readers to replace the paper's fading traditional base of blue-collar New Yorkers, who had been fleeing the city for decades. Felker hired magazine writers for his "Manhattan" section of the *News* and assigned staffers like Susan to explain how to pick up a date at the Metropolitan Museum of Art or where to find the best Latin American cuisine. Susan had trouble producing at a newspaper pace, and Felker and his editors felt that her radical mood swings and her haughty response to criticism made her a liability they could do without.

Susan was interviewed for a job at *Women's World*, where Maris Cakars, the old Gordon family boyfriend, was managing editor. Maris and her Vassar friend Susan Kent had lived north of the city for several years, in a small town on the Hudson where they continued to put out *WIN*, the pacifist magazine. Now they were back in Brooklyn, with two children, and Maris had a job in the publishing mainstream. Susan Kent and Maris didn't see Susan Lydon anymore, but he was still happy to set up an appointment for her with his magazine's editor-in-chief.

Susan showed up late and announced that she had to go to the bathroom. When she came back, Maris and his boss noted that everything about her had changed from hard to soft—the tone of her voice, the pace of her delivery, the look in her eye.

She didn't get the job.

* * *

But then, Susan already had a job. She'd joined the less than ten percent of the populace Ronald Reagan lauded so often as the salvation of the battered American economy. Susan was an entrepreneur.

Recently Shuna had accompanied her mother to Rockefeller Center on a sales call. They moved through the crowd in the bustling lobby of one of the buildings and took an elevator up to the executive offices of NBC. Shuna followed her mom into a room dominated by a huge square table. It was surrounded by men in dark business suits. Susan walked to the head of the table and handed one of them a bag of cocaine. He smiled and all the other men took out their wallets at the same time and began to count out money.

An upcoming article in *Rolling Stone* would argue that heroin, Susan's powder of preference, had returned as a "pastime of the boring eighties." The writer quoted a doctor at New York's Payne Whitney Psychiatric Clinic: "Heroin hit a few years ago. The people who were able to handle cocaine—which is most people, after all—began saying 'I can handle this.'" Some said the growing "social acceptability" of heroin had to do with all the "Euro-trash" in New York, young jet-setters and asset-laden refugees from confiscatory foreign tax policies or fallen monarchies like Iran. These svelte newcomers were now to be seen at every trendy venue.

The funny thing about being a junkie and a dealer was that people on the outside thought you'd lost all "self-discipline" when in fact retaining your customer base and staying alive required unyielding discipline and a commando's sense of logistics. Susan was developing the street smarts of a good pimp and the expertise of a pharmacology professor. In less than an hour she could collect ten thousand dollars in cash—but then it always seemed that some connection was owed twelve thousand. It was the money pressure that made her experiment with getting clean.

Susan and her current boyfriend, an overweight part-time chef and nearly full-time dealer, talked often about kicking heroin. They dreamed of a cure almost as Sheila and Peter Probst had dreamed of buying a piece of land in California. One time they even went to an addiction counselor together. But of the hundreds of junkies Susan knew who had tried to kick, she could name only two who were still clean. One of them, also a writer, had gone to a treatment center in Palm Beach, Florida, that cost twenty-five hundred dollars a week.

"So much," Susan said when he returned.

"Cheaper than my habit," the writer replied.

Susan tried a methadone program. Methadone was a drug designed to fill in the gaping holes, just as heroin was originally synthesized to help morphine addicts come down easy. But the methadone just cranked open Susan's need. She found that a particularly pure strain of opium available out on the street slipped right past methadone's chemical blockade. The opium lit her up and laid her way back. Then she was fearless again, the envy of her friends.

Methadone could be circumvented; detox programs were expensive; waiting lists everywhere, even for local methadone programs, were long. And besides, "Once a junkie, always a junkie," as Susan would say. "I've tried, but all I can do is make the best of a bad situation."

Susan claimed she could parachute onto any city street in the world and scare up a score inside an hour. She said she could spot a junkie a block away. Junkies loved to peruse the popular culture in search of kindred spirits. "Look at her. Look at him....One of ours." They'd watch known or rumored junkies (or in Susan's case, various celebrity customers) on TV, and they'd talk a junkie lingo as distinct as any ethnic dialect.

Prowling the Lower East Side, Susan thought a lot about her father and her oddly symmetrical connection to his struggle to survive on the same streets as a boy. Sam had worked the streets too. Wasn't he hustling in the netherworld to this day, still on the lookout for the discarded brick or movable tree?

One night Susan inhaled a pile of dope not a hundred feet from the frigid railroad flat on East Eleventh Street where Sam once wondered if it was worth a beating to steal a lump of coal. The streets near Second Avenue, the old Jewish Rialto, blocks like the one that had horrified Sam when Lorraine decided to live poor, were now carnival alleys housing a new kind of shooting gallery. Much of the area looked like it had recently been bombed. But Susan felt the family history down on the Lower East Side, and it gave her a strange comfort when she thought about what she was up to now and who she had become.

Shuna posed for the photograph that ran with her mother's "Bag Writer" article thinking all the while that this was the real future of her little family. They would have no place to live, and her mother would stand on street corners raving like a madwoman.

"You used to dress in beautiful colors. You were the most beautiful dresser ever," Shuna would say. She couldn't stand to see her mother in dirty clothes. Sometimes Susan wore things inside out or with the labels in front. Shuna hated the way her greenish-gray skin sweat all the time now. Her mother smelled. And the house smelled too.

"Everyone will know!" Shuna would plead when her reeking, disheveled mom left the house.

Susan would laugh and walk out. The strange thing was that she was right. Nobody noticed what was happening.

Toward the end of 1981, Shuna told her father that her mother was on drugs. But Michael didn't invite her to move into the tiny apartment he shared with Ellen, a place where Shuna always felt like an intrusive guest. Michael believed it was "not natural" for an ex-husband to "stay in touch" with his ex-wife. Michael could not mention Susan's name in conversation. He called her "your mother" or "Shuna's mother."

After Shuna's revelation, Michael came by more often to take her shopping for food. He gave her money when he saw her (as did Eve). But all Michael had to say about the drug life his daughter described was, "I don't want you to go driving around the city with your mother and her boyfriend."

But Shuna did go out with her mother and her boyfriend, while they conducted business. It seemed better than always being alone. Occasionally they'd find that the connection was gone, maybe in jail or dead. The boyfriend almost broke Susan's ribs once after she got burned on a deal. Another time they fought because Susan refused to sell a girl some Quaaludes.

"She's depressed. Don't you understand she's going to kill herself with that buy?"

"It was a good deal," the boyfriend said.

He had a gun, this boyfriend of her mom's. For a time he also had a bandage around his neck because someone reached into his car and cut his throat. He drove right over to the emergency room and got it stitched up.

Now that Shuna was fourteen her "thinking" was changing. She imagined that she was beginning to think like an adult. She thought about the nature of air. She considered jumping out the window—not to kill herself or anything, but just to be, you know, part of the air.

Every single day, Shuna chose to take a hard-boiled egg to school. At lunch, she'd peel the egg in exactly the same way, always in the same posture and the same seat. Then she'd go to the ice cream parlor and eat the same kind of ice cream cone. This way lunch had a specific form. You could count on a lunch like this.

Sometimes Shuna didn't see her mother awake for days. Every so often her mom would wake her up at four or five o'clock in the morning and give her instructions, things about the house, but Shuna never remembered what she'd said.

There was always a lot of money around the house, but her mother never stopped talking about being broke. Shuna thought that if she would just stop hanging out with rich Aricans and rich customers who went around in limousines, then she wouldn't have to think about money so much. Shuna went with her mom to Betsey Bunky Nini, a fancy Madison Avenue store where Susan bought a beautiful sweater. Shuna was so confused.

Sometimes, if Susan was really complaining, Shuna would wait until she was asleep. Then, as Susan had once given Eve five dollars to buy a black-and-white taffeta skirt, Shuna would slip some money she'd saved into her mother's purse.

During the summer, after Shuna and Susan were evicted from the big apartment on East Seventy-first Street and had to move to the West Side apartment that gave Shuna nightmares because it always seemed like people were trying to get in, Gina Schick came to New York to attend an Arican convention held at an upstate resort called Sugar Maples. Oscar Ichazo called the gathering Metamorphosis. He announced that the Arica family needed to be subdivided into eight-person "octagons." Everyone present would be "initiated" into an octagon for what sounded to Gina like the same reasons that revolutionary movements and terrorist gangs, or perhaps the early Christians during the years of persecution, tended to break up into cells. For most Aricans, Sugar Maples marked the end of their collective life as a family. Not long after the convention, Oscar moved to Hawaii.

At one point Gina noticed a skeletal-looking woman who seemed to be trying to get her attention. The woman came closer, calling Gina's name over and over, but even when she was right in front of her, Gina wasn't sure who it was. "It's Susan!" the woman screamed. "What's the matter with you?"

Back home, Gina's phone would ring very late at night. Susan's voice was usually weak. "Help me. Please help," she'd say. Gina helped by sending Susan money, and Susan would send heroin back through the mail. Gina would shake her head because the counts were skimpy and the dope far from pure. But then, she hadn't sent the money because she wanted to get high.

* * *

At the end of the year Susan told several friends she would have to learn Yiddish in order to understand enough about her life to re-create it in an autobiography. Susan kept a vigil at the Selectric, trying to connect an unwritten life to a ravaged one.

Shuna loved to hear the family stories Susan had managed to retrieve. It was good to see how her fascination with her Russian forebears brought her face back to life. But the smiles didn't make up for Susan's talk of suicide, and they didn't ease Shuna's constant worry about her mother going up in flames. One time Susan had nodded out and her cigarette ignited the sleeve of her blouse. Twice the wrinkled sheets where she spent so much time in a weirdly impenetrable sleep momentarily caught fire.

Shuna would go to Susan's room in the morning and find her asleep at the typewriter, her cheek pressed to the opening above the steel ball element. Her slender, dark arms would be hugging the machine. Shuna would slip a pillow under her mother's head and put a blanket over her back. Then she'd get her egg and go to school.

————◆————

Parenting.

It seems that child psychologist Fitzhugh Dodson was the first to take a word whose root refers to a simple biological act and turn it into a morally freighted gerund. By 1982 "parenting" had come to symbolize a generation's anxious determination to give their offspring childhoods psychologically and developmentally superior to their own. Sheila, along with millions of other women who'd postponed the experience of child-rearing about a decade longer than their mothers, read Dodson's definition of the new verb in the early pages of his 1970 best-seller, *How to Parent*, still going strong in paperback: "To parent...to use, with tender loving care, all the information science has accumulated about child psychology in order to raise happy and intelligent human beings."

By the time Sheila actually read Dodson, it would have taken a year for a baby-boom mother to absorb not *all* the child-raising literature but just that portion with the buzzword in the title. New guides now arrived in bookstores by the week: *Creative Parenting, Quality Parenting, Natural Parenting, Whole-Life Parenting, Self-Reparenting.*

"You're doing fine. You've been a wonderful mother to Dani, Sheila," Eve kept reassuring her fearful daughter, whose own daughter had just turned three. "You're old enough to handle it. When I had Susan I was much too young. I really wasn't ready to be a mother."

"I never realized what Mom did," Sheila would later say to the veteran mother Lorraine. "You can't possibly know what it's like to have children until you do it."

Though Sheila had not replicated certain aspects of Lorraine's parenting—such as breast-feeding her children until they could announce in full sentences that they were hungry and help their mother unbutton her blouse—she believed Lorraine was in many ways a model mother. But even if Sheila could copy the best of Eve and Lorraine, she doubted that would be enough to assure that Danielle would enter her adult years unimpaired by her upbringing.

Perhaps because she was older, as Eve said—and so much more widely read on the subject than mothers of previous generations—Sheila gazed into her little daughter's future like a first-year medical student suddenly stunned by a world rife with killer diseases. Sheila was bound and determined to create something much better than a habitable future for her Danielle. Dani would never weep on the stairs because she believed nobody cared. Dani would go to the senior prom Sheila had missed. Dani would learn to "actualize" the "unique potential self within," as Dodson put it, and thus be spared the crippling denial of her true feelings. Sheila, like so many others intent on parenting with grace and love and advanced technique, wanted to be a master among moms. But she wasn't exactly sure how.

Dodson, and by now hundreds of other specialists, contended that the first five years of a child's life were by far the most essential for emotional and even intellectual development. Dodson said that every child was equipped from birth with a pair of psychological "eyeglasses" that filtered experience to form a lasting sense of self and a "basic outlook on life." The environment parents created before the changing lenses of a young child would determine whether that child could trust and be happy. In order to be properly nurturing, parents had to turn inward and back to their own childhoods. "You must re-establish contact with the child within yourself, the child you once were," Dodson wrote, for "without the feel of childhood we adults will misuse and distort the scientific facts because we will be viewing them entirely through adult eyes." Without a strong sense of the child you were, you would "know the words of parenting, but lack the tune."

The Swiss psychoanalyst Alice Miller, author of *Prisoners of Childhood*—a new book being passed around among committed parents of a psychoanalytic bent (and among Sheila, Lorraine, and Ricky)—took the ocular metaphor of a child's earliest formative perceptions to an even more terrifying level from the perspective of a new parent. Borrowing from British psychoanalyst and pediatrician D. W. Winnicott, Miller described a baby staring into a mother's eyes and seeing, as if in a mirror, an image of itself. That was fine, Miller said, "provided that the mother is really looking at the unique, small, helpless being and not projecting her own…expectations, fears, and plans" onto the child. If the child saw the mother's psychological agenda, he would "remain without a mirror, and for the rest of his life would be seeking this mirror in vain."

Miller argued that beyond denying a child self-confidence and spirit, a psychologically undeveloped mother lost in a pit of selfishness—"narcissistic cathexis"—could rob the child of his or her very soul. If the mirror was clouded, the "mirroring function" warped by unpredictability, insecurity, anxiety, or hostility, there would surely be a "disturbance."

Alice Miller's popular book was salted with childhood traumas suffered by many highly creative adults. Hermann Hesse, whose own mother was "broken at the age of four" by her parents, was shipped off to "an institution for the care of epileptics and defectives" at the age of fifteen because he was obstreperous. Balzac's mother rejected him in favor of his coddled brother, so he "courted his mother in the guise of different women" all his life. Igor Stravinsky suffered in the mirrored eye of a distant father and unloving mother, and Ingmar Bergman once wet his pants and was forced to wear a red dress all day "so that everybody would know what he had done." Several years later Miller would write that *Prisoners of Childhood* (retitled *The Drama of the Gifted Child*) was informed by her own childhood, by "the child in me, condemned to silence long ago—abused, exploited, and turned to stone—who finally found her feelings and along with them her speech, and then told me, in pain, her story."

It came as no great surprise to Ricky's sisters and friends that he now spoke of Alice Miller's book in terms usually reserved for holy writ. Her theories and the moving disclosure of his beloved Stravinsky's childhood trauma helped him recognize the prison yard of Harbor Isle and the psychic jail of 221 Lincoln for what they were. As he angrily rehashed the past with Richard Trachtman for just under two hours each week, Ricky saw the terrified child, circa 1964, who inhabited him. He was living in 1982 disguised as a sensitive young man when in fact he was a prisoner of his childhood.

Sheila would gaze hard into Dani's bright blue eyes, if not with perfect insight, then with near-perfect love. Public debate now raged over the "superwoman" dilemma facing mothers who acknowledged their children's need for them but were torn by their own need for the psychic or economic gratifications of work. Sheila could afford to be a full-time mother, so parenting would be her job for a while. But the more she read and the more Ricky bombarded her with machine-gun insights from therapy—the more she looked at Dani and saw herself, crying her eyes out on the landing at 221 Lincoln and resolving to be the best little girl in the world so she could win her parents' love—the more she realized that just being there was not enough. The parenting books were not enough. Not even more than a decade of cultural preoccupation with becoming a free and happy adult through self-discovery seemed to offer enough information to raise a free and happy child.

Sheila began what would be a six-year course of regular psychotherapy with a neo-Freudian (there were more than two hundred variations on Freud by now) intellectually grounded in the work of the German-born psychiatrist Karen Horney. If Harry Stack Sullivan, whose writings guided Lorraine's therapist in the late 1960s, distinguished himself by concentrating on cultural forces and interpersonal relations in which Freud had little interest, Karen Horney made her mark by asserting that Freud failed to account for the psychological toll of simply living in a culture where women, in particular, were "subordinated" and lonely, though not necessarily alone. When Horney came to the United States in 1932, she noticed for the first time "compliant trends" in her patients' personalities. In reaction to such cultural phenomena as "the ever-precarious self-respect" of men, many women became practiced in the art of deference, yearning only to be unselfish and good and able to please at the expense of their own needs. In Horney's view, women often served men who were deeply afraid of the power of motherhood.

Not long after Sheila entered therapy, she discovered that her tiniest gesture contained her past. She always waited a few seconds before swinging the refrigerator door shut. This, she now realized, was aimed at her mother, for whom a refrigerator door held open longer than "necessary" was a mortal sin. "I don't understand a wife who tells her husband they have to go out for dinner. Wives should cook," Eve always said, so Sheila and Jon, both skilled and creative cooks, went out to dinner and ate take-out food all the time.

Through her new psychological eyeglasses, Sheila looked around. She saw that she'd married someone who knew how to fix and build things and was never unnerved. In Lamaze class, Jon had horrified the other expectant parents with terrible stories he'd heard about births that went wrong. He wasn't very interested in psychological subtleties, though he said he was finally "getting used to being a father." He was the kind of man who thought you could make anything work out as long as you were strong—not unlike Sam.

The more Sheila concentrated her considerable maternal energies on her daughter, and the more the delicate leaves of memory unfolded during therapy, the more she realized the depth of her jealousy. She envied her parents, her siblings, and almost everyone she knew. She had so much, yet she was jealous.

All her life, Sheila had heard her father say that he had never envied another human being. One day she decided to ask him for an update. "Daddy, are you ever jealous of other people?"

"Nobody," Sam said mechanically, his neck and shoulders stiffening pridefully. "Except," he added in a softer voice, "for people with happy family lives. Sometimes I get jealous of people like that."

———◦———

Sam listened intently as one parent after another described children who'd turned into liars and cheats and thieves and junkies. Everybody at the Pill-Anon meeting in the cafeteria at Mercy Hospital had a child who'd "broken down"—the term Sam applied in its most mechanistic and least psychological sense to the behavior of his daughter Susan. It seemed that every time Sam Gordon turned around, another kid had cracked up or gone haywire or generally pulled off the highway with severe engine trouble. And all these kids apparently had parents who wanted to take you aside and tell you their sad tale.

Sam had recently done a job for a wealthy lady who started telling him out of the blue that she had big-time family problems. "First I noticed that my fifteen-year-old son kept twenty or thirty radios and stereos in his bedroom," she said, as if discussing the weather. The kid went on to set up a full-scale robbery in which his own father got cold-cocked with a blunt instrument. The story continued for quite a while from there. The kid was home, then away at a hospital, then back home again. He couldn't stop. "Finally," the lady said, still calm, still relating the saga to Sam as if it had happened to somebody other than herself, "I got a phone call to come down to the morgue and identify the body." After a brief pause, meeting his eyes, she added, "And I'm still not sure which is better, Sam. That's the strange thing. I still can't say whether it's better to have a son who's dead or a son who takes drugs."

Drugs had now invaded Eve's mah-jongg game. Stories about needles and pills were traded at gas stations, hardware stores, and beauty parlors. A Harbor Isle couple lost their twenty-year-old child to drugs. Drugs got to the Kennedy kids. Within a few years Patty Duke, who always seemed so depressed to Lorraine's sidekick, Ellen Levy, would reveal that her childhood misery led to years of drug and alcohol abuse and attempted suicides. Little Lauren Chapin, "Kitten" on the 1950s family idyll *Father Knows Best*, grew up into a major drug habit. Billy Gray, the actor who played Bud, Kitten's older brother, began a long struggle with drugs in 1962. And Robert Young, the paradigm of the self-possessed television dad, the father who knew best, was treated for alcoholism and severe depression.

Tommy Rettig, who played Timmy on *Lassie*, faced cocaine smuggling charges in the 1970s, and Desi Arnaz, Jr., son of Lucille Ball, told the readers of *Good Housekeeping* that he'd been hooked for sixteen years. Drew Barrymore, one of the stars of this year's smash movie, Steven Spielberg's *E.T.*, would admit during a spate of similar confessions in the later 1980s that she began abusing alcohol and drugs at the age of nine. Wall Street brokers, senior Senate aides with security clearance, technicians monitoring the dials at the nation's nuclear plants, cops—lots of cops—all had problems with "substance abuse," and most had parents trying to sort out how much of it was their fault. Not long before Sheila and Jon dragged Sam and Eve to the Pill-Anon meeting at Mercy Hospital, a father in Florida went public to complain that his kid should have received a much stiffer sentence.

Sam Gordon knew he stood accused of various mistakes and derelictions of paternal duty. He didn't give out compliments readily enough. He wasn't there enough. He blew his top too often when Lorraine and Susan were young. But a kid on drugs made your whole life come back at you like a boomerang. Sam was transfixed during the meeting when another rich lady—he could tell a rich lady when he saw one—stood up to "share" the story of her fourteen-year-old, who stole money from her and ran away looking for dope. "I have to learn it isn't my fault," the woman said, "but I haven't learned it yet."

Parent after parent kept talking about feelings of "shame." Shame wasn't the same as guilt. Guilt was generated by the breach of a vow, a violation of one's own standards. Shame was a condition, an involuntary state. It couldn't be rectified or assuaged as easily as guilt—or such seemed to be the distinction in this world of heartbreaking narratives. Shame was a dark stain on your heart.

Eve had only agreed to attend the Pills Anonymous meeting because Susan crossed the line and asked Sam for money.

"You gotta face it, Eve," her son-in-law, Jon, had been saying for months before Susan went to Sam. "You've got a junkie for a daughter.

She cleaned out our medicine chest the other day. I know she steals from you every time she comes. I just hope you hide your jewelry."

"You...you don't know what the fuck you're talking about!" Eve sputtered at the mention of the jewelry collection Sam had been building up with regular gifts for several years. "Who the hell are you to say such a thing? Money, money, money. All you talk about is money. Who gives a shit about money! It's all about gold and jewels to you, and you don't...you don't know everything!"

Before she heard that Sam and Eve had agreed to attend the Pill-Anon meeting, Lorraine had all but given up on convincing her mother or Sheila that Susan was a professional drug addict. "She's not tired, Mom. That's called nodding out," she'd say. "She's using drugs—heavily."

"No," Eve persisted. "She's...under pressure."

Eve and Sheila agreed that Lorraine's viewpoint might be distorted. They both thought Lorraine and Susan were still vying for maternal attention. If one wrecked a car, the other would have a crash soon afterward. Lorraine admitted that she and Susan were bound together unnaturally, as if parts of their psyches were somehow shared. "But what I'm trying to tell you now," Lorraine persisted to Eve and Sheila, "is that Susan is going to die."

"Why are you making trouble for me? You've always made trouble for me!" Susan spat at Lorraine over the phone.

Then, finding herself nearly two thousand dollars behind on her rent, she went to Sam after Eve refused her the money, and in so doing, she breached basic if unwritten family laws.

"I don't know what to do, Daddy. Please!"

Sam called Eve on the phone. "Write a check," he instructed.

"You went to *him!*" Eve screamed at Susan. "How dare you! After all I've given you. How *dare* you! You aren't my daughter anymore....And I don't want to see you again."

Later, calm and guilty, Eve phoned Susan to ask how she felt.

"To tell you the truth, I'm real dope-sick," Susan said. "I'm so sick I feel ready to die."

As Eve wept quietly beside him at the Pill-Anon meeting, Sam could feel the weight of his own remorse ease a bit. The experience was different from spilling your guts to a rabbi. The idea, he now saw, was to "line your own story up against other family stories, and then you look at yourself again." In the camaraderie of disappointment forged among anonymous strangers in the cafeteria, Sam felt release. As Masons gathered to discuss the trials and complexities of true manhood, parents of damaged children came together here to muster the will to go on.

In a time when unhappiness was private, many of these same people had once gathered to plant suburban saplings and build their new towns. Now they'd reassembled to share the troubles that had befallen them. In these painful, heartfelt stories, Sam saw the sameness again, the old community that had left the city for a normal life—badly battered, perhaps, but here.

Sam glanced over at Eve, who cried through every story, and he could tell that for her it was different.

Some parents got up to talk about what they called "tough love," a term that had lately spread from the rehab professionals to the hundreds of new support groups for those affected by drugs but not addicted themselves. Tough love, first introduced in the drug treatment programs developed by the Synanon organization, meant that to love addicts was to deny them. You couldn't help them. You couldn't give them money. If your love was tough love—the love they really needed—you couldn't even let them in the door.

"Can you believe this?" Eve whispered to Sam. "This is what these people call love."

"I was an enabler," said a mother at the meeting. An "enabler," it appeared, was someone who helped the addict or alcoholic avoid the consequences of his or her actions. The enabler slipped the addict money, bailed the addict out of jail, kept the sickness going by insulating the addict.

Eve listened with her mouth agape. *Enabler!* she wanted to scream at these heartless, defeated people. *I am a mother!* She couldn't believe what she was hearing. An enabler was a bad person who saved a child from hitting bottom? An enabler refused to step on a child like she was no better than a cockroach?

"I have a daughter who is *alive!*" Eve raged to Sam after the meeting. "I am not an enabler. I am a mother!"

A mother, Eve kept telling herself bitterly, long into another night of lurid thoughts. A mother to a daughter who sold drugs to the children of other mothers. A daughter who did this and probably other things that no human being should be allowed to do and live. A daughter who didn't sound or act or even look like the daughter she once knew.

"Listen, hon, I got a lot out of the meeting, but it's a busy time," Eve told Sheila. "You know, even if all those people have the same problem I have, that doesn't mean they're like me."

Eve never went back to Pill-Anon, and because she didn't, neither did Sam.

1983

In the early fall the Gordons convened a formal meeting to discuss the perambulating social problem that was their eldest daughter and sister. The agenda included forcing Susan to choose once and for all between family and drugs. Ricky refused to attend, but the others gathered in the living room at the boatyard. With tears in his eyes, Sam sat rigid in the antique barber's chair. Sheila sat between Lorraine and Eve on one wing of the big green couch. Jon sat next to Shuna, who sobbed against his shoulder on the other wing. Susan sat in the crux, where the sofa curved.

If the curators of Madame Tussaud's museum had decided to display a forty-year-old New York City junkie fresh off the streets of 1983, the paraffin effigy would have looked more alive than Susan Gordon Lydon did right now. Her eyes, black and fathomless as the crawl space, seemed to have receded into her head. Shortly before Eve finally withdrew the last impediment to family action—her own adamant refusal to look at what was happening and see it—she'd stared at her daughter and said, "You're haunted. I've finally figured out what it is. You're possessed."

Susan was doing two full "bundles"—some twenty bags of quality heroin—every day. Her habit cost over three thousand dollars a week and represented a pharmaceutical intake that would have killed two average junkies twice her size. She'd spent much of the past cold winter wandering the upper and lower corners of Manhattan with plastic garbage bags lining her boots, huddling around fires in old oil drums to exchange reconnaissance updates on the whereabouts of "the man." In the wake of Ronald Reagan's declaration of a "war on drugs" during a speech in October 1982, a local police operation called Pressure Point had reduced the supply. One night the cops burned down one of Susan's regular scoring spots, a Lower East Side drug shop called the Executive. But by the next morning there was already a fresh tunnel leading from a contiguous abandoned tenement back into the basement, where business was being conducted as usual.

Connections were always dying, but by the summer many of them were running away. By then, Susan had seen the blades of a few knives and the barrels of several guns pointed her way. But impending violence, like the weather and the twenty-four-hour days, was in the job description. This was what Susan did, who she was, though she preferred to travel under a code name. "I'm a survivor," she'd say.

The confrontational one-act about to begin in the living room of the boatyard closely resembled a therapeutic maneuver known in addiction treatment circles as an "intervention." As the brief moment of social acceptance of hard drugs passed (the largest epidemiological psychiatric survey ever conducted, a study of nearly seventeen thousand individuals sponsored by the National Institute of Mental Health, had recently revealed that drug and alcohol dependence, not depression as was previously thought, was now the nation's leading "mental ailment,"), the word "intervention" began to refer to something other than military adventurism. Family interventions meant drawing together to tell a beloved member that he or she needed help, and that from now on no quarter would be given.

The technique of penetrating a dependent person's "denial system" through confrontation was first developed in the 1960s at the Johnson Institute, an alcoholism and addiction research center in Minneapolis. But by far the most famous and widely copied intervention occurred on April 1, 1978, when a seriously alcoholic, pill-popping wife and mother named Betty Ford opened her front door to find her family standing there with two professional "crisis interventionists." "We want to present to her, lovingly but firmly, brief facts about two things," Dr. Joe Pursch had explained to Jerry Ford and the rest of the family before the meeting. "How her illness is affecting and destroying her, and how her illness is affecting and destroying you."

"We're here, Susan," Jon said, "because we all think you need help. Something has to be done. You've stopped taking care of your daughter as well as yourself."

At this, Shuna saw her mother turn and stare at her with what she would always remember as loathing. The gaze was much worse than her mother's usual "you don't love me anymore" face.

As Shuna burst into tears and buried her face in Jon's shoulder, Susan looked at her sisters and parents and measured their resolve. She could choose the family or the dope, and as much as it tore at her heart, she believed drugs were a part of her life she simply could not live without.

The family meeting surprised Shuna, because she'd given up on anyone else ever seeing what was happening. Her grandmother had walked right into the laundry room while her mother was snorting a huge mound of heroin from the top of the washing machine, and Shuna knew that Eve had simply turned around and walked out. Shuna also knew that Nanny continued to give her mother money after that. Eve gave Shuna money too, which Shuna interpreted as a way of saying that there was nothing she could do.

It was Jon who'd kept asking Shuna to tell him about her life at home, and finally she did. Soon after, Michael Lydon received a phone call from Sheila in which he "was told," as he later put it, that the Gordons had decided Shuna should come to Harbor Isle. He subsequently drove his daughter and her belongings out to the boatyard.

Shuna sometimes assumed her father hadn't rescued her because he lived in such a small apartment. In New York people decided not to have families because their apartments were too small. Marriages stayed together because of the vagaries of the real estate market. But other times Shuna figured her father didn't come to save her because nobody could.

Before Shuna left the city, she had something to say to her mother. Lately Susan had been trying to force Shuna to scream at her and call her names. She would badger Shuna into scolding her, and then she would interrupt the feeble tirade with a singsong "I…can't…hear you." In reaction to this strange ritual, Shuna's natural speaking voice had become an affectless whisper whenever she was in her mom's presence, but the day she left the apartment on the Upper West Side, she looked from her packed bags into the hollows of her mother's eyes and heard herself say quite clearly, "I am leaving you now. You are not my mother anymore."

Eve could barely make out what was said at the beginning of the family meeting. The conversation was too loud. There was too much happening at once. There had been too much happening for a while.

Not only was Shuna living with Sam and Eve, more moody and in need than ever, but Maggie, now a freshman at Hunter College, was also in residence at the boatyard. So was Lorraine—now Mrs. Curt "Mohan" Wenzel of Yogaville, Virginia—who had turned up with Ram and Shiva and was pregnant again.

Sheila had called Sam and Eve the previous autumn to say that Lorraine was getting married and moving from Charlottesville to the ashram. "Who does she know to marry?" Eve had asked. "A few weeks ago she was complaining she didn't know any men."

Mohan, the groom, was a fifty-year-old former policeman and Broadway dancer who could be seen as part of the chorus in reruns of the 1954 film *Seven Brides for Seven Brothers*. The flourishing Yogaville community included six of Mohan's children by two previous marriages. Four of them were teenage boys, which made the trailer home Lorraine managed for the new family of ten a bit cramped. On the phone, Lorraine told Sam that Mohan was a "plumbing contractor," which was a more than slight exaggeration of his general handiness.

When Eve finally met her new son-in-law, she looked him up and down. Mohan had long gray hair and facial stubble like the popular country singer Willie Nelson. He was as preternaturally thin as a Giacometti. Sotto voce, Eve said to Ricky, "Doesn't look like a cop to me. And skinny? *Oy vey.*"

"What do you expect?" said Ricky. "The man's been on a diet for twenty years."

"This," Eve whispered back, "is like a bad dream."

And then Lorraine showed up in Harbor Isle, pregnant and unhappy with her new marriage. Mohan and his boys had "no respect for women." She was tired of the trailer, tired of shopping for ravenous males on a meager budget, and tired of being treated "like a slave." She promptly dumped an unsorted load of laundry in the machine.

"Thirty-six years old and you still don't separate darks from whites!" Eve screamed.

Eve knew that Lorraine's arrival meant that Susan would soon phone her in need. She did, asking if she could come stay at the house, but her request was denied.

Seven-year-old Ram—Eve always called him Gabe—loved to help his grandmother with the mammoth shopping trips required to feed the resident refugee population at the boatyard. Whenever they went to the supermarket, Eve's tall, tow-headed grandson made a beeline for the butcher's counter, where he would stand transfixed for half an hour at a time, staring longingly at the cuts of meat.

In April Sheila had her second child, a boy she named Daryl. She'd had to spend six weeks in bed because of the possibility of a miscarriage, and Eve had been taking care of her and her family. It was around then that Lorraine announced her plans to have her fourth child "at home" in the boatyard.

"I've found a midwife who will do it right here," Lorraine said with the gooey, dreamy expression that gave Eve the creeps. "I think it will be a wonderful experience for all of us."

"Oh God, no," Eve begged. "No. No, Lorraine. You're killing me. You're all killing me. Please don't finish me off. If you have a baby in my house, I will have a heart attack and die. I promise I will, Lorraine."

So Gopal Joshua Wenzel came into the world at the home of some friends of Lorraine's who were born-again Hasidic Jews and had to get special rabbinical permission to answer the phone and use other technological conveniences on the day Lorraine went into labor. By the end of the fruitful summer of 1983, Sam and Eve's extended tribe officially numbered fifteen.

One afternoon a few weeks later, Lorraine was talking to Sheila about going back to Mohan. Eve was in the kitchen with them, and in a loud voice she asked her daughters if they'd like to hear a joke she'd recently told at her mah-jongg game. Without waiting for a reply, Eve drew an appropriate accent from her quiver and let fly with a vaudeville turn.

"So someone asks this lady, 'How's your lovely daughter?' 'Oh, she's fine. Married to a doctor,' says the lady. 'Wasn't she also married to a lawyer?' asks the first. 'That's right.' 'And wasn't she also married to a banker?' 'That's right.' 'Oy,' says the first, 'so much happiness from one daughter!'"

Sheila doubled over with laughter, but Lorraine just sat there, gloomily staring out at the water.

Lorraine often pondered how her history of serial monogamy must look to her mother and others with more traditional lives. In conversation with the good shopkeepers of Buckingham County, she was always far more conscious of her connubial background than she was concerned with what the locals might make of her spiritual life. (Word around Buckingham was that Yogaville residents liked to suck towels in through their noses and pull them out of their mouths.)

"Lorraine, you're paying a big price," Eve would always say, and Lorraine knew she wasn't referring to a life marred by bad luck or the forces of karmic reaction. From the time of Lorraine's pitched battles with her father as a teenager, Eve had contended that all the trouble in her life could be traced to a single source—her aggressiveness toward men.

After Sheila stopped laughing at Eve's joke, Lorraine turned her attention back to her mother and sister. "I can't be like either of you," she said glumly. "You defer to men, and I can't. I won't. I will never compromise like both of you do."

"You're bragging about this?" Eve snapped. "This is your problem, and you act proud?"

"What do you mean?" Lorraine asked.

Eve raised her voice. "You know damn well what I mean! You should have learned by now to just shut your mouth. You think you stand up for yourself, and what have you got—three former husbands, that's what!"

"Two," said Lorraine.

"Okay then, two," Eve allowed.

"Still. I will not defer."

Though she deferred every day to the will and wisdom of her guru, Lorraine was still something of a Goldflower. In terms of the intellectual schism between radical feminists and the women they disdained as "liberal integrationists"—a long-standing dispute that was back in the news again—Lorraine still held to the radical vision of family and sexual relationships as inherently oppressive unless women constantly fought back in the name of equality.

A year into what the *New York Times* called the "postfeminist" 1980s, and twenty years after the publication of *The Feminine Mystique*, Betty Friedan had come out with a new book called *The Second Stage*. In it she argued that American women had moved past the "first stage" of feminism—having achieved "full participation, power and voice in the mainstream"—and must now cooperate with men in "restructuring institutions and transforming the nature of power itself." American women were now governors of states, partners in law firms, conductors of orchestras, astronauts, and Rhodes Scholars. A woman had refereed one of Muhammad Ali's heavyweight title bouts. Shirley Temple became a U.S. ambassador. In 1984 Geraldine Ferraro would run for vice president of the United States. Friedan said that the new feminist frontier was the family. Feminism needed to endorse the forms of human intimacy inherent in family life. The movement's "extreme vision," Friedan implied, focused too much on dissecting conflicts between men and women and criticizing the family.

Not surprisingly, radical feminists almost universally accused Friedan of executing the classical liberal ploy of cozying up just to the left of the "pro-family" views held by the likes of Jerry Falwell in an effort to attract support. At the opposite pole from Friedan, Alison Jagger argued in a new book, *Feminist Politics and Human Nature,* that far from seeking integration, women could now look forward to the "ultimate transformation of human nature." Technology, Jagger reported, held the promise of a genderless world in which women would be capable of insemination, and men of bearing children.

"Just compromise," Eve would tell her daughters, passing along for the thousandth time her personal mantra. "You have to compromise."

If she were young again in 1983, Eve thought she probably wouldn't give up her singing career as she had forty years ago. But she would still compromise. She would never desire everything at once like her girls. She would always be able to bend, because bending was how families survived. Every family needed a bough that would bend but never break.

"And you know what else?" Eve said to Lorraine during another of their debates that difficult summer. "*I'm* the holy one in the family. I'm holy because when push comes to shove, I take all the responsibility." Eve paused and looked around the encampment inside her little house by the water. "Sam's holy too, because he goes along with this. How many guys would have gone along? Most guys would say, 'It's the kids' problem. It's their responsibility. Leave me alone.' He's a good guy, your father. He really is. Sam deserves to live a long life with his horse."

Galloping along the ribbon-thin trails of Old Westbury, the forest on both sides a blur of many greens, Sam felt loosed within time. In control of the mighty force below him, one with the spirit of his horseman father, Sam was at his best.

One Sunday Sam was riding along when he spotted an unnatural shade of blue on the ground. It looked to be a piece of denim, perhaps a pair of blue jeans. He thought nothing of it until he passed the bit of cloth on the way back. He paused and was quickly surrounded by an odor he hadn't smelled since the European war so long ago.

Under a tree a few feet off the trail, he saw a naked girl. Maybe sunbathing. Sam waited for her to move. He dismounted and approached her. She was quite young—possibly a student at the nearby college— and she was dead. It would turn out that she'd gone for a ride on a white motorcycle with a man recently out of prison. He'd raped her and killed her and left her under the tree.

By the time the police arrived, Sam was wondering if he'd have to slap another rider who'd stopped at the scene and was nearly hysterical. The guy, about Sam's age, bummed one cigarette after another from the cops, clearly on the verge of losing it. "I have two daughters," he kept saying. "You don't understand."

Sam had realized early on that a parent couldn't afford to think about the kids too much. Once you started, once you allowed all the things that could hurt them to invade your daily consciousness, you became obsessed. The fear became everything—especially if you had girls.

All those clamorous needs and desires, all the pushing and pulling that could toss a man around a family like a helpless doll—none of it meant a thing when you considered what could happen. A father could wait almost forty years for a daughter finally to accept him and love him in a way he could feel, and suddenly some asshole on a motorcycle could come by and leave her dead under a tree.

Just before Father's Day, Susan sat down beneath a halo of fine white heroin she'd snared. She'd recently read in "Dear Abby" that a letter is often a serviceable vehicle of family reconciliation. So Susan began to write to her father out of her memories and deepest feelings. She wrote the entire letter in longhand, at a single sitting. She didn't need to go back and correct a single word.

Dear Dad,

Mark Twain once said that when he was 14 he was embarrassed by his father's ignorance, but when he was 21, he was amazed to see how much the old man had learned in a few short years. Dad, I'm really impressed with your education progress over the past few years! And at your advanced age, too!

Seriously, though, the older I get, the more I appreciate you—your advice and counsel, your intelligence (which I've been lucky enough to inherit), your strength and determination, and the way you have always been there for me when I need your help. Now that my own daughter is 14, I've been getting some insight into how I must have seemed to you, and I shudder to think of some of the things I said and did to you. What I really regret, though, was how ungrateful I appeared for my education, when it meant so much to me. I have to write these things down because if I tried to say them I'd be so emotionally hysterical that I couldn't get them out.

Nowadays psychologists talk about the importance of "bonding," the attachment formed between the parents and child at the moment of the child's birth. Due to circumstances beyond our control, we got a late start in our relationship, and God knows, we had our ups and downs and difficulties. I was so desperate to please you and win your love when I was a kid that I think I alienated you instead. We're so much alike in so many ways, and, being the oldest, I felt I had to go head to head with you to prove that I could be as intelligent and competent as the son I felt you would have preferred. Now that I have to go out in the world and make a living to support my family, I have far more empathy for the pressures you faced and the terrific job you did, but as a kid I couldn't have been more ignorant and insensitive about your situation—provoking you to anger when I just wanted you to be proud of me and respect and love me.

Daddy, I love you more than I could ever express in words, and though, through hurt and rejection and confusion, I tried to hide my feelings behind a mask of arrogance and bravado, your opinion of me has always been deeply, profoundly important to me. Your approval of something I did could elevate me to cloud 9—your disapproval could (as it still can) plunge me to the depths of despair—and my relationship with you has colored every aspect of my life—from my most basic feelings of self-worth or worthlessness, to my sometimes problematic relationships with other men. I struggled to prove myself intellectually, an area which I thought you respected, and was stupid enough to believe the bullshit of my teachers and argue with you from their points of view (as my daughter now does to me), though secretly I believed you were the most brilliant man in the world, a genius, and that I could never live up to your high standards.

I thank God that we both survived long enough to try to iron out some of the problems between us. I know there are scars and mistrust on both sides—sometimes I can feel the awkwardness you feel with me—and the fear that we'll create another explosion if we are not careful—and I still overreact to your criticism of me. I think both of us try our best to hide our sensitive natures under a wall of toughness, and I pray that someday we'll be able to be as easy and relaxed with each other, as close and expressive of the deep love we feel, as I always craved as a child and still long for.

We are products of heredity and history. Heredity determines our basic characteristics, the raw material we have to work with as we make our way in the world. History intervenes, as it did between us when I was born, and sometimes buffets us with forces that can affect our lives as strongly as our genetic inheritance. The women's movement, a strong historical current, made itself felt in me from an early age—though it wasn't something I could articulate at that time, and since you were the most important man in my life, I competed with you to find my own power & equality.

Problems can be an advantage, a challenge to overcome. I really feel grateful for the progress we have made toward understanding each other in the past ten years, and I really respect your willingness to open up to your children and grandchildren more than you could when you had the support of 6 or 7 people at a time on your shoulders. Knowing how you started with nothing and worked your way up to a position of financial security and material comfort by sheer hard work, long hours, and unshakable determination, I respect you much more than someone who starts out with silver spoon advantages in life and just improves upon them. Dad, I hope this doesn't embarrass you, my pouring out my heart to you like this, but it's so important to me—one of the top priorities in my life, in fact—that I am willing to risk appearing ridiculous to tell you how I feel.

Mostly on this father's day, I want to tell you how much I love you, more than ever, and how grateful I feel for the progress we've made in straightening out our problems. You're the greatest, Dad, a real mensch in the truest sense of the word, and I'm very proud to be your daughter.

Many years of health and happiness to you and

> All my love forever,
> Susan

"To: Mr. Samuel Gordon, Dad Extraordinaire," read the envelope, "from: his #1 daughter, Susan, with mucho love and kisses from the"— and here there was a picture of a heart. "Personal (—Very!)—please read in private," she wrote, and then, in various lettering, "Patriarch of the Gordon clan," "#1 father," "Founder of a Dynasty," "Paterfamilias," "Heap Big Chief," "Father Knows Best!!" "The Peerless Père," "Fabulous Father," "Gonsa Grandpa," "Dynamite Daddy."

———❖———

"Count me out," Ricky said ten weeks later when Eve called to invite him to the Gordon family meeting. "I've had enough of all this already."

Ricky had spirited Susan's Father's Day missive out of Sam's dresser drawer. He wasn't sure if it was the pathos or the dishonesty he perceived that bothered him more.

Ricky was now determined to stop "taking in the family pathology," as he put it. He'd recently thrown his back out after a fight with Eve. At home, he decided, he "became his mother" by "internalizing her pain." He boycotted the family meeting because he wanted to focus on his own problems, not because he feared conflict. Conflict, with an assist from a particularly emotional stage of psychotherapy, had become Ricky's middle name—as he'd recently demonstrated during an encounter with his eminently successful fellow composer and longtime hero Stephen Sondheim.

Work had been going well for Ricky. He'd completed a number of song cycles for major singers and several ballets for a small modern dance company. The previous year he'd been an artist-in-residence in Denver, where he'd written a score for Bertolt Brecht's A Man's a Man. Broadway producers Dore Schary and Cheryl Crawford had heard and complimented his rich, complex music.

Sondheim, on the other hand, had recently created a work that New York Times theater critic Frank Rich called "a shambles." Merrily We Roll Along was a musical about three friends who reach the pinnacle of show business success only to discover that they've lost the ideals and spirit that animated them in the first place. Nineteen eighty-three may not have been the best time to examine the dark side of the American success story and the show quickly closed, but Ricky was moved by many of the songs and wrote Stephen Sondheim a letter, reminding him that he was the kid who'd vomited in his bathroom some years ago.

Sondheim wrote back, and in a few days Ricky found himself quavering on his hero's doorstep again, wearing an olive-green suit selected after forty-eight straight hours of fashion despair.

After several glasses of wine out on the terrace in back of Sondheim's brownstone, a discussion of the avant-garde operas of Philip Glass flowed easily into talk of obscure film scores. Ricky and Stephen talked on and on, fellow artists—peers.

Then Ricky heard himself say, "So Stephen, tell me what happened with *Merrily We Roll Along*."

"When did you see it?" Sondheim asked calmly.

"In first previews," Ricky answered.

Sondheim's voice got louder. "Don't you think it's a bit presumptuous to form an opinion from a first preview?"

Ricky admitted that he should have seen the show again after the previews, and he reiterated his love of the score.

"You know, it's people like you who are the reason I'm getting out of the theater!"

At first Ricky wondered if he was dreaming. But suddenly the Ricky Gordon who'd had just about enough of internalizing other people's pathologies spoke up. "People like *me!*" he screamed at his hero. "People like *me!* People like me have seen everything you've ever done six times over! People like me can play every song you've ever written from memory! You can't project your shit onto me. *I* am your fan!"

They yelled at each other all the way out of the house and onto Forty-ninth Street, where Ricky bellowed at the top of his lungs, "You...are...not...my father!"

And with that, Stephen Sondheim turned his back and stomped away.

So it wasn't confrontation *per se* that caused the veteran family witness in Ricky to pass up the Susan meeting. If anything, it was the sadness sure to be born of the confrontation that he couldn't bear right now. It wasn't so much that Susan would claim once again that she'd kept a vigil over the family, raised her siblings, and been denied her father's love; it was his fear of the look on his father's face when she said it. Ricky knew that Susan's Father's Day epistle had touched Sam deeply. It would remain in the top drawer of his dresser, hidden beneath his socks, for many years to come. Ricky didn't want to see his father retreat in pain.

Not long ago Ricky and Sam had argued about the movie *Gandhi* after Sam's verdict that "Gandhi was a nut."

"*Gandhi?* Gandhi was a nut!" Ricky cried. "I mean, is that all you have to say? Gandhi was a nut?"

But for some reason Sam wouldn't take the bait. Ricky's leonine dad just sat there, hurt, as if he'd lost his instinct for the fray. "I'm not into fighting anymore, you know," Sam said later.

More recently, Sam had confided to Ricky, "You know, the suburbs backfired on me." Ricky found the statement so painful that he was able to contemplate it only as a line he would someday have to set to music.

So when Eve invited him to the family meeting, Ricky said, "Count me out." Some family Waterloos would have to pass unobserved.

———◆———

"We're here, Susan," Jon said again, "because we all think you need help."

In his can-do way Jon had discovered that Susan could probably finance a stay at a drug rehabilitation center. Since the previous November, she had been working a night job at a type and print shop owned by Reverend Moon's Unification Church. Moon was in jail now on tax fraud and conspiracy charges (under oath at his trial, he had declared, "I have the possibility of becoming the real Messiah"), but his young flower-brandishing "Moonies" still plied city streets all over the country for contributions, and the managers of the Unification Church's significant store of accrued assets continued to invest in print shops, New England fishing fleets, and various publishing operations, including D.C.'s daily *Washington Times*. Thanks to the benefits package extended to employees of the possible real Messiah, Susan had health insurance, and Jon wanted her to use it to go into treatment.

"What I need," Susan said, "is a black box."

It was said that several famous British rockers had cleaned up with a black box, an electronic device designed to emit sonic vibrations that would quell addicts' cravings by producing the endorphins they no longer produced naturally. New research on the brain chemistry of drug addicts now focused on a nodal cluster of cells at the base of the brain called the locus coeruleus, a chunk of bluish-colored matter that was thought to be the engine of anxiety and fear. There were also rumors on the street and in addiction recovery circles that soon a new drug would address the needy opiate receptors in this section of the brain. And if you were a rich enough junkie, you could go off to one of several clinics in Western Europe to have your blood replaced like so much dirty motor oil.

Lorraine shook her head at the mention of the black box. "Oh, come on," she said, looking at Sheila.

Until Shuna told Jon what was going on at home, Sheila had remained almost as steadfast as Eve in her refusal to consider Susan an addict. "It's a weekend thing," she'd say. "She just pops pills." Now, as she sat on the couch looking at her fidgeting sister, Sheila saw a woman who'd lost her apartment, was having parenting problems with her daughter, and had trouble holding down a job. Susan, Sheila thought, was a girl in need of her family's love.

Sam sat in the barber's chair in the same single-pocket T-shirt he always wore, staring helplessly at Susan while Jon tried to get her attention. Sam would later be unable to recall how the family meeting came about, but he always remembered that he'd never felt so utterly powerless in all his life.

When the day came that Sam could no longer align himself with Eve's denial that Susan had a serious problem, his one instinct had been to take her to the police and turn her in. Sam knew from his experience with horses that drugs could make you strong and drugs could make you weak, but a person needed drugs all the time only when life stopped having any meaning. Sam had no idea what to do about Susan, so for now he sat stricken in the barber chair while his son-in-law wielded the family scepter.

"What we want to suggest," Jon continued, "is that—"

"None of you can possibly understand this!" Susan cried. "I'm not the same as any of you. I *feel* things more. I'm too sensitive. I have all this pain—"

"Spare us the junkie talk, Susan," Lorraine cut in, her voice rising. "Let's not fall into some kind of routine here. Let's just try to focus on your addiction, not on your excuses for it."

Jon attempted to retake the floor, but Susan bolted to her feet, flailing her finger at him. "You! You! Before you came along, *I* was the one in this family that everybody looked up to." She turned and swept the finger around the family circle until it was pointing back at Jon. "He just came in and scarfed up all of my father's attention. He just took over my role in the family! He scarfed it up!"

Now Sheila was on her feet, her big eyes bright. "Even if that's true, Susan," she said, "don't blame Jon because your father doesn't pay attention to you!"

Everyone turned to Sam. With tears brimming in his eyes, he looked to Lorraine like an older version of the man in the windbreaker who once stared at her from a doorway at Bellevue Hospital. Lorraine looked at her father and saw a man bravely doing what he could for his family just by being there, just by staying there in his chair.

Shuna looked and saw a grandfather who didn't care. *He doesn't want to be here,* she thought.

Sheila looked and saw an unfamiliar Sam. *Maybe he's not always brave. Maybe Daddy can be as terrified by the emotions that come out of people as I am.*

Sheila spoke up again. "I think we all know that Susan has a serious problem. We should talk about the options available to someone who wants to get off drugs." She mentioned Jon's discovery that various "chemical dependency" facilities would accept Susan's health insurance. She and Jon would pay for her transportation.

"I think the place James Taylor went would be really good," Shuna said weakly. She couldn't read the look her mother gave her.

Susan had occasionally seen James Taylor standing in line on her erstwhile trips to Manhattan methadone clinics. The gifted songwriter and singer had grown up with "all the advantages," as the saying went. His father once said, "We quite consciously set out to raise our children free of the hang-ups we see in ourselves and our generation." James's brother said they'd been raised to believe "that simply because you were a Taylor, you could and should be able to accomplish anything." Accomplished in the extreme, by his generation's standards, James Taylor stood in line with everyone else to wait for his methadone. Susan watched him, tall and gaunt, hunching down into his long raincoat in a futile attempt to disappear. But some teen junkie always came up to him with a pen. "Hey, James! Could you please autograph my take-out slip?"

Taylor had also sought rehabilitation at one of the expensive inpatient facilities now flourishing around the country. When Shuna mentioned "the place James Taylor went," Lorraine assumed she had heard Susan claim that she deserved a lavish means of kicking drugs.

"There's no such thing as a middle-class junkie," Lorraine said, staring at Susan. "A junkie's a junkie." Lorraine's voice was heavy with experience. "You know that better than I do, Susan."

Unable to imagine losing either her family or her heroin, Susan finally agreed to go away for treatment. With that, the family meeting was adjourned.

As Sam pried himself from the barber chair, Lorraine came and stood by his side. "You did a really good job tonight," he said. "Thanks."

Lorraine turned away quickly, trying to remember another instance when she'd ever pleased her father. All that came back were a few silent nods offered when she'd handed over the right tool at age five.

Eve, who hadn't said a word during the meeting, went immediately to her bedroom. Susan followed her. "So now you know."

"So now I know," Eve said, almost whispering.

"Now that you know, how about giving me seventy bucks so I won't be sick?"

Susan was broke and had little left to sell. An emerald-and-diamond ring that the family appraiser, Aunt Sylvia, valued at around eight thousand dollars had recently gone to a pawnbroker for fifteen hundred. The lone cherished possession from all the trunks and boxes Susan used to cart from dwelling to dwelling like some high Victorian tourist was the strand of pearls Sam had given her when Shuna was born.

Eve went to her dresser and got her purse.

Two weeks separated the family meeting and Susan's departure for one of the nunneries to which junkies had been getting themselves for several years now. On most of those fourteen mornings, Shuna awoke surprised that the night had passed without news of her mother's death. But then she remembered that *she* was the one who was dead. Shuna found that she could make herself believe she was dead with the same facility her mother brought to believing she was a rat.

Shuna was about to enter the famous New York High School for the Performing Arts, where she would develop her natural flair for drawing. It was decided that she would commute to school from Harbor Isle.

Four days before Susan left for Minneapolis and St. Mary's Hospital, Shuna went downtown after school to visit her father. Strolling down St. Marks Place, she passed a spot she'd visited often because one of her mother's dope connections hung out there, an enterprising young man who moonlighted as a pimp. Shuna was looking straight ahead, trying to ignore the spot, when she thought she heard her mother's voice coming from a parked car. "Shuna, it's me." She walked a bit faster, locking her gaze hard into the distance. *I am dead*, she thought. *Just walk ahead, Shuna. Just be dead.*

1984

"**S**ome of 'em gotta be here hiding out from the cops," Sam said on his first day at the ashram. He had an elaborate theory about Yogaville being little more than a latter-day Hole-in-the-Wall. "Perfectly situated in Asshole, Virginia. Think about it," he'd say. "Who'd ever think to look there?"

During lunch that first day of Sam and Eve's visit, he inspected the interior of Siviananda Hall, a multi-use auditorium and cafeteria, well enough constructed and currently filling up with a lot of hungry suspects, each of whom, to the man, woman, and whispering child, gave Sam a jangling case of the heebie-jeebies. The ashram dwellers waited to pass in front of a table offering rice, yogurt, wheat germ, a curry concoction, and a stainless steel vat of what looked to be stewed kelp. Then most of them went to kneel at one of several long tables with legs no more than two feet high. They hunkered devoutly over their bowls, obviously satisfied, Sam thought, by something that had nothing at all to do with food. He had to force himself to stop staring at all their pious, apple-cheeked faces.

Over the doorway leading out of Siviananda Hall into a lobby where you were allowed to talk, Sam saw a huge photograph depicting the aging swami on top of a mountain, eyeballing a nearby cloud. The walls were lined with hyperreal portraits of Jesus and Buddha and various modern spiritual dignitaries. On a large stage at one end of the hall loomed a life-sized full-color cardboard cutout of Lorraine's guru, cross-legged in his saffron robes. On the other side of the stage sat a throne, an honest-to-God wooden throne. Citizens of Buckingham County who came to check out what "the Hindus" of Yogaville were up to always went away talking about the throne.

But Sam couldn't stop looking at the faces on the ashram regulars, each a mask stretched tight around something utterly pathetic. Or dangerous—Sam wasn't quite sure which. These were loser faces of long standing. These were people who'd fallen off their horses a long, long time ago and would never manage to remount. They'd come to a riverbank haven "unchanged since the Pilgrims," Sam said, because here the world stood still and all you had to do to fit in was stay calm.

"That smile," Sam whispered to Eve. "Check out that smile."

Eve cocked her head and mimicked the smile expertly.

By the end of the day, Eve was furious. She resented deeply that the goal of "yogi shit" was to run as far as possible from the "real shit" everyone else had to wade through. Real life was being sixty-three years old and managing a family still mired in a forty-two-year run of turmoil. Real life was having two complicated teenagers on your hands, both of them looking for constant care in recompense for what they'd been through.

At the turn of the year, demographers had reported that millions of American children Shuna's or Maggie's age or a bit older were either staying at home or moving back home. In Detroit, a study by the Advance Mortgage Corporation showed a huge increase in local apartment vacancies because children were "doubling up" with their parents, a phenomenon not seen since the young husbands and wives of the immediate postwar years moved in with their urban parents. In the poorer sections of many cities, families were even tripling up—a result of the Reagan administration's radical cuts in affordable housing allotments, according to some public policy experts.

Maggie and Shuna, as their grandmother was quick to point out, were not her children. By the end of the 1980s the significant percentage of mothers who were bringing up their children's children would finally draw public attention, but in 1984, to the extent the trend was noticed at all, it was thought to be confined to the black ghettos.

Often, after Sam went to sleep, Eve—whom the grandchildren called Nanny without reference to the hired caretakers of the idealized Victorian family—would cry for hours. She kept hearing voices.

Why should you? one said.

Because you have to. You love them, said another.

But why you? Let somebody else do it! It's too goddamn hard. You know you don't want to. Aren't you entitled to a life?

No. I mean yes. I have to. I can handle it. Besides, I have an open kitchen now. I have a view.

Whatever else might be said of this Mohan, the husband with whom Lorraine was attempting a reconciliation, Sam could tell within five minutes that he was no professional contractor. Sam watched Mohan and a friend work on one of the many mobile homes that full-time ashramites lived in. Mohan stood on one side of the trailer, struggling with sheets of aluminum he thought would insulate the flimsy dwellings from the temperatures outside. Every so often he'd throw his hammer over the top of the trailer to his friend on the other side. Sam watched the performance with his mouth open. Finally he retrieved one of his own hammers from his extensive traveling tool kit. "Here," he said. "So no one should get killed."

When Sam and Eve got back from the construction site that would someday be LOTUS, Sam found his hammer near a puddle, caked with mud. He stood there glowering as if it were the grand old flag smoldering on the ground. Eve looked at him and knew he was crossing yet another son-in-law off his list. With each blink of her husband's offended eyes, Mohan Wenzel was plummeting further into the void.

Once again Sam and Eve were confronted with the painful sight of their Lorraine in poverty. It was even worse now because of the three young boys who loved to hang from Sam's neck. This time Lorraine had found a hillbilly style of downtroddenness that reminded her parents of Walker Evans photographs and magazine pictures of ragged Okies on the move from the Depression.

"Another loser place," said Sam.

"No," said Eve. "This is poverty beyond the pale."

The ashram was located in one of the poorest parts of the country. The unemployment rate in Buckingham County was perennially twice the Virginia state average. One fifth of the three thousand or so people in the forested hills and valleys of the geographically immense county lived in poverty.

While Satchidananda had many prosperous devotees (the guru noted with pleasure that "where there had once been hippies" there were now "doctors, lawyers, administrators," and other professionals in his flock), a significant proportion of the several hundred members who lived on the grounds of the Yogaville ashram—among them "householders" who were expected to pay their own way, unlike the resident renunciants training to be swamis—had to scrounge for money.

The young swamis of the *sannyas* order had taken the seemingly contradictory vows of "detachment and devotion" ("detachment" from cars, houses, and trust funds often liquidated for the sake of "devotion"). The ritual abnegations of the *sannyasin* included a pledge to "dedicate my entire life and renounce all the things which I call mine at the feet of Sri Gurudev. This includes my body, mind, emotions, intellect and all the material goods in my possession." Though they weren't expected to pay for basics like food and lodging, they were relegated to rickety trailers sometimes infested with mice or lice.

By 1984, alternative lifestyles like the one in evidence at Yogaville—which ten years earlier might have been ranked in the forefront of cultural rebellion—were widely regarded as "marginal," and the people who lived them as declassed "refugees from the 1960s," a dismissive phrase favored by peers who'd scrambled for a spot in the economic mainstream. "Guru" had now entered the vocabulary as a title for aerobics masters and stock market seers. The "world teacher" Satchidananda had an audience with Pope John Paul II in May (Swamiji gave the Pope a lotus pin, and the Pope gave Swamiji an apostolic medallion), but several Integral Yoga schools had closed down. Yogaville and an ashram in California (as well as a two-thousand-acre "sister community" in Australia) were now the swami's mainstay.

Lorraine watched Ram and Shiva climb all over Sam, giggling and screaming as he tossed them into the air like toys.

"I wonder if we'll ever hear any good news from Lorraine," Sam said as he and Eve were leaving.

"Well, there's her children," said Eve.

"Beautiful kids," he agreed. "Some of the best kids in the whole world."

"If you can judge a person's life by their kids—and God knows people do—then Lorraine's doing okay."

After stopping for some "real food," Sam and Eve drove to Monticello, home of an American who believed that the world belonged to the living, not to some revolving cast of recycled souls. Thomas Jefferson lost four of his six children to the early death so common in his era, and his beloved wife died young (he was so long beside her sickbed that his patriotism was publicly questioned). One of his two surviving daughters gave him ten grandchildren. President, philosopher, scientist, architect, undoubtedly one of the busier husbands, fathers, and grandfathers of his time, Jefferson said toward the end, "The happiest moments of my life have been the few which I have passed at home in the bosom of my family."

Sam had to wonder if Jefferson got flak from his kids at the end of a long day building the nation.

Michael Reagan, the current president's son by his first marriage, complained in *People* magazine that his father had yet to invite him to the White House ("It seems Nancy's are the real kids"). But on Father's Day, during his weekly radio address, the president once again called for a return to "traditional family values." A few weeks later, the evangelical guardians of those values all but overran the Republican National Convention in Dallas, where many more crosses than elephants were on display as Ronald Reagan did his best to make the pro-family forces feel at home. He told them that politics and morality could not be separated in a decent nation. "We need religion as a guide. We need it because we are imperfect." He said he wanted to put God "back in the classroom."

Sam was less keen on Reagan now, largely because his policies seemed to favor the rich and invite economic concentrations on the order of the old monopolies. Reagan would turn out to be the fourth president in a row Sam would later regret voting for. Though he supported him again in November as "the least of two evils," he barely cared enough to vote at all. By now it was just a habit, and Sam felt both proud and sad to think that there had once been a time when you could vote for a man because you believed he could be truly great.

Sam and Eve drove all over Virginia, the first of the Thirteen Colonies. They stopped so Sam could examine the overgrown stations where General Lee's fleeing troops had rested their horses. They stopped wherever Sam spotted evidence of superior craftsmanship from a time when people had respect. He found a cemetery with some of the most intricate and artistic ironwork he'd ever come across. "Eve! Look. I can't believe what I'm seeing," he said. "And nobody bothers to notice. Everyone probably just walks by."

When he traveled around the country, Sam was always touched most by things that hadn't changed. He and Eve pulled into a southern town where everyone was so worked up over a high school basketball game that all the stores were closed and the motel rooms filled with out-of-town relatives. Sam's kids had never been excited about something as simple as a basketball game—but then, neither had he. His children had apparently been born aspiring to something far different from the school spirit he'd never had time to enjoy.

"You know what really gets me about the ashram?" Eve said as they headed north. "It's that they all believe they can change things simply by running away to someplace new. They don't know that there's really no Nirvana—I think that's what they call it. There's no such place as Shangri-la."

━━◆◆━━

Ricky was performing at the Grand Casino des Bains des Mers, an aristocratic fortress in the principality of Monaco. Beyond the stage was an audience liberally strewn with European royalty who'd come to Monte Carlo for the Grand Prix. Dark men in perfect tuxedos sat beside women in long gowns with surgically taut faces.

Before the curtain went up, Ricky would entertain members of the twenty-piece orchestra he was conducting. Accompanying himself on piano, he'd sing his densely melodic settings of Yeats, May Sarton, and W. S. Merwin, turning and lowering his head slightly as he often did when he played, his eyes closed tight. The musicians loved it, and one night Ricky heard one of them say "genius" in French just as four dancers in silver lamé jumpsuits took their positions on stage.

The curtain rose, Ricky raised his baton, and the orchestra blasted out the opening strains of "Maniac," the hit song from the movie *Flashdance*. In an instant, the crowd was roaring. Princelings and peers of assorted realms went wild.

On his day off, Ricky was talking to one of the lean dancers on a train headed for Milan. He'd become obsessed with the young man, who was blond, blue-eyed, and beautifully muscled. In the middle of an intellectually strenuous point, Ricky saw the dancer's eyes go dead, as if he'd suddenly heard "Maniac" rolling down from an Apennine hilltop. His head turned mechanically toward the window.

Ricky took out his notebook and wrote what would later become lyrics to a song, "Bright Red Flowers": "All the pretty fields are full of bright red flowers / Staring out the window's pane for miles and hours /…Somewhere you were rude to me…Rude you were, you turned your head away…"

Back home, it didn't take more than half a therapy session for the incident and lyrics to open onto a jolting moment of Oedipal byplay. Down the stairs he'd bounded, five years old and happy, leaping into his father's arms. But his father turned away.

Ricky no longer slept with a hammer under his pillow. The dragons of the unconscious had fallen before therapy and experience. Ricky sat down to attend to some unsettled business.

Dear Dad, This letter is to let you know that I love you. I don't know if you know that.

Dad, sometimes I feel like it makes you upset that I spend more time with mom than with you. I'm used to her—we have a lot in common, mom and I.

Once you told me you were not interested in getting angry anymore, but I guess in a lot of ways, you were very angry when we were little, dad. I understand it. You were working your ass off all day and there were four screaming kids when you came home. I was mad though, mad and upset. I didn't feel like you spent enough time with me. There were only women to be with, so they were all I was used to. But I have turned out OK.

Dad, I'm gay—so what. I love someone who loves me. We get along. That's more than I can say for most people.

...I know from little things you've told me that there were problems with your father. Listen, father and son relationships are hard. I am not the same kind of man as you, dad—I never was—but I am a man. I admire your strength and persistence, but I love myself for being sensitive and perceptive. I think there is room in the world for all kinds, and I'm happy to be here.

I love you dad—no matter what happens. Don't ever forget that.

Ricky

P.S. We once had a talk in a truck about how the suburbs backfired on you in terms of your kids. The opening to the musical I'm writing about a family is about that. I appreciate your input.

A few weeks after Ricky sent his letter, he and his new boyfriend, a singer named Jim Mahady, went to Sheila's house for Thanksgiving dinner. Before everyone gathered around the table, Sam plopped down next to his son on the couch and leaned toward him as he had in Ricky's dream, when they were together in the gay bar.

"Got your letter," Sam said, his voice gruff and thick. After a moment he said, "Thanks." Then Sam got up slowly to take his place at the head of the dinner table.

———◆———

It had now been a year since Susan left New York, a full year since she had an animated conversation with herself all the way to Minnesota. Susan had begun jabbering away in full voice in the departure lounge at LaGuardia, her lines supplied by a combination of some extremely pure heroin she'd stuffed up her nose in the ladies' room and disparate bits and pieces of her fragmented personality that floated to the surface now and again.

The veteran chemical dependency (CD) professionals at St. Mary's who treated Susan after she arrived in Minneapolis tended to regard

West Coast operations like the new Betty Ford Center and the place in Rancho Mirage that had reconstituted Elizabeth Taylor earlier in the year as upstarts. St. Mary's had its own star-studded clientele, including actor Dick Van Dyke and Robert Kennedy's son David, who later overdosed in Florida. St. Mary's had matriculated a sufficient number of CEOs, Wall Street traders, and similar sorts to fill up a large room at Manhattan's Harvard Club for the hospital's annual fund-raiser. In the hallways of St. Mary's it was often whispered that a recent registrant was a senior soldier shipped in from a New York Mafia family because he'd become too personally involved with his stock-in-trade. A very good drug customer of Susan's had made the trip to St. Mary's—a rambling red-brick campus rising dramatically on a high bluff overlooking the Mississippi—and had returned to New York an ex-customer. She told Susan that if you had to kick, St. Mary's was the way to go, though as most veteran addicts correctly understood, the success rates at even the most elite detox programs were depressingly low.

Minneapolis had become the Mecca of addicts and alcoholics looking to make a change. By 1984 the CD "business" there was being likened to the advertising or financial services industries in New York. Barely five minutes of radio time in the Twin Cities area passed without mention of the well-known names and 800 numbers of several of the more than twenty chemical dependency facilities.

The local human turnaround business was in part nurtured by an early 1970s state law requiring insurance companies to provide some coverage for chemical dependency treatment. The presence in one city of elite repair shops like Hazelden (retreat of many famous alcoholics, Liza Minnelli being a recent example), the Johnson Institute (home of the "intervention" technique and other adaptations of family therapy), and the hospital programs at Willmar State and St. Mary's (considered the source of the "Minnesota Model" of addiction treatment) may also have owed something to a local faith in programmatic approaches to health and welfare, the result, perhaps, of the area's Scandinavian heritage.

The Minnesota Model wedded neurological and medical research into the chemistry of addiction to the "modalities" of recovery pioneered by Alcoholics Anonymous. A patient at St. Mary's was invited into the "lifelong process" of recovering from addiction through a complex and delicate treatment designed to restore physical, mental, social, familial, and spiritual well-being.

Many members of the large clinical and support staff at St. Mary's had kicked monster addictions of their own, but Susan's two-bundle-a-day habit made them step back with something like respect. This New York City girl with the street mouth had a jones as big as the Ritz.

Susan didn't sleep much for the first three weeks of detox. Counselors would come in and sit with her through some of the worst moments. They explained that she had a serious chronic disease that was nevertheless amenable to something like a cure, but first she would have to stop taking drugs—all drugs. This was the first of a series of Minnesota Model modalities that irritated the hell out of Susan. Her problem was with heroin, not with the many lesser and far more socially acceptable substances that had been a part of her life since she was a young girl.

In subsequent group therapy sessions at the hospital, fellow patients and professionals told Susan that she had to admit and accept the extent of her problem. Now was the time to clarify and reassess her most basic values. Staff "spiritual counselors" explained the precepts of twelve-step programs like those of Alcoholics Anonymous or Narcotics Anonymous. The idea seemed to be that once you admitted that you were a hopeless addict, that you couldn't handle your life by yourself, that drugs had so enhanced your capacity for selfishness that you no longer gave a hoot about anyone else, you could join the fraternity of the sick and attempt to get straight "one day at a time."

"For most people, growing up is a natural process," said one of the Narcotics Anonymous pamphlets Susan was given. "As addicts, however, we seem to falter along the way. We never seem to outgrow the self-centeredness of the child. We never seem to find the self-sufficiency that others do....We become self-obsessed; our wants and needs become our demands."

Many of Susan's fellow patients participated in an elaborate "family program." Entire families showed up for a full week of group therapy, lectures, and "communications workshops." Susan would later think that if only her family had come, then perhaps all the time and money invested in her at St. Mary's might have come to something more.

The actual stay at St. Mary's was short. Only a few years earlier rehabilitation patients would stay for two months, but with the insurance companies checking the records and asking for evidence of recovery every day, treatment now lasted only twenty-eight days.

Susan had spent her fortieth birthday at a St. Mary's halfway house. Gina Schick sent a mug that said "I'd rather be forty than pregnant." Ricky sent a flannel shirt to keep Susan warm during a Minnesota winter that forever emblazoned the term "wind chill" on the memories of addicts from milder climes. By the time the thaw came, Susan was sneaking out of the halfway house as easily as she used to sneak out of 221 Lincoln Avenue. She would smoke pot beside the Mississippi River or at her new job as a proofreader for a small printing shop. The pot, Susan believed, was keeping her straight.

As the weather turned cold again in the fall, some people from *Life* magazine tracked Susan down in Minneapolis. By then she was pumping a couple of cooked-up loads of a controlled narcotic analgesic called Dilaudid into her arm every day. *Life* offered to fly Susan to San Francisco as part of the magazine's plan to reunite important figures from the Berkeley scene in the 1960s. Twenty-five leaders of the Berkeley Free Speech Movement were duly located and assembled on the steps of the University of California administration building. Jerry Rubin ("46, a New York businessman," his photo caption reported), Black Panther leader Bobby Seale ("48, director of a Philadelphia youth program...still a political revolutionary by principle"), the surviving members of the Grateful Dead, and the surviving members of Janis Joplin's band, Big Brother and the Holding Company—including the drummer, David Getz ("44, a silk-screen artist")—all agreed to pose for a retrospective ode to the town "where the sixties were born."

Proud as she was of her junkie boast about dropping into any city in the world and scaring up a fix before the sweats kicked in, Susan was glad that a Minneapolis buddy, an actor who starred in porno movies, had given her the name of a Bay Area connection. Throughout the reunion, the photo shoot, her interview about her memories of the sixties, and a late-night conversation with her old CR group friends Nancy Bardacke and Consie Miller (during which she told them about her drug problems and said she was now getting straight), Susan was blasted, high as could be.

On the sixth page of the *Life* spread, which appeared in early 1985, was a photograph of eight members of Berkeley's first women's group below the headline "Struggling for Sisterhood and Liberation." Susan Lydon (41, occupation not reported) sat in the front row. She was slumped to one side with her head resting on the shoulder of her friend Suzy Nelson, a rising star of the northern California restaurant scene. At first glance, Susan's pose appeared to be one of sisterly affection. But if you looked closer, you could see something strange about her eyes.

Ironically, Minneapolis had recently eclipsed Berkeley as a citadel of radical feminism. In January the thoughtful mayor of Minneapolis, Donald Fraser, had vetoed an amendment to the city's Civil Rights Ordinance that would have redefined certain kinds of pornography as "the sexually explicit subordination of women, explicitly depicted." Fraser contended that the definition, written by University of Minnesota law professor Catharine MacKinnon and feminist Andrea Dworkin, was so broad and vague as to raise constitutional issues he could not ignore. By midsummer the city council was once again debating a similar ordinance, and a twenty-three-year-old woman had doused herself with gasoline and set herself on fire because, she told friends, pornography and sexual exploitation had ruined her life. But Susan wasn't even aware of the imbroglio. Her friend in the porno business, as it happened, was actually one of the more pleasant and honest people she knew.

Not long after she returned from Berkeley, Susan took up with a boyfriend who held knives to her throat and beat her with his heavy boots. She'd never expected Ahmad to become her boyfriend when she met him in a grocery store, but when another downtown street hustler she'd been hanging with was sent to prison, she felt the need of male companionship and protection—especially protection, because Susan was a woman, and also because she'd adapted to local market conditions by severely "stepping on," or diluting, the heroin she sold. Cutting a package until there was hardly any drug at all left inside, and generally conning customers and adventurous tourists—known as "wopping" along the downtown Minneapolis thoroughfare Hennepin Avenue— was a risky business made less so if a girl had a friend like Ahmad.

Ahmad was a handsome, sexy man. He had skin of an almost adobe hue that looked burnished under the dim lights he favored. He had powerful, bulging muscles from lifting weights day after day while in prison. His eyes, at peace or in rage, were red. After a while, Susan moved in with him. She'd accompany him to the dice houses, where she would stand at his shoulder for hours.

Ahmad was a gambler, a pimp, and a leading member of the underground chamber of commerce composed of black street hustlers who had trained in places like Detroit, Chicago, Memphis, Kansas City, and even New York before coming to Minneapolis, Minnesota, there to exploit some of the whitest and most naïve people in the civilized—and thus connable—world. Compared to the fully criminalized street gangs that terrorized many urban neighborhoods, most of the jolly Robin Hoods of Hennepin Avenue, with their wop cocaine or heroin and trade in tricks that did or did not exist, were law-abiding citizens. Sometimes the boys would dispense with salesmanship and steal people's money outright, but mostly they only lied and cheated and retailed illegal goods and services.

Susan could find street friends along "the Avenue" twenty-four hours a day. Named for Louis Hennepin, the Franciscan friar who came upon the "dark and inexorable" Mississippi with La Salle, it was now lined with seedy movie houses, seedy bookstores, and shops displaying mechanized dildos and an array of fascinating steel objects.

If Susan appeared in the doorway of a Hennepin Avenue bar called Moby's, home of "whale-sized drinks," one of Ahmad's colleagues might call out to her by her street nickname, "Yo, New York." She usually arrived at Moby's with several shopping bags full of fancy perfumes and colognes, expensive clothes, and other fashion accessories. She'd learned how to "boost" these goods from racks and shelves of up-market local shops. Shoplifting seemed the most appropriate supplement to her continued work in the print shop and her wopping. At the print shop she made three hundred a week. Shoplifting, she made three hundred in a day—not that this was enough, since nothing ever was. But boosting was a middle-class job for which Susan had a lifetime of applicable shopping experience.

Sometimes, after a fix, Susan would wander into one of the many bookstores in the reader's town of Minneapolis—a city of 500,000 inhabitants, a little more than twice the number of junkies in New York—and find the paperbacks she knew bore little blurbs drawn from reviews she'd written for the *Village Voice*. Then she would turn around and trudge back toward the Avenue.

<hr />

Eve had been taking piano lessons for six months when Susan called just after Thanksgiving to say she was coming home to visit. Eve was "already with the pedals" and playing well enough to accompany herself on a couple of songs. Playing made her feel good. It was something she was doing just for herself "for a change," like a trip to the casinos.

A guy Susan knew from dealing and methadone lines picked her up at LaGuardia and drove her straight to the South Bronx. Susan said she wanted to see the old neighborhood—and cop.

More than a quarter of the South Bronx had become a ravaged moonscape. A few years earlier, during the World Series, sportscaster Howard Cosell had looked at a flaming video image sent into the heartland from the Goodyear Blimp over Yankee Stadium and reported, "The Bronx is on fire."

Now the arsonists were finished, and Susan led her friend past demolished and gutted buildings, expecting to see the storybook neighborhood of her imagined youth in ruins. It was two in the morning when they passed the infamous bunkered police station known as Fort Apache and turned onto Hunt's Point Avenue. There, not two blocks from the apartment houses that occupied her dreams, Susan saw women wheeling bundled babies along the street, people hurrying through the unseasonable warmth of the evening to the Laundromat, young men in small groups playing conga drums. Whole families sat on the stoops of coral-colored buildings, looking safe and happy in a place most New Yorkers were much too afraid to go. Then Susan saw the telltale curve on Hunt's Point Avenue up ahead, and she began to remember everything. She later told her friend that she felt her grandparents walking with them on the ghostly, lively streets of the Bronx that night.

Copping was another story. In response to President Reagan's constant rhetoric, police pressure had been stepped up since Susan left town. Federal contributions to New York drug rehabilitation programs had actually diminished in the last two years, from over thirty-four million to just over nineteen million, and the New York police commissioner, Benjamin Ward, said his forces had arrested some four thousand "low-level" dealers in a single year to demonstrate to Reagan and Mayor Koch that rhetoric was not enough. But all this meant to the junkies was that it was harder to find the drug bazaars and the all-essential connection.

Early the next morning, Eve peeked into the spare bedroom and found Susan lying on her back in her bathrobe. Her arms and legs extended unnaturally from her torso, like the limbs of a battle casualty. Her head was at an odd angle, and her mouth was hanging open.

Eve put her hand to her heart. She was sure her daughter was dead. But Susan's neck was warm when Eve slipped her arm around her and hoisted her into a sitting position. Eve looked down and saw bright white dust all over the bed.

"Is that drugs?" she asked, her lips close to Susan's ear.

Susan opened one eye and glanced at the powder. "Ummm, no."

"You said you didn't do this anymore!" Eve screamed. "How many times can you kill a person, Susan? How many times can you stick a knife in a person?"

Susan's eyes were shut again. "You're...overreacting," she mumbled.

"Overreacting! Listen to me! Just go get a gun and shoot yourself, Susan. Make it easier, Susan. Please!"

Eve couldn't remember ever hearing her own voice so loud.

When Susan got back to Minneapolis she told Ahmad and some of the street hustlers at Moby's that her mother was finally through with her. "It's all over," she said. "I have no place to go."

Eve called her piano teacher after Susan left to say that she wouldn't be able to come by anymore.

1985

Out of the odd dream-light of a fitful sleep and into the darkness of her Harbor Isle bedroom, Shuna was already sitting up when she opened her eyes. It was three in the morning. She was panting hard and sobbing. The echoes of a scream she'd heard in the dream were still reverberating in her ears.

Something was wrong. Shuna knew she had to find her mother.

Eve had written Susan's latest telephone number in her address book at the bottom of a page with so many crossed-out lines that it looked like an accountant's log. Shuna didn't phone her mother often. One time she'd called to tell Susan that she was thinking about killing herself—something she talked about all the time since coming to Harbor Isle, as Eve could attest. "I am too," her mother moaned. "I'm thinking about the same thing."

Shuna went off to Minneapolis for a brief visit one time, and she came back with her head full of brand-new nightmares. In Minneapolis she'd met her mother's handsome boyfriend, whose face came back to her now like some terrible mask carved on a totem pole. Shuna thought her mother shared this boyfriend with another woman who lived in the same scary place.

"But how *was* she?" Eve kept asking when Shuna returned.

"Fine," Shuna would say. "She's fine."

One day Shuna looked up at the Empire State Building and thought she saw herself floating down from the top. Not long after, she began to see a psychotherapist in Manhattan. During the early sessions, Shuna found that if she really concentrated, she could turn her life into a slide show. She could render a mental image—of her maternal grandmother's face, for instance—static and amenable to closer study, like the pictures she captured so skillfully with her camera.

All her life, Shuna had considered herself a serious student of grown-ups, in all their glory and astounding fatuity, but after her therapist helped her isolate and concentrate on a particular person, she began to see much more. She noticed that if Eve wasn't singing or talking, her face naturally fell into an angry frown.

"Do you have, like, a Gordon voice in your head?" Shuna asked Maggie. "I mean, just the sound of their voices without the words? When I think about the Gordon voice in my head, it sounds like the way people sound when they say, 'I hate you.'"

"I hear it too sometimes," Maggie said.

But Maggie was twenty years old now to Shuna's seventeen. Maggie was on the verge of transcending the family altogether. She was a student of modern literature. She had a mother who did things Maggie was able to consider "just silly."

The night Shuna found herself hyperventilating in her bed, she wanted her mother—no matter how deeply silly or depraved her mother had become.

"Yeah, she was here," said someone at the new drug rehabilitation hospital after Shuna dialed the most recent number in Eve's address book. "But now she's in jail."

"Why?" Shuna asked, still panting. "Where?"

"Well, it's weird," said the woman in Minnesota. "The cops just came right in here and took her to the county jail."

<hr>

On first sighting, the retired motorcycle bandit who was the new man in Lorraine's life made people jumpy. Bill Behny rose six feet five inches into the air and sported an enormous black beard that covered much of his handsome face and descended like a luxurious sable bib to just below his solar plexus. Along arms that appeared to conceal braided steel cord and pneumatic tubing were tattoos Bill had commissioned at various times: a rose in full bloom, a skull with a snake slithering out of an empty eye socket, a glaring black panther, the cartoon character Speedy Gonzalez. Big ornate block letters formed the words "GARBAGE GUT," and not far away, a dog was engaged in the evidently existential act of urinating on the pronoun "IT."

Recently pastoralized though he was, Bill Behny still looked like exactly what he'd been for half of his thirty-eight years—a member of a notorious biker gang that marauded through most midwestern states under the name and colors of the Hell's Henchmen. "Garbage Gut" Behny's dad, a suburban Chicago management consultant and father of six other children, had ordered his wildest and oldest boy out of the house when he was just thirteen. By the time he was fifteen, Bill could assemble a motorcycle from spare parts. By the time he was seventeen, he was a full-fledged Henchman. By August of 1968, when the members of the South Side chapter of the Hell's Henchmen decided to ride downtown to Grant Park to see what the cops and the hippie protesters were up to, Garbage Gut was chapter president.

As Bill recalled it, he and his buddies heard that the Democratic National Convention had brought "a whole lot of fuckin' braless hippie chicks" to town who were looking to "dispense free love." Instead, the Henchmen found the hippies in Grant Park fleeing before an army of frenzied Chicago cops in full charge. The bikers joined the protesters at the front lines for much of the first night of rioting. "We were used to being harassed by the Chicago police," Bill said, "but that night gangs of cops were dragging women and people walking down the street into alleys and doorways, just beating them over and over again."

Bill would always contend—revisionist rationalization though it might have been—that the bloody night in Grant Park began a process of alienation that would eventually turn his motorcycle club into the outlaw horde so many law-abiding citizens had since come to fear. By the time he decided to sell his several Harley-Davidsons and take early retirement from the gang's officer corps, the Henchmen were active in business sectors attended by the strong probability of a lengthy jail sentence. Bill told his buddies he was weary of the road, and like so many unhorsed highwaymen of his generation, he began to search far and wide for a piece of land to call home.

Beneath the Visigoth veneer, Bill was an animated, articulate talker who might have been known as a "charming conversationalist" if not for the residue of violence behind his smile and his eyes. Bill still tended to call women "bitches" (he would explain that the macho reference was just "a bad habit left over" from the biker life), and his reaction to the violation of his property or his person might not have been to phone the police, but he'd come to settle down not eight miles from Yogaville determined to be a good neighbor, a man of peace.

Less than a month after he found Buckingham County, Bill ventured down the road to help the "toe suckers" at the ashram put up a new building at the Integral Yoga school. He was excited to see Yogaville, in part because he had an old road buddy who'd gone yogi and moved there some months earlier, and also because he was intrigued by the idea of a self-sufficient community connected by faith, loyalty, and mutual respect. But as soon as he strolled across the gravel parking lot next to Siviananda Hall, Bill noticed ashram residents stopping in mid-stride to stare at him. Bill stopped and stared back. Each face was less friendly, healthy, or well fed than the last. Everyone he saw in Yogaville resembled a ravaged victim of something—cancer or famine.

Finally a skinny, wiry girl with long thick hair and glasses flashed him a smile. Toward the end of the day, Bill approached her. "I think you're beautiful," he said in his deep voice. "You don't seem to fit into this place. You look to me like a person who wants to be free."

<hr />

"Yeah," said a laconic attendant at the third jail Shuna called, "she's here."

"May I speak to her please?" Shuna asked politely. "She's my mother."

"Nope."

Shuna pleaded to no avail. She asked if she could leave a message for her mother.

"Nope."

Shuna managed to awaken Eve, but she couldn't stop crying. "They won't let you talk to her either," Shuna assured her.

"Yeah? Just watch me," Eve said as she threw on a robe.

At first Eve was polite and businesslike with the prison matron who answered the phone. "I am her mother!" Eve finally screamed. "And I...have...colon cancer! I have to talk to my girl. Right *now!*"

Like Ronald Reagan, Eve had recently entered the hospital to have a small early malignancy removed. She'd emerged with a clean bill of health. Shuna was astounded when she played the cancer card. She stood by fuming while Eve waited to talk to Susan—even though it had been *Shuna's* hallucinatory "gut instinct" that launched this most recent rescue effort.

Susan was sound asleep in her cell when the matron went to get her. She came to the phone and began to apprise her mother of the details of the latest miscarriage of American justice that had reunited her with prisoners and prison guards of her previous acquaintance.

Conversing with Susan Gordon Lydon ("a/k/a Susan C. Lydon, a/k/a Susan Carol Gordon," as she was now known in the Minnesota criminal justice system) had become a startling experience for anyone who'd

known her during any of her previous forty-one years. "Ah go' tell ya,
honey, ah juzz ain' go' doot!" she'd say in a declamatory falsetto. In her
diction and inflections Susan had come 180 degrees from her old
Katharine Hepburn/Vassar delivery. Now she spoke a pure, rhythmic
strain of street jive, heavily laced with the older sounds of the cotton
fields. Her voice was full of music, of struggle and flight.

The Gordons didn't sound like they all came from the same family.
You could hear the Lower East Side in Sam's speech, and Eve's East
Harlem childhood in hers. Ricky's accent was far more bleached of Long
Island than Sheila's, and Lorraine had no apparent accent at all, though
she slowly enunciated each syllable of each word as if she were waiting
for the sound of finger cymbals to syncopate a phrase. And now there
was Susan, the former Scarlett O'Hara of the Gordon clan, with her
street-hardened, fast-hustle variant on the dialect of Scarlett's beloved if
excitable black maid.

"She *is* a black person now," Eve announced to various members of
the family after another surreal phone call to Minnesota. "She sounds
like she's gonna break right into 'Swing Low, Sweet Chariot.'"

Susan's new dialect was in part utilitarian. Like the protective coloration offered by the less than fashionable wardrobe she now favored, a
mastery of the rich idiom of the urban ghettos was essential to work and
love on Hennepin Avenue. But the jive was also like a lifetime pass to
an endless show at the Apollo Theater, a means of moving closer to her
Minnesota family, and audible proof of citizenship in the downtown
democracy of junkies and hustlers and whores Susan had come to love.
To Susan's ear the street idiom sounded like real Americans talking. If
the rest of America would just emerge from the cloistered privacy of
modern life and take a look around, everyone would want to reclaim
this wonderful jargon, so theatrical and mimetic. When junkie oration
was pouring forth at its nonstop best, Susan felt part of something. She
was part of the family of cool, a thing she'd been chasing for many years.

Wisdom on Hennepin Avenue was a hybrid of the ability to stay
alive and the ability to play a serviceable Socrates when it was your turn
to address the outdoor academy. Junkies, Susan believed, were the color-
blind egalitarians of every white liberal's fantasy. Blacks called each
other "nigger" here and it meant nothing, because their connections as
brothers and sisters went deeper than words. Susan referred to one of
her dealer colleagues as "the most dishonest white man in the world,"
and the black street hustlers just smiled and agreed.

One time Susan was assigned to a halfway house in rural St. Cloud, a town full of great big German-Catholic Americans so blond and white you couldn't see them when it snowed. All she could think about was getting back to Minneapolis, to its perfect round lakes with names like Hiawatha and Nokomis, where a girl could sit on a bench in peace. Most of all she missed the warmth of the neon-lit stage on Hennepin Avenue, and she longed for all the tall talk a white Jewish junkie girl in blackface would never find in St. Cloud.

Like all Americans, the hustlers told each other stories about their families. And not one of those families resembled the Huxtables.

Some thirty million people now sat down each week to watch comedian Bill Cosby be a good father to a good family. Nothing at all like the black cockalorums of recent TV fame (the roosterish George Jefferson of *The Jeffersons*, Fred Sanford of *Sanford and Son*), Cosby's character was authoritative but never distant. Dr. Cliff Huxtable set limits for his kids, but he allowed them to see that he struggled to abide by limits himself. His family values were traditional and moral, but not moralistic. If the Huxtables were cushioned by an affluence statistically infrequent among blacks, then as Cosby said when his show was attacked for not being "black enough," all he'd ever intended to do was portray "parents who love their children, who give them understanding." Writing from a sociological perspective at the end of the decade, the black scholar Henry Louis Gates, Jr., took a different view, arguing that the Huxtable family was part of a historical process: "When American society could not successfully achieve the social reformation it sought in the '60s through the Great Society, television solved the problem simply by inventing symbols of that transformation in the '80s....the social vision of *Cosby*...reassuringly throws the blame for black poverty back onto the impoverished."

Susan preferred the harrowing stories she heard on the streets to the good black family on TV. Her close friend Jimmy came from one of those troubled black families intellectuals and academics—notably social scientist Charles A. Murray and former professor Daniel P. Moynihan, senator from New York—had been arguing over in public for much of the year. Had the "anvil" of the American black family been tossed overboard as a result of perverse government social policies originating in LBJ's Great Society (Murray), or had the black family begun its disintegration before that, in response to mysterious forces rooted in some aspect of culture (Moynihan)?

Jimmy grew up very poor in a matriarchal household in the South.

Like one in ten black men in most American states, he'd done time in prison—in his case, most of the time between his twentieth and recent thirty-fifth birthdays.

Susan considered her buddy Jimmy one of Hennepin Avenue's finest con men and most prescient social critics. Once she told him that her continued submersion in her family past had led her to read up on Hasidism, which she described as a rich and mystical kind of Judaism that addressed all the spiritual concerns ignored by the suburban Judaism of her youth. Jimmy listened attentively, noting that he'd seen many of these religious Jews when he worked the streets of Chicago. Susan launched into something of a dissertation upon the Hasidic experience in the eighteenth century, the wellspring of their deep adherence to a powerful tradition.

"Well, yeah, maybe so," Jimmy said, nodding his head. "But up in Chicago they're also a buncha big-time pussy-buying motherfuckers too."

This was what Susan loved about the Avenue.

The violence of a man like Ahmad, on the other hand, was a part of the hustling life she didn't like at all. Ahmad was "a psycho," Susan said. Not only did he beat her up, but one night when Susan was in jail he gave the pearls Sam had bought her to another woman. "I just hocked 'em to her 'cause she loaned me a hunnert bucks," he explained.

Susan still worked some outright cons on the streets and sold her wop cocaine. Once she got busted with a bag of very good heroin and a lot of her wop merchandise. She managed to do up the good bag before emptying her pockets at the station house.

"What's this?" a cop said, holding up the remaining bags of white powder.

"Well, it sho' ain't dope," Susan said. And the lab report concurred.

The wopping and the conning were okay. The beatings were terrible. The busts were terrifying because they meant being away from the supply, but an odd trick was like nothing, like going on automatic pilot.

Susan had by now gone pro as a booster. When Minneapolis police officers Kortan and Spehn responded to a call from the security manager at the Dayton's department store in the Brookdale Shopping Center, they discovered that a female customer had entered a fitting room with four dresses and emerged empty-handed. A shoplifting harness was connected to the alleged perpetrator's tights (owning such a device is a felony in Minnesota). They also found three receipts indicating that other merchandise had been returned to Dayton's within the last ten days in exchange for $471.20. You stole it, you returned it.

Susan, if the truth be told, had worked a similar scam as a student at

Vassar College. Shoplifting had always been the crime of choice of people as abidingly middle-class as Susan and her brother (Ricky had lifted more than a few items of desired clothing in his time) and certain friends of Eve's.

Susan and Ahmad got busted while boosting a grocery store in Minnetonka, and Susan joined a half million other Americans currently in jail. The first time she spent the night in a cell, she heard women screaming like they were being tortured. She thought jails only sounded like that in South America.

After the Dayton's bust, Susan was sentenced to a two-month cleanup program at Willmar State Hospital, which she feared just as much as going to prison. By now she could more easily imagine dying than doing without her drugs. The first time a urinalysis showed traces of marijuana in her system at Willmar State, Susan explained to the addiction counselors that she'd been out on an evening release with some people who'd lit up a joint in a car. When a subsequent urinalysis revealed narcotics, one of the shrinks at Willmar said, "Well, Susan, looks like some people in a car were smoking barbiturates." Luckily, Willmar had a network of tunnels running underneath its buildings, and if you were careful, you could go down there and shoot up Dilaudids.

It was when Susan was at Willmar State that the policemen came and took her back to jail. They told her to clean out her cubicle, and they led her away in leg irons and handcuffs. The whole thing was screwy, as Susan assured Eve on the phone. The system had gone haywire.

Eve called Susan's lawyer the morning after she talked to her daughter in jail. Mark Luther was a seasoned Minneapolis criminal attorney who understood the symbiotic relationship between the Minnesota penal system and the chemical dependency scene. Luther had maintained a working relationship with Ahmad for several years, but he didn't have too many clients with résumés like Susan's.

Eve ascertained in an instant that Luther was a Jew. "Oh, please. Please get her out for the High Holidays, Mr. Luther. It's so important that we're together for the New Year."

Shuna stared at her grandmother as she had the night before, with her "I'm nauseated" face.

"People leave hospitals for the holidays if they're not dying. Can't they leave a jail? You see, I just had surgery…for cancer, and I need my daughter home for the holidays."

Eve hung up, rather impressed with her own performance.

Susan was released shortly thereafter.

1986

The Light of Truth Universal Shrine was almost done. The fifteen-acre lake was dug and filled with water. The long reflecting pond in front of LOTUS duly mirrored the cotton-candy-colored mosaic tiles on the gigantic architectural flower petals. The petals were closed against a large baby-blue mammary dome from whose top rose a gold cupola reminiscent of a minaret, a "cosmic antenna" that Swamiji himself had directed into place while sitting beside the crane operator. LOTUS, Swamiji told the excited residents of Yogaville, would help people "learn to love the whole world as their family."

The celebration marking the close of six years of LOTUS building served to distract ashram habitants from the tensions and murmurings so evident in Yogaville these days. The community had been rocked by revelation of the untimely pregnancy of a sixteen-year-old householder, and residents were stunned once again when they learned that the man involved was a Yogaville husband and father of long standing.

The scandal came in the wake of considerable concern in senior ashram circles over the dire national publicity generated by reports of multimillion-dollar counterfeit product scams, kidnappings, beatings, and even murder at the Hare Krishna outpost in rural Martinsburg, West Virginia (the leader of the sect, Kirtanananda Swami Bhaktipada, would later receive a thirty-year sentence for mail fraud and racketeering, a charge that included authorizing the violence perpetrated by his devotees). Outside churches and ballfields in Buckingham County there was now talk of the crimes of Bhagwan Shree Rajneesh, an Indian guru who had purchased a significant portion of a rural Oregon county and was deported for immigration fraud amid rumors concerning a long list of his personal depravities. The departed Bhagwan used to drive around in a different Rolls-Royce every day. By the time he was run out of town, he had around eighty-five of them, including thirteen that were "artistically" painted over with images of flying cranes and lightning bolts. Life at the Bhagwan's ashram, according to defectors, was not morally pure.

One of the rumors making the rounds in Buckingham County had it that Satchidananda faked his Indian accent and was really from Detroit. The stories about Yogaville swamis swallowing beach towels and threading them out of various orifices became more prevalent and graphic all the time. A great many locals would have been happy to turn the "Get the Hindus out of Buckingham" refrain into a crusade.

From the perspective of those close to Satchidananda, Yogaville was under siege. A "crass" external culture was at the gate, and just as in hundreds of other American communities of a more secular cast, the ashram leaders responded with a call for the protection of the family, better care of the children, and a return to the authority and traditions basic to a decent yoga life.

Senate hearings and talk shows were now frequent forums for parents concerned that American popular culture contained too many sparks that could ignite the worst of youthful passions. Rock lyrics in particular were being analyzed for pornographic and even demonic suggestions. Incensed upon hearing the word "masturbation" as her eleven-year-old daughter listened to a song by the rock singer Prince, Tipper Gore, wife of Senator Albert Gore of Tennessee, helped found the Parents' Music Resource Center in May 1985. The group called for formal scrutiny, warning labels, and even censorship of lyrics that might contain lines glorifying sex, violence, drugs, suicide, and satanism. By the middle of 1986, twelve state legislatures were considering laws that would make it a crime to sell "obscene" records to minors.

On the ashram, where alcohol and drugs had long been strictly controlled, dozens of onetime children of rock 'n' roll sat down to make lists of "offensive" songs and television shows to be banned within Yogaville's borders. Soon after, dating between ashram children was banned through the end of high school. Then all children attending the ashram school were asked to sign a document pledging that they would not date, have sexual contact, listen to restricted music, or watch restricted television shows.

Satchidananda never came forth to comment formally on the new restrictions, but residents understood that the rules carried his implied imprimatur. The guru often decried the breakdown of the extended family in the United States. Without grandparents to raise them, children were now being robbed of their mothers too. Satchidananda referred to baby-sitters and day-care employees as "money-sitters" who worked for gain instead of love. He said he would rather see a Yogaville mother "in rags" than have her leave her children behind to go to work.

Satchidananda was asked if the postwar experience of Americans who had moved to suburbs they thought would be safer and better for their children, only to watch those children grow up and rebel, was cause for concern about the future of a protected community like Yoga-ville. "Rebelliousness," the swami replied, "comes not when you force children to do something. It comes from them not knowing why you are asking them to do it. If you explain and convince them, then they accept rules as their own ideas. Then it becomes easy for them to follow. Then there is no need to rebel."

When it was announced that a committee was forming to identify the specific songs, bands, and shows that would no longer be suffered by ashramites, Lorraine volunteered to serve. Though she'd warbled "Tired of bastards fuckin' over me" countless times before large audiences, Lor-raine was frankly shocked and offended by the rock lyrics she heard on the radio. As the head of a family living on a tight budget, she also dis-approved of the powerful commercials that turned kids into avid con-sumers so quickly. But like many ashram parents, Lorraine worried that her desire to protect her children might come into conflict with her belief in fundamental civil liberties and the right of free expression.

When one group of ashramites reported another for listening to a Bruce Springsteen album, Lorraine was incensed. "So what are we say-ing here?" she asked during a subsequent committee debate, sounding like a Lorraine out of mothballs, a woman the friends of "Leela" had never met before. "Are we saying, maybe, that truth is one, paths are many, but step off *my* path, come around *my* daughter, and you'd better watch out?"

"It was all so democratic, so...level at first," Lorraine told Bill Behny shortly after their first date. "The teachings are still there. The teachings are still pure."

"Yes, but let's look at what's really happened here," said the scary-looking biker, passing his gaze over the inside of the trailer Lorraine had lived in since she and the boys left Mohan for good. "A lot of cheap labor was needed to get this ashram going. Now that phase is ending. This is the single most class-conscious place I've ever seen. Your guru has a fancy house and lots of cars, and his people don't provide work for you or take care of you at all. Yogaville is designed for the rich yogis who come on retreats or the people who want to retire here. People like you are no longer welcome."

In the meetings Lorraine attended, meat, tobacco, certain books, and the fraternization of adolescents of the opposite sex outside of school were added to the long list of proscriptions, and written vows were required. "Hey, Lynchburg's just down the road, guys," Lorraine volunteered during one session. "I cannot believe we're talking loyalty oaths and censorship at Yogaville. Let's go tell Jerry Falwell. He'll be proud."

When Lorraine was first spied in the company of the meat-eating, cigarette-smoking ex-Henchman, some of her ashram friends came up to say, "We're so worried about you. What's happening to you?" By the time she was seen with "three jugs of liquor" (actually two jugs of apple juice, and yes, one jug of white wine—Gallo), most of her ashram friends had stopped approaching her altogether.

Bill moved into the trailer with Lorraine and the boys, though his loathing of the "yoga police" was becoming hard to contain. In a loud voice he was often heard to address Mohan Wenzel, Gopal's father, as "Moron," which he didn't hesitate to yell across an open field.

Three-year-old Gopal had turned out to be what the parenting books charitably referred to as an "active" child. Gopal bounced face-first off walls and did somersaults down staircases even in his low-key mode. Though Lorraine would sometimes joke that her youngest would excel as an attorney one day, most of the time his perpetual and precocious defiance taxed the good humor of the most patient adults.

One day Bill, whose love of guns and loud machines made him appear to Gopal like some gigantic black-bearded god, swatted Gopal once on the butt. A few hours later Gopal took one of his regular falls, from the considerable height of a bar-style stool onto the unforgiving surface of a brick floor. When he went to his father's trailer for a visit that night, Mohan noticed a bruise on one of his buttocks. Mohan and several of Lorraine's friends were already worried about Gopal's possible pollution by Bill, and as soon as Mohan saw the bruise he went to visit an ashram resident who was a social worker "on the outside." The next day a report was phoned in to the state Child Protective Services office in Buckingham, the hamlet that served as the county seat, alleging child abuse. Shortly thereafter Mohan filed papers requesting custody of Gopal.

In the last three years the once unspeakable crimes of physically and sexually abusing children had emerged so conspicuously from behind family walls and out of the darkness of "private matters" that almost any household or schoolroom now seemed a potential torture chamber for innocents. Accusations that the operators of a preschool in Los Angeles had been sexually abusing their charges for ten years had led to a thousand long-overdue examinations of places where parents left their children in trust. In August 1985 a *Los Angeles Times* poll indicated that twenty-two percent of all Americans had experienced sexual abuse as children.

The families of origin of troubled adults were now being plumbed for evidence of abuse that might explain their psychological problems or their own propensity to abuse their kids. Magazine articles asked parents to consider the more subtle "verbal abuse" that could also leave children scarred or injured. Social service organizations set up child-abuse hotlines and other reporting systems so that concerned citizens could help stop the epidemic of abuse. But with the rise in anonymous reports of abuse, some observers discerned abuse of the new reporting systems. According to a study conducted at the conservative American Enterprise Institute, thirty-five percent of reported cases of child abuse were judged unprovable, well intended but wrong, or purely malicious back in 1983. By 1986, the number was up to sixty-five percent. Officials in Buckingham County estimated that two of three abuse claims fell into the same categories. The specialists there suspected that local lawyers routinely suggested to clients that phoning in an anonymous charge of child abuse wouldn't hurt a subsequent custody case.

"Give me back my son," Lorraine said to her onetime friend, the social worker.

Gopal had been placed in the woman's custody by internal Yogaville decree until the hearing. As soon as Lorraine found out where he was, she'd rushed over.

"This is nothing but a vendetta. This is because of Bill, and you know it."

"Leela, Mohan is a better parent," the woman said. "He lives the yogic life you've repudiated. Gopal would be better off with his father. This is not about you. It's for your son."

At this, Lorraine scooped Gopal into her arms and started to leave, but the woman—one of the few Yogaville residents possessed of substantial girth—forcibly restrained her. Lorraine felt something pure and wild overtake her as she fought back. For all her spiritual discipline, she was suddenly aware that if she had a bit more strength she would be capable of murder when it came to protecting her kids. She finally had to leave the house empty-handed.

Before the preliminary court hearing Ram and Shiva were kicked out of the ashram school for refusing to take the new vows, and also, Lorraine learned more informally, because Bill had not chosen to alter his personal habits. Meanwhile, the Yogaville Girl Scout troop was purged of those who were not abiding by the moral rules.

Under oath, Maggie Shapiro declared that her mother never beat her children. She said she'd come all the way from New York to assure the authorities that Lorraine was a good mother. Six of Lorraine's ashram friends were still willing to back Maggie's testimony. The magistrate listened to Bill describe the swat he gave Gopal. Bill was told that if anything similar happened again, he would face criminal prosecution. Gopal, it was decided, would continue to live with his mother.

Lorraine felt like a good American the day she left Yogaville, some sixteen years after she stopped a Vietnamese woman on the way to a college class to apologize for being a citizen of a nation of war criminals. She was leaving the ashram, a place she loved, as a matter of principle.

Lorraine, Bill, and the boys moved into a rented farmhouse just past the small white clapboard church five miles down the road that led to the ashram. Built in 1747, the house sat beneath the lower boughs of an ancient box elder and in the shade of a row of much taller oaks. Their new home had no hot water, and no telephone line ran in from the road. There was a large cleared field where Bill—and now Lorraine—dreamed of raising pheasants and other wild birds.

Shortly after arriving in the poverty-stricken county of Buckingham, Bill had noted the irony that it was contiguous with Albemarle County, home to the highest concentration of millionaires, on a per capita basis, in the state or the nation.

Only in America, it seemed, could a former Hell's Henchman make the acquaintance of an Albemarle resident he called Patty, though she was known in the gossip columns as Mrs. John Kluge, the much younger wife of a seventy-one-year-old German-born businessman who'd come away from one of the recent leveraged buyout deals conjured up on Wall Street with no less than $1.4 billion dollars of his own. Bill and Lorraine met Patty Kluge because she was something of a huntress. She employed an English-born gamekeeper Bill knew, and she often roamed the six thousand acres of her Virginia estate in search of birds to shoot out of the air.

The fleet, meaty game birds hunters preferred cost almost nothing as baby chicks. Raised to maturity, however, they could be sold to sportsmen at around seven dollars apiece. Bill read that during some elite hunting parties in England, five thousand birds were often killed in a day. The American game-bird market was much smaller, but Bill still planned to build a business capable of selling at least twenty thousand birds a season.

It wasn't a life that Bill's white-collar dad would have understood, but it was a way to live on the land and build something up from scratch. Lorraine worked hard to ignore the karmic implications of a business dedicated to the careful raising of beautiful animals so they could fly fast to their deaths. She also averted her gaze from the guns all over the house. She tried not to hear Bill's primitive references to women, concentrating instead on the sight of her boys following him everywhere, learning his man's skills like fishing and hunting and building.

Lorraine would rise very early in the morning now and braid her long hair. She'd pull on her jeans and dusty boots and trudge through the woods to an old pump house to get water, pausing for just a few minutes of meditation at a mossy spot where a clear stream broke musically over some rocks. She'd lug the water back and work until she fell from exhaustion at night. She'd build fences and chop wood. She began to cook and eat meat. She served her man and her boys like a pioneer wife.

Lorraine loved Bill Behny in a way she hadn't loved any of the other, less assured men in her life, though she'd read enough psychology to know that some of his allure was connected to her father. Bill worked as hard as Sam to keep his feelings inside, and as with Sam, Lorraine still knew those feelings just by looking at his face. Sometimes Bill barked out bloody-minded opinions that sounded like bigotry pure and simple, but he would stop his truck to offer an old black man a ride and help him in and take him wherever he wanted to go. Bill was ruled and overruled by absurd manly codes and by a brutal biker dogma no more malleable than the axioms of Masonry.

When Sam and Eve came to visit Lorraine and the boys, Eve inspected Bill and said, "You look like the guy who breaks people's legs when they don't pay their debts," and Sam asked him about birds and building projects. Lorraine watched Bill and her father walking together, talking, broad shoulders at ease. Sam would later announce that Lorraine had finally found herself "a human being," a man who knew how to shake hands and look you in the eye and care for tools. Best of all, this one, this Bill, planned to make something of himself.

The first time Lorraine gave Bill a brief history of the Gordon family, he shrugged and said, "Sounds typical to me. Your father got a house. He got too busy with makin' a buck to be around, and when he was home the kids got on his nerves. The kids ran off in a million directions and saw a fair amount of action. That's just what happened to a lot of families."

One of Bill's brothers was prominent in the gay community in San Francisco; another was an artist. He had two "yuppie" siblings working in the booming financial services industry in New York, and a father and mother recently retired to a sunny part of southern California.

"Families have to grow up," Bill said. "Sometimes it takes a while."

Lorraine acknowledged the paradoxes of a feminist and devout yogi settling down to a lifestyle outmoded for much of a century, as "old lady" to an ex-biker who reminded her of her father. And yet she'd never felt so "normal."

Ricky was surprised to receive a long letter from Lorraine in which she described how much she loved being a Gordon. "I'm proud of it," she wrote, "proud to be a part of it. We have all learned a lot and we've had courage to go through it all."

◆————◆

A student of supply lines and logistical management since World War II, Sam was impressed with the dope dealers of midtown Manhattan. He noticed that the pusher making primary connections in Bryant Park behind the New York Public Library would never actually carry the goods. The drugs were kept in doorways along nearby side streets. The assistant holding the stash would watch another guy across the street with a clear view of the transaction and potential trouble. Assuming the coast was clear, a hand signal indicating the size of a customer order would set the wheels of commerce in motion—fast and furious motion that Sam noticed was getting faster all the time. The drug business made the streets too active, he thought. Everybody was getting jumpy.

Sam was walking down Thirty-eighth Street one afternoon when a sprinting man carrying a briefcase was tackled and dragged to the sidewalk at his feet. Instantly, people began screaming and running, while not five feet away from where Sam stood, the downed man, probably a drug dealer, battled viciously with another man who was trying to steal his wares. At one point the dealer broke free and struggled to his feet. He staggered back and turned to glare into Sam's eyes. "You Jew bastard!" the man hissed.

Sam stood his ground for a few moments. *How does he know I'm Jewish?* he kept thinking. For want of an answer, the next thing that came to Sam was, *What in the hell am I doing in the middle of a fight that could involve guns any second?*

The fight escalated, and Sam quickly crossed the street, though he couldn't stop marveling at the stunning historical compression he'd observed—the hand-to-hand street combat and even the anti-Semitic taunt of his earliest memories juxtaposed in an instant to the modern world of drugs, source of his current torment.

Sam later asked several people he considered streetwise if they'd noticed how wild the city had become, wilder than ever before. Several of them told him the madness was due to a new substance, something called crack.

———❦———

Ricky stared at the ceiling from the floor of his hotel room in Milwaukee. From the next room he could hear the hysterical voice of Teri Mitzi, the producer of his second musical, *Toby Tyler* (the first was a musical version of Marlowe's *Dr. Faustus* that he'd written at Carnegie Mellon). Ricky was scheduled to conduct *Toby Tyler* for the Milwaukee-based Great American Children's Theater Company in a few days. Teri was trying to whisper, but her distress kept breaking through like little cries of pain. "I'm trying to tell you that my composer and musical director has gone crazy. He's lying on his back in the middle of the floor surrounded by little magic rocks and gemstones. He refuses to speak!"

A severe back spasm brought on by a high-intensity, high-impact aerobics class Ricky attended at dawn had laid him low by mid-morning. Now he was stuck in Milwaukee with a cast of singers who couldn't sing, his "epic tragedy"—the opus based on the Gordon family—still unfinished back home, and a pain emanating from a gap between two lower vertebrae was telegraphing bolts of much worse pain down to his heels.

Thank God—in the cosmic, energy-rich, life-force form in which Ricky now envisaged the Deity—that he'd at least remembered to bring his "sacred minerals," his crystals, his tiny engines of curative power and divine light. Arrayed around his painfully contracted form were Ricky's rose quartz ("Calms the heart," said the New Age texts, "relates well to the kidneys, increases feelings of self-worth and love"), his potent double-terminated clear crystal, and his tourmaline. The "crystal bed" Ricky constructed on the floor of his hotel room also included his amethyst, which "brings integration between three healing systems of the body—the physical, mental, and emotional and spiritual."

Some one hundred million dollars was in the process of being expended during 1986 on quartz nuggets that promised New Age believers not only healing powers but the chance to raise "the levels" of their souls. Crystals amplified and transmitted the energy stored in the boundlessness of the mind, and since New Age theory held that the purest of that energy was of divine essence, the pieces of quartz could therefore deliver spiritual power like pocket-sized superchargers.

According to Ricky's new psychic, a Long Island housewife named Barbara Stabiner, a half-inch-long, unsmudged quartz crystal of only middling purity "projects an energy field up to three feet." A concentrated mind could direct energy through a crystal as light becomes a laser. A pretty rock collection, properly understood and carefully "programmed," could supply energy, store information, awaken the mind, perform "psychic surgery," and provide inner sight not unlike the elusive third eye, the *ajna chakra*, into which New Age seekers allowed acupuncturists to plunge tiny needles in order to open a passageway to the soul.

Ricky now slept with crystals pointed at his head. He worked at his piano with the tips of powerful crystals aimed at his heart. He wore them on little chains around his neck and carried them in his pockets (crystal mavens recommended their placement on the collars of beloved pets, near plants, under mattresses—for "totally unified" lovemaking—near the baby's crib, and even taped to the gas line of your car). For a while Ricky believed one of his crystals had halted the slow retreat of his hairline, but then a "knowing crystal person" informed him sadly that he'd bought the wrong rock. (Four years earlier Ricky had participated in a preliminary test of the hair-growth drug minoxidil at New York University Hospital; only peach fuzz had appeared, the drug cost ninety dollars a bottle, and Ricky got heart palpitations when he read a document enumerating the risks.)

Never one to tread softly in pursuit of a new passion, Ricky piled into the New Age like a fullback. His knowledge of astrology was already voluminous, though his star studies paled before his skillful practice of numerology, an arcane and ancient psychic science in which various numerical manipulations generated an analysis of an individual's multileveled state and future path. Offered only a name and precise birth date, Ricky would "do" your numbers, describing in the course of an hour your talents, personality, and fate.

The letters of sister Susan's name, Ricky explained, fell into the numerological category called "soul's urge" as the number fourteen. Fourteen was connected both to temperance and to the tendency to learn only through experience. And wasn't that, when all was said and done, an amazingly clear analysis of Susan's problems?

Sam Gordon was born on the second day of the second month of the year, which, once formulized, "came out" a two, which meant that Sam had lived the first half of his life under the number four, which was depicted as a box—the box of limitation and hard work! Four was limitation; five was freedom. Abraham Lincoln was a five. Unfortunately for poor Sam, the name Goldenberg came out an eight, which was the number of power and money. This, clearly, was why Uncle Freddy, a Goldenberg still, had done so very well in business.

Ricky began to tell his family and friends that he was seriously considering changing the spelling of his middle name. The numerological outlook of Ricky Iaan Gordon was sufficiently superior to that of Ricky Ian that he believed the confusing Welsh look of the new name might be worth the trouble.

Changing the spelling of your name was certainly easier than subduing the unruly extremes of your personality through psychotherapy. As Ricky continued to analyze his psychological formation, the apparently scientific approach to his psyche was forever uncorking emotions that felt tethered to forces much larger and more profound than his mother and father. "The pain and the joy I can feel seems like it's a thousand years old," Ricky would say. "There has to be more to existence than the history of me." So Ricky turned to an increasingly convenient store of literature, expertise, and sacred goods all dedicated to the proposition that the key to the universe was locked away in his mind.

While Lorraine was in New York for a brief family visit, Ricky drew her into his bedroom with one of his New Age friends and insisted she try an experiment with them. "So the three of us just sat there with these stainless steel pyramids on top of our heads," Lorraine reported to Eve. "Even I thought it was strange."

Before he discovered pyramids, crystals, astrology, numerology, and Barbara Stabiner, Ricky attended a lecture given by the famous Swami Muktananda. After trying to quit smoking for two years with Richard Trachtman's help, Ricky found himself standing in a long line waiting to hand over his cigarettes to the old guru. He was meditating on his bed shortly thereafter when he began to feel himself enclosed within "a bubble." He looked around and noticed that the intensity of the light in his bedroom had changed. Then he thought, knowing the thought to be slightly strange, "I look like an angel." Ricky walked down to one of his favorite stores on Columbus Avenue, a shop specializing in hand-painted antique knickknacks and exotic European cheeses. Ricky believed everyone in the shop was looking at him, at his angel face and protective bubble of perfect light. The sensation transcended any feeling of emotional release he'd ever experienced in therapy.

Ricky never did smoke cigarettes again, but the passivity of medita-tion and his Sam-like abhorrence of being "a follower" led him to fur-ther exploration. By now a vast smorgasbord of "paranormal" experi-ences, reinvigorated theosophy, and venerable occult practices was spread before the questers of the mid-1980s under the rubric of the New Age. Ricky paid Barbara Stabiner $200 for a reading, and he paid a man $150 to balance and adjust his aura. Barbara defined an aura as "the electrical life energy" that surrounds all living things. Some people claimed that they could see other people's auras. Ricky now said that when he crossed his eyes, he could see the color of his friends' auras. Whatever they thought privately, most of his better friends could only nod their assent before so pervid and joyous a pursuit of answers.

Ricky's aura balancer laid him down on a table. As the man circled him, Ricky could hear a loud crackling, like the sound of a wool sweater discharging static electricity. Then Ricky felt waves of heat rushing around him. "There is a blockage," the aura man said, and punched his hand into Ricky's belly. Ricky gasped and began to wail. It was a long time before he could stop. The aura adjuster explained that he'd removed a significant psychic barrier, a blockage composed, he said, of "sadness."

For another two years Ricky would study and work hard to believe in New Age alternatives to mainstream religion. All the variations he practiced derived from the assumption that life was part of an ordered universe, that existence was as carefully orchestrated and balanced as a symphony.

As an acolyte of the paranormal, Ricky, unlike a yogi or an Arican, could simply reach for the Yellow Pages and locate a New Age techni-cian who would provide progress reports on the spirit that now inhab-ited his little piece of the mortal coil. While educated young people all over Asia were abandoning their religious traditions and scorning the ancient belief in reincarnation, in the America of the mid-1980s, as the debunking science writer Martin Gardner pointed out, an astonishingly powerful fad had brought reincarnation into hundreds of thousand of middle-class American lives. The president of the United States and his wife were secretly consulting a West Coast astrologer, and twenty-five to thirty percent of Americans, according to recent polls, claimed to have experienced a "past life" at one time or another.

"Channeling" was a profitable subcalling among clairvoyants. Channelers would give you access to your previous and future souls by actually *becoming* "discarnated" spirits. Shirley MacLaine, once peed upon by Shuna Lydon, accessed the "astral plane" via a woman named J.

Z. Knight of Yelm, Washington, a farming town south of Seattle. In exchange for four hundred dollars, an observer could watch J.Z. mount a stage and become "Ramtha," a being who had lived some thirty-five thousand years ago in the lost civilization of Atlantis, and among other things, had "invented war." J. Z. Knight was in the process of making millions of dollars in 1986, and some of her followers even moved to the Northwest to be close to her—close enough, in some cases, to notice her practicing her Ramtha takes without benefit of a deep trance.

Some channelers became ancient Venetian traders, and one, a certain Jamic Sams, became a Venutian, an interplanetary soul named Leah who would live six centuries hence on Earth's sister planet. Ricky's clairvoyant, Barbara Stabiner, would go into a trance from which she could "regress" clients back beyond the edge of conscious and even subconscious selves. In a thick Long Island accent she would reveal the truth of former lives.

A pleasant if harried woman, Barbara Stabiner often found the weight of near-complete insight difficult to bear. According to Washington, D.C., journalist Mary Davis, wife of a congressman from Michigan, Barbara phoned her on January 27, 1986, to say that she felt a disaster coming on. "It feels like a giant explosion," Davis recalled Stabiner saying. "I see America in mourning...fire and explosion." The next day the space shuttle *Challenger* blew up.

The first time Ricky went to Barbara Stabiner, he watched a woman who might have stepped right out of Arlene's Beauty Parlor in Island Park fall into a deep trance. In a low voice, Barbara told Ricky that though he was surrounded by a cocoon of white light, his aura was "cracked." Others were thus allowed to "sap" his vital energy. Barbara said she believed the crack was the result of some horrible experience with drugs.

Ricky immediately thought of his childhood LSD trip. He thought of his compulsion to entertain, to be a friend to everyone, to keep putting out energy day and night.

Then Barbara identified Ricky's spirit guide. Did he by any chance have a late relative called "I, something I"?

"Irving," Ricky said, naming a cousin who had been killed by a car when they were both young.

Yes. Irving, Barbara reported, was "stuck" and needed Ricky's help to join their grandmother and the others in the afterlife. Ricky was stunned. Barbara went on in subsequent sessions to inform him that he had been Napoleon and had written the words to "The Star-Spangled Banner" as Francis Scott Key. Once, to his pure delight, she told him that Wolfgang Amadeus Mozart was present in the room. He'd come to help Ricky with certain "personality issues."

From eternity's multitude of souls, Barbara, like so many psychics, communicated primarily with a handful of historical figures familiar to anyone with a liberal arts education. When Ricky's insistent phone calls finally persuaded Lorraine to see Barbara Stabiner, she learned that she was once, among other people, the martyred Joan of Arc.

Barbara had done a double take when Ricky first showed her some family pictures and she came to Lorraine. "This one is going through so much," Barbara said, shaking her head. "Your sister is living through all her past lifetimes in a single lifetime. She was on a slave ship once; somebody did voodoo on her in the past; she was a prophet in a country where nobody would listen, and she went insane. A thread of spirituality bonds you to Lorraine, Ricky, a golden thread that means you can climb rainbows together."

Ricky was deeply moved.

Barbara also told Ricky that there had been many times in her current life when his mother could have gone insane. He nodded, because he'd always thought so himself.

Eve told Ricky that none of his new "Shirley MacLaine stuff" came to her as a surprise. "All my life people have called when I thought they would or walked into the room when I knew they would," she said—news that came to *him* as a surprise. One recent evening she'd seen a huge orange ball "bigger than the sun" float past the boatyard window and down the next block. "I'm the daughter of a mother whose dreams came true," she said. "I'm the mother of children whose whimpers and cries I can hear in my head when they are thousands of miles away."

Barbara Stabiner believed that people were only drawn to psychics and the exploration of things unseen by the experience of serious trouble. "Pain," she would write in *The Unseen World*, published in 1989, "is one sure way to change a person's life." She had never utilized her own paranormal gifts until her twenty-one-year-old brother died, the loss followed quickly by the deaths of several other family members. She said she realized she could either psychologically close the door on her tragedy and pretend all was well, or she could try to follow the beloved lost spirits in search of meaning. Eventually Barbara saw that there were others—millions of them—who needed to move beyond their troubles by tapping into the universe.

One afternoon in early September, Eve Gordon called the Island Park Police Department and asked them to come take Susan away. "She's not my daughter anymore. She's a monster. Please come."

Susan had returned to Harbor Isle after a Minnesota judge, Henry McCarr, told her in court that if she didn't complete a treatment program and for three years "abstain from the use of all addicting chemicals and drugs, including alcohol," he reserved the right to impose an extremely stiff prison sentence.

"What's the sentence?" Susan asked Judge McCarr.

"Sentencing is stayed during your probation," he said, staring down at Susan. "If you do not comply, if there is any failure to comply, you will very likely end up in jail on this. Do you understand *that*?"

"Yeah," Susan said.

Susan was living with Jimmy, the philosophical Hennepin Avenue hustler, in a small apartment house crawling with junkies. Women turned tricks in the halls and in the alley out back.

"Sue, you must think you're a pincushion," Jimmy would say. "You gotta do something, Sue. Call your mother."

"She won't take me back."

But the apparent inevitability of a dopeless prison cell finally inspired Susan to act. "Ma, do I still have the option to come home and live with you while I go back on methadone? Otherwise they're gonna send me to prison."

Eve got off the phone and called Susan's probation officer to arrange for a visit.

Susan, the steely-eyed old pro, thought she had experienced every possible drug sensation until she tried this new stuff, a smokable cocaine distillation called crack. With that first hit, Susan felt encircled by an exhilaration that came whipping and winding around her like a cyclone, a spinning, frothy, soaring state of ecstasy. The feeling rose up like a vast, thrilling orgasm, again and again, head to toe, the peak like some perfect plateau set against the best of all red sunsets. The high felt so endless and complete that she pictured the drug massaging her pleasure centers. Light glowed glorious and warm. It was better than heroin, sex, food—better even than those oceanic memories of the infant bliss stolen from her at the end of World War II.

But crack also had a dark side more frightening than anything Susan had known before. If you didn't force yourself to save a hit to nurse your mourning psyche when you came back down, you felt like you wanted to die. You'd sweat rivers, even in front of an air conditioner running full blast. On the downside of a crack high, you could probably kill somebody and not really care. Susan quickly understood why crack-heads sprayed streets full of people with gunfire. Even a little of life without crack was like being awake inside your worst Nazi dream. You had to score. You just had to score to make the dark side go away.

In New York City five-buck vials of crack had changed the drug life the way warfare alters daily life. Not long after she came home, Susan copped on Lincoln Place, a well-known crack street in Brooklyn. The dealers there sold beat crack—breadcrumbs, crushed peanuts, Ivory Snow, anything they could pulverize—but as if in some nightmare version of the wopping scene back in Minneapolis, swindled customers returned with Uzis. Crackheads would light up a street like Lincoln Place until it looked like a movie depiction of Vietnam. Crackheads killed their moms. Crack moms smashed their babies against walls.

Before long, Susan was down to eighty pounds. She smelled. She was often so weak that she couldn't walk unless she got high. An article she managed to write for the *Voice* about hairstyles was reprinted in *Cosmopolitan*. With the reprint payment she bought a ticket and flew to see Jimmy in Minneapolis. Jimmy was free-basing coke now, but he wasn't hip to crack. "You look like a damned Ethiopian, Sue," he said.

Back in New York again, Susan came into some investment-grade heroin, but all she wanted to do was trade it for crack. She borrowed Eve's Chevette one night and drove to the black section of Freeport, a town not far from Harbor Isle. When she got back to the boatyard, all the windows in the car were gone, and so was Susan's purse.

Sam came home and walked around the car twice before going upstairs. "Get her the hell out of here," he said, breathing hard. "Get her locked up!"

So Eve called the police. An officer came to the phone to explain that a smashed-up car wasn't sufficient proof of crime to warrant an arrest.

Eve hung up. She'd heard that the Romans killed their children. Eve wanted her daughter to die.

"I want to kill Susan," Eve told Lorraine numbly on the phone. "I have prayed for her death. What should I do?"

Lorraine had recently taken a job processing patient information at a drug rehabilitation hospital in Charlottesville. After talking with several chemical dependency counselors on the staff, she began to make calls. Within an hour she phoned Eve with the name of a rehab hospital near Albany, New York. Lorraine gave her mother the number of Conifer Park's Manhattan office.

The next day Eve and Susan went to see a former addict named Jerry Lopez. "What can you pay?" he asked.

"I don't know, maybe a thousand," said Eve.

Lopez said thirty days of treatment at Conifer Park would cost eleven thousand dollars—about as much as four years of tuition when Susan went to Vassar. "Maybe we can help," he added.

"You mean like a scholarship?" Eve said.

Lopez looked at the serious case sitting beside the terrified lady from Long Island. The rehab programs were all reporting absurd recidivism rates among crack smokers. Crackheads slipped back at least six times more often than heroin addicts. Two years earlier, only one in ten drug addicts preferred cocaine, but crack was changing everything. Public hysteria over drug abuse was at such a pitch that two-thirds of respondents to a recent poll said they would pay higher taxes if pushers could be put away or—if television talk show sentiments were any indication of public opinion—lined up against a wall and shot.

"We can help you out," Lopez said, and turned to Susan. "Go wait outside, will ya?"

"Don't give up on her," he told Eve after Susan was gone. "You've gotta keep yourself hoping. Try to have faith."

On Saturday, September 13, while waiting to board the train for Albany at Grand Central Station, Susan began to quiver and weep and beg. "One more, Ma. Please! I gotta run out for one more!"

Eve looked at Susan with an expression that would have scared ravening lions away. Susan said nothing more. She just cried.

The next day Ronald Reagan appeared on television to talk about the national epidemic of drug abuse. The president called drugs a menace to society, a force that threatened American values and institutions. Drugs also killed children, he said, calling for a "crusade" against drugs. Then he turned the microphone over to his wife, the nation's First Lady and First Mother. Nancy Reagan wanted to extend a personal message to American youth. "There's a big wonderful world our there for you. It belongs to you. It's exciting and stimulating and rewarding," Mrs. Reagan said. "Don't cheat yourselves out of this promise. Our country needs you. But it needs you to be clear-eyed and clear-minded….Say yes to your life. And when it comes to drugs and alcohol, just say no."

1987

Three hours before dawn in Fort Lauderdale, Sam looked down through the window of his Florida condominium and shuddered at the sight of so many dozens of his fellow retirees walking aimlessly through the night. "Like zombies," Sam would tell Eve in the morning, the senior citizens wandered on pathways that snaked around perfectly shaped man-made lakes. Wielding their aluminum walkers, they hobbled past glassy swimming pools with thatched "Tiki huts" at poolside. They held to their sluggish pace as they rounded the nine-foot-tall bronze statue of the eternally jaunty Red Buttons, who was born Aaron Chwatt three days after Sam Gordon in 1919 and lived a few blocks away on what he would later call "a pretty tough block," even by the Lower East Side standards of the time.

Chwatt went north to the Borscht Circuit hotels two years before the young singer Eve Samberg. After adopting the catchy stage name—a reference to a doorman's uniform he once wore, and his second professional sobriquet (the first was "Little Skippy")—Red Buttons became a dependable if minor star of stage and screen, garnering the lion's share of his exposure on television late in his career. Since 1969 he had been delivering sales pitches that had filled up some four thousand apartments at Century Village at Pembroke Pines, where Sam and Eve had recently decided to move, as well as several thousand units at three other Century Village outposts.

The morning after Sam first discovered the village insomniacs on the march, he told Eve that he'd seen many ambulances gliding down the litter-free, high-security Century Village thoroughfares, which by day were clogged with air-conditioned maxibuses ferrying residents around the complex. Sam said it wasn't so much the number of sick or dead being taken beyond the security gatehouse during the night that bothered him, it was that "none of these people who've retired from life could manage to so much as turn their heads when an ambulance went by."

Like the original houses in Harbor Isle, the sixty-six barrackslike pastel buildings at Century Village all looked the same. Where the mortgage and down payment plans available from Harbor Isle developers were based on GI Bill allotments, the mortgage and maintenance plans at Century Village were keyed to maximum Social Security payments. As the Harbor Isle pioneers were led, almost to a household, by war veterans, Century Village was designed for the "active" retiree.

"But it's not like coming to Harbor Isle, because nobody in this country will ever feel what we felt when we moved out of the city," Sam said. "That was our special time. We had the American Dream going then. I don't even think there is an American Dream anymore."

Eve thought this over for a few moments. "Well, Sam," she said, "at least there's condos."

Frustrated by the preference of some eighty-five percent of older Americans to "age in place" instead of partaking of the glory of packaged "senior living," marketing experts serving the thirty-year-old retirement community industry had recently segmented the marketplace according to levels of service. Century Village was designed for the "active older adult." Many Century Villagers started out as "snowbirds" who purchased their condos while still in their fifties and came south only for a few weeks during "the season" until retirement later on. "CV," as residents called their walled enclave, was an "active living" environment, as opposed to facilities promoted as "life care," "continuing care," and "assisted living" communities for seniors in need of closer observation. For all the talk and fear of nursing homes, less than five percent of Americans ever ended up in them.

When the first planned retirement community opened in 1960 in Sun City, Arizona, Margaret Mead declared that building "special preserves" for old people was like building "ghettos" for unwanted portions of the populace. Under the weird late-night light of spherical halogen lamps, Century Village indeed conjured for Sam images of the unspeakable camps where millions of European ghetto dwellers perished, but this latter-day ghetto for retirees was certainly comprised of men and women who were by and large far wealthier and healthier than they ever dreamed they'd be at this stage of life. Most of them, at least by day, appeared to be having a ball.

For many Americans, this was the best of all times to be elderly. Men born the same year as Sam now had a statistical probability of living some fourteen years past the sixty years actuarially allotted in 1919. A study conducted at the Hoover Institution at Stanford University showed that the average per capita income of retirees now exceeded the family income of middle-aged working people. Americans over sixty-five represented twelve percent of the population and controlled forty percent of financial assets. Thirty percent of the total federal budget was now directed at older Americans, as compared to just twelve percent twenty-five years earlier and two percent at the beginning of World War II. The number of elderly poor had dropped by nearly half since 1970, while the number of children living in poverty doubled over the same stretch of time.

Like six of ten Americans over sixty-five, Sam and Eve owned their home and the boatyard free and clear. Sam shook the hand of the boatyard's new owner (his wife couldn't get over the view: "The light. Look at the light," she said), and was given a check for more than six times what he'd paid for it. The size of the check made Sam think about his former partner, the intransigent Louis, who'd balked at a real estate transaction that would have made both of them rich. SGE Electric had ceased to exist the day Sam left Harbor Isle. Without a suitably skilled and dedicated heir—since so many of his clients depended not on the business but on him—SGE was reduced to the hundreds of tools Sam took along with him to Florida. Sam had worked himself crazy for the better part of half a century and didn't have a dime to show for it (Eve reckoned that the kids had cost about $400,000), yet he had enough capital to retire and move to Century Village just from sitting on some real estate and shares of stock in the local utility.

The small two-bedroom condo was only forty-thousand dollars but Sam kept reminding Eve that retirement meant that "from here on out, every dollar we spend will be gone forever." He figured that his emotional difficulty over abandoning his business and the little island village he'd help settle thirty-seven years earlier must be a sign that he was getting old. Once he'd prided himself on making quick decisions and never looking back. But for months after the move, Sam couldn't quell his agitation.

Eve had a much easier time of it. She had a whole new audience for her best jokes, and a couple of the mah-jongg players weren't half bad.

The hub of life at Century Village was the Clubhouse, a huge building rising behind the monument to Red Buttons. An enormous chandeliered lobby led back to rooms filled with acres of card tables and rooms where the Bronxite Club, the Brooklyn Club, and various trade union and religious groups held meetings. The Clubhouse also included a thousand-seat auditorium where residents could see first-run movies and live shows. There was even a dance hall, by day the scene of constant low-impact aerobics-style classes and the inevitable mass hokey-pokey sessions.

The Clubhouse was the only place Eve had ever been where her taste in clothing seemed subdued. If Eve was of a mind to feel youthful and downright svelte, all she had to do was go to one of the pools. "I'm going to look at a thousand pounds distributed between three people in bathing suits," she'd tell Sam, towel in hand.

"And the conversation!" Eve would tell the kids on the phone. "Forget Jim and Tammy Bakker and the stock market. What you've got to know down here is 'early bird special.' Three in the afternoon, and they're all in line for dinner at the restaurants so it should always be a good deal."

Still, Eve kind of liked the place. "Come on, Sam," she'd say when some new discovery about the village scared or depressed him. "We've been private too long. Honey, it's good for us to people around again."

Sam enjoyed the dances at the Clubhouse. Eve thought about Roseland and the old beach clubs of the South Shore as he guided her artfully around the halting couples on the floor. Sometimes other residents would stop to watch them. Bold women would cut in, and Eve would nod and yield her husband, a man so attractive to women still. When she was back in his arms, she could tell that people were talking about how Sam looked at her as they swirled around the hall. On the dance floor Eve stopped being a worried mother. She wasn't sixty-six years old or any age. She was a dancer, moving to the music and being loved by Sam.

But later he'd be up again watching the night-stalkers with terrible fascination. "Half of them have been dumped here by their kids. The place is so nice, kids don't have to feel guilty. They don't have to see their parents either," Sam said. "These people have dropped everything in their lives. All they have left is time to sleep, and look at them. They can't even do that."

Back when work owned too much of him, Sam was sure that retirement would be the "living death" he'd heard other men talk about. But he'd gradually come off the need for constant labor. He'd taught himself to substitute projects and new hobbies. Sam was prepared to live without "making a living," but he couldn't abide not living. Not yet.

"You know, Eve, I've been asking around, and if we bought ourselves a place just a few miles inland, we could afford some land. It's zoned out there for animals."

And from that point on Eve knew that her future held yet another role. She would soon be called away from the endless mah-jongg game of retirement at Century Village to take up her position as wife to a rancher.

———•◦•———

Ricky marched in the annual Gay and Lesbian Pride Parade down Fifth Avenue beside a man he'd dreamed of seducing for years. The man was holding a large sign that said LIVING WITH AIDS FOR TWO YEARS AND TWO MONTHS—NO THANKS TO RONALD REAGAN.

Though there was still plenty of color at this year's parade—Witches and Pagans for Gay Rights, Dykes on Bikes, outrageous downtown drag queens, furious "counterdemonstrators" stationed in front of St. Patrick's Cathedral—the tone seemed far more subdued than in the past. Some thought that the health crisis facing the gay community had propelled a more conservative look and style to the cultural forefront, since a gay investment banker or a gay legislator was more likely to attract press coverage, funding, and government support for the cause. Others said AIDS was simply chasing gays back into the closet. Still others said that whatever the sociological effect on gay life, the AIDS crisis required gay men and lesbians to march down Fifth Avenue more proudly than ever before.

Ricky had no intention of finding out if he was among the more than one million Americans estimated to be infected with the virus that had already killed six thousand people, including some of Ricky's good friends. He forced himself to read up on what was known about the dread disease. He wrote and donated a song that Jim Mahady, his erst-while boyfriend and best friend of several years, sang in his pure, big tenor on the soundtrack of a safe-sex film that Gay Men's Health Crisis was now showing in gay bars. Ricky had signed up for training to be a counselor to the very sick, but it would be another year or two before he could handle a vigil at the bedside of a dying friend. Sometimes Ricky didn't know what to do with the anxiety, the guilt, and the rage engendered by this insidious plague.

At every funeral Ricky pondered the same irony. If he'd been only half as desirable or self-confident as he'd always wanted to be, if he'd participated fully in the great sexual awakening that should have been his by right of the timing of his birth—if he'd *been there* in the way Lorraine and Susan had carried the flag into the best of their times—then by now he might very well be dead. Always a much better witness than participant, even now something of the little boy who once drilled through walls to look at his sisters undressing, Ricky watched fellow musicians and friends get sick and sicker and die, and it made him yearn to understand why he'd been spared.

Ricky considered himself an unsuccessful homosexual. Because of that, and not because of all the dying, he'd been wondering lately if he'd become gay out of some sense of despair. He speculated on the cumulative effect of seeing his sexy sisters naked so often when he was young. He recalled how obsessed he once was with Jody Pilchik. Why had this changed? His several attempts at heterosexual lovemaking, beginning in his senior year of high school, had been failures in every way. And yet women still gave him so much. He counted many beautiful women among his best friends, and at times he still felt he wanted them—but he wanted men more, especially men who didn't love him or men who were so introverted and sexually repressed that they'd never be able to tell him they loved him even if they did.

"Maybe by being gay, another man can represent my masculinity as…you know, an *otherness*," Ricky said to Jim Mahady over muffins one morning. "This way I don't assume the role of the masculine and thereby become my father."

According to a recent report on the "the sissy boy syndrome" by psychologist Richard Green, a fifteen-year study showed that seventy-five percent of men who had exhibited effeminacy as boys (playing with dolls, dressing in girls' clothes, playing exclusively with girls) indeed became bisexual or homosexual. The study did not support the old assumption that a domineering mother and a distant father made for a gay child, nor did any particular "parenting style" seem to lead to gayness, though Dr. Green allowed that his results might still "frighten some parents of young boys." Another new study indicated that homosexuality seemed to "clump" within families, though the researchers, a psychiatrist and a psychobiologist, noted that their findings did not substantively address the debate over whether the origins of homosexuality were environmental or genetic. At the end of 1991 an extensive examination of twins published in the *Archives of General Psychiatry* would indicate that fifty-two percent of identical twin brothers of gay men were also gay, compared with twenty-two percent of fraternal twin brothers and eleven percent of adopted brothers. The evidence, wrote the two researchers who conducted the study—psychologist Michael Bailey of Northwestern University and psychiatrist Richard Pillard of the Boston University School of Medicine—indicated that homosexuality was "innate."

"It's not heredity," Aunt Sylvia often assured any member of the Gordon family who cared to listen. "At least in *my* family the boys were boys and the girls were girls. They all got married and had beautiful, bee-*yoo*-tiful families."

For all their comparative enlightenment and ability to be accepting, Lorraine and Sheila both believed, however unfashionably, that Ricky's homosexuality was the result of deficient early tutoring in the basic manly arts. Ignoring the heterosexual masculinity of so many orphans and children from fatherless households, both sisters thought that if Sam had only spent more time teaching Ricky to throw balls and build things and fight (Lorraine, in particular, still wished that just once Sam had showed Ricky how to pound one of the Harbor Isle bullies into the pavement), then their adored brother might not have grown up to be gay and now so much at risk.

Recently Lorraine had overheard some of her neighbors suggest tossing all the AIDS-infected gays into camps. There was talk in Buckingham County, as there was in Greenwich Village, about the possibility that mosquitoes might spread the disease, like malaria. Lorraine prayed for Ricky and was always scared he'd get sick.

Sheila, like Sam, still entertained fantasies of Ricky marrying a nice girl. After Ricky badgered her incessantly, she finally gave in and went for a reading with Barbara Stabiner, who assured her from a deep trance that Ricky was not homosexual. "He is androgynous, a balanced soul comfortable in either and in or." When Sheila's son, Daryl, asked her to paint his nails and do his hair as she often did for Danielle, Jon went out immediately and spent two hundred dollars on GI Joe dolls, water guns, and various other masculine paraphernalia. Sheila had to admit that she felt better every time Jon took Daryl shopping at the hardware store.

When Sam said, "He could snap out it. He might find the right girl and get married," Eve would just nod. In many ways Eve's acceptance of Ricky's lifestyle was complete. (Before Susan went upstate for treatment, while Ricky was visiting the boatyard with a female friend, he overheard his mother talking on the phone: "How am I? I'm fine. I'm sitting here with a lesbian, a gay, and a junkie sleeping on the couch.") But Eve was far too agitated now over news of the terrible gay plague to indulge in any retrospective analyses of her son's sexuality.

From the start of his relationship with Jim Mahady, Ricky noticed that Sam accepted and even welcomed Jim as he had welcomed no other non-Jewish boyfriend of a Gordon child before. Sam called his ruddy-faced midwestern pal "Jimmy," and he always made a point of talking to him. For several years—as lovers and then as friends—Ricky and Jim slept in the same bed at the boatyard, and Sam never batted an eye.

When Ricky retrieved early images of his father from the shadowy past—that phantom presence looming in the background while his mother bathed him in a small tub—he often felt that in some ways he'd rejected Sam all along. His father was scary because he was so strong, and the fear was magnified by Sam's inability to balance that strength with expressions of love. Sam had turned his children into little adults when they were still young. In doing so, Ricky now believed, he'd given his children the power to destroy him. The result was family chaos.

With a lot of therapy under his belt, with much of a cathartic musical work about his family down on paper, and—after a year's obsession with New Age dogma—with the assurance of Barbara Stabiner and other psychics that his long and harrowing family saga, in Barbara's words, had "a happy ending," Ricky was able to see that he'd inherited his father's seriousness and intensity of mind. Whatever Lorraine might think, Sam had taught him perseverance and bequeathed him his strong will.

Ricky was standing in a crowded car on a Long Island Rail Road train, on his way to Oceanside to see Sheila, Jon, and the kids. He tried to stand his ground, but a hulking young man began to edge him up against the door as soon as the train pulled out of Penn Station. Ricky looked at this macho character and marveled that so much coiffed hair and neck-borne jewelry, an earring, and even a blousy silk shirt opened suggestively to a point just above the navel should bedeck such a muscle-bound lug.

Eventually the guy really started hassling Ricky. "Say, buddy," he said, his pectorals bulging under his silk shirt, "you got a problem?"

Ricky turned his back, but not before he heard himself say, "I don't have to talk to you, asshole."

Then Ricky felt a hand on his shoulder, and suddenly he'd been rotated 180 degrees. It occurred to him that the guy looked something like Sylvester Stallone as Rambo—only taller and broader. "Whud you say!" he bellowed, grabbing Ricky and lifting him in the air by his collar as the other passengers began to move away.

As Ricky stared back, the man turned into every neighborhood bully and gay-baiter. He became the anonymous harasser on all the streets and trains. From his new height nearly two feet above the floor of the crowded car, Ricky suddenly felt like that great white hunter of the urban jungle, the New York subway gunman Bernhard Goetz. This guy was in for a surprise.

Ricky leaned close, as if he had a secret to share. "I said," he hissed, "I don't have to talk to you, you complete *asshole*." And without waiting for a reaction, he twisted free of the iron grasp, put his head down, and drove the Stallone clone back against the door. His fists whirled like a cartoon character's, pummeling the hulk's face. He backed up and charged again, howling like a soldier in a war movie, but now several passengers moved in to separate them. As they were being pulled apart, Ricky reached over, red-faced and grunting, and grabbed hold of the fancy silk shirt. In one motion he ripped it in half, and in another he tore the pieces off his would-be tormentor's back.

The guy looked like he was going to cry. "Look," he said. "Look what he did to my shirt. He's crazy!"

"And he was such a gorgeous little boy," Aunt Sylvia would say if even the most tangential remark gave her an opening. "But what little boy notices a woman's bathing suit? That was my first inkling, when he was five. But I never said anything then, *nev*-er, not to anybody at all...."

———≪≫———

According to a spring poll conducted by *Parents* magazine sixty-two percent of all American parents—or at least middle-class parents who were readers of *Parents*—believed their children's childhoods were "more satisfactory" than their own. "People may be saying by this, 'I'm a much more active and involved and loving parent than those I had in my home as I grew up,'" postulated Peter Wish of the New England Institute of Family Relations when he saw the poll. Nicholas Zill, director of Child Trends, a nonprofit research organization in Washington, D.C., wondered if the superior physical health of children as compared to the 1940s and 1950s accounted for the poll results, along with the fact that children now had "many more material goods...from toys to technology."

Between the window of Sheila's kitchen and the picturesque inland waterway beyond her Oceanside backyard were a dock, a very big motorboat, a smaller motorboat, a fiberglass water craft with foot pedals, a sailboat, a Weber gas grill, and a splinter-resistant, pressure-treated deck (a word that rarely referred to playing cards anymore in the suburbs) bearing a redwood hot tub. The yard held an aboveground pool, matching lawn chairs, a hammock wide enough for two adults, a large swing for adults, smaller swings for the kids, a jungle gym, a wooden hobbyhorse, sports equipment of all kinds, and a scattering of those bulbous, blow-molded Tiny Tykes plastic toys replicating in vivid primary colors steam shovels, trains, sports cars, and various other machines used in adult work and play. The great shiny chalice of a satellite dish rose high above the back of Sheila and Jon's house, as if elevated in a rousing after-dinner toast to times like these.

Jon now housed a collection of fine wines down in the basement. He could recognize the odor of burning mesquite in the air as easily as he could distinguish fresh rosemary from coriander, with the same olfactory acuity by which hundreds of kids from suburbs like Oceanside once distinguished Acapulco Gold from Lebanese blond hashish.

Dani, now eight years old, took regular tennis lessons at the exclusive, elegant Middle Bay Country Club and would soon be playing at a level that earned her a state ranking. Sheila had allowed her to junk the flowered, canopied decor of her bedroom, which now had the sleek, high-tech, shiny look of a newly constructed airport concourse. Dani had her own TV with a built-in VCR, an unusual special feature.

Eve considered it "a bit much" when Sheila changed all the expensive carpeting in her house, not because it was worn out, but because "on a whim" she preferred a different color. Eve had wanted the floor of the playroom painted over even though Sam assured her that the battleship-red linoleum would "last a lifetime," but the paint job had probably cost less than a yard of Sheila's new carpet. "Sheila enjoys her money," Eve occasionally felt it incumbent upon her to admit, "but she's the type who could go back to having nothing and not be destroyed."

Sheila hosted a family Passover celebration before Sam and Eve moved south. Like nearly nine of ten married Jewish couples, Sheila and Jon had decided that they wanted to retain certain ritual aspects of Judaism, so Sheila laid out the symbolic platters and cooked the traditional meal. At dinner she noticed Shuna glaring at her as soon as everyone sat down. Shuna had gone away the previous fall to study art at the State University of New York in the Hudson River town of New Paltz. Her father had weighed in with paternal assistance when it came to selecting a college and seeing to the financial aid forms. Now she was a most serious-minded freshman.

The conversation turned briefly to recent acquisitions, as family table talk often did, and Sheila saw her nineteen-year-old niece's face harden with disapproval.

"I just wonder," Shuna interrupted. "When we're done discussing *money*, can we move on to another topic?"

"Sheila's changed," Shuna said later when Ricky asked her about her outburst. Her kind, happy aunt, who'd cared for her back in Berkeley, had been "lobotomized by money." Shuna went so far as to use the most damning epithet in her arsenal. "Sheila has turned into a yuppie."

Because of Jon's savvy management of his family business and his ownership of a mid-Manhattan building Sam had rewired and helped restore, Sheila and Jon were among the five percent of the population that owned fifty percent of the wealth. Sheila didn't mind being young and rich, but she refused to shoulder the opprobrium of the dismissive label "yuppie". By the most widely accepted demographic definition—"professionals" born between 1945 and 1959 who earned over forty thousand dollars a year and lived in a city—only 1.5 million Americans actually qualified as "yuppies," but in its two short years of life the term had been seized upon as a comfortable reduction. It was employed by conservatives who argued that a generation of former rebels had finally seen the capitalist light, and more recently as a cutting rebuke to baby-boomers who had allegedly repudiated their old morally superior values.

Sheila insisted she was not a yuppie. Articles like a recent *New York Times* piece about a family cutting corners because their yearly income was only $600,000 appalled her. She thought of yuppies as younger—lawyers and junior financial types who wore impeccable suits and floppy or not so floppy silk ties, depending on gender. "A yuppie tries to act super-sophisticated," Sheila said, "even if he or she is not. And I'm not rich," she'd add.

"Face it," Ricky said from the big hammock. "You're rich, Sheila. You are rich."

"Okay," she'd say. "I'm rich."

When people stared at her manicured nails or the rich leather interior of her Volvo, Sheila knew she was being pegged as a "rich housewife." But she really didn't feel rich. Rich was being so much a part of your wealth that you no longer worried. Rich was a unity, an enclosure. Sheila went to the country club and watched the truly wealthy roam their artificial preserve like carefree children. She felt so far removed from their self-satisfaction and ease that she sometimes wondered if she was going insane. The plane of privilege inhabited by these apparently lucky husbands and wives struck her as no less treacherous than the humbler levels of family life.

When Sheila watched TV these days, she skipped the admirable, communicative Cosby show in favor of the frosted upper-class intrigues of *Dallas* and *Knots Landing*. She studied the morally supple characters on *Dallas*—in particular the cowboy Iago J.R.—to learn more about the entrepreneurial life that Jon had apparently mastered so completely over the past few years. *Knots Landing*, the show Jerry Falwell loathed, which amplified weekly the astonishing array of seamy, complex dramas emanating from one suburban cul-de-sac, offered an hour of therapeutic escape. Not unlike the oil paintings and watercolors Sheila was beginning to concentrate on in her free time, *Knots Landing* let you leave your life without running away.

Sheila vividly remembered watching her father watch his cowboy shows and sensing how much he wanted to climb inside the box and disappear in the Western dust. She took solace from the fact that the traumas of Val and Abby and Karen and Gary on *Knots Landing* were at least different from her own. For an hour she didn't have to worry about her family. For an hour she didn't have to feel as overwhelmed as she often did, and as her own mother must have felt when she broke plates, or the time she briefly ran away.

From Sheila's agitated perspective, her backyard bulged with items that social scientists had taken to calling "signifiers" of family status in part because of a media-transmitted consumer ethos that made many of her daughter's friends as fearful of buying the wrong brand as Sheila and her sisters had been of the crawl space and nuclear war. Across a huge economic gulf, Sheila concurred with Lorraine, and across a significant political gulf, she even agreed with the "pro-family" forces of the New Right: advertising and marketing were turning children into more avid consumers than their parents. In a series of interviews conducted by writer and family specialist Barbara Dafoe Whitehead, "focus groups" of parents would soon identify "materialism" as the single most pernicious force in the culture. In some areas of the country middle-class parents who grew up at a time when uniforms were considered an affront to individuality at best and a sign of authoritarianism at worst were banding together to demand uniforms in the public schools as a means of curbing the crazed consumerism that had overtaken their kids.

But Sheila also thought that her backyard museum of outdoor artifacts was a response to the perpetual trumpeting of kidnappings, molestations, hit-and-run accidents, and any number of other current dangers that had relegated roaming bands of happy suburban children to the ash heap along with maternal peace of mind. A Mayo Clinic survey would soon indicate that seventy-two percent of parents feared their children would be abducted by strangers, though the statistical probability of such an event was about one in 1.5 million. And that was only one of a host of parental anxieties at a time when the same affluence and adroit marketing that had created millions of youthful shopping addicts seemed to have turned all the candy-store hoodlums, high school sluts, and teenage anarchists into anomic "burnouts," ritual suicides, and heavy-metal satanists. If you could equip a home with a sufficient number of items to intrigue the kids and keep them busy, then perhaps—just perhaps—they might be safe.

But would they be kind? Would they learn how to care and truly feel? Sheila wondered hard and long into many sleepless nights. Would Dani and Daryl turn out like the high school and college kids surveyed each year, the ones in the majority that now found it much less important to "help people" or "have a meaningful philosophy of life" than to acquire larger and larger quantities of expensive things? Would they become the warped children of "narcissistic entitlement" that psychiatrist Robert Coles wrote about?

"Maybe we should move to a place where having a new Guess jeans outfit isn't quite so important," Sheila sometimes said to Jon.

Sheila's Oceanside neighbor Sarah had been a youth counselor at a synagogue in a much wealthier suburb for ten years. Sarah was an ideal mother in Sheila's book, a role model. "It's not the things, Sheila," Sarah would counsel. "It's whether the things stand in for love or guidance. Plenty of poor people spoil their children. Go ahead and buy them things, but be there too."

Sheila's careful study of the art of creating an injury-free childhood had become less bookish and more clinical in light of the challenge of real kids. Calling the fuzzy afghans Eve knitted for the grandchildren "transitional objects" and referring to verbal interchanges softer than a bellow as "dialoguing" during "quality time" seemed less important than getting through the day. Daryl was a handful, spinning like a top, too often losing control. The job of being a mother made Sheila feel like she was exploding with pleasure at times, even as new worries cropped up by the day. Would Dani so entirely appropriate the argot of a Valley Girl that she perceived the world as either totally tubular or grody to the max? Would her children love her or blame her in the end?

Yuppie or not, Sheila's generosity and nurturing instinct had allowed her to assume Eve's household mantle gracefully. Ricky now came regularly to Oceanside with friends to watch Jon's videos on a huge screen, devour the contents of her refrigerator, and talk for hours. Lorraine liked to emerge from the wilderness for R and R at Sheila's, and Susan, who was so devastated by Sam and Eve's move to Florida that she told her rehabilitation counselors she was "homeless" on top of everything else, would soon feel up to sitting happily on Sheila's dock.

Even Eve had learned to enjoy relinquishing her longtime monopoly on the family dinner table. Though Sam had his troubles with Jon's brash style, he always marveled at the mother Sheila had become. "Do you see how she is with those kids? She's like their friend. It's beyond mother and daughter and mother and son. She really explains things, and those kids really love her."

Sheila's was the last Long Island outpost now. As the canonical normal family of postwar lore became increasingly elusive, she was anointed keeper of Gordon tradition and tender of the hearth. Her parents, siblings, nieces, and especially her own children came to Sheila to feel warmed and loved.

Sheila would try to tell Eve and Ricky and her sisters that there were times when her home life seemed to spin out of control, times when she wanted to run away. She said she didn't feel rich at all, and that she worried too much. It was impossible to find a baby-sitter, and her life was a clutter. Her husband could be as trying as he was helpful, and no matter what you did to protect them, your children remained at risk.

Sheila, the one to whom everyone came, sometimes thought she was the angriest Gordon child of all.

Toward the end of the summer Sheila decided it was time Dani understood that terrible things could happen to a family. In the spirit of progressive parenting, she made Dani privy to one of the most difficult legal decisions responsible parents must make. "Dani," she said forcing herself to look into her pretty daughter's eyes, "it won't happen, of course, but if Daddy and I die, who would you want to live with?"

Dani thought. Of course she'd want the person who did her hair so well at family gatherings, who told her stories and used a black doll and a white doll to explain racial prejudice to her when she was six. Dani shot her mother a look such as only an exasperated eight-year-old can summon. It was so-o-o-o obvious. She clucked her tongue. "Susan," she said. "I'd want to live with Susan."

<hr />

The stock market crash of October 19 was one of the few events of the fall that failed to make Susan Lydon weep with grief. Greeting cards, TV commercials, phone calls, family pictures, the passing memory of the smell of Eve's typewriter in the SGE Electric building back on Austin Boulevard, that long PBS documentary about the war in Vietnam, the stories she heard at the hundreds of meetings of anonymous addicts she attended every day and every night—everything made Susan cry. Sometimes she couldn't believe how often and long she was able to cry. Endings did her in—endings of conversations, of her profoundly limited excursions, of books, chapters in books, sentences, the setting of the sun at the end of the day. Every ending was cause for renewed lamentation.

But Wall Street and the disappearance of five hundred billion dollars in stockholder equity in the course of a single day were of little interest to anyone at Women Inc., a looming Victorian residence in a scary Boston neighborhood near Roxbury and Dorchester, a place where some of the most hardened street junkies were sent to see if they could find a reason not to die. A fenced-in yard on one side of the dingy clapboard white elephant housing Women Inc. contained jungle gyms, climbing ropes, children at play, and women with hard, almost exclusively Afro-American faces, street-warrior faces, jail-cell faces. The day Susan arrived from her four-week rehab at Conifer Park, many of those faces stared a hole into the white girl with a lot of white in her dark hair.

Susan was soon known around the halls of Women Inc. as "Lucci," because some of the other residents thought she looked like Susan Lucci of daytime soap opera fame. By the fall of 1987, after nearly a year at Women Inc. without her beloved drugs, Susan was once again barely recognizable to anyone who hadn't seen her for a while. The transfiguration was more profound than the addition of thirty pounds. As emaciated as she'd been, Susan's skin had always remained smooth. As a junkie she'd had a weird, angel-faced glow, like those tubercular red-lipped children of a hundred years earlier. Now she look weathered, like denim and leather and furnishings "stressed" for designer effect. From the contours of her face to her carriage and the texture of her hair, the change was dramatic, as though something in the drugs had kept Susan in stasis, like an arctic organism encased for years in ice. All of a sudden, she had aged.

Sitting at a table draped with a banner that read HOPE WITHOUT DOPE, Susan occasionally "shared" portions of her story. "I'm like Rip Van Winkle," she said one night, and many of her listeners grinned and nodded at the image. "I look like a grown-up, but I'm really a teenager. I have teenage emotions and teenage social skills, and it's so hard....But it's an adventure too."

In the large audience someone said, "Amen, Susan. Amen."

Though the hacienda-style rehab hospital called Conifer Park was surrounded by thirty-two acres of forest, playing fields, barbecue pits, and picnic tables, many of the counselors who worked there had logged plenty of street time in Harlem and on the Lower East Side. No bunch of Valium-munching amateurs, like so many of her fellow patients, some of them were former dope fiends who could spot a serious attitude like Susan's at a hundred paces.

Susan was detoxed and placed "in silence" so she could concentrate on her feelings. Soon she began to remember things about her family past—terrible things. She went to her group sessions and paid attention. She missed her drugs more than she'd missed anything else in her life, but by the time her month was up, she was finally listening.

A continuing-care counselor broke the news that while everyone else in her unit was going home to some sort of out-patient mainte-nance program, the Conifer Park staff felt that the only logical place for a hard-core case like Susan was Women Inc., a residential therapeutic program in Boston, like the one made famous by Phoenix House—a highly regimented environment designed for more committed and less sophisticated junkies than Susan believed herself to be. Whereas the bill for a month at an elite treatment center like St. Mary's could now run as high as twenty-eight thousand dollars, a month at Women Inc. cost fifty-five dollars.

When Susan heard that she wouldn't be allowed to go home, she felt as if she'd flunked. "They won't let me go," she sobbed to another patient in her unit. "They want to put me in a halfway house."

"Cheer up, Sue," the fellow said. "Maybe you'll be the one who makes it."

Susan went back to the continuing-care counselor's office and asked if she could look through a book listing residential programs to see if there was one "near home" in New York. But most of the programs for women were designed for alcoholics or were otherwise unsuitable.

"How about this one?" she'd say, pointing to an address.

"No way," said the counselor, who hailed from Harlem. "Place has a shooting gallery out back the house."

"But my family's in New York," Susan cried.

"I'm afraid they're going to let her out," Eve told Lorraine on the phone. Lorraine was designated to call Conifer Park and report that Susan's family did not want her released. She was assured that a stay at Women Inc. was a long way from freedom.

Since addicted celebrities rarely choose to get straight at Women Inc., the program's impressive track record since its beginnings in 1973 remains little known, even within chemical dependency circles. Women Inc. includes an AIDS outreach program and a day-care center. The tough recovery program is designed to keep addicted mothers and their children together throughout the healing process, whose central goal is a "change in social habits." To break through the "chronically thoughtless, self-absorbed" habits that encase a seasoned junkie, the women who run Women Inc. seek to "stress" the addict by imposing a discipline of boot-camp severity.

"It's very, very hard here," a Women Inc. counselor explained to Susan when she arrived. "For a while you'll think you're living in hell, but I can promise you it leads to some relief. You won't be allowed to read at first, and you can forget about using the phone for a few months too."

One of the few activities condoned and demanded of new residents at Women Inc. was housework. As she moved a bucket along a few inches at a time, scrubbing down one surface after another, Susan often pondered the orbit of her life and wondered what her mother might think if she could see her. Susan was ordered down into the catacomb-like cellar of the rambling old mansion, there to scour its damp and terrifying expanse. Any individual decision or action not previously ordained by the daily plan had to be formally cleared. Almost every request was denied.

Soon after Susan arrived, it appeared that some of the other women were determined to check her out—in street talk, to "fuck with" her, to taunt and intimidate her in various ways many of them had learned in prison. There was even a street-hardened counselor who rode her. At first Susan stood her ground. She mustered her junkie pride. "Don't worry 'bout me, honey," she'd say if somebody suggested that she should watch her back. "I'm jus' like cream. I'm boun' to rise to the top." But when she spoke, her voice would quaver and break. She couldn't make it through a conversation without crying, and once she started crying she couldn't stop. It was hard to be tough.

After several months, the hazing began to subside, and the regimentation eased a bit. Susan was allowed to take brief excursions around the crime-ridden neighborhood, though when she returned, her urine was immediately tested for drugs.

Out for a walk one day, Susan discovered an old Jewish temple, big as a cathedral. Weeds and vines grew in and out of every crevice. Shattered windows opened into impenetrable blackness, as if the panes were covered with black construction paper. Back in her room, Susan wrote Ricky a letter describing the synagogue. "The building's like me...grand but ruined. You know perfectly well how terrified I am of my own pain, and how long and how hard I've been running. I know you backed away from me when I was a failure because it reflected your own fears.…But God, Ricky, am I ever sick of being a drug addict!"

"I feel homeless, hopeless, helpless, and stupid," she wrote in another letter to Ricky. "My daughter is so mad at me—she talks about me like I talk about Daddy. Can you imagine? And we didn't even have a crawl space!…Can you believe our family? Sometimes it really boggles the imagination, how such a seemingly normal family could be such a snake pit of emotional depravity."

At Women Inc., in sessions with a veteran addiction counselor named Diane Wood—while Diane sometimes held Susan in her arms—Susan would talk about Kelly Street and the world of her grandparents, which for some reason had always constituted her truest image of home. While at Conifer Park, Susan had recalled a terrible incident that helped explain her lifelong idealization of the Bronx home that all studies of early childhood cognitive development indicated she couldn't possibly remember so vividly. If that imagined world free of men had imbued her with a perfect sense of trust, she was now beginning to remember that her maternal grandfather, the hard-drinking Simon Samberg, had "done something" to her when she was very young and so had impaired her capacity ever to trust fully again.

Years later, when Susan would talk about bits and pieces of a broken taboo that surfaced during her recovery, it turned out that Lorraine was just beginning to lift the shrouds covering a similar memory. Little by little, the details came back to her. She was three, and she was sitting on her grandfather's lap. He hurt her, and he broke her doll. Lorraine thought Simon had told her that he would kill her if she ever told. And then—this was by far the most powerful and resonating part of the story for Lorraine, a part she immediately connected to her wealth of phobias and the many mysteries of her relationships with men—she remembered her grandfather telling her that the incident was her own fault. By sitting on his lap—in the lap of family, of safety, of love—Lorraine had caused a terrible thing to occur.

As if something alien and alive had risen from within, Susan and Lorraine, separately, began to believe that they'd been sexually victimized—like three of ten girls, according to current estimates. Incestuous abuse comprises only a portion of all instances of child sexual abuse, but that portion represents millions of people. Even a former Miss America from the halcyon family year of 1958 would eventually come forward to tell her story of incestuous abuse. Shocking tales of incest and the molestation of children aired on talk shows every week.

From Conifer Park Susan tried to tell her mother about her agonizing recollection, but Eve clammed up and couldn't respond. For a time, especially according to Susan, Simon's sick abuse became "the answer" to everything—but then, the single answer had been needed and sought and never quite found by a variety of Gordons for a long time.

A large crowd gathered for the twelve-step meeting where Susan was scheduled to speak. Several hundred people from all over the Boston area traveled in the spirit of fellowship and recovery to a blighted stretch of Dorchester, to settle into folding chairs arrayed in twenty-five long arcs across a big linoleum floor. Many ardent crackheads from Roxbury and other poor parts of the city turned out, but at least half of those who'd come to be "in the room" the evening of Susan's address were downtown executives in designer ties or youthful rockers wearing bandannas, earrings, and carefully torn jeans. Preppies accoutered in the latest offerings from L. L. Bean shared a row with little old ladies in frilly collars. There were Cambridge intellectuals wearing those thick, plastic-rimmed, smart-people glasses that once signified a certain social ineptitude but had lately become popular with young movie stars.

Susan sat in front. It was her night to speak at length, to "qualify." Through the mist rising from gallons of hot coffee and scores of cigarettes, she began by telling the crowd that her name was Susan—just Susan—and that she was without doubt addicted to many things.

"Hi, Susan," the audience called back. For some the greeting was clearly a rote utterance that had become part of life, like saying thank you when someone holds a door open, but others offered it with genuine feeling, so that it sounded like the "Go, man, go!" of a beat poetry reading or the "Right on!" of movement days.

"I know I'm a dope fiend—a dope fiend down to the bone—and if *I* can get clean, anybody can."

Susan had shed her Charlie Parker cool delivery and her bravura patter. Her voice was flat. It betrayed almost no emotion save a tiny trace of irony. She said she'd been thinking a lot about her high school days, about when she first heard that smoking pot led to using heroin, an admonition transmitted by "the voice of authority." "Because I never believed anything a person of a.uthority ever said to me, I scoffed at the idea. Besides, drugs were a lot of fun."

"That's right!" someone yelled.

"Truth is," Susan continued, "drugs were the best sort of fun in the world for a long, long time."

Susan pined for drugs every minute of every day. Their loss was like all your friends and lovers dying at the same time, she said. Diane Wood kept telling her that if she was to recover this time around, all those gaping holes in her heart had to scar over. Never again could she plug them with chemicals. "Believing that God is watching would help too," Diane said.

It was a rare day when Susan didn't learn something new about how to be alive from the miracle workers of Women Inc. In the autumn, she moved to an apartment not far from the big old house and began to work in a local print shop, though she attended meetings in her free time and went regularly to have her urine checked. By then she saw that her life had once again been graced by access to an elite institution. Addicts came to Women Inc. to be "raised from the dead." Women Inc. was the Vassar of human salvage operations.

If Susan still found herself working overtime to protect the purity of her suffering and the sanctity of the various reasons her life had been derailed, then at least she knew she wasn't far away from a house full of women who really understood her, who could make her feel safe and less alone.

One of Susan's counselors at Women Inc. said, "You know, the thing about you is that you feel the pain of the world like it's personal."

Lately it seemed like millions of people did.

The phrase "one day at a time" or a passing reference to "my program" or "my meeting" was by now immediately recognizable to many Americans beyond the estimated fifteen million who regularly attended the meetings offered by Alcoholics Anonymous, Narcotics Anonymous, or dozens of smaller programs like Pills Anonymous, where Sam and Eve had once sought help.

That the sounds of recovery often resembled the confessional out-pourings of born-again Christians was no doubt due to the models of personal renewal that inspired a "hopeless drunk" named Bill Wilson to create Alcoholics Anonymous back in 1935. Wilson had apparently looked into the work of a British-based organization called Moral Rear-mament, which at the time was energetically spreading a gospel of Christian temperance and anti-Communism. In the early years of AA, psychoanalyst Carl Jung observed to a physician working with Wilson that he couldn't imagine an escape from the jail of alcohol without the help of a "spiritual experience." (In Yogaville, senior swamis noted that serious devotees had at some point been "zapped" with "kundalini energy." They'd felt elevated and outside themselves and wanted to feel it again through yoga.)

It was Bill Wilson who formulated the "twelve steps" Susan first heard about and quickly rejected back at St. Mary's. Step one (admitting powerlessness in the face of addiction), step two ("We came to believe that a Power greater than ourselves could restore us to sanity"), and step three ("We made a decision to turn our will and our lives over to the care of God as we understand Him") provided the underpinnings of the decidedly religious though nonsectarian tone of AA meetings. "Awareness, acceptance, and action" were the sequential triumvirate fostered by the twelve steps, the "action" phase heavily emphasizing the importance of eventually "making amends."

In "the rooms"—as twelve-steppers called the various meeting places of the late 1980s, in churches, hospitals, and community centers—recovery groups became modern theaters of human suffering and spiritual rebirth. Alcoholics and addicts came to learn and draw strength from the stories of others. They came to feel uplifted just by showing up. They came to hear a hundred people say hi and refuse to disapprove of them no matter how many times they "slipped" back into drugs or generally screwed up. At the meetings, people would always, always be waiting, less like perfect friends than perfect mothers. One revealing recovery program acronym was AWOL—A Way of Life. Part town meeting, part Bible study group, be-in, and consciousness-raising group, and large part family dinner table of a child's dreams, the rooms were now the Masonic Halls and mah-jongg tables and barrooms and TV rooms of millions. So many battered ships in out of the fog, moored together in a boatyard of anonymity, just trying to get through a day or an hour of a day or a piece of a long night.

"…But then came heroin," Susan continued. "Heroin made me so dead inside, so cold. Like, you know, like…like I can remember walking down the street and feeling my heart had just turned all black. I feel like I'm trying to learn how to live all over again after doing drugs for so long. But it's really hard. Like I feel I got to be this age in a night. Yesterday I was a teenager, and today I'm in my forties, and…I just don't even know what the fuck to do with myself."

"Amen," said someone in the crowd.

"If it gets hot outside, I really want to get high. If it gets cold or snowy, well, I still really want to get high. If I get tired, if I have too much energy, all I want to do is get high. But just because I wanna get high—"

And here the audience joined her in a raucous chorus: "THAT DON'T MEAN I HAVE TO GET HIGH!"

The surgeon general of the United States, Ahab-bearded C. Everett Koop, came to give a talk at Women Inc. Susan was impressed by the obvious compassion and commitment showing through Koop's technocratic delivery, but she was also terrified by what he said. Dr. Koop figured that ninety percent of the junkies in New York City, and almost every drug user who'd ever shared a needle, carried the HIV virus. And everyone who carried the virus, Koop said, would probably develop AIDS and die.

Susan steeled herself and went for a blood test at a local clinic. She rolled up both sleeves, and though the technicians executed a variety of maneuvers, they couldn't seem to locate a working vein. Susan had mine disasters for arms. Glancing up, she caught two clinic employees exchanging looks. Susan turned and ran from the room, tears filling her eyes. She went back to her little apartment for another long cry.

1988

Lorraine now had something of a backwoods twang. The family grapevine carried news that she'd taken to calling Ram, Shiva, and Gopal "boy," as in "Git over here, boy." The foremost Gordon pacifist now watched her sons emerge from the forest looking feral and joyous, bearing axes and guns on their shoulders. It was further reported by Maggie after a visit that the living quarters beside the Blue Ridge Pheasantry were infested with insects large and small and several species of worms.

Eighty-seven of Bill and Lorraine's game birds were slaughtered by a frenzied weasel early in the year, but under the watchful tutelage of an honest-to-God titled Englishman who helped manage the hunting preserve at a nearby estate, the cages were soon restocked with ring necks, versicolors, white wings, jumbos, pea fowls, and a couple of exquisitely colored Orientals that glowed like the posters Lorraine and Ricky used to put on their bedroom walls. Soon Bill and Lorraine would begin construction of a flying pen large enough to keep a thousand birds in shape.

Every so often Lorraine would sneak over to the cages and allow a few of the doomed creatures to fly away. She also chanted on the sly. Lorraine could tell that Bill already considered her weak—"sniveling," as he put it—largely because of the way she chose to handle her health problems. If Bill realized how much she missed the comfort of yoga, he might criticize her in front of the boys, who might decide she was even weaker and less like a man—their new standard of merit—than she imagined they thought she was now.

When Lorraine was first told that she had a malignant tumor hugging her thyroid gland, she addressed the problem with macrobiotic curatives. For over two years she had paid a New Age practitioner in Rockville, Maryland, $150 an hour for consultations, dietary recommendations, and herbal prescriptions, but lately she had become thin and weak, though her tumor flourished.

Eve listened to Lorraine describe her exotic therapies. "Have a goddamn operation like a normal person, Lorraine. You're killing yourself and you're killing me."

On four separate occasions Eve and Sam had packed to be in attendance during the surgery, and each time Lorraine backed out. "Surgery is unnatural. It's invasive," she said.

Eve was much less put off by the psychic stuff the kids were into than by some of the other ideas they'd espoused in the past, but Lorraine was playing with her life. The popular comedian Andy Kaufman, a Long Island boy made good, went off to have his lung cancer treated in the Philippines by "psychic surgeons." Back in the States, Kaufman was buoyant during an interview with the *National Enquirer,* proclaiming that "the doctors don't know everything." Within a few weeks he was dead at thirty-five.

Lorraine told Eve that "intuition" had led her to switch to a different New Age practitioner. "You know what kind of people get a lot of intuition coming their way, Lorraine?" Eve said. "People who are about to die. They get plenty intuitive."

When the tumor approached Lorraine's vocal cords, causing her to fear that she'd soon lose her ability to speak and sing, Lorraine contacted a homeopathic healer in Ireland who began to treat her according to a remote diagnosis made from a photograph. A few weeks later, Bill decided he'd had enough. "This corks it! Get the operation or we're through!"

"Get the fucking operation, Lorraine!" Eve agreed from Florida. "I can't put my life on hold anymore. Just do it."

A senior physician on the staff of the University of Virginia Hospital in Charlottesville examined Lorraine and agreed with her mother and boyfriend. Sensing her ambivalence, the surgeon wrote Lorraine a letter imploring her to have the tumor removed.

Lorraine phoned her guru. Satchidananda overlooked her waywardness of late and took the call. "Do it," he said.

"What's the most auspicious day for the surgery, Gurudev?"

"Just do it, Leela."

Sam took a sledgehammer down to the basement of Lorraine and Bill's ancient farmhouse and bludgeoned a hole in the foundation large enough for a new sump pump. An impressive population of fleas had made him think twice about joining the dogs on the living room sofa for a nap, and besides, work was good for the tension.

The surgeon finally came into the waiting room to tell Eve that the tumor and over ninety percent of Lorraine's thyroid gland were gone. He said it would shortly have choked her to death.

Eve went to her daughter's bedside. "Lorraine, you look like shit warmed over," she said.

During her recuperation, Lorraine kept thinking about the choking sensation she'd experienced since she was a little girl. Was it the earliest manifestation of the tumor that had almost strangled her? Or was the tumor the manifestation of the choking? The family psychic, Barbara Stabiner, did a reading for Lorraine over the phone. Barbara said that the choking was the result of her spirit guides trying to open a channel through which Lorraine could "speak the truth about things she didn't want to reveal to herself."

And so the mystery persisted. Was it simply cells gone wild, perhaps a by-product of an environment sullied with poisons that triggered cancer? Was it a visit from a strangler from a past life? Or was it the suffocating hands of men—a physical sign of her fear of the true will of Bobby and Harry and Mohan and Bill, who was acting more like a macho biker all the time, and of Sam, and of her grandfather Simon, who Lorraine was now quite sure had threatened to kill her if she ever told what happened when she was only three?

Lorraine would touch the mafioso's scar above her jugular vein and wonder. There was so much cause for wonder.

Before Maggie graduated with honors from City College and left for England on a scholarship to Oxford University, she went to Buckingham to say good-bye to her mother and half-brothers. Magdalena Shapiro was twenty-three, petite, pretty, and extremely bright. Her academic specialty (within a few months she would say "speciality," British-style) was William Butler Yeats, a poet who believed in the reincarnation of souls and selves. By now a highly practical sort, Maggie was not impressed by this particular aspect of the Irishman's metaphysics.

What bothered Maggie about Gordons, yogis, Aricans, and New Agers (though she got a big kick out of Ricky's crystals and numerology) was their shared tendency to "look at life and ask only, What am I supposed to learn from this? What am I supposed to take away from this moment?" Such a "self-centered viewpoint" necessarily led to places like ashrams, in Maggie's opinion. How else could "one," as she put it, stand to live in a world so overburdened with meaning, if not within some cloistered Oxford for the addicted, the wealthy, the retired, or the generally overwhelmed? No wonder the Gordon family was rife with gurus and psychics and gods. After spending a week with Lorraine while she was recovering from her surgery, Maggie observed that her mother would do well to "get to know herself a little better," but she was also wary of presuming that she could ever really know what another person was going through.

Maggie stayed only a day or two at the Blue Ridge Pheasantry. Then she went off to live in a place where most citizens eschewed speculation about the inner life both of others and of themselves. In England, as Maggie discovered, a person either coped or failed to cope, like a machine that either worked or did not. Maggie easily "went native" amid the spires of Oxford. She adopted a refined accent and a prim manner with an alacrity that stunned even a family used to rapid costume changes.

On the phone or over meals, the Gordons marveled that Lorraine should have produced a daughter whose personal style and preferences seemed modeled on Mrs. Miniver's. Maggie fit right in among the Brits because she was hell-bent and determined to cope.

———◆———

"You *have* to finish it," Aunt Syl would counsel when Susan phoned her in tears. "Write your article, *Su*-san, it'll be nice—such a ca-*tharsis* for you."

"Do it, Susan," one of her favorite counselors at Women Inc. told her. "Remember that the road to recovery is paved with a whole lot of storytelling."

Susan was struggling to write an article about her addiction. She'd landed an assignment from the magazine section of the *Boston Globe*, but several deadlines had already passed. Writing, it turned out, was not a bit easier when you were clean and sober. Like a painter too long away from the basics of the craft, Susan was taking a writing course in Boston taught by novelist Dennis McFarland, who would soon publish *The Music Room*, a beautifully crafted work widely read in recovery circles as "a novel about alcoholism" or "an alcoholic family story." The huge book-reading population of recuperating substance abusers now scoured texts in search of addiction and dependency the way English majors looked for Christian symbolism and Marxists for evidence of historical determinism.

One of Susan's many drafts of her article began with a Narcotics

Anonymous–style admission that she'd been a drug user for years. "By the grace of God I survived, and this is why I tell the story now. Because a survivor is one who lives to tell the tale." But then Susan would seize up, right at the point where before she would have reached for the dope and now there were only cigarettes and coffee. It was as hard as when she'd tried to tell the family story in her autobiography. She just couldn't abide all the pain.

When she wasn't working at the Ink Spot print shop, or trying to write her story, or telling her story in meetings, or rehashing her story on the phone as a gifted adviser to other addicted women, Susan was reading book after new book about how to stop feeling so much personal pain. All around her pleasant wood-trimmed apartment towered piles of books, almost all of them by or about women with stories to tell. In less than a week she'd recently devoured four books about troubled women: *The Wounded Woman*, *Women Who Love Too Much*, *On the Way to the Wedding*, and *Escape from Intimacy*.

The quantity of books about addiction and recovery—and especially about the "dysfunctional family" that so many authors identified as the root of dependency—now dwarfed the new books on parenting techniques and strategies for insuring healthy, happy childhoods. The "child within" suffering adults had knocked the child out of the cultural spotlight. The self-help shelves in bookstores multiplied as if by spontaneous generation, threatening to drive all the other books into the basement.

This hugely successful new genre was an adjunct to all the groups and meetings to which Americans now flocked, whether they could pinpoint a specific addiction or not. "Finding a group" was now perceived, especially in urban centers, as a developmental prerequisite to finding yourself. As citizens of other nations risked life and limb in the streets to demand democratic political institutions, Americans were rallying around a new democracy of psychological experience, a democracy of shared pain.

Robin Norwood, the author of *Women Who Love Too Much*, said there were "over one hundred varieties of Anonymous programs" now available. "I've never yet encountered a troubled individual who didn't qualify," she added. Back in Susan's old stamping ground, Minneapolis, there were now at least forty types of self-help, support, and Anonymous groups. Alcoholics Anonymous (which doubled its membership in the 1980s to nearly two million) and Narcotics Anonymous were now mainstream granddaddies of groups for victims of eating disorders and premenstrual syndrome. Anonymous addicted shoppers gathered to tell their stories down the block from the compulsive shoplifters' group. In

New York, one variation on the twelve-step model brought together mothers of daughters who refused to speak to them. No entrance fees, no down payments were required to join these groups. The key to admission was that you'd suffered and were willing to talk about it. "Without my suffering," proclaimed John Bradshaw, the famous leader of hundreds of meetings, "I would not be able to bear witness."

Outside the meeting rooms, candidates for public office hooked into the public appetite for personal confession. Deep feeling—evidenced by the capacity to exhibit tears—was now a campaign requirement as essential as emotional toughness had been before. Senator Edmund Muskie had lost a shot at the presidency because he wept publicly during a 1972 snowstorm after hearing a slight to the good name of his wife. In 1988 any politician worth his salt could choke up on cue.

Almost all the current candidates for president had moving family stories to tell. Some were descended from immigrants who'd suffered inordinately but managed to survive. Setbacks were matched everywhere by recoveries, star-spangled all-American comebacks. Jesse Jackson, born in poverty to a teenage single mother, won five Democratic primaries on "Super Tuesday." George Bush, who had lost a child to disease, was running hard for his party's nomination. Michael Dukakis was heir to the traditions of an underappreciated immigrant minority. (And Kitty Dukakis was an addict by any definition, though her substance abuse was revealed after her husband lost the November election.)

For Americans so old-fashioned that they still reacted to trouble— in the world or within themselves—with anger instead of remorse, a broad avenue of rage had now opened into foreign jungles and haunts of billionaire drug dealers. "The plague...the national scandal...the $25 billion-a-year drain on our national wealth...reaching from the board room to the assembly line and study hall," according to *Newsweek*, was not addiction and its behavioral complications but the drugs themselves. Drugs would soon be declared a central focus of American foreign policy. In December 1989, on the orders of President George Bush, American troops would invade the tiny nation of Panama, ostensibly to oust its drug-dealing head of state, General Manuel Antonio Noriega.

But the latter-day Great Fear over drugs was overshadowed as the personal comeback through self-help methods became a secular road to salvation. Addiction was now the reigning cultural metaphor for sadness, loneliness, emptiness, and feelings of drift. The long search for an interpretive framework by which to understand personal history and its attendant pain had spawned hundreds of spiritual, psychological, and frequently profitable paths to clarity via self-help and previously esoteric psychological concepts. Few of the pathologies and methodologies described in the self-help books or groups were new. They were simply made available—democratized—just as corporate bonds and other high-priced financial instruments were now accessible to every American through money-market mutual funds.

The eloquent popularizers now writing books and filling lecture halls explained that the problem with American life was not the fact of drugs, as the angry people said, nor the specific addictions and compulsions that robbed individuals of their souls. To a man and woman, all the popularizers had been addicted to one or more substances or activities and had "recovered" from their addictions, only to find that "the problem" was still there. The true problem in America was the "dysfunctional family," a description that applied to ninety-six percent of American families, according to that inspired preacher of the new dogma of human unhappiness John Bradshaw, whose book *Bradshaw On: The Family* sold millions of copies, and whose 1986 ten-part PBS series of the same name had become a mainstay of VCR play, recovery program viewing, prison viewing, and public television viewing during fund-raising drives.

Bradshaw "put the cork" in the source of his own primary addiction on December 11, 1965. Before that, he attempted to tame his drinking and addiction to brothel visits by becoming a "perfect" celibate seminarian in the company of the Basilian Fathers of Toronto. But eventually Bradshaw left the seminary and started drinking again. He drank himself into a hospital in Austin, Texas, and soon thereafter discovered the twelve steps and recovery. He became a professional addiction counselor, assisting the daughter of comedian Carol Burnett, among others, though all the while he says he knew he was not really cured. "My helping people was more about me than about people....I was still out of touch with my feelings, grandiose and compulsive."

It wasn't long before John Bradshaw—sallow and bearded, just shy of fifty, with greased-back hair that would soon be telegenically blow-dried, clad in polyester disarray that would yield to designer suits—could be found on stages everywhere, standing before weeping Americans who'd paid upwards of $250 to hear him free-associate brilliantly and with great emotion about the mythical haven of family. Bradshaw said that the biological structure called family was almost invariably antagonistic to the true "needs of individuals." The family was the secret engine of human disorder, the cause of "the war within ourselves." And the American family, John Bradshaw and dozens of other psychological popularizers warned (not for the first time, but arguably to the widest audience ever, wider even than the Reverend Falwell's a few years earlier), was "in crisis."

The family dysfunction gurus held that individuals constrict and twist and deny their true selves in order to accommodate the geometry of emotional forces that dominates the life of a family. Consequently, the products of modern American families had grown up empty, in constant pain, riddled with addictive and compulsive behaviors adopted in an effort to escape the pain. The dysfunctional family, Bradshaw said— borrowing heavily from earlier clinical studies of multigenerational pathologies by Murray Bowen and others—created people who lived by the "don't trust, don't feel rules" they'd learned during childhood. The dysfunctional family not only engendered addictions to drugs, alcohol, and sex, Bradshaw claimed, but also produced what he called "rage-aholics" and "sad-aholics," as well as the ninety-seven to ninety-eight percent of Americans who couldn't make a diet work. There were "a hundred million people who look like adults, talk and dress like adults, but are actually adult children. These adult children run our schools, our churches, and our government. They also create our families." An "otherness" would control these individuals until they finally located that "injured child within" and began to recover.

Bradshaw sprinkled his talks with quotations from English poets and European thinkers like Kierkegaard and Sartre. He quoted his own somewhat disapproving mother and distant children. He invoked the work of Erik Erikson and Sigmund Freud. Bradshaw occasionally acknowledged that his purpose was to popularize some thirty-five years of research conducted under rubrics such as "family systems theory," "family structure theory," and "conjoint family therapy." Bradshaw's lectures owed their intellectual force to psychiatrists and social scientists like Bowen, Nathan Ackerman, Lyman Wynne, Virginia Satir, Gregory Bateson, Jay Haley, Salvatore Minuchin, David H. Olsen, and numerous others who were searching for a conceptual and scientific model of human behavior based on the general assumption that people's thoughts, feelings, and actions were the result of complex emotional processes and connections.

The family, these theorists and John Bradshaw agreed, was an enclosed system that could pass psychological balances and imbalances along as an inheritance. In opposition to the Freudian conception of the sovereign self, and in refutation of an analysis favored by several Gordons and millions of others who thought that the outbreak of family trouble from World War II to the present had something to do with "the times," family systems theories blamed the family itself for the problems that reappeared in "the gardens" of children and grandchildren.

Thanks to Bradshaw and his fellow lecturers and authors, the ideas of Bowen and his colleagues about the multigenerational dimension of family psychology were now so well known that millions of addicted and otherwise unhappy Americans were reexamining their family histories, not for nostalgic tidbits, but for signs of pathology. The discrete profile of the "alcoholic family"—another construct drawn from the multigenerational research of the family systems specialists—was now studied as intensively as "the Irish family" or "the Jewish family" had been before.

Where Bowen, Haley, and the other family systems investigators were as yet not satisfied that they'd hit upon a fully integrative theory, no such doubts afflicted John Bradshaw and the rest. "Are you from a dysfunctional family?" asked one of Bradshaw's printed fliers. "Did your family exhibit any of the following traits—chemical, physical, or emotional abuse, eating disorders, perfectionism, or extreme moral or religious rigidity? Did you experience the abandonment of a workaholic, physically or emotionally ill, or deceased parent? If, as a child you—like so many of us—experienced any of these compulsive behaviors or forms of abandonment, you probably carry with you behavioral traits that seriously interfere with your ability to function as a happy, fulfilled adult."

Some of America's favorite families were now openly dysfunctional. It would soon turn out that the family of Ronald and Nancy Reagan—at least according to their daughter, Patti Davis—was highly dysfunctional. Michael Reagan, in the course of a book about his own estrangement and angst, revealed that he was molested by a camp counselor as a boy. Patti Davis claimed that family communication was so inadequate at the Reagan home that she never had a clue who her mother really was. "I saw the same dynamic in our family—a dysfunctional family—mirrored in the country in the 1980s," Davis told a writer for *Vanity Fair*. "If you take this family, and you put them up there as the First Family—if you look at what the dynamic is in the family—you might have a pretty good sense of how it's going to trickle down."

"Everyone is responsible," John Bradshaw would tell his audiences. "But no one is to blame."

Like so many others, Susan pored through book after self-help book, feeling a little healthier by the page. "Can you imagine how different it could have been if this kind of information and support was around when we were young?" she asked Sheila on the phone.

Susan was now convinced that the family of Sam and Eve Gordon, the family of Yetta and Joe Goldenberg, and the family of Simon and Rebecca Samberg were all severely dysfunctional. The template of dysfunction fit like a glove, right down to the popularizers' schema of individual family roles, or "functioning positions." In the alcoholic, addicted, or dysfunctional family as described by Wayne Kritsberg, president of Family Integration Systems in Austin, Texas, the oldest child was usually the family hero, the overachiever; the second was the troublemaker and occasional scapegoat; the third was the lost child, the keeper of family tensions, who had a hard time establishing a separate identity; and the fourth was the comedian, the child equipped with radar, who internalized every family nuance.

Didn't that fit the Gordons to a tee?

Susan argued to her siblings during phone calls that their mother was the child of an abusive alcoholic father and his suicidal wife. "What could Mom ever have known about a normal family?" Sam came from a home full of rage. "To him, normal was just coming home at night. No wonder he was a workaholic," she said, and then, invoking the action and reaction theory of the family structuralists, she added, "No wonder so many of us have problems and issues with work. Our father used his work addiction to escape the family, and he only showed us his rage."

Susan recalled the day Yetta had verbally attacked her on Sam's boat. She ran to Sam for solace, but he acted like *she* was the unreasonable one. Sam couldn't spend five minutes with his mother. He knew better than anyone how difficult Yetta was, yet he'd turned it all around on Susan. "This is what people who talk about alcoholic and dysfunctional families refer to as 'the elephant in the living room.' Something big and obvious right there that nobody will acknowledge," Susan explained.

When Sheila's marriage to Peter was failing, what did she always say? That at least it was "exciting, at least not boring." This was right from the books. She was compensating in an attempt to reestablish stability within her family system, and she was able to do so because she was still involved in a "triangle" with Sam and Eve. Lorraine, with her serial head-over-heels relationships with men, was also one for the books.

And Eve. Eve was what Ricky called "the Queen of Denial." All that anxious quieting of the day's turmoil in preparation for Sam's arrival at dinner, all that clinging to the reins of family power. Susan remembered the day Cleo the dog was run over in front of the house on Lincoln Avenue. "This is too much," Eve said when Susan wept. "We'll never have another dog." Normal, to Eve, was not grieving; normal was the dysfunctional curtailment of her own feelings. As Susan saw it, Eve, getter of her father's wine jugs and slipper of cash to her junkie daughter, was the family's paramount "codependent."

"Scratch an addict," went a saying popular in addiction and dysfunction circles, "and you find a codependent." Melody Beattie, who was to codependency what John Bradshaw was to family dysfunction, defined the affliction as addiction to another human being. In her 1987 book, *Codependent No More*, which would sell over four million copies by 1990, Beattie wrote that a "codependent person is one who has let another person's behavior affect him or her and who is obsessed with controlling that person's behavior." Another codependency authority, Sharon Wegscheider-Cruse, quoted in an article in *Seven Days* magazine, extended the definition to anyone in love with or married to an alcoholic, anyone who had one or more alcoholic parents or grandparents, and anyone who grew up in an emotionally "repressive" family. Wegscheider-Cruse estimated that ninety-six percent of the general population was codependent—the same as Bradshaw's figure for the number of dysfunctional families, and an astonishing statistic when you considered that more than five percent of the population was younger than the rather dependent age of four.

Melody Beattie was now thirty-nine years old. She had been the victim of a sexual attack at five. She worked as a stripper and was a full-time drug addict until, like Susan, she found herself in front of a Minneapolis judge who offered her a choice between jail and rehab. During treatment at one of the bastions of the Minnesota Model of recovery, Beattie had a "spiritual experience" on the lawn of the hospital. The sky turned purple and she "knew there was a God."

As with John Bradshaw, sobriety did not solve her problems. Beattie was still codependent. She went on public assistance to support her family and wrote *Codependent No More*. Where Bradshaw drew his inspiration from psychologists and academics, Beattie said she was influenced by the work of Richard Bach, author of *Jonathan Livingston Seagull*. She later told a reporter for the *New York Times* that as she worked on her book she "kept thinking of Sylvester Stallone, penniless and writing *Rocky* because he believed in it." *Codependent No More* listed some two hundred codependent tendencies like "feels anxiety and guilt when others have a problem." The catchall nature of the now ubiquitous term was probably why the tens of thousands of new groups gathering under the Codependents Anonymous or similar banners were the fastest-growing of all.

Asked about her apparently extreme disregard of existing psycholog-ical theory and research, Beattie replied, "We're talking about a group of people like myself who bottomed out so badly that we didn't have time to waste on things like penis envy."

For all her study of these powerful new interpretive approaches, Susan was still struggling to get her own story down on paper. For all the com-fort she drew from having a context for her grandfather's terrible viola-tion, and for what she called the "ball of pain," the "nuclear nightmare" that was her family of origin, each time she gave even a verbal version of "the story" of her addiction, the reason she got hooked in the first place changed.

Sometimes the reason Susan's life had veered off course was that Sam came home from the war a stranger and brushed her aside. Other times it was never "truly feeling loved" or "smart enough" or "pretty enough." She said she became an addict in the early seventies because writing was so hard, or in the mid-sixties under the glow of painkillers administered after the traumatic loss of her baby in London, or in the late sixties because drugs were so much fun. She once posited that she shot heroin a few years later because she "never should have left Berke-ley for Marin County."

So many traumas and enticements to recover from; so many answers, yet not one of them clear and complete enough to crystallize on paper. Susan's incestuous sexual victimization as a child was clearly rife with implications for herself, her siblings, and her mother—who might have suffered her own childhood traumas. The self-help phe-nomenon had given the public greater access to clinical expertise on incest and child abuse than ever before. Most current thinking indi-cated that the healing process could eventually lead victims beyond "getting over" the effects of abuse, neglect, and serious family dysfunc-tion. "When survivors heal from child sexual abuse," specialist Ellen Bass wrote, "they become people who have thoroughly explored them-selves; their strengths and their weaknesses, their hopes and their fears, their values and commitments." But for Susan, at this point in her recovery, being a "survivor" still meant knocking a big enough hole in the thick tomb of her life to give her the light to see.

Susan finally submitted to the *Boston Globe* an article composed in the "just the facts" style of speakers at Anonymous meetings. She felt the police-blotter tone was appropriate because the drama in her story was supplied by the unadorned truth. Susan sent an advance copy to Shuna. Then she took a deep breath and sent another copy to Eve and Sam.

Shuna had always loved reading her mother's prose, and ever since she took a writing course at college, she'd appreciated her mother's early work all the more. But Shuna didn't like the *Globe* article. "It's just more NA stuff. 'I took a lot of these pills. I shot some of that. I smoked some crack.' That stuff just doesn't faze me anymore."

Shuna reacted similarly to the Adult Children of Alcoholics meetings she'd attended a few times after accompanying her mother to a Narcotics Anonymous meeting in Boston. The meetings made Shuna fantasize about jumping to her feet and shouting, "Yes, this is what you did to yourself, but how did it make you *feel?* So you smoked crack, so what! What did it do to your spirit?...*What did it do to your kid?*"

Shuna read the *Boston Globe* article looking for the paragraph about the surprise birthday party she'd thrown for Susan. Where was the part about how her addict mother had turned to her after the guests were gone and screamed, "Where is my present!" The party hadn't been enough. Where was the description of the card her mother had the nerve to send her from Conifer Park, the one that said, "Hi, I'm up here because I sort of got into crack, but I'm cleaning up. Bye." One lousy sentence on a "fucking Hallmark card." When Shuna opened it she tried to make herself laugh, but she couldn't because she knew she no longer cared about her mother enough to locate the irony. Shuna now believed she hated her mother completely.

At the end of 1987, Shuna had traveled from New Paltz to Boston to see her mother. During a visit that included moments of warmth and a memorable screaming match, Susan said, "Well, at least one thing I was able to pass along to you is a sense of pride." Shuna shot back a look of astonishment. "Not in a million years," she said.

Shuna Lydon was so slender and graceful that she looked much taller than she really was. The words "willowy" or "lovely" might easily have come to an onlooker's mind as she walked by if not for her short-cropped hair colored in vivid shades of bright violet and exotic plum set off by lemon-yellow and magenta stripes. After Shuna let the clean-shaven crescents located on either side of an ice-blue Mohawk grow out, she got an early Harbor Isle little boy's crew cut with a bit of frontal fringe, almost like a "Princeton cut" from the 1940s, except that she dyed the hair in front chartreuse and the rest of it Kelly green. Then she had a friend carefully crosshatch the field of green with a checkerboard pattern done in a bright shade of red. Shuna's cranium stopped pedestrians dead on every street and tended to distract from her fluid gait. Questioned by bold strangers, Shuna would often say, "It's better than doing drugs," and leave it at that.

After Shuna's Boston visit, Susan called Ricky, and in what the rest of the family subsequently received as an indication that "the old Susan" was far from lost, she said to her brother, "Have you seen Shuna's hair? Ricky, what have I done wrong?"

Shuna wasn't ashamed or embarrassed about her family, but when people asked questions, she often replied, "There's not much to say." If she really trusted the person, she'd tell the truth. "Well, I lived with my grandparents for a long time, so I'm really close to them. My grandmother is neurotic. My aunt Lorraine is a yogi, and my uncle Ricky is gay. My aunt Sheila is just this total JAP, and my mother, well, she's a drug addict. My father's still a hippie, but that's another story. All my cousins have funny names. We're all real intense people, and we're all real close."

Shuna had by now read and heard enough about the model alcoholic and dysfunctional family to know that a "real close" family was not necessarily considered conducive to emotional health and well-being. In fact, tight-knit families more often appeared to indicate serious pathology to expert and amateur family-watchers alike.

The first time she got up to speak at an Adult Children of Alcoholics meeting, Shuna noticed that her voice sounded small and distant. But the story still held together, and even from what seemed like a perch outside herself, just telling it in front of strangers made Shuna feel released, wonderful and warm.

Some twenty-three million children of alcoholics were the original focus of ACOA or ACA, as it was known, but when Shuna tried to find a group for children of drug addicts, she was told that the format of almost all the meetings was the same. ACOA regulars were beginning to notice that at a meeting of two hundred people, less than one hundred might be able to identify a single alcoholic or chemically dependent person in their families of origin. AA veterans told of a new flood of "toast burners" showing up at meetings, people who had not truly bottomed out (they'd been pushed "over the edge" by something like burning a piece of toast while drunk) and were not "ready," according to those who knew what they were talking about. NA veterans similarly complained that crack was causing a false bottoming-out that masked an unreadiness to change. Twelve-steppers all over the country lamented to one another that the meetings were becoming social scenes.

Chemical dependency professionals began to come forward to express displeasure and skepticism at the self-help movement's appropriation of specific recovery models, including the twelve steps. One senior executive of Narcotics Anonymous, noting the proliferation of spin-off groups, wondered "whether participants are clear what they want to recover from." An addiction counselor at the Johnson Institute in Minneapolis said, "These modalities are designed for addicts—for people with specific responses—down to the timing of their adrenaline rush. The twelve steps are being used by non-addicts who probably won't respond."

A "more diseased than thou" phenomenon was fracturing the recovery world, just as competing definitions of "liberal" and "radical" and "revolutionary" once aroused passionate debate in the movement. Meanwhile, popular practitioners worked to minimize the schisms and enlarge the flock by asserting that anyone who was a member of a family could rightfully claim a disease.

Murray Bowen, one of the father figures of family systems theory, was disturbed by the popular conflation of pathologies. According to Bowen, troubled people and addicted people were not the same. Not long before his death in 1989, Bowen would say that though he always expected family systems theory to be packaged for public consumption, he disapproved of the metaphors of addiction and disease now being applied wholesale across the psychic landscape as a simplistic vision of the human condition. Similarly, it wasn't surprising that battle-scarred addiction counselors and abusers who'd fought the war of getting clean occasionally looked askance at codependent twelve-steppers seeking to "make amends" and "recover" from loving or caring or sacrificing too much for others, however painful such habitual emotional responses might be.

Parts of family systems theory made sense to Shuna. She thought her grandmother probably felt neglected because her children all craved acceptance from Sam. But Sam couldn't give it—"He just couldn't say, 'Hey, I love you,'" Shuna said—so her mother never got what she wanted. "In a funny way my mom got from Nanny what she really wanted from Grandpa, but it was never what she needed, so she never let go of the family."

Shuna was almost ready to let go of her family and grow up. She continued to attend ACOA and Codependents Anonymous meetings for a while, but for all the pleasure and insight of her early experiences, she soon began to feel uncomfortable. There was something eerie about all these lost souls speaking their intimate truths into a vacuum. No action was meant to result from these soapbox addresses. Everyone in the room, Shuna saw, was there for the sake of one person—the little child within. By the time she stopped going, she'd decided that this rendered the whole experience strangely empty.

By claiming to be diseased, the anonymous sharers seemed to embrace a tragic sense that the world around them could not be changed. Shuna, who was "getting more political all the time," noticed an absence in the rooms of any suggestion that these problems argued for changes in society. If the meetings, as many feminist twelve-steppers argued, were indeed reincarnations of the consciousness-raising groups Shuna's mother had told her so much about, where was the essential assumption that personal stories were also political? What about the material and moral environment in which so many people and families were working to be repaired? Shuna had lately become very concerned about the homeless people she saw on the streets. She knew what it was like to feel homeless, but the feeling came back to her now as empathy for those too poor to have a home. Shuna had grown up with the sound of movements all around her. Now there were only programs, and it just didn't seem like enough. After a while the meetings struck Shuna as kind of irresponsible.

The basic pledge of the codependent seeking to be reborn—"I am not going to get into your problems anymore"—was hardly a good thing for society as a whole, nor was it, according to the academic family systems theorists, a neutral act. Sending an article about your addiction to your daughter and your parents was a strong statement in family systems terms. It was a reach for control that the family, the system, would field as a change in equilibrium that required a systemic response.

During the summer, some Arican friends with whom Shuna was still in touch helped her get a job caring for a six-year-old boy named Darien who suffered from cerebral palsy and epilepsy. She went to live with Darien and his close-knit family in Los Angeles. Shuna loved Darien, and she loved to watch his gentle, patient parents. She came back from Los Angeles convinced that there must be thousands of families that worked. Darien's family made the culture of codependency hard to take. "There's just too much to do and see in the world to sit around in meetings," Shuna said.

Like the people in the meetings, Shuna's family was full of people who wanted to be reborn—some of them had been looking for quite a while. But Shuna felt ready to go on with life such as she had it. She was not an addict, though she'd certainly been denied important aspects of a normal childhood, and she would rather feel dependent and needy at times if recovering from dependency meant regarding moral outrage, loyalty, and even love as symptoms of a disease. As she assured inquisitive friends, for all that had happened inside her family, it was still a "close family," and Shuna refused to see this as pathology and nothing more.

Susan phoned Shuna one night and said that she was thinking a lot about their Berkeley days. "When I'm done here, how would you feel about going back and, you know, living there again?"

Shuna replied that she enjoyed her art and design courses at New Paltz but Berkeley had been on her mind too. "I've been thinking that someday I want to go back to northern California and take courses at the California College of Fine Arts in Oakland. Maybe we can go together," Shuna said.

A pause ensued.

"Maybe we can," Susan managed. "After all, Berkeley was the last place where things were okay."

Shuna hung up the phone feeling excited and scared.

After the conversation Susan stared at the walls of her small apartment. They were covered with pictures of Sam and Eve, alone and with various grandchildren. There were photographs of Shuna as a little girl. Drawings and prints and elegant cards Shuna had made were tacked and taped everywhere. "I love you, but I'm worried about you," was written on one. A card on the refrigerator door said, "I'm proud of you. Love, Shuna."

John Bradshaw tended to pause before the point in a speech when he said, "Watch your children. You will learn more from your children than from your parents."

⤜◆⤏

Sam finished reading the newspaper and trudged out into the midday Florida sun to fork some manure around the trunks of his new fruit trees, "to give them a break." He wasn't at his chores more than five minutes before he felt a strange, expansive sensation in his chest, the result, he figured, of the healthy quantity of lox he'd eaten at lunch. At the next tree, he felt like something was sitting on his chest. His teeth started to hurt; his jaw felt sore too. Sam's shoulders suddenly flashed with pain. He shook his head like a reeling fighter trying to clear the cobwebs.

Sam allowed that it must be hotter than he'd realized.

* * *

The newspaper was still full of items about the presidential election. Though Sam had judged Michael Dukakis "a nobody," he was already certain that he'd look back on his vote for George Bush as a big mistake. Sam regretted every Republican vote he'd ever cast. Reagan had turned out to be another of the "princes of privilege," as Harry Truman labeled Republicans back in 1948. If it hadn't become such a habit, Sam probably wouldn't have voted at all.

Along with millions of other Americans, Sam was enjoying all the news stories about sleazy evangelists caught with their hands in the till—or in other unexpected places. He was also getting a big kick out of the state of Florida. Now that he and Eve had a house out near the alligator lanes (they only went back to the contrived preserve of Century Village to dance or play cards), he'd met dozens of wholly entertaining Floridians—con men, bunko artists, guys posing as plumbers, roofers, handymen, and even electricians. Sam said the Florida version of an electrician made him feel smarter than Thomas Edison. "They got people down here trying scams that stopped selling in New York City fifty years ago," he said, not without appreciation. Native Floridians came by to offer bushel baskets full of tomatoes and swollen cucumbers—"real gestures," said Sam. Florida, he thought, was a neighborly sort of rogues' gallery, and it was zoned in some spots for farm animals. Sam liked it fine.

He was fencing off the new property, and he'd already built coops for the chickens and geese. He'd finished a big paddock and a dock that protruded fifteen feet into a brackish pond covered over by a thick, teeming, lima-bean-colored algal brocade. All the work finished and in progress was Sam's own except for the new roof on the stable, and he'd hired that job out in the name of expediency. Being almost seventy had nothing to do with it at all. Sam was a rancher now, and he felt strong as a young bull. He felt utterly renewed.

His plan for the day was to finish spreading the manure around the fruit trees and get to work on some cages and pens for a planned menagerie worthy of Noah's Ark. But the pain in his jaw wouldn't go away, and the ache in one of his shoulders was getting worse. Sam decided to go inside and get some Ben-Gay.

Ricky was visiting his parents at their new spread. He sat with Eve inside the cool, capacious living room. A stone fireplace was set between two large glass doors that opened onto a screened area housing a swimming pool and various tropically tough-looking plants. A little fountain contraption rose from the middle of the pool, throwing out a thin stream of water. From the living room the sound of the water falling and the blinding whiteness of the sun beyond created the hot and cool sense of tranquillity offered by an Italian piazza in a small village.

A copy of Susan's article sat on the coffee table. Eve had read it several times when it arrived, and she cried each time. Beyond her own feelings of guilt, she was overwhelmed by the consistency of suffering that had apparently characterized her daughter's life from the beginning. "You know why we never took drugs?" Eve said to Sam. "It was because we never had enough time for all the suffering."

"I knew plenty of times when I thought my parents didn't love me," Eve told Ricky. "But who didn't? Isn't that just part of life?"

Eve was thankful that there was no hint in Susan's article of the "incest thing," which Lorraine had also mentioned by now. Eve felt so responsible for such an act on her father's part that she still couldn't acknowledge that it had occurred.

When Susan first told Sam about her article, he asked about her fee. But he didn't read the article, and he never would.

Through his sisters, Ricky had heard that a song he sang Eve from his family piece had upset her. Apparently a trio he wrote for the three sisters was too full of "family stuff," even for Eve.

Ricky had become interested in the dysfunctional family models Susan was always talking about. The way he applied what he'd read in *Women Who Love Too Much* and other books, Eve protected Sam, who was never allowed to see things like how terrified Ricky had been to be left at home when he was young. In one of his journals Ricky made a list of family "addictions":

> *Ricky—food, men, his looks*
> *Sheila—food, own lack of self-esteem*
> *Lorraine—food (control), illness, men*
> *Susan—drugs, men, books, shopping*
> *Mother—father, coffee, sugar, jokes*
> *Father—work, sex*

Ricky discovered a twelve-step group called Arts Anonymous and attended a meeting, but he would soon seek solace, camaraderie, and better health by abjuring both his afternoon reveries about the first cocktail of the evening and the cocktail itself. Along with a significant percentage of his friends and colleagues in New York, Ricky joined AA. This new reconsideration of his life suddenly revealed a potential answer to several lasting mysteries—getting sick at Stephen Sondheim's house the first time after drinking, fighting with Sondheim the second time after drinking, passing out at dinner back at Carnegie Mellon. And why was it that his unconscious vision of a heart-to-heart talk and final reconciliation with his distant tough-guy father had come to him in a dream set in a bar?

Few of Ricky's friends could ever recall seeing him drunk, but they all saw how calm and concentrated his association with AA allowed him to be. Ricky's absorption in his family past shifted from comic, Freudian, New Age, or self-help constructs to the Promethean musical composition he now called *The Family Eyes*. When he wasn't coaching Broadway singers or writing ballets or song cycles (he would soon be courted by Metropolitan Opera soprano Teresa Stratas, who would leave breathtaking renditions of Ricky's songs on his answering machine), he was writing music to accompany the story of an American family struggling to make sense of lives that hadn't quite turned out as any of them had expected. The piece featured three variously talented and injured sisters, a mother (a former singer) who steps back from the footlights early on to "a tidy home inside this house/To claim the kitchen my domain," and a dark, brooding father ("I ride away on my horse that never knows how many things to be sorry for there are"). There was also a young brother, the narrator who observes the action from the side of the stage.

On the basis of four selections from the work in progress, Ricky was awarded a grant from the National Institute for Music Theater. Playwright John Guare told Ricky the songs were "self-pitying," and an actress friend asked him if he would ever "stop blaming your parents for everything," but Ricky was much less the "stripped screw," as he'd once described himself, for his experience of writing *The Family Eyes*, and if his mother was not ready to hear it, then he would sit beside her in her new house and talk of other things.

The Ben-Gay didn't help, so Sam went in to lie down. When he woke up, he felt like a large animal was crouching on his chest, and there were pains shooting down his arms.

It seemed that everyone in the Gordon family had "almost had a heart attack" at one time or another. It was an expression Eve had often used to draw attention to the cause of her distress: Ricky smoking in the bushes, Susan lying on her bed like she was dead. But heart attacks *per se* were not among the family's healthy store of obsessions. Sam scoffed at the *alte cockers* over at Century Village who cut the skin off their chicken. He thought a pain in your tooth was a toothache, not an indi- cation of the onset of a myocardial infarction of the sort that killed some 540,000 Americans every year.

On the way to the hospital, Sam began a brief inventory of his life—"just like in a movie." It was a life that had already stretched out some eight years longer than he thought it would. Papa Joe, after all, had died at sixty-two. Sam wondered whether he might have lived longer if he'd learned to delegate work. And he couldn't help thinking about all the aggravation he'd known.

Eve came out of the intensive care unit and told Ricky that the doctors were hopeful. "He wants to talk to you," she said.

Ricky approached the bed where his father lay connected to the kinds of wires and tubes Ricky associated with Sam's whole life. "Lis- ten," Sam said. "I want you to take care of things if something happens to me. I want your mother to sell the house, and Ricky, I'd really appre- ciate it if you'd come down to help her if I die."

Sam told Ricky where he kept the safe deposit keys and important documents. Then he stopped talking and just looked at his son with eyes so full of love that both of them had to look away.

1989

Not long after Sam's heart attack and the publication of Susan's article in the *Boston Globe*, Lorraine inched her little red Subaru into the middle of an empty rural crossroads and was blindsided by a delivery truck traveling at over fifty miles an hour. Lorraine staggered out of her car and lay down on the warm tarmac. She was still half-consciously pondering the relative brevity of the opportunity to chisel a mark into a fleeting soul when she heard the consummately terrestrial voice of Bill Behny, her partner in business and life.

"You think it's totaled?" Bill was asking the policeman who'd phoned him with news of the crash. Lorraine saw Bill's long legs pass in the direction of the pay phone at the corner store. Bill did not join Lorraine in the ambulance; nor did he come to her bedside in the hospital until he'd tended to the car.

Lorraine was lucky in that her injuries were slight. But she checked out of the hospital and went home to tell her boys that it was time once again to be a family without a man.

In San Francisco, Gina Schick added Lorraine's car crash to her accounting of other Gordon events of recent weeks. For more than a quarter century, Gina—who now preferred her Sufi name, Rahima—had tracked and analyzed the nuances of Gordon family progress with the zeal of a sports fan. Gina inventoried the transcontinental confluence of Susan's public confessional, Sam's coronary, and Lorraine's car crash, and she marked the "coincidence" as typical of the subconscious human animations that had so fascinated her grandfather and his Freudian friends, typical of the transcendent cosmic valences that bind a family together, and typical of the Gordons—a clan Gina always pictured riding through time in a small boat. Whenever too many members of the family went to one side to look into the sea, the water would rush in over the side.

Gina was currently preoccupied with a project she hoped would right her own family boat. She was by now the strong-willed, thrice-divorced mother of two good kids—a boy named Ben, who was attending college, and a girl named Zena, seventeen. But she was also the mother of the child she'd given up for adoption twenty-four years earlier when she and Lorraine lived in Greenwich Village. She'd finally come to believe that some fundamental balance was missing from her family life because—like so many thousands of other "birth mothers" of her generation—she'd relinquished not only her baby but the right to know who he was.

Some twenty states now had protocols by which official agencies would assist in the "reunification" of adopted children and their families of blood, but almost all the procedures were predicated on the "mutually voluntary" efforts of parents and child. Some services would assist a searching child, but a parent usually had to turn to an underground investigative network for help.

Gina located a Santa Barbara–based private detective—called a "finder" in underground argot—a woman who had a reputation for getting information out of the particular New York adoption agency that had placed Gina's son. Her finder refused to begin a search until Gina "fronted" half of the three-hundred-dollar fee, and she said she wouldn't send the birth certificate she eventually turned up until payment was rendered in full. ("It's like buying dope," Gina told her friends.) The document included the adoptive father's name and occupation, which led Gina to a professional directory, which in turn led to a town in a county only half an hour away, to a high school records office where Gina posed as a would-be employer, and eventually to one of the humanities departments at the University of California at Berkeley, where Gina's son had recently earned a degree. Once Gina was convinced that her son was alive and healthy and probably lived within two miles of her house, she decided to stop short of making contact. She wasn't sure what he had been told, and she found that knowing he existed granted her peace.

Gina took a part-time job with a local law firm that served "surrogate mothers." For a fee, usually around ten thousand dollars—less than a third of what the prospective parents often spent on their cars, as Gina would point out to the firm's clients—women were now having children to make families for others. Gina tried to help potential surrogates understand how strong the force of family could be, so strong that even if they never spoke a word to their child and the child never knew they existed, that child would always have a place in their hearts.

Such was the awesome, secret power of family love.

Ricky was strolling up the street across from Central Park on one of those spring afternoons so full of crystalline sunlight that it was difficult to imagine the park as the site of the "preppy" strangulation murder and the rape of an innocent jogger by a gang of "wilding" youths. He glanced at a passing reflection of himself in a picture window and was instantaneously depressed. Framed by the dense tree line of the park behind him and backlit by the brilliant sun was the stark image of his own balding head.

"I would have traded it all," Albert Einstein reportedly said, "if I could only have kept all my hair."

Ricky stared at his reflection and wondered what his father would think about a man looking for his hair in a picture window. "You'll always be lovable and cute to me, bald or not," Lorraine wrote to her brother. "Just try to realize that Daddy's abandonment was out of his inability to express his love to you as a son and man. Maybe he feared homosexuality. The love was there, but not the expression...which is what I always missed so much too."

Ricky turned away and crossed the street. At the edge of the park, he noticed an old man whose face was composed into one of the most beautiful and loving looks Ricky had ever seen. The old man's eyes were riveted on a little girl with blond hair who was skipping rope at his feet. Her back was turned to Ricky, but he saw that she was wearing a frilly pink party dress and shiny patent-leather shoes. The man was clearly the girl's grandfather, and Ricky couldn't get over how the sight of her spread so pure an expression of love across his face.

Ricky kept watching until his eyes filled with tears. The trees were thick with leaves, and the spring day was full of perfect family love.

Ricky walked toward the old gentleman, and as he passed he glanced over his shoulder at the little girl, at a face that made him gasp. This blond angel of a grandchild had the most grotesquely ruined and bloated visage he'd ever seen. The little girl's face was like the Elephant Man's in the movie, only so much more tortured and difficult to behold. But Ricky knew that when she looked at her grandfather, all she could see in the mirrors of his eyes was love.

At seventy-five Sri Swami Satchidananda could still glide gracefully across a room in his flowing robes. His long white hair rose from a spot farther back on his brow than before, though the change only enhanced his leonine aspect. His long beard was cottony white. He carried reading glasses for fine print.

Satchidananda had recently been featured in a magazine because of his obsession with personal computers. He had one for business and another for his own use. He enjoyed using advanced AutoCad engineering programs to create three-dimensional design images for Yogaville buildings of the future. One structure in the planning stages was the guru's huge mausoleum. Another was a life-sized statue of the guru just a foot or so shorter than the likeness of Red Buttons at Century Village. Talk of his computers or his mausoleum caused Swamiji's eyes to light up, whereas the endless predicaments of his followers made him look like a weary parent at the end of his rope.

As far as Swami Satchidananda was concerned, a devotee like Leela, who'd come hammering on his door in search of forgiveness, had failed to "follow me one hundred percent," as he put it. Lorraine always *said* she loved him—he knew that, of course—but then she was always going off to experiment on her own. "This is natural. My food is not the only good food," the guru acknowledged. "Maybe it gets stale after a time." But Lorraine, "she tries to do things for my approval, *just* for my approval."

Never once during all of Lorraine's more than fifteen years of devotion had her guru sat down to chat with her, but he was nonetheless quite sure that Lorraine's was a life filled with lessons as yet unlearned.

Lorraine felt like her car drove itself to Yogaville.

It turned onto a private drive and continued all the way to the end, where the road circled in front of a big house that hung high over the James River and looked like the house in Alfred Hitchcock's *North by Northwest*.

I don't care if he kicks my head in, Lorraine thought.

How could she have been such a fool? She had everything a human being could ask for at the ashram, and she'd thrown it away for a demon biker who cussed and smoked and ate meat and sold harmless animals to people who took pleasure in killing. If Lorraine had been playing Eve Gordon to Bill Behny's Sam, then that particular psychological theater was now closed.

Gurudev's personal secretary showed her inside the house and asked her business. She left and returned almost immediately. "I'm sorry, Leela. Gurudev cannot see you."

Lorraine drove over to LOTUS and climbed the stairs leading into the dimness of the central dome's interior. When Lorraine had LOTUS to herself like this, she was sure she could feel vibrations. She knelt down on one of the soft pads on the floor inside the dome and fell into the gentle night of meditation. When she opened her eyes, she felt protected. She knew she was finally back home.

After Lorraine and the boys left Bill and moved back into a trailer at the ashram, she met and quickly fell in love with a newcomer to Yogaville named Jai Heard, a forty-five-year-old healer and former Texas firefighter who stood out among the white- and saffron-clad disciples because of his dusty blue jeans, his much dustier cowboy boots, his very long white hair, and one of those total-lip-coverage scrub-brush mustaches that made it seem he could throw his voice like a ventriloquist. Jai had a trail-weary, good-ole-boy conversational style of the sort more suited to discussions of horses or beer or women than of the exotic varieties of metaphysical and spiritual experience that dominated Jai Heard's thoughts.

Jai's father had been killed in action in 1944. He still carried a picture of his dad clutching the infant Jai—who was Jay then—during his last time home on leave. "Growin' up fatherless in Texas when Ah did meant that people thought Ah was a potential homosexual. It wadn't normal," Jai said. "And it wadn't easy."

Until the latter half of 1976, Jai was a Texas redneck and proud of it. He had a master's degree in education and had done a bit of teaching, but he'd spent most of his working life fighting fires. He was assistant chief of the fire department down in Huntsville, Texas, a prison town south of Houston. He also trained firefighters and emergency medical units for the city of Houston. His idea of fun was to swear and spit and drink and play dominoes in a cowboy bar with his state trooper buddies. He loved to drive a road like Interstate 45 drunk in a police cruiser at 150 miles an hour, running a few speeding truckers to ground while he was at it, maybe squeezing off a few rounds at animals out the car windows, whooping away. In 1972 Jai cast an enthusiastic vote for Richard Nixon. In 1975 he tried marijuana for the first time.

But all that was before Jai picked up a book about yoga and realized that never once, not for a second in his entire life, had he been happy. Within a few months he was living at the Satchidananda Ashram in Santa Barbara, California, where one day he found himself picking up the telephone to call his guru in Virginia.

"Yes, what is it, Jai?" the swami said.

"Well, Gurudev, I would like to be a pre-*sannyasin*," the rookie yogi drawled. He wanted to enter the period of renunciation and training that would eventually lead to initiation into the monkish life of a full-time swami.

"Is that all, Jai?" Satchidananda asked. Jai wasn't sure, but he thought he heard the guru say, "Carry on," before the receiver clattered down.

Jai felt so rejected that he went back to Texas, to another fire department. He returned to California after a while and took a job with a local homeopath, a practitioner of therapeutic techniques developed by an eighteenth-century German named Hahnemann, who was influenced by the works of Hippocrates, Paracelsus, and other ancient masters of the healing arts. Under the shadow of the American medical establishment, homeopathy—the practice of administering organic compounds as chemical antidotes to the toxic sources of disease—was promoted by a tiny dissenting sect until the New Age resuscitated it as one of many alternative disciplines.

The homeopath Jai worked for in California treated more than fifty patients each day in his two offices. Jai ran one office and studied the voluminous *materia medica* texts essential to a vision of healing that he said should be imagined as the careful withdrawal of "the corkscrew" of disease. Homeopathy was the science of gradually removing the screw; modern technological medicine, Jai explained to Lorraine and others who came to him to be "worked on," recklessly "ripped the corkscrew right out." Jai said he'd seen the California homeopath cure many cases of herpes and at least one case of rectal cancer with his elixirs and herbs.

In the meantime, Jai had developed a taste for marijuana and cocaine. He also began to drink heavily and stay out all night in search of women and kicks. But the teachings of Swami Satchidananda eventually regained their hold on him, and he spent several years working as something of a missionary, dispensing yoga and homeopathic cures to homeless people in Santa Barbara (a man on the docks once tried to slit his throat). By the time Jai packed his fireman's helmet and tall rubber boots into his yellow Volkswagen van and headed for Yogaville, he'd come to believe that he'd somehow acquired powers of divination and insight that enabled him to heal much more effectively than any drug.

Lorraine would sit under a tree with Jai and listen to him explain that drug addiction was the result of "a systemic bodily craving caused by problems with people's livers and other organs." He said that gold and silver fillings accounted for tremendous numbers of medical problems, just as vaccinations had made "a generation of children deranged."

Fluoridated water also had a lot to do with the course of modern disease. Lorraine decided to take Ram off the pills a neurologist in Charlottesville had prescribed for his terrible headaches, and after a few weeks drinking Jai's alternative mixtures and following his dietary advice, Ram felt much better.

Gabriel Hughes, tall and blond and thirteen, had his own views of the family's move back to an ashram trailer with a kitchen at one end, a room for the three boys in the middle, and an empty meditation room at the other end. He and his brothers were still attending public school, where he asked to be called Ram, though not out of any devotion to yoga. ("Out here nobody's named Gabe. They have names like Ron and Mike around here. My nickname's Rambo, so call me Ram.") As soon as he crossed the Yogaville border, Ram headed for the nearest radio to listen to Guns N' Roses. Full of defiance, he returned from a Boy Scout jamboree not long after they'd left Bill—whom all the boys missed— and announced that he'd eaten a hot dog. Lorraine was furious. Jai said he'd get a bad headache soon, and he did.

Jai listened to Lorraine's detailed description of nearly a half century of Gordon family tribulation. He heard the worst of it—drugs, drinking, fights, flying plates and phones, cancer, a bit of promiscuity here and there, homosexuality, shyness, brazenness, on and on—and to story after story, he ascribed a biological genesis. For each and every aspect of family trouble there was a homeopathic reason why.

Lorraine was dazzled. Jai was a man who'd taken to an alternative path and had no intention of turning back. He'd been celibate for years, which made the touch of his big hand around hers all the more electric as they strolled the beautiful grounds, talking away hours and days, meditating side by side, and chanting in the evening with the boys "like a real yoga family," as nine-year-old Shiva said.

Jai took up the secular task of organizing a Yogaville firefighting brigade equipped to serve the Buckingham community beyond the ashram. He wore a beeper connected to the headquarters of the local emergency services and rescue squad, and unlike most other ashramites, he numbered as close friends many of the locals who gathered at the tiny, old-fashioned general store at a nearby crossroads called Winjina. Lorraine would sit beside Jai in the store as he tipped back his chair like an old hand, winding out stories with men and women who would have jumped up and run if they knew about all the power he believed he had in his hands. He didn't tell them he was sure that energy emanating from the third eye, a highly developed *chakra*, coursed through his fingers, and that he had the power to heal.

"Well, what I don't understand is how can you give up the traditions and practices of your childhood," one lady in the Winjina store circle said to Jai and Lorraine. "I mean, Leela, dontcha-all at least call yerself Joosh?"

Lorraine flinched. "We...practice and celebrate the traditions of all religions," she replied.

But in truth, Lorraine often regretted the loss of traditions that had seemed so important to her grandparents when she was young. She occasionally found herself falling into a "pit of self-pity and lament" over how seldom she had conformed even with her own idealized vision of the good granddaughter or daughter or wife or member of a spiritual community—or member of a family. Looking only for the truth and the best in people's hearts, rejecting at every turn the smallness of people's minds, refusing to acknowledge that people or things could not be set right, she'd been married three times, and she was still left wondering what she was supposed to have learned.

Lorraine was well aware that Susan and Ricky considered her a "woman who loves too much," but she dismissed such mechanistic analyses of human motivation. "You've been talking about Daddy for ten years," Lorraine said to Sheila, who now had nearly a decade of psychotherapy under her belt, "and you know as well as I do you still go mad from PMS." Lorraine agreed with Eve that an "enabler" was hard to distinguish from a good mother. And she wasn't impressed with the urban vogue for turning life into one long meeting, because the self-help movement seemed to create new addictions—to meetings and books.

Whatever people thought about the way she lived, Lorraine was still able to imagine a perfect love between a man and a woman, a love that was indissoluble and forever. She was just old-fashioned that way.

A few months after they met, Lorraine and Jai were married. Ram, Shiva, and Gopal joined two Integral Yoga ministers and a few friends in the meditation room at the far end of the trailer for a ceremony that all present found warm and hopeful.

When Lorraine turned to her new husband, a phrase came to her that she'd never applied to any previous association with a man. She looked into Jai's soft blue eyes, and she thought, with more love than she'd ever felt before, *This is it. This is the way it should always have been.*

◆

When Shuna met new people after she and her mother moved to California, she wasn't shy about letting them know her politics. She sometimes wore an iridescent pink T-shirt bearing an image of former President Reagan with AIDSGATE emblazoned underneath, and she had a button that said, "Housing Is a Right," though she did not believe that "simply wearing something on your body necessarily means you're doing something for the cause."

The previous summer, before leaving New York, Shuna had wandered into the middle of what many eyewitnesses and journalists at the scene judged a full-scale "police riot." On a Saturday night she was walking with some friends near Tompkins Square Park, where Lorraine used to sit with baby Maggie, where Goldflower presented free concerts, where Ricky first saw Hare Krishna dancers and barefoot hippie girls with flowers in their hair. A block from the park she saw a mounted policeman dragging a disheveled man along by his hair. The cop dumped the man on the sidewalk in front of Stromboli Pizza, and he lay there bleeding. A police helicopter buzzed overhead, and Shuna heard screams coming from the park, where a tiny demonstration of no more than a hundred people protesting "yuppies and real estate developers" in the neighborhood had escalated into a riot. People out to get an early edition of the Sunday paper were being beaten and chased by the police.

As Shuna disappeared into the fray, her friends ran away and shouted at her over the noise to come with them. "No!" Shuna yelled back. "Look what they're doing! This is these people's neighborhood!" Billy clubs and pieces of the street were flying all around her. Shuna went up to a cop and began to scream louder than she'd ever heard herself scream. She hadn't been able to raise her voice much since her mother forced her to yell at her when they lived in their "drug house," but now she was bellowing obscenities at a cop whose wild eyes flashed fearful beneath his Plexiglas visor. She saw people staring out of windows in the surrounding buildings, and she thought they were looking down to see who could possibly be screaming so loud.

Shuna's friends finally dragged her away from the Tompkins Square riot of July 1988, an event that would lead to accusations and counter-accusations and mayoral statements in the press for several weeks. Shuna had thrown herself in front of furious club-wielding policemen on charging horses—just as her aunt Lorraine had done more than twenty years earlier, and just as her great-grandmother Yetta had tried to stand her ground before men on horses some seventy years before that. When she told her father what she'd seen and done, Michael Lydon said, "One thing about a demonstration—even a peaceful one. You have to believe. You have to believe one hundred percent in the reason you are there. Like a soldier ready to die for a cause, you have to know why you're out there."

Shuna knew that Michael had witnessed the glory days of street politics from the Freedom Summer of 1964 through the antiwar demonstrations. She knew he'd watched events that Shuna studied in history class, always with his notebook in hand, the narrator of other people's heartfelt rage. Shuna believed her father had never been truly committed to anything until he became a "serious hippie," a description that fit him to this day. Michael wore his shoulder-length gray-and-white hair in a thick ponytail. He and his wife, Ellen, performed their gentle musical send-ups around the Village, often at the same club and during the same week as the up-and-coming singer-songwriter Eddie Hughes, known to his former relatives as Harry Hughes.

In Shuna's view, a "teenage factor" was behind the marriage of Michael Lydon and Susan Gordon, an event apparently erased from history except for the fact of herself. Shuna could imagine her mother all geared to be cool and confident, so sexy and crazy to be liked, and her father, kind of "wimpy and nerdy and smart and ready to be swept off his feet" by a sexually sophisticated woman, as Shuna was sure Susan was. In many ways, Shuna believed, neither of them had changed.

Shuna couldn't understand why Michael refused to speak the name of a woman he had married and fathered a child with. Because she was planning to visit Maggie in England, she tried to ask Michael about his London days. "I can't remember a thing. That was before I met Ellen," her father said in a tone that implied he was surprised Shuna didn't understand that his history began several years after she was born. What Shuna did understand was that just because you had a child, that didn't mean you were a parent. And just because you were close to fifty, that didn't mean you were a grown-up.

Sometimes Shuna wished she had just one photograph of her parents together.

Shuna thought often about her childhood after she moved to Oakland, because so many adults—especially adults her mother's and father's age—would ask her what it was like to be a child in the sixties, though she was not yet two when the decade ended. They always seemed to be checking her out, to see how she had "survived."

One day Susan, Shuna, and Gina drove to Marin County, just to look up the hill at the house full of memories. David Getz was living in Los Angeles, Susan said, so Shuna was shocked when she raced up the stairs and saw him at the door, with gray hair and an infant in his arms.

David insisted they all come inside. David's daughter Alzara, with whom Shuna once shared the house in Fairfax, was now a Russian lit major. David, a member of AA for a decade, was remarried and the full-time father of a small child. David said he'd decided to do the whole "parenting thing" differently this time around. This time the kid came first. He was well aware that his second chance to be a better father was something of a biological and economic luxury, one much coveted by many women of his age and general experience.

"You know I prayed for you, Susan," David said. "At the end of the AA meetings. You know, when they ask for a moment of silence for those who still suffer, I always prayed for you. Each time; for ten years."

Shuna could tell that her mother didn't say anything because she was trying not to cry.

Then David asked Shuna about the sixties. "You know, have you ever thought about how being a little kid then affected you?"

In truth Shuna sometimes resented her vague recollections of the legendary sixties. She couldn't remember much about hippies or all the famous people her mother knew, just a continuum of different people, different families, and different houses.

"Well," she said, "I won't smoke cigarettes or take drugs. I guess that comes from growing up the way I did. And I think I was lucky to be around so many people. All the people in the communes and at Blue Fairyland, all the Aricans who were like a hundred mothers and fathers when I needed them. It was like having so many parents to depend on."

If Shuna had never known a stable home, then at least she'd known that the boundaries of home did not define the world. But her experience of so many living arrangements that were "like families" had left her committed to a traditional vision of nuclear family life, like David Getz, a man with a second chance. Since her fragile mother was sitting beside her, Shuna didn't tell David until she saw him again some months later about two other oaths she'd taken after much reflection upon her childhood. "If I ever get married, it will be forever," she said. "And I will never believe for a second that having a kid is the same thing as being a parent."

Susan and Shuna hunted down original Blue Fairyland parents, commune buddies, and women's movement friends still living in the Bay Area. Susan would tell them a short version of "her story" since leaving town, and the old friends would touch her shoulder or nod without surprise. They asked Shuna questions, and one after another they offered progress reports on their own children, who were invariably described as having "good values." They talked about "sensitive," "aware," "likable," and even "cool" children who, for all the things their parents had done wrong, had not grown up to be Republicans or wealth-obsessed automatons or burnouts or even kids who blamed everything on Mom and Dad.

"Abbie always said that not one of his kids grew up to be a self-involved yuppie," Susan observed. "Abbie said that at least at that he was a success."

During the summer of 1988, Abbie Hoffman had attended a conference in Chicago commemorating the twentieth anniversary of the Democratic Convention of 1968 and a "police riot" much better known than the one in Tompkins Square because it was watched, as people said out on Michigan Avenue at the time, by the "whole world." When it was Hoffman's turn to speak, he said he believed that the protests of 1968 had passed along to the entire nation the "energy" contained until then within the relatively small antiwar movement.

Hoffman was once asked what he thought had happened to the fiery spirit of the sixties children who tried to revitalize democracy and stop a war. "We became numb," he said. When it was reported in 1989 that he had taken 150 pills and was dead at the age of fifty-two, many Americans wept because—though it was difficult to make some people understand in 1989, even their own children—Abbie Hoffman had been one of their heroes.

Still something of a Rip Van Winkle, Susan mentioned to a journalist writing a business article that if he wanted a radical viewpoint, he ought to get in touch with David Horowitz, her old colleague at *Ramparts*. Because Susan had been working the streets of Minneapolis and getting into crack at the time, she didn't know that Horowitz and another former radical named Peter Collier had published articles explaining why they'd voted for Ronald Reagan and had essentially repudiated what they called the political errors of their misspent youth. Beneath headlines like "Lefties for Reagan" and "Good-bye to All That," Horowitz and Collier contended that a pro-Soviet and totalitarian sensibility had motivated all the sixties activists, from the Weather Underground to the pacifist antiwar marchers. Susan didn't know that her old friend had chosen to be reborn during the 1980s, though not as a recovering addict or an evangelical Christian. David Horowitz had recovered from the sixties and been reborn as John Wayne.

In 1987, tens of millions of otherwise accomplished middle-aged Americans had discovered that not one of them, by the high standards of the times, was morally fit to serve as a justice of the United States Supreme Court. Ronald Reagan had nominated a forty-one-year-old conservative, Douglas H. Ginsburg, to a seat on the nation's highest court, but when it was discovered that Ginsburg had once *smoked pot*, he was forced to withdraw. "What serious forty-year-old public figure—or journalist, doctor, lawyer, professor, film maker, or corporation executive—doesn't have behind him or her at least some familiarity with nonalcoholic drugs, unorthodox sex, cohabitation, abortion, divorce and political demonstrations?" asked Todd Gitlin and a co-writer, Ruth Rosen, on the Op Ed page of the *New York Times*.

The highest-ranking baby-boomer in the land was now Dan Quayle, the beaming vice president, who on a recent trip to Samoa had grinned into a crowd of islanders and said, "You all look like happy campers to me. Happy campers you are....Happy campers you will always be."

A few years back, when she was still haunting the streets of New York, Susan had once dropped in on Sam while he was doing some electrical work in Manhattan. "I had a long talk with one of your people this morning," Sam said to his daughter. "This...black guy, he was telling me about his marching days in the civil rights movement. So I was telling him about all those marches and freedom rides and CORE meetings you used to run off to." Susan could hear an undertone of pride in his voice.

Her people. This was a part of the story of her life too—the part that was about other people's freedom. The civil rights movement was now something of a nostalgic cliché trotted out annually in recollections of Martin Luther King, and compressed into a few hundred pages of laws and regulations dedicated to making American life fair. It was easy to forget that people had once fought and died for those laws, that more than fifty million baby-boomers had been born into a time when black citizens were denied entrance to voting booths, and that many young whites who knew little else about black America had responded with infectious moral outrage.

Some eighty courses about "the sixties" were now being taught at American universities, in some cases broken down into early sixties and late, hard political history and sociological considerations of the counterculture. New books about the sixties were appearing one after another—about Freedom Summer, the political events of 1968, Woodstock. Former student leaders Todd Gitlin and Tom Hayden published reminiscences that captured—consciously or not—the sadness of so many children of the baby boom. The common lament was rarely articulated except among old friends, but it had to do with the loss of a moment of youthful unity, of a sense of community based on the way politics or drugs or the music made you feel, and on urgencies spawned from a shared belief that the world could indeed be transformed.

But as Shuna observed with disdain, movements were now over-shadowed by programmatic personal salvage operations. Advertisers paid a fortune for the use of Beatles songs to promote cars, shoes, and even cookies. The war in Vietnam was either a history course or an infantryman in a flak jacket moving across a jungle on a television screen to the strains of a Buffalo Springfield song.

Susan hunted down dozens of old Berkeley friends. Suzy Nelson, who let Susan rent the little garden house behind her big home in Oakland, was now a renowned restaurateur, owner of Berkeley's Fourth Street Grill and a pioneer of "California cuisine." Several of the other women from the consciousness-raising group had shed their men and were still without husbands, unlike the now suburbanized Aricans Susan found, many of whom had barely changed. The Aricans had cared well for themselves and were pushing middle age out into the future like football line-men at a blocking sled. Some of them told Susan they worried that Oakland was much too dangerous a place for a single woman to live.

Susan called an old Arica boyfriend, now a successful screenwriter in Hollywood. She found a former Harbor Isle playmate in Berkeley named Peter Mitchell. "Peter," she said with wonder when they got together. "I am *forty-five years old*." "It happens," said Peter, a divorced father of two boys. Susan and Peter talked about their neighborhood friend Randy Watson, who as Randall Forsberg had organized the huge nuclear freeze demonstrations of 1982. Susan mentioned Nancy Siegel, a high school friend who married a rich lawyer, got hooked on pills, and was now dead and gone. Nancy had once showed up at Susan's apart-ment on the East Side in a limousine, and they'd ridden around Man-hattan chewing on Percodans like girlfriends sharing a bag of M&Ms.

Many of Susan's more recent friends were dead or in jail. Susan knew that one Minneapolis companion had OD'd in Shokopee Women's Prison, and that another had been murdered over a quarter ounce of cocaine. But the sixties crowd in the Bay Area was amazingly intact, though none of them appeared to be completely "over" the old times. When stories were told of successful families, or children who'd grown up healthy, or jobs that didn't entirely compromise earlier con-victions, they would all nod, because it was such good news that still another had survived.

Susan and Shuna went back to the Med, the old hangout on Tele-graph Avenue. An astrologist Susan had known came up to say hello, but in the middle of a sentence Susan suddenly stopped speaking. She explained a few minutes later that she'd had a vision, a "flashback to the sixties, if that's not too trite a thing to say. I thought it was 1972, and Shuna"—she turned to her daughter—"I could see you out on the street. You were four years old, talking to the street people. You were laughing in the sun."

People kept asking Shuna about her memories of the sixties and early seventies. They inquired, it seemed, because so few of them knew exactly what to think about that stretch of time themselves. *Newsweek* devoted an entire issue to the question "Will We Ever Get Over the Sixties?" but the succinct answer was no. Even if it was only to shiver a bit at the documentary snippets aired on television on the anniversary of the Tet offensive, the Democratic Convention in Chicago, or the definitive cultural experience recently boiled down to a series of "Woodstock Moments," the answer was no. Even if it was only to cry a little at the sight of that infantryman running across the screen or at the sound of the Beatles or Buffalo Springfield, or to find it strangely impossible to include that absurdly thick leather belt with the peace symbol on the buckle in the Salvation Army pile, millions of Americans born in the decade that followed World War II would never "get over" the sixties, because it was such a destructive and magnificent time to be young.

<hr/>

Before Susan got into the ancient Oldsmobile Aunt Sylvia had given her and drove to California, she joined Ricky, Sheila and Lorraine, who was up for a visit, for what would be the last dinner at a Gordon family dwelling on Long Island. Sheila and Jon and their children would soon be moving to a Florida community forty-five miles away from Sam and Eve.

During dinner, Sheila did her Aunt Sylvia imitation and everyone howled. Sheila reported that she'd seen her ex-husband, Peter Probst, who was still as drop-dead handsome as always. He was married to a Jamaican woman, the father of three kids and stepfather of another.

Lorraine told them about her perfect marriage to Jai and about her own encounter with her ex-husband. Yesterday she'd gone to a club in the Village to see "Eddie" Hughes—by day, Dr. Harold Hughes, a psychopharmacologist conducting an experiment designed to determine whether massive quantities of cocaine were good for the health and well-being of pregnant lab rats. Harry was still handsome too, and he was still single. He wore an earring in one ear and sang haunting songs about war, about "gunships above," and about suburban boys dreaming of being free.

After his set, Lorraine told Harry that Gabe had recently won fourth place in the Virginia State Spelling Bee. "You'd be proud of him, Harry," she said. "I wish you could spend more time with him."

Harry admitted that it was the abiding power of guilt that kept him away from his son. They picked a date for him to visit Buckingham, and though Harry showed up, he did not "parent" by any definition of the term. He said he was not proud of his record of attentiveness but that at least Gabe was lucky to have such a good mother.

Susan and Lorraine both considered the men they had married failures as fathers, though neither was sure whether this was the result of their own poor choices or a general lack of paternal involvement in the aftermath of so many broken marriages. More than twice the number of children were now growing up without fathers than in 1960. One of every four children did not live with his or her father, and a study conducted by a researcher at the University of Pennsylvania indicated that over half of those children had never visited their fathers' homes and over forty percent saw their fathers less than once a year.

Susan reported that Maris Cakars and Susan Kent were living happily together in a Brooklyn brownstone with their two teenage children. Maris was now editor of the New York City Fire Department's publications; Susan was an editor of psychology books. Lorraine said that her old friend Ellen Levy Hine was managing a fancy restaurant in Boulder, Colorado. Ellen and Marty, now a restorer of antique horse-drawn vehicles, lived on a ranch outside town with their five children, three of them adopted and of Korean descent. Ricky told of Peter Randsman's success as an agent for international opera singers. Peter was almost always in attendance when Ricky's music was performed.

Susan listened to the updates on old family friends wearing her best Cheshire Cat grin. Through the cloud of cigarette smoke that surrounded her at all times, one of her older hairstyles was evident, the one with straight bangs falling to her clear dark-brown eyes. Susan was wearing makeup again and was looking rather chic.

At one point during dinner, when Susan was talking about her years of addiction, she started to cry. "You know, I always wanted to protect you guys. I really did. I wanted to make everything okay."

None of her siblings bothered to refute the statement.

Out in Berkeley, there would be plenty of twelve-step meetings for Susan to attend. "You just better take real good care of yourself," Susan's counselor and friend at Women Inc., Diane Wood, warned her when she left town. "'Cause I got a nickel in that dime, Sue."

Shuna's dorm room at the California School of Fine Arts was only a few minutes from the house Susan rented from Suzy Nelson. Susan and Shuna got together often, though they tended to argue about the true nature of various events they'd shared during their lives. Shuna let it be known that she felt she was owed something by her mother, though she couldn't say exactly what. But more often Susan and Shuna talked about love and clothes.

Susan knew she would be in recovery for the rest of her life. She was trying hard to shake off the self-pity and remorse, and belatedly she was trying to be a parent to Shuna, to begin what child psychologist Urie Bronfenbrenner called that "escalating ping-pong game between two people who are crazy about each other."

One night Shuna came over for dinner and said, "You know what, Mom? I feel so special because I have you as a mother. You're a great person." And once again Susan's eyes filled with tears.

Shuna came over another night and told Susan that after attending Maggie's wedding to her British boyfriend, she planned to stay on in London for several months, maybe longer. When she left, Susan couldn't stop crying. The news hurt so badly that Susan felt herself begin to unhook the new bindings. She wanted to put down her ping-pong paddle and retreat to the safety of detachment, to become numb until the abandonment stopped hurting her. She "loved too much." She needed to back away so it wouldn't hurt. *I can't miss her this much*, Susan thought.

But without drugs, without a countercultural ethos supportive of maternal self-involvement, the pain lingered. *I can really feel it*, Susan thought. *I can feel how much I really love her.* Then Susan wondered if maybe that had been it all along—maybe the secret had always been that pain was just the other side of love.

———◆———

Eve looked out at the strange sight of her husband not working. Sam was swimming in the pool, diving under the water and emerging again, looking trim and youthful, with a large, square nitroglycerin patch stuck to the skin over his heart.

Eve knew that Sam planned to live well past his heart attack when he drove up in a new van, a huge Ford Aerostar that came with a state-of-the-art stereo system, lots of toggle switches, a captain's chair for the driver, and enough thick pile carpeting to cover a living room. This, Eve was quite sure, was not the van of a man who believed he was about to die.

The way Sam understood it, the electrical impulses that controlled the valves in his heart were shorting out. His problem was not that the veins and arteries were sludged up. It was a wiring problem.

Eve reread a recent letter from Maggie. At the bottom of the aerogram there was a postscript: "By the way, Nanny, what *is* my mother's last name these days?"

"*Vey iz mir*, Lorraine!" Eve had said when she heard about her daughter's most recent marriage. "I didn't even know you were divorced from the last one."

"I am sorry," Eve said to Sam. "A woman with three children has no business marrying a man without money. I know I'm too practical...I know, I know, I know. But who's gonna end up supporting them?"

"It's too perfect," Eve said when she'd calmed down. "She's a hypochondriac and he's a healer. It's like the old Yiddish line, *Zey hobn zikh beyde farlibt—er mit zikh un zi mit zikh*." They're both in love—he with himself, she with herself.

Sam and Eve weren't any more supportive of Susan's return to California. Sam couldn't keep the sarcasm out of his voice on the phone. "Oh, you're goin' back 'cause you did so good there the first time?"

Aunt Sylvia, even though she offered the old car, said that Susan was returning to "her Waterloo."

It was often hard to imagine that family changes would turn out for the best. "And can you blame us?" Eve asked. "Sam Gordon and I have gotten the shaft so often we should invest in Vaseline."

On a Sunday morning the phone rang too early. Eve was already prepared for something terrible before she heard Lorraine's voice.

Jai Heard had tended professionally to many victims of heart attacks, but when his own came neither his emergency training nor his healing insight helped him know what to do about the strange pain in his chest. It was more out of confusion than fear that Jai decided to telephone his guru for the first time since his call of thirteen years earlier had ended so abruptly.

Lorraine actually made the call for him, because Jai was lying down. She explained to Satchidananda's secretary that something was happening to her husband's "physical body" and he felt the need for special guidance.

The secretary returned with a message. "Gurudev said, 'If Jai has faith in me, he will know he doesn't need to speak with me. I will keep him in my prayers.'" Then she added, "If you think he needs medical help, Leela, tell him to seek it."

"I'll drive you to the hospital," Lorraine said.

"And what do you think they'll do there?" Jai asked calmly.

"I suppose they'll keep you, put you in intensive care."

"Yes, and they'll give me drugs and take my blood and undo every-thing I've tried to do and stand for as a healer."

So Jai continued to lie in bed, and after a while he said he felt bet-ter. The phone rang in the other room, but when Lorraine picked it up, nobody was there. When she went back into the bedroom Jai was dead.

"Whatever I thought about the way she got married, she loved him," Eve said to Sam, her face full of pain.

"I'm going to work," Sam said. He grabbed a rake and hiked out toward the fifteen-hundred-square-foot plot where he planned to plant melons once he'd pulled out the rocks and tilled the soil.

1990 and Beyond

Visitors to the Gordon Ponderosa near the Everglades were struck by the vitality of spirit that imbued the little ranch and the stunning good health on display there. Sam and Eve's children could feel a regenerative aura, a "life force," a sense of peace.

Eve glowed youthful and rubescent, still the woman whose blush once caused a soldier to fall in love with a glossy tacked to the side of a khaki footlocker. She said she missed the card tables of Century Village but would "live Sam's dream for a while, and then take my own turn." Sam looked regal and at ease atop Viscount Lady, his muscular oak-colored Tennessee walking horse. He could often be seen smiling as he tended to the racing pigeons he'd bred to be driven over one hundred miles away and set free to fly home faster than the wind.

Sam could also be seen grumbling at the evening news. "Between taxes and recession, the middle class is disappearing. We're turning into Europe—just the rich and the poor....Bush lets Saddam get away, and then he gives himself parades bigger than the ones after World War II." Sam had trouble accepting that a Patriot now meant a piece of explosive hardware. He noted that ever since the time of his own war, all the talk of Great Americans had been matched by the impossibility of finding any. The 1991 hearings on the nomination of Clarence Thomas to the Supreme Court were depressing, in Sam's estimation. He believed the accuser, Anita Hill.

But for the most part Sam Gordon was buoyant, jaunty as a cowboy at the end of a cattle drive. "And Sammy laughs now," Eve would say. She'd begun to call him Sammy again, as if she'd retrieved the name like a forgotten memento from the attic. "He does. Sammy laughs all the time. You never notice that the laughing has stopped until it comes back again."

The same week that one of Sam's noisy geese bit Eve on the leg, two personal checks made out to Eve Gordon arrived in the mail on the same day. In markets and coffee shops all along Eve's two-mile hiking circuit, various residents of south Florida knew all about the goose attack ("I'd just fed the damned things…"), but "the miracle" of the two checks—simultaneous repayments of loans to Susan and Lorraine—was too difficult for even a veteran storyteller like Eve Gordon to convey to outsiders with appropriate effect.

"You know what's so strange about it?" Eve said, showing the checks to Sam. "It just doesn't feel…normal."

Nor, at first, did the sedate tenor of the constant family visits to Florida seem normal. Family arrived, and yet the floors didn't creak under the imported weight of their adversities, their anger, and their overabundance of accumulated pain. "They don't even bring their laundry anymore," Eve told some of the mah-jongg ladies with whom she still played once or twice a week over at Century Village.

The children and grandchildren came not to be rescued or even to fight. The family gravity that pulled them in no longer seemed to issue from things that should have happened and did not, or from those that should never have happened but did. The family bindings were as tenacious as ever, they were just a lot more elastic now.

Eve could still see her visitors' battle scars, of course—even the subcutaneous ones—much more so on the faces of her four children than upon those of her seven grandchildren. But then, didn't every member of any family bear some evidence of the toll of the campaign? Who knew how many postwar families had at least been nicked or sprained, if not broken?

Sam and Eve found that younger parents tended to ask them for advice, not because the questioners knew much about Gordon family history, but because Sam and Eve had an air of experience and parental wisdom.

"Spend as much time as you can with them," Sam said. "Always be there when presents are handed out. And try not to take what happens too personally."

Ricky phoned his father for advice one day, not about family quandaries but because he felt overwhelmed. Too many challenges had arisen all at once, he told Sam, and the coming week looked like a battlefield.

"You know what, Ricky, if I've learned one thing about getting through the tough times in my life, it's that all you really have to do is show up. When the counting's done, what matters is whether or not you were there."

"The trick is to get through it," Eve would tell young parents. "You have to understand that it's all part of life, natural. You can't know all the answers, and you won't even understand all the questions. You think you will at the beginning, but you won't. If what eventually happens isn't like your dreams, you have to learn that this is not a tragedy, because after a while you see that your dreams come from somewhere too."

"Try to be the same mother to all your children," she would add. "I made a lot of mistakes, but at least I didn't confuse them by not being myself. At least they had that."

To those in pain because of family trouble, Eve might philosophize, "Having an easy life doesn't always make for a good one. Sometimes you go through adversity and you're better for it. Then again, sometimes you're up shit creek."

"Listen to advice," Sam would chip in if he was there, "but don't let yourself feel judged. Anybody who sits in judgment about another family—especially in this day and age—is just plain out of his mind."

<hr />

A leading member of the expert class, family sociologist David Popenoe—whose father, family expert Paul Popenoe, had worried publicly about the future of the family through much of the middle part of the century—reported at the beginning of the nineties that according to a simple mathematical extrapolation from trends over the past thirty years, the American family would be in ruins by the end of the century. Most marriages would end in divorce, adultery would become "the norm" within the few marriages that lasted, and the birth rate would drop well below the level necessary to replace the population. Evidently the family decline and fall predicted by Carle Zimmerman of Harvard in the late forties, and by the other Cassandras before and after him, would finally come true.

Never had there been more evidence of "fear to bring children into the world," as Bob Dylan said in "Masters of War." A National Opinion Research Center poll revealed that six of ten Americans believed it was "not fair to bring a child into the world." Eight of ten, according to the Gallup organization, believed raising a family was more difficult now than when their own parents were raising them. And yet more babies were born in America in 1989 than ever before in a single year.

On the political plane—despite, or perhaps because of, a raft of alarming statistics about poverty, drug abuse, crime, and suicide rates among children and teenagers, and amid fears that America was producing a generation with the moral foundations of the average terrorist, as pediatrician T. Barry Brazelton put it—there was less of the moralistic fury evident back in 1980, when the White House Conference on the Family was so riven with emotionally charged disagreement over what an American family *was* that participants voted to change the name of the proceedings to the White House Conference on Families and accomplished little else. Reverend Falwell's Moral Majority had gone out of business in 1988, and by the early nineties, previously unimaginable alliances had been forged in the name of the family and the welfare of children.

Colorado congresswoman Pat Schroeder, a liberal proponent of "national family policy," joined with Phyllis Schlafly, the archconservative advocate of "family values," to argue for divorce laws that discouraged separation and promoted the continuing responsibility of both parents, for parental leave programs so working mothers and fathers could care for infants, for better day care, better parenting education programs, and better and more widely available prenatal care.

In 1991, in the afterglow of the popular war in the Persian Gulf, the bipartisan National Commission on Children—with a membership ranging from staunch Reaganites to Democratic progressives—would propose a fifty-six-billion-dollar plan to provide tax credits, health insurance, day care, and a host of other services to American children. "I am convinced," the president of the conservative Family Research Council was heard to say during a congressional hearing, "that the politics of saving the family will be the politics of the nineties."

If television was any guide, family would continue to be a cultural obsession in coming years. By 1990 tens of millions of Americans were tuning in daily to a nightmare vision of family. Talk shows presented a harrowing litany of the appalling things that happened when families went wrong. In any given week, viewers could hear stories of children who were simply sold by their parents as if at a yard sale, of children who were suing their parents for ruining their lives, of children regularly and terribly abused, psychologically, physically, and/or sexually, by their own parents or grandparents, of children who were mothers of their own fathers' children. People appeared on television to reveal that they were abused by their parish priests, or that their mothers had spirited away their boyfriends, or that their mothers were now men or their fathers women.

But like the sad stories told in recovery groups and self-help meetings, public visions of family darkness could comfort those in pain. Americans stared into the hell of other families like rubber-necking motorists fascinated by a bloody traffic accident. They saw dark allegories in other people's wrong turns. They experienced relief that they and their loved ones weren't lying there on the road, and they felt sympathy—a human connection—that offered a kind of strength to continue.

After choking for two years on guilt over her father's transgressions against her two oldest daughters, Eve began to read magazine articles and books about children who were abused and hurt by their families. She was greatly moved by her reading of *Keeping Secrets*, TV actress Suzanne Somers's book about her childhood in an alcoholic family. There were no answers or models in these stories, but they helped Eve see that what her father had done was not her fault.

For all the often shocking details, there was something liberating about the real families of true-life confession and revelation. Unlike the exemplary "normal families" of the era when the Gordons were starting out (the Nelsons, the Andersons, the Eisenhowers), these families and their stories suggested that no family should be held to a "norm," and that a family did not have to be "normal" to be strong.

Far from normal by the definition Sam and Eve took to Harbor Isle was the family of Roseanne Conner, the prime-time mother on the hit show *Roseanne*, who occasionally instructed her children to "stick a fork in your tongue." Roseanne, a minimum-wage-earning wife of a great big blue-collar baby-boomer ("Is there anything I can do to make you feel better without actually touching you?" she asked her husband one night), would have liked to be a writer, one episode revealed, like the poet who inspired her when she was young, Ricky's heroine Sylvia Plath.

Like the cartoon Simpsons, a dysfunctional family right off the self-help shelves ("Kiss you?" bug-eyed Bart once scoffed. "But Dad, I'm your kid"), the members of Roseanne's family weren't very nice to each other much of the time, but they always seemed to love each other. If the wise-cracking children were depicted as more sophisticated and quick-witted than their parents at times, then their parents did not seem to risk psychic destruction during dinner table onslaughts of the sort that had ripped so many families apart two decades earlier. As far from Ozzie and Harriet and the early 1980s "pro-family" paradigm as they could possibly be, and dysfunctional by any number of definitions, the Conner family was nonetheless connected. They were deeply rooted to a place and a community. They seemed to accept that family trouble was a given, that family pain was part of life, and that the best a family hurtling together through time could possibly do was to love and stay close.

———◆◆———

Sam, Eve, and Maggie grinned at the sight of Shuna and Ricky dancing together one evening at Century Village. Sporting a spring-green Mohawk, Shuna spun and posed with Isadora abandon amid the sea of halting box-steppers. "Yeah, she's a gorgeous kid all right," Sam said as Villagers came by for a grandparental verdict. "Now, I do happen to think she's ruinin' her head. You can ruin a head a' hair pretty damned easy, you know."

Magdalena Shapiro had come to Florida to introduce her husband. Martin and Maggie were about to migrate to Australia. She said she planned to get a job in business after they found a house. "I guess when it comes down to it," Maggie told her grandparents, "I want a pretty traditional life."

Shuna and Ricky seemed horrified that Maggie now considered her passionate love of poetry "an indulgence." After Maggie visited her in Virginia, Lorraine noted that her daughter had adopted viewpoints and plans "in reaction, in counterpoint to my own life…because," she said, her voice growing soft and small, "she doesn't want to be me."

But as grandparents who'd finally laid claim to the emotional distance grandparents were always said to enjoy, Sam and Eve were happy that Maggie seemed happy. They only regretted her decision to move so far away.

During a visit in 1990 Ricky was surprised to find himself watching while Eve sang "What Are You Doing for the Rest of Your Life?" His mother now knew how to accompany herself on the piano—the result of a new round of lessons—so it was no longer necessary for him to play for her while she leaned on his shoulders. Ricky was thrilled finally to stand back and appreciate "the gift" of his mother's phrasing and the imaginative, uninhibited way—even after she entered her eighth decade at the end of 1990—Eve could still take a song and make it her own.

Ricky sat out on the dock and told Sam about being a birth coach for an old friend whose husband was squeamish about such things. He said he attended Lamaze courses with the woman and was there telling her to breathe when the baby's tiny head emerged.

The Gordon "line" begun the day Sam had stopped being Sam

Goldenberg would certainly end with Ricky, but at least Ricky knew what it was like to help a life start, as he now knew how it felt to help a life draw to a close. Ricky's exposure to so many spiritual explanations of death and dying was useful when it came time to help his good friend Bart move past his fierce struggle with AIDS. As Bart came closer to death, Ricky stayed by his side, realizing that he would never be able to consider death without thinking of the description of the hereafter once offered him by the philosopher Eve Gordon, who said that when people died they went to a place not unlike the Harbor Isle Beach Club circa 1962, where mothers sat at tables in the sun clicking mah-jongg tiles and cracking jokes.

"He's like a whirl of energy," Sam would say when Ricky left after his visits. On the phone, Sam always asked Ricky to pick the next date, to come back soon. He never told Ricky that during his convalescence from his coronary he could "feel his heart healing" when his son played the piano, nor that he no longer wished Ricky would become an electrician or give him a hand with the ranch. At the end of a visit during the spring of 1992, Ricky was stunned when his father leaned over and kissed him. "I'm really gonna miss you a lot," Sam Gordon said to his son.

Ricky enjoyed sitting out in back with his parents, watching the evening sun go down. From the nearby swamp, huge clouds of insects would rise into the dusk blotting out the vista and the colors of the day. The sight reminded Ricky of a scene in the 1985 film version of E. M. Forster's *A Room with a View*, when the senior Mr. Emerson offers to give up his view of the river Arno in Florence. "I don't care what I see outside. My vision is within. *Here* is where the birds sing!" he cries, jabbing his fork in the direction of his heart. "*Here* is where the sky is blue!"

Ricky had played with the idea of changing the name of his work so long in progress from *The Family Eyes* to *It's Not Outside You*. By the time Ricky won—somewhat ironically, considering their last personal contact—the 1991 Stephen Sondheim Award, given to the nation's best up-and-coming musical theater composer, the name of the piece was *Mah-Jongg: The House Sparrow*. In one of the recent songs he'd written for his family musical, the three sisters and the parents turn in unison to the narrator, the youngest child and only son. "You have to release us, and let us become who we are," they sing. One of the sisters complains that the brother has shaped them to conform to his own emotional requirements, but now, the lyrics continue, "you have to let us go."

The brother replies, "I release you. Now go."

Nothing was as yet clear or simple about a life dedicated to being creative or about the prospect of living it alone, but Ricky was able to write, and now he could listen to a range of human melodies composed from experiences extending from birth to death, and he could hear—instead of the discordant notes of a painfully different and lacerating childhood or of a family in trouble—music that simply sounded like life.

Ricky came often to Florida to sing with his mother and sit quietly while his father talked to him as he talked to other men he respected. Ricky loved to visit his parents and look out at the still pond, and to bask in the warm sensation of being on the brink of a thousand things.

The first time Eve saw one of Sheila's skillful oil paintings, she said, "Why didn't you tell me? How come I never knew? You…you kept all of this inside?" She stared at her daughter's richly colored canvases, which to Eve were no less than Rembrandts. To the somewhat more critical teachers at the Art Students League in New York, Sheila's work bore evidence of a solid and marketable talent, and by the end of 1991 Sheila had received several commissions for portraits and had gone pro.

The first time Sam saw her paintings, his eyes filled with tears. "I was always…well, good at drawing," he said. "I never got to do anything with it, but maybe it's here. Maybe you got this from me."

Sheila said that every painting was "like a new beginning." As soon as she began to carve out a portion of each day to work at her easel, Sheila found that the intensity of the drama and struggle of daily family life seemed to subside in contrast to the intensity of her work.

When Jai Heard died, Sheila had gone to Yogaville to be with Lorraine. She found that she was jealous of the ashram dwellers she met. Believing as they did that they lived "in the lap of God"—like the acolytes of the twelve-step programs who'd given up the responsibilities and anxieties of the past "to a higher power"—they reminded Sheila of the siren song of freedom and release originating outside the circle of family, mocking the countervailing pull of family. The call away had been in the background of her life for as long as she could remember. The culture within which carefully tended families like hers dwelled was not friendly to those families, and the culture of release was but a step away.

But as soon as her painting became such a serious facet of her life, Sheila felt at home. It no longer mattered where her family lived. Since Jon was weary of his business life, they sold their house in Oceanside for eight times what they paid for it and moved to Boca Raton, less than an hour's drive from Sam and Eve's menagerie and home.

When Sheila went to see her parents, she'd sit with her mother while Sam sent Daryl, or one of the neighbor boys who loved to follow him around, into the garage for tools. If Ram, Shiva, and Gopal were there, Sam would roughhouse with the cousins or join in a round of "poo-poo" jokes or a burping contest. Sitting there watching Sam patiently tend to her son and nephews, Sheila felt that the vision "made up for some of the things I lacked."

Less jealous and angry than before, and less convinced that sufficient wisdom existed to create a family without turmoil and pain, Sheila had decided that a normal family was one in which "everybody is allowed to fall apart now and then." The new dining room in the house she and Jon began to build in 1991 was designed to accommodate a table big enough for all the members of the extended family to have a chair. Sheila looked forward to the gatherings of her clan, to the chance to just "be family"—whatever that might mean.

Lorraine and her boys moved off the ashram to a pretty little house on a quiet block in a small southern city. The boys attended public school, and Lorraine worked as a freelance copy editor for New York publishing houses and as a freelance "healer" and massage therapist. Nothing about being a single mother of three active boys was easy. Jai had left her no money, but he did leave a sense of commitment to serving others that Lorraine managed to turn into a way to support herself and her kids.

After Jai died, Lorraine read all his books about homeopathy, and she studied formally and informally a variety of alternative disciplines dedicated to alleviating illness and pain. A successful healer could charge as much as a hundred dollars an hour, and after two decades of training and just about enough poverty, Lorraine had also "gone pro."

Though her mother and her sisters scoffed at Lorraine's contention that a gifted New Age practitioner could "see" an internal medical problem, many of her patients—like so many of her friends and the members of her family—felt their spirits renewed and their physical strength enhanced simply by talking about life with Lorraine Gordon Shapiro Hughes Wenzel Heard. Even strangers found that Lorraine was capable of a peculiarly penetrating empathy.

A few days after Lorraine lost her husband, Swami Satchidananda had alluded to Yogaville's loss during an evening *satsang*. In his soft, calm voice, the old guru reminded his followers that death was but "changing vehicles." He offered a simile of birth to describe death, likening it to a chick finally throwing off its shell.

Lorraine tried to weigh the image of a tiny newborn bird against the mountain of her grief. She and Jai were perfect together. They were supposed to grow old together.

"Just cry for a few minutes and then get up and go do something," Satchidananda recommended to the widow.

Lorraine cried for more than a few minutes. Eventually she found the will to seek out professional grief counseling, the sort of help that would have made growing up so much less traumatic, she often thought, had it been widely available when she was a troubled little girl. As she got stronger, Lorraine finally began to take a close, hard look at the Satchidananda Ashram. She saw, as the biker Bill Behny had seen from the start, a community as profoundly divided between poor and rich— between the trailer dwellers who lived an hour's drive from a day's wages and the followers who built woody, burled homes and could afford luxuries and gifts of automobiles for the swami—as any of the cities her parents' generation had fled in search of a new democracy where everyone was middle-class and everyone was the same.

Lorraine watched from the doorway of LOTUS one morning as Satchidananda ushered Lauren Hutton into the shrine. The guru smiled at Hutton and told her funny little stories. Lorraine was standing beside one of his Cadillacs (he had an antique pink one now, a white one, a green one, and a cherry-red Rolls-Royce) when the beautiful model and the guru came out and climbed inside. Satchidananda did not acknowledge Lorraine's presence except to glare at her and bark in his irritated-father voice, "Don't slam the door!"

Not long after, Lorraine decided that she had "given too much power to the guru" for too long. When her family asked why she had left the ashram, she said, "I've just outgrown it." Though Lorraine still believed that human beings were capable of constructing a political and spiritual community predicated on fairness, universal acceptance, and a quality of love as compelling as the best moments of family life, she saw now that Satchidananda was just a man, not the angry father she might somehow please, and certainly not a god. But like someone leaving a bad marriage that still held profound emotions, Lorraine left Yogaville saying that she would love the guru forever, in a different way.

In her new home, Lorraine planned to maintain the ashram's strict ban on dating until after high school. "Until then," the former "boy-crazy" teen explained to her children, "boys and girls have trouble seeing each other as people." Gopal spent precious little time with his father at the ashram, though he often went to the countryside to see Bill Behny, who had traded in his dream of raising game birds for medical training and a job with the Buckingham emergency medical team.

For a brief time, in the wake of Jai's death, Lorraine thought about moving to Florida to be close to Sam and Eve. But the urge passed, and so she came as a visitor, like the others, to be close to a loving mother and father. Neither the "old" fearless and furious Lorraine nor the pious and fear-riddled woman of later years, a durable and relaxed Lorraine would come to sit with her mother and father and look out at Sam's spread. "I'm still a fighter," she said. "I just think I'm going to pick my fights better in the future.

Lorraine would occasionally look over at Eve and wonder, *Can I ever be as much to my children as she's been? Can I ever be as unselfish?*

"You know what I think?" Eve said during one of Lorraine's visits. "I think the trick of complete happiness is to always be ready. If you could be completely ready to be born, ready to be married, and ready to be a parent, I think you could be happy. The trick of getting old is to be ready to die. But I can't die yet, because I'm not ready. I don't have the right gown. So when I find the right outfit I'm gonna call you, Lorraine, and then you call the others."

The first time Susan came to Florida, Eve was waiting at the gate. Susan wore expensive glasses in an antique frame, a careful application of makeup, and a new perfume.

"You look good," Eve said. In Florida, she had noticed, people usually said a person looked good when they meant they looked better than expected.

They walked toward the large waiting room at the end of the Fort Lauderdale airport's main concourse. Framed within a distant aperture at the end of the tunnel was her father. Susan recognized Sam's powerful hands curled around the edges of an open newspaper, which tipped forward as she approached.

Sam looked into Susan's eyes and saw that they were alive with love. The look in his daughter's eyes was the thing he remembered from that strange day when he came home from the war and was told by a two-year-old girl to go away. But now, as she moved toward him, her eyes drew him to her.

Susan heard Sam's voice snag in his throat when he tried to speak. He just kept grinning at her, staring into her eyes.

For all of a week they did things together like a little storybook family. Sam, Eve, and Susan went to visit friends. They went to the famous

Florida malls, and Susan tried to remember if she'd ever been in a mall or even a store with her father.

"Let's go to the beach," Sam said after they'd returned from an outing, and Susan followed him back to the big van in a daze—because it all felt so new, because it *was* so new.

In the evening, Sam drove Susan to a local drug treatment center so she could attend a meeting. Several years clean and sober, Susan still thought about getting high. The vision of some perfect high would float past her, and she'd feel that savage force driving up from inside, urging her to grab it, but she was too far along to let that happen. She admitted that she was often bored by the communal storytelling of the addicted, as bored as she was at times by the story of her own life with drugs. But still, in front of her new computer, Susan worked to turn her story of drug addiction into a book. She was also freelancing for San Francisco publications and writing a shopping column for the *Berkeley Monthly*, and she'd even moved to the literary cutting edge by "authoring" a computer disk of boilerplate letters (letters of complaint, of condolence, of love) that an old Arica friend planned to market through his computer software company.

Susan attended a reunion of Aricans in Honolulu. Six hundred people came to reminisce, meditate, and take a look at white-haired Oscar Ichazo, who startled his longtime students by having grown old. Susan still contended that without Arica she would have plunged even more deeply into the death grip of drugs than she did. Shuna agreed that this was true. College, marriage, motherhood, material abundance, fame, political commitment—nothing, save perhaps the recovery experience crowned by her time at Women Inc.—had ever stayed the pain like the complex ego-dampening disciplines of Arica.

Susan occasionally traveled to Minneapolis to see her friends there, some recovered from the streets and some not. At one point she went back to help her philosophical friend Jimmy into a treatment program. Jimmy lived with her in Berkeley for a while, and Susan enjoyed telling friends that she had two children, Shuna and Jimmy. Jimmy eventually went back to Hennepin Avenue, though this time he stayed clean.

By the end of 1990, Susan had come to terms with her grandfather's terrible assault on her childhood. She now likened the pain that must have inspired his abuse and his drinking to the pain that motivated her own psychological abuse of those she loved while she was a slave to the drugs. "Sick, like me," she wrote at the end of a poem about Simon Samberg. "I love you. Rest in peace."

Susan became much less dogmatic about the structural genesis of family dysfunction, in part because her painful reconciliation with Shuna and with her parents allowed her to see that the ties that hold a family together in conflict are inextricably braided with those that bind a family in support and endless love.

In Florida on another visit, taking a break from her work on those anonymous personal letters for computer owners, Susan noticed in Sam's open dresser drawer the fervid Father's Day letter she'd written seven years earlier. She shuddered at the thought of the delusion wound around the core of love in that letter, but she knew that she would have kept such a letter too.

"Maybe he loved me all along," Susan said as she drew closer to her fiftieth year. She considered a childhood that had left her father unable to field the rejection of a two-year-old. She thought of his desire to have a normal family and of what the poor man got instead.

Back in Berkeley after yet another Florida journey, Susan found a brief letter from Sam. It came with a little box bearing delicate gold hoop earrings. "This might be the first letter I've written in fifty years. I'm sending you this with much love."

"It was his idea," Eve said on the phone. "Went and picked them out and everything."

Like her brother and sisters, Susan loved to come to Florida to enjoy the backyard paradise behind her parents' home. Around the time Sam completed a big corral for Viscount Lady—the fence wrought from the same rough-hewn lumber Sam had only been able to make into an inviolate corner back in Harbor Isle—Susan went inside the house to write a poem.

> In the cool damp dark south Florida air.
> My mother drinks decaf; I work on my knitting;
> The pool glows aqua, lit from below ...
> Dense, textured, black southern night
> Enfolds the little oasis of light
> Where my mother and I,
> Two old broads,
> Bound by blood and oceans of knowing,
> Are having ourselves a time.

———◆———

Eve preferred organic floral metaphors of family triumph. What a wife and mother wanted in the end was for everybody to bloom. They were late bloomers, her kids, but bloom all of them finally did. Not a season passed when Gordon children hadn't reached for the sun, sometimes so strong and accomplished along the way, but they'd somehow never really bloomed until now.

That so varied a garden should spring from the same earth and roots still mystified Sam and Eve. Eve would think about the trajectory of her children's departures and returns, about their passions and sadnesses, their heroes and spirits and godlings, the sound of their music, their costume changes, and she would come back to whether or not it was "the times."

Eve realized that back when her children were born, not one aspect of what they had each become even existed, either as an acceptable way of being or as a thought in her own head. Who had ever heard of a Vassar-educated feminist and reformed street junkie; of an American yogi healer with kids named Magdalena Shapiro and Shiva; of a good mother who painted a lot and dwelt wealthy yet unaffected at the upper edge of a middle class that nobody could possibly have imagined back then? And who could ever have dreamed that a young man of talent could be openly homosexual? Some of it had to be "the times," some of it was the children and parents she and Sam had been during their own lives, and some of it was a big secret.

Young parents might ask questions, but the model of a good family was not a simple thing. It moved in great circles, endlessly re-created through constant trial and error, a thing made of the clarity of certain experiences and the dreamy obscurity of others. There was so much Sam and Eve would have liked to know and do at various points in their family lives. A willingness to make adjustments, they would advise, was essential. The only constants were commitment and effort, the will to feel everything as real, and the immutable determination to stay in love.

"I give a lot of credit to Sammy," Eve would say. "He was brought up to believe that life was different from every single thing the children threw his way. He took it. Not always gracefully. But he took it."

"Yeah, but I still feel like I missed so much. I never got to know my children," Sam told Eve on several occasions, usually after Susan, Lorraine, Sheila, or Ricky had gone back to their homes.

"Let's be happy we can all love each other now," Eve replied. "We're lucky because now we can just love our children until we die."

During the final weeks of 1991, Sam's sister Sylvia died after a long bout with cancer. Sheila was in her aunt's hospital room when she noticed Sylvia raise her head off the pillow. "Puh-*lease!*" Sylvia barked in obvious irritation.

Three days later, at the funeral, Sam found himself pondering the trials of his early life. As Sam got older, memories of his childhood poverty tended to overwhelm him with emotion. Though he could sit in a traffic jam these days and not even sweat, visions of his childhood really got to him. How much did his own freezing, sleepless Depression nights and the tiger fights of his earliest family memories have to do with the job he did as a parent? How much did the quality of that job have to do with what happened later on? How much did these questions matter now...or even then?

With the miasma of crisis finally clearing, Sam and Eve often looked around at families so deeply gored that the love had drained away. At some point all the ruined families had lost the capacity to enter the holding pattern of simply *being family*, and so they'd lost their basic faith that the most wounded of families could eventually heal.

Sam and Eve agreed that their clan had moved dizzyingly close to the edge of ruin more than once, but they never stopped being family. And the two of them had never stopped being in love.

One evening Sam and Eve were out back, the air thick with citrus smells and the scent of oleander.

"I had a good life with you, Eve," Sam said, turning to his wife. "Without you I wouldn't have survived."

"We made some mistakes. That's for sure," Eve said. "Our life was totally *meshuga* at times, but at least everyone survived. I've had a good life with you too."

And they both turned and looked quietly at the vista outside their house as the insects rose into the coming night.

ACKNOWLEDGMENTS

The written record of American events since World War II is almost as rich as it is voluminous. Though most of my research concentrated on contemporaneous and eyewitness source materials, I wish to acknowledge here the work of several authors whose books—and in some cases, whose personal assistance—were particularly helpful as I labored to construct a historical chassis for the preceding family events.

I read Godfrey Hodgson's *America in Our Time* upon its publication more than fifteen years ago, and I continue to admire the mix of analysis and reportage Hodgson brought to his treatment of the years between the end of the war and the Nixon presidency. Eric F. Goldman's *The Crucial Decade: America, 1945–1955* was extremely helpful, as were Joseph C. Goulden's *The Best Years: 1945–1950*, Murray Kempton's collection *America Comes of Middle Age*, and Marty Jezer's tendentious but insightful *The Dark Ages: Life in the United States 1945–1960*. I often relied on J. Ronald Oakley, whose *God's Country: America in the Fifties* is an essential key to an understanding of that era. Bernie Bookbinder, journalist and historian of Long Island, was another valuable and gracious resource.

Daniel J. Boorstin's 1961 *The Image: A Guide to Pseudo-Events in America* is not precisely a "sixties book," but its prescient critique provides a fascinating context for the wealth of sixties literature that followed. As a part of my research for the chapters dealing with the 1960s I read or reread *The Year of the Barricades* by David Caute, *Gates of Eden: American Culture in the Sixties* by Morris Dickstein, *The Sixties: Years of Hope, Days of Rage* by Todd Gitlin, *Reporting the Counterculture* by Richard Goldstein, *Reunion: A Memoir* by Tom Hayden, *Moving Through Here* by Don McNeil, *Dream Time* by Geoffrey O'Brien, *The Angry Decade: The Sixties* by Paul Sann, and *Storming Heaven: LSD and the American Dream*, Jay Stevens' underappreciated tour de force. I also drew from various writings about the 1960s by Taylor Branch, Robert Christgau, Joan Didion, Robert Draper, Paul Goodman, David Halberstam, Michael Harrington, Charles Kaiser, J. Anthony Lukas, Norman Mailer, James Miller, Kate Millett, Abe Peck, Robert Shelton, Ronald Sukenick, Milton Viorst, Irving Welfeld, and Tom Wolfe.

Books about the 1970s are much more difficult to come by. Peter N. Carroll's *It Seemed Like Nothing Happened* certainly reveals that a great deal happened over the course of the decade after all. I read with fascination many publications of the Integral Yoga Institute and the Arica Institute Press. The best histories of the 1970s and 1980s are undoubtedly forthcoming, but I found books about the 1980s by Gary Wills, Barbara Ehrenreich, and Haynes Johnson to be first-rate.

An array of "time line" historical surveys was essential to this project. Among the best is my late professor Bernard Grun's *The Timetables of History*, Alan Gordon and Lois Gordon's *American Chronicle: Seven Decades in American Life*, Gorton Carruth's *The Encyclopedia of American Facts and Dates*, and the *Facts on File Weekly World News Digest*.

Though I have attempted to invoke academic, clinical, and professional analysis of the family only insofar as it filtered into the popular culture and became available to middle-class families, I consider my background reading in this realm essential to my efforts. I thank Christopher Lasch for his time and his splendid writing about the American family. The work of Mary Jo Bane, Steven Bayme, Robert N. Bellah, David Blankenhorn, Murray Bowen, Ernest W. Burgess, Urie Bronfenbrenner, Robert Coles, John Demos, Barbara Ehrenreich (*For Her Own Good: 150 Years of the Experts' Advice to Women*, cowritten with Deirdre English, is fascinating), Jean Bethke Elshtain, Erik H. Erikson, Gerald Handel, Jules Henry, Kenneth Keniston (*All Our Children* and *Young Radicals* in particular), Mike Lew, Margaret Mead, William F. Ogburn, David Popenoe, David Riesman, Bertrand Russell (*Marriage and Morals*), Maggie Scarf, Edward Shorter, Frank Tannenbaum, Paul Wachtel, Barbara Dafoe Whitehead, D. W. Winnicott, Carle C. Zimmerman, and many others helped to inform the historical and psychological "state of the family" motif underlying this tale. Barbara H. Solomon's collection of American short stories, *American Families*, offered a series of fascinating family vistas of another sort.

The special skills of many hardworking individuals were essential to the creation of this book. Mark Padnos has burrowed expertly and quickly through New York's libraries for years on my behalf. Linda Williams at Time Warner, Andrea Basora at Yale, Brian Patton at Vassar, Paul McEnroe in Minneapolis, Robin Paxton in London, and Bill Boles in Boston all helped provide research assistance. Glenda Lagradelle, Kim Davis, Lara Courtien, Kim Larson, and Gwen Hargreve each waded into an avalanche of archival material with diligent filing assistance. Dina Schrivanich provided late typing assistance, and the incomparable Jean Kidd typed, transcribed hundreds of tapes, gently suggested, and offered valued words of support throughout all four years of this project. Fred Smoler—professor, writer, reader, and best sort of friend for more than twenty years—commented on early drafts. My agent, Amanda Urban, protectively shepherded this project from the moment she heard the idea. Aaron Asher and Joy Johannessen are two remarkably talented editors, and I have had the great luck and honor of their brilliant efforts. Bill Shinker and other executives at HarperCollins invited me and my book into their publishing house late during the writing process, and they have lavished care and enthusiasm on it ever since. My beloved children and my wife and ever sharp-eyed first reader, Leslie Larson, were unbelievably patient with my long absence from my own family as I wrote about another.

Once more, I want to thank the Gordon family for allowing me to attempt a depiction of the world not as it is—as the Talmud puts it—but as we are.